Y0-CLZ-254

6 4962

DISCARDED

This Volume was reproduced
from an original in the
North Carolina Collection,
The Library,
University of North Carolina,
Chapel Hill, N. C.

"History of the Colony and Ancient Dominion of Virginia", by Charles Campbell, is part of a series of reprints on the early history both of Virginia and the other 13 Colonies.

Another, and very rare, early Virginia volume, "The History of the First Discovery and Settlement of Virginia", by William Stith, is also available.

A Heritage Series of reprints was started five years ago on South Carolina and now includes the following nine volumes: J. B. O. Landrum's Colonial and Revolutionary History of Upper South Carolina and History of Spartanburg County; John H. Logan's History of the Upper Country of South Carolina; Alexander Hewatt's Historical Account of the Rise and Progress of the Colonies of South Carolina and Georgia, 2 volumes; David Ramsay's History of South Carolina, 2 volumes; and the South Carolina, 1790, First Census; Alexander Gregg's History of The Old Cheraws.

Books available in a similar North Carolina Heritage Series include: R. B. Creecy's Grandfather's Tales of North Carolina History, Francis L. Hawks' History of North Carolina, 2 volumes, and the North Carolina, 1790, First Census.

In addition to the South and North Carolina 1790 Census volumes, Reprint Company has completed the volumes available on the other 10 states: Virginia, Pennsylvania, Maine, Rhode Island, Vermont, New Hampshire, Maryland, New York, Massachusetts and Connecticut.

Two books are currently available on Georgia. They are: Dr. Charles C. Jones "History of Georgia", Vols. 1 and 2. These are recognized by leading authorities as among the best works on the aboriginal, colonial and revolutionary epochs of the state.

THE REPRINT COMPANY
154 W. Cleveland Pk. Dr.
Spartanburg, S.C., 29303
November, 1965.

HISTORY

OF THE

COLONY AND ANCIENT DOMINION

OF

VIRGINIA.

BY

CHARLES CAMPBELL.

PHILADELPHIA
J. B. LIPPINCOTT AND CO.
1860.

Entered, according to Act of Congress, in the year 1859, by
CHARLES CAMPBELL,
In the Clerk's Office of the District Court of the United States for the Eastern District of Virginia.

PREFACE.

ALTHOUGH Virginia must be content with a secondary and unpretending rank in the general department of history, yet in the abundance and the interest of her historical materials, she may, without presumption, claim pre-eminence among the Anglo-American colonies. While developing the rich resources with which nature has so munificently endowed her, she ought not to neglect her past, which teaches so many useful lessons, and carries with it so many proud recollections. Her documentary history, lying, much of it, scattered and fragmentary, in part slumbering in the dusty oblivion of Transatlantic archives, ought to be collected with pious care, and embalmed in the perpetuity of print.

The work now presented to the reader will be found to be written in conformity with the following maxim of Lord Bacon: "It is the office of history to represent the events themselves, together with the counsels, and to leave the observations and conclusions thereupon, to the liberty and faculty of every man's judgment."

I avail myself of this occasion to express my acknowledgments to Hugh B. Grigsby, Esq., (who has contributed so much to the illustration of Virginia history by his own writings,) for many valuable suggestions, and for having undergone the trouble of revising a large part of the manuscript of this work.

PETERSBURG, VA., *September 2d*, 1859.

SUMMARY OF CONTENTS.

Chapter I.—Early Voyages of Discovery. Sir Walter Raleigh's Colony of Virginia.. 17
II.—Early Life and Adventures of Captain John Smith............... 30
III.—Landing at Jamestown and Settlement of Virginia proper. Wingfield, President of Council. Ratcliffe, President......... 35
IV.—Smith's Explorations. Smith, President........................... 55
V.—Smith's Adventures with the Indians. His Administration of the Colony. His Departure. His Character and Writings.. 70
VI.—The Indians of Virginia... 85
VII.—Sufferings of the Colonists. Wreck of the Sea-Venture. Miscellaneous Affairs. Percy, President. Lord Delaware, Governor. Percy, Acting Governor. Sir Thomas Dale, High Marshal. Sir Thomas Gates, Governor............................. 92
VIII.—Pocahontas visits England. Her Death. Yeardley, Deputy Governor... 112
IX.—Argall, Governor. His Administration. Powhatan's Death.. 124
X.—Sir Walter Raleigh.. 132
XI.—First Assembly of Virginia. Powell, Deputy Governor. Yeardley, Governor... 138
XII.—Negroes imported into Virginia. Yeardley, Governor.......... 143
XIII.—London Company. George Sandys, Treasurer. Wyat, Governor... 149
XIV.—Tobacco.. 153
XV.—East India School... 158
XVI.—Massacre of 1622... 160
XVII.—Extermination of Indians... 166
XVIII.—Dissolution of Charter of Virginia Company. Earl of Southampton, Nicholas Ferrar, and Sir Edwin Sandys................ 169
XIX.—Royal Government established in Virginia. Yeardley, Governor. West, Governor. Pott, Governor. Sir John Harvey, Governor... 179
XX.—Maryland settled. Contest between Clayborne and Lord Baltimore... 187
XXI.—Virginia during Harvey's Administration. He is recalled and succeeded by Wyatt.. 198

(xiii)

SUMMARY OF CONTENTS.

CHAPTER XXII.—Virginia during the Civil War of England. Berkley, Governor. Kemp, Governor... 199

XXIII.—Virginia during the Commonwealth of England. Bennet, Governor 210

XXIV.—Maryland during the Protectorate.. 222

XXV.—Virginia during the Protectorate. Digges, Governor. Matthews, Governor.. 233

XXVI.—Virginia under Richard Cromwell and during the Interregnum. Berkley, Governor... 240

XXVII.—Loyalty of Virginia. Miscellaneous Affairs. Morrison, Governor. Berkley, Governor.. 249

XXVIII.—Scarburgh's Report of his Proceedings in establishing the Boundary Line between Virginia and Maryland. "The Bear and the Cub," an extract from the Accomac Records 259

XXIX.—Miscellaneous Affairs.. 263

XXX.—Berkley's Statistics of Virginia 271

XXXI.—Threatened Revolt 274

XXXII.—Rev. Morgan Godwyn's Account of the Condition of the Church in Virginia 277

XXXIII.—Indian Disturbances. Disaffection of Colonists............. 280

XXXIV.—Bacon's Rebellion.. 283

XXXV.—Bacon's Rebellion, continued.. 293

XXXVI.—Bacon's Rebellion, continued.. 308

XXXVII.—Closing Scenes of the Rebellion.. 313

XXXVIII.—Punishment of the Rebels. Berkley's death. Succeeded by Jeffreys... 319

XXXIX.—Chicheley, Governor. Culpepper, Governor.................... 326

XL.—Statistics of Virginia.. 331

XLI.—Effingham, Governor. Death of Beverley. Effingham's Corruption and Tyranny 335

XLII.—William and Mary proclaimed. College chartered. Andros, Governor.. 343

XLIII.—Condition of Virginia. Powers of Governor. Courts and State Officers. Revenue.. 349

XLIV.—Administration of Andros. Nicholson again Governor.... 356

XLV.—Assembly held in the College. Ceremony of Opening. Governor's Speech.. 364

XLVI.—Church Affairs. Nicholson recalled. Huguenots.......... 367

XLVII.—Rev. Francis Makemie. Dissenters... 371

XLVIII.—Nott, Lieutenant-Governor. Earl of Orkney, Governor-in-chief.. 375

XLIX.—Spotswood, Governor.. 378

L.—Indian School 384

LI.—Spotswood's Tramontane Expedition 387

LII.—Virginia succours South Carolina. Disputes between Spotswood and the Burgesses. Blackbeard................ 391

CHAPTER LIII.—Spotswood's Administration reviewed. His subsequent Career and Death. His Family.................................. 398
LIV.—Drysdale, Governor. Robert Carter, President............ 411
LV.—Gooch's Administration. Carthagena Expedition........... 414
LVI.—Settlement of the Valley. John Lewis....................... 423
LVII.—Rev. James Blair. Governor Gooch and the Dissenters. Morris. Davies. Whitefield.. 433
LVIII—Gooch resigns. Robinson, President. Lee, President. Burwell, President.. 444
LIX.—Dinwiddie, Governor. Davies and the Dissenters. George Washington. Fairfax... 452
LX.—Hostilities with the French. Death of Jumonville. Washington surrenders at Fort Necessity................................ 460
LXI.—Dinwiddie's Administration, continued. Braddock's Expedition.. 469
LXII.—Davies. Waddell. Washington................................ 482
LXIII.—Settlers of the Valley. Sandy Creek Expedition. Dinwiddie succeeded by President Blair............................ 488
LXIV.—Fauquier, Governor. Forbes captures Fort Du Quesne... 500
LXV.—"The Parsons' Cause." Patrick Henry's Speech........... 507
LXVI.—Patrick Henry.. 519
LXVII.—Rev. Jonathan Boucher's Opinions on Slavery. Remarks... 526
LXVIII.—Disputes between Colonies and Mother Country. Stamp Act. Speaker Robinson, Randolph, Bland, Pendleton, Lee, Wythe... 530
LXIX.—Stamp Act opposed. Loan-Office Scheme. Robinson's Defalcation. Stamp Act Repealed. Offices of Speaker and Treasurer separated. Family of Robinson................ 538
LXX.—Bland's Inquiry.—Death of Fauquier. Persecution of Baptists. Blair's tolerant Spirit..................................... 549
LXXI.—Botetourt, Governor. Parliamentary Measures resisted. Death of Botetourt. Nelson, President. American Episcopate.. 556
LXXII.—Rev. Devereux Jarratt.. 563
LXXIII.—Duty on Tea. Dunmore, Governor. Revolutionary Proceedings.. 568
LXXIV.—Dunmore's Administration. Revolutionary Proceedings.. 572
LXXV.—Richard Henry Lee. Congress at Philadelphia. Patrick Henry. Washington... 577
LXXVI.—Battle of Point Pleasant. General Andrew Lewis. Cornstalk... 582
LXXVII.—Logan. Kenton. Girty. Dunmore's ambiguous Conduct 590
LXXVIII.—Daniel Boone.. 595
LXXIX.—Second Virginia Convention. Henry's Resolutions and Speech.. 599
LXXX.—Thomas Jefferson... 603

SUMMARY OF CONTENTS.

CHAPTER LXXXI.—Dunmore removes the Gunpowder. Revolutionary Commotions. Patrick Henry extorts Compensation for the Powder from the Governor 607
LXXXII.—The Mecklenburg Declaration 615
LXXXIII.—Dunmore retires from Williamsburg. Washington made Commander-in-chief. 618
LXXXIV.—Committee of Safety. Carrington, Read, Cabell. Death of Peyton Randolph. The Randolphs of Virginia... 624
LXXXV.—Dunmore's War. Battle of Great Bridge. Committee of Safety and Colonel Henry.................................. 632
LXXXVI.—Dunmore's War, continued. Colonel Henry resigns..... 639
LXXXVII.—Convention at Williamsburg. Declaration of Rights and Constitution of Virginia. Patrick Henry, Governor. George Mason.. 644
LXXXVIII.—Declaration of Independence. George Wythe. Benjamin Harrison, Jr., of Berkley. Thomas Nelson......; 652
LXXXIX.—Richard Henry Lee. Francis Lightfoot Lee. Carter Braxton.. 659
XC.—Dunmore retires from Virginia. Events of the War in the North. Death of General Hugh Mercer............. 664
XCI.—Death of Richard Bland. The Bland Genealogy. Petitions concerning Church Establishment. Scheme of Dictator. Hampden Sidney College. The Virginia Navy 670
XCII.—Examination of Charges against Richard Henry Lee. His Honorable Acquittal 681
XCIII.—Events of the War in the North. General Clark's Expedition to the Northwest 685
XCIV.—Convention Troops removed to Charlottesville. Church Establishment abolished. Events of the War in the South. Battle of King's Mountain. Jefferson, Governor... 693
XCV.—Arthur Lee. Silas Deane. Dr. Franklin. James Madison 701
XCVI.—Logan. Leslie's Invasion. Removal of Convention Troops 706
XCVII.—Arnold's Invasion.. 710
XCVIII.—Battle of the Cowpens and of Guilford. Phillips and Arnold invade Virginia...................................... 715
XCIX.—Cornwallis and La Fayette in Virginia. Nelson, Governor... 726
C.—Capture of the Patriot. The Barrons and Captain Starlins. Battle of the Barges............................ 738
CI.—Washington in the North. Cornwallis occupies Yorktown. Battle of Eutaw Springs. Henry Lee. Washington invests Yorktown. Cornwallis surrenders..... 742

HISTORY OF THE COLONY

AND

ANCIENT DOMINION OF VIRGINIA.

CHAPTER I.

1492-1591.

Early Voyages of Discovery—Sir Humphrey Gilbert—Walter Raleigh—Expedition of Amadas and Barlow—They land on Wocokon Island—Return to England—The New Country named Virginia—Grenville's Expedition—Colony of Roanoke—Lane, Governor—The Colony abandoned—Tobacco—Grenville returns to Virginia—Leaves a small Colony at Roanoke—Sir Walter Raleigh sends out another Expedition—City of Raleigh chartered—White, Governor—Roanoke found deserted—Virginia Dare, first Child born in the Colony—White returns for Supplies—The Armada—Raleigh assigns the Colony to a Company—White returns to Virginia—Finds the Colony extinct—Death of Sir Richard Grenville—Gosnold's Voyage to New England.

THE discoveries attributed by legendary story to Madoc, the Welsh prince, have afforded a theme for the creations of poetry; those of the Northmen of Iceland, better authenticated, still engage the dim researches of antiquarian curiosity. To Columbus belongs the glory of having made the first certain discovery of the New World, in the year 1492; but it was the good fortune of the Cabots to be the first who actually reached the main land. In 1497, John Cabot, a Venetian merchant, who had become a resident of Bristol in England, with his son Sebastian, a native of that city, having obtained a patent from Henry the Seventh, sailed under his flag and discovered the main continent of America, amid the inhospitable rigors of the wintry North. It was subsequent to this that Columbus, in his third voyage, set his foot on the main land of the South. In the following year, Sebastian Cabot again crossed the Atlantic, and coasted from the fifty-eighth degree of north latitude, along the shores of the United States, perhaps as far as to the southern boundary of Maryland. Portuguese, French, and Spanish navigators now visited North America.

Dreadful circumstances attended the foundation of the ancient St. Augustine. The blood of six hundred French Protestant refugees has sanctified the ground at the mouth of St. John's River, where they were murdered "not as Frenchmen, but as heretics," by the ruthless Adelantado of Florida, Pedro Menendez, in the year 1565.

In the summer of the ensuing year he sent a captain, with thirty soldiers and two Dominican monks, "to the bay of Santa Maria, which is in the latitude of thirty-seven degrees," together with the Indian brother of the cacique, or chief of Axacan, (who had been taken thence by the Dominicans, and baptized at Mexico, by the name of the Viceroy Don Luis de Velasco,) to settle there, and undertake the conversion of the natives. But this expedition sailed to Spain instead of landing.

This region of Axacan comprised the lower part of the present State of North Carolina. The Spanish sound of the word is very near that of Wocokon, the name of the place, according to its English pronunciation, where the colony sent out by Raleigh subsequently landed.*

In the year 1570 Father Segura and other Jesuit missionaries, accompanied by Don Luis, visited Axacan, but were treacherously cut off by him. In the same year, or the following, the Spaniards repaired to the place of their murder and avenged their death.†

In 1573 Pedro Menendez Morquez, Governor of Florida, explored the Bay of Santa Maria, "which is three leagues wide,

---

* Memoir on the first discovery of the Chesapeake Bay. Communicated by Robert Greenhow, Esq., to the Virginia Historical Society, May, 1848, in Early Voyages to America, (edited by Conway Robinson, Esq., and published by the Society,) p. 486. Mr. Greenhow cites for authority the Ensayo Chronologico Para la Historia de la Florida of Barcia, (Cardenas.)

† MS. letter of John Gilmary Shea, Esq., author of "History of the Catholic Missions among the Indian Tribes of the United States," citing Barcia and Alegambe.

and is entered toward the northwest. In the bay are many rivers and harbors on both sides, in which vessels may anchor. Within its entrance on the south the depth is from nine to thirteen fathoms, (about five feet nine inches English,) and on the north side from five to seven; at two leagues from it in the sea, the depth is the same on the north and the south, but there is more sand within. In the channel there are from nine to thirteen fathoms; in the bay fifteen, ten, and six fathoms; and in some places the bottom cannot be reached with the lead." Barcia describes the voyage of Morquez from Santa Helena "to the Bay of Santa Maria, in the latitude of thirty-seven degrees and a half,"* and makes particular mention of the shoal running out from what is now Cape Lookout, and that near Cape Hatteras, the latitude and distances given leaving no doubt but that the Bay of Santa Maria is the same with the Chesapeake.† Ten years will probably include the period of these early Spanish visits to Axacan and the Chesapeake; and these explorations appear to have been unknown to the English, and Spain made no claim on account of them. Had she set forth any title to Virginia, Gondomar would not have failed to urge it, and James the First would have been, probably, ready to recognize it.

In the year 1578 Sir Humphrey Gilbert obtained from Queen Elizabeth letters patent, authorizing him to discover and colonize remote heathen countries unpossessed by any Christian prince. After one or two unsuccessful expeditions, Sir Humphrey again set sail in 1583, from Plymouth, with a fleet of five small vessels. The largest of these, the bark Raleigh, was compelled in two days to abandon the expedition, on account of an infectious disease that broke out among the crew.

After Cabot's discovery, for many years the vessels of various flags had frequented the northern part of America for the purpose of fishing, and when Sir Humphrey reached St. John's Harbor, the thirty-six fishing vessels found there at first refused

---

* "A 37 grados y medio." Alegambe says: "Axaca ab æquatore in Boream erecta 37°."

† In a map found in a rare work, in French, dated 1676, entitled "Tourbe Ardante," shown me by Townsend Ward, Esq., Librarian of Pennsylvania Hist. Society, the Chesapeake is called St. Mary's Bay.

him admittance; but upon his exhibiting the queen's commission they submitted. He then entered the harbor, landed, and took formal possession of the country for the crown of England.

As far as time would admit, some survey of the country was made, the principal object of which was the discovery of mines and minerals; and the admiral listened with credulity to the promises of silver. The company being dispersed abroad, some were taken sick and died; some hid themselves in the woods, and others cut one of the vessels out of the harbor and carried her off. At length the admiral, having collected as many of his men as could be found, and ordered one of his vessels to remain and take off the sick, set sail with three vessels, intending to visit Cape Breton and the Isle of Sable; but one of his vessels being lost on a sand-bank, he determined to return to England. The Squirrel, in which he had embarked for the survey of the coast, was very small and heavily laden, yet this intrepid navigator persisted in remaining on board of her, notwithstanding the urgent entreaties of his friends in the other and larger vessel, the Hind; in reply to which, he declared, that he would not desert his little crew on the homeward voyage, after having with them passed through so many storms and perils. And after proceeding three hundred leagues, the little bark, with the admiral and all her crew, was lost in a storm. When last seen by the company of the Hind, Sir Humphrey, although surrounded by imminent perils, was seated composedly on the deck with a book in his hand, and as often as they approached within hearing was heard to exclaim: "Be of good cheer, my friends; it is as near to heaven by sea as by land." At midnight the lights of the little vessel suddenly disappeared, and she was seen no more. Sir Humphrey Gilbert was descended from an ancient family in Devonshire; his father was Otho Gilbert, Esq., of Greenway, and his mother, Catharine, daughter of Sir Philip Champernon, of Modbury. He was educated at Oxford, and became distinguished for courage, learning, and enterprise. Appointed colonel in Ireland, he displayed singular energy and address. In the year 1571 he was a member of the House of Commons from Compton, his native place. He strenuously defended the queen's prerogative against the charge of monopoly, alleged by a Puritan member against an exclusive grant made to some merchants. He was the author of several publications on cosmography and navigation. Having attracted the attention of the queen in his boyhood, she at length knighted him, and gave him one of her maids of honor in marriage. When he was preparing for his voyage she sent him a golden anchor with a large pearl at the peak, which he ever after prized as a singular honor. Raleigh accompanied this present, which was sent through his hands with this letter: "I have sent you a token from her majesty—an anchor guided by a lady, as you see; and farther, her highness willed me to send you word that she wished you as great hap and safety to your ship as if herself were there in person, desiring you to have care of yourself as of that which she tendereth. Farther, she commandeth that you leave your picture with me."

Not daunted by the fate of his heroic kinsman, Raleigh adhered to the design of effecting a settlement in America, and being now high in the queen's favor, obtained letters patent for that purpose, dated March, 1584. Aided by some gentlemen and merchants, particularly by his gallant kinsman Sir Richard Grenville, and Mr. William Sanderson, who had married his niece, Raleigh succeeded in providing two small vessels. These were put under the command of Captains Philip Amadas and Arthur Barlow. Barlow had already served with distinction under Raleigh in Ireland. The two vessels left the Thames in April, 1584, and pursuing the old circuitous route by the Canaries, reached the West Indies. After a short stay there they sailed north, and early in July, as they approached the coast of Florida, the mariners were regaled with the odors of flowers wafted from the fragrant shore. Amadas and Barlow, proceeding one hundred and twenty miles farther, landed on the Island of Wocokon, in the stormy region of Cape Hatteras, one of a long series of narrow, low, sandy islands—breakwaters apparently designed by nature to defend the mainland from the fury of the ocean. The English took possession of the country in the queen's name. The valleys were wooded with tall cedars, overrun with vines hung in graceful festoons, the grapes clustering in rich profusion on the ground and trailing in the murmuring surges of the sea. For two days no inhabitant was seen; on the third a canoe with three men approached, one of whom was readily persuaded to come on board, and some presents gained his confidence. Going away, he began to fish, and having loaded his canoe, returned, and dividing his cargo into two parts, signified that one was for the ship, the other for the pinnace. On the next day they were visited by some canoes, in which were forty or fifty men, among whom was Granganameo, the king's brother. The king Wingina himself lay at his chief town, six miles distant, confined by wounds received in a recent battle. At this town the English were hospitably entertained by Granganameo's wife. She was small, pretty, and bashful, clothed in a leathern mantle with the fur turned in; her long dark hair restrained by a band of white coral; strings of beads hung from her ears and reached to her waist. The manners of the natives were composed; their disposition seemed gentle; presents and traffic soon conciliated their good will. The country was called Wingandacoa.* The soil was productive; the air mild and salubrious; the forests abounded with a variety of sweet-smelling trees, and oaks superior in size to those of England. Fruits, melons, nuts, and esculent roots were observed; the woods were stocked with game, and the waters with innumerable fish and wild-fowl.

After having discovered the Island of Roanoke on Albemarle Sound, and explored as much of the interior as their time would permit, Amadas and Barlow sailed homeward, accompanied by two of the natives, Manteo and Wanchese. Queen Elizabeth, charmed with the glowing descriptions of the new country, which the enthusiastic adventurers gave her on their return, named it, in allusion to her own state of life, VIRGINIA. As hitherto all of North America as far as discovered was called Florida, so henceforth all that part of it lying between thirty-four and forty-five degrees of north latitude came to be styled Virginia, till gradually by different settlements it acquired different names.†

Raleigh was shortly after returned to Parliament from the County of Devon, and about the same time knighted. The queen

---

* Wingan signifies "good."
† Smith's History of Virginia, i. 79. Stith's History of Virginia, 11.

granted him a patent to license the vending of wines throughout the kingdom. Such a monopoly was part of the arbitrary system of that day. Nor was Sir Walter unconscious of its injustice, for when, some years afterwards, a spirit of resistance to it showed itself in the House of Commons and a member was warmly inveighing against it, Sir Walter was observed to blush. He voted afterwards for the abolition of such monopolies, and no one could have made a more munificent use of such emoluments than he did in his efforts to effect the discovery and colonization of Virginia. He fitted out, in 1585, a fleet for that purpose, and entrusted the command to his relative, Sir Richard Grenville. This gallant officer, like Cervantes, shared in the famous battle of Lepanto, and after distinguishing himself by his conduct during the Irish rebellion, had become a conspicuous member of Parliament. He was accompanied by Thomas Cavendish, afterwards renowned as a circumnavigator of the globe; Thomas Hariot, a friend of Raleigh and a profound mathematician; and John Withe, an artist, whose pencil supplied materials for the illustration of the works of De Bry and Beverley. Late in June the fleet anchored at Wocokon, but that situation being too much exposed to the dangers of the sea, they proceeded through Ocracock Inlet to the Island of Roanoke, (at the mouth of Albemarle Sound,) which they selected as the seat of the colony. The colonists, one hundred and eight in number, were landed there. Manteo, who had returned with them, had already been sent from Wocokon to announce their arrival to his king, Wingina. Grenville, accompanied by Lane, Hariot, Cavendish and others, explored the coast for eighty miles southward, to the town of Secotan, in the present County of Craven, North Carolina. During this excursion the Indians, at a village called Aquascogoc, stole a silver cup, and a boat being dispatched to reclaim it, the terrified inhabitants fled to the woods, and the English, regardless alike of prudence and humanity, burned the town and destroyed the standing corn. Grenville in a short time re-embarked for England with a valuable cargo of furs, and on his voyage captured a rich Spanish prize.

Lane extended his discoveries to the northward, as far as the town of Chesapeakes, on Elizabeth River, near where Norfolk stands, and about one hundred and thirty miles from the Island of Roanoke. The Chowan River was also explored, and the Roanoke, then known below the falls as the Moratoc. Lane, although a good soldier, seems to have wanted some of the qualities indispensable in the founder of a new plantation. The Indians grew more hostile; conspiracies were entered into for the destruction of the whites, and the rash and bloody measures employed to defeat their machinations aggravated the mischief. The colonists, filled with alarm, became impatient to escape from a scene of so many privations and so much danger. Owing to a scarcity of provisions, Lane distributed the colonists at several places. At length Captain Stafford, who was stationed at Croatan, near Cape Lookout, descried twenty-three sail, which proved to be Sir Francis Drake's fleet. He was returning from a long cruise—belligerent, privateering, and exploratory—and, in obedience to the queen's orders, now visited the Colony of Virginia to render any necessary succor. Upon learning the condition of affairs, he agreed to furnish Lane with vessels and supplies sufficient to complete the discovery of the country and to insure a safe return home, should that alternative be found necessary. Just at this time a violent storm, raging for four days, dispersed and shattered the fleet, and drove out to sea the vessels that had been assigned to Lane. The tempest at length subsiding, Drake generously offered Lane another vessel with supplies. But the harbor not being of sufficient depth to admit the vessel, the governor, acquiescing in the unanimous desire of the colonists, requested permission for them all to embark in the fleet, and return to England. The request was granted; and thus ended the first actual settlement of the English in America.

During the year which the colony had passed at Roanoke, Withe had made drawings from nature illustrative of the appearance and habits of the natives; and Hariot had accurately observed the soil and productions of the country, and the manners and customs of the natives, an account of which he afterwards published, entitled, "A briefe and true report of the new found land of Virginia." He (Lane) and some others of the colonists learned from the Indians the use of a narcotic plant called by them uppowoc; by the English tobacco. The natives smoked it;

sprinkled the dust of it on their fishing weirs, to make them fortunate; burned it in sacrifices to appease the anger of the gods, and scattered it in the air and on the water to allay the fury of the tempest. Lane carried some tobacco to England, supposed by Camden to have been the first ever introduced into that kingdom. Sir Walter Raleigh, by his example, soon rendered the use of this seductive leaf fashionable at court; and his tobacco-box and pipes were long preserved by the curiosity of antiquaries. It is related, that having offered Queen Elizabeth some tobacco to smoke, after two or three whiffs she was seized with a nausea, upon observing which some of the Earl of Leicester's faction whispered that Sir Walter had certainly poisoned her. But her majesty in a short while recovering, made the Countess of Nottingham and all her maids smoke a whole pipe out among them. It is also said that Sir Walter made a wager with the queen, that he could calculate the weight of the smoke evaporated from a pipeful of tobacco. This he easily won by weighing first the tobacco, and then the ashes, when the queen acknowledged that the difference must have gone off in smoke. Upon paying the wager, she gayly remarked, that "she had heard of many workers in the fire who had turned their gold into smoke, but that Sir Walter was the first that had turned his smoke into gold." Another familiar anecdote is, that a country servant of Raleigh's, bringing him a tankard of ale and nutmeg into his study as he was intently reading and smoking, was so alarmed at seeing clouds of smoke issuing from his master's mouth, that, throwing the ale into his face, he ran down stairs crying out that Sir Walter was on fire.

Sir Walter Raleigh never visited Virginia himself, although it has been so represented by several writers. Hariot's "Report of the new found land" was translated by a Frenchman * into Latin, and this translation refers to those "qui generosum D. Walterum Raleigh in eam regionem comitati sunt." The error of the translator in employing the words "comitati sunt," has been pointed out by Stith, and that error probably gave rise to the mistake which has been handed down from age to age, and is still prevalent. A few days after Drake's departure, a vessel arrived at

---

* De Bry.

Roanoke with supplies for the colony; but finding it abandoned, she set sail for England. Within a fortnight afterwards, Sir Richard Grenville, with three relief vessels fitted out principally by Raleigh, arrived off Virginia; and, unwilling that the English should lose possession of the country, he left fifteen men on the island, with provisions for two years. These repeated disappointments did not abate Raleigh's indomitable resolution. During the ensuing year he sent out a new expedition of three vessels to establish a colony chartered by the title of "The Governor and Assistants of the City of Raleigh in Virginia." John White was sent out as governor with twelve counsellors, and they were directed to plant themselves at the town of Chesapeakes, on Elizabeth River. Reaching Roanoke near the end of July, White found the colony deserted, the bones of a man scattered on the beach, the fort razed, and deer couching in the desolate houses or feeding on the rank vegetation which had overgrown the floor and crept up the walls. Raleigh's judicious order, instructing White to establish himself on the banks of Elizabeth River, was not carried into effect, owing to the refusal of Ferdinando, the naval-officer, to co-operate in exploring the country for that purpose.

One of the English having been slain by the savages, a party was dispatched to avenge his death, and by mistake unfortunately killed several of a friendly tribe. Manteo, by Raleigh's direction, was christened, and created Lord of Roanoke and Dassamonpeake. On the eighteenth of August, the governor's daughter, Eleanor, wife to Ananias Dare, one of the council, gave birth to a daughter, the first Christian child born in the country, and hence named *Virginia*. Dissensions soon arose among the settlers; and, although not in want of stores, some, disappointed in not finding the new country a paradise of indolent felicity, as they had fondly anticipated, demanded permission to return home; others vehemently opposed; at length all joined in requesting White to sail for England, and to return thence with supplies. To this he reluctantly consented; and setting sail in August, 1587, from Roanoke, where he left eighty-nine men, seventeen women, and eleven children, he arrived in England on the fifth of November.

He found the kingdom wholly engrossed in taking measures of

defence against the threatened invasion of the Spanish Armada, and Raleigh, Grenville, and Lane assisting Elizabeth in her council of war—a conjuncture most unpropitious to the interests of the infant colony. Raleigh, nevertheless, found time even in this portentous crisis of public affairs to dispatch White with supplies in two vessels. But these, running after prizes, encountered privateers, and, after a bloody engagement, one of them was so disabled and plundered that White was compelled to put back to England, while it was impossible to refit, owing to the urgency of more important matters. But, even after the destruction of the Armada, Sir Walter Raleigh found it impracticable to prosecute any further his favorite design of establishing a colony in Virginia; and in 1589 he formed a company of merchants and adventurers, and assigned to it his proprietary rights. This corporation included among its members Thomas Smith, a wealthy London merchant, afterwards knighted; and Richard Hakluyt, dean of Westminster, the compiler of a celebrated collection of voyages. He is said to have visited Virginia, and Stith gives it as his opinion that he must have come over in one of the last-mentioned abortive expeditions. Raleigh, at the time of making this assignment, gave a hundred pounds for propagating Christianity among the natives of Virginia. After experiencing a long series of vexations, difficulties, and disappointments, he had expended forty thousand pounds in fruitless efforts for planting a colony in Virginia. At length, disengaged from this enterprise, he indulged his martial genius, and bent all his energies against the colossal ambition of Spain, who now aspired to overshadow the world.

More than another year was suffered to elapse before White returned to search for the long-neglected colony. He had now been absent from it for three years, and felt the solicitude not only of a governor, but also of a parent. Upon his departure from Roanoke it had been concerted between him and the settlers, that if they should abandon that island for another seat, they should carve the name of the place to which they should remove on some conspicuous object; and if they should go away in distress, a cross should be carved above the name. Upon his arrival at Roanoke, White found not one of the colonists; the houses had been dismantled and a fort erected; goods had been buried in the earth, and in part disinterred and scattered; on a post within the fort the word CROATAN was carved, without a cross above it. The weather proving stormy, some of White's company were lost by the capsizing of a boat; the stock of provisions grew scanty; and no further search was then made. Raleigh, indeed, sent out parties in quest of them at five different times, the last in 1602, at his own charge; but not one of them made any search for the unfortunate colonists. None of them were ever found; and whether they perished by famine, or the Indian tomahawk, was left a subject of sad conjecture. The site of the colony was unfortunate, being difficult of access, and near the stormy Cape Hatteras, whose very name is synonymous with peril and shipwreck. Thus, after many nobly planned but unhappily executed expeditions, and enormous expense of treasure and life, the first plantation of Virginia became extinct.

In the year 1591 Sir Richard Grenville fell, in a bloody action with a Spanish fleet near the Azores. Mortally wounded, he was removed on board one of the enemy's ships, and in two days died. In the hour of his death he said, in the Spanish language, to those around him: "Here I, Richard Grenville, die with a joyous and quiet mind, for that I have ended my life as a true soldier ought to do, fighting for his country, queen, religion, and honor, my soul willingly departing from this body, leaving behind the lasting fame of having behaved as every valiant soldier is in his duty bound to do." His dying words may recall to mind the familiar verses of Campbell's Lochiel:—

"And leaving in death no blot on my name,
Look proudly to heaven for a death-bed of fame."

Sir Richard Grenville was, next to his kinsman, Sir Walter Raleigh, the principal person concerned in the first settlement of Virginia.

In 1602, the forty-third and last year of the reign of Queen Elizabeth, Captain Bartholomew Gosnold, deviating from the usual oblique route by the Canaries and the West Indies, made a direct voyage in a small bark across the Atlantic, and in seven weeks reached Massachusetts Bay. It was on this occasion that Englishmen, for the first time, landed on the soil of New England. Gosnold returned to England in a short passage of five weeks. In these early voyages the heroism of the navigators is the more admirable when we advert to the extremely diminutive size of their vessels and the comparative imperfection of nautical science at that day. Encouraged by Gosnold's success, the mayor, aldermen, and merchants of Bristol sent out an expedition under Captain Pring, in the same direction, in 1603, the year of the accession of James I. to the throne. During the same year a bark was dispatched from London under Captain Bartholomew Gilbert, who fell in with the coast in latitude 37°, and, as some authors say, ran up into the Chesapeake Bay, where the captain and four of his men were slain by the Indians.

In 1605 Captain Weymouth came over under the auspices of Henry, Earl of Southampton, and Lord Thomas Arundel.

CHAPTER II.

1579-1604.

Early Life and Adventures of Captain John Smith—Born at Willoughby—At Thirteen Years of Age undertakes to go to Sea—At Fifteen Apprentice to a Merchant—Visits France—Studies the Military Art—Serves in the Low Countries—Repairs to Scotland—Returns to Willoughby—Studies and Exercises—Adventures in France—Embarks for Italy—Thrown into the Sea—His Escape—Joins the Austrians in the Wars with the Turks—His Gallantry—Combat with Three Turks—Made Prisoner at Rottenton—His Sufferings and Escape—Voyages and Travels—Returns to England.

In 1606 measures were taken in England for planting another colony; but preliminary to a relation of the settlement of Virginia proper, it is necessary to give some history of Captain John Smith, "the father of the colony." He was born at Willoughby, in Lincolnshire, England, in 1579, being descended on his father's side from an ancient family of Crudley, in Lancashire; on his mother's, from the Rickands at Great Heck, in Yorkshire. After having been some time a scholar at the free schools of Alford and Louth, when aged thirteen, his mind being bent upon bold adventures, he sold his satchel, books, and all he had, intending to go privately to sea; but his father's death occurring just then prevented the execution of that scheme. Having some time before lost his mother, he was now left an orphan, with a competent hereditary estate, which, being too young to receive, he little regarded. At fifteen he was bound apprentice to Thomas Sendall, of Lynn, the greatest merchant of all those parts; but in a short time, disgusted with the monotony of that life, he quit it, and accompanied a son of Lord Willoughby to France. Within a month or six weeks, he was dismissed, his service being needless, with an allowance of money to take him back to England; but he determined not to return. At Paris, meeting with a Scottish gentleman, David Hume, he received from him an additional supply of money and letters, which might recommend him to the favor of James the Sixth of Scotland.

Young Smith, proceeding to Rouen, and finding his money nearly all gone, made his way to Havre de Grace, and there began to learn the military art, during the reign of the warlike Henry the Fourth. From France the adventurer went to the Low Countries, where he served for four years under the standard of the patriot army against Spain, in the war that eventuated in their independence. Embarking thence for Scotland, with the letters of recommendation previously given to him, and after suffering shipwreck and illness, Smith at length reached Scotland, where he was hospitably entertained "by those honest Scots at Kipweth and Broxmouth," but finding himself without money or means to make himself a courtier, he returned to his native place, Willoughby. Here he soon grew weary of much company; and indulging a romantic taste, retired into a forest, and in its recesses, near a pretty brook, he built for himself a pavilion of boughs, where he studied Machiavel's Art of War, and Marcus Aurelius, and amused his leisure by riding, throwing the lance, and hunting. His principal food was venison, which he thus provided for himself, like Shakespeare, with but little regard for the game-laws; and whatever else he needed was brought to him by his servant. The country people wondered at the hermit; and his friends persuaded an Italian gentleman, rider to the Earl of Lincoln, to visit him in his retreat; and thus he was induced to return to the world, and after spending a short time with this new acquaintance at Tattersall's, Smith now repaired a second time to the Low Countries. Having made himself sufficiently master of horsemanship, and the use of arms and the rudiments of war, he resolved to go and try his fortunes against the Turks, having long witnessed with pain the spectacle of so many Christians engaged in slaughtering one another.

Proceeding to St. Valery, in France, by collusion between the master of the vessel and some French gallants, his trunks were plundered there in the night, and he was forced to sell his cloak to pay for his passage. The other passengers expressed their indignation against this villany, and one of them, a French soldier, generously supplied his immediate necessities, and invited Smith to accompany him to his home in Normandy. Here he was kindly welcomed by his companion and the Prior of the ancient abbey of St. Stephen, (where repose the remains of William the Conqueror,) and others; and the story of his misfortunes reaching the ears of some noble lords and ladies, they replenished his purse; and he might have enjoyed their hospitality as long as he pleased, but this suited not his restless, energetic and independent spirit. Wandering now from port to port in quest of a man-of-war, he experienced some extraordinary turns of fortune. Passing one day through a forest, his money being spent, worn out with distress of mind, and cold, he threw himself on the ground, at the side of a fountain of water, under a tree, scarce hoping ever to rise again. A farmer finding him in this condition, relieved his necessities, and enabled him to pursue his journey. Not long afterwards, meeting in a grove one of the gallants who had robbed him, without a word on either side, they drew their swords, and fought in view of the inmates of a neighboring antique ruinous tower. In a short while the Frenchman fell, and, making confessions and excuses, Smith, although himself wounded, spared his life. Directing his course now to the residence of "the Earl of Ployer," with whom he had become acquainted while in the French service, he was by him better refurnished than ever.

After visiting many parts of France and Navarre, he came to Marseilles, where he embarked for Italy, in a vessel carrying a motley crowd of pilgrims of divers nations, bound for Rome. The winds proving unfavorable, the vessel was obliged to put in at Toulon, and sailing thence the weather grew so stormy that they anchored close to the Isle of St. Mary, opposite Nice, in Savoy. Here the unfeeling provincials and superstitious pilgrims showered imprecations on Smith's head, stigmatizing him as a Huguenot, and his nation as all pirates, and Queen Elizabeth as a heretic; and, protesting that they should never have fair weather as long as *he* was on board, they cast him into the sea to propitiate heaven. However, he swam to the Islet of St. Mary, which he found inhabited by a few cattle and goats. On the next day he was taken up by a privateering French ship, the captain of which, named La Roche, proving to be a neighbor and friend of the Earl of Ployer, entertained him kindly. With him, Smith visited Alexandria in Egypt, Scanderoon, the Archipelago, and coast of Greece. At the mouth of the Adriatic Sea, a Venetian argosy, richly laden, was captured and plundered, after a desperate action, in which Smith appears to have participated. He landed in Piedmont with five hundred sequins and a box of jewels, worth about as much more—his share of the prize. Embarking for Leghorn, he travelled in Italy, and here met with his friends, Lord Willoughby and his brother, both severely wounded in a recent bloody fray. Going to Rome, Smith surveyed the wonders of the Imperial City, and saw the Pope, with the cardinals, ascend the holy staircase, and say mass in the Church of St. John de Lateran. Leaving Rome, he made the tour of Italy, and embarking at Venice, crossed over to the wild regions of Albania and Dalmatia. Passing through sterile Sclavonia, he found his way to Gratz, in Styria, the residence of the Archduke Ferdinand, afterwards Emperor of Germany. Here he met with an Englishman and an Irish Jesuit, by whose assistance he was enabled to join a regiment of artillery, commanded by Count Meldritch, whom he accompanied to Vienna, and thence to the seat of war. At this time, 1601, there was a bloody war going on between Germany and the Turks, and the latter had gained many signal advantages, and the Crescent, flushed with victory, was rapidly encroaching upon the confines of Christendom. Canissia having just fallen, it was at the siege of Olympach, beleaguered by the Turks, that Smith first had an opportunity of displaying the resources of his military genius, for which he was put in command of two hundred and fifty horse.

That siege being raised, after some interval of suspended hostilities, the Christian forces, in their turn, besieged Stowle Wessenburg, which soon fell into their hands. Mahomet the Third, hearing of this disaster, dispatched a formidable army to retrieve or avenge it; and in the bloody battle that ensued on the plains of Girke, Smith had a horse shot under him, and was badly wounded. At the siege of Regal he encountered and slew, in a tournament, three several Turkish champions, Turbashaw, Grualgo, and Bonny Mulgro. For these exploits he was honored with a triumphal procession, in which the three Turks' heads were borne on lances. A horse richly caparisoned was presented to him, with a cimeter and belt worth three hundred ducats; and he was promoted to the rank of major.

3

In the bloody battle of Rottenton, he was wounded and made prisoner. With such of the prisoners as escaped massacre, he was sold into slavery at Axiopolis, and fell into the hands of the Bashaw Bogall, who sent him, by way of Adrianople, to Constantinople, a present to his youthful mistress, Charatza Tragabigzanda. Captivated with her prisoner, she treated him tenderly; and to prevent his being sold again, sent him to remain for a time with her brother, the Tymour Bashaw of Nalbritz, in Tartary, who occupied a stone castle near the Sea of Azof. Immediately on Smith's arrival, his head was shaved, an iron collar riveted on his neck, and he was clothed in hair-cloth. Here long he suffered cruel bondage; at length one day, while threshing in a barn, the Bashaw having beaten and reviled him, he turned and slew him on the spot, with the threshing bat; then put on his clothes, hid his body in the straw, filled a sack with corn, closed the doors, mounted the Bashaw's horse, and rode off. After wandering for some days, he fell in with a highway, and observing that the roads leading toward Russia were indicated by a cross, he followed that sign, and in sixteen days reached Ecopolis, a Russian frontier post on the Don. The governor there took off his irons, and he was kindly treated by him and his wife, the lady Callamata. Traversing Russia and Poland, he returned to Transylvania in December, 1603, where he met many friends, and enjoyed so much happiness that nothing less than his desire to revisit his native country could have torn him away.

Proceeding through Hungary, Moravia, and Bohemia, he went to Leipsic, where he found Prince Sigismund, who gave him fifteen hundred golden ducats to repair his losses. Travelling through Germany, France, and Spain, from Gibraltar he sailed for Tangier, in Africa, and to the City of Morocco. Taking passage in a French man-of-war, he was present in a terrible sea-fight with two Spanish ships; and after touching at Santa Cruz, Cape Goa, and Mogadore, he finally returned to England in 1604.*

---

* "The True Travels, Adventures, and Observations of Captain John Smith," in his History of Virginia. Hillard's Life of Smith, in Sparks' American Biography. Simms' Life of Smith.

CHAPTER III.

1606-1608.

Gosnold, Smith, and others set on foot another Expedition—James I. issues Letters Patent—Instructions for Government of the Colony—Charter granted to London Company for First Colony of Virginia—Sir Thomas Smith, Treasurer—Government of the Colony—Three Vessels under Newport sail for Virginia—The Voyage—Enter Chesapeake Bay—Ascend the James River—The English entertained by the Chief of the Quiqoughcohanocks—Landing at Jamestown—Wingfield, President—Smith excluded from the Council—Newport and Smith explore the James to the Falls—Powhatan—Jamestown assaulted by Indians—Smith's Voyages up the Chickahominy—Murmurs against him—Again explores the Chickahominy—Made prisoner—Carried captive through the country—Taken to Werowocomoco—Rescued by Pocahontas—Returns to Jamestown—Fire there—Rev. Mr. Hunt—Rage for Gold-hunting—Newport visits Powhatan—Newport's Departure—Affairs at Jamestown.

BARTHOLOMEW GOSNOLD was the prime mover, and Captain John Smith the chief actor, in the settlement of Virginia. Gosnold, who had already, in 1602, made a voyage to the northern parts of Virginia, afterwards called New England, for many years fruitlessly labored to set on foot an expedition for effecting an actual settlement. At length he was reinforced in his efforts by Captain Smith; Edward Maria Wingfield, a merchant; Robert Hunt, a clergyman, and others; and by their united exertions certain of the nobility, gentry, and merchants, became interested in the project, and King James the First, who, as has been before mentioned, had, in 1603, succeeded Elizabeth, was induced to lend it his countenance. April 10th, 1606, letters patent were issued, authorizing the establishment of two colonies in Virginia and other parts of America. All the country from 34° to 45° of north latitude, then known as Virginia, was divided into two colonies, the First or Southern, and the Second or Northern.

The plantation of the Southern colony was intrusted to Sir Thomas Gates and Sir George Somers, knights; Richard Hackluyt, clerk, prebendary of Westminster; Edward Maria Wingfield, and others, mostly resident in London. This company was authorized to plant a colony wherever they might choose between 34° and 41° of north latitude; and the king vested in them a right of property in the land extending along the sea-coast fifty statute miles on each side of the place of their first plantation, and reaching into the interior one hundred miles from the sea-coast, together with all islands within one hundred miles of their shores. The Second, or Northern colony of Virginia, was in like manner intrusted to Thomas Hanham, and others, mostly residents of Bristol, Exeter, and Plymouth. These were authorized to plant a colony wherever they might choose between 38° and 45° of north latitude, and he gave to them a territory of similar limits and extent to that given to the first colony. He provided, however, that the plantation of whichever of the said two colonies should be last effected, should not be within one hundred miles of the other that might be first established. The company of the Southern colony came to be distinguished as the London company, and the other as the Plymouth company. But eventually these names were dropped; and the name of Virginia, which had been at first common to the two colonies, was appropriated to the Southern colony only; while the Northern colony was now called New England.*

In the charter granted to Sir Thomas Gates and his associates, it was provided that the colony should have a council of its own, subject to a superior council in England. The subordinate council was authorized to search for and dig mines, coin money, carry over adventurers, and repel intruders. The president and council were authorized to levy duties on foreign commodities; the colonists were invested with all the rights and privileges of English subjects, and the lands granted to settlers in free and common soccage.†

On the 20th of November, 1606, instructions were given by the crown for the government of the two colonies, directing that the council in England should be appointed by the crown; the local council by the superior one in England; the local one to

---

* See charter in Stith's Hist. of Va., Appendix; "Notes as to the Limits of Virginia," by Littleton Waller Tazewell, in Va. Hist. Register, No. 1.

† Hening's Statutes at Large, i. 57.

choose a president annually from its own body; the Christian religion to be preached; lands to descend as in England; trial by jury secured in criminal causes; and the council empowered to determine all civil actions; all produce and goods imported to be stored in magazines; a clerk and treasurer, or cape-merchant, to be appointed for the colony. The stockholders, styled adventurers, were authorized to organize a company for the management of the business of the colony, and to superintend the proceedings of the local council. The colonists were enjoined to treat the natives kindly, and to endeavor by all means to convert them to Christianity.* Sir Thomas Smith was appointed treasurer of the company, and the chief management of their affairs intrusted to him. He was an eminent London merchant; had been chief of Sir Walter Raleigh's assignees; was about this time governor of the East India Company, and had been ambassador to Russia.†

The frame of government thus provided for the new colony was cumbrous and complicated, the legislative and administrative powers being so distributed between the local council, the crown, and the company, as to involve the danger of delays, uncertainty, conflict, and irresponsibility. By the words of the charter the colonists were invested with the rights of Englishmen; yet, as far as political rights were concerned, there being no security provided by which they could be vindicated, they might often prove to be of no more real value than the parchment on which they were written. However, the government of such an infant colony must, of necessity, have been for the most part arbitrary; the political rights of the colonists must, for a time, have lain in abeyance. Their civil rights were protected in criminal causes by the trial by jury, and lands were to be held by a free tenure.

At length three vessels were fitted out for the expedition, one of twenty tons, one of forty, the third of one hundred tons, and they were put under the command of Captain Christopher Newport, a navigator experienced in voyages to the New World. Orders being put on board inclosed in a sealed box, not to be opened until their arrival in Virginia, they set sail from Black-

---

* Hen. 67; Stith, 36, and in Appendix. † Stith, 42.

wall on the 19th of December, 1606. For six weeks they were detained by headwinds and stormy weather in the Downs, within view of the English coast, and during this interval, disorder, threatening a mutiny, prevailed among the adventurers. However, it was suppressed by the interposition of the clergyman, Robert Hunt. The winds at length proving favorable, the little fleet proceeded along the old route by the Canaries, which they reached about the twenty-first of April, and on the twenty-sixth sailed for the West Indies, upon arriving at which it appears that Captain Smith was actually in command of the expedition, for,* writing afterwards in 1629, he says: "Because I have ranged and lived among those islands, what my authors cannot tell me, I think it no great error in helping them to tell it myself. In this little Isle of Mevis, more than twenty years ago, I have remained a good time together, to wood and water, and refresh *my men*." This isle was, on this occasion, the scene of a remarkable incident in his life, and one which appears to have escaped the notice of our historians. "Such factions here we had as commonly attend such voyages, that a pair of gallows was made; but Captain Smith, for whom they were intended, could not be persuaded to use them. But not any of the inventors but their lives by justice fell into his power to determine of at his pleasure, whom, with much mercy, he favored, that most basely and unjustly would have betrayed him."

After passing three weeks in the West Indies they sailed in quest of Roanoke Island, and having exceeded their reckoning three days without finding land, the crew grew impatient, and Ratcliffe, captain of the pinnace, proposed to steer back for England.

At this conjuncture a violent storm, compelling them to scud all night under bare poles, providentially drove them into the mouth of Chesapeake Bay. The first land that they came in sight of, April 26th, 1607, they called Cape Henry, in honor of the Prince of Wales, eldest son of King James, as the opposite point, Cape Charles, was named after the king's second son, then Duke of York, afterwards Charles the First. A party of twenty

---

* Smith's Hist. of Va., ii. 276.

or thirty, with Newport, landing here, found a variety of pretty flowers and goodly trees. While recreating themselves on the shore they were attacked by five of the savages, who came creeping upon all-fours from the hills like bears, and with their arrows wounded two, but retired at the discharge of muskets.*

That night the sealed box was opened, when it appeared that the members of council appointed were—Bartholomew Gosnold, John Smith, Edward Maria Wingfield, Christopher Newport, John Ratcliffe, John Martin and George Kendall. They were instructed to elect, out of their own number, a president for one year; he and the council together were invested with the government; affairs of moment were to be examined by a jury, but determined by the council.

Seventeen days were spent in quest of a place for the settlement. A point on the western side of the mouth of the Chesapeake Bay they named Point Comfort, because they found a good harbor there, which, after the recent storm, put them in good comfort. Landing there, April 30th, they saw five Indians, who were at first alarmed; but seeing the captain lay his hand upon his heart, they came boldly up and invited the strangers to Kecoughtan, now Hampton, their town, where they were entertained with corn-bread, tobacco and pipes, and a dance. May 4th, the explorers were kindly received by the Paspaheghs. The chief of a neighboring tribe sent a guide to conduct the English strangers to his habitation. Percy calls them the Rappahannas; but as no such tribe is mentioned by Smith as being near the James River, they were probably the Quiqoughcohanocks, who dwelled on the north side of the river, about ten miles above Jamestown.† Upon the arrival of the English this chief stood on the bank of the river to meet them, when they landed, "with all his train," says Percy, "as goodly men as any I have seen of savages, or Christians, the Werowance [chief] coming before them, playing on a flute made of a reed, with a

---

* Narrative (in Purchas' Pilgrims, iv. 1685,) by George Percy, brother of the Earl of Northumberland, and one of the first expedition. See Hillard's Life of Smith in Sparks' Amer. Biog., 211 and 214 in note. (Hillard in the main follows Stith.) Smith's Newes from Virginia.

† Smith, i. 140–41.

crown of deer's hair, colored red, in fashion of a rose, fastened about his knot of hair, and a great plate of copper on the other side of his head, with two long feathers, in fashion of a pair of horns, placed in the midst of his crown. His body was painted all with crimson, with a chain of beads about his neck; his face painted blue, besprinkled with silver ore, as we thought; his ears all behung with bracelets of pearl, and in either ear a bird's claw through it, beset with fine copper or gold. He entertained us in so modest a proud fashion, as though he had been a prince of civil government, holding his countenance without laughter, or any such ill behavior. He caused his mat to be spread on the ground, where he sate down with a great majesty, taking a pipe of tobacco, the rest of his company standing about him. After he had rested awhile he rose, and made signs to us to come to his town: he went foremost, and all the rest of his people and ourselves followed him up a steep hill, where his palace was settled. We passed through the woods in fine paths having most pleasant springs, which issued from the mountains [hills.] We also went through the goodliest corn-fields that ever were seen in any country. When we came to Rappohanna town, he entertained us in good humanity." While this hospitable, unsophisticated chief was piping a welcome to the English strangers, how little did he anticipate the tragic scenes of war and blood which were so soon to ensue!

On the 8th of May the English went farther up the river to the country of the Appomattocks, who came forth to meet them in a most warlike manner, with bows and arrows, and formidable war-clubs; but the whites, making signs of peace, were suffered to land unmolested.* At length they selected for the site of the colony a peninsula lying on the north side of the James River, and about forty miles from its mouth. The western end of this peninsula, where it is connected by a little isthmus with the main land, was the spot pitched upon for the erection of a town, which was named, in honor of the king, Jamestown. Some contention occurred between Wingfield and Gosnold in regard to the selection of this place, Gosnold objecting to it. Smith conceived it a

---

* Percy's Narrative.

fit place for a great city. Gosnold exhibited in this matter the better judgment. The situation, eligible in some points, was extremely unhealthy, being low and exposed to the malaria of extensive marshes covered with water at high-tide. The bank of the river there is marked by no striking or picturesque feature. According to the terms of the charter, the territory now appropriated to the colony comprised a square of a base of one hundred miles, and including an area of ten thousand square miles, of which Jamestown was the centre, so to speak.

The settlers landed at Jamestown on the 13th day of May, 1607. This was the first permanent settlement effected by the English in North America, after the lapse of one hundred and ten years from the discovery of the continent by the Cabots, and twenty-two years after the first attempt to colonize it, made under the auspices of Walter Raleigh. Upon landing, the council took the oath of office; Edward Maria Wingfield was elected president, and Thomas Studley, cape-merchant or treasurer of the colony.* Smith was excluded from the council upon some false pretences. Dean Swift says: "When a great genius appears in the world, the dunces are all in confederacy against him."

All hands now fell to work, the council planning a fort, the rest clearing ground for pitching tents, preparing clapboard for freighting the vessels, laying off gardens, and making fishing-nets. The Indians frequently visited them in a friendly way. The president's overweening jealousy would allow no military exercise or fortification, save the boughs of trees thrown together in a semicircle by the energy of Captain Kendall.

On the fourth of June, Newport, Smith, and twenty others were dispatched to discover the head of the river on which they were seated, called by the Indians, Powhatan, and by the English, the James. The natives everywhere received them kindly, dancing, and feasting them with bread, fish, strawberries, and mulberries, for which Newport requited them with bells, pins, needles, and looking-glasses, which so pleased them that they followed the strangers from place to place. In six days they reached a town

---

* Stith, 46.

called Powhatan, one of the seats of the great chief of that name, whom they found there. It consisted of twelve wigwams, pleasantly situated on a bold range of hills overlooking the river, with three islets in front, and many corn-fields around. This picturesque spot lies on the north bank of the river, about a mile below the falls, and still retains the same name.

On the day of their arrival, the tenth of June, the party visited the falls, and again on the day following, Whitsunday, when they erected a cross there to indicate the farthest point of discovery. Newport, in return for Powhatan's hospitality, presented him with a gown and a hatchet. Upon their return, the Indians first gave occasion for distrust at Weyanoke, within twenty miles of Jamestown. Arriving there on the next day, June the twentieth, they found that a boy had been killed, and seventeen men, including the greater part of the council, had been wounded by the savages; that during the assault a cross-bar shot from one of the vessels had struck down a bough of a tree among them and made them retire, but for which all the settlers there would probably have been massacred, as they were at the time of the attack planting corn in security, and without arms. Wingfield now consented that the fort should be palisaded, cannon mounted, and the men armed and exercised. The attacks and ambuscades of the natives were frequent, and the English, by their careless straggling, were often wounded, while the fleet-footed savages easily escaped.

Thus the colonists endured continual hardships, guarding the workmen by day and keeping watch by night. Six weeks being passed in this way, Newport was now about to return to England. Ever since their departure from the Canaries, save for a while in the West Indies, Smith had been in a sort of duress upon the false and scandalous charges of some of the principal men in the expedition, who, envying his superiority, gave out that he intended to usurp the command, murder the council, and make himself king; that his confederates were distributed in the three vessels; and that divers of them, who had revealed it, would confirm it. Upon these accusations Smith had been arrested, and had now lain for several months under the cloud of these suspicions. Upon the eve of Newport's departure, Smith's accusers affecting through pity to refer his case to the council in England, rather than overwhelm him on the spot by an exposure of his criminal designs, he defied their malice, defeated their base machinations, and so bore himself throughout the whole affair, that all saw his innocence and the malignity of his enemies. The very witnesses suborned to accuse him charged his enemies with subornation of perjury. Kendall, the ringleader of them, was adjudged to pay him two hundred pounds in damages, which Smith contributed to the common stock of the colony. During these disputes Hunt, the chaplain, used his exertions to reconcile the parties, and at his instance Smith was admitted into the council on the twentieth day of June, and on the next day they all received the communion. The Indians now sued for peace, and two days after Newport weighed anchor, leaving at Jamestown one hundred settlers, with provisions sufficient, as was supposed, for more than three months.*

Not long after his departure a fatal sickness began to prevail at Jamestown, engendered by the insalubrity of the place, the exposure of the settlers, and the scarcity and bad quality of their food. Hitherto they had procured provisions from the vessels, but now, for some time, the daily allowance of each man was a pint of damaged wheat or barley. "Our drink was water, and our lodgings castles in the air." By September fifty of them, being one-half of the colony, died; the rest made out to subsist upon sturgeon and crabs. Among the victims of disease was Bartholomew Gosnold, the projector of the expedition, whose name is well worthy to be ranked with Smith and Raleigh. The sick, during this calamitous season, received the faithful attentions of Thomas Wotton, surgeon-general.

Wingfield, the president, after engrossing, as it was alleged, the public store of provisions to his own use, attempted to escape from the colony in the pinnace, and return to England. This baseness roused the indignation even of the emaciated survivors, and they deposed him, and appointed Captain John Ratcliffe in

---

* Smith, i. 153; Newes from Virginia; Anderson's History of the Colonial Church, i. 217.

his place, and displaced Kendall, a confederate of Wingfield, from the council.

In a manuscript journal of these early incidents, written by Wingfield himself, and preserved in the Lambeth Library, he undertakes to exculpate himself from the charge of engrossing the common store in the following terms: "As I understand, by report, I am much charged with starving the colony; I did always give every man his allowance faithfully, both of corn, oil, aquavitæ, etc., as was by the council proportioned; neither was it bettered after my time, until toward the end of March a biscuit was allowed to every workingman for his breakfast, by means of the provision brought us by Captain Newport, as will appear hereafter. It is further said I did much banquet and riot; I never had but one squirrel roasted, whereof I gave a part to Mr. Ratcliffe, then sick; yet was that squirrel given me. I did never heat a flesh-pot but when the common-pot was so used likewise; yet how often Mr. Presidents and the councillors have, night and day, been endangered to break their backs, so laden with swans, geese, ducks, etc. How many times their flesh-pots have swelled, many hungry eyes did behold, to their great longing; and what great thieves and thieving there hath been in common store since my time, I doubt not but is already made known to his majesty's council for Virginia."

At length their stores were almost exhausted, the small quantity of wine remaining being reserved for the communion-table; the sturgeon gone, all further effort abadoned in despair, and an attack from the savages each moment expected. At this hopeless conjuncture, a benignant Providence put it into the hearts of the Indians to supply the famished sufferers with an abundance of fruits and provision. Mankind, in trying scenes, render an involuntary homage to superior genius. Ratcliffe, the new president, and Martin, finding themselves incompetent and unpopular, intrusted the helm of affairs to Smith, who, acting as cape-merchant, set the colonists to work, some to mow, others to build houses and thatch them, he himself always performing the heaviest task. In a short time habitations were provided for the greater part of the survivors, and a church was built. Smith next embarked in a shallop to go in quest of supplies. Igno rance of the Indian language, the want of sails for the boat, and of clothing for the men and their small force, were discouraging impediments, but they did not dishearten him. With a crew of six or seven he went down the river to Kecoughtan, a town of eighteen cabins. Here he replied to a scornful defiance, by a volley of musketry and capturing their okee—an idol stuffed with moss, and painted and adorned with copper chains—so terrified them, that they quickly brought him a supply of venison, wild-fowl, and bread. Having procured a supply of corn, on his return he discovered the town and county of Warrasqueake, where he procured a further supply. After this, in several journeys, he explored the borders of the Chickahominy River. During his absence, Wingfield and Kendall, leaguing with the sailors and others, seized the pinnace in order to escape to England; but Smith, returning unexpectedly, opened so hot a fire upon them as compelled them to stay or sink. For this offence Kendall was tried by a jury, convicted, and shot.* Not long after, Ratcliffe and Captain Gabriel Archer made a similar attempt, and it was foiled by Smith's vigilance and resolution.

At the approach of winter the rivers of Virginia abounded with wild-fowl, and the English now were well supplied with bread, peas, persimmons, fish, and game. But this plenty did not last long; for what Smith carefully provided the colonists carelessly wasted. The idlers at Jamestown, including some of the council, now began to mutter complaints against Smith for not having discovered the source of the Chickahominy, it being supposed that the South Sea or Pacific Ocean lay not far distant, and that a communication with it would be found by some river running from the northwest. The Chickahominy flowed in that direction, and hence the solicitude of these Jamestown cosmographers to trace that river to its head. To allay this dissatisfaction of the council, Smith made another voyage up that river, and proceeded until it became necessary, in order to pass, to cut away a large tree which had fallen across the stream. When at last the barge could advance no farther, he returned eight miles and moored her in a wide bay out of danger, and leaving orders

---

* Newes from Va., 7.

to his men not to venture on shore until his return, accompanied by two of his men and two Indian guides, and leaving seven men in the barge, he went still higher up in a canoe to the distance of twenty miles. In a short time after he had parted from the barge the men left in her went ashore, and one of them, George Cassen, was surprised and killed. Smith, in the mean while, not suspecting this disaster, reached the marshy ground toward the head of the river, "the slashes," and went out with his gun to provide food for the party, and took with him one of the Indians. During his excursion his two men, Robinson and Emry, were slain; and he himself was attacked by a numerous party of Indians, two of whom he killed with a pistol. He protected himself from their arrows by making a shield of his guide, binding him fast by the arm with one of his garters. Many arrows pierced his clothes, and some slightly wounded him. Endeavoring to reach the canoe, and walking backward with his eye still fixed on his pursuers, he sunk to his waist in an oozy creek, and his savage with him. Nevertheless the Indians were afraid to approach, until, being now half-dead with cold, he threw away his arms, when they drew him forth, and led him to the fire where his two companions were lying dead. Here the Indians chafed his benumbed limbs, and having restored the vital heat, Smith inquired for their chief, and they pointed him to Opechancanough, the great chief of Pamunkey. Smith presented him a mariner's compass; the vibrations of the mysterious needle astonished the untutored sons of the forest. In a short time they bound the prisoner to a tree, and were about to shoot him to death, when Opechancanough holding up the compass, they all laid down their bows and arrows. Then marching in Indian file they led the captive guarded, by fifteen men, about six miles, to Orapakes, a hunting town in the upper part of the Chickahominy swamp, and about twelve miles northeast from the falls of James River (Richmond.) At this town, consisting of thirty or forty houses, built like arbors and covered with mats, the women and children came forth to meet them, staring in amazement at Smith. Opechancanough and his followers performed their military exercises, and joined in the wardance. Smith was confined in a long house under a guard, and an enormous quantity of bread and venison was set before him, as if to fatten him for sacrifice, or because they supposed that a superior being required a proportionately larger supply of food. An Indian who had received some toys from Smith at Jamestown, now, in return, brought him a warm garment of fur—a pleasing instance of gratitude, a sentiment often found even in the breast of a savage. Another Indian, whose son had been mortally wounded by Smith, made an attempt to kill him in revenge, and was only prevented by the interposition of his guards.

Opechancanough meditating an assault upon Jamestown, undertook to entice Smith to join him by offers of life, liberty, land, and women. Being allowed to send a message to Jamestown, he wrote a note on a leaf of a book, giving information of the intended assault, and directing what means should be employed to strike terror into the messengers, and what presents should be sent back by them. Three men dispatched with the note returned with an answer and the presents, in three days, notwithstanding the rigor of the season; it being the midst of the winter of 1607, remarkable for its extraordinary severity, and the ground being covered with snow. Opechancanough and his people looked upon their captive as some supernatural being, and were filled with new wonder on seeing how the "paper could speak." Abandoning the design of attacking Jamestown, they conducted Smith through the country of the Youghtanunds, Mattapanients, Payanketanks, Nantaughtacunds, and Onawmanients, on the banks of the Rappahannock, and Potomac. Thence he was taken to Pamaunkee, at the junction of the Matapony and Pamunkey—the residence of Opechancanough. Here, for three days, they engaged in their horrid orgies and incantations, with a view to divine their prisoner's secret designs whether friendly or hostile. They also showed him a bag of gunpowder, which they were reserving till the next spring, when they intended to sow it in the ground, as they were desirous of propagating so useful an article.

Smith was hospitably entertained by Opitchapan, (Opechancanough's brother,) who dwelt a little above, on the Pamunkey. Finally, the captive was taken to Werowocomoco, probably signifying chief place of council, a favorite seat of Powhatan, on the York River, then called the Pamaunkee or Pamunkey. They found this chief in his rude palace, reclining before the fire, on a sort of throne, resembling a bedstead, covered with mats, his head adorned with feathers and his neck with beads, and wearing a long robe of raccoon skins. At his head sate a young female, and another at his feet; while, on each side of the wigwam, sate the men in rows, on mats; and behind them as many young women, their heads and shoulders painted red, some with their heads decorated with the snowy down of birds, and all with strings of white beads falling over their shoulders. On Smith's entrance they all raised a terrific yell; the queen of Appomattock brought him water to wash, and another, a bunch of feathers for a towel. After feasting him, a long consultation was held. That ended, two large stones were brought, and the one laid upon the other, before Powhatan; then as many as could lay hold, seizing Smith, dragged him to the stones, and laying his head on them, snatched up their war-clubs, and, brandishing them in the air, were about to slay him, when Pocahontas, Powhatan's favorite daughter, a girl of only twelve or thirteen years of age,* finding all her entreaties unavailing, flew, and, at the hazard of her life, clasped the captive's head in her arms, and laid her own upon his. The stern heart of Powhatan was touched —he relented, and consented that Smith might live.

Werowocomoco, the scene of this celebrated rescue, lies on the north side of York River, in the County of Gloucester, about twenty-five miles below the fork of the river, and on a bay into which three creeks empty.† This is Timber-neck Bay, on the east bank of which stands a remarkable old stone chimney, traditionally known as "Powhatan's chimney," and its site corresponds exactly with the royal house of that chief, as laid down on Smith's Map of Virginia. Werowocomoco is only a few miles distant from the historic field of Yorktown, which is lower down the river, and on the opposite side. The lapse of time will continually heighten the interesting associations of Werowocomoco, and in ages of the distant future the pensive traveller will linger

---

* Smith, ii. 30. In Newes from Va., Smith calls her "a child of ten years old." This was a mistake.

† Stith, 53; Newes from Virginia, 11.

at the spot graced with the lovely charms of nature, and endeared by recollections of the tender heroism of Pocahontas.

Within two days after Smith's rescue, Powhatan suffered him to return to Jamestown, on condition of sending him two great guns and a grindstone, for which he promised to give him the country of Capahowosick, and forever esteem him as his own favorite son Nantaquoud. Smith, accompanied by Indian guides, quartered at night in some old hunting cabins of Paspahegh, and reached Jamestown on the next morning about sunrise. During the journey, as ever since his capture, he had expected at almost every moment to be put to death. Returning, after an absence of seven weeks, he was joyfully welcomed back by all except Archer and two or three of his confederates. Archer, who had been illegally admitted into the council, had the insolent audacity to indict Smith, upon a chapter of Leviticus, for the death of his two men slain by the Indians on the Chickahominy. He was tried on the day of his return, and sentenced to be hanged on the next day, or the day after the next, when Newport's opportune arrival on the very night after Smith's return, providentially saved him from this ignominious fate. Wingfield attributes the saving of *his* life likewise to Newport, who released him from the pinnace, where he was in duress.*

Smith now treated his Indian guides kindly, and showing Rawhunt, a favorite servant of Powhatan, two pieces of cannon and a grindstone, gave him leave to carry them home to his master. A cannon was then loaded with stones, and discharged among the boughs of a tree hung with icicles, when the Indians fled in terror, but upon being persuaded to return, they received presents for Powhatan, his wives and children, and departed.

At the time of Smith's return to Jamestown, he found the number of the colonists reduced to forty. Of the one hundred original settlers,† seventy-eight are classified as follows: fifty-four gentlemen, four carpenters, twelve laborers, a blacksmith, a

---

* Anderson's History of the Colonial Church, i. 221, referring to Wingfield's MS. Journal.

† List of the first planters, Smith, i. 153.

sailor, a barber, a bricklayer, a mason, a tailor, a drummer, and a "chirurgeon." Of the gentlemen, the greater part were indolent, dissolute reprobates, of good families; and they found themselves not in a golden El Dorado, as they had fondly anticipated, but in a remote wilderness, encompassed by want, exposure, fatigue, disease, and danger.

The return of Smith, and his report of the plenty that he had witnessed at Werowocomoco, and of the generous clemency of Powhatan, and especially of the love of Pocahontas, revived the drooping hopes of the survivors at Jamestown. The arrival of Newport at the same juncture with stores and a number of additional settlers, being part of the first supply sent out from England by the treasurer and council, was joyfully welcomed. Pocahontas too, with her tawny train of attendants, frequently visited Jamestown, with presents of bread, and venison, and raccoons, sent by Powhatan for Smith and Newport. However, the improvident traffic allowed between Newport's mariners and the natives, soon extremely enhanced the price of provisions, and the too protracted detention of his vessel made great inroads upon the public store. Newport, not long after his arrival, accompanied by Smith, Scrivener, newly arrived, and made one of the council, and thirty or forty picked men, visited Powhatan at Werowocomoco. Upon their arrival, Smith landed with a party of men, and after crossing several creeks on bridges of poles and bark, (for it appears that he had mistaken the right landing place, having probably passed up a little beyond the mouth of Timberneck Bay,) they were met and escorted to the town by Opechancanough, Nantaquaus, Powhatan's son, and two hundred warriors. Powhatan was found seated on his bedstead throne of mats, with his buckskin pillow or cushion, embroidered with beads. More than forty trays of bread stood without, in rows on each side of the door. Four or five hundred Indians were present. Newport landed on the next day, and some days were past in feasting, and dancing, and trading, in which last Powhatan exhibited a curious mixture of huckstering cunning, and regal pride. Smith gave him a suit of red cloth, a white greyhound, and a hat. Charmed with some blue beads, for one or two pounds of them he gave in exchange two or three hundred bushels of corn.

Newport presented him a boy named Thomas Salvage, in return for an Indian named Namontack. Smith acted as interpreter.

The English next visited Opechancanough, at his seat, Pamunkey. The blue beads came to be in great request, and none dared to wear them save the chiefs and their families. Having procured a further supply of corn at this place, Newport and his party returned to Jamestown, which was now destroyed by an accidental fire. Originating in the public storehouse, the flames spread rapidly over the cabins, thatched with reeds, consuming even the palisades, some eight or ten yards distant. Arms, apparel, bedding, and much of their private provision, were consumed, as was also a temporary church, which had been erected. "The minister, Hunt, lost all his library, and all that he had but the clothes on his back; yet none ever heard him repine at his loss. Upon any alarm he was as ready for defence as any, and till he could not speak, he never ceased to his utmost to animate us constantly to persist; whose soul, questionless, is with God."* As no further mention is made of him at Jamestown, it is probable that he did not live long after this fire. Dr. Hawks, however, conjectures that he survived long enough to officiate in the first marriage in Virginia, which took place in the year 1608.† He appears to have resided in the County of Kent, England, where, in January, 1594, he was appointed to the vicarage of Reculver, which he resigned in 1602. But he probably still continued to reside there, or to consider that his home, until he embarked for Virginia, because when in the Downs, which are opposite to Kent, he was only twenty miles "from his habitation." Of his appointment as chaplain to the expedition, Wingfield, in his journal referred to before, gives the following account: "For my first work, (which was to make a right choice of a spiritual pastor,) I appeal to the remembrance of my Lord of Canterbury's Grace, who gave me very gracious audience in my request. And the world knoweth whom I took with me, truly a man, in my opinion, not any way to be touched with the rebellious humor of a papist spirit, nor blemished with the least suspicion of a fac-

---

* Purchas, iv. 1710, cited in Anderson's History Col. Church, i. 222.
† Hawks' Contributions, 22.

tious schismatic." My Lord of Canterbury was that persecuting prelate, Archbishop Bancroft, who persecuted the Puritan dissenters till they desired to come over to Virginia to get out of his reach, and which they were prohibited from doing by a royal proclamation, issued at his instance. Rev. Robert Hunt, by all the notices of him that are given, appears to have been a pious, disinterested, resolute, and exemplary man.

When the English first settled at Jamestown, their place of worship consisted of an awning, or old sail, suspended between three or four trees, to protect them from the sun; the area covered by it was inclosed by wooden rails; the seats were unhewed trees, till plank was cut; the pulpit was a wooden crosspiece nailed to two neighboring trees. In inclement weather an old decayed tent served for the place of worship. After awhile, by the zeal of the minister Hunt, and the assistance of Newport's seamen, a homely structure like a barn was erected, "set upon crachets, covered with rafts, sedge, and earth," as likewise were the sides, the best of the houses being constructed after the same fashion, and the greater part of them worse than the church, so that they were but a poor defence against wind or rain. Nevertheless, the service was read daily, morning and evening, and on Sunday two sermons were preached, and the communion celebrated every three months, till the Rev. Mr. Hunt died. After which prayers were still said daily, and a homily read on Sunday, and so it continued until the arrival of other preachers some two or three years afterwards. The salary allowed Mr. Hunt appears to have been £500 a year, appropriated by the council of the Virginia Company in England, consented to by the council in Virginia, and confirmed by the Archbishop of Canterbury in 1605, to Richard Hackluyt, Prebend of Westminster, who, by his authority, sent out Mr. Hunt, "an honest, religious, and courageous divine, during whose life our factions were oft qualified, our wants and greatest extremities so comforted, that they seemed easy in comparison of what we endured after his memorable death."*

---

* Captain John Smith's "Advertisements for the Unexperienced Planters of New England, or anywhere," etc. A rare pamphlet, written at the house of Sir

The stock of provisions running low, the colonists at Jamestown were reduced to a diet of meal and water, and this, together with their exposure to cold, after the loss of their habitations, cut off upwards of one-half of them. Their condition was made still worse by a rage for gold that now seized them. "There was no talk, no hope, no work, but dig gold, wash gold, refine gold, load gold." Smith, not indulging in these empty dreams of imaginary wealth, laughed at their infatuation in loading "such a drunken ship with gilded dust."

Captain Newport, after a delay of three months and a half, being now ready to sail for England, and the planters having no use for parliaments, places, petitions, admirals, recorders, interpreters, chronologers, courts of plea, nor justices of the peace, sent Master Wingfield and Captain Archer home with him, so that they, who had ingrossed all those titles to themselves, might seek some better place of employment. Newport carried with him twenty turkeys, which had been presented to him by Powhatan, who had demanded and received twenty swords in return for them. This fowl, peculiar to America, had been many years before carried to England by some of the early discoverers of North America.*

After Newport's departure, Ratcliffe, the president, lived in ease, peculating on the public store. The spring now approaching, Smith and Scrivener undertook to rebuild Jamestown, repair the palisades, fell trees, prepare the fields, plant and erect another church. While thus engaged they were joyfully surprised by the arrival of the Phœnix, commanded by Captain Nelson, who had left England with Newport, about the end of the year 1607, and after coming within sight of Cape Henry, had been driven off to the West Indies. He brought with him the remainder of the first supply, which comprised one hundred and twenty settlers. Having found provisions in the West Indies, and having economically husbanded his own, he im-

---

Humphrey Mildmay, in the Parish of Danbery, Essex County, England, dedicated to the excellent Archbishop Abbot, and published in 1631. Cited in Anderson's History of Col. Church, ii. 747.

* Grahame's Col. Hist. U. S., Amer. ed., i. 28, in note.

parted them generously to the colony, so that now there was accumulated a store sufficient for half a year.

Powhatan having effected so advantageous an exchange with Newport, afterwards sent Smith twenty turkeys, but receiving no swords in return, he was highly offended, and ordered his people to take them by fraud or force, and they accordingly attempted to seize them at the gates of Jamestown. The president and Martin, who now ruled, remained inactive, under pretence of orders from England not to offend the natives; but some of them happening to meddle with Smith, he handled them so roughly, by whipping and imprisonment, as to repress their insolence.

Pocahontas, in beauty of feature, expression, and form, far surpassed any of the natives; and in intelligence and spirit "was the nonpareil of her country." Powhatan, hearing that some of his people were kept prisoners at Jamestown, sent her, with Rawhunt, (who was as remarkable for his personal deformity, but shrewd and crafty,) with presents of a deer and some bread to sue for their ransom. Smith released the prisoners, and Pocahontas was dismissed with presents. Thus the scheme of Powhatan to destroy the English with their own swords, was happily frustrated.

The Phœnix was freighted with a cargo of cedar, and the unserviceable, gold-hunting Captain Martin, concluded to return with her to England. Of the 120 settlers brought by Newport and Nelson, there were 33 gentlemen, 21 laborers, (some of them only footmen,) 6 tailors, 2 apothecaries, 2 jewellers, 2 gold-refiners, 2 goldsmiths, a gunsmith, a perfumer, a surgeon, a cooper, a tobacco-pipe maker, and a blacksmith.*

---

* Smith, i. 170.

CHAPTER IV.

1608.

Smith's First Exploring Voyage up the Chesapeake Bay—Smith's Isles—Accomac—Tangier Islands—Wighcocomoco—Watkins' Point—Keale's Hill—Point Ployer—Watts' Islands—Cuskarawaok River—The Patapsco—Potomac—Quiyough—Stingray Island—Smith returns to Jamestown—His Second Voyage up Chesapeake Bay—The Massawomeks—The Indians on the River Tockwogh—Sasquesahannocks—Peregrine's Mount—Willoughby River—The Patuxent—The Rappahannock—The Pianketank—Elizabeth River—Nansemond River—Return to Jamestown—The Hudson River Discovered—Smith, President—Affairs at Jamestown—Newport arrives with Second Supply—His Instructions—The First English Women in Virginia—Smith visits Werowocomoco—Entertained by Pocahontas—His Interview with Powhatan—Coronation of Powhatan—Newport Explores the Monacan Country—Smith's Discipline—Affairs at Jamestown—Newport's Return—Smith's Letter to the Council—The First Marriage in Virginia—Smith again visits Powhatan.

ON the second day of June, 1608, Smith, with a company of fourteen, consisting of seven gentlemen (including Dr. Walter Russel, who had recently arrived,) and seven soldiers, left Jamestown, for the purpose of exploring the Chesapeake Bay. The party embarked in an open barge of less than three tons, and dropping down the James River, parted with the Phœnix off Cape Henry, and crossing over thence to the Eastern Shore, discovered and named, after their commander, "Smith's Isles." At Cape Charles they met some grim, athletic savages, with bone-headed spears in their hands, who directed them to the dwelling-place of the Werowance of Accomac, who was found courteous and friendly, and the handsomest native that they had yet seen. His country pleasant, fertile, and intersected by creeks, affording good harbors for small craft. The people spoke the language of Powhatan. Smith pursuing his voyage, came upon some uninhabited isles, which were then named after Dr. Russel, surgeon of the party, but now are known as the Tangier Islands. Searching there for fresh water, they fell in with the River Wighcomoco, now called Pocomoke; the northern point was named

Watkins' Point, and a hill on the south side of Pocomoke Bay, Keale's Hill, after two of the soldiers in the barge. Leaving that river they came to a high promontory called Point Ployer, in honor of a French nobleman, the former friend of Smith. There they discovered a pond of hot water. In a thunder-storm the barge's mast and sail were blown overboard, and the explorers, narrowly escaping from the fury of the elements, found it necessary to remain for two days on an island, which they named Limbo, but it is now known as one of Watts' Islands. Repairing the sails with their shirts, they visited a river on the Eastern Shore called Cuskarawaok, and now, by a singular transposition of names, called Wighcocomoco. Here the Indians ran along the banks in wild amazement, some climbing to the tops of trees and shooting their arrows at the strangers. On the following day a volley of musquetry dispersed the savages, and the English found some cabins, in which they left pieces of copper, beads, bells and looking-glasses. On the ensuing day a great number of Indians, men, women, and children, thronged around Smith and his companions with many expressions of friendship. These savages were of the tribes Nause, Sarapinagh, Arseek, and Nantaquak, of all others the most expert in trade. They were of small stature like the people of Wighcocomoco; wore the finest furs, and manufactured a great deal of Roenoke, or Indian money, made out of shells. The Eastern Shore of the bay was found low and well wooded; the Western well watered, but hilly and barren; the valleys fruitful, thickly wooded, and abounding in deer, wolves, bears, and other wild animals. A navigable stream was called Bolus, from a parti-colored gum-like clay found on its banks, it is now known as the Patapsco.

The party having been about a fortnight voyaging in an open boat, fatigued at the oar, and subsisting on mouldy bread, now importuned Smith to return to Jamestown. He at first refused, but shortly after, the sickness of his men, and the unfavorable weather, compelled him reluctantly to turn back, where the bay was about nine miles wide and nine or ten fathoms deep. On the sixteenth of June they fell in with the mouth of the Patawomeke, or Potomac, where it appeared to be seven miles wide; and the tranquil magnificence of that majestic river reanimated their drooping spirits, and the sick having now recovered, they agreed to explore it.

About thirty miles above the mouth, near the future birthplace of Washington, two Indians conducted them up a small creek, toward Nominy, where the banks swarmed with thousands of the natives, who, with their painted bodies and hideous yells, seemed so many infernal demons. Their noisy threats were soon silenced by the glancing of the English bullets on the water and the report of the muskets re-echoing in the forests, and the astonished red men dropped their bows and arrows, and, hostages being exchanged, received the whites kindly. Toward the head of the river they met some canoes laden with bear, deer, and other game, which the Indians shared with the English.

On their return down the river, Japazaws, chief of Potomac, having furnished them with guides to conduct them up the River Quiyough, at the mouth of which he lived, (supposed by Stith* to be Potomac Creek,) in quest of Matchqueon, a mine, which they had heard of, the party left the Indian hostages in the barge, secured by a small chain, which they were to have for their reward. The mine turned out to be worthless, containing only a sort of antimony, used by the natives to paint themselves and their idols, and which gave them the appearance of blackamoors powdered with silver-dust. The credulous Newport had taken some bags of it to England as containing silver. The wild animals observed were the beaver, otter, mink, marten, and bear; of fish they met with great numbers, sometimes lying in such schools near the surface that, in absence of nets, they undertook to catch them with a frying-pan; but, plenty as they were, they were not to be caught with frying-pans. The barge running aground at the mouth of the Rappahannock, Smith amused himself "spearing" them with his sword, and in taking one from its point it stung him in the wrist. In a little while the symptoms proved so alarming that his companions concluded his death to be at hand, and sorrowfully prepared his grave in a neighboring island by his directions. But by Dr. Russel's judicious treatment the patient quickly recovered, and supped that evening

---

* Stith, 65.

upon the offending fish. This incident gave its name to Stingray Island. The fish was of the ray species, much like a thornback, but with a long tail like a horse-whip, containing a poisoned sting with a serrate edge.

The party returned to Jamestown late in July, and found sickness and discontent still prevalent there. Ratcliffe, the president, was deposed in favor of Smith, who, of the council, was next entitled to succeed; but Smith substituted Scrivener in his stead, and embarked again to complete his discoveries.

On the twenty-fourth of July he set out for the Chesapeake Bay, his company consisting of six gentlemen, including Anthony Bagnall, surgeon, and six soldiers. Detained some days at Kecoughtan, (Hampton,) they were hospitably entertained by the Indians there, who were astonished by some rockets thrown up in the evening. Reaching the head of the bay, the explorers met some canoes manned by Massawomeks, who, after their first alarm being propitiated by the present of two bells, presented Smith with bear's meat, venison, fish, bows, arrows, targets, and bearskins. Stith supposed this nation to be the same with the Iroquois, or Five Nations.*

On the River Tockwogh (now Sassafras) Smith came to an Indian town, fortified with a palisade and breastworks, and here men, women, and children, came forth to welcome the whites with songs and dances, offering them fruits, furs, and whatever they had, spreading mats for them to sit on, and in every way expressing their friendship. They had tomahawks, knives, and pieces of iron and copper, which, as they alleged, they had procured from the Sasquesahannocks, a mighty people dwelling two days' journey distant on the borders of the Susquehanna. Suckahanna, in the Powhatan language, signifies "water."†

Two interpreters being dispatched to invite the Sasquesahannocks to visit the English, in three or four days sixty of that gigantic people arrived, with presents of venison, tobacco-pipes three feet long, baskets, targets, bows and arrows. Five of their chiefs embarked in the barge to cross the bay. It being Smith's custom daily to have prayers with a psalm, the savages were

---

* Stith, 67.   † Smith, i. 147.

filled with wonder at it, and in their turn performed a sort of adoration, holding their hands up to the sun, and chanting a wild unearthly song. They then embraced Captain Smith, adoring him in the like manner, apparently looking upon him as some celestial visitant, and overwhelming him with a profusion of presents and abject homage.

The highest mountain seen by the voyagers to the northward they named Peregrine's Mount; and Willoughby River derived its name from Smith's native town. At the extreme limits of discovery crosses were carved in the bark of trees, or brass crosses were left. The tribes on the Patuxent were found very tractable, and more civil than any others. On the banks of the picturesque Rappahannock, Smith and his party were kindly treated by the Moraughtacunds; and here they met with Mosco, one of the Wighcocomocoes, who was remarkable for a bushy black beard, whereas the natives in general had little or none. He proved to be of great service to the English in exploring the Rappahannock. Mr. Richard Fetherstone, a gentleman of the company, died during this part of the voyage, and was buried on the sequestered banks of this river, where a bay was named after him. The river was explored to the falls, (near Fredericksburg,) where a skirmish took place with the Rappahannocks.

Smith next explored the Pianketank, where the inhabitants were, for the most part, absent on a hunting excursion, only a few women, children, and old men being left to tend the corn. Returning thence the barge encountered a tremendous thunderstorm in Gosnold's Bay, and running before the wind, the voyagers could only catch fitful glimpses of the land, by the flashes of lightning, which saved them from dashing to pieces on the shore, and directed them to Point Comfort. They next visited Chesapeake, now Elizabeth River, (on which Norfolk is situated,) six or seven miles from the mouth of which they came upon two or three cultivated patches and some cabins. After this they sailed seven or eight miles up the Nansemond, and found its banks consisting mainly of oyster-shells. Skirmishing here with the Chesapeakes and Nansemonds, Smith procured as much corn as he could carry away. September the 7th, 1608, the party arrived at Jamestown, after an absence of upwards of three months, and found some of the colonists recovered, others still sick, many dead, Ratcliffe, the late president, under arrest for mutiny, the harvest gathered, but the stock of provisions damaged by rain.

During that summer, Smith, with a few men, in a small barge, in his several voyages of discovery traversed a distance of not less than three thousand miles.* He had been at Jamestown only three days in three months, and had, during this interval, explored the whole of Chesapeake Bay and of the country lying on its shores, and made a map of them.

In the year 1607 the Plymouth Company, under the direction of Lord Chief Justice Popham, dispatched a vessel to inspect their territory of North Virginia. That vessel being captured by the Spaniards, Sir John Popham, at his own expense, sent out another, which, having returned with a favorable report of the country, he was enabled to equip an expedition for the purpose of effecting a settlement there. Under the command of his brother, Henry Popham, and of Raleigh Gilbert, a nephew of Sir Humphrey Gilbert, a hundred emigrants, embarking May, 1607, in two vessels, repaired to North Virginia, and seated themselves at the mouth of the River Sagahadock, where they erected Fort St. George. However, after enduring a great deal of sickness and hardship, and losing several of their number, including their president, Henry Popham, and hearing by a supply-vessel of the death of their chief patrons, Sir John Popham, and Sir John Gilbert, (brother of Raleigh Gilbert,) they gladly abandoned the colony, and returned to England in the spring of 1608.

It was in this year that Henry Hudson, an Englishman, employed by the Dutch East India Company, after entering the Chesapeake, and remarking the infant settlement of the English, discovered the beautiful river which still retains the name of that distinguished navigator. The Dutch afterwards erected near its mouth, and on the Island of Manhattan, the fort and cabins of New Amsterdam, the germ of New York.

Smith had hitherto declined, but now consented, September, 1608, to undertake the office of president. Ratcliffe was under arrest for mutiny; and the building of the fine house which he

---

* Smith, i. 191.

had commenced for himself in the woods, was discontinued. The church was repaired, the storehouse newly covered, magazines for supplies erected, the fort reduced to a pentagon figure, the watch renewed, troops trained; and the whole company mustered every Saturday in the plain by the west bulwark, called "Smithfield." There, sometimes, more than a hundred dark-eyed and dark-haired tawny Indians would stand in amazement to see a file of soldiers batter a tree, where a target was set up to shoot at.

Newport arrived with a second supply, and brought out also presents for Powhatan, a basin and ewer, bedstead and suit of scarlet clothes. Newport, upon this voyage, had procured a private commission in which he stood pledged to perform one of three impossibilities; for he engaged not to return to England without either a lump of gold, a certainty of the South Sea, or one of Sir Walter Raleigh's lost colonists. Newport brought also orders to discover the Manakin (originally Monacan) country, and a barge constructed so as to be taken to pieces, which they were to carry beyond the falls, so as to convey them down by some river running westward to the South Sea or Pacific Ocean. Vasco Nunez, in 1513, crossing the Isthmus of Darien, from the summit of a mountain discovered, beyond the other side of the continent, an ocean, which, from the direction in which he saw it, took the name of the "South Sea."

The cost of this last supply brought out by Newport was two thousand pounds, and the company ordered that the vessels should be sent back freighted with cargoes of corresponding value, and threatened, in case of a failure, that the colonists should be left in Virginia as banished men. It appears that the Virginia Company had been deeply incensed by a letter received by Lord Salisbury, (Sir Robert Cecil,) Secretary of State, reporting that the planters intended to divide the country among themselves. It is altogether improbable that they had conceived any design of appropriating a country which so few of them were willing to cultivate, and from which so many of them were anxious to escape. The folly of the instructions was only surpassed by the inhumanity of the threat, and this folly and inhumanity were justly exposed by Smith's letter in reply.*

---

* Stith, 82; Smith, 200.

Newport brought over with him Captains Peter Wynne and Richard Waldo, two veteran soldiers and valiant gentlemen; Francis West, brother of Lord Delaware; Raleigh Crashaw; Thomas Forest with Mrs. Forest, and Anne Burras, her maid; the first English women that landed at Jamestown.* Some Poles and Germans were sent out to make pitch, tar, glass, soap, ashes, and erect mills. Waldo and Wynne were admitted into the council; and Ratcliffe was restored to his seat.

The time appointed for Powhatan's coronation now drawing near, Smith, accompanied by Captain Waldo, and three others, went overland to a point on the Pamaunkee (York) River, opposite Werowocomoco, to which they crossed over in an Indian canoe. Upon reaching Werowocomoco, Powhatan being found absent, was sent for, and, in the mean time, Smith and his comrades were being entertained by Pocahontas and her companions. They made a fire in an open field, and Smith being seated on a mat before it, presently a hideous noise and shrieking being heard in the adjoining woods, the English snatched up their arms, and seized two or three aged Indians; but Pocahontas immediately came, and protested to Smith that he might slay her if any surprise was intended, and he was quickly satisfied that his apprehensions were groundless. Then thirty young women emerged from the woods, all naked, save a cincture of green leaves, their bodies being painted; Pocahontas wearing on her head a beautiful pair of buck's horns, an otter's skin at her girdle and another on her arm; a quiver hung on her shoulder, and she held a bow and arrow in her hand. Of the other nymphs, one held a sword, another a club, a third a pot-stick, with the antlers of the deer on their heads, and a variety of other savage ornaments. Bursting from the forest, like so many fiends, with unearthly shrieks, they circled around the fire singing and dancing, and thus continued for an hour, when they again retired to the woods. Returning, they invited Smith to their habitations, where, as soon as he entered, they all crowded around, hanging about him with cries of "Love you not me? love you not me?" They then feasted their guest; some serving, others singing and dancing, till at last, with blazing torches of light-wood, they escorted him to his lodging.

---

* Smith, i. 193.

On the next day, Powhatan having arrived, Smith informed him of the presents that had been sent out for him; restored to him Namontack, who had been taken to England, and invited the chief to visit Jamestown to accept the presents, and with Newport's aid to revenge himself upon his enemies, the Monacans. Powhatan, in reply, refused to visit Jamestown, saying that he, too, was a king; but he consented to wait eight days to receive presents; as for the Monacans, he was able to avenge his grievances himself. In regard to the salt water beyond the mountains, of which Smith had spoken, Powhatan denied that there was any such, and drew lines of those regions on the ground. Smith returned to Jamestown, and the presents being sent round to Werowocomoco by water, near a hundred miles, Newport and Smith, with fifty men, proceeded thither by the direct route across the neck of land that separates the James from the York.

All being assembled at Werowocomoco, the ensuing day was set for the coronation, when the presents were delivered to Powhatan—a basin, ewer, bed, and furniture ready set up. A scarlet cloak and suit of apparel were with difficulty put upon him, Namontack, meanwhile, insisting that it would not hurt him. Still more strenuous efforts were found necessary to make him kneel to receive the crown, till, at last, by dint of urgent persuasions, and pressing hard upon his shoulders, he was induced, reluctantly, to stoop a little, when three of the English placed the crown upon his head. At an appointed signal a volley of musketry was fired from the boats, and Powhatan started up from his seat in alarm, from which, however, he was in a few moments relieved. As if, by way of befitting satire upon so ridiculous a ceremony, Powhatan graciously presented his old moccasins and mantle to Newport, and some corn; but refused to allow him any guides except Namontack. The English having purchased, in the town, a small additional supply of corn, left Werowocomoco, and returned to Jamestown.

Shortly afterwards Newport, contrary to Smith's advice, undertook to explore the Monacan country, on the borders of the upper James River, with one hundred and twenty picked men, commanded by Captain Waldo, Lieutenant Percy, Captain Wynne, Mr. West, and Mr. Scrivener. Smith, with eighty or ninety men, some sick, some feeble, being left at Jamestown; Newport and his party, embarking in the pinnace and boats, went up to the falls of the river, where, landing, they marched forty miles beyond on the south side in two days and a half, and returned by the same route, discovering two towns of the Monacans—Massinacak, and Mowchemenchouch. The natives, "the Stoics of the woods," evinced neither friendship nor enmity; and the English, out of abundant caution, took one of their chiefs, and led him bound at once a hostage and a guide. Having failed to procure any corn from the Indians, Newport's party returned from the exploration of this picturesque, fertile, well-watered region, more than half of them sick or lame, and disheartened with fatigue, stinted rations, and disappointed hopes of finding gold.

Smith, the president, now set the colonists to work; some to make glass, others to prepare tar, pitch, and soap-ashes; while he, in person, conducted thirty of them five miles below the fort to cut down trees and saw plank. Two of this lumber-party happened to be young gentlemen, who had arrived in the last supply. Smith sharing labor and hardship in common with the rest, these woodmen, at first, became apparently reconciled to the novel task, and seemed to listen with pleasure to the crashing thunder of the falling trees; but when the axes began to blister their unaccustomed hands, they grew profane, and their frequent loud oaths echoed in the woods. Smith taking measures to have the oaths of each one numbered, in the evening, for each offence, poured a can of water down the offender's sleeve; and this curious discipline, or water-cure, was so effectual, that after it was administered, an oath would scarcely be heard in a week. Smith found that thirty or forty gentlemen who volunteered to work, could do more in a day than one hundred that worked by compulsion; but, he adds, that twenty good workmen would have been better than the whole of them put together.

Smith finding so much time wasted, and no provisions obtained, and Newport's vessel lying idle at heavy charge, embarked in the discovery barge, taking with him eighteen men and another boat, and leaving orders for Lieutenant Percy to follow after him, went up the Chickahominy. Being overtaken by Percy, he procured a supply of corn. Upon his return to Jamestown, Newport and Ratcliffe, instigated by jealousy, attempted to depose Smith from the presidency, but he defeated their schemes. The colony suffered much loss at this time by an illicit trade carried on between the sailors of Newport's vessel, dishonest settlers, and the Indians. Smith threatened to send away the vessel and to oblige Newport to remain a year in the colony, so that he might learn to judge of affairs by his own experience, but Newport submitting, and acknowledging himself in the wrong, the threat was not executed. Scrivener visiting Werowocomoco, by the aid of Namontack procured another supply of corn and some puccoons, a root which it was supposed would make an excellent dye, as the Indians used its red juice to stain their faces.

Newport at last sailed for England, leaving at Jamestown two hundred souls, carrying a cargo of such pitch, tar, glass, and soap-ashes as the colonists had been able to get ready. Ratcliffe, whose real name was discovered to be Sicklemore, was sent back at the same time. Smith in his letter to the council in England, exhibited, in caustic terms, the preposterous folly of expecting a present profitable return from Virginia. He sent them also his map of the country, drawn with so much accuracy, that it has been taken as the groundwork of all succeeding maps of Virginia.

Not long after Newport's departure, Anne Burras was married at Jamestown to John Laydon, the first marriage in Virginia. Smith finding the provisions running low, made a voyage to Nansemond, and afterwards went up the James, and discovered the river and people of Appomattock, who gave part of their scanty store of corn in exchange for copper and toys.

About this time Powhatan sent an invitation to Smith to visit him, and a request that he would send men to build him a house, and give him a grindstone, fifty swords, some guns, a cock and hen, with much copper, and many beads, in return for which he promised to load his vessel with corn. Having dispatched by land a party of Englishmen and four Dutchmen to build the house, Smith, accompanied by the brave Waldo, set out for Werowocomoco on the twenty-ninth of December, with the pinnace and two barges manned with forty-six men. Smith went in a barge with six gentlemen and as many soldiers, while in the pinnace were Lieutenant Percy and Francis West, with a number of gentlemen and soldiers. The little fleet dropping down the James arrived on the first night at Warrasqueake, from which place Sicklemore, a veteran soldier, was dispatched with two Indian guides in quest of Sir Walter Raleigh's lost company, and of silk grass. Smith left Samuel Collier, his page, at Warrasqueake to learn the language. The party being detained, by inclement weather, a week at Kecoughtan, spent the holidays there among the natives, feasting on oysters, venison, wild-fowl, and good bread, enjoying also excellent fires in the dry, smoky cabins. While here Smith and two others killed one hundred and forty-eight wild-fowl in three shots.

At Kiskiack, (now Chescake, pronounced Cheese-cake,) the severity of the cold again compelled the English to take shelter in the Indian wigwams. On the twelfth day of January they reached Werowocomoco. The York River being frozen over near half a mile from the shore, Smith, to lose no time, undertook to break his way through the ice; but the tide ebbing, left the barge aground on a shoal. In this dilemma, although the cold was extreme, Smith jumping into the icy river, set the example to his men of wading near waist deep to the shore, where, quartering in the first cabins that they reached, they sent to Powhatan for provisions. On the following day he supplied them abundantly with bread, wild turkeys, and venison. Like Nestor of old, he told Smith somewhat extravagantly, that he had seen the death of all of his people thrice; that he was now old and must ere long die; that his brothers, Opitchapan, Opechancanough, and Kekataugh, his two sisters, and their two daughters, were to be his successors. He deprecated war, and declared that when he and his people, forced to fly by fear of the English, lay in the woods, exposed to cold and hunger, if a twig but broke, every one cried out, "There comes Captain Smith." At length, after a long dialogue, Powhatan still obstinately insisting that the English should lay aside their arms, Smith gave orders privately to his people in the boat to approach and capture him. Discovering their design he fled with his women and children, while his warriors beset the cabin where Smith was. With pistol, sword, and target, he rushed out among them and fired; some fell one over another, the rest escaped.

Powhatan, finding himself in Smith's power, to make his peace sent him, by an aged orator, a large bracelet and a string of beads, and in the mean while the savages, goodly, well-formed fellows, but grim-looking, carried the corn on their backs down to the boats. The barges of the English being left aground by the ebb-tide, they were obliged to wait till the next high-water; and they returned ashore to lodge in some Indian wigwams.

Powhatan, and the treacherous Dutchmen who had been sent to build him a house, and who were attracted by the abundant good cheer that they enjoyed at Werowocomoco, now together plotted Smith's destruction. But Pocahontas, the chieftain's dearest jewel, in that dark night, passing through the gloomy woods, told Smith that great cheer would soon be sent to him, but that her father with all his force would quickly come and kill him and all the English, with their own weapons, while at supper; that therefore, if he would live, she wished him to go at once. Smith would have given her such toys as she delighted in; but, with tears streaming down her cheeks, she said that she would not dare to be seen to have them, for if her father should know it she would die; and so she ran away by herself as she had come. The attempt to surprise Smith was accordingly soon after made; but, forewarned, he readily defeated the design.

Upon the return of the tide, Smith and his party embarked for Pamaunkee, at the head of the river, leaving with Powhatan Edward Boynton, to kill fowl for him, and the Dutchmen, whose treachery was not as yet suspected, to finish his house. As the party sent forward to build the house had been there about two weeks, and as the chimney is erected after the house, it may be probably inferred that "Powhatan's Chimney" was built by the Dutchmen. It indeed looks like a chimney of one of those Dutch houses described by Irving in his inimitable "Legend of Sleepy Hollow." It is the oldest relic of construction now extant in Virginia, and is associated with the most interesting incident in our early history. This chimney is built of stone found on the banks of Timberneck Bay, and easily quarried; it is eighteen and a half feet high, ten and a half wide at the base, and has a double flue. The fire-place is eight feet wide, with an oaken beam across. The chimney stands on an eminence, and is conspicuous from every quarter of the bay; and itself a monumental evidence of no inconsiderable import. That the colonists would construct for Powhatan's house a durable and massive chimney there is every reason to believe, and here is such a one still extant, and still retaining, through all the mutations of time, the traditional name of "Powhatan's Chimney." There is no other such chimney in all that region, nor the remains of such a one. At the foot of the yard, and at a short distance from the chimney, which is still in use, being attached to a modern farm-house, is a fine spring, formerly shaded by a venerable umbrageous red-oak, of late years blown down. In the rivulet that steals along a ravine from the spring, Pocahontas sported in her childhood. Her name, according to Heckwelder, signifies "a rivulet between two hills," but this is denied by others.

In the early annals of Virginia, Werowocomoco is second only to Jamestown in historical and romantic interest; as Jamestown was the seat of the English settlers, so Werowocomoco was the favorite residence of the Indian monarch Powhatan. It was here that, when Smith was about to meet his fate,

"An angel knelt in woman's form
And breathed a prayer for him."

It was here that Powhatan was crowned by the conceited Newport; here that supplies for the colony were frequently procured; here that occurred so many interviews and rencontres between the red men and the whites. Here, two centuries and a half ago, dwelt the famous old Powhatan, tall, erect, stern, apparently beardless, his hair a little frosted with gray. Here he beheld, with barbarous satisfaction, the scalps of his enemies recently massacred, suspended on a line between two trees, and waving in the breeze; here he listened to recitals of hunting and blood, and in the red glare of the council-fire planned schemes of perfidy and revenge; here he sate and smoked, sometimes observing

Pocahontas at play, sometimes watching the fleet canoe coming in from the Pamaunkee. Werowocomoco was a befitting seat of the great chief, overlooking the bay, with its bold, picturesque, wood-crowned banks, and in view of the wide majestic flood of the river, empurpled by transient cloud-shadows, or tinged with the rosy splendor of a summer sunset.

CHAPTER V.

1608-1609.

Smith visits Pamaunkee—Seizes Opechancanough—Goes back to Werowocomoco—Procures Supplies—Returns to Jamestown—Smith's Rencontre with Chief of Paspahegh—Fort built—"The Old Stone House"—Colonists dispersed to procure Subsistence—Tuckahoe-root—Smith's Discipline—New Charter—Lord Delaware appointed Governor—Fleet dispatched for Virginia—Sea-Venture; cast away on Island of Bermuda—Seven Vessels reach Virginia—Disorders that ensued—Smith's Efforts to quell them—He Embarks for England—His Character, Life, and Writings.

SMITH and his party had no sooner set sail from Werowocomoco, up the river, than Powhatan returned, and dispatched two of the Dutchmen to Jamestown. The two emissaries, by false pretences and the assistance of some of the colonists, who confederated with them, succeeded in procuring a supply of arms and ammunition, which were conveyed to Powhatan by some of his people who were at hand for that purpose. In the mean time the other Dutchman, who had been retained by Powhatan as a hostage, provided him with three hundred stone tomahawks. Edward Boynton and Thomas Savage, discovering the treachery, attempted to make their escape back to Jamestown, but were apprehended and taken back, and expected every moment to be put to death.

During this interval, Smith having arrived at Pamunkey, at the junction of the Pamunkey and the Matapony, landed with Lieutenant Percy and others, to the number of fifteen, and proceeded to Opechancanough's residence, a quarter of a mile back from the river. The town was found deserted by all, except a lame man and a boy, and the cabins stripped of everything. In a short time the chief of the warlike Pamunkies returned, accompanied by some of his people, armed with bows and arrows. After some conference, Smith finding himself deceived as to the supply of corn which had been promised, reproached the chief for his treachery. Opechancanough, to veil his designs, agreed to sell what scanty commodities he then had, at Smith's own price, and promised to bring on the morrow a larger supply. On the next day Smith, with the same party, marched again up to Opechancanough's residence, where they found four or five Indians, who had just arrived, each carrying a large basket. Soon after the chief made his appearance, and with an air of frankness began to tell what pains he had been at to fulfil his promise, when Mr. Russel brought word that several hundred of the Indians had surrounded the house where the English were. Smith, perceiving that some of his party were terrified, exhorted them "to fight like men and not die like sheep." Reproaching Opechancanough for his murderous designs, he challenged him to decide the dispute in single combat on a neighboring island. The wily chief declining that mode of settlement, endeavored to inveigle Smith into an ambuscade, when his treachery being manifest, the president seized him by the forelock, and with a cocked pistol at his breast, led him, trembling, in the midst of his own people. Overcome with terror, Opechancanough surrendered his vambrace, bow, and arrows; and his dismayed followers threw down their arms. Men, women, and children, now brought in their commodities to trade with the English. Smith, overcome with fatigue, retired into a cabin to rest; and while he was asleep, a party of the Indians, armed with swords and tomahawks, made an attempt to surprise him, but starting up at the noise, he, with the help of some of his comrades, soon put the intruders to flight.

During this time, Scrivener, misled by letters received from England, began to grow ambitious of supplanting Smith, who was cordially attached to him; and setting out from Jamestown for Hog Island, on a stormy day, in company of Captain Waldo, Anthony Gosnold, and eight others, the boat was sunk and all were lost. When no one else could be found willing to convey this intelligence to Smith, Richard Wyffin volunteered to undertake it. At Werowocomoco he was shielded from danger by Pocahontas, who, in every emergency, still proved herself the tutelary angel of the colony. Wyffin having overtaken Smith at Pamunkey, he concealed the news of the recent disaster from his party, and, releasing Opechancanough, returned down the river. On the following morning, a little after sunrise, the bank of the river swarmed with Indians, unarmed, carrying baskets, to tempt Smith ashore, under pretence of trade. Smith, landing with Percy and two others, was received by Powhatan at the head of two or three hundred warriors formed in two crescents; some twenty men and a number of women carrying painted baskets. Smith attempted to inveigle Powhatan into an ambuscade, but the savages, on a nearer approach, discovering the English with arms in their hands, fled. However, the natives, some days afterwards, from all parts of the country, within a circuit of ten or twelve miles, in the snow brought, on their naked backs, corn for Smith's party.

Smith next went up the Youghtanund (now Pamunkey) and the Matapony. On the banks of this little river the poor Indians gave up their scanty store of corn with such tears and lamentations of women and children as touched the hearts of the English with compassion.*

Returning, he descended the York as far as Werowocomoco, intending to surprise Powhatan there, and thus secure a further supply of corn; but Powhatan had abandoned his new house, and had carried away all his corn and provisions; and Smith, with his party, returned to Jamestown. In this expedition, with twenty-five pounds of copper and fifty pounds of iron, and some beads, he procured, in exchange, two hundred pounds of deer suet, and delivered to the Cape-merchant four hundred and seventy-nine bushels of corn.

At Jamestown the provision of the public store had been spoiled by exposure to the rain of the previous summer, or eaten by rats and worms. The colonists had been living there in indolence, and a large part of their implements and arms had been trafficked away to the Indians. Smith undertook to remedy these disorders by discipline and labor, relieved by pastimes and recreations; and he established it as a rule, that he who would not work,

---

* The word Matapony is said to signify "no bread at all." The four confluents of this river, on modern maps, are whimsically named Ma, Ta, Po, and Ny, being the four component syllables of the word. Captain Smith calls it the Matapanient.

should not eat. The whole government of the colony was now, in effect, devolved upon him—Captain Wynne being the only other surviving councillor, and the president having two votes. Shortly after Smith's return, he met the Chief of Paspahegh near Jamestown, and had a rencontre with him. This athletic savage attempting to shoot him, he closed and grappled, when, by main strength, the chief forced him into the river to drown him. They struggled long in the water, until Smith, grasping the savage by the throat, well-nigh strangled him, and, drawing his sword, was about to cut off his head, when he begged for his life so piteously that Smith spared him, and led him prisoner to Jamestown, where he put him in chains. He was daily visited by his wives, and children, and people, who brought presents to ransom him. At last he made his escape. Captain Wynne and Lieutenant Percy were dispatched, with a party of fifty, to recapture him, failing in which they burned the chief's cabin, and carried away his canoes. Smith now going out to "try his conclusions" with "the salvages," slew some, and made some prisoners, burned their cabins, and took their canoes and fishing weirs. Shortly afterwards the president, passing through Paspahegh, on his way to the Chickahominy, was assaulted by the Indians; but, upon his firing, and their discovering who he was, they threw down their arms, and sued for peace. Okaning, a young warrior, who spoke in their behalf, in justifying the escape of their chief from imprisonment at Jamestown, said: "The fishes swim, the fowls fly, and the very beasts strive to escape the snare, and live." Smith's vigorous measures, together with some accidental circumstances, dismayed the savages, that from this time to the end of his administration, they gave no further trouble.

A block-house was now built in the neck of the Jamestown Peninsula; and it was guarded by a garrison, who alone were authorized to trade with the Indians; and neither Indians nor whites were suffered to pass in or out without the president's leave. Thirty or forty acres of land were planted with corn; twenty additional houses were built; the hogs were kept at Hog Island, and increased rapidly; and poultry was raised without the necessity of feeding. A block-house was garrisoned at Hog Island for the purpose of telegraphing shipping arrived in the river. Captain Wynne, sole surviving councillor, dying, the whole government devolved upon Smith. He built a fort, as a place of refuge in case of being compelled to retreat from Jamestown, on a convenient river, upon a high commanding hill, very hard to be assaulted, and easy of defence. But the scarcity of provisions prevented its completion.* This is, no doubt, the diminutive structure known as "the Old Stone House," in James City County, on Ware Creek, a tributary of York River. It stands about five miles from the mouth of the creek, and twenty-two from Jamestown. It is built of sandstone found on the bank of the creek, and without mortar. The walls and chimney still remain. This miniature fortress is eighteen and a half feet by fifteen in size, and consists of a basement under ground, and one story above. On one side is a doorway, six feet wide, giving entrance to both apartments. The walls are pierced with loop-holes, and the masonry is exact. This little fort stands in a wilderness, on a high, steep bluff, at the foot of which Ware Creek meanders. The Old Stone House is approached only by a long, narrow ridge, surrounded by gloomy forests and dark ravines overgrown with ivy. It is the oldest house in Virginia; and its age and sequestered situation have connected with it fanciful stories of Smith and Pocahontas, and the hidden treasures of the pirate Blackbeard.

The store of provisions at Jamestown was so wasted by rats, introduced by the vessels, that all the works of the colonists were brought to an end, and they were employed only in procuring food. Two Indians that had been some time before captured by Smith, had been until the present time kept fettered prisoners, but made to perform double tasks, and to instruct the settlers in the cultivation of corn. The prisoners were released for want of provision, but were so well satisfied as to remain. For upwards of two weeks the Indians from the surrounding country supplied the colony daily with squirrels, turkeys, deer, and other game, while the rivers afforded an abundance of wild-fowl. Smith also bought from Powhatan half of his stock of corn. But, nevertheless, it was found necessary to distribute the settlers in dif-

---

* Smith, i. 227.

ferent parts of the country to procure subsistence. Sergeant Laxon, with sixty or eighty of them, was sent down the river to live upon oysters; Lieutenant Percy with twenty, to find fish at Point Comfort; West, brother of Lord Delaware, with an equal number, repaired to the falls, where, however, nothing edible was found but a few acorns. Hitherto the whole body of the colonists had been provided for by the courage and industry of some thirty or forty.

The main article of their diet was, for a time, sturgeon, an abundant supply of which was procured during the season. It not only served for meat, but when dried and pounded, and mixed with herbs, supplied the place of bread. Of the spontaneous productions of the soil, the principal article of sustenance was the tuckahoe-root, of which one man could gather enough in a day to supply him with bread for a week. The tockawhoughe, as it is called by Smith, was, in the summer, a principal article of diet among the natives. It grows in marshes like a flag, and resembles, somewhat, the potato in size and flavor. Raw it is no better than poison, so that the Indians were accustomed to roast it, and eat it mixed with sorel and corn-meal.* There is another root found in Virginia called tuckahoe, and confounded with the flag-like root described above, and erroneously supposed by many to grow without stem or leaf. It appears to be of the convolvulus species, and is entirely unlike the root eaten by the Jamestown settlers.†

Such was the indolence of the greater number of the colonists, that it seemed as if they would sooner starve than take the trouble of procuring food; and at length their mutinous discontents arose to such a pitch that Smith arrested the ringleader of the malecontents, and ordered that whoever failed to provide daily as much food as he should consume, should be banished from Jamestown as a drone. Of the two hundred settlers, many were billeted among the Indians, and thus became familiar with their habits and manner of life.

---

* Smith, i. 123; Beverley's Hist. of Va., iii. 15. I refer to the first edition of 1705, which does not differ materially from the second edition of 1722.

† Farmer's Register for April, 1839, ix. 3; Jefferson's Notes on Va., 33; Rees' Cyclopædia, art. Tuckahoe; Fremont's Report, 135, 160.

Sicklemore, who had been dispatched to Chowanock, returned, after a fruitless search for Sir Walter Raleigh's people. He found the Chowan River not large; the country generally overgrown with pines; pemminaw, or silk-grass growing here and there. Two other messengers, sent to the country of the Mangoags in quest of the lost settlers, learned that they were all dead. Guides had been supplied by the hospitable chief of the Quiyoughcohannocks to convoy the messengers. This chief was of all others most friendly to the whites; although a superstitious worshipper of his own gods, yet he acknowledged that they were as inferior to the English God in power as the bow and arrow were inferior to the English gun; and he often sent presents to Smith, begging him "to pray to the English God for rain, else his corn would perish, for his gods were angry."

The Virginia Company in England, mainly intent on pecuniary gain and quick returns, were discouraged by the disasters that had befallen the colony, and disappointed in their visionary hopes of the discovery of gold mines, and of a passage to the South Sea. They therefore took measures to procure from King James a new charter, abrogating the existing one, and investing them with ampler powers. Having associated with themselves a numerous body of additional stockholders, or adventurers, as they were then styled, including many persons of rank, and wealth, and influence, they succeeded in obtaining from the king a new charter, dated May 23d, 1609, transferring to the Company several important powers before reserved to the crown. By this charter the extent of Virginia was much enlarged, the eastern boundary being a line extending two hundred miles north of Point Comfort, and two hundred miles south of it, the northern and southern boundaries being parallels drawn through the extremities of the eastern boundary back to the South Sea or Pacific—the western boundary being the Pacific.

By the provisions of the new charter the Virginia Company became indeed apparently more independent and republican, but under the new system the governor of the colony was indued with arbitary power, and authorized to declare martial-law; and the condition of the colonists became even worse than before. This sudden repeal of the former charter evinced an ingratitude for the services of Smith and his associates, who, under it, had endured the toil, and privations, and dangers of the first settlement.

The Supreme Council in England, now chosen by the stockholders themselves, appointed Sir Thomas West, Lord Delaware, Governor and Captain-General of Virginia. He was the third Lord Delaware, and the present (1843) Earl Delaware, John George West, is his lineal descendant. Sir Thomas Gates was appointed Lieutenant-Governor, and Sir George Somers, Admiral. Sir George was a member of Parliament, but upon being appointed to a colonial post his seat was declared vacant.

Nine vessels were speedily fitted out, with supplies of men and women, five hundred in number, and provisions and other stores for the colony. Newport, who was entrusted with the command of the fleet, and Gates and Somers, were each severally authorized, whichever might happen first to reach Jamestown, to supersede the existing administration there until the arrival of Lord Delaware, who was not to embark for several months, and who did not reach Virginia until the lapse of more than a year. This abundant caution defeated itself, for Newport, and the lieutenant-governor, and the admiral, finding it impossible to adjust the point of precedence among themselves, embarked together by way of compromise, in the same vessel, the Sea-Venture.*

The expedition sailed from Plymouth toward the end of May, 1609, and going, contrary to instructions, by the old circuitous route, via the Canaries and the West Indies, late in July, when in latitude thirty degrees north, and, as was supposed, within eight days' sail of Virginia, they were caught "in the tail of a hurricane," blowing from the northeast, accompanied by an appalling darkness, that continued for forty-four hours. Some of the vessels lost their masts, some their sails blown from the yards, the sea breaking over the ships.

---

* The following is a list of the vessels and their commanders: the Sea-Adventure, or Sea-Venture, Admiral Sir George Somers, with Sir Thomas Gates and Captain Christopher Newport; the Diamond, Captain Ratcliffe and Captain King; the Falcon, Captain Martin and Master Nelson; the Blessing, Gabriel Archer and Captain Adams; the Unity, Captain Wood and Master Pett; the Lion, Captain Webb; the Swallow, Captain Moon and Master Somers. There were also in company two smaller craft, a ketch and a pinnace.

> "When rattling thunder ran along the clouds,
> Did not the sailors poor and masters proud
> A terror feel, as struck with fear of God?"*

A small vessel was lost, July twenty-fourth, and the Sea-Venture, with Newport, Gates, Somers, and one hundred and fifty settlers, destined for Virginia, was separated from the other vessels of the expedition. The other vessels, shattered by the storm, and having suffered the loss of the greater portion of their supplies, and many of their number by sickness, at length reached Jamestown in August, 1609. They brought back Ratcliffe, or Sicklemore, who had been remanded to England on account of his mutinous conduct, also Martin and Archer, together with sundry other captains, and divers gentlemen of good means and high birth, and about three hundred settlers, the greater part of them profligate youths, packed off from home to escape ill destinies, broken-down gentlemen, bankrupt tradesmen, and the like, "decayed tapsters, and ostlers trade-fallen, the cankers of a calm world and long peace."

Upon the appearance of this fleet near Jamestown, Smith, not expecting such a supply, took them to be Spaniards, and prepared to encounter them, and the Indians readily offered their assistance. The colony had already, before the arrival of the fleet, been threatened with anarchy, owing to intelligence of the premature repeal of the charter, brought out by Captain Argall, and the new settlers had now no sooner landed than they gave rise to new confusion and disorder. The factious leaders, although they brought no commission with them, insisted on the abrogation of the existing charter, rejected the authority of Smith, whom they hated and feared, and undertook to usurp the government. Their capricious folly equalled their insolence; to-day the old commission must rule, to-morrow the new, the next day neither— thus, by continual change, plunging all things into anarchy.

Smith, filled with disgust, would cheerfully have embarked for England, but seeing little prospect of the arrival of the new commission, (which was in the possession of Gates on the Island of Bermudas,) he resolved to put an end to these incessant plots and

---

* Smith's Hist of Va.

machinations. The ringleaders, Ratcliffe, Archer, and others, he arrested; to cut off another source of disturbance, he gave permission to Percy, who was in feeble health, to embark for England, of which, however, he did not avail himself. West, with one hundred and twenty picked men, was detached to the falls of James River, and Martin, with nearly the same number, to Nansemond. Smith's presidency having expired about this time, he had been succeeded by Martin, who, conscious of his incompetency, had immediately resigned it to Smith. Martin, at Nansemond, seized the chief, and, capturing the town, occupied it with his detachment; but owing to want of judgment, or of vigilance, he suffered himself to be surprised by the savages, who slew many of his party, rescued the chief, and carried off their corn. Martin not long after returned to Jamestown, leaving his detachment to shift for themselves.

Smith going up the river to West's settlement at the falls, found the English planted in a place not only subject to the river's inundation, but "surrounded by many intolerable inconveniences." To remedy these, by a messenger he proposed to purchase from Powhatan his seat of that name, a little lower down the river. The settlers scornfully rejected the scheme, and became so mutinous that Smith landed among them and arrested the chief malecontents. But overpowered by numbers, being supported by only five men, he was forced to retire on board of a vessel lying in the river. The Indians daily supplied him with provisions, in requital for which the English plundered their corn, robbed their cultivated ground, beat them, broke into their cabins, and made them prisoners. They complained to Captain Smith that the men whom he had sent there as their protectors, "were worse than their old enemies, the Monacans." Smith embarking, had no sooner set sail for Jamestown than many of West's party were slain by the savages.

It so happened, that before Smith's vessel had dropped a mile and a half down the river, she ran aground, whereupon, making a virtue of necessity, he summoned the mutineers to a parley, and they, now seized with a panic, on account of the assault of a mere handful of Indians, submitted themselves to his mercy. He again arrested the ringleaders, and established the rest of the party at Powhatan, in the Indian palisade fort, which was so well fortified by poles and bark as to defy all the savages in Virginia. Dry cabins were also found there, and nearly two hundred acres of ground ready to be planted, and it was called Nonsuch, as being at once the strongest and most delightful place in the country. Nonsuch was the name of a royal residence in England.

When Smith was now on the eve of his departure, the arrival of West again threw all things aback into confusion. Nonsuch was abandoned, and all hands returned to the falls, and Smith, finding all his efforts abortive, embarked in a boat for Jamestown. During the voyage he was terribly wounded while asleep, by the accidental explosion of a bag of gunpowder, and in the paroxysm of pain he leapt into the river, and was well-nigh drowned before his companions could rescue him. Arriving at Jamestown in this helpless condition, he was again assailed by faction and mutiny, and one of his enemies even presented a cocked pistol at him in his bed; but the hand wanted the nerve to execute what the heart was base enough to design.

Ratcliffe, Archer, and their confederates, laid plans to usurp the government of the colony, whereupon Smith's faithful soldiers, fired with indignation at conduct so infamous, begged for permission to strike off their heads; but this he refused. He refused also to surrender the presidency to Percy. For this, Smith is censured by the historian Stith, who yet acknowledges that Percy was in too feeble health to control a mutinous colony. Anarchy being triumphant, Smith probably deemed it useless to appoint a governor over a mob. He at last, about Michaelmas, 1609, embarked for England, after a stay of a little more than two years in Virginia,* to which he never returned.

Here, then, closes the career of Captain John Smith in Virginia, "the father of the colony," and a hero like Bayard, "without fear and without reproach." One of his comrades, in deploring his departure, describes him as one who, in all his actions, made justice and prudence his guides, abhorring baseness, idleness, pride, and injustice; that in no danger would he send others where

---

* Smith, i. 239.

he would not lead them himself; that would never see his men want what he had, or could by any means procure; that would rather want than borrow, and rather starve than not pay; that loved action more than words, and hated falsehood and avarice worse than death; "whose adventures were our lives, and whose loss our deaths." Another of his soldiers said of him:—

> "I never knew a warrior but thee,
> From wine, tobacco, debts, dice, oaths, so free."

From the time of Smith's departure from Virginia to the year 1614, little is known of him. In that year he made his first voyage to New England. In the following year, after many disappointments, sailing again in a small vessel for that country, after a running fight with, and narrow escape from, two French privateers, near Fayal, he was captured, near Flores, by a half-piratical French squadron. After long detention he was carried to Rochelle, in France, and there charged with having burned Port Royal, in New France, which act had been committed by Captain Argall. Smith, at length, at the utmost hazard, escaped from his captors, and being assisted by several of the inhabitants of Rochelle, especially by Madame Chanoyes, he was enabled to return to England. The protective sympathy exhibited toward him, at several critical conjunctures, is thus mentioned in some complimentary verses prefixed to his History of Virginia:—

> "Tragabigzanda, Callamata's love,
> Deare Pocahontas, Madam Shanoi's too,
> Who did what love with modesty could do."

In 1616 Smith published his "Description of New England," composed while he was a prisoner on board of the French piratical vessel, in order, as he says, to keep his perplexed thoughts from too much meditation on his miserable condition. The Plymouth Company now conferred upon him the title of Admiral of New England. It was during this year that Pocahontas visited England. After this time, Smith never again visited America. When, in 1622, the news of the massacre reached England, he proposed to come over to Virginia with a proper force to reduce the savages to subjection, but his proposal was not accepted.

Captain Smith received little or no recompense for his colonial
discoveries, labors, and sacrifices; and after having spent five years,
and more than five hundred pounds, in the service of Virginia
and New England, he complains that in neither of those countries
has he one foot of land, nor even the house that he built, nor the
ground that he cultivated with his own hands, nor even any content or satisfaction at all, while he beheld those countries bestowed
upon men who neither could have them, nor even know of them
but by his descriptions. It is remarkable that in his "Newes
from Virginia," published in 1608, no allusion is made to his
rescue by Pocahontas. In 1612 appeared his work entitled "A
Map of Virginia, with a Description of the Country, Commodities, People, Government, and Religion, etc.," and in 1620,
"New England Trials." In 1626 was published his "General
History of Virginia, New England, and the Summer Isles," the
greater part of which had already been published in 1625, by
Purchas, in his "Pilgrim." The second and sixth books of this
history were composed by Smith himself; the third was compiled
by Rev. William Simons, Doctor of Divinity, and the rest by
Smith from the letters and journals of about thirty different
writers. During the year 1625 he published "An Accidence, or
the Pathway to Experience necessary for all young Seamen," and
in 1627 "A Sea Grammar." In 1630 he gave to the public
"The True Travels, Adventures, and Observations of Captain
John Smith, in Europe, Asia, Africa, and America, from 1593
to 1629." This work, together with "The General History," was
republished by Rev. Dr. John H. Rice, in 1819, at Richmond,
Virginia. The copy is exact and complete, except some maps
and engravings of but little value. The obsolete orthography and
typography of the work confines it to a limited circle of readers.
It is now out of print and rare. In 1631 Smith published "Advertisements for the unexperienced planters of New England, or
anywhere," etc., said to be the most elaborate of his productions.
The learned, judicious, and accurate historian, Grahame, considers
Smith's writings on colonization, superior to those of Lord
Bacon. At the time of his death, Smith was engaged in composing a "History of the Sea." So famous was he in his own
day, that he complains of some extraordinary incidents in his life

having been *mis*represented on the stage. He was gifted by nature with a person and address of singular fascination. He married, and the author of a recent interesting English book of travels, a lineal descendant, refers with just pride to his distinguished ancestor: "On the upper waters of the Alt, near the celebrated Rothen Thurm, (or Red Tower,) several severe engagements ushered in the seventeenth century. It was at this time that the wave of Mohammedan conquest rolled on, and broke over Hungary, Transylvania, and Wallachia, and, whether advancing or retiring, swept those unfortunate lands with equal severity. Sigismund Bathori, after holding his own for awhile in Transylvania against the emperor, was obliged to succumb; the Voyvode of Wallachia, appointed by the Porte, aroused, by his cruelties, an insurrection against him, and the moment appeared favorable for thrusting back the Turkish power beyond the Danube. The Austrian party not only appointed a new Voyvode, but marched a large army, chiefly Hungarian, into the country, and were at first victorious, in a well-contested battle. But, at length, between the river and the heights of the Rothen Thurm range, the Christian army was attacked with impetuosity by a far greater number, composed principally of Tartars, and was entirely cut to pieces. In this catastrophe several English officers, serving with the Hungarian army, were slain; and *an ancestor of the author's*, who was left for dead on the field, after describing this 'dismall battell,' gives their names, and observes that 'they did what men could do, and when they could do no more, left there their bodies in testimony of their mind.'"[*]

Captain John Smith died at London, 1631, in the fifty-second year of his age. He was buried in St. Sepulchre's Church, Skinner Street, London; and from Stowe's Survey of London, printed in 1633, it appears there was a tablet erected to his memory in that church, inscribed with his motto, "Vincere est vivere," and the following epitaph:—

>Here lies one conquered that hath conquered kings,
>Subdued large territories, and done things
>Which, to the world, impossible would seem,
>But that the truth is held in more esteem.

---

[*] A Year with the Turks, by Warington W. Smyth, A.M., 27.

> Shall I report his former service done
> In honor of God and Christendom,
> How that he did divide from pagans three
> Their heads and lives, types of his chivalry;
> For which great service, in that climate done,
> Brave Sigismundus, (King of Hungarion,)
> Did give him a coat of arms to wear,
> Those conquered heads got by his sword and spear?
> Or shall I tell of his adventures since
> Done in Virginia, that large continent,
> How that he subdued kings unto his yoke,
> And made those heathens fly as wind doth smoke,
> And made their land, being of so large a station,
> A habitation for our Christian nation,
> Where God is glorified, their wants supplied,
> Which else for necessaries might have died?
> But what avails his conquest? now he lies
> Interred in earth, a prey for worms and flies.
> O may his soul in sweet Elysium sleep
> Until the Keeper, that all souls doth keep,
> Return to judgment, and that after thence
> With angels he may have his recompense.

The tablet was destroyed by the great fire in the year 1666, and all now remaining to the memory of Captain Smith is a large flat stone, in front of the communion-table, engraved with his coat of arms, upon which the three Turks' heads are still distinguishable.* The historian Grahame concludes a notice of him in these words: "But Smith's renown will break forth again, and once more be commensurate with his desert. It will grow with the growth of men and letters in America, and whole nations of its admirers have yet to be born." A complete edition of his works would be a valuable addition to American historical literature. The sculptor's art ought to present a fitting memorial of him and of Pocahontas, in the metropolis of Virginia.

---

* Godwin's Churches of London, i. 9.

CHAPTER VI.

The Indians of Virginia—Their Form and Features—Mode of wearing their Hair—Clothing—Ornaments—Manner of Living—Diet—Towns and Cabins—Arms and Implements—Religion—Medicine—The Seasons—Hunting—Sham-fights—Music—Indian Character.

The mounds—monuments of a primitive race, found scattered over many parts of North America, especially in the valley of the Mississippi—have long attracted the attention of men curious in such speculations. These heir-looms of dim, oblivious centuries, seem to whisper mysteriously of a shadowy race, populous, nomadic, not altogether uncivilized, idolatrous, worshipping "in high places." The Anglo-Saxon ploughshare is busy in obliterating these memorials, but many yet survive, and many, perhaps, remain yet to be discovered. Whether they were the work of the progenitors of the Indians, or of a race long since extinct, is a question for such as have taste and leisure for such abstruse inquiries. The general absence of written language and of architectural remains, indicates a low grade of civilization, and yet the relics that have been disinterred, and the enormous extent of some of their earth-works, would argue a degree of art, and of collective industry, to which the Indians are entire strangers. We may, at the least, conclude that either they, in the lapse of ages, have greatly degenerated, or that the mound-makers were a distinct and superior race. Some of these mounds are found in Virginia. The most remarkable of these is the Mammoth Mound, in the County of Marshall. Mr. Jefferson[*] was of opinion that there is nothing extant in Virginia deserving the name of an Indian monument, as he would not dignify with that name their stone arrow-points, tomakawks, pipes, and rude images. Of labor on a large scale there is no remain, unless it be the barrows, or mounds, of which many are found all over this country.

---

[*] Notes on Va., 104, ed. 1853.

They are of different sizes; some of them constructed of earth, and some of loose stones. That they were repositories of the dead is obvious, but on what occasion they were constructed is a matter of doubt. Mr. Jefferson opened one of them near Monticello, and found it filled with human bones. The Mammoth Mound in Marshall County is 69 feet high, 900 in circumference at the base; in shape the frustrum of a cone, with a flat top 50 feet in diameter. An oak standing on the top has been estimated to be five hundred years old. In the interior have been discovered vaults, with pieces of timber, human skeletons, ivory beads, and other ivory ornaments, sea-shells, copper bracelets around the wrists of skeletons, with laminated mica, and a stone with hieroglyphic characters inscribed on it, in the opinion of some, of African origin. The whole mass of the mound is studded with blue spots, supposed to have been occasioned by deposites of the remains of human bodies consumed by fire. Seven lesser mounds are connected with the main one by low entrenchments. Some rude towers of stone, greatly dilapidated, are also found in the neighborhood. Porcelain beads are picked up, and a stone idol has been found, as also tubes of lead, blue steatite, syphon-like, drilled, twelve inches long, and finely polished.

The places of habitation of the Indians may yet be identified along the banks of rivers, by the deposites of shells of oysters and muscles, which they subsisted upon, as also of ashes and charred wood, arrow-points, fragments of pottery, pipes, tomahawks, mortars, etc. Vestiges may be traced of their moving back their cabins when urged by the accumulation of shells and ashes. Standing on such a spot one's fancy may almost repeople it with the shadowy forms of the aborigines, and imagine the flames of the council-fire projecting its red glare upon the face of the York or the James, and hear their wild cries mingling with the dash of waves and the roar of the forest. Here they rejoice over their victories, plan new enterprises of blood, and celebrate the war-dance by the rude music of the drum and the rattle, commingled with their own discordant yells.

The Indians of Virginia were tall, erect, and well-proportioned, with prominent cheek-bones; eyes dark and brilliant, with an animal expression, and a sort of squint; their hair dark and straight. The chiefs were distinguished by a long pendant lock. The Indians had little or no beard, and the women served as barbers, eradicating the beard, and grating away the hair with two shells. Like all savages, they were fond of toys and tawdry ornaments. The principal garment was a mantle, in winter dressed with the fur in, in summer with it out; but the common sort had scarce anything to hide their nakedness, save grass or leaves, and in summer they all went nearly naked. The females always wore a cincture around the middle. Some covered themselves with a mantle of curiously interwoven turkey feathers, pretty and comfortable. The greater part went barefoot; some wore moccasins, a rude sandal of buckskin. Some of the women tattooed their skins with grotesque figures. They adorned the ear with pendants of copper, or a small living snake, yellow or green, or a dead rat, and the head with a bird's wing, a feather, the rattle of a rattlesnake, or the hand of an enemy. They stained the head and shoulder red with the juice of the puccoon.

The red men dwelt for the most part on the banks of rivers. They spent the time in fishing, hunting, war, or indolence, despising domestic labor, and assigning it to the women. These made mats, baskets, pottery, hollowed out stone-mortars, pounded the corn in them, made bread, cooked, planted corn, gathered it, carried burdens, etc. Infants were inured to hardship and exposure. The Indians kindled a fire quickly "by chafing a dry pointed stick in a hole of a little square piece of wood, which, taking fire, sets fire to moss, leaves, or any such dry thing." They subsisted upon fish, game, the natural fruits of the earth, and corn, which they planted. The tuckahoe-root, during the summer, was an important article of diet in marshy places. Their cookery was not less rude than their other habits, yet *pone* and *hominy* have been borrowed from them, as also, it is said, the mode of *barbecuing* meat. *Pone*, according to the historian Beverley, is derived "not from the Latin panis, but from oppone," an Indian word; according to Smith, *ponap* signifies meal-dumplings. The natives did not refuse to eat grubs, snakes, and the insect locust. Their bread was sometimes made of wild oats, or the seed of the sunflower, but mostly of corn. Their salt was only such as could be procured from ashes. They were fond of roasting ears of corn, and they welcomed the crop with the festival of the green-corn dance. From walnuts and hickory-nuts, pounded in a mortar, they expressed a liquid called pawcohiccora. The hickory-tree is indigenous in America. Beverley has fallen into a curious mistake in saying that the peach-tree is a native of this country. Indian-corn and tobacco, although called indigenous, appear to have grown only when cultivated. They are never found of wild spontaneous growth. In their journeys the Indians were in the habit of providing themselves with rockahominy, or corn parched and reduced to a powder.

They dwelt in towns, the cabins being constructed of saplings bent over at the top and tied together, and thatched with reeds, or covered with mats or bark, the smoke escaping through an aperture at the apex. The door, if any, consisted of a pendant mat. They sate on the ground, the better sort on matchcoats or mats. Their fortifications consisted of palisades ten or twelve feet high, sometimes encompassing an entire town, sometimes a part. Within these enclosures they preserved, with pious care, their idols and relics, and the remains of their chiefs. In hunting and war they used the bow and arrow—the bow usually of locust, the arrow of reed, or a wand. The Indian notched his arrow with a beaver's tooth set in a stick, which he used in the place of a file. The arrow was winged with a turkey-feather, fastened with a sort of glue extracted from the velvet horns of the deer. The arrow was headed with an arrow-point of stone, often made of white quartz, and exquisitely formed, some barbed, some with a serrate edge. These are yet to be found in every part of the country. For knives the red men made use of sharpened reeds, or shells, or stone; and for hatchets, tomahawks of stone, sharpened at one end or both. Those sharpened only at one end, at the other were either curved to a tapering point, or spheroidally rounded off, so as to serve the purpose of a hammer for breaking or pounding. In the middle a circular indenture was made, to secure the tomahawk to the handle. They soon, however, procured iron hatchets from the English. Trees the Indians felled by fire; canoes were made by dint of burning and scraping with shells and tomahawks. Some of their canoes were not less than forty or fifty feet long. Canoe is a West Indian word, the Powhatan word is quintan, or aquintan.* The women manufactured a thread, or string of bark, or of a kind of grass called pemminaw, or of the sinews of the deer. A large pipe, adorned with the wings of a bird, or with beads, was the symbol of friendship, called the pipe of peace. A war-chief was styled werowance, and a war-council, matchacomoco. In war, like all savages, they relied mainly on surprise, treachery, and ambuscade; in the open field they were timid; and their cruelty, as usual, was proportionate to their cowardice.

The Virginia Indians were of course idolatrous, and their chief idol, called Okee, represented the spirit of evil, to appease whom they burnt sacrifices. They were greatly under the influence and control of their priests and conjurors, who wore a grotesque dress, performed a variety of divinations, conjurations, and enchantments, called powwowings, after the manner of wizards, and by their superior cunning and shrewdness, and some scanty knowledge of medicine, contrived to render themselves objects of veneration, and to live upon the labor of others. The superstition of the savages was commensurate with their ignorance. Near the falls of the James River, about a mile back from the river, there were some impressions on a rock like the footsteps of a giant, being about five feet apart, which the Indians averred to be the footprints of their god. They submitted with Spartan fortitude to cruel tortures imposed by their idolatry, especially in the mysterious and horrid ordeal of huskanawing. The avowed object of this ordeal was to obliterate forever from the memory of the youths subjected to it all recollection of their previous lives. The house in which they kept the Okee was called Quioccasan, and was surrounded by posts, with human faces rudely carved and painted on them. Altars on which sacrifices were offered, were held in great veneration.

The diseases of the Indians were not numerous; their remedies few and simple, their physic consisting mainly of the bark and roots of trees. Sweating was a favorite remedy, and every town was provided with a sweat-house. The patient, issuing from

---

* Strachey's Virginia Britannica.

the heated atmosphere, plunged himself in cold water, after the manner of the Russian bath.

The Indians celebrated certain festivals by pastimes, games, and songs. The year they divided into five seasons, Cattapeak, the budding time of spring; Messinough, roasting ear time; Cohattayough, summer; Taquitock, the fall of the leaf; and Popanow, winter, sometimes called Cohonk, after the cry of the migratory wild-geese. Engaged from their childhood in fishing and hunting, they became expert and familiar with the haunts of game and fish. The luggage of hunting parties was carried by the women. Deer were taken by surrounding them, and kindling fires enclosing them in a circle, till they were killed; sometimes they were driven into the water, and there captured. The Indian, hunting alone, would stalk behind the skin of a deer. Game being abundant in the mountain country, hunting parties repaired to the heads of the rivers at the proper season, and this probably engendered the continual hostilities that existed between the Powhatans of the tide-water region and the Monacans, on the upper waters of the James, and the Mannahoacks, at the head of the Rappahannock. The savages were in the habit of exercising themselves in sham-fights. Upon the first discharge of arrows they burst forth in horrid shrieks and the war-whoop, so that as many infernal hell-hounds could not have been more terrific. "All their actions, cries, and gestures, in charging and retreating," says Captain Smith, "were so strained to the height of their quality and nature, that the strangeness thereof made it seem very delightful." For their music they used a thick cane, on which they piped as on a recorder. They had also a rude sort of drum, and rattles of gourds or pumpkins. The chastity of their women was not held in much value, but wives were careful not to be suspected without the consent of their husbands.

The Indians were hospitable, in their manners exhibiting that imperturbable equanimity and uniform self-possession and repose which distinguish the refined society of a high civilization. Extremes meet. Yet the Indians were in everything wayward and inconstant, unless where restrained by fear; cunning, quick of apprehension, and ingenious; some were brave; most of them timorous and cautious; all savage. Not ungrateful for benefits, they seldom forgave an injury. They rarely stole from each other, lest their conjurors should reveal the offence, and they should be punished.*

---

* Smith, ii. 129, 137; Beverley, B. iii.; Drake's Book of the Indians; Thatcher's Lives of the Indians; Bancroft's History of U. S., vol. iii. cap. xxii.

CHAPTER VII.

1609-1614.

Condition of the Colony at the time of Smith's Departure—Assaults of Indians—"The Starving Time"—The Sea-Venture—Situation of the English on the Island of Bermuda—They Embark for Virginia—Arrive at Jamestown—Jamestown abandoned—Colonists meet Lord Delaware's Fleet—Return to Jamestown—Delaware's Discipline—The Church at Jamestown—Sir George Somers—Delaware returns to England—Percy. Governor—New Charter—Sir Thomas Dale, Governor—Martial Laws—Henrico Founded—Plantations and Hundreds settled—Argall makes Pocahontas a Prisoner—Dale's expedition up York River—Rolfe visits Powhatan—Dale returns to Jamestown—Rolfe marries Pocahontas—The Chickahominies enter into Treaty of Peace—Community of Goods abolished—Argall's Expeditions against the French in Acadia—Captures Fort at New Amsterdam.

CAPTAIN SMITH, upon embarking for England, left at Jamestown three ships, seven boats, a sufficient stock of provision, four hundred and ninety odd settlers, twenty pieces of cannon, three hundred muskets, with other guns, pikes, swords, and ammunition, and one hundred soldiers acquainted with the Indian language, and the nature of the country.* The settlers were, for the most part, poor gentlemen, serving-men, libertines; and with such materials the wonder is, not that the settlement was retarded by many disasters, but that it was effected at all. Lord Bacon says: "It is a shameful and unblessed thing to take the scum of people, wicked, condemned men, with whom you plant; and not only so, but it spoileth the plantation, for they will ever live like rogues, and not fall to work, but be lazy and do mischief; spend victuals and be quickly weary."† Immediately upon

---

* The colony was provided with fishing-nets, working tools, apparel, six mares and a horse, five or six hundred swine, with some goats and sheep. Jamestown was strongly fortified with palisades, and contained fifty or sixty houses. There were, besides, five or six other forts and plantations. There was only one carpenter in the colony; three others were learning that trade. There were two blacksmiths and two sailors.

† Bacon's Essays, 123.

Smith's departure the Indians renewed their attacks. Percy, the Earl of Northumberland's brother, for a time administered the government; but it soon fell into the hands of the seditious malecontents. Provisions growing scarce, West and Ratcliffe embarked in small vessels to procure corn. Ratcliffe, inveigled by Powhatan, was slain with thirty of his companions, two only escaping, of whom one, a boy, Henry Spilman, a young gentleman well descended, was rescued by Pocahontas, and he afterwards lived for many years among the Patawomekes, acquired their language, and often proved serviceable as an interpreter for his countrymen. He was slain by the savages, on the banks of the Potomac, in 1622. The loss of Captain Smith was soon felt by the colonists: they were now continually exposed to the arrow and the tomahawk; the common store was consumed by the commanders and the savages; swords and guns were bartered with the Indians for food; and within six months after Smith's departure the number of English in Virginia was reduced from five hundred to sixty men, women, and children. These found themselves in a starving condition, subsisting on roots, herbs, acorns, walnuts, berries, and fish. Starch became an article of diet, and even dogs, cats, rats, snakes, toadstools, and the skins of horses. The body of an Indian was disinterred and eaten; nay, at last, the colonists preyed on the dead bodies of each other. It was even alleged that a husband murdered his wife for a cannibal repast; upon his trial, however, it appeared that the cannibalism was feigned, to palliate the murder. He was put to death—being burned according to law. This was long afterwards remembered as "the starving time." Sir Thomas Smith, treasurer of the Virginia Company, was bitterly denounced by the sufferers for neglecting to send out the necessary supplies. The happiest day that many of them expected ever to see, was when the Indians had killed a mare, the people wishing, while the carcass was boiling, "that Sir Thomas was upon her back in the kettle." It seemed to them as if the Earl of Salisbury's threat of abandoning the colony to its fate, was now to be actually carried into effect; but it is to be recollected that a large portion of ample supplies, that had been sent out from England for the colony, had been lost by storm and shipwreck.

It has before been mentioned, that toward the end of July, 1609, in a violent tempest, the Sea-Venture, with Newport, Gates, and Somers, and one hundred and fifty souls, had been separated from the rest of the fleet. Racked by the fury of the sea, she sprang a leak, and the water soon rose in her hold above two tiers of hogsheads that stood over the ballast, and the crew had to stand up to their waists in the water, and bail out with buckets, baricos, and kettles. They continued bailing and pumping for three days and nights without intermission, yet the water appeared rather to gain upon them than decrease; so that all hands, being at length utterly exhausted, came to the desperate resolution to shut down the hatches and resign themselves to their fate; and some having "good and comfortable waters fetched them, and drank to one another as taking their last farewell." During all this time the aged Sir George Somers, sitting upon the quarter-deck, scarce taking time to eat or sleep, bearing the helm so as to keep the ship as upright as possible, but for which she must have foundered,—at last descried land. At this time many of the unhappy crew were asleep, and when the voice of Sir George was heard announcing "land," it seemed as if it was a voice from heaven, and they hurried up above the hatches to look for what they could scarcely credit. On finding the intelligence true, and that they were, indeed, in sight of land,—although it was a coast that all men usually tried to avoid,—yet they now spread all sail to reach it. Soon the ship struck upon a rock, till a surge of the sea dashed her off from thence, and so from one to another till, at length, fortunately, she lodged (July twenty-eighth) upright between two rocks, as if she was laid up in a natural dry-dock. Till this, at every lurch they had expected instant death; but now, all at once, the storm gave place to a calm, and the billows, which at each successive dash had threatened destruction, were stilled; and, quickly taking to their boats, they reached the shore, distant upwards of a league, without the loss of a single man out of upwards of one hundred and fifty. Their joy at an escape so unexpected and almost miraculous, arose to the pitch of amazement. Yet their escape was not more wonderful in their eyes than their preservation after they had landed on the island; for the Spaniards had always looked upon it as more frightful than purgatory itself; and all seamen had reckoned it no better than an enchanted den of Furies and devils—the most dangerous, desolate, and forlorn place in the whole world; instead of which it turned out to be healthful, fertile, and charming.

The Bermudas are a cluster of islands lying in the Atlantic Ocean, at the distance of six hundred miles from the American Continent, extending, in crescent form, from east to west; in length, twenty miles; in breadth, two and a half. On the coast of the principal of these islands, Bermuda, the Sea-Venture was wrecked; and, on landing, the English found, instead of those gloomy horrors with which a superstitious fancy had invested it, a terrestrial paradise blessed with all the charms of exquisite scenery, luxuriant vegetation, and a voluptuous atmosphere, which have since been celebrated in the verse of a modern poet. Here they remained for nearly a year. Fish, fowl, turtle, and wild hogs supplied the English with abundant food; the palmetto leaf furnished a cover for their cabins. They had daily morning and evening prayers, and on Sunday divine service was performed and two sermons preached by the chaplain, the Rev. Mr. Bucke. He was a graduate of Oxford, and received the appointment of chaplain to the Virginia expedition upon the recommendation of Dr. Ravis, Bishop of London. Mr. Bucke was the second minister sent out from England to Virginia, being successor to Rev. Robert Hunt. The company of the Sea-Venture were summoned to worship by the sound of the church-going bell, and the roll was called, and absentees were duly punished. The clergyman performed the ceremony of marriage once during the sojourn on the island, the parties being Sir George Somers' cook and a maid-servant, (of one Mrs. Mary Horton,) named Elizabeth Persons. The communion was once celebrated. The infant child of one John Rolfe—a daughter, born on the island—was christened, February eleventh, by the name of Bermuda, Captain Newport, the Rev. Mr. Bucke, and Mrs. Horton being witnesses. It would seem from this, that John Rolfe was a widower when he afterwards married Pocahontas. Another infant, born on the island, a boy, was christened by the name of Bermudas. Six of the company, including the wife of Sir Thomas Gates, died there.

Living in the midst of peace and plenty in this sequestered and delightful place of abode, after escaping from the yawning perils of the deep, many of the English lost all desire ever to leave the island, and some were even mutinously determined to remain there. Gates, however, having decked the long-boat of the Sea-Venture with the hatches, dispatched the mate, Master Raven, an expert mariner, with eight men, to Virginia for succor; but the boat was never more heard of. Discord and insubordination found a place among the exiles of the Bermudas; and even the leaders, Gates and Somers, lived for awhile asunder. At length, while Somers was engaged in surveying the islands, Gates completed a vessel of about eighty tons, constructed somewhat after the manner of Robinson Crusoe, partly from the timber of the Sea-Venture, and the rest of cedar. A small bark was also built under the direction of Sir George Somers, of cedar, without the use of any iron, save a bolt in her keel. These two vessels were named, the one the "Patience," the other the "Deliverance." Finally, on the 10th day of May, 1610, after the lapse of nine months spent on the island, and nearly a year since their departure from England, harmony being restored, and the leaders reconciled, they embarked in these cedar vessels for Virginia.

The name of Sir Thomas West, afterwards Lord la Ware, or De la War, or Delaware, appears in the commission appointed in the year of James the First, for inquiring into the case of all such persons as should be found openly opposing the doctrines of the Church of England. Such was the spirit of that age, by which standard the men of that age ought to be judged. Lord Delaware was, nevertheless, distinguished for his virtues and his generous devotion to the welfare of the infant colony of Virginia—a man of approved courage, temper, and experience. The Rev. William Crashaw, father of the poet of that name, at the period of Lord Delaware's appointment to the place of Governor of Virginia, was preacher at the Temple; and he delivered a sermon before his lordship, and others of his majesty's council for the Colony of Virginia, and the rest of the adventurers or stockholders in that plantation, upon occasion of his lordship's embarkation for Virginia, on the 21st day of February, 1609–10. The text was from Daniel, xii. 3: "They that turn many to righteousness shall shine as the stars forever and ever." This sermon was printed by William Welby, and sold in Paul's Churchyard, at the sign of the Swan, 1610, and is the first missionary sermon preached in England to any of her sons embarking for Virginia. Crashaw, in this discourse, urges it warmly upon his countrymen to aid the enterprise of planting the colony; rejects, with indignant scorn, the more sordid motives of mere lucre, and appeals to loftier principles, and the more elevated motives of Christian beneficence. But although he rejects motives of mere profit, he tells his auditors that if they will pursue their object, animated by these enlarged views, they will probably find the plantation eventually a source of pecuniary profit, the soil being good, the commodities numerous and necessary for England, the distance not great, and the voyage easy, so that God's blessing was alone wanting to make it gainful. In his peroration, the preacher, apostrophizing Lord Delaware, excites his generous emulation by a personal appeal, reminding him of the gallant exploit of his ancestor, Sir Roger la Warr, who, assisted by John de Pelham, captured the King of France at the battle of Poictiers. In memory of which exploit, Sir Roger la Warr—Lord la Warr according to Froissart—had the crampet or chape of his sword for a badge of that honor. Crashaw bitterly denounces the Papists, and the Brownists, and factious separatists, and exhorts the Virginia Company not to suffer such to have any place in the new colony. Rome and Geneva were the Scylla and Charybdis of the Church of England.* Lord Delaware sailed in February for Virginia.

Gates and Somers, after leaving the Bermudas in May, in fourteen days reached Jamestown, where they found only sixty miserable colonists surviving. Sir Thomas Gates, Lieutenant-Governor, landing on the twenty-fourth of May, caused the church-bell to be rung; and such as were able repaired thither, and the Rev. Mr. Bucke delivered an earnest and sorrowful prayer upon their finding so unexpectedly all things so full of misery and misgovernment. At the conclusion of the religious service the new commission of Gates was read; Percy, the acting president,

---

* Anderson's Hist. of Col. Church, i. 232.

scarcely able to stand, surrendered up the former charter and his commission. The palisades of the fort were found torn down; the ports open; the gates distorted from the hinges; the houses of those who had died, broken up and burned for firewood, and their store of provision exhausted. Gates reluctantly resolved to abandon the plantation, and to return to England by way of Newfoundland, where he expected to receive succor from English fishing vessels. June seventh, they buried their ordnance and armor at the gate of the fort, and, at the beat of drum, embarked in four pinnaces. Some of the people were, with difficulty, restrained from setting fire to the town; but Sir Thomas Gates, with a select party, remained on shore until the others had embarked, and he was the last man that stepped into the boat. They fired a farewell volley; but not a tear was shed at their departure from a spot associated with so much misery. How often is the hour of despair but the deeper darkness that immediately precedes the dawn! At noon they reached Hog Island, and on the next morning, while anchored off Mulberry Island, they were met by a long-boat with dispatches from Lord Delaware, who had arrived with three vessels, after a voyage of three months and a half from England.* Upon this intelligence Gates, with his company, returned up the river to, Jamestown on the same day. Lord Delaware arrived there with his three vessels on the ninth, and on the morning of the following day (Sunday) he landed at the south gate of the fort, and although the Lieutenant-Governor, Sir Thomas Gates, with his company, were drawn up to meet him, he fell on his knees, and remained for some time in silent prayer. After this he repaired to the church, and heard a sermon delivered by the Rev. Mr. Bucke. A council was then called, and the governor delivered an address to the colonists. The hand of a superintending and benignant Providence was plainly manifested in all these circumstances. The arrival of Sir Thomas Gates rescued the colony from the jaws of famine; his prudence preserved the fort at Jamestown, which the unhappy colonists, upon abandoning the place, wished to destroy, so as to cut off all possibility of a return; had their return been longer delayed, the

---

* Anderson's Hist. of Col. Church, i. 263.

savages might have destroyed the fort; had they set sail sooner, they would probably have missed Lord Delaware's fleet, as they had intended to sail by way of Newfoundland, in a direction contrary to that by which Lord Delaware approached.*

---

* The wreck of the Sea-Venture appears to have suggested to Shakespeare the groundwork for the plot of "The Tempest," several incidents and passages being evidently taken from the contemporary accounts of that disaster, as narrated by Jordan and the Council of the Virginia Company.

"Boatswain, down with the top-mast, yare
Lower, lower; bring her to try with the main course."

Captain Smith, in his Sea-Grammar, published 1627, under the article how to handle a ship in a storm, says: "Let us lie as try with our main course—that is, to haul the tack aboard, the sheet close aft, the boling set up, and the helm tied close aboard." Again, the boatswain says: "Lay her a-hold, a-hold; set her two courses." The two courses are the mainsail and the foresail; and to lay a ship a-hold is to bring her to lie as near the wind as she can. These, and other nautical orders, are such as the brave old Somers probably gave when trying to keep the ship as upright as possible.

"We are merely cheated of our lives by drunkards."

This was suggested to the poet by the recorded incident of part of the crew of the Sea-Venture having undertaken to drown their despair in drunkenness.

"Farewell, my wife and children!
Farewell, brother!
Ant. Let's all sink with the king.
Seb. Let's take leave of him."

These answer to the leave-taking of the Sea-Venture's crew. Jordan, in his narrative, says: "It is reported that this land of Bermudas, with the islands about it, are enchanted and kept by evil and wicked spirits," etc. Shakespeare accordingly employs Prospero, Ariel, and Caliban to personate this fabled enchantment of the island. Ariel's task is, at Prospero's bidding—

"To fly,
To swim, to dive into the fire, to ride
On the curled clouds."

The tempest, in which the ship was wrecked, is thus described by Ariel:—

"I boarded the king's ship; now on the beak,
Now in the waist, the deck, in every cabin,
I flamed amazement: sometimes I'd divide,
And burn in many places; on the top-mast,
The yards, and bowsprit, would I flame distinctly,
Then meet and join; Jove's lightnings, the precursors

Lord Delaware, Governor and Captain-General, was accompanied by Sir Ferdinand Waynman, Master of the Horse, who died shortly afterwards; Captain Holcroft; Captain Lawson; and

> O' the dreadful thunder-claps, more momentary
> And sight-outrunning were not; the fire, and cracks
> Of sulphurous roaring, the most mighty Neptune
> Seemed to besiege, and make his bold waves tremble."

Again :—

> "Not a soul
> But felt a fever of the mad and played
> Some tricks of desperation."

The almost miraculous escape of all from the very jaws of impending death, is thus alluded to by Ariel in her report to Prospero:—

> "Not a hair perished;
> On their sustaining garments not a blemish,
> But fresher than before: and as thou bad'st me,
> In troops I have dispersed them 'bout the isle."

The particular circumstances of the wreck are given quite exactly in the familiar verses:—

> "Safely in harbor
> Is the king's ship; in the deep nook, where once
> Thou call'st me up at midnight to fetch dew
> From the still-vexed Bermoothes, there she's hid."

Bermoothes, the Spanish pronunciation of Bermudas, or Bermudez, the original name of the island, taken, as is said, from that of a Spanish captain wrecked there. Another real incident is referred to in the following verses, the time only being transposed:—

> "The mariners all under hatches stowed;
> Whom, with a charm joined to their suffered labor,
> I have left asleep."

The return of the other seven vessels of the fleet is described with a change, however, of the sea in which they sailed, and in their place of destination:—

> "And for the rest of the fleet,
> Which I dispersed, they all have met again;
> And are upon the Mediterranean flote,
> Bound sadly home for Naples;
> Supposing that they saw the king's ship wrecked
> And his great person perish."

For nearly a year after the Sea-Venture's separation from the fleet, it was believed, in Virginia and in England, that she and her company were lost. Smith

other gentlemen. Lord Delaware was the first executive officer of Virginia with the title of Governor; and the titles of Governor and Captain-General were ever after given to the colonial chief magistrates of Virginia. Under Lord Delaware's discreet and energetic management, discipline and industry were speedily restored, the hours of labor being set from six o'clock in the morning to ten, and from two to four in the afternoon. The store of provisions that he had brought over with him was sufficient to supply four hundred men for twelve months. He gave orders for repairing the church. Its length was sixty feet, and its breadth twenty-four, and it was to have a chancel of cedar and a communion-table of black-walnut, and the pews of cedar, with handsome wide windows, to shut and open according to the weather, made of the same wood; as also a pulpit with a font hewed out hollow like a canoe, with two bells at the west end. The building was so constructed as to be very light within; and the Lord Governor and Captain-General caused it to be kept passing sweet, and trimmed up with divers flowers. There was also a sexton belonging to it. Every Sunday there were two sermons delivered, and every Thursday one—there being two preachers who took their weekly turns. In the morning of every day, at the ringing of the bell at ten o'clock, the people attended prayers; and also again at four in the afternoon, before supper.

---

and Pocahontas may have suggested some materials for the characters of Ferdinand and Miranda.

Shakespeare, after abandoning the stage, in 1607 or 1608, about the time of the first landing at Jamestown, remained in London for some four or five years. Smith, and the early colonists of Virginia, had many of them probably witnessed the theatrical performances at the Globe or Black Fryars; Beggars' Bush, now Jordan's Point, an early plantation on the James River, derived its name from a comedy of Fletcher's. Shakespeare was, no doubt, quite familiar with the more remarkable incidents of the first settlement of the colony: the early voyages; the first discovery; the landing; Smith's rencontres with the Indians; his rescue by Pocahontas; the starving time, etc. Smith, indeed, as has been before mentioned, complained of his exploits and adventures having been misrepresented on the stage, in London. That Shakespeare makes few or no allusions to these incidents, is because they occurred after nearly all his plays had been composed. "The Tempest," however, was written several years after the landing at Jamestown, being one of his latest productions—a creation of his maturest intellect.

On Sunday, when the Governor went to church, he was accompanied by the councillors, officers, and all the gentlemen, with a guard of halberdiers in his lordship's livery, handsome red cloaks, to the number of fifty on each side, and behind him. In the church his lordship had his seat in the choir, in a green velvet chair, with a cloth, and also a velvet cushion laid on the table before him on which he knelt. The council and officers sate on each side of him, and when he returned to his house he was escorted back in the same manner. The newly appointed council consisted of Sir Thomas Gates, whose title was changed from that of Lieutenant-Governor to that of Lieutenant-General; Sir George Somers, Admiral; Captain George Percy; Sir Ferdinando Wayman, Master of the Ordnance; Captain Newport, Vice-Admiral; and Mr. Strachey, Secretary and Recorder. Strachey, who appears to have been a scholar, published an interesting account of the colony at this period. Some of the houses at Jamestown were covered with boards; some with Indian mats. They were comfortable, and securely protected from the savages by the forts. Lord Delaware was a generous friend of the colony; but it was as yet quite too poor and too much in its infancy to maintain the state suitable to him and his splendid retinue. The fashions of a court were preposterous in a wilderness. On the ninth of June, Sir George Somers was dispatched, in compliance with his own suggestion, in his cedar vessel to the Bermudas, accompanied by Argall in another vessel, to procure further supplies for the colony. Captain Argall, in consequence of adverse winds and heavy fogs, returned to Jamestown. Sir George Somers, after much difficulty, reached his destination, where he shortly after died, at a spot on which the town of St. George commemorates his name. The islands themselves received the designation of his surname, and were afterwards called the Summer Islands. It is said that the Bermudas were at first named in England "Virginiola," but shortly after the "Summer Islands," partly in allusion to their temperature, and partly in honor of Sir George.* It was remarked of him that he was "a lamb upon land; a lion at sea." As his life had been divided between the

---

* Court and Times of James the First, 160.

Old World and the New, so after his death his remains were buried, part at Bermuda, part at Whitchurch, Dorsetshire, in England.

Lord Delaware dispatched Captain Argall to the Potomac for corn, which he succeeded in procuring by the aid of the youthful prisoner, Henry Spilman. His lordship erected two forts, called Henry and Charles, after the king's sons. These forts were built on a level tract bordering Southampton River, and it was intended that settlers arriving from England should first land there, to refresh themselves after the confinement of the voyage. Sir Thomas Gates, who had before sent his daughters back to England, now returned there himself, in order to render to the council an account of all that had happened. Captain Percy was dispatched with a party to chastise the Paspaheghs, for some depredations; they fled before the English, who burnt their cabins, captured their queen and her children, and shortly after barbarously slew them. Lord Delaware, visiting the falls with a party of soldiers, was attacked by the Indians, who killed some of his men.

His lordship having suffered much sickness, and finding himself in a state of extreme debility, embarked,* in company of Dr. Bohun and Captain Argall, and about fifty others, for the Island of Mevis, in the West Indies. Contrary winds drove them to the north, and having put in at the mouth of a large river, then called Chickohocki, it hence derived its name of the Delaware.

Lord Delaware upon leaving the colony, committed the charge of it to Captain George Percy, an honorable and resolute gentleman, but in infirm health, and deficient in energy. The number of colonists was at this period about two hundred; the stock of provisions sufficient for ten months, and the Indians peaceable and friendly. Before Lord Delaware reached England, the Virginia Council, discouraged by so many disasters and disappointments, were at a loss to decide whether they should use any further efforts to sustain the ill-fated colony, or should abandon the enterprise, and recall the settlers from Virginia. But Sir Thomas Gates made so strenuous an appeal in favor of sustaining the plantation, that Sir Thomas Dale was dispatched with three

---

* March 28th, 1611.

vessels, cattle, hogs, and other supplies. The title given to Dale was that of High Marshal of Virginia, indicative of the martial authority with which he was invested. He was a military man, and had served in the Low Countries, and he brought over with him an extraordinary code of "laws divine, moral, and martial," compiled by William Strachey, secretary of the colony, for Sir Thomas Smith, from the military laws observed during the wars in the Low Countries. This code was sent over by Sir Thomas Smith, treasurer or governor of the Virginia Company, without the company's sanction, as it has been alleged; but since the company in no way interposed its authority in contravention to the new code, their sanction of it may be presumed. Several of these laws were barbarous, inhuman, written in blood.

Arriving in Virginia in the month of May, 1611, Dale touched at Kiquotan, and set all hands there to planting corn. Reaching Jamestown on the tenth of May, he found the settlers busily engaged in their usual occupation, playing at bowls in the streets. He set them to work felling trees, repairing houses, and providing materials for enclosing the new town, which he proposed to build. To find a site for it he surveyed the Nansemond River and the James as far as the falls, and finally pitched upon a high ground, with steep banks, on the north side of the river, near Arrohattock, and about twelve miles below the falls of the river. The site was on a peninsula, known as Farrar's Island, in Varina Neck. Sir Thomas was prevented for a time from founding the new town by the disturbances that prevailed in the colony, and to restore order he enforced martial law with rigor. Eight of the colonists appear to have been convicted of treasonable plots and conspiracies, and executed by cruel and unusual modes, before midsummer. Among these was Jeffrey Abbot, who had served long in the army in Ireland and in the Netherlands; had been a sergeant of Captain John Smith's company in Virginia, who avers that he never knew there a better soldier or more loyal friend of the colony. It must be acknowledged that rigorous measures were necessary, and it was fortunate for the colony that the cruel and despotic code of laws, to which it was now subjected, was administered by so discreet and upright a governor as Dale.

Early in August, 1611, Sir Thomas Gates, commissioned to

take charge of the government of the colony, came over with six vessels, three hundred men, and abundant supplies. He was accompanied by the Rev. Mr. Glover, an approved preacher in Bedford and Huntingdonshire, a graduate of Cambridge, in easy circumstances, and somewhat advanced in years. Arriving at Jamestown early in August, during the sickly season, he soon after died.

Dale, relieved from the cares of the chief post, cheerfully occupied a subordinate position, and now turned his attention to the establishment of new settlements on the banks of the James, at some distance above Jamestown. Furnished by Gates with three hundred and fifty men, he sailed up the river early in September, and on the spot selected before, he founded the town of Henrico, so called in honor of the heir-apparent, Prince Henry, eldest son of James the First. The peninsula on which it was built is formed by a remarkable bend, styled the "Dutch Gap," where the river, after sweeping a circuit of seven miles, returns within one hundred and twenty yards from the point of departure. The site commands an extensive and picturesque view of the winding river, which in this part of it is called the "Corkscrew." The fertile tract of land there produced tobacco nearly resembling the Spanish Varinas, and hence received the appellation of Varina, the name of a well-known plantation. This was afterwards the residence of the Rev. William Stith, the best of our early historians, who dates the preface of his History of Virginia there, in 1746.

The peninsula, surrounded on three sides by the river, was impaled across the isthmus from water to water. There were three streets of well-framed houses, a handsome church of wood completed, and the foundation laid of a better one to be built of brick, besides store-houses, watch-houses, etc. Upon the river edge there were five houses, in which lived "the honester sort of people," as farmers in England, and they kept continual watch for the town's security. About two miles back from the town was a second palisade, near two miles in length, from river to river, guarded by several commanders, with a good quantity of corn-ground impaled, and sufficiently secured.

The breastwork thrown up by Sir Thomas Dale is still to be

traced, and vestiges of the town are indicated by scattered bricks, showing the positions of the houses.* Burk† and Keith‡ have fallen into singular mistakes as to the situation of this town.

On the south side of the river a plantation was established, called Hope in Faith and Coxendale, with forts, named, respectively, Charity, Elizabeth, Patience, and Mount Malady, and a guest-house for sick people, on the spot where afterwards, in Stith's time, Jefferson's church stood. On the same side of the river the Rev. Alexander Whitaker, sometimes styled the "Apostle of Virginia," established his parsonage, a well-framed house and one hundred acres of land, called Rock Hall.§

The work of William Strachey, already referred to, entitled "The History of Travel into Virginia Britannia," etc., appears to have been written before 1616, and two manuscripts of it exist, one in the British Museum, the other in the Ashmolean manuscripts at Oxford.‖

Sir Thomas Dale, when he came over to Virginia, was accompanied by Rev. Alexander Whitaker, the son of Dr. William Whitaker, Master of St. John's College, Cambridge, and also Regius Professor of Divinity there. The doctor distinguished himself by his controversial writings against the Church of Rome, and took a leading part in framing and maintaining the Lambeth Articles, which were Calvinistic, and had they been established, might have gone far toward healing the divisions between the Church of England and the Presbyterians. Rev. Alexander

---

* Va. Hist. Reg., i. 161.   † Hist. of Va., i. 166.   ‡ Hist. of Va., 124.

§ Stith, 124; Keith, 124; Beverley, i. 25; South. Lit. Messr. for June, 1845; Hawks' Narrative, 29.

‖ It has been of late years printed for the first time by the Hakluyt Society in England. The work is illustrated by etchings, comprising fac-similes of signatures, Captain Smith's map, and several engravings from De Bry. It contains also a copious glossary of Indian words. The first book comprises the geography of the country, with a full and admirable account of the manners and customs of Powhatan and his people. It is an important authority, but as it was printed only for the use of the members of the Hakluyt Society, it is but little known in this country. The second book treats of Columbus, Vespucius, Cabot, Raleigh, and Drake, with notices of the early efforts to colonize Northern Virginia, or New England. The period to which Strachey's History of Virginia relates includes 1610, 1611, and 1612. The same author published a map of Virginia at Oxford, in 1612. Mr. Peter Force has a MS. copy of it.

Whitaker, when he reached Virginia, had been a graduate of Cambridge some five or six years, and had been seated in the North of England, where he was held in great esteem. He had property of his own and excellent prospects of promotion; but, animated by a missionary spirit, he came over to Virginia. The voyage is described as speedy and safe, "being scarce eight weeks long."

The Appomattox Indians having committed some depredations, Sir Thomas Dale, about Christmas, 1611, captured their town, near the mouth of the Appomattox River where it empties into the James. The town was five miles distant from Henrico. Sir Thomas, pleased with the situation, established a plantation there, and called it Bermudas, the third town erected in Virginia, now known as Bermuda Hundred, the port of Richmond for ships of heavy burden. He laid out several plantations there, the Upper and Lower Rochdale, West Shirley, and Digges' Hundred. In conformity with the code of martial law each hundred was subjected to the control of a captain. The Nether Hundred was enclosed with a palisade two miles long, running from river to river, and here, within a half mile of each other, were many neat houses already built. Rochdale, or Rock's Dale, enclosed by a palisade four miles in length, was dotted with houses along the enclosure; here the hogs and cattle enjoyed a range of twenty miles to graze in securely. About fifty miles below these settlements stood Jamestown, on a fertile peninsula, with two rows of framed houses, some of them with two stores and a garret, and three large storehouses. The town was well enclosed, and it and the neighboring region were well peopled. Forty miles below Jamestown, at Kiquotan, the settlers enjoyed an abundance of fish, fowl, and venison.*

Captain Argall now arriving from England, in a vessel with forty men, was sent to the Potomac to trade for corn, and he contrived to ingratiate himself with Japazaws, a friendly chief, and from him learned that Pocahontas was there. She had never visited Jamestown since Smith's departure, and on the remote banks of the Potomac she thought herself unknown. Japazaws,

---

* Smith, ii. 13.

easily bribed, betrayed the artless and unsuspecting girl into Argall's hands. When she discovered the treachery she burst into tears. Argall, having sent a messenger to inform Powhatan that his favorite daughter was a prisoner, and must be ransomed with the men and arms, conveyed her to Jamestown. Three months thereafter Powhatan restored seven English prisoners and some unserviceable muskets, and sent word that if his daughter was released he would make restitution for all injuries, and give the English five hundred bushels of corn, and forever remain in peace and amity.* They refused to surrender Pocahontas until full satisfaction was rendered.

Powhatan was deeply offended, and nothing more was heard from him for a long time. At length Governor Dale, with Argall's vessel and some others, manned with one hundred and fifty men, went up the York River, taking the young captive with him, to Werowocomoco. Here, meeting with a scornful defiance, the English landed, burnt the cabins, and destroyed everything. On the next day Dale, proceeding up the river, concluded a truce with the savages. He then sailed up to Matchot, another residence of Powhatan, on the south side of the Pamunkey, where it unites with the Matapony. Matchot is supposed to be identical with Eltham, the old seat of the Bassets, in the County of New Kent, and which borrows its name from an English seat in the County of Kent. At this place, where several hundred warriors were found, the English landed, and the savages demanded a truce till Powhatan could be heard from, which being granted, two of Powhatan's sons went on board the vessel to see their sister Pocahontas. Finding her well, contrary to what they had heard, they were delighted, and promised to persuade their father to make peace, and forever be friends with the English.

John Rolfe, and another of the Englishmen named Sparks, were dispatched to let Powhatan know these proceedings. He entertained them hospitably, but would not admit them into his presence; they, however, saw his brother Opechancanough, who engaged to use his influence with Powhatan in favor of peace. It now being April, the season for planting corn, Sir Thomas

---

* Court and Times of James the First, i. 262.

Dale returned to Jamestown, intending not to renew hostilities until the next crop was made.

March 12th, 1612, another charter was granted to the Virginia Company, extending the boundaries of the colony, so as to include all islands lying within three hundred leagues of the continent. The object of this extension was to embrace the Bermudas, or Summer Islands; but the Virginia Company shortly afterwards sold them to one hundred and twenty of its own members, who became incorporated into a distinct company.*

On the 4th of November, 1612, died Henry, Prince of Wales, a gallant and generous spirit, the friend of Raleigh, and the idol of the nation; and his premature death was deplored like that of the Black Prince before, and the Princess Charlotte in more modern times. He appears to have been a warm friend of the infant plantation of Virginia, and Sir Thomas Dale speaks of him "as his glorious master, who would have enamelled with his favors the labors which were undertaken for God's cause," and laments that the "whole frame of the enterprise seemed fallen into his grave."

Mr. John Rolfe, a worthy gentleman, who appears to have been a widower, had been for some time in love with Pocahontas, and she with him; and, agitated by the conflicting emotions of this singular and romantic attachment, in a letter he requested the advice of Sir Thomas Dale, who readily gave his assent to the proposed union. Pocahontas likewise communicated the affair to her brother; so that the report of the marriage soon reached Powhatan, and it proved likewise acceptable to him. Accordingly, within ten days he sent Opachisco, an aged uncle of Pocahontas, and her two brothers, to attend the wedding, and fill his place at the ceremony. The marriage took place early in April, 1613, at Jamestown, and the rites were no doubt performed by the Rev. Mr. Whitaker.†

---

* Hen. Stat., i. 98; Stith, 126, and Appendix No. 3.

† A letter was written by Dale on the occasion, dated in June, 1614, and addressed to a friend in London; another of Rolfe to Dale, before mentioned, was published in London, 1615, by Ralph Hamor, in his work entitled, "A True Discourse of the Present State of Virginia," etc.; Rev. Alexander Whitaker addressed a letter on the same subject to a cousin in London. These letters were

This remarkable union became a happy link of peace and harmony between the red man and the white; and the warlike Chickahominies now came to propose a treaty of peace.* This fierce and numerous tribe, dwelling on the borders of the Chickahominy River, and near neighbors to the English, had long maintained their independence, and refused to acknowledge the sceptre of Powhatan. They now sent two runners to Governor Dale with presents, apologizing for all former injuries, and offering to submit themselves to King James, and to relinquish the name of Chickahominies, and be called Tassautessus (English.) They desired, nevertheless, still to be governed by their own laws, under the authority of eight of their own chiefs. Governor Dale, with Captain Argall and fifty men, on the banks of the Chickahominy, concluded a treaty of peace with them, and they ratified it by acclamation. An aged warrior then arose and explained the treaty, addressing himself successively to the old men, the young, and the women and children. The Chickahominies, apprehensive of being reduced under the despotism of Powhatan, sheltered themselves under the protection of the whites—a striking proof of the atrocious barbarity of a race whose imaginary virtues have been so often celebrated by poets, orators, and historians, and who have been described as renewing the golden age of innocent felicity.

The system of working in common, and of being provided for out of the public store, although unavoidable at first, had hitherto tended to paralyze industry, and to retard the growth of the colony. An important alteration in this particular was now effected; Sir Thomas Dale allotted to each man three acres of cleared ground, from which he was only obliged to contribute to the public store two and a half barrels of corn. These regulations, raising the colonists above the condition of absolute dependence, and creating a new incentive to exertion, proved very acceptable and beneficial.†

---

republished in this country in 1842, in a pamphlet explanatory of Chapman's picture of the Baptism of Pocahontas.

* Stith, 131.

† Chalmers, Introduction, i. 10; Grahame's Colonial Hist. U. S., i. 64. Compare Belknap's Amer. Biog., ii. 151.

Early in the year 1614 Sir Thomas Gates returned again to England, and Sir Thomas Dale reassumed the government of the colony. The French settlers of Acadia had, as early as 1605, built the town of Port Royal, on the Bay of Fundy; St. Croix was afterwards erected on the other side of the bay. Dale, looking upon these settlements as an encroachment upon the territory of Virginia, which extended to the forty-fifth degree of latitude, dispatched his kinsman, Argall, an enterprising and unscrupulous man, with a small force, to dislodge the intruders. The French colony was found situated on Mount Desert Island, near the Penobscot River, and within the bounds of the present State of Maine. The French, surprised while dispersed in the woods, soon yielded to superior force, and Argall, as some accounts say, furnished the prisoners with a fishing vessel, in which they returned to France, except fifteen, including a Jesuit missionary, who were brought to Jamestown. According to other accounts, their vessels were captured, but the colonists escaped, and went to live among the Indians. On his return, Argall visited the Dutch settlement near the site of Albany, on the Hudson, and compelled the governor there to surrender the place; but it was reclaimed by the Dutch not long afterwards, and during the next year they erected a fort on Manhattan Island, on which is now seated the commercial metropolis of the United States.

CHAPTER VIII.

1614-1617.

Hamor visits Powhatan—Richard Hakluyt—Pocahontas Baptized—Fixed Property in the Soil established—Dale Embarks for England accompanied by Pocahontas—Yeardley, Deputy Governor—Culture of Tobacco introduced—Pocahontas in England—Tomocomo—Death of Pocahontas—John and Thomas Rolfe—Smith and Pocahontas.

RALPH HAMOR* having obtained permission from Sir Thomas Dale to visit Powhatan, and taking with him Thomas Savage, as interpreter, and two Indian guides, started from Bermuda (Hundred) in the morning, and reached Matchot (Eltham) on the evening of the next day. Powhatan recognizing the boy Thomas Savage, said to him: "My child, I gave you leave, being my boy, to go see your friends; and these four years I have not seen you nor heard of my own man, Namontack, I sent to England, though many ships have been returned from thence." Turning then to Hamor, he demanded the chain of beads which he had sent to Sir Thomas Dale at his first arrival, with the understanding that whenever he should send a messenger, he should wear that chain about his neck; otherwise he was to be bound, and sent home. Sir Thomas *had* made such an arrangement, and on this occasion had directed his page to give the necklace to Hamor; but the page had forgotten it. However, Hamor being accompanied by two of Powhatan's own people, he was satisfied, and conducted him to the royal cabin, where a guard of two hundred bowmen stood always in attendance. He offered his guest a pipe of tobacco, and then inquired after his brother, Sir Thomas Dale, and his daughter, Pocahontas, and his unknown son-in-law, Rolfe, and "how they lived and loved." Being answered that Pocahontas was so well satisfied, that she would never live with him again, he

---

* Smith, ii. 19. There appears to be a mistake in affixing William Parker's name to the account of this visit, for it was evidently written by Hamor.

laughed, and demanded the object of his visit. Hamor gave him to understand that his message was private, to be made known only to him and to Papaschicher, one of the guides who was in the secret. Forthwith Powhatan ordered out all his people, except his two queens "that always sit by him," and bade Hamor deliver his message. He then, by his interpreter, let him know that Sir Thomas Dale had sent him pieces of copper, strings of white and blue beads, wooden combs, fish-hooks, and a pair of knives, and would give him a grindstone, when he would send for it; that his brother Dale, hearing of the charms of his younger daughter, desired that he would send her to Jamestown, as well because he intended to marry her, as on account of the desire of Pocahontas to see her, and he believed that there could be no better bond of peace and friendship than such a union. While Hamor was speaking, Powhatan repeatedly interrupted him, and when he had ended, the old chief replied: "I gladly accept your salute of love and peace which, while I live, I shall exactly keep. His pledges thereof I receive with no less thanks, although they are not so great as I have received before. But, for my daughter, I have sold her within these few days to a great werowance, three days journey from me, for two bushels of rawrenoke." Hamor: "I know your highness, by returning the rawrenoke, might call her back again, to gratify your brother, Sir Thomas Dale, and the rather because she is but twelve years old. Besides its forming a bond of peace, you shall have in return for her, three times the value of the rawrenoke, in beads, copper, and hatchets." Powhatan: "I love my daughter as my life, and though I have many children, I delight in none so much as her, and if I should not often see her I could not possibly live, and if she lived at Jamestown I could not see her, having resolved on no terms to put myself into your hands, or go among you. Therefore, I desire you to urge me no further, but return my brother this answer: I desire no firmer assurance of his friendship than the promise he hath made. From me he *has* a pledge, one of my daughters, which, so long as she lives, shall be sufficient; when *she* dies, he shall have another. I hold it not a brotherly part to desire to bereave me of my two children at once. Further, tell him that though he had no pledge at all, he need not fear any injury from me or my people; there have been too many of his men and mine slain; and, by my provocation, there never shall be any more, (I who have power to perform it, have said it,) even if I should have just cause, for I am now old, and would gladly end my days in peace; if you offer me injury, my country is large enough for me to go from you. This, I hope, will satisfy my brother. Now, since you are weary and I sleepy, we will here end." So Hamor and his companions lodged at Matchot that night. While there they saw William Parker, who had been captured three years before at Fort Henry. He had grown so like an Indian in complexion and manner, that his fellow-countrymen recognized him only by his language. He begged them to intercede for his release, but upon their undertaking it, Powhatan replied: "You have one of my daughters, and I am satisfied; but you cannot see one of your men with me, but you must have him away, or break friendship; but if you must needs have him, you shall go home without guides, and if any evil befall you, thank yourselves." They answered him that if any harm befell them he must expect revenge from his brother Dale. At this Powhatan, in a passion, left them; but returning to supper, he entertained them with a pleasant countenance. About midnight he awoke them, and promised to let them return in the morning with Parker, and charged them to remind his brother Dale to send him ten large pieces of copper, a shaving-knife, a frowl, a grindstone, a net, fish-hooks, and other such presents. Lest they might forget, he made them write down the list of articles in a blank book that he had. They requesting him to give them the book, he declined doing so, saying, "it did him much good to show it to strangers."*

During the year 1614 Sir Walter Raleigh published his "History of the World;" Captain John Smith made a voyage to North Virginia, and gave it the name of New England; and the Dutch, as already mentioned, effected a settlement near the site of Albany, on the Hudson River. Sir Thomas Gates, upon his return to England, reported that the plantation of Virginia would fall to the ground unless soon reinforced with supplies.† Martin, a lawyer, employed by the Virginia Company to recommend some

---

* Smith, ii. 21.   † Court and Times of James the First, i. 311.

measure to the House of Commons, having spoken disparagingly of that body, was arraigned at the bar of the House; but, upon making due acknowledgment upon his knees, was pardoned.* During this year died Richard Hakluyt, the compiler of a celebrated collection of voyages and discoveries. He was of an ancient family in Herefordshire, and, after passing some time at Westminster School, was elected to a studentship at Oxford, where he contracted a friendship with Sir Philip Sydney, to whom he inscribed his first collection of Voyages and Discoveries printed in 1582. Having imbibed a taste for the study of geography and cosmography from a cousin of the same name, a student of law at the Temple, he applied himself to that department of learning with diligence, and was at length appointed to lecture at the University on that subject. He contributed valuable aid in fitting out Sir Humphrey Gilbert's expedition. Soon after, taking holy orders, he proceeded to Paris as chaplain to Sir Edward Stafford, the English Ambassador. During his absence he was appointed to a prebendal stall at Bristol, and upon his return to England he frequently resided there. He was afterwards preferred to the rectory of Witheringset, in Suffolk. In 1615 he was appointed a prebendary of Westminster, and became a member of the council of the Virginia Company. He continued to watch over the affairs of the colony until his death. He was buried in Westminster Abbey. Hakluyt's Voyages consist of five volumes, folio.

Pocahontas was now carefully instructed in the Christian religion, and such was the change wrought in her, that after some time she lost all desire to return to her father, and retained no longer any fondness for the rude society of her own people. She had already, before her marriage, openly renounced the idolatry of her country, confessed the faith of Christ, and had been baptized. Master Whitaker, the preacher, in a letter dated June 18th, 1614, expresses his surprise that so few of the English ministers, "that were so hot against the surplice and subscription," came over to Virginia, where neither was spoken of. At the end of June Captain Argall returned to England with tidings of the more auspicious state of affairs. The Virginia Company

---

* Court and Times of James the First, i. 317.

now proceeded to draw the lottery, which had been made up to promote the interests of the colony, and twenty-nine thousand pounds were thus contributed; but Parliament shortly after prohibited this pernicious practice. It has been said that this is the first instance of raising money in England by lottery;* but this is erroneous, for there had been a lottery drawn for the purpose of repairing the harbors of the kingdom as far back as 1569.†

The year 1615 is remarkable in Virginia history for the first establishment of a fixed property in the soil, fifty acres of land being granted by the company to every freeman in absolute right.‡ This salutary reform was brought about mainly by the influence of Sir Thomas Dale, one of the best of the early governors. Sir Thomas having now, after a stay of five years in Virginia, established good order at Jamestown, appointed George Yeardley to be deputy governor in his absence, and embarked for England, accompanied by John Rolfe and his wife, the Princess Pocahontas, and other Indians of both sexes. They arrived at Plymouth on the 12th of June, 1616, about six weeks after the death of Shakespeare, who died on the twenty-third of April. The arrival is thus noticed in a news-letter: "Sir Thomas Dale is arrived from Virginia, and brought with him some ten or twelve old and young of that country, among whom is Pocahontas, daughter of Powhatan, a king or cacique of that country, married to one Rolfe, an Englishman. I hear not of any other riches or matter of worth, but only some quantity of sassafras, tobacco, pitch, tar, and clapboard—things of no great value, unless there were plenty and nearer hand. All I can hear of it is, that the country is good to live in, if it were stored with people, and might in time become commodious. But there is no present profit to be expected."§

Reverting to the condition of affairs in the colony, it is to be observed, that the oligarchical government of the president and council, with all its odious features, had long before this come to an end; order and diligence had now taken the place of confu-

---

* Chalmers' Annals, 33.   † Anderson's Hist. Col. Church, i. 27, in note.
‡ Chalmers' Introduc., i. 10.
§ Court and Times of James the First, i. 415.

sion and idleness; peace with the Indians had given rise to a free trade with them, and the English acquired their commodities by lawful purchase instead of extorting them by force of arms. The places inhabited by the whites, at this time, were Henrico and the limits, Bermuda Nether Hundred, West and Shirley Hundred, Jamestown, Kiquotan, and Dale's Gift. At Henrico there were thirty-eight men and boys, of whom twenty-two were farmers. The Rev. William Wickham was the minister of this place. It was the seat of the college established for the education of the natives; they had already brought hither some of their children, of both sexes, to be taught. At Bermuda Nether Hundred (Presquile) the number of inhabitants was one hundred and nineteen. Captain Yeardley, deputy governor, lived here for the most part. The minister here was Master Alexander Whitaker. At West and Shirley Hundred there were twenty-five men under Captain Madison. At Jamestown fifty, under Captain Francis West; the Rev. Mr. Bucke minister. At Kiquotan Captain Webb commanded; Rev. Mr. Mease the minister. Dale's Gift, on the sea-coast, near Cape Charles, was occupied by seventeen men under Lieutenant Cradock. The total population of the colony, at this time, was three hundred and fifty-one.* Yeardley directed the attention of the colony to tobacco, as the most saleable commodity that they could raise, and its cultivation was introduced into Virginia in this year, 1616, for the first time. The English now found the climate to suit their constitutions so well, that fewer people died here in proportion than in England. The Chickahominies refusing to pay the tribute of corn agreed upon by the treaty, Yeardley went up their river with one hundred men, and, after killing some and making some prisoners, brought off much of their corn. On his return he met Opechancanough at Ozinies, about twelve miles above the mouth of the Chickahominy. In this expedition Henry Spilman, who had been rescued from death by Pocahontas, now a captain, acted as interpreter.

---

* Sir Thomas Dale, at one haul with a seine, had caught five thousand fish, three hundred of which were as large as cod, and the smallest of the others a kind of salmon-trout, two feet long. He durst not adventure on the main school, for fear it would destroy his nets.

In the mean time Pocahontas was kindly received in London; by the care of her husband and friends she was, by this time, taught to speak English intelligibly; her manners received the softening influence of English refinement, and her mind was enlightened by the truths of religion. Having given birth to a son, the Virginia Company provided for the maintenance of them both, and many persons of quality were very kind to her. Before she reached London, Captain Smith, who was well acquainted at court, and in especial favor with Prince Charles, in requital for her former preservation of his life, had prepared an account of her in a small book, and he presented it to Queen Anne. But, at this time, being about to embark for New England, he could not pay her such attentions as he desired and she well deserved. Nevertheless, learning that she was staying at Brentford, where she had repaired in order to avoid the smoke of the city, he went, accompanied by several friends, to see her. After a modest salutation, without uttering a word, she turned away, and hid her face, as if offended. In that posture she remained for two or three hours, her husband and Smith and the rest of the company having, in the mean while, gone out of the room, and Smith now regretting that he had written to the queen that Pocahontas could speak English. At length she began to talk, and she reminded Captain Smith of the kindness she had shown him in her own country, saying: "You did promise Powhatan what was yours should be his, and he the like to you; you called him father, being in his land a stranger, and for the same reason so I must call you." But Smith, on account of the king's overweening and preposterous jealousy of the royal prerogative, felt constrained to decline the appellation of "father," for she was "a king's daughter." She then exclaimed, with a firm look: "Were you not afraid to come into my father's country, and cause fear in him and all his people (but me,) and fear you here that I should call you father? I tell you then I will, and you shall call me child, and I will be forever and ever your countrywoman. They did tell us always you were dead, and I knew no other till I came to Plymouth; yet Powhatan did command Uttomattomakkin to seek you, and know the truth, because your countrymen will lie much." It is remarkable that Rolfe, her husband, must have been privy to the deception thus practised on her; are we to attribute this to his secret apprehension that she would never marry him until she believed that Smith was dead?

Tomocomo, or Uttamattomakkin, or Uttamaccomack, husband of Matachanna, one of Powhatan's daughters, being a priest, and esteemed a wise and knowing one among his people, Powhatan, or, as Sir Thomas Dale supposed, Opechancanough, had sent him out to England, in company of Pocahontas, to number the people there, and bring back to him an account of that country. Upon landing at Plymouth he provided himself, according to his instructions, with a long stick, and undertook, by notching it, to keep a tally of all the men he could see; but he soon grew weary of the task, and gave it out in despair. Meeting with Captain Smith in London, Uttamattomakkin told him that Powhatan had ordered him to seek him out, that he might show him the English God, the king, queen, and prince. Being informed that he had already seen the king, he denied it; but on being convinced of it, he said: "You gave Powhatan a white dog, which Powhatan fed as himself; but your king gave me nothing, and I am better than your white dog." On his return to Virginia, when Powhatan interrogated him as to the number of people in England, he is said to have replied: "Count the stars in the heavens, the leaves on the trees, the sands on the sea-shore." Whether this and other such figurative expressions attributed to the Indians, were actually uttered by them, or whether they have received some poetical embellishment in the course of interpretation, the judicious reader may determine for himself.

During Smith's brief stay in London, many courtiers and others of his acquaintance daily called upon him for the purpose of being introduced to Pocahontas, and they expressed themselves satisfied that the hand of Providence was manifest in her conversion, and declared that they had seen many English ladies worse favored, proportioned, and behaviored. She was presented at Court by Lady Delaware, attended by the lord her husband, and other persons of quality, and was graciously received. Her modest, dignified, and graceful deportment, excited the admiration of all, and she received the particular attentions of the king and queen.

It is said, upon the authority of a well-established tradition, that King James was at first greatly offended at Rolfe for having presumed to marry a princess without his consent; but that upon a fuller representation of the matter, his majesty was pleased to express himself satisfied. There is hardly any folly so foolish but that it may have been committed by "the wisest fool in Christendom."

"The Virginia woman, Pocahontas, with her father counsellor, have been with the king, and graciously used, and both she and her assistant well placed at the masque."* She was styled the "Lady Pocahontas," and carried herself "as the daughter of a king." Lady Delaware and other noble persons waited on her to masquerades, balls, plays, and other public entertainments. Purchas, the compiler of Voyages and Travels, was present at an entertainment given in honor of her by the Bishop of London, Doctor King, which exceeded in pomp and splendor any other entertainment of the kind that the author of "The Pilgrim" had ever witnessed there.

Sir Walter Raleigh, after thirteen years' confinement in the Tower, had been released on the seventeenth of March preceding, and, upon gaining his liberty, he went about the city looking at the changes that had occurred since his imprisonment. It is not improbable that he may have seen Pocahontas.

Early in 1617 John Rolfe prepared to embark for Virginia, with his wife and child, in Captain Argall's vessel, the George. Pocahontas was reluctant to return. On the eve of her embarkation it pleased God to take her unexpectedly from the world. She died at Gravesend, on the Thames, in the latter part of March. As her life had been sweet and lovely, so her death was serene, and crowned with the hopes of religion.

"The Virginia woman, whose picture I sent you, died this last week at Gravesend, as she was returning home."* The parish register of burials at Gravesend, in the County of Kent, contains the following entry: "1616, March 21, Rebecca Wrothe,

---

* Court and Times of James the First, i. 388.

† Letter of John Chamberlain to Sir Dudley Carleton, dated at London, March, 1617, in Court and Times of James the First, ii. 3.

wyffe of Thomas Wrothe, Gent. A Virginia Lady borne, was buried in the Chancell." The date, 1616, corresponds with the historical year 1617. It appears that there was formerly a family of the name of Wrothe resident near Gravesend. This name might therefore easily be confounded with that of Rolfe, the sound being similar. Nor is the mistake of Thomas for John at all improbable. Gravesend Church, in which Pocahontas was buried, was destroyed by fire in 1727, and no monument to her memory remains, if any ever existed.*

According to Strachey, a good authority, the Indians had several different names given them at different times, and Powhatan called his favorite daughter when quite young, Pocahontas, that is, "Little Wanton," but at a riper age she was called Amonate. According to Stith,† her real name was Matoax, which the people of her nation concealed from the English, and changed it to Pocahontas from a superstitious fear, lest, knowing her true name, they should do her some injury. Others suppose Matoax to have been her individual name, Pocahontas her title. After her conversion she was baptized by the name of Rebecca, and she was sometimes styled the "Lady Rebecca." The ceremony of her baptism has been made the subject of a picture, (by Chapman,) exhibited in the rotundo of the Capitol at Washington.

Of the brothers of Pocahontas, Nantaquaus, or Nantaquoud, is especially distinguished for having shown Captain Smith "exceeding great courtesy," interceding with his father, Powhatan, in behalf of the captive, and he was the "manliest, comeliest, boldest spirit," Smith ever saw in a savage.

Of the sisters of Pocahontas two are particularly mentioned, Cleopatre and Matachanna. Strachey has recorded the names of the numerous wives and children of Powhatan, the greater part of which are harsh and guttural, and apparently almost incapable of being pronounced by the vocal organs of civilized man.

Smith says that Pocahontas, "with her wild train, visited Jamestown as freely as her father's habitation." In these visits

---

* Letter of C. W. Martin, Leeds Castle, England, to Conway Robinson, Esq., in Va. Hist. Reg., ii. 187.

† Stith, 136 and 285.

she had to cross the York River, some two miles wide, in a canoe, ("quintan" in the Powhatan language,) and then walk some ten or twelve miles across to Jamestown. She is described as "being of a great spirit, however her stature;" from which it may be inferred that she was below the middle height.* She died at the age of twenty-two, having been born about the year 1595. Her infant son, Thomas Rolfe, was left for a time at Plymouth, under the care of Sir Lewis Stukely, Vice-Admiral of Devon, who afterwards, by his base treachery toward Sir Walter Raleigh, covered himself with infamy, and by dishonest and criminal practices reduced himself to beggary. The son of Pocahontas was subsequently removed to London, where he was educated under the care of his uncle, Henry Rolfe, a merchant.†

Thomas Rolfe came to Virginia and became a person of fortune and note in the colony. It has been said that he married in England a Miss Poyers; however that may have been, he left an only daughter, Jane Rolfe, who married Colonel Robert Bolling. He lies buried at Farmingdale, in the County of Prince George.‡ This Colonel Robert Bolling was the son of John and Mary Bolling, of Alhallows, Barkin Parish, Tower Street, London. He was born in December, 1646, and came to Virginia in October, 1660, and died in July, 1709, aged sixty-two years. Colonel Robert Bolling, and Jane Rolfe, his wife, left an only son, Major John Bolling, father of Colonel John Bolling and several daughters, who married respectively, Col. Richard Randolph, Colonel John Fleming, Doctor William Gay, Mr. Thomas Eldridge, and Mr. James Murray.

Censure is sometimes cast upon Captain Smith for having failed to marry Pocahontas; but history no where gives any just ground for such a reproach. The rescue of Smith took place in

---

* Smith, ii. 31; Beverley, B. i. 27. † Stith, 144; Beverley, B. i. 34.

‡ Of Farmingdale, or Farmingdell, John Randolph of Roanoke said, in a letter dated 1832: "But the true name is Kippax, called after the village of Kippax and Kippax Park, adjacent thereto, the seat of my maternal ancestors, the Blands, of the West Riding of York." Bland, of Kippax, County York, anciently seated at Bland's Gill, in that county, was raised to the degree of baronet in 1642. The present representative (1854) is Thomas Davison Bland, of Kippax Park, Esq. Gill signifies dell or valley.

the winter of 1607, when he was twenty-eight years of age, and she only twelve or thirteen.* Smith left Virginia early in 1609, and never returned. Pocahontas was then about fourteen years of age; but if she had been older, it would have been impossible for him to marry her unless by kidnapping her, as was done by the unscrupulous Argall some years afterwards—a measure which, if it had been adopted in 1609, when the colony was so feeble, and so rent by faction, would probably have provoked the vengeance of Powhatan, and overwhelmed the plantation in premature ruin. It was in 1612 that Argall captured Pocahontas on the banks of the Potomac, and from the departure of Smith until this time she never had been seen at Jamestown, but had lived on the distant banks of the Potomac. In the spring of 1613 it is stated, that long before that time "Mr. John Rolfe had been in love with Pocahontas, and she with him." This attachment must, therefore, have been formed immediately after her capture, if it did not exist before; and the marriage took place in April, 1613. It is true that Pocahontas had been led to believe that Smith was dead, and in practising this deception upon her, Rolfe must have been a party; but Smith was in no manner whatever privy to it; he cherished for her a friendship animated by the deepest emotions of gratitude; and friendship, according to Spenser, a cotemporary poet, is a more exalted sentiment than love.

Pocahontas appears to have regarded Smith with a sort of filial affection, and she accordingly said to him, in the interview at Brentford, "I tell you then, I *will* call you father, and you *shall* call me child." The delusion practised on her relative to Smith's death would, indeed, seem to argue an apprehension on the part of Rolfe and his friends that she would not marry another while Smith was alive, and the particular circumstances of the interview at Brentford would seem to confirm the existence of such an apprehension. Yet, however that may have been, the honor and integrity of Smith remain untarnished.

---

* Inscription of date on Smith's likeness, prefixed to his history; Stith, 55, 127.

CHAPTER IX.

1617-1618.

Argall, Governor—Condition of Jamestown—Death of Lord Delaware—Name of Delaware River—Argall's Martial Law—Brewster's Case—Argall leaves Virginia—His Character—Powhatan's Death—His Name, Personal Appearance, Dominions, Manner of Life, Character—Succeeded by Opitchapan.

LORD RICH, an unscrupulous and corrupt head of a faction in the Virginia Company, having entered into partnership with Captain Samuel Argall, (a relative of Sir Thomas Smith, the Treasurer or Governor of the Company,) by his intrigues contrived to have him elected Deputy-Governor of Virginia and Admiral of that country and the seas adjoining. He sailed for Virginia early in 1617, accompanied by Ralph Hamor, his vice-admiral, and arrived at Jamestown in May. Argall was welcomed by Captain Yeardley and his company, the right file of which was led by an Indian. At Jamestown were found but five or six habitable houses, the church fallen, the palisades broken, the bridge foundrous, the well spoiled, the storehouse used for a church; the market-place, streets, and other vacant ground planted with tobacco; the savages as frequent in the houses as the English, who were dispersed about as each man could find a convenient place for planting corn and tobacco. Tomocomo, who (together with the other Indians that had gone out to England in the suite of Pocahontas, as may be presumed, although the fact is not expressly mentioned,) had returned with Argall, was immediately, upon his arrival, sent to Opechancanough, who came to Jamestown, and received a present with great joy and thankfulness. But Tomocomo denounced England and the English in bitter terms, especially Sir Thomas Dale. Powhatan having some time before this resigned the cares of government into the hands of Opechancanough, went about from place to place, still continuing in friendship with the English, but greatly lamenting the death of Pocahontas. He rejoiced, nevertheless, that her child was living, and he and Opechancanough both expressed much desire to see him. During this year a Mr. Lambert introduced the method of curing tobacco on lines instead of in heaps, as had been the former practice.* Argall's energetic measures procured from the Indians, by trade, a supply of corn. The whole number of colonists now was about four hundred, with numerous cattle, goats, and swine. The corn contributed to the public store was about four hundred and fifty bushels, and from the tributary Indians seven hundred and fifty, being considerably less than the usual quantity. Of the "Company's company" there remained not more than fifty-four, including men, women, and children. Drought, and a storm that poured down hailstones eight or nine inches in circumference, greatly damaged the crops of corn and tobacco.

The following is found among the early records:—

"BY THE ADMIRAL, ETC.

"To all to whom these presents shall come, I, Samuel Argall, Esq., admiral, and for the time present principal Governor of Virginia, send greeting in our Lord God everlasting, si'thence in all places of wars and garrison towns, it is most expedient and necessary to have an honest and careful provost marshall, to whose charge and safe custody all delinquents and prisoners of what nature or quality soever their offences be, are to be committed; now know ye that for the honesty, sufficiency, and carefulness in the execution and discharge of the said office, which I conceived of William Cradock, I do by these presents nominate, constitute, ordain, and appoint the said William Cradock to be provost marshall of the Bermuda City, and of all the Hundred thereto belonging, giving and granting unto the said William Cradock, all power and authority to execute all such offices, duties, and commands belonging to the said place of provost marshall; with all privileges, rights, and preëminences thereunto belonging, and in all cases which require his speedy execution of his said office, by virtue of these presents, he shall require all captains, officers, soldiers, or any other members of this colony, to be aiding and

---

* Stith, 147.

assisting to him, to oppose all mutinies, factions, rebellions, and all other discords contrary to the quiet and peaceable government of this Commonwealth, as they will answer the contrary at their peril.

"Given at Bermuda City this twentieth of February, in the 15th year of the reign of our Sovereign Lord James, by the Grace of God, King of England, and of Scotland the 51st, and in the 11th year of this Plantation. Anno Domini, 1617.

"Extract and recorded per John Rolf, Sec'y and Recorder Genl.

["Copia. Test. R. Hickman, Ck. Secy's office."]

To reinforce the colony the Company sent out a vessel of two hundred and fifty tons, well stored, with two hundred and fifty people, under command of Lord Delaware. They set sail in April, 1618; during the voyage thirty died, and among them Lord Delaware, a generous friend of the colony. The intelligence of his death reached London October fifth. Stith* says: "And I think I have somewhere seen that he died about the mouth of Delaware Bay, which thence took its name from him." Stith fell into a mistake on this point, and Belknap, equally distinguished for his general accuracy, has followed him.† Delaware Bay (the mouth of the river called by the Indians Chihohocki) and River were named as early as 1611, when Lord Delaware put in there, during his homeward voyage.‡ According to Strachey, the bay was discovered in 1610, by Captain Argall, and he named Cape Delaware, "where he caught halibut, cod, and ling fish, and brought some of them to Jamestown."

His lordship's family name was West, and persons descended from the same stock are yet found in Virginia bearing the name. West-Point, at the head of York, derived its name from the same source, and it was at first called Delaware. Lord Delaware married, in 1602, the daughter of Sir Thomas Shirley, of Whiston; and, perhaps, the name of Shirley, the ancient seat on James River, may be traced to this source.

---

* Stith, 147. † Belknap, ii. 115.
‡ Anderson's Hist. of Col. Church, i. 271–311.

Martial law had already been established in Virginia by Dale; Argall came over invested with powers to make the government still more arbitrary and despotic, and bent upon acquiring gain by all possible means of extortion and oppression. He decreed that goods should be sold at an advance of twenty-five per cent., and tobacco rated at the Procrustean value of three shillings—the penalty for rating it either higher or lower being three years slavery to the colony; that there should be no trade or intercourse with the Indians, and that none of them should be taught the use of fire-arms; the penalty for violating which ordinance was death to teacher and learner. Yet it has been contended by some, that the use of fire-arms by the savages hastened their extermination, because they thus became dependent on the whites for arms and ammunition; when their guns came to be out of order they became useless to them, for they wanted the skill to repair them; and, lastly, fire-arms in their hands when effective, were employed by hostile tribes in mutual destruction.

> "The white faith of history cannot show
> That e'er a musket yet could beat a bow."*

Argall also issued edicts that no one should hunt deer or hogs without his leave; that no man should fire a gun before a new supply of ammunition, except in self-defence, on pain of a year's slavery; absence from church on Sundays or holidays, was punished by confinement for the night and one week's slavery to the colony; for the second offence the offender should be a slave for a month; and for the third, for a year and a day. Several of these regulations were highly judicious, but the penalties of some of them were excessive and barbarous, and the vigorous enforcement of these, and his oppressive proceedings, rendered Argall odious to the colony, and a report of his tyranny and extortions having reached England, Sir Thomas Smith, Alderman Johnson, deputy treasurer, Sir Lionel Cranfield, and others of the council, addressed a letter dated August 23, 1618, to him, in which they recapitulated a series of charges against him of dishonesty, corruption, and oppression. At the same time a letter,

---

* Cited in Logan's Scottish Gaël, 223.

of the same purport, was written to Lord Delaware, and he was told, that such was the indignation felt by the stockholders in the Virginia Company against Argall that they could hardly be restrained from going to the king, although on a distant progress, and procuring his majesty's command for recalling him as a malefactor. The letter contained further instructions to Lord Delaware to seize upon all the goods and property in Argall's possession. These letters, by Lord Delaware's death, fell into Argall's hands, and finding his sand running low, he determined to make the best of his remaining time, and so he multiplied his exactions, and grew more tyrannical than ever. The case of Edward Brewster was a remarkable instance of this. A person of good repute in the colony, he had the management of Lord Delaware's estate. Argall, without any rightful authority, removed the servants from his lordship's land, and employed them on his own. Brewster endeavored to make them return, and upon this being flatly refused by one of them, threatened him with the consequences of his contumacy. Brewster was immediately arrested by Argall's order, charged with sedition and mutiny, and condemned to death by a court-martial. The members of the court, however, and some of the clergy, shocked at such a conviction, interceded earnestly for his pardon, and Argall reluctantly granted it on condition that Brewster should depart from Virginia, with an oath never to return, and never to say or do anything to the disparagement of the deputy governor. Brewster, nevertheless, upon his return to England, discarding the obligation of an oath extorted under duress, appealed to the Company against the tyranny of the deputy governor, and the inhuman sentence was reversed. John Rolfe, a friend of Argall, made light of the affair.[*]

During this year, 1618, a ship called the Treasurer was sent out from England by Lord Rich, who had now become Earl of Warwick, a person of great note afterwards in the civil wars, and commander of the fleet against the king. This ship was manned with recruits from the colony, and dispatched on a semi-piratical cruise in the West Indies, where she committed some depredations on the Spanish possessions.

---

[*] Smith, ii. 37.

Upon receiving intelligence of the death of Lord Delaware, the Virginia Company appointed Captain George Yeardley, who was knighted upon this occasion, Governor and Captain-General of Virginia. Before his arrival in the colony Argall embarked for England, in a vessel laden with his effects, and being a relation of Sir Thomas Smith, and a partner in trade of the profligate Earl of Warwick, he escaped with impunity. In 1620 Argall commanded a ship-of-war in an expedition fitted out against the Algerines, and in 1623 was knighted by King James. Argall's character has been variously represented; he appears to have been an expert mariner of talents, courage, enterprise, and energy, but selfish, avaricious, unscrupulous, arbitrary and cruel.

In April, 1618, Powhatan died, being upwards of seventy years of age. He was, perhaps, so called from one of his places of residence;* he was also sometimes styled Ottaniack, and sometimes Mamanatowick,† but his proper name was Wahunsonacock. The country subject to him was called Powhatan, as was likewise the chief river, and his subjects were called Powhatans. His hereditary domain consisted only of Powhatan, Arrohattox, Appamatuck, Youghtanund, Pamunkey, and Matapony, together with Werowocomoco and Kiskiack. All the rest were his conquests, and they consisted of the country on the James River and its branches, from its mouth to the falls, and thence across the country to the north, nearly as high as the falls of all the great rivers over the Potomac, as far as to the Patuxent in Maryland. Some nations on the Eastern Shore also owned subjection to this mighty werowance. In each of his several hereditary dominions he had houses built like arbors, thirty or forty feet long, and whenever he was about to visit one of these, it was supplied beforehand with provision for his entertainment. The English first met with him at a place of his own name, (which it still retains,) a short distance below the falls of James River, where now stands the picturesque City of Richmond.‡ His favorite residence was Werowocomoco, on the east

---

* Stith, 53.   † Strachey.

‡ In an act, dated 1705, found in the old "Laws of Virginia," mention is made of a ferry from Powhatantown to the landing at Swineherd's. The site of this

bank of what is now known as Timberneck Bay, on York River, in the County of Gloucester; but in his latter years, disrelishing the increasing proximity of the English, he withdrew himself to Orapakes, a hunting-town in the "desert," as it was called, more properly the wilderness, between the Chickahominy and the Pamunkey. It is not improbable that he died and was buried there, for a mile from Orapakes, in the midst of the woods, he had a house where he kept his treasure of furs, copper, pearl, and beads, "which he storeth up against the time of his death and burial."* This place is about twelve miles northeast from Richmond.

At the time of the first settlement of the colony, Powhatan was usually attended, especially when asleep, by a body-guard of fifty tall warriors; he afterwards augmented the number to about two hundred. He had as many wives as he pleased, and when tired of any one of them, he bestowed her on some favorite. In the year 1608, by treachery, he surprised the Payanketanks, his own subjects, while asleep in their cabins, massacred twenty-four men, and made prisoners their werowance with the women and children, who were reduced to slavery. Captain Smith, himself a prisoner, saw at Werowocomoco the scalps of the slain suspended on a line between two trees. Powhatan caused certain malefactors to be bound hand and foot, then a great quantity of burning coals to be collected from a number of fires, and raked round in the form of a cock-pit, and the victims of his barbarity thrown in the midst and burnt to death.† He was not entirely destitute of some better qualities; in him some touches of princely magnanimity are curiously blended with huckstering cunning, and the tenderness of a doating father with the cruelty of an unrelenting despot.

Powhatan was succeeded by his second brother, Opitchapan, sometimes called Itopatin, or Oeatan, who, upon his accession, again changed his name to Sasawpen; as Opechancanough, upon

---

Powhatantown is on the upper part of Flower de Hundred Plantation. Numerous Indian relics have been found there, and earthworks, evidently thrown up for fortification, are still extant. The name of Powhatantown was given to this spot by the whites. Near Jamestown is the extensive Powhatan Swamp.

* Smith, i. 143. † Smith, i. 144.

the like occasion, changed his to Mangopeomen. Opitchapan being decrepid in body and inert in mind, was in a short time practically superseded in the government by his younger, bolder, and more ambitious brother, the famous Opechancanough; though for a time he was content to be styled the Werowance of Chickahominy. Both renewed the assurances of continued friendship with the English.

CHAPTER X.

Sir Walter Raleigh—His Birth and Parentage—Student at Oxford—Enlists in Service of Queen of Navarre—His stay in France—Returns to England—At the Middle Temple—Serves in Netherlands and Ireland—Returns to England—His Gallantry—Undertakes Colonization of Virginia—Member of Parliament—Knighted—In Portuguese Expedition—Loses Favor at Court—Retires to Ireland—Spenser—Sir Walter in the Tower—His Flattery of the Queen—She grants him the Manor of Sherborne—His Expedition to Guiana—Joins Expedition against Cadiz—Wounded—Makes another Voyage to Guiana—Restored to Queen's Favor—Contributes to Defeat of Treason of Essex—Raleigh made Governor of Jersey—His Liberal Sentiments—Elizabeth's Death—Accession of James the First—Raleigh confined in the Tower—Found guilty of High Treason—Reprieved—Still a Prisoner in the Tower—Devotes himself to Study—His Companions—His "History of the World"—Lady Raleigh's Petition—Raleigh Released—His Last Expedition to Guiana—Its Failure—His Son killed—Sir Walter's Return to England—His Arrest, Condemnation, Execution, Character.

DURING the same year, 1618, died the founder of Virginia colonization, the famous Sir Walter Raleigh. He was born at Hayes, a farm in the Parish of Budley, Devonshire, 1552, being the fourth son of Walter Raleigh, Esq., of Fardel, near Plymouth, and Catharine, daughter of Sir Philip Champernon, and widow of Otho Gilbert, of Compton, Devonshire. After passing some time at Oriel College, Oxford, about the year 1568, where he distinguished himself by his genius and attainments, at the age of seventeen he joined a volunteer company of gentlemen, under Henry Champernon, in an expedition to assist the Protestant Queen of Navarre. He remained in France five years, and while in Paris, under the protection of the English embassy, he witnessed the massacre of St. Bartholomew's day. On returning to England he was for a while in the Middle Temple; but whether as a student is uncertain. His leisure hours were devoted to poetry. In the year 1578 he accompanied Sir John Norris to the Netherlands. In the following year he joined in Sir Humphrey Gilbert's first and unsuccessful voyage. Now, when at the age of twenty-seven, it is said that of the twenty-four hours he allotted four to study and only five to sleep; but this is rather improbable, for so much activity of employment as always characterized him, demanded a proportionate degree of repose. In 1580 he served in Ireland as captain of horse, under Lord Grey, and became familiar with the dangers and atrocities of civil war. In 1581, the following year, he became acquainted with the poet Spenser, then resident at Kilcolman. Disgusted with a painful service, Raleigh returned to England during this year, and it was at this period that he exhibited a famous piece of gallantry to the queen. She, in a walk, coming to a "plashy place," hesitated to proceed, when he "cast and spread his new plush cloak on the ground" for her to tread on. By his graceful wit and fascinating manners, he rose rapidly in Elizabeth's favor, and "she took him for a kind of oracle." His munificent and persevering efforts in the colonization of Virginia ought to have moderated the too sweeping charge of levity and fickleness brought against him by Hume.

During the year 1583 Raleigh became member of Parliament for Devonshire; was knighted, and made Seneschal of Cornwall and Warden of the Stanneries. Engaged in the expedition whose object was to place Don Antonio on the throne of Portugal, Sir Walter for his good conduct received a gold chain from the queen. The rivalship of the Earl of Essex having driven Raleigh into temporary exile in Ireland, he there renewed his acquaintance with the author of the "Faëry Queen," who accompanied him on his return to England.

Sir Walter was arrested in 1592, and confined in the Tower, on account of a criminal intrigue with one of the maids of honor, who was imprisoned at the same time; and this incident is alluded to in Sir Walter Scott's "Fortunes of Nigel." The lady was Elizabeth, daughter of Sir Nicholas Throckmorton, and a celebrated beauty, whom Raleigh afterwards married. In a letter written from the Tower, and addressed to Sir Robert Cecil, Raleigh indulged in a vein of extravagant flattery of the queen: "I that was wont to behold her riding like Alexander, hunting like Diana, walking like Venus—the gentle wind blowing her fair hair about her pure cheeks like a nymph; sometime sitting in the shade like a goddess; sometime singing like an angel; sometime playing like Orpheus." Elizabeth was at this time about sixty years old.

In 1593 she granted him the Manor of Sherborne, in Dorsetshire. About this period he distinguished himself in the House of Commons. In 1595 he commanded an expedition to Guiana, in quest of the golden El Dorado, and another in the following year. In an expedition against Cadiz he led the van in action, and received a severe wound in the leg. Upon his return to England he embarked in his third voyage to Guiana. In 1597 he was restored to his place of captain of the guard, and entirely reinstated in the queen's favor.

Essex having engaged in a rash treasonable conspiracy, the object of which was to seize upon the queen's person, so as thereby to control the government, Raleigh aided in defeating his designs. But after the execution of his popular rival, Raleigh's fortune began to wane. Nevertheless, in 1600 he was made Governor of the Isle of Jersey. In the following year, in a speech made in Parliament on an act for sowing hemp, Sir Walter said: "For my part, I do not like this constraining of men to manure or use their grounds at our wills, but rather let every man use his ground to that which it is most fit for, and therein use his discretion." Queen Elizabeth died in 1603, and Raleigh's happiness ended with her life.

James the First came to the throne of Great Britain prejudiced against Raleigh. He was also at this time extremely unpopular, and especially odious to the friends of the highly gifted, but rash and unfortunate Earl of Essex. In three months after the arrival of King James in England, Sir Walter was arrested on a charge of high treason, in conspiring with the Lords Cobham and Grey to place the Lady Arabella Stuart on the throne. Arraigned on charges frivolous and contradictory, tried under circumstances of insult and oppression, he was found guilty without any sufficient evidence. By their conduct on this occasion, Sir Edward Coke, Lord Chief Justice Popham, and Sir Robert Cecil proved themselves fit tools for the abject and heartless James. Raleigh, though reprieved, remained a prisoner in the Tower at the king's mercy.

Lady Raleigh and her son were not excluded from the Tower,

and Carew, the youngest, was born there. During his long confinement, Sir Walter devoted himself to literature and science, and enjoyed the society of a few friends, among them Hariot and the Earl of Northumberland, who was likewise a State prisoner. Sir Walter was also frequently visited by Prince Henry, the heir-apparent, who was devotedly attached to him, and who said that "none but his father would keep such a bird in a cage." Prince Charles, on the contrary, appears to have entertained a strong dislike to him. In the Tower Raleigh composed his great work, the "History of the World," the first volume of which appeared in the year 1614; it extended from the creation to the close of the Macedonian war, and embraced a period of about four thousand years. It was dedicated to Prince Henry. Raleigh intended to compose two other volumes, but owing to the untimely death of that prince, and to the suppression of it by King James, on the ground that it censured princes too freely, and perhaps to the magnitude of the task, he proceeded no further than the first volume. Oliver Cromwell recommended this work to his son.

During his confinement the king gave away Raleigh's estate of Sherborne to his favorite, Sir Robert Carr, afterwards the infamous Viscount Rochester and Earl of Somerset, who swayed the influence at Court from 1611 to 1615, when he was supplanted by the equally corrupt George Villiers, Duke of Buckingham.

When Lady Raleigh, with her children around her, kneeling in tears, besought James to restore this estate, the only answer she received was, "I maun have the land, I maun have it for Carr." At length, owing in part to the death of some of his enemies, and in part to the influence of money, Sir Walter Raleigh was released from the Tower for the purpose of making another voyage to Guiana. The expedition failed in its object, and Sir Walter, after losing his son in an action with the Spaniards, returned to England, where he was arrested.

James was now wholly bent on effecting a match between his son, Prince Charles, afterwards Charles the First, and the Spanish Infanta, and to gratify the Court of Spain and his own malignity, he resolved to sacrifice Raleigh. He was condemned, after a most eloquent defence, under the old conviction of 1603, notwithstanding that he had been recently commissioned commander of a fleet and Governor of Guiana, which had unquestionably annulled that conviction. "He was condemned (said his son Carew) for being a friend of the Spaniards, and lost his life for being their bitter enemy."

Queen Anne, then in declining health, interceded for him, not long before his execution, in the following note, addressed to the Marquis of Buckingham:—

"My Kind Dog:—

"If I have any power or credit with you, in dealing sincerely and earnestly with the king, that Sir Walter Raleigh's life may not be called in question. If you do it so that the success answer my expectation, assure yourself that I will take it extraordinarily kindly at your hands, and rest one that wisheth you well, and desires you to continue still (as you have been) a true servant to your master.

"ANNE R."*

Sir Walter Raleigh was executed on the twenty-ninth day of October, 1618, in the Old Palace Yard. He died with Christian heroism. Distinguished as a navigator and discoverer, a naval and military commander, an author in prose and verse, a wit, a courtier, a statesman and philosopher, there is perhaps in English history no name associated with such lofty and versatile genius, so much glorious action, and so much wise reflection. He was indeed proud, fond of splendor, of a restless and fiery ambition, sometimes unscrupulous. An ardent imagination, excited by the enthusiasm of an extraordinary age, infused an extravagance and marvellousness into some of his relations of his voyages and discoveries, that gave some occasion for distrust. The ardor of his temperament and an over-excited imagination involved him in several projects that terminated unhappily. But with his weaknesses and his faults he united noble virtues, and Virginia will ever be proud of so illustrious a founder.†

---

* Miss Strickland's Lives of Queens of England, vii. 357.

† Oldy's Life of Raleigh, 74; Belknap, i. art. Raleigh, 289, 370; "A Brief Relation of Sir Walter Raleigh's Troubles," Harleian Mis., No. 100. There are also lives of Raleigh by Birch, Cayley, Southey, and Mrs. Thompson.

The Queen Anne, of Denmark, who had in vain employed her kind offices in his behalf, did not long survive him; she died in March, 1619. Without any extraordinary qualities, she was accomplished, distinguished for the easy elegance of her manners, amiable, and the generous friend of the oppressed and unfortunate.

CHAPTER XI.

1619.

Sir Edwin Sandys, Treasurer of London Company—Powell, Deputy Governor—Sir George Yeardley, Governor—First Assembly meets—Its Proceedings.

SIR THOMAS SMTIH, Treasurer or Governor of the Virginia Company, was displaced in 1618, and succeeded by Sir Edwin Sandys.* This enlightened statesman and exemplary man was born in Worcestershire, in 1561, being the second son of the Archbishop of York. Educated at Oxford under the care of "the judicious Hooker," he obtained a prebend in the church of York. He afterwards travelled in foreign countries, and published his observations in a work entitled "Europæ Speculum, or a View of the State of Religion in the Western World." He resigned his prebend in 1602, was subsequently knighted by James, in 1603, and employed in diplomatic trusts. His appointment as treasurer gave great satisfaction to the colony; for free principles were now, under his auspices, in the ascendant. His name is spelt sometimes Sandis, sometimes Sands. Sir Thomas Smith was shortly after reappointed, by the Virginia Company, President of the Somers Islands.

When Argall, in April, stole away from Virginia, he left for his deputy, Captain Nathaniel Powell,† who had come over with Captain Smith in 1607, and had evinced courage and discretion. He was one of the writers from whose narratives Smith compiled his General History. Powell held his office only about ten days, when Sir George Yeardley, recently knighted, arrived as Governor-General, bringing with him new charters for the colony. He added to the council Captain Francis West, Captain Nathaniel

---

* Court and Times of James the First, i. 161.   † A Welsh name.

Powell, John Rolfe, William Wickham, and Samuel Macock.* John Rolfe, who had been secretary, now lost his place, probably owing to his connivance at Argall's malepractices, and was succeeded by John Pory. He was educated at Cambridge, where he took the degree of Master of Arts, in April, 1610. It is supposed that he was a member of the House of Commons. He was much of a traveller, and was at Venice in 1613, at Amsterdam in 1617, and shortly after at Paris. By the Earl of Warwick's influence he now procured the place of Secretary for the Colony of Virginia, having come over in April, 1619, with Sir George Yeardley, who appointed him one of his council.

In June, Governor Yeardley summoned the first legislative assembly that ever met in America. It assembled at James City or Jamestown, on Friday, the 30th of July, 1619, upwards of a year before the Mayflower left England with the Pilgrims. A record of the proceedings is preserved in the London State Paper Office, in the form of a Report from the Speaker, John Pory.†

John Pory, Secretary of the Colony, was chosen Speaker, and John Twine, Clerk. The Assembly sate in the choir of the church, the members of the council sitting on either side of the Governor, and the Speaker right before him, the Clerk next the Speaker, and Thomas Pierse, the Sergeant, standing at the bar.

---

* Macocks, the seat on James River, opposite to Berkley, was called after this planter, who was the first proprietor.

† This interesting document, discovered by Mr. Bancroft, was published by the New York Historical Society in 1857, and a number of copies were sent to Richmond by George Henry Moore, Esq., Secretary of that Society, for distribution among the members of the Assembly. The attention of Virginians was first drawn to the existence of this document by Conway Robinson, Esq., Chairman of the Executive Committee of the Virginia Historical Society.

The number of burgesses was twenty-two. For James City, Captain William Powell, Ensign William Spense; for Charles City, Samuel Sharpe and Samuel Jordan: for the City of Henricus, Thomas Dowse, John Polentine; for Kiccowtan, Captain William Tucker, William Capp; for Martin-Brandon, Captain John Martin's Plantation, Mr. Thomas Davis, Mr. Robert Stacy; for Smythe's Hundred, Captain Thomas Graves, Mr. Walter Shelley; for Martin's Hundred, Mr. John Boys, John Jackson; for Argall's Gift, Mr. Pawlett, Mr. Gourgainy; for Flowerdieu Hundred, Ensign Rossingham, Mr. Jefferson; for Captain Lawne's Plantation, Captain Christopher Lawne, Ensign Washer; for Captain Ward's Plantation, Captain Ward, Lieutenant Gibbes.

Before commencing business, prayer was said by Mr. Bucke, the minister. Each burgess then, as called on, took the oath of supremacy. When the name of Captain Ward was called, the Speaker objected to him as having seated himself on land without authority. Objection was also made to the burgesses appearing to represent Captain Martin's patent, because they were, by its terms, exempted from any obligation to obey the laws of the colony. Complaint was made by Opochancano, that corn had been forcibly taken from some of his people in the Chesapeake, by Ensign Harrison, commanding a shallop belonging to this Captain John Martin, "Master of the Ordinance." The Speaker read the commission for establishing the Council of State and the General Assembly, and also the charter brought out by Sir Thomas Yeardley. This last was referred to several committees for examination, so that if they should find anything "not perfectly squaring with the state of the colony, or any law pressing or binding too hard," they might by petition seek to have it redressed, "especially because this great charter is to bind us and our heirs forever." Mr. Abraham Persey was the Cape-merchant. The price at which he was to receive tobacco, "either for commodities or upon bills," was fixed at three shillings for the best and eighteen pence for the second rate. After inquiry the burgesses from Martin's patent were excluded, and the Assembly "humbly demanded" of the Virginia Company an explanation of that clause in his patent entitling him to enjoy his lands as amply as any lord of a manor in England, adding, "the least the Assembly can allege against this clause is, that it is obscure, and that it is a thing impossible for us here to know the prerogatives of all the manors in England." And they prayed that the clause in the charter guaranteeing equal liberties and immunities to grantees, might not be violated, so as to "divert out of the true course the free and public current of justice." Thus did the first Assembly of Virginia insist upon the principle of the Declaration of Rights of 1776, that "no man or set of men are entitled to exclusive or separate emoluments or privileges from the community, but in consideration of public services." Certain of the instructions sent out from England were "drawn into laws" for protection of the Indians from injury, and regulating intercourse with them, and educating their children, and preparing some of the most promising boys "for the college intended for them; that from thence they may be sent to that work of conversion;" for regulating agriculture, tobacco, and sassafras, then the chief merchantable commodities raised. Upon Captain Powell's petition, "a lewd and treacherous servant of his" was sentenced to stand for four days with his ears nailed to the pillory, and be whipped each day. John Rolfe complained that Captain Martin had made unjust charges against him, and cast "some aspersion upon the present government, which is the most temperate and just that ever was in this country—too mild, indeed, for many of this colony, whom unwonted liberty hath made insolent, and not to know themselves." On the last day of the session were enacted such laws as issued "out of every man's private conceit." "It shall be free for every man to trade with the Indians, servants only excepted upon pain of whipping, unless the master will redeem it off with the payment of an angel." "No man to sell or give any of the greater hoes to the Indians, or any English dog of quality, as a mastiff, greyhound, bloodhound, land or water spaniel." Any man selling arms or ammunition to the Indians, to be hanged so soon as the fact is proved. All ministers shall duly "read divine service, and exercise their ministerial function according to the ecclesiastical laws and orders of the Church of England, and every Sunday, in the afternoon, shall catechise such as are not ripe to come to the communion." All persons going up or down the James River were to touch at James City, "to know whether the governor will command them any service." "All persons whatsoever, upon the Sabbath days, shall frequent divine service and sermons, both forenoon and afternoon; and all such as bear arms shall bring their pieces, swords, powder, and shot."

Captain Henry Spellman, charged by Robert Poole, interpreter, with speaking ill of the governor "at Opochancano's court," was degraded from his rank of captain, and condemned to serve the colony for seven years as interpreter to the governor. Paspaheigh, embracing three hundred acres of land, was also called Argallstown, and was part of the tract appropriated to the governor. To compensate the speaker, clerk, sergeant, and provost marshal, a pound of the best tobacco was levied from every male above sixteen years of age. The Assembly prayed that the treasurer, council, and company would not "take it in ill part if these laws, which we have now brought to light, do pass current, and be of force till such time as we may know their further pleasure out of England; for otherwise this people (who now at length have got their reins of former servitude into their own swindge) would, in short time, grow so insolent as they would shake off all government, and there would be no living among them." They also prayed the company to "give us power to allow or disallow of their orders of court, as his majesty hath given *them* power to allow or reject *our* laws." So early did it appear, that from the necessity of the case, the colony must in large part legislate for itself, and so early did a spirit of independence manifest itself. Owing to the heat of the weather, several of the burgesses fell sick, and one died, and thus the governor was obliged abruptly, on the fourth of August, to prorogue the Assembly till the first of March.* There being as yet no counties laid off, the representatives were elected from the several towns, plantations, and hundreds, styled boroughs, and hence they were called burgesses.

---

* Proceedings of the First Assembly of Virginia, in 1619.

CHAPTER XII.

1619-1621.

The New Laws—Yeardley, Governor—Affairs of the Colony—Landing of the Pilgrims at Plymouth—Negroes Imported into Virginia—Supplies sent out from England—Wives for the Colonists—The Bishops directed to take up Collections for aid of the Colony in erecting Churches and Schools—England claims a Monopoly of Virginia Tobacco—Charitable Donations.

THUS after eleven years of suffering, peril, discord, and tyranny, intermingled with romantic adventure, bold enterprise, the dignity of danger, virtuous fortitude, and generous heroism, were at length established a local legislature and a regular administration of right. The Virginia planters expressed their gratitude to the company, and begged them to reduce into a compend, with his majesty's approbation, such of the laws of England as were applicable to Virginia, with suitable additions, "because it was not fit that his subjects should be governed by any other rules than such as received their influence from him." The acts of the Assembly were transmitted to England for the approval of the treasurer and company. They were thought to have been very judiciously framed, but the company's committee found them "exceeding intricate and full of labor." There was granted to the old planters an exemption from all compulsory service to the colony, with a confirmation of their estates, which were to be holden as by English subjects.

It is remarkable, that from about 1614, for some seven years, James the First had governed England without a parliament; and the Virginia Company was during this period a rallying point for the friends of civil and religious freedom, and the colony enjoyed the privilege, denied to the mother country, of holding a legislative assembly.

Yeardley finding a scarcity of corn, undertook to promote the cultivation of it, and this year was blessed with abundant crops of grain. But an extraordinary mortality carried off not less than three hundred of the people. Three thousand acres of land were allotted to the governor, and twelve thousand to the company. The Margaret, of Bristol, arrived with some settlers, and "also many devout gifts." The Trial brought a cargo of corn and cattle. The expenditure of the Virginia Company at this period, on account of the colony, was estimated at between four and five thousand pounds a year.

A body of English Puritans, persecuted on account of their nonconformity, had, in 1608, sought an asylum in Holland. In 1617 they conceived the design of removing to America, and in 1619 they obtained from the Virginia Company, by the influence of Sir Edward Sandys, the treasurer, "a large patent," authorizing them to settle in Virginia. They embarked in the latter part of the year 1620, in the Mayflower, intending to settle somewhere near the Hudson River, which lay within the Virginia Company's territory. The Pilgrims were, however, conducted to the bleak and barren coast of Massachusetts, where they landed on the twenty-second day of December, (new style,) 1620, on the rock of Plymouth. Thus, thirteen years after the settlement of Jamestown, was laid the foundation of the New England States. The place of their landing was beyond the limits of the Virginia Company.

In the month of August, 1619, a Dutch man-of-war visited Jamestown and sold the settlers twenty negroes, the first introduced into Virginia. Some time before this, Captain Argall sent out, at the expense of the Earl of Warwick, on a "filibustering" cruise to the West Indies, a ship called the Treasurer, manned "with the ablest men in the colony," under an old commission from the Duke of Savoy against the Spanish dominions in the western hemisphere. She returned to Virginia after some ten months, with her booty, which consisted of captured negroes, who were not left in Virginia, because Captain Argall had gone back to England, but were put on the Earl of Warwick's plantation in the Somer Islands.*

---

* Belknap, art. Argall, citing Declaration of Va. Council, 1623, and Burk's Hist. of Va., i. 319; Smith, ii. 39, where Rolfe gives the true date, 1619; Stith, 171; Beverley, B. i. 37; Chalmers' Annals, 49; Burk, i. 211, and Hening, i.

It is probable that the planters who purchased the negroes from the Dutch man-of-war reasoned but little on the morality of the act, or if any scruples of conscience presented themselves, they could be readily silenced by reflecting that the negroes were heathens, descendants of Ham, and consigned by Divine appointment to perpetual bondage.* The planters may, if they reasoned at all on the subject, have supposed that they were even performing a humane act in releasing these Africans from the noisome hold of the ship. They might well believe that the condition of the negro slave would be less degraded and wretched in Virginia than it had been in their native country. This first purchase was probably not looked upon as a matter of much consequence, and for several ages the increase of the blacks in Virginia was so inconsiderable as not to attract any special attention. The condition of the white servants of the colony, many of them convicts, was so abject, that men, accustomed to see their own race in bondage, could look with more indifference at the worse condition of the slaves.

The negroes purchased by the slavers on the coast of Africa were brought from the interior, convicts sold into slavery, children sold by heathen parents destitute of natural affection, kidnapped villagers, and captives taken in war, the greater part of them born in hereditary bondage. The circumstances under which they were consigned to the slave-ship evince the wretchedness of their condition in their native country, where they were the victims of idolatry, barbarism, and war. The negroes imported were usually between the ages of fourteen and thirty, two-thirds of them being males. The new negro, just transferred from the wilds of a distant continent, was indolent, ignorant of the modes and implements of labor, and of the language of his master, and perhaps of his fellow-laborers.† To tame and domesticate, to instruct in the modes of industry, and to reduce to

---

146, all (as Bancroft, i. 177, remarks,) rely on Beverley. It may be added, that they were all misled by him in making the date 1620. I was enabled to rectify this date by an intimation from the Rev. Dr. Wm. H. Foote, author of "Sketches of Virginia."

* Burk, i. 211. † Bancroft, iii. 402.

subordination and usefulness a barbarian, gross, obtuse, perverse, must have demanded persevering efforts and severe discipline.

While the cruel slave-trade was prompted by a remorseless cupidity, an inscrutable Providence turned the wickedness of men into the means of bringing about beneficent results. The system of slavery, doubtless, entailed many evils on slave and slave-holder, and, perhaps, the greater on the latter. These evils are the tax paid for the elevation of the negro from his aboriginal condition.

Among the vessels that came over to Virginia from England, about this time, is mentioned a bark of five tons. A fleet sent out by the Virginia Company brought over, in 1619, more than twelve hundred settlers.* The planters at length enjoyed the blessings of property in the soil, and the society of women. The wives were sold to the colonists for one hundred and twenty pounds of tobacco, and it was ordered that this debt should have precedence of all others. The price of a wife afterwards became higher. The bishops in England, by the king's orders, collected nearly fifteen hundred pounds to build a college or university at Henrico, intended in part for the education of Indian children.†

---

* They were disposed of in the following way: eighty tenants for the governor's land, one hundred and thirty for the company's land, one hundred for the college, fifty for the glebe, ninety young women of good character for wives, fifty servants, fifty whose labors were to support thirty Indian children; the rest were distributed among private plantations.

† The following is a copy of the letter addressed by the king on this occasion to the archbishops, authorizing them to invite the members of the church throughout the kingdom to assist in the establishment of the college, and such works of piety. The exact date of the letter has not been ascertained; but it was about the year 1620. It has never been published until recently, and is the first document of the kind ever issued in England for the benefit of the colonies. It is as follows:—

"Most reverend father in God, right, trusty, and well-beloved counsellor, we greet you well. You have heard ere this time of the attempt of divers worthy men, our subjects, to plant in Virginia, (under the warrant of our letters patents,) people of this kingdom as well as for the enlarging of our dominions, as for the propagation of the gospel amongst infidels: wherein there is good progress made and hope of further increase; so as the undertakers of that plantation are now in hand with the erecting of some churches and schools for the education of the children of those barbarians, which cannot but be to them a very great charge and above the expense which, for the civil plantation, doth

In July, 1620, the population of the colony was estimated at four thousand. One hundred "disorderly persons" or convicts, sent over during the previous year by the king's order, were employed as servants.* For a brief interval the Virginia Company had enjoyed freedom of trade with the Low Countries, where they sold their tobacco; but in October, 1621, this was prohibited by an order in council; and from this time England claimed a monopoly of the trade of her plantations, and this principle was gradually adopted by all the European powers as they acquired transatlantic settlements.†

---

come to them. In which we doubt not but that you and all others who wish well to the increase of Christian religion, will be willing to give all assistance and furtherance, you may, and therein to make experience of the zeal and devotion of our well-minded subjects, especially those of the clergy. Wherefore we do require you, and hereby authorize you to write your letters to the several bishops of the dioceses in your province, that they do give order to the ministers and other zealous men of their dioceses, both by their own example in contribution and by exhortation to others to move our people within their several charges to contribute to so good a work, in as liberal a manner as they may; for the better advancing whereof our pleasure is, that those collections be made in all the particular parishes, four several times within these two years next coming; and that the several accounts of each parish, together with the moneys collected, be returned from time to time to the bishops of the dioceses, and by them be transmitted half yearly to you; and so to be delivered to the treasurer of that plantation to be employed for the godly purposes intended, and no other." (*Anderson's Hist. of Col. Church*, i. 315; *Stith's Hist. of Va.*, 159.)

* Mr. Jefferson appears to have fallen into a mistake as to the period of time when malefactors were first shipped over to this country from England, for he says: "It was at a late period of their history that the practice began." (*Writings of Jefferson*, i. 405.)

† Chalmers' Introduc., i. 15. The following letter accompanied a shipment of marriageable females sent out from England to Virginia:—

"LONDON, *August* 21, 1621.

"We send you a shipment, one widow and eleven maids, for wives of the people of Virginia: there hath been especial care had in the choice of them, for there hath not one of them been received but upon good commendations.

"In case they cannot be presently married, we desire that they may be put with several householders that have wives, until they can be provided with husbands. There are nearly fifty more that are shortly to come, and are sent by our honorable lord and treasurer, the Earl of Southampton, and certain worthy gentlemen, who, taking into consideration that the plantation can never flourish till families be planted, and the respect of wives and children for their people on the soil, therefore having given this fair beginning; reimbursing of whose

Two persons unknown presented plate and ornaments for the communion-table at the college, and at Mrs. Mary Robinson's Church, so called because she had contributed two hundred pounds toward the founding of it. Another person unknown gave five hundred and fifty pounds for the education of Indian children in Christianity; he subscribed himself "Dust and Ashes;" and was afterwards discovered to be Mr. Gabriel Barber, a member of the company.

---

charges it is ordered that every man that marries them, give one hundred and twenty pounds of best leaf tobacco for each of them.

"We desire that the marriage be free according to nature, and we would not have those maids deceived and married to servants, but only to such freemen or tenants as have means to maintain them. We pray you, therefore, to be fathers of them in this business, not enforcing them to marry against their wills." (*Hubbard's note in Belknap,* art. ARGALL.)

CHAPTER XIII.

Proceedings in London of Virginia Company—Lord Southampton elected Treasurer—Sir Francis Wyat appointed Governor—New frame of Government—Instructions for Governor and Council—George Sandys, Treasurer in Virginia—Notice of his Life and published Works—Productions of the Colony.

Sir Edwin Sandys held the office of treasurer of the company but for one year, being excluded from a re-election by the arbitrary interference of the king. The election was by ballot. The day for it having arrived, the company met, consisting of twenty peers of the realm, near one hundred knights, together with as many more of gallant officers and grave lawyers, and a large number of worthy citizens—an imposing array of rank, and wealth, and talents, and influence. Sir Edwin Sandys being first nominated as a candidate, a lord of the bedchamber and another courtier announced that it was the king's pleasure not to have Sir Edwin Sandys chosen; and because he was unwilling to infringe their right of election, he (the king) would nominate three persons, and permit the company to choose one of them. The company, nevertheless, voted to proceed to an election, as they had a right to do under the charter. Sir Edwin Sandys withdrew his name from nomination, and, at his suggestion it was finally agreed that the king's messengers should name two candidates, and the company one. Upon counting the ballots, it was ascertained that one of the royal candidates received only one vote, and the other only two. The Earl of Southampton received all the rest.

The Virginia Company was divided into two parties, the minority enjoying the favor of the king, and headed by the Earl of Warwick; the other, the liberal, or opposition, or reform party, headed by the Earl of Southampton. The Warwick faction were greatly embittered against Yeardley, and their virulence was increased by his having intercepted a packet from his own secretary, Pory, containing proofs of Argall's misconduct, to be used against him at his trial, which the secretary had been bribed by his friend, the Earl of Warwick, to convey to him. The mild and gentle Yeardley, overcome by these annoyances, at length requested leave to retire from the cares of office. His commission expired in November, 1621; but he continued in the colony, was a member of the council, and enjoyed the respect and esteem of the people. During his short administration, many new settlements were made on the James and York rivers; and the planters, being now supplied with wives and servants, began to be more content, and to take more pleasure in cultivating their lands. The brief interval of free trade with Holland had enlarged the demand for tobacco, and it was cultivated more extensively.

Sir George Yeardley's term of office having expired, the company's council, upon the recommendation of the Earl of Southampton, appointed Sir Francis Wyat governor, a young gentleman of Ireland, whose education, family, fortune, and integrity, well qualified him for the place. He arrived in October, 1621, with a fleet of nine sail, and brought over a new frame of government constituted by the company, and dated July the 24th, 1621, establishing a council of State and a general assembly—vesting the governor with a negative upon the acts of the assembly; this body to be convoked by him in general once a year, and to consist of the council of State and of two burgesses from every town, hundred, or plantation; the trial by jury secured; no act of the assembly to be valid unless ratified by the company in England; and, on the other hand, no order of the company to be obligatory upon the colony without the consent of the assembly. This last feature displays that spirit of constitutional freedom which then pervaded the Virginia Company. A commission bearing the same date with the new frame of government recognized Sir Francis Wyat as the first governor under it; and this famous ordinance became the model of every subsequent provincial form of government in the Anglo-American colonies.*

---

* Chalmers' Introduc., i. 13–16; Belknap, art. SIR FRANCIS WYAT. Belknap is an excellent authority, as accurate as Stith without his diffuseness; and Hubbard's notes are worthy of the text. The ordinance and commission may be seen in Hening's Statutes at Large, i. 110–113.

Wyat brought with him also a body of instructions intended for the permanent guidance of the governor and council. He was to provide for the service of God in conformity with the Church of England as near as may be; to be obedient to the king, and to administer justice according to the laws of England; not to injure the natives, and to forget old quarrels now buried; to be industrious, and to suppress drunkenness, gaming, and excess in clothes; not to permit any but the council and heads of hundreds to wear gold in their clothes, or to wear silk, till they make it themselves; not to offend any foreign prince; to punish pirates; to build forts; to endeavor to convert the heathen; and each town to teach some of the Indian children fit for the college which was to be built; to cultivate corn, wine, and silk; to search for minerals, dyes, gums, and medicinal drugs, and to draw off the people from the excessive planting of tobacco; to take a census of the colony; to put 'prentices to trades and not let them forsake them for planting tobacco, or any such useless commodity; to build water-mills; to make salt, pitch, tar, soap, and ashes; to make oil of walnuts, and employ apothecaries in distilling lees of beer; to make small quantity of tobacco, and that very good.

Wyat, entering on the duties of his office on the eighteenth of November, dispatched Mr. Thorpe to renew the treaties of peace and friendship with Opechancanough, who was found apparently well affected and ready to confirm the pledges of harmony. A vessel from Ireland brought in eighty immigrants, who planted themselves at Newport's News. The company sent out during this year twenty-one vessels, navigated with upwards of four hundred sailors, and bringing over thirteen hundred men, women, and children. The aggregate number of settlers that arrived during 1621 and 1622 was three thousand five hundred.

With Sir Francis Wyat came over George Sandys, treasurer in Virginia, brother of Sir Edwin Sandys, treasurer of the company in England. George Sandys, who was born in 1577, after passing some time at Oxford, in 1610, travelled over Europe to Turkey, and visited Palestine and Egypt. He published his travels, at Oxford, in 1615, and they were received with great favor. The first poetical production in Anglo-American literature was composed by him, while secretary of the colony; and in the midst of the confusion which followed the massacre of 1622,—"by that imperfect light which was snatched from the hours of night and repose,"—he translated the Metamorphoses of Ovid and the First Book of Virgil's Æneid, which was published in 1626, and dedicated to King Charles the First. He also published several other works, and enjoyed the favor of the literary men of the day. Dryden pronounced Sandys the best versifier of his age. Pope declared that English poetry owed much of its beauty to his translations; and Montgomery, the poet, renders his meed of praise to the beauty of the Psalms translated by him. Having lived chiefly in retirement, he died in 1643, at the house of Sir Francis Wyat, in Bexley, Kent. A fine copy of the translation of Ovid and Virgil, printed in 1632, in folio, elegantly illustrated, once the property of the Duke of Sussex, is now in the library of Mr. Grigsby. Mr. Thomas H. Wynne, of Richmond, also has a copy of this rare work.

CHAPTER XIV.

Use of Tobacco in England—Raleigh's Habits of Smoking—His Tobacco-box—Anecdotes of Smoking—King James, his Counterblast—Denunciations against Tobacco—Amount of Tobacco Imported.

In 1615 twelve different commodities had been shipped from Virginia; sassafras and tobacco were now the only exports. During the year 1619 the company in England imported twenty thousand pounds of tobacco, the entire crop of the preceding year. James the First endeavored to draw a "prerogative" revenue from what he termed a pernicious weed, and against which he had published his "Counterblast;" but he was restrained from this illegal measure by a resolution of the House of Commons. In 1607 he sent a letter forbidding the use of tobacco at St. Mary's College, Cambridge.

Smoking was the first mode of using tobacco in England, and when Sir Walter Raleigh first introduced the custom among people of fashion, in order to escape observation he smoked privately in his house, (at Islington,) the remains of which were till of late years to be seen, as an inn, long known as the Pied Bull. This was the first house in England in which it was smoked, and Raleigh had his arms emblazoned there, with a tobacco-plant on the top. There existed also another tradition in the Parish of St. Matthew, Friday Street, London, that Raleigh was accustomed to sit smoking at his door in company with Sir Hugh Middleton. Sir Walter's guests were entertained with pipes, a mug of ale, and a nutmeg, and on these occasions he made use of his tobacco-box, which was of cylindrical form, seven inches in diameter and thirteen inches long; the outside of gilt leather, and within a receiver of glass or metal, which held about a pound of tobacco. A kind of collar connected the receiver with the case, and on every side the box was pierced with holes for the pipes. This relic was preserved in the museum of Ralph Thoresby, of

Leeds, in 1719, and about 1843 was added, by the late Duke of Sussex, to his collection of the smoking utensils of all nations.*

Although Sir Walter Raleigh first introduced the custom of smoking tobacco in England, yet its use appears to have been not entirely unknown before, for one Kemble, condemned for heresy in the time of Queen Mary the Bloody, while walking to the stake smoked a pipe of tobacco. Hence the last pipe that one smokes was called the Kemble pipe.

The writer of a pamphlet, supposed to have been Milton's father, describes many of the play-books and pamphlets of that day, 1609, as "conceived over night by idle brains, impregnated with tobacco smoke and mulled sack, and brought forth by the help of midwifery of a caudle next morning." At the theatres in Shakespeare's time, the spectators were allowed to sit on the stage, and to be attended by pages, who furnished them with pipes and tobacco.

About the time of the settlement of Jamestown, in 1607, the characteristics of a man of fashion were, to wear velvet breeches, with panes or slashes of silk, an enormous starched ruff, a gilt-handled sword, and a Spanish dagger; to play at cards or dice in the chamber of the groom-porter, and to smoke tobacco in the tilt-yard, or at the playhouse.

The peers engaged in the trial of the Earls of Essex and Southampton smoked much while they deliberated on their verdict. It was alleged against Sir Walter Raleigh that he used tobacco on the occasion of the execution of the Earl of Essex, in contempt of him; and it was perhaps in allusion to this circumstance that when Raleigh was passing through London to Winchester, to stand his trial, he was followed by the execrations of the populace, and pelted with tobacco-pipes, stones, and mud. On the scaffold, however, he protested that during the execution of Essex he had retired far off into the armory, where Essex could not see him, although he saw Essex, and shed tears for him. Raleigh used tobacco on the morning of his own execution.

As early as the year 1610 tobacco was in general use in Eng-

---

* Introduction to "A Counterblast to Tobacco, by James the First, King of England," published at Newcastle-upon-Tyne, 1843.

land. The manner of using it was partly to inhale the smoke and blow it out through the nostrils, and this was called "drinking tobacco," and this practice continued until the latter part of the reign of James the First. In 1614 the number of tobacco-houses in or near London was estimated at seven thousand. In 1620 was chartered the Society of Tobacco-pipe Makers of London; they bore on their shield a tobacco-plant in full blossom.

The "Counterblast against Tobacco," attributed to James the First, if in some parts absurd and puerile, yet is not without a good deal of just reasoning and good sense; some fair hits are made in it, and those who have ridiculed that production might find it not easy to controvert some of its views. King James, in his Counterblast, does not omit the opportunity of expressing his hatred toward Sir Walter Raleigh, in terms worthy of that despicable monarch. He continued his opposition to tobacco as long as he lived, and in his ordinary conversation oftentimes argued and inveighed against it.

The Virginia tobacco in early times was imported into England in the leaf, in bundles, as at present; the Spanish or West Indian tobacco in balls. Molasses or other liquid preparation was used in preparing those balls. Tobacco was then, as now, adulterated in various ways. The nice retailer kept it in what were called lily-pots, that is, white jars. The tobacco was cut on a maple block; juniper-wood, which retains fire well, was used for lighting pipes, and among the rich silver tongs were employed for taking up a coal of it. Tobacco was sometimes called the American Silver Weed.

The Turkish Vizier thrust pipes through the noses of smokers; and the Shah of Persia cropped the ears and slit the noses of those who made use of the fascinating leaf. The Counterblast says of it: "And for the vanity committed in this filthy custom, is it not both great vanity and uncleanness, that at the table—a place of respect of cleanliness, of modesty—men should not be ashamed to sit tossing of tobacco-pipes and puffing of smoke, one at another, making the filthy smoke and stink thereof to exhale athwart the dishes, and infect the air, when very often men who abhor it are at their repast? Surely smoke becomes a kitchen far better than a dining-chamber; and yet it makes the kitchen oftentimes in the inward parts of man, soiling and infecting them with an unctuous and oily kind of soot, as hath been found in some great tobacco-takers that after their deaths were opened."

"A Counterblast to Tobacco," by James the First, King of England, was first printed in quarto, without name or date, at London, 1616. In the frontispiece was engraved the tobacco-smoker's coat of arms, consisting of a blackamoor's head, cross-pipes, cross-bones, death's-head, etc. It is not improbable that it was intended to foment the popular prejudice against Sir Walter Raleigh, who first introduced the use of tobacco into England, and who was put to death in the same year, 1616. King James alludes to the introduction of the use of tobacco and of Raleigh as follows: "It is not so long since the first entry of this abuse among us here, as that this present age cannot very well remember both the first author and the form of the first introduction of it among us. It was neither brought in by king, great conqueror, nor learned doctor of physic. With the report of a great discovery for a conquest, some two or three savage men were brought in together with this savage custom; but the pity is, the poor wild barbarous men died, but that vile barbarous custom is still alive, yea, in fresh vigor; so as it seems a miracle to me how a custom springing from so vile a ground, and brought in by a father so generally hated, should be welcomed upon so slender a warrant."

The king thus reasons against the Virginia staple: "Secondly, it is, as you use or rather abuse it, a branch of the sin of drunkenness, which is the root of all sins,* for as the only delight that drunkards love any weak or sweet drink, so are not those (I mean the strong heat and fume) the only qualities that make tobacco so delectable to all the lovers of it? And as no man loves strong heavy drinks the first day, (because nemo repente fuit turpissimus,) but by custom is piece and piece allured, while in the end a drunkard will have as great a thirst to be drunk as a sober man to quench his thirst with a draught when he hath need of it; so is not this the true case of all the great takers of tobacco, which therefore they themselves do attribute to a bewitching quality in

---

* And one from which the king himself was not free.

it? Thirdly, is it not the greatest sin of all that you, the people of all sorts of this kingdom, who are created and ordained by God to bestow both your persons and goods for the maintenance both of the honor and safety of your king and commonwealth, should disable yourself to this shameful imbecility, that you are not able to ride or walk the journey of a Jew's Sabbath but you must have a reeky coal brought you from the next poor-house to kindle your tobacco with? whereas he cannot be thought able for any service in the wars that cannot endure oftimes the want of meat, drink, and sleep; much more then must he endure the want of tobacco." A curious tractate on tobacco, by Dr. Tobias Venner, was published at London in 1621. The author was a graduate of Oxford, and a physician at Bath, and is mentioned in the Oxoniæ Athenienses.*

The amount of tobacco imported in 1619 into England, from Virginia, being the entire crop of the preceding year, was twenty thousand pounds. At the end of seventy years there were annually imported into England more than fifteen millions of pounds of it, from which was derived a revenue of upwards of £100,000.†

In April, 1621, the House of Commons debated whether it was expedient to prohibit the importation of tobacco entirely; and they determined to exclude all save from Virginia and the Somer Isles. It was estimated that the consumption of England amounted to one thousand pounds per diem. This seductive narcotic leaf, which soothes the mind and quiets its perturbations, has found its way into all parts of the habitable globe, from the sunny tropics to the snowy regions of the frozen pole. Its fragrant smoke ascends alike to the blackened rafters of the lowly hut, and the gilded ceilings of luxurious wealth.

---

* A copy of this rare pamphlet was lent me by N. S. Walker, Esq., of Richmond.
† Chalmers, Introduc. to Hist. of Revolt of Amer. Colonies, i. 18.

CHAPTER XV.

1621-1622.

Silk in Virginia—Endowment of East India School—Ministers in Virginia—Sermon at Bow Church—Corporation of Henrico.

IN November and December, 1621, at an assembly held at James City, acts were passed for encouraging the planting of mulberry-trees, and the making of silk; but this enterprise, so early commenced in Virginia, and so earnestly revived of late years, is still unsuccessful; and it may be concluded that the climate of Virginia is unpropitious to that sort of production.

The Rev. Mr. Copeland, Chaplain on board of the Royal James, East Indiaman, on the return voyage from the East Indies, prevailed upon the officers and crew of that ship to contribute seventy pounds toward the establishment of a church and school in Virginia, and Charles City County was selected as the site of it, and it was to be called the East India School, and to be dependent upon the college at Henrico. The Virginia Company allotted one thousand acres of land for the maintenance of the master and usher, and presented three hundred acres to Mr. Copeland. Workmen were accordingly sent out early in 1622, to begin the building. The clergymen in Virginia at this time were Messrs. Whitaker, Mease, Wickham, Stockham, and Bargrave.*

The following is found in the early records:—

THE CORPORATION OF HENRICO.

On the northerly ridge of James River, from the falls down to Henrico, containing ten miles in length, are the public lands, surveyed and laid out; whereof, ten thousand acres for the university lands, three thousand acres for the company's lands, with other lands belonging to the college. The common land for that corporation, fifteen hundred acres.

On the southerly side, beginning from the falls, there are there patented, viz.:—

Early in 1622 very favorable intelligence from Virginia reached England, and upon this occasion, on the seventeenth of April, the Rev. Mr. Copeland, by appointment, preached before the Virginia Company, at Bow Church. He was shortly afterwards appointed a member of the Virginia Council and rector of the college established for the conversion of the Indians; but all these benevolent purposes and hopeful anticipations were suddenly darkened and defeated by the news of a catastrophe which had, in a few hours, blasted the labors of so many years.

	Acres.		Acres.
John Petterson	100	Peter Nemenart	110
Anthony Edwards	100	William Perry	100
Nathaniel Norton	100	John Plower	100
John Proctor	200	Surveyed for the use of the iron-work.	
Thomas Tracy	100		
John Vithard	100	Edward Hudson	100
Francis Weston	300	Thomas Morgan	150
Phettiplace Close	100	Thomas Sheffield	150
John Price	150		

Cosendale, within the Corporation of Henrico:—

	Acres.		Acres.
Lieut. Edward Barckley	112	Peter Nemenart	40
Richard Poulton	100	Thomas Tindall	100
Robert Analand	200	Thomas Reed	100
John Griffin	50	John Laydon	200

CHAPTER XVI.

1622.

The Massacre—Its Origin, Nemattanow—Opechancanough—Security of Colonists—Perfidy of the Indians—Particulars of Massacre—Its Consequences—Brave Defence of some—Supplies sent from England—Captain Smith's Offer.

On the twenty-second day of March, 1622, there occurred in the colony a memorable massacre, which originated, as was believed, in the following circumstances: There was among the Indians a famous chief, named Nemattanow, or "Jack of the Feather," as he was styled by the English, from his fashion of decking his hair. He was reckoned by his own people invulnerable to the arms of the English. This Nemattenow coming to the store of one of the settlers named Morgan, persuaded him to go to Pamunkey to trade, and murdered him by the way. Nemattanow, in two or three days, returned to Morgan's house, and finding there two young men, Morgan's servants, who inquired for their master, answered them that he was dead. The young men, seeing their master's cap on the Indian's head, suspected the murder, and undertook to conduct him to Mr. Thorpe, who then lived at Berkley, on the James River, since well known as a seat of the Harrisons, and originally called "Brickley." Nemattanow so exasperated the young men on the way that they shot him, and he falling, they put him into a boat and conveyed him to the governor at Jamestown, distant seven or eight miles. The wounded chief in a short time died. Feeling the approaches of death, he entreated the young men not to disclose that he had been mortally wounded by a bullet: so strong is the desire for posthumous fame even in the breast of a wild, untutored savage!

Opechancanough, the ferocious Indian chief, agitated with mingled emotions of grief and indignation at the loss of his favorite Nemattanow, at first muttered threats of revenge; but the retorted defiance of the English made him for a time smother his resentment and dissemble his dark designs under the guise of friendship. Accordingly, upon Sir Francis Wyat's arrival, all suspicion of Indian treachery had died away; the colonists, in delusive security, were in general destitute of arms; the plantations lay dispersed, as caprice suggested, or a rich vein of land allured, as far as the Potomac River;* their houses everywhere open to the Indians, who fed at their tables and lodged under their roofs. About the middle of March, a messenger being sent upon some occasion to Opechancanough, he entertained him kindly, and protested that he held the peace so firm that "the sky should fall before he broke it." On the twentieth of the same month, the Indians guided some of the English safely through the forest, and the more completely to lull all suspicion, they sent one Brown, who was sojourning among them for the purpose of learning their language, back home to his master. They even borrowed boats from the whites to cross the river when about holding a council on the meditated attack. The massacre took place on Friday, the twenty-second of March, 1622. On the evening before, and on that very morning, the Indians, as usual, came unarmed into the houses of the unsuspecting colonists, with fruits, fish, turkeys, and venison for sale: in some places they actually sate down to breakfast with the English. At about the hour of noon the savages, rising suddenly and everywhere at the same time, butchered the colonists with their own implements, sparing neither age, nor sex, nor condition; and thus fell in a few hours three hundred and forty-nine men, women, and children. The infuriated savages wreaked their vengeance even on the dead, dragging and mangling the lifeless bodies, smearing their hands in blood, and bearing off the torn and yet palpitating limbs as trophies of a brutal triumph.

Among their victims was Mr. George Thorpe, (a kinsman of Sir Thomas Dale,) who had been of the king's bedchamber, deputy to the college lands, and one of the principal men of the colony —a pious gentleman, who had labored zealously for the conversion of the Indians, and had treated them with uniform kindness. As an instance of this, they having at one time expressed their fears of the English mastiff dogs, he had caused some of them

---

* Beverley, 89.

to be put to death, to the great displeasure of their owners. Opechancanough inhabiting a paltry cabin, Mr. Thorpe had built him a handsome house after the English manner.* But the savage miscreants, equally deaf to the voice of humanity and the emotions of gratitude, murdered their benefactor with every circumstance of remorseless cruelty. He had been forewarned of his danger by a servant, but making no effort to escape, fell a victim to his misplaced confidence. With him ten other persons were slain at Berkley.

Another of the victims was Captain Nathaniel Powell, one of the first settlers, a brave soldier, and who had for a brief interval filled the place of governor of the colony. His family fell with him. Nathaniel Causie, another of Captain Smith's old soldiers, when severely wounded and surrounded by the Indians, slew one of them with an axe, and put the rest to flight. At Warrasqueake a colonist named Baldwin, by repeatedly firing his gun, saved himself and family, and divers others. The savages at the same time made an attempt upon the house of a planter named Harrison, (near Baldwin's,) where were Thomas Hamor with some men, and a number of women and children. The Indians tried to inveigle Hamor out of the house, by pretending that Opechancanough was hunting in the neighboring woods and desired to have his company; but he not coming out, they set fire to a tobacco-house; the men ran toward the fire, and were pursued by the Indians, who pierced them with arrows and beat out their brains. Hamor having finished a letter that he was writing, and suspecting no treachery, went out to see what was the matter, when, being wounded in the back with an arrow, he returned to the house and barricaded it. Meanwhile Harrison's boy, finding his master's gun loaded, fired it at random, and the Indians fled. Baldwin still continuing to discharge his gun, Hamor, with twenty-two others, withdrew to his house, leaving their own in flames. Hamor next retired to a new house that he was building, and there defending himself with spades, axes, and brickbats, escaped the fury of the savages. The master of a vessel lying

---

* The chief was so charmed with it, especially with the lock and key, that he locked and unlocked the door a hundred times a day.

in the James River sent a file of musqueteers ashore, who recaptured from the enemy the Merchant's store-house. In the neighborhood of Martin's Hundred seventy-three persons were butchered; yet a small family there escaped, and heard nothing of the massacre until two days after.

Thus fell in so short a space of time one-twelfth part of the colonists of Virginia, including six members of the council. The destruction might have been universal but for the disclosure of a converted Indian, named Chanco, who, during the night preceding the massacre, revealed the plot to one Richard Pace, with whom he lived. Pace, upon receiving this intelligence, after fortifying his own house, repaired before day to Jamestown, and gave the alarm to Sir Francis Wyat, the Governor; his vigilance saved a large part of the colony from destruction.* Eleven were killed at Berkley, fifty at Edward Bonit's plantation, two at Westover, five at Macocks, four on Appomattox River, six at Flower-de-Hundred, twenty-one of Sir George Yeardley's people at Weyanoke, and seventy-three at Martin's Hundred, seven miles from Jamestown.

The horrors of famine threatened to follow in the train of massacre, and the consternation of the survivors was such that twenty or thirty days elapsed before any plan of defence was concerted. Many were urgent to abandon the James River, and take refuge on the eastern shore, where some newly settled plantations had escaped. At length it was determined to abandon the weaker plantations, and to concentrate their surviving population in five or six well fortified places, Shirley, Flower-de-Hundred, Jamestown, with Paspahey, and the plantations opposite to Kiquotan, and Southampton Hundred. In consequence a large part of the cattle and effects of the planters fell a prey to the enemy. Nevertheless, a planter, "Master Gookins," at Newport's News, refused to abandon his plantation, and with thirty-five men resolutely held it.

The family of Gookins is ancient, and appears to have been found originally at Canterbury, in Kent, England. The name

---

* Purchas, his Pilgrim, iv. 1788; Smith, ii. 65: a list of the slain may be found on page 70.

has undergone successive changes—Colkin, Cockin, Cockayn, Cocyn, Cokain, Cokin, Gockin, Gokin, Gookin, Gookins, Gooking, and others. The early New England chroniclers spelled it "Goggin."* Daniel Gookin removed to County Cork, in Ireland, and thence to Virginia, arriving in November, 1621, with fifty men of his own and thirty passengers, exceedingly well furnished with all sorts of provision and cattle, and planted himself at Newport's News. In the massacre he held out with a force of thirty-five men against the savages, disregarding the order to retire. It is probable that he affected to make a settlement independent of the civil power of the colony, and it appears to have been styled by his son a "lordship." It was above Newport's News, and was called "Mary's Mount."†

To return to the incidents of the massacre. Samuel Jordan, with the aid of a few refugees, maintained his ground at Beggar's Bush;‡ as also did Mr. Edward Hill, at Elizabeth City. "Mrs. Proctor, a proper, civil, modest gentlewoman," defended herself and family for a month after the massacre, until at last constrained to retire by the English officers, who threatened, if she refused, to burn her house down; which was done by the Indians shortly after her withdrawal. Captain Newce, of Elizabeth City, and his wife, distinguished themselves by their liberality to the sufferers. Several families escaped to the country afterwards known as North Carolina, and settled there.§

When intelligence of this event reached England, the king granted the Virginia Company some unserviceable arms out of

---

* ARMS. Quarterly: First, gules, a chevron ermine between three cocks or, two in chief, one in base, Gookin. Second and third, sable, a cross crosslet, ermine. Fourth, or, a lion rampant, gules between six crosses fitchée. CREST. On a mural crown, gules, a cock or, beaked and legged azure, combed and wattled gu.

† Article by J. Wingate Thornton, Esq., of Boston, in Mass. Gen. and Antiq. Register, vol. for 1847, page 345, referring, among other authorities, to Records of General Court of Virginia.

‡ Afterwards called and still known as Jordan's Point, in the County of Prince George, the seat of the revolutionary patriot Richard Bland. Beggar's Bush, as already mentioned, was the title of one of Fletcher's comedies then in vogue in England. (*Hallam's Hist. of Literature*, ii. 210.)

§ Martin's Hist. of North Carolina, i. 87.

the Tower, and "*lent* them twenty barrels of powder;" Lord St. John of Basing gave sixty coats of mail; the privy council sent out supplies, and the City of London dispatched one hundred settlers.*

One effect of the massacre was the ruin of the iron-works at Falling Creek, on the south side of the James River, (near Ampthill in the present County of Chesterfield,) where, of twenty-four people, only a boy and girl escaped by hiding themselves.† Lead was found near these iron-works. King James promised to send over four hundred soldiers for the protection of the colony; but he never could be induced to fulfil his promise. Captain John Smith offered, if the company would send him to Virginia, with a small force, to reduce the savages to subjection, and protect the colony from future assaults. His project failed on account of the dissensions of the company, and the niggardly terms proposed by the few members that were found to act on the matter. The Rev. Jonas Stockham, in May, 1621, previous to the massacre, had expressed the opinion that it was utterly in vain to undertake the conversion of the savages, until their priests and "ancients" were put to the sword. Captain Smith held the same opinion, and he states that the massacre drove all to believe that Mr. Stockham was right in his view on this point.‡ The event justified the policy of Argall in prohibiting intercourse with the natives, and had that measure been enforced, the massacre would probably have been prevented. The violence and corruption of such rulers as Argall serve to disgrace and defeat even good measures; while the virtues of the good are sometimes perverted to canonize the most pernicious.

---

* Smith, ii. 79; Chalmers' Introduction, i. 19; Belknap, art. WYAT.
† Beverley, 43.
‡ Anderson's Hist. of Col. Church, i. 343; Smith, 139; Stith, 233.

CHAPTER XVII.//
1622.

Crashaw and Opechancanough—Captain Madison massacres a Party of the Natives—Yeardley invades the Nansemonds and the Pamunkies—They are driven back—Reflections on their Extermination.

DURING these calamitous events that had befallen the colony, Captain Raleigh Crashaw had been engaged in a trading cruise up the Potomac. While he was there, Opechancanough sent two baskets of beads to Japazaws, the chief of the Potomacs, to bribe him to slay Crashaw and his party, giving at the same time tidings of the massacre, with an assurance that "before the end of two moons" there should not be an Englishman left in all the country. Japazaws communicated the message to Crashaw, and he thereupon sent Opechancanough word "that he would nakedly fight him, or any of his, with their own swords." The challenge was declined. Not long afterwards Captain Madison, who occupied a fort on the Potomac River, suspecting treachery on the part of the tribe there, rashly killed thirty or forty men, women, and children, and carried off the werowance and his son, and two of his people, prisoners to Jamestown. The captives were in a short time ransomed.

When the corn was ripe, Sir George Yeardley, with three hundred men, invaded the country of the Nansemonds, who, setting fire to their cabins, and destroying whatever they could not carry away, fled; whereupon the English seized their corn, and completed the work of devastation. Sailing next to Opechancanough's seat, at the head of York River, Yeardley inflicted the same chastisement on the Pamunkies. "In New England it was said: "Since the news of the massacre in Virginia, though the Indians continue their wonted friendship, yet are we more wary of them than before, for their hands have been embrued in much English blood, only by too much confidence, but not by force."*

---

* Purchas, iv. 1840.

The red men of Virginia were driven back, like hunted wolves, from their ancient haunts. While their fate cannot fail to excite commiseration, it may reasonably be concluded that the perpetual possession of this country by the aborigines would have been incompatible with the designs of Providence in promoting the welfare of mankind. A productive soil could make little return to a people so destitute of the art and of the implements of agriculture, and habitually indolent. Navigable rivers, the natural channels of commerce, would have failed in their purpose had they borne no freight but that of the rude canoe; primeval forests would have slept in gloomy inutility, where the axe was unknown; and the mineral and metallic treasures of the earth would have remained forever entombed. In Virginia, since the aboriginal population was only about one to the square mile, they could not be justly held occupants of the soil. However well-founded their title to those narrow portions which they actually occupied, yet it was found impossible to take possession of the open country, to which the savages had no just claim, without also exterminating them from those particular spots that rightfully belonged to them. This inevitable necessity actuated the pious Puritans of Plymouth as well as the less scrupulous settlers of Jamestown; and force was resorted to in all the Anglo-American settlements except in that effected, at a later day, by the gentle and sagacious Penn. The unrelenting hostility of the savages, their perfidy and vindictive implacability, made sanguinary measures necessary. In Virginia, the first settlers, a small company, in an unknown wilderness, were repeatedly assaulted, so that resistance and retaliation were demanded by the natural law of self-defence. Nor were these settlers voluntary immigrants; the bulk of them had been sent over, without regard to their choice, by the king or the Virginia Company. Nor did the king or the company authorize any injustice or cruelty to be exercised toward the natives: on the contrary, the colonists, however unfit, were enjoined to introduce the Christian religion among them, and to propitiate their good will by a humane and lenient treatment. Smith and his comrades, so far from being encouraged to maltreat the Indians, were often hampered in making a necessary self-defence, by a fear of offending an arbitrary government at home.

It has been remarked by Mr. Jefferson,* that it is not so general a truth, as has been supposed, that the lands of Virginia were taken from the natives by conquest, far the greater portion having been purchased by treaty. It may be objected, that the consideration was often inadequate; but a small consideration may have been sufficient to compensate for a title which, for the most part, had but little validity; besides, a larger compensation would oftentimes have been thrown away upon men so ignorant and indolent. Groping in the dim twilight of nature, and slaves of a gross idolatry, their lives were circumscribed within a narrow uniform circle of animal instincts and the necessities of a precarious subsistence. Cunning, bloody, and revengeful, engaged in frequent wars, they were strangers to that Arcadian innocence and the Elysian scenes of a golden age of which youthful poets so fondly dream. If an occasional exception occurs, it is but a solitary ray of light shooting across the surrounding gloom. Yet we cannot be insensible to the many injuries they have suffered, and cannot but regret that their race could not be united with our own. The Indian has long since disappeared from Virginia; his cry no longer echoes in the woods, nor is the dip of his paddle heard on the water. The exterminating wave still urges them onward to the setting sun, and their tribes are fading one by one forever from the map of existence. Geology shows that in the scale of animal life, left impressed on the earth's strata, the inferior species has still given place to the superior: so likewise is it with the races of men.

---

* Notes on Va., 102.

CHAPTER XVIII.

1622-1625.

James the First jealous of Virginia Company—Gondomar—The King takes Measures to annul the Charter—Commissioners appointed—Assembly Petitions the King—Disputes between Commissioners and Assembly—Butler's Account of the Colony—Nicholas Ferrar—Treachery of Sharpless, and his Punishment—The Charter of Virginia Company dissolved—Causes of this Proceeding—Character of the Company—Records of the Company—Death of James the First—Charles the First succeeds him—The Virginia Company—Earl of Southampton—Sir Edwin Sandys and Nicholas Ferrar—The Rev. Jonas Stockham's Letter—Injustice of the Dissolution of the Charter—Beneficial Results—Assembly of 1624.

THE Court of James the First, already jealous of the growing power and republican spirit of the Virginia Company, was rendered still more inimical by the malign influence of Count Gondomar, the Spanish ambassador, who was jealous of any encroachment on the Spanish colony of Florida. He remarked to King James, of the Virginia Company, that "they were deep politicians, and had further designs than a tobacco-plantation; that as soon as they should get to be more numerous, they intended to step beyond their limits, and, for aught he knew, they might visit his master's mines." The massacre afforded an occasion to the enemies of the company to attribute all the calamities of the colony to its mismanagement and neglect, and thus to frame a plausible pretext for dissolving the charter.

Captain Nathaniel Butler, a dependent of the Earl of Warwick, had, by his influence, been sent out Governor of Bermudas for three years, where he exercised the same oppression and extortion as Argall had exhibited in Virginia. Upon finding himself compelled to leave those islands, he came to Virginia, in the midst of the winter succeeding the massacre. He was hospitably entertained by Governor Wyat, which kindness he proved himself wholly unworthy of, his conduct being profligate and disorderly.

(169)

He demanded a seat in the council, to which he was in no way entitled. He went up the James as far as to the mouth of the Chickahominy, where "he plundered Lady Dale's cattle;" and after a three months' stay, he set sail for England. Upon his return, Butler was introduced to the king, and published "The Unmasked Face of our Colony in Virginia, as it was in the Winter of 1622," in which he took advantage of the misfortunes of the colony, and exaggerated its deplorable condition. The Rev. William Mease, (who had been for ten years resident in the colony,) with several others, replied to this defamatory pamphlet.*

The company was divided into two parties, the one headed by the Earl of Southampton, Lord Cavendish, Sir Edward Sackville, Sir John Ogle, Sir Edwin Sandys, with several others of less note; on the other side, the leaders were the Earl of Warwick, Sir Thomas Smith, Sir Nathaniel Rich, Sir Henry Mildmay, Alderman Johnson, etc. They appeared before the king, the Earl of Warwick's faction presenting their accusations against the company, and the other side defending it; and Sir Edward Sackville used such freedom of language that "the king was fain to take him down soundly and roundly." However, by the lord treasurer's intervention, the matter was reconciled on the next day.†

In May, 1623, a commission was issued authorizing Sir William Jones, a justice of the common pleas, Sir Nicholas Fortescue, Sir Francis Goston, Sir Richard Sutton, Sir William Pitt, Sir Henry Bourchier, and Sir Henry Spilman,‡ to inquire into the affairs of the colony. By an order of the privy council the records of the company were seized, and the deputy treasurer, Nicholas Ferrar, imprisoned, and on the arrival of a ship from Virginia, her packets were seized and laid before the privy council.

Nicholas Ferrar, Jr., was born in London in 1592, educated at Cambridge, where he was noted for his talents, acquirements,

---

* Stith, 243, 268.
† Court and Times of James the First, ii. 389.
‡ Stith calls him Spilman; Burk, Spiller. (See *Belknap*. art. WYAT.)

and piety.* Upon leaving the university he made the tour of Europe, winning the esteem of the learned, passing through many adventures and perils with Christian heroism, and maintaining everywhere an unsullied character. Upon his return to England, in 1518, he was appointed king's counsel for the Virginia Plantation. In the year 1622 he was chosen deputy treasurer of the Virginia Company, (which office his brother John also filled for some years,) and so remained till its dissolution. In the House of Commons he distinguished himself by his opposition to the political corruption of that day, and abandoned public life when little upwards of thirty years of age, "in obedience to a religious fancy he had long entertained," and formed of his family and relations a sort of little half-popish convent, in which he passed the remainder of his life.†

Carlyle‡ thus describes this singular place of retirement: "Crossing Huntingdonshire in his way northward, his majesty§ had visited the establishment of Nicholas Ferrar, at Little Gidding, on the western border of that county. A surprising establishment now in full flower, wherein above fourscore persons, including domestics, with Ferrar and his brother, and aged mother at the head of them, had devoted themselves to a kind of Protestant monachism, and were getting much talked of in those times. They followed celibacy and merely religious duties; employed themselves in binding of prayer-books, embroidering of hassocks, in almsgiving also, and what charitable work was possible in that desert region; above all, they kept up, night and day, a continual repetition of the English liturgy, being divided into relays and watches, one watch relieving another, as on shipboard, and never allowing at any hour the sacred fire to go out."

In October, 1623, the king declared his intention to grant a new charter modelled after that of 1606. This astounding order

---

* His father, of the same name, a London merchant, was one of the leading stockholders in the Virginia Company. Sir Walter Raleigh, Sir John Hawkins, Sir Francis Drake, Sir Edwin Sandys, and the like, were frequent guests at his table.

† Belknap, art. WYAT, in note; Foster's Miscellanies, 368.

‡ Letters and Speeches of Oliver Cromwell, i 69.

§ Charles the First.

was read three times, at a meeting of the company, before they could credit their own ears; then, by an overwhelming vote, they refused to relinquish their charter, and expressed their determination to defend it.

The king, in order to procure additional evidence to be used against the company, appointed five commissioners to make inquiries in Virginia into the state and condition of the colony. In November, 1623, when two of these commissioners had just sailed for Virginia, the king ordered a writ of *quo warranto* to be issued against the Virginia Company.

In the colony, hitherto, the proclamations of the governors, which had formed the rule of action, were now enacted into laws; and it was declared that the governor should no more impose taxes on the colonists without the consent of the Assembly, and that he should not withdraw the inhabitants from their private labor to any service of his; and further, that the burgesses should be free from arrest during the session of the Assembly. These acts of the legislature of the infant colony, while under the control of the Virginia Company, render it certain that there was more of constitutional and well-regulated freedom in Virginia then, than in the mother country.

Of the commissioners appointed to make inquiries in Virginia, John Harvey and John Pory arrived there early in 1624; Samuel Matthews and Abraham Percy were planters resident in the colony, and the latter a member of the House of Burgesses; John Jefferson, the other commissioner, did not come over to Virginia, nor did he take any part in the matter, being a hearty friend to the company.* Thomas Jefferson, in his memoir of himself,† says that one of his name was secretary to the Virginia Company. The Virginia planters at first looking on it as a dispute between the crown and the company, in which they were not essentially interested, paid little attention to it; but two petitions, defamatory of the colony and laudatory of Sir Thomas Smith's arbitrary rule, having come to the knowledge of the Assembly, in February, 1624, that body prepared spirited replies, and drafted a petition to the king, which, with a letter to

---

* Stith, 297. † Writings of Jefferson, i. 1.

the privy council, and other papers, were entrusted to Mr. John Pountis, a member of the council.* He died during the voyage to England. The letter addressed to the privy council prayed "that the governors may not have absolute power, that they might still retain the liberty of popular assemblies, than which nothing could more conduce to the public satisfaction and public utility." At the same time the Virginia Company, in England, presented a petition to the House of Commons against the arbitrary proceedings of the king; but although favorably received, it was withdrawn as soon as the king's disapprobation was announced.

In Virginia the commissioners refused to exhibit their commission and instructions, and the Assembly therefore refused to give them access to their records. Pory, one of the commissioners, who had formerly lost his place of secretary of the colony by betraying its secrets to the Earl of Warwick, suborned Edward Sharpless, clerk of the council, to expose to him copies of the journal of that body, and of the House of Burgesses. Sharpless being convicted of this misdemeanor was sentenced to the pillory, with the loss of his ears.† Only a part of one ear was actually cut off.

The commissioners, having failed to obtain from the Assembly a declaration of their willingness to submit to the king's purpose of revoking the charter, made a report against the company's management of the colony and the government of it, as too popular, that is, democratic, under the present charter. The king, by a proclamation issued in July, suppressed the meetings of the company, and ordered for the present a committee of the privy council, and others, to sit every Thursday, at the house of Sir Thomas Smith, in Philpot Lane, for conducting the affairs of the colony. Viscount Mandeville was at the head of this committee: Sir George Calvert, Sir Ferdinando Gorges, Sir Samuel Argall, John Pory, Sir John Wolstenholme, and others, were members. At the instance of the attorney-general, to enable the company to make a defence, their books were restored and the deputy treasurer released. In Trinity term, 1624, the writ of *quo war-*

---

* Hening, i. 120. † Stith, 315.

ranto was tried in the Court of King's Bench, and the charter of the Virginia Company was annulled. The case was determined only upon a technicality in the pleadings.

In one of the hearings against the company, before the privy council, the Marquis of Hamilton said of the letters and instructions of the company, written by Nicholas Ferrar, Jr.: "They are papers as admirably well penned as any I ever heard." And the Earl of Pembroke remarked: "They all deserve the highest commendation: containing advices far more excellent than I could have expected to have met with in the letters of a trading company. For they abound with soundness of good matter and profitable instruction, with respect both to religion and policy; and they possess uncommon elegance of language."*

The company had been long obnoxious to the king's ill will for several reasons; it had become a nursery for rearing and training leaders of the opposition, many of its members being likewise members of parliament. It was a sort of reform club. The king, in a speech, swore that "the Virginia Company was a seminary for a seditious parliament." The company had chosen a treasurer in disregard of the king's nomination; and in electing Carew Raleigh, a member, they had made allusions to his father, Sir Walter Raleigh, which were doubtless unpalatable to the author of his judicial murder. The king was greedy of power and of money, which he wanted the sense and the virtue to make a good use of; and he hoped to find in Virginia a new field for extortion. Fortunately for the history of the colony, copies of the company's records were made by the precaution of Nicholas Ferrar: these being deposited in the hands of the Earl of Southampton, after his death, which took place in 1624, descended to his son. After his death, in 1667, they were purchased from his executors, for sixty guineas, by the first Colonel William Byrd, then in England. From these two folio volumes, in possession of Sir John Randolph, and from the records of the colony, Stith compiled much of his History of Virginia, which comes down to the year 1624.†

---

* Hist. Mag., ii. 34.

† It has been said that these folios were sent back to England by John Randolph of Roanoke, (*Belknap*, art. WYAT;) but it appears that they came into

On the sixth day of April, 1625, died King James the First, aged fifty-nine, after a reign of twenty years. By his consort, Anne of Denmark, he had issue, Henry and Robert, who died young, Charles, his successor, and Elizabeth, who married Frederic the Fifth, elector Palatine. Charles the First succeeding to the crown and the principles of his father, took the government of Virginia into his own hands.

The company thus dissolved, had expended one hundred and fifty thousand pounds in establishing the colony, and had transported nine thousand settlers without the aid of government. The number of stockholders was about one thousand; and the annual value of exports from Virginia was, at the period of the dissolution of the charter, only twenty thousand pounds.

The company embraced much of the rank, wealth, and talents of the kingdom—near fifty noblemen, several hundred knights, and many gentlemen, merchants, and citizens. Among the leaders in its courts were Lord Cavendish, afterwards Earl of Devonshire; Sir Edwin Sandys; and Sir Edward Sackville, afterwards the celebrated Earl of Dorset; and, above all, the Earl of Southampton, the friend of Essex, and the patron of Shakespeare. Henry Wriothesley, third Earl of Southampton, in 1601, was implicated with the Earl of Essex in his hair-brained and abortive conspiracy to seize the person of Queen Elizabeth. Essex lost his life. Southampton was convicted, attainted and imprisoned during the queen's life. Upon the accession of James the First he was liberated, and restored in 1603. He was afterwards made Captain of the Isle of Wight and Governor of Carisbroke Castle; and in 1618 a member of the privy council.

---

possession of Congress as part of Mr. Jefferson's library, and are now in the Law Library at Washington. There is to be found there also a volume of papers and records of the Virginia Company, from 1621 to 1625. (See article by J. Wingate Thornton, Esq., of Boston, in Hist. Mag., ii. 33, recommending that these documents should be published by Congress.) There are also valuable MS. historical materials in Richmond which ought to be published. The recent destruction of the library of William and Mary College shows the precarious tenure by which the collections of the Virginia Historical Society, and the records preserved in the State Capitol, are held.

Brave and generous, but haughty and impetuous, he was by no means adapted to the court and cabinet of James, where fawning servility and base intrigue were the ordinary stepping-stones of political advancement.

About the year 1619, the Earl of Southampton was imprisoned through the influence of Buckingham, "whom he rebuked with some passion for speaking often to the same thing in the house, and out of order." In 1620 he was chosen Treasurer, or Governor of the Virginia Company, contrary to the king's wishes; but he, nevertheless, continued in that office until the charter was dissolved, and at its meetings, and in parliament, opposed the measures of a feeble and corrupt court. He and Sir Edwin Sandys, the leaders, together with the bulk of the members of the company, shared largely in the spirit of civil and religious freedom, which was then manifesting itself so strongly in England. In the hostile course pursued against the company, the attacks were especially directed against the earl and his associates Sir Edwin Sandys and Nicholas Ferrar. These three were celebrated: Lord Southampton for wisdom, eloquence, and sweet deportment; Sir Edwin Sandys for great knowledge and integrity; and Nicholas Ferrar for wonderful abilities, unwearied diligence, and the strictest virtue.* The earl and Sir Edwin were particular objects of the king's hatred. Sir Edwin, a member of the House of Commons, was arbitrarily imprisoned in 1621, during the session of parliament; and the earl was arrested after its dissolution. Spain had, at this time, acquired the ascendancy in the English Court, and this malign influence was skilfully maintained by the intrigues of her crafty ambassador, Count Gondomar. It was believed by many that James was even willing to sacrifice the interests of the English colonies for the benefit of those of Spain. The Rev. Jonas Stockham, a minister in Virginia, in a letter dated in May, 1621, and addressed to the Council of the Virginia Company, said: "There be many Italianated and Spaniolized Englishmen envies our prosperities, and by all their ignominious scandals they can

---

* Peckard's Life of Ferrar—a work which throws much light on the early history of Virginia.

devise, seeks to dishearten what they can those that are willing to further this glorious enterprise. To such I wish, according to the decree of Darius, that whosoever is an enemy to our peace, and seeketh either by getting monipolical patents, or by forging unjust tales to hinder our welfare—that his house were pulled down, and a pair of gallows made of the wood, and he hanged on them in the place."

The Earl of Southampton was grandson of Wriothesley, the famous Chancellor of Edward the Sixth, father to the excellent and noble Treasurer Southampton, grandfather to Rachel Lady Russel. In his later years he commanded an English regiment in the Dutch service, and died in the Netherlands, 1624. Shakespeare dedicated some of his minor poems to him; the County of Southampton, in Virginia, probably also took its name from him. Captain Smith, who had been unjustly displaced by the company, approved of the dissolution of their charter. Yet, as no compensation was rendered for the enormous expenditure incurred, it can be looked upon as little better than confiscation effected by chicane and tyranny. A parliamentary committee, of which Sir Edwin Sandys was a member, in the same year, 1624, drew up articles of impeachment against Lord Treasurer Cranfield for his agency in bringing about the dissolution of the charter.* Nevertheless, the result was undoubtedly favorable to the colony, as is candidly acknowledged by that honest chronicler, Stith, although no one could be more strenuously opposed to the arbitrary means employed.

An Assembly had been held in March, 1624, and its acts are preserved: they are brief and simple, coming directly to the point, without the redundancy of modern statutes; and refer mainly to agriculture, the church establishment, and defence against the Indians.† The following is a list of the members of this early Assembly:—

Sir Francis Wyat, Knt., Governor, etc.

Captain Francis West,	John Pott,
Sir George Yeardley,	Captain Roger Smith,
George Sandys, Treasurer,	Captain Ralph Hamor,

And John Pountis, *of the Council.*

---

* Belknap. † Hening's Statutes, i. 119, 129.

BURGESSES.

William Tucker,
Jabez Whitakers,
William Peeine,
Raleigh Crasnaw,
Richard Kingsmell,
Edward Blany,
Luke Boyse,
John Pollington,
Nathaniel Causey,
Robert Adams,
Thomas Harris,
Richard Stephens,

BURGESSES.

Nathaniel Bass,
John Willcox,
Nicolas Marten,
Clement Dilke,
Isaac Chaplin,
John Chew,
John Utie,
John Southerne,
Richard Bigge,
Henry Watkins,
Gabriel Holland,
Thomas Morlatt,
R. Hickman, *Clerk.*

CHAPTER XIX.

1624-1632.

Charles the First commissions Sir Thomas Wyat, Governor—Assemblies not allowed—Royal Government virtually established in Virginia—Other Colonies on Atlantic Coast—Wyat returns to Ireland—Succeeded by Yeardley—Yeardley succeeded by West—Letter of Charles the First directing an Assembly to meet—Assembly's Reply—John Pott, Governor—Condition of Colony—Statistics—Diet—Pott superseded by Harvey—Dr. John Pott Convicted of Stealing Cattle—Sir John Harvey—Lord Baltimore visits Virginia—Refuses to take the Oaths tendered to him—Procures from Charles the First a Grant of Territory—Acts relative to Ministers, Agriculture, Indians, etc

In August, 1624, King Charles the First granted a commission appointing Sir Thomas Wyat Governor, with a council during pleasure, and omitting all mention of an assembly, thinking so "popular a course" the chief source of the recent troubles and misfortunes. The eleven members of the council were, Francis West, Sir George Yeardley, George Sandys, Roger Smith, Ralph Hamor, who had been of the former council, with the addition of John Martin, John Harvey, Samuel Matthews, Abraham Percy, Isaac Madison, and William Clayborne. Several of these were then, or became afterwards, men of note in the colony. This is the first mention of William Clayborne, who was destined to play an important part in the future annals of Virginia.

Thus in effect a royal government was now established in Virginia; hitherto she had been subject to a complex threefold government of the company, the crown, and her own president or governor and council.*

---

* Chalmers' Introduction, i. 22. Beverley, B. i. 47, says expressly that an assembly was allowed. Burk, ii. 15, asserts that "assemblies convened and deliberated in the usual form, unchecked and uninterrupted by royal interference, from the dissolution of the proprietary government to the period when a regular constitution was sent over with Sir W. Berkeley in 1639." For authority reference is made to a document in the Appendix, which document, however, is not to be found there. The opinions of Chalmers—who, as clerk of the privy

From 1624 to 1628 there is no mention in the statute-book of Virginia, or in the journal of the Virginia Company, of any assembly having been held in the colony, and in 1628 appeals were made to the governor and council; whereas had there been an assembly, it would have been the appellate court.

The French had established themselves as early as 1625 in Canada; the Dutch were now colonizing the New Netherlands; a Danish colony had been planted in New Jersey; the English were extending their confines in New England (where New Plymouth numbered thirty-two houses and one hundred and eighty settlers) and Virginia; while the Spaniards, the first settlers of the coast, still held some feeble posts in Florida.

Sir Thomas Wyat, the governor of the colony of Virginia, on the death of his father, Sir George Wyat, returning, in 1626, to Ireland, to attend to his private affairs there, was succeeded by Sir George Yeardley. He, during the same year, by proclamation, which now again usurped the place of law, prohibited the selling of corn to the Indians; made some commercial regulations, and directed houses to be palisaded. Yeardley dying, was succeeded in November, 1627, by Francis West, elected by the council. He was a younger brother of Lord Delaware.*

At a court held at James City, November the sixteenth, Lady Temperance Yeardley came and confirmed the conveyance made by her late husband, Sir George Yeardley, knight, late governor, to Abraham Percy, Esq., for the lands of Flowerdieu Hundred, being one thousand acres, and of Weanoke, on the opposite side of the water, being two thousand two hundred acres. This lady's Christian name is Puritanical; another such was Obedience Robins, a burgess of Accomac in 1630.

James the First had extorted a revenue from the tobacco of Virginia by an arbitrary resort to his prerogative, and in violation of the charter. Charles the First, in a letter dated June, 1628, proposed that a monopoly of the tobacco trade should be granted to him, and recommended the culture of several new pro-

---

council, had access to the archives in England—and Hening, confirmed by a corresponding hiatus in the records, appear conclusive against the unsupported statements of Beverley and Burk.

* Belknap, art. WYAT, errs in making Sir John Harvey the successor.

ducts, and desired that an assembly should be called to take these matters into consideration. The ensuing assembly replied, demanding a higher price and more favorable terms than his majesty was disposed to yield. As to the introduction of new staples, they explained why, in their opinion, that was impracticable. This letter was signed by Francis West, Governor, five members of the council, and thirty-one members of the House of Burgesses.

Sir George Yeardley, the late governor, with two or three of the council, had resided for the most part at Jamestown; the rest of the council repaired there as occasion required. There was a general meeting of the governor and council once in every three months. The population of the colony was estimated at not less than fifteen hundred; they inhabited seventeen or eighteen plantations, of these the greater part, lying toward the falls of the James River, were well fortified against the Indians by means of palisades. The planters dwelling above Jamestown, found means to procure an abundant supply of fish. On the banks of that river the red men themselves were now seldom seen, but their fires were occasionally observed in the woods.*

There was no family in the colony so poor as not to have a sufficient stock of tame hogs. Poultry was equally abundant; bread plenty and good. For drink the colonists made use of a home-made ale; but the better sort of people were well supplied with sack, aqua-vitæ, and good English beer. The common diet of the servants was milk-hominy, that is, bruised Indian-corn, pounded and boiled thick, and eaten with milk. This dish was also in esteem with the better sort. Hominy, according to Strachey, is an Indian word; Lord Bacon calls it "the cream of maize," and commends it as a nutritious diet. The planters were generally provided with arms and armor, and on every holiday each plantation exercised its men in the use of arms, by which means, together with hunting and fowling, the greater part of them became excellent marksmen. Tobacco was the only staple cultivated for sale. The health of the country was greatly im-

---

* The number of cattle amounted to several thousand head; the stock of goats was large, and their increase rapid; the forests abounded with wild hogs, which were killed and eaten by the savages.

proved by clearing the land, so that the sun had power to exhale up the humid vapors. Captain Francis West continued governor till March, 1628, and he then being about to embark for England, John Pott was elected governor by the council.

In the year 1629 most of the land about Jamestown was cleared; little corn planted; but all the ground converted into pasture and gardens, "wherein doth grow all manners of English herbs and roots and very good grass." Such is the cotemporaneous statement, but after the lapse of more than two centuries Eastern Virginia depends largely on the Northern States for her supply of hay. The greater portion of the cattle of the colony was kept near Jamestown, the owners being dispersed about on plantations, and visiting Jamestown as inclination prompted, or, at the arrival of shipping, come to trade. In this year the population of Virginia amounted to five thousand, and the cattle had increased in the like proportion. The colony's stock of provisions was sufficient to feed four hundred more than its own number of inhabitants. Vessels procured supplies in Virginia; the number of arrivals in 1629 was twenty-three. Salt fish was brought from New England; Kecoughtan supplied peaches.

Mrs. Pearce, an honest industrious woman, after passing twenty years in Virginia, on her return to England reported that she had a garden at Jamestown, containing three or four acres, where in one year she had gathered a hundred bushels of excellent figs, and that of her own provision she could keep a better house in Virginia, than in London for three or four hundred pounds a year, although she had gone there with little or nothing. The planters found the Indian-corn so much better for bread than wheat, that they began to quit sowing it.

An assembly met at Jamestown in October, 1629; it consisted of John Pott, Governor, four councillors, and forty-six burgesses, returned from twenty-three plantations. Pott was superseded in the same year by Sir John Harvey, at some time between October and March. In March, the quarter court ordered an assembly to be called, to meet Sir John Harvey on the twenty-fourth of that month; and nothing was done in Pott's name after October, so far as can be found in the records.

The late governor was, during the ensuing year, Rob-Roy-like, convicted of stealing cattle. The trial commenced on the ninth of July, 1630; the number of jurors was thirteen, of whom three were members of the council. The first day was wholly spent in pleading, the next in unnecessary disputations, Dr. John Pott endeavoring to prove Mr. Kingsmell, one of the witnesses against him, a hypocrite by the story of "Gusman of Alfrach, the Rogue." Pott was found guilty, but in consideration of his rank and station, judgment was suspended until the king's pleasure should be known; and all the council became his security.

Sir John Harvey, the new governor, had been one of the commissioners sent out by King James to Virginia, in 1623, for the purpose of investigating the state and condition of the colony, and of procuring evidence which might serve to justify the dissolution of the charter of the Virginia Company. Harvey had also been a member of the provisional government in the year 1625. Returning now to Virginia, no doubt with embittered recollections of the collisions with the assembly in which he had been formerly involved, he did not fail to imitate the arbitrary rule that prevailed "at home," and to render himself odious to the inhabitants of the colony.

Sir George Calvert, the first Lord Baltimore, descended from a noble family in Flanders, born at Kipling, in Yorkshire, England, was educated partly at Trinity College, Oxford, and partly on the continent. Sir Robert Cecil, lord treasurer, employed him as his secretary, and he was promoted to the clerkship of the council. In 1618 he was knighted, and in the succeeding year he was made a secretary of state, and one of the committee of trade and plantations, with a pension of one thousand pounds. Through the influence of Sir Thomas Wentworth, afterwards Earl of Strafford, he was chosen a member of Parliament. Receiving a patent for the southeastern peninsula of Newfoundland, he undertook to establish, in 1621, the plantation of Ferryland, which he called the Province of Avalon—a name derived from some mediæval legend. In 1624 he professed the Romish faith, and resigned his place of secretary of state; but James the First still retained this strenuous defender of royal prerogative as a member of his privy council, and created him[*] Baron of Balti-

---

[*] 1625.

more, in the County of Longford, in Ireland, he being at this time the representative of the University of Oxford in the House of Commons. Still bent upon establishing a colony in America, for the promotion of his private interests, and to provide an asylum for the unmolested exercise of his religion, embarking in a ship lent him by King Charles the First, he came over to Virginia in the year 1629.

Virginia was founded by men devoted to the principles of the Reformation, amid vivid recollections of the persecutions of Mary, the Spanish armada, and the recent gunpowder plot, and when horror of papists was at its height. The charter of the colony expressly required that the oaths of allegiance and supremacy should be taken for the purpose of guarding against "the superstitions of the Church of Rome."*

The assembly being in session at the time of Lord Baltimore's arrival, proposed these oaths to him and those with him. He declined complying with the requisition, submitting, however, a form which he was ready to accept, whereupon the assembly determined to refer the matter to the privy council. The virtues of this able and estimable nobleman did not secure him from personal indignity. In the old records is found this entry: "March 25th, 1630, Thomas Tindall to be pilloried two hours for giving my Lord Baltimore the lie, and threatening to knock him down."†

Finding the Virginians unanimously averse to the very name of papist, he proceeded to the head of Chesapeake Bay, and observing an attractive territory on the north side of the Potomac River unoccupied, returned to England, and, in violation of the territorial rights of Virginia, obtained from Charles the First a grant of the country, afterwards called Maryland,‡ but died before the sealing of his patent.

During the session of 1629–30 ministers were ordered to conform themselves in all things "according to the canons of the Church of England." It would appear that Puritanism had begun to develope itself among the clergy as well as the laity of the colony. Measures were adopted for erecting a fort at Point

---

* Burk, ii. 25; Hen., i. 73, 97. † 1 Hen., 552.
‡ Belknap, iii. 206; Allen's Biog. Dic., art. CALVERT.

Comfort; new-comers were exempted from military service during the first five years after their arrival; engrossing and forestalling were prohibited. For the furtherance of the production of potashes and saltpetre, experiments were ordered to be made; to prevent a scarcity of corn, it was enacted that two acres of land, or near thereabouts, be planted for every head that works in the ground; regulations were established for the improvement of the staple of tobacco. An act provided that the war commenced against the Indians be effectually prosecuted, and that no peace be concluded with them.*

The first act of the session of February, 1632, provides that there be a uniformity throughout this colony, both in substance and circumstance, to the canons and constitution of the Church of England, as near as may be, and that every person yield ready obedience to them, upon penalty of the pains and forfeitures in that case appointed. Another act directs that ministers shall not give themselves to excess in drinking, or riot, spending their time idly, by day or night, playing at dice, cards, or any other unlawful game. Another order was, that all the council and burgesses of the assembly shall in the morning be present at divine service, in the room where they sit, at the third beating of the drum, an hour after sunrise. No person was suffered to "tend" above fourteen leaves of the tobacco-plant, nor to gather more than nine leaves, nor to tend any slips of old stalks of tobacco, or any of the second crop; and it was ordained that all tobacco should be taken down before the end of November. No person was permitted to speak or parley with the Indians, either in the woods or on any plantation, "if he can possibly avoid it by any means." The planters, however, were required to observe all terms of amity with them, taking care, nevertheless, to keep upon their guard. The spirit of constitutional freedom exhibited itself in an act declaring that the governor and council shall not lay any taxes or impositions upon the colony, their land, or commodities, otherwise than by authority of the grand assembly, to be levied and employed as by the assembly shall be appointed.

Act XL. provides, that the governor shall not withdraw the

---

* 1 Hening, 149.

inhabitants from their private labors to service of his own, upon any color whatsoever. In case of emergency, the levying of men shall be ordered by the governor, with the consent of the whole body of the council. For the encouragement of men to plant a plenty of corn, it was enacted, that the price shall not be restricted, but it shall be free for every man to sell it as dear as he can. Men were not allowed to work in the grounds without their arms, and a sentinel on guard; due watch to be kept at night when necessary; no commander of any plantation shall either himself spend, or suffer others to spend, powder unnecessarily, that is to say, in drinking or entertainments. All men fit to bear arms were required to bring their pieces to the church on occasion of public worship. No person within the colony, upon any rumor of supposed change and alteration, was to presume to be disobedient to the present government, nor servants to their private officers, masters, and overseers, at their uttermost peril. No boats were permitted to go and trade to Canada or elsewhere that be not of the burthen of ten tons, and have a flush deck, or fitted with a grating and a tarpauling, excepting such as be permitted for discovery by a special license from the governor.*

---

* 1 Hening, 155, 175.

CHAPTER XX.

1632-1635.

Charles the First appoints Council of Superintendence for Virginia—Acts of Assembly—William Clayborne authorized by the Crown to make Discoveries and Trade—George Lord Baltimore dies—The Patent of Territory granted is confirmed to his Son Cecilius, Lord Baltimore—Virginia remonstrates against the grant to Baltimore—Lord Baltimore employs his Brother, Leonard Calvert, to found the Colony of Maryland—St. Mary's Settled—Harvey visits Calvert—Clayborne's Opposition to the New Colony—Character of Baltimore's Patent—Contest between Clayborne and the Marylanders—He is convicted of High Crimes—Escapes to Virginia—Goes to England for trial of the Case.

IN the year 1632 King Charles issued a commission appointing a Council of Superintendence over Virginia, empowering them to ascertain the state and condition of the colony. The commissioners were Edward, Earl of Dorset, Henry, Earl of Derby, Dudley, Viscount Dorchester, Sir John Coke, Sir John Davers, Sir Robert Killegrew, Sir Thomas Rowe, Sir Robert Heath, Sir Kineage Tench, Sir Dudley Diggs, Sir John Holstenholm, Sir Francis Wyat, Sir John Brooks, Sir Kenelm Digby, Sir John Tench, John Banks, Esq., Thomas Gibbs, Esq., Samuel Rott, Esq., George Sands, Esq., John Wolstenholm, Esq., Nicholas Ferrar, Esq., Gabriel Barber, and John Ferrar, Esquires.*

Elaborate acts passed by the Colonial Legislature at this period, for improving the staple of tobacco and regulating the trade in it, evince the increasing importance of that crop. Tithes were imposed of tobacco and corn; and the twentieth "calfe, kidd of goates and pigge" granted unto the minister. During the year 1633 every fortieth man in the neck of land between the James River and the York, (then called the Charles,) was directed to repair to the plantation of Dr. John Pott, to be employed in building of houses and securing that tract of land lying between Queen's Creek, emptying into Charles River, and Archer's Hope

---

* 2 Burk's Hist. of Va., 35.

Creek, emptying into James River. This was Middle Plantation, (now Williamsburg,) so called as being midway between the James River and the York. Each person settling there was entitled to fifty acres of land and exemption from general taxes. All newcomers were ordered to pay sixty-four pounds of tobacco toward the maintenance of the fort at Point Comfort.* Thus far, under Harvey's administration, the Assembly had met regularly, and several judicious and wholesome acts had been passed.

The Chesapeake Bay is supposed to have been discovered by the Spaniards as early as the year 1566 or before, being called by them the Bay of Santa Maria.† It was discovered by the English in 1585, when Ralph Lane was Governor of the first Colony of Virginia. In 1620 John Pory made a voyage of discovery in the Chesapeake Bay, and found one hundred English happily settled on its borders, (in what particular place is not known,) animated with the hope of a very good trade in furs.‡ During the years 1627, 1628, and 1629 the governors of Virginia gave authority to William Clayborne, "Secretary of State of this Kingdom," as the Ancient Dominion was then styled, to discover the source of the bay, or any part of that government from the thirty-fourth to the forty-first degree of north latitude.§ In May, 1631, Charles the First granted a license to "our trusty and well-beloved William Clayborne," one of the council and Secretary of State for the colony, authorizing him to make discoveries, and to trade. This license was, by the royal instructions, confirmed by Governor Harvey; and Clayborne shortly afterwards established a trading post on Kent Island, in the Chesa-

---

* 1 Hening, 188, 190, 199, 208, 222. The pay of the officers at Point Comfort was at this time:—

	Lbs. Tobacco.	Bbls. Corn.
To the captain of the fort	2000	10
To the gunner	1000	6
To the drummer and porter	1000	6
For four other men, each of them 500 pounds of tobacco, 4 bbls. corn	2000	16
Total	6000	38

† Early Voyages to America, 483.   ‡ Chalmers' Polit. Annals, 206.
§ Chalmers' Annals, 227.

peake Bay, not far from the present capital of Maryland, Annapolis; and subsequently another at the mouth of the Susquehanna River. In the year 1632 a burgess was returned from the Isle of Kent to the Assembly at Jamestown.* In 1633 a warehouse was established in Southampton River for the inhabitants of Mary's Mount, Elizabeth City, Accomac, and the Isle of Kent.

In the mean time, George, the elder Lord Baltimore, dying on the fifteenth of April, 1632, aged fifty, at London, before his patent was issued, it was confirmed June twentieth of this year, to his son Cecilius, Baron of Baltimore. The new province was named Maryland in honor of Henrietta Maria, Queen Consort of Charles the First of England, and daughter of Henry the Fourth of France. For eighteen months from the signing of the Maryland charter, the expedition to the new colony was delayed by the strenuous opposition made to the proceeding. The Virginians felt no little aggrieved at this infraction of their chartered territory; and they remonstrated to the king in council in 1633, against the grant to Lord Baltimore, alleging that "it will be a general disheartening to them, if they shall be divided into several governments." Future events were about to strengthen their sense of the justice of their cause. In July of this year the case was decided in the Star Chamber, the privy council, influenced by Laud, Archbishop of Canterbury, and the Earl of Strafford, deeming it fit to leave Lord Baltimore to his patent and the complainants to the course of law "according to their desire," recommending, at the same time, a spirit of amity and good correspondence between the planters of the two colonies. So futile a decision could not terminate the contest, and Clayborne continued to claim Kent Island, and to abnegate the authority of the proprietary of Maryland.

At length, Lord Baltimore having engaged the services of his brother, Leonard Calvert, for founding the colony, he with two others, one of them probably being another brother, were appointed commissioners. The expedition consisted of some twenty gentlemen of fortune, and two or three hundred of the

---

* 1 Hening, 154.

laboring class, nearly all of them Roman Catholics. Imploring the intercession of the Blessed Virgin, St. Ignatius, and all the guardian angels of Maryland, they set sail from Cowes, in the Isle of Wight, in November, 1633, St. Cecilia's day. The canonized founder of the order of the Jesuits, Ignatius Loyola, was the patron saint of the infant Maryland. February twenty-seventh, 1634, they reached Point Comfort, filled with apprehensions of the hostility of the Virginians to their colonial enterprise. Letters from King Charles and the chancellor of the exchequer conciliated Governor Harvey, who hoped, by his kindness to the Maryland colonists, to insure the recovery of a large sum of money due him from the royal treasury. The Virginians were at this time all under arms expecting the approach of a hostile Spanish fleet. Calvert, after a hospitable entertainment, embarked on the third of March for Maryland. Clayborne, who had accompanied Harvey to Point Comfort to see the strangers, did not fail to intimidate them by accounts of the hostile spirit which they would have to encounter in the Indians of that part of the country to which they were destined. Calvert, on arriving in Maryland, was accompanied in his explorations of the country by Captain Henry Fleet, an early Virginia pioneer, who was familiar with the settlements and language of the savages, and in much favor with them; and it was under his guidance and direction that the site of St. Mary's, the ancient capital of Maryland, was selected.* White, a Jesuit missionary, says of Fleet: "At the first he was very friendly to us; afterwards, seduced by the evil counsels of a certain Clayborne, who entertained the most hostile disposition, he stirred up the minds of the natives against us."† White mentions that the Island of Monserrat, in the West Indies, where they touched, was inhabited by Irishmen who had

---

* White's Relation, 4; Force's Hist. Tracts.

† White's Relation of the Colony of the Lord Baron of Baltimore in Maryland, near Virginia, and a Narrative of the Voyage to Maryland, was copied from the archives of the Jesuit's College at Rome, by Rev. William McSherry, of Georgetown College, and translated from the Latin. An abstract of it may be found in chapter first of History of Maryland, by James McSherry. The first part of the Relation is a description of the country, and appears to have been written at London previous to the departure of Calvert; the remainder details the incidents of the voyage and the first settlement of the colony, especially of the proceedings of the Jesuit missionaries down to the year 1677.

been expelled by the English of Virginia "on account of their profession of the Catholic faith."

In a short time after the landing of Leonard Calvert in Maryland, Sir John Harvey, Governor of Virginia, visited him at St. Mary's. His arrival attracted to the same place the Indian chief of Patuxent, who said: "When I heard that a great werowance of the English was come to Yoacomoco, I had a great desire to see him; but when I heard the werowance of Pasbie-haye was come thither also to see him, I presently start up, and without further counsel came to see them both."*

In March, 1634, at a meeting of the governor and council, Clayborne inquired of them how he should demean himself toward Lord Baltimore and his deputies in Maryland, who claimed jurisdiction over the colony at Kent Isle. The governor and council replied that the right of his lordship's patent being yet undetermined in England, they were bound in duty and by their oaths to maintain the rights and privileges of the colony of Virginia. Nevertheless, in all humble submission to his majesty's pleasure, they resolved to keep and observe all good correspondence with the Maryland new-comers.†

The Maryland patent conferred upon Lord Baltimore, a popish recusant, the entire government of the colony, including the patronage and advowson of all churches, the same to be dedicated and consecrated according to the ecclesiastical law. This charter was illegal, inasmuch as it granted powers which the king himself did not possess; the grantee being a papist could not conform to the ecclesiastical laws of England; and, therefore, the provisions of this extraordinary instrument could not be, and were not designed to be, executed according to the plain and obvious meaning. Such was the character of the instrument by which King Charles the First despoiled Virginia of so large a portion of her territory. It is true, indeed, that the Virginia charter had been annulled, but this was done upon the condition explicitly and re-

---

* Anderson's Hist. of Col. Church, ii. 120, referring to "Relation of the successful beginnings of the Lord Baltimore's Plantation, in Maryland," signed by Captain Wintour, and others, adventurers in the expedition, and published in 1634.

† Chalmers' Annals. Chalmers is the more full and satisfactory in his account of Maryland, because he had resided there for many years.

peatedly declared by the royal government, that vested rights should receive no prejudice thereby.*

Clayborne, rejecting the authority of the new plantation, Lord Baltimore gave orders to seize him if he should not submit himself to the proprietary government of Maryland. The Indians beginning to exhibit some indications of hostility toward the settlers, they attributed it to the machinations of Clayborne, alleging that it was he who stirred up the jealousy of the savages, persuading them that the new-comers were Spaniards and enemies to the Virginians, and that he had also infused his own spirit of insubordination into the inhabitants of Kent Island. A trading vessel called the Longtail, employed by Clayborne in the Indian trade in the Chesapeake Bay, was captured by the Marylanders. He thereupon fitted out an armed pinnace with a crew of fourteen men under one of his adherents, Lieutenant Warren, to rescue the vessel. Two armed pinnaces were sent out by Calvert under Captain Cornwallis; and in an engagement that ensued in the Potomac, or, as some accounts have it, the Pocomoke River, one of the Marylanders fell, and three of the Virginians, including Lieutenant Warren. The rest were carried prisoners to St. Mary's. Clayborne was indicted although not arrested, and convicted of murder and piracy, constructive crimes inferred from his opposition. The chief of Patuxent was interrogated as to Clayborne's intrigues among the Indians.†

Harvey, either from fear of the popular indignation, or from some better motive, refused to surrender the fugitive Clayborne to the Maryland commissioners, and according to one authority‡ sent him to England, accompanied by the witnesses. Chalmers, good authority on the subject, makes no allusion to the circumstance, and it appears more probable that Clayborne having appealed to the king, went voluntarily to England.§ It is certain that he was not brought to trial there.

---

* Force's Hist. Tracts, ii.; Virginia and Maryland, 7 et seq.; and Anderson's Hist. of Col. Church, ii. 113.

† McSherry's Maryland, 40; Chalmers' Annals, 211, 232; Force's Historical Tracts, ii. 13.

‡ Burk's Hist. of Va., ii. 41, referring to "Ancient Records" of the London Company.

§ Force's Hist. Tracts, ii.; Maryland and Virginia, 22.

CHAPTER XXI.

1635-1639.

Eight Shires—Harvey's Grants of Territory—His Corrupt and Tyrannical Administration—The Crown guarantees to the Virginians the Rights which they enjoyed before the Dissolution of the Charter—Burk's Opinion of Clayborne—Governor Harvey deposed—Returns to England—Charles the First reinstates him—Disturbances in Kent Island—Charles reprimands Lord Baltimore for his Maltreatment of Clayborne—The Lords Commissioners decide in favor of Baltimore—Threatening State of Affairs in England—Harvey recalled—Succeeded by Sir Francis Wyat.

IN the year 1634 Virginia was divided into eight shires: James City, Henrico, Charles City, Elizabeth City, Warrasqueake, Charles River, and Accomac. The original name of Pamaunkee, or Pamunkey, had then been superseded by Charles River, which afterwards gave way to the present name of York. Pamunkey, at first the name of the whole river, is now restricted to one of its branches. The word Pamaunkee is said to signify "where we took a sweat."

The grant of Maryland to Lord Baltimore opened the way for similar grants to other court-favorites, of lands lying to the north and to the south of the settled portion of the Ancient Colony and Dominion of Virginia. While Charles the First was lavishing vast tracts of her territory upon his favorites, Sir John Harvey, a worthy pacha of such a sultan, in collusion with the royal commissioners, imitated the royal munificence by giving away large bodies not only of the public, or crown lands, but even of such as belonged to private planters.* In the contests between Clayborne and the proprietary of Maryland, while the people of Virginia warmly espoused their countryman's cause, Harvey sided with Baltimore, and proved himself altogether a fit instrument of the administration then tyrannizing in England. He was extor-

---

* Beverley, B. i. 50.

tionate, proud, unjust, and arbitrary; he issued proclamations in derogation of the legislative powers of the assembly; assessed, levied, held, and disbursed the colonial revenue, without check or responsibility; transplanted into Virginia exotic English statutes; multiplied penalties and exactions, and appropriated fines to his own use; he added the decrees of the court of high commission of England to the ecclesiastical constitutions of Virginia. The assembly, nevertheless, met regularly; and the legislation of the colony expanded itself in accordance with the exigencies of an increasing population. Tobacco was subjected, by royal ordinances, to an oppressive monopoly; and in those days of prerogative, a remonstrance to the Commons for redress proved fruitless.

At length, in July, 1634, the council's committee for the colonies, either from policy or from compassion, transmitted instructions to the governor and council, saying: "That it is not intended that interests which men have settled when you were a corporation, should be impeached; that for the present they may enjoy their estates with the same freedom and privilege as they did before the recalling of their patents," and authorizing the appropriation of lands to the planters, as had been the former custom.*

Whether these concessions were inadequate in themselves, or were not carried into effect by Harvey, upon the petition of many of the inhabitants, an assembly was called to meet on the 7th of May, 1635, to hear complaints against that obnoxious functionary. There is hardly any point on which a people are more sensitive than in regard to their territory, and it may therefore be concluded, that one of Harvey's chief offences was his having sided with Lord Baltimore in his infraction of the Virginia territory.

Burk, in his History of Virginia, has stigmatized Clayborne as "an unprincipled incendiary" and "execrable villain;" other writers have applied similar epithets to him. It appears to have been only his resolute defence of his own rights and those of Vir-

---

* By the words "for the present," was probably intended "at present," "now," otherwise their interests might be impeached at a future day, although not immediately. Chalmers, Hist. of Revolt of Amer. Colonies, 36, so interprets the expression.

ginia that subjected him to this severe denunciation. He was long a member of the council; long filled the office of secretary; was held in great esteem by the people, and was for many years a leading spirit of the colony. Burk* denounces Sir John Harvey for refusing to surrender the fugitive Clayborne to the demand of the Maryland Commissioners, and adds: "But the time was at hand when this rapacious and tyrannical prefect (Harvey) would experience how vain and ineffectual are the projects of tyranny when opposed to the indignation of freemen." Thus the governor, who excited the indignation of the Virginians by his collusion with the Marylanders, was afterwards reprobated by historians for sympathizing with Clayborne in his defence of the rights of Virginia, and opposition to the Marylanders. If Harvey, in violation of the royal license granted to Clayborne in 1631, had surrendered him to the Maryland Commissioners, he would have exposed himself to the royal resentment; and nothing could have more inflamed the indignation of freemen than such treatment of the intrepid vindicator of their territorial rights.

Before the assembly (called to hear complaints against the governor) met, Harvey, having consented to go to England to answer them, was "thrust out of the government" by the council on the 28th of April, 1635, and Captain John West was authorized to act as governor until the king's pleasure should be known. The assembly having collected the evidence, deputed two members of the council to go out with Harvey to prefer the charges against him. It was also ordered that during the vacancy in the office of governor, the secretary (Clayborne) should sign commissions and passes, and manage the affairs of the Indians.†

King Charles the First, offended at the presumption of the council and assembly, reinstated Sir John, and he resumed his place, in or before the month of January, 1636. Chalmers‡ says that he returned in April, 1637. Thus the first open resistance to tyranny, and vindication of constitutional right, took place in the colony of Virginia; and the deposition of Harvey foreshadowed the downfall of Charles the First. The laws that had

---

* Hist. of Va., ii. 40.   † Hen., i. 223.
‡ Hist. of Revolt of Amer. Colonies, i. 36.

been enacted by the first assembly of Maryland, having been sent over to England for his approval, he rejected them, on the ground that the right of framing them was vested in himself; and he directed an assembly to be summoned to meet in January, 1638, to have his dissent announced to them.

Early in 1637 a court was established by the Maryland authorities, in Kent Island, and toward the close of that year Captain George Evelin was appointed commander of the island. Many of Clayborne's adherents there refused to submit to the jurisdiction of Lord Baltimore's colony, and the governor, Leonard Calvert, found it necessary to repair there in March, 1638, in person, with a military force, to reduce to submission these Virginia malecontents. The Maryland legislature, convened in compliance with Lord Baltimore's orders, refused to acquiesce in his claim of the legislative power, and in the event they gained their point, his lordship being satisfied with a controlling influence in the choice of the delegates, and his veto.

The Virginians captured by Cornwallis in his engagement with Warren, had been detained prisoners without being brought to trial, there being no competent tribunal in the colony. At length Thomas Smith, second in command to Warren, was brought to trial for the murder of William Ashmore, (who had been killed in the skirmish,) and was found guilty, and sentenced to death; but it is not certain that he was executed. Clayborne was attainted, and his property confiscated; and these proceedings probably produced those disturbances in Kent Island which required the governor's presence.

Harvey, after his restoration, continued to be governor of Virginia for about three years, during which period there appears to have been no meeting of the assembly, and of this part of his administration no record is left.

In July, 1638, Charles the First addressed a letter to Lord Baltimore, referring to his former letters to "Our Governor and Council of Virginia, and to others, our officers and subjects in these parts, (in which) we signified our pleasure that William Clayborne, David Morehead, and other planters in the island near Virginia, which they have nominated Kentish Island, should in no sort be interrupted by you or any other in your right, but rather be encouraged to proceed in so good a work." The king complains to Baltimore that his agents, in spite of the royal instructions, had "slain three of our subjects there, and by force possessed themselves by night of that island, and seized and carried away both the persons and estates of the said planters." His majesty concludes by enjoining a strict compliance with his former orders.*

In 1639 Father John Gravener, a Jesuit missionary, resided at Kent Island. In April of this year the Lords Commissioners of Plantations, with Laud, Archbishop of Canterbury, at their head, held a meeting at Whitehall, and determined the controversy between Clayborne and Lord Baltimore. This decision was made in consequence of a petition presented in 1637 by Clayborne to the king, claiming, by virtue of discovery and settlement, Kent Island and another plantation at the mouth of the Susquehanna River, and complaining of the attempts of Lord Baltimore's agents there to dispossess him and his associates, and of outrages committed upon them. The decision was now absolute in favor of Baltimore; and Clayborne, despairing of any peaceable redress, returned to Virginia, and having in vain prayed for the restoration of his property, awaited some future opportunity to vindicate his rights, and to recover property amounting in value to six thousand pounds, of which he had been despoiled.†

The Governor of Maryland, engaged in hostilities with the Indians, obtained a supply of arms, ammunition, and provision from the Governor of Virginia.

Charles the First, bred in all the arts of corrupt and arbitrary government, had now for many years governed England by prerogative, without a parliament, until at length his necessities constrained him to convene one; and his apprehensions of that body, and the revolt of the Scotch, and other alarming ebullitions of discontent, admonished him and his advisers to mitigate the highhanded measures of administration. The severity of colonial rule was also relaxed, and in November, 1639, the unpopular Sir

---

* Chalmers' Annals, 232.

† Clayborne is the same name with Claiborne; it is found sometimes spelt Claiborn, and sometimes Cleyborne.

John Harvey was displaced, and succeeded by Sir Francis Wyat.* But Harvey remained in Virginia, and continued to be a member of the council. About this time mention is made of the exportation of cattle from Virginia to New England.

---

* 1 Hening's Stat. at Large, 4. Burk, Hist. of Va., ii. 46, erroneously makes Sir William Berkley succeed Harvey.

CHAPTER XXII.

1640-1644.

Alarming State of Affairs in England—The Long Parliament summoned—In Virginia Stephen Reekes pilloried—Sir William Berkley made Governor—Assembly declare against Restoration of Virginia Company—The King's Letter—Puritans in Virginia—Act against Non-conformists—Massacre of 1644—Opechancanough captured—His Death—Civil War in England—Sir William Berkley visits England—Clayborne expels Calvert from Maryland, and seizes the Government—Treaty with Necotowance—Statistics of the Colony.

THE spirit of constitutional freedom awakened by the Reformation, and which had been long gradually gaining strength, began to develope itself with new energy in England. The arbitrary temper of Charles the First excited so great dissatisfaction in the people, and such a strenuous opposition in parliament, as to exact at length his assent to the "Petition of Right." The public indignation was carried to a high pitch by the forced levying of ship-money, that is, of money for the building of ships-of-war, and John Hampden stood forth in a personal resistance to this unconstitutional mode of raising money. The Puritans found within the pale of the Established Church, as well as without, were arrayed against the despotic rule of the crown and the hierarchy; and Scotland was not less offended against the king, who undertook to obtrude the Episcopal liturgy upon the Presbyterian land of his birth. In the year 1640 Charles the First found himself compelled to call together the Long Parliament. Virginia meantime remained loyal; the decrees of the courts of high commission were the rule of conduct, and the authority of Archbishop Laud was as absolute in the colony as in the fatherland. Stephen Reekes was pilloried for two hours, with a label on his back signifying his offence, fined fifty pounds, and imprisoned during pleasure, for saying "that his majesty was at confession with the Lord of Canterbury," that is, Archbishop Laud.

In May, 1641, the Earl of Strafford was executed, and Archbishop Laud sent to the Tower, where he was destined to remain until he suffered the same fate. The massacre of the Protestants in Ireland occurring in the latter part of this year, rendered still more portentous the threatening storm. January tenth, the king left London, to which he was not destined to return till brought back a prisoner.

In February, 1642, Sir Francis Wyat gave way to Sir William Berkley, whose destiny it was to hold the office of governor for a period longer than any other governor, and to undergo extraordinary vicissitudes of fortune. His commission and instructions declared that it was intended to give due encouragement to the plantation of Virginia, and that ecclesiastical as well as temporal matters should be regulated according to the laws of England; provision was also made for securing to England a monopoly of the trade of the colony. By some salutary measures which Sir William Berkley introduced shortly after his arrival, and by his prepossessing manners, he soon rendered himself very acceptable to the Virginians.

In April, 1642, the assembly made a declaration against the restoration of the Virginia Company then proposed, denouncing the company as having been the source of intolerable calamities to the colony by its illegal proceedings, barbarous punishments, and monopolizing policy. They insisted that its restoration would cause them to degenerate from the condition of their birthright, and convert them from subjects of a monarchy to the creatures of a popular and tumultuary government, to which they would be obliged to resign their lands held from the crown; which they intimate, if necessary, would be more fitly resigned to a branch of the royal family than to a corporation. They averred that the revival of the company would prove a death-blow to freedom of trade, "the life-blood of a commonwealth." Finally, the assembly protested against the restoration of the company, and decreed severe penalties against any who should countenance the scheme.*

At a court holden at James City, June the 29th, 1642, present Sir William Berkley, knight, governor, etc., Captain John West, Mr. Rich. Kemp, Captain William Brocas, Captain Christo-

---

* 1 Hening, 230; Burk, ii. 68.

pher Wormley, Captain Humphrey Higginson. The commission for the monthly court of Upper Norfolk was renewed, and the commissioners appointed were, Captain Daniel Gookin, commander, Mr. Francis Hough, Captain Thomas Burbage, Mr. John Hill, Mr. Oliver Spry, Mr. Thomas Den, Mr. Randall Crew, Mr. Robert Bennett, Mr. Philip Bennett. The captains of trained bands: Captain Daniel Gookin, Captain Thomas Burbage.*

Among the converts made by one of the New England missionaries, named Thompson, was Daniel Gookin (son of the early settler of that name.) He removed to Boston in May, 1644, being probably one of those who were driven away from Virginia for non-conformity. He went away with his family in a ship bought by him from the governor, and was received with distinction at Boston. He soon became eminent in New England, and afterwards enjoyed the confidence of Cromwell, of whom he was a devoted adherent. He was author of several historical works. He died in March, 1686–7†.

The alarming crisis in the affairs of Charles the First strongly dictated the necessity of a conciliatory course; and the remonstrance, together with a petition, being communicated to him, then at York, just on the eve of the "Grand Rebellion," he replied to it, firmly engaging never to restore the Virginia Company.

The following is a copy of the king's letter:—

"C. R.

"Trusty and well-beloved, we greet you all. Whereas, we have received a petition from you, our governor, council and burgesses of the grand assembly in Virginia, together with a declaration and protestation of the first of April, against a petition presented in your names to our House of Commons in this our kingdom, for restoring of the letters patent for the incorporation of the late treasurer and council, contrary to our intent and meaning, and against all such as shall go about to alienate you from our immediate protection. And whereas, you desire by

---

* Art. by J. Wingate Thornton, Esq., in Mass Gen. and Antiq. Register for 1847, page 348. † Ibid., 352.

your petition that we should confirm this your declaration and protestation under our royal signet, and transmit the same to that our colony; these are to signify, that your acknowledgments of our great bounty and favors toward you, and your so earnest desire to continue under our immediate protection, are very acceptable to us; and that as we had not before the least intention to consent to the introduction of any company over that our colony; so we are by it much confirmed in our former resolutions, as thinking it unfit to change a form of government wherein (besides many other reasons given, and to be given,) our subjects there (having had so long experience of it) receive so much content and satisfaction. And this our approbation of your petition and protestation we have thought fit to transmit unto you under our royal signet.

"Given at our Court, at York, the 5th of July, 1642.

"To our trusty and well-beloved our Governor, Council, and Burgesses of the Grand Assembly of Virginia."*

It was in this year that the name of Charles City County was changed into York.

As early as 1619 a small party of English Puritans had come over to Virginia; and a larger number would have followed them, but they were prevented by a royal proclamation issued at the instance of Bancroft, the persecuting Archbishop of Canterbury. In 1642 a deputation was sent from some Virginia dissenters to Boston, soliciting a supply of pastors from the New England churches; three clergymen were accordingly sent, with letters recommending them to the governor, Sir William Berkley. On their arrival in Virginia they began to preach in various parts of the country, and the people flocked eagerly to hear them. The following year the assembly passed the following act: "For the preservation of the purity of doctrine and unity of the church, it is enacted, that all ministers whatsoever, which shall reside in the colony, are to be conformable to the orders and constitutions of the Church of England and the laws therein established; and not otherwise to be admitted to teach or preach, publickly or

---

* Chalmers' Annals, 133.

privately; and that the governor and council do take care, that all non-conformists, upon notice of them, shall be compelled to depart the colony with all convenience."* Sir William Berkley, equally averse to the religious tenets and political principles of the Puritan preachers, issued a proclamation in consonance with this exclusive act. Mather says of the three New England missionaries: "They had little encouragement from the rulers of the place, but they had a kind entertainment with the people;" and Winthrop: "Though the State did silence the ministers, because they would not conform to the order of England, yet the people resorted to them in private houses to hear them." In a short time the preachers returned to their own country.

The Indians, whose hatred to the whites, although dissembled, had never been abated, headed by Opechancanough, committed a second massacre on the 18th day of April, 1644. It was attributed to the encroachments made upon them by some of Sir John Harvey's grants; but it was suspected by some that Opechancanough was instigated to this massacre by certain of the colonists themselves, who informed him of the civil war then raging in England, and of the dissensions that disturbed the colony, and told him, that now was his time or never, to root out all of the English. This is improbable. Had the Indians followed up the first blow, the colonists must have all been cut off; but after their first treacherous onslaught, their courage failed them, and they fled many miles from the settlements. The colonists availed themselves of this opportunity to gather together, call an assembly, secure their cattle, and to devise some plan of defence and attack.

Opechancanough, the fierce and implacable enemy of the whites, was now nearly a hundred years old, and the commanding form, which had so often shone conspicuous in scenes of blood, was worn down by the fatigues of war, and bending under the weight of years. No longer able to walk, he was carried from place to place by his warriors in a litter. His body was emaciated, and he could only see when his eyelids were opened by his attendants. Sir William Berkley at length moving rapidly with a party of

---

* 1 Hening, 277.

horse, surprised the superannuated chief at some distance from his residence, and he was carried a prisoner to Jamestown, and there kindly treated. He retained a spirit unconquered by decrepitude of body or reverse of fortune. Hearing one day footsteps in the room where he lay, he requested his eyelids to be raised, when, perceiving a crowd of persons attracted there by a curiosity to see the famous chief, he called for the governor, and upon his appearance, said to him: "Had it been my fortune to take Sir William Berkley prisoner, I would have disdained to make a show of him." He, however, had made a show of Captain Smith when he was a prisoner. About a fortnight after Opechancanough's capture, one of his guards, for some private revenge, basely shot him in the back. Languishing awhile of the wound, he died at Jamestown, and was probably buried there. His death brought about a peace with the Indian savages, which endured for many years without interruption.

Sir William Berkley left Virginia for England in June, 1644, and returned in June, 1645, his place being filled during his absence by Richard Kemp.

The spirit of freedom long gaining ground, like a smothered fire, began now to flame up and burst forth in England. Charles the First, incomparably superior to his father in manners, habits, and tastes—a model of kingly grace and dignity, yet was a more determined and dangerous enemy to the rights of the people. On the 19th of March, 1642, having escaped from insurgent London, he reached the ancient capital, York, and on the twenty-fifth day of August raised his standard, under inauspicious omens, at Nottingham. The royal forces under Prince Rupert suffered a disastrous defeat at Marston Moor, July 2d, 1644; and while Sir William Berkley was crossing the Atlantic, the king was overthrown at Naseby, on the 4th of June, 1645. In this eventful year, and so disastrous to the king, of whom the Berkleys were such staunch supporters, Gloucester, the chief city of the county where they resided, and which had been ravaged and plundered by Rupert, was now in the hands of the parliamentary forces, and Cromwell had been early in the year convoying ammunition thither.* A sad time for the visit of the loyal Berkley!

---

* Carlyle's Cromwell, i. 144.

During the troubles in England the correspondence of the colony was interrupted, supplies reduced, trade obstructed; and the planters looked forward with solicitude to the issue of such alarming events.

In the mean while Lord Baltimore, taking advantage of the weakness of the crown, had shown some contempt for its authority, and had drawn upon himself the threat of a *quo warranto*.

Early in 1645, Clayborne, profiting by the distractions of the mother country, and animated by an indomitable, or, as his enemies alleged, a turbulent spirit, and by a sense of wrongs long unavenged, at the head of a band of insurgents, expelled Leonard Calvert, deputy governor, from Maryland, and seized the reins of government. In the month of August, 1646, Calvert, who had taken refuge in Virginia, regained command of Maryland. Nevertheless, Clayborne and his confederates, with but few exceptions, emerged in impunity from this singular contest.

Opechancanough was succeeded by Necotowance, styled "King of the Indians," and in October, 1646, a treaty was effected with him, by which he agreed to hold his authority from the King of England, (who was now bereft of his own,) while the assembly engaged to protect him from his enemies; in acknowledgment whereof, he was to deliver to the governor a yearly tribute of twenty beaver skins at the departure of the wild-geese.* By this treaty it was further agreed, that the Indians were to occupy the country on the north side of York River, and to cede to the English all the country between the York and the James, from the falls to Kiquotan; death for an Indian to be found within this territory, unless sent in as a messenger; messengers to be admitted into the colony by means of badges of striped cloth; and felony for a white man to be found on the Indian hunting-ground, which was to extend from the head of Yapin, the Blackwater, to the old Mannakin town, on the James River; badges to be received at Fort Royal and Fort Henry, alias Appomattox. Fort Henry had been established not long before this, at the falls of the Appomattox, now site of Petersburg; Fort Charles at the falls of the James; Fort James on the Chickahominy. This

---

* Cohonk, the cry of the wild-geese, was an Indian term for winter.

one was under command of Lieutenant Thomas Rolfe, son of Pocahontas.* Fort Royal was on the Pamunkey.

The colony bore a natural resemblance to the mother country, no little modified by new circumstances, and followed her, yet not with equal step. The government and the people were apparently, in the main, loyal, but there was a growing Puritan party, and William Clayborne appears to have been at the head of it. In 1647 certain ministers, refusing to read the Common Prayer on the Sabbath, were declared not entitled to tythes. Two years before, mercenary attorneys had been, by law, expelled from the courts, and now attorneys were prohibited from receiving any compensation for their services, and the courts were directed not to allow any professional attorneys to appear in civil causes. In case there appeared danger of a party suffering in his suit by reason of his weakness, the court was directed to appoint some suitable person in his behalf from the people. It has been suggested in modern times, as an improvement in the administration of justice, to allow the parties to make their own statements.

There were in Virginia, in 1648, about fifteen thousand English, and of negroes that had been imported, three hundred good servants. Of cows, oxen, bulls, and calves, "twenty thousand, large and good;" and the colonists made plenty of butter and good cheese. The number of horses and mares, of good breed, was two hundred; of asses fifty. The sheep numbered three thousand, producing good wool; there were five thousand goats. Hogs, tame and wild, innumerable, and the bacon excellent; poultry equally abundant. Wheat was successfully cultivated. The abundant crop of barley supplied malt, and there were public brew-houses, and most of the planters brewed a good and strong beer for themselves. Hops were found to thrive well. The price-current of beef was two pence halfpenny (about five cents) a pound, pork six cents. Cattle bore about the same price as in England; most of the vessels arriving laid in their stores here. Thirty different sorts of river and sea fish were caught. Thirty species of birds and fowls had been observed, and twenty kinds of quad-

---

* Toward the end of 1641 he had petitioned the governor for permission to visit his kinsman, Opechancanough, and Cleopatre, his aunt.

rupeds; deer abundant. The varieties of fruit were estimated at fifteen, and they were comparable to those of Italy. Twenty-five different kinds of trees were noticed, suitable for building ships, houses, etc. The vegetables were potatoes, asparagus, carrots, parsnips, onions, artichokes, peas, beans, and turnips, with a variety of garden herbs and medicinal flowers. Virginia (or Indian) corn yielded five hundred fold; it was planted like gardenpeas; it made good bread and furmity, and malt for beer, and was found to keep for seven years. It was planted in April or May, and ripened in five months. Bees, wild and domestic, supplied plenty of honey and wax. Indigo was made from the leaves of a small tree, and great hopes were entertained that Virginia would in time come to supply all Christendom with the commodity which was then procured "from the Mogul's country." The Virginia tobacco was in high esteem, yet the crop raised was so large that the price was only about three pence, or six cents, a pound. A man could plant enough to make two thousand pounds, and also sufficient corn and vegetables for his own support. The culture of hemp and flax had been commenced. Good iron-ore was found, and there were sanguine anticipations of the profits to be derived from that source. There were windmills and water-mills, horse-mills and hand-mills: a saw-mill was greatly needed, it being considered equivalent to the labor of twenty men. There came yearly to trade above thirty vessels, navigated by seven or eight hundred men. They brought linens, woollens, stockings, shoes, etc. They cleared in March, with return cargoes of tobacco, staves, and lumber. Many of the masters and chief mariners of these vessels had plantations, houses, and servants, in the colony. Pinnaces, boats, and barges were numerous, the most of the plantations being situated on the banks of the rivers. Pitch and tar were made. Mulberry-trees abounded, and it was confidently believed that silk could be raised in Virginia as well as in France. Hopeful anticipations of making wine from the native grape were entertained, but have never been realized. Virginia was now considered healthy; the colonists being so amply provided with the necessaries and comforts of life, the number of deaths was believed to be less, proportionally, than in England. The voyage from England to Virginia occupied about six weeks; the outward-bound voyage averaging about twenty-five days.

At this time a thousand colonists were seated upon the Accomac shore, near Cape Charles, where Captain Yeardley was chief commander. The settlement was then called Northampton; the name of Accomac having been changed in 1643 to Northampton, but the original name was afterwards restored. Lime was found abundant in Virginia; bricks were made, and already some houses built of them. Mechanics found profitable employment, such as turners, potters, coopers, sawyers, carpenters, tilemakers, boatwrights, tailors, shoemakers, tanners, fishermen, and the like. There were at this time twelve counties. The number of churches was twenty, each provided with a minister, and the doctrine and orders after the Church of England. The ministers' livings were worth one hundred pounds, or five hundred dollars, per annum, paid in tobacco and corn. The colonists all lived in peace and love, happily exempt by distance from the horrors of civil war that convulsed the mother country. The Virginia planters were intending to make further discoveries to the south and west. A colony of Swedes had made a settlement on the banks of the Delaware River, within the limits of Virginia, and were carrying on a profitable traffic in furs. The Dutch had also planted a colony on the Hudson River, within the Virginia territory, and their trade in furs amounted to ten thousand pounds per annum. Cape Cod was then looked upon as the point of demarcation between Virginia and New England. Cattle, corn, and other commodities were shipped from Virginia to New England. Sir William Berkley had made an experiment in the cultivation of rice, and found that it produced thirty fold, the soil and climate being well adapted to it, as the negroes affirmed, who, in Africa, had subsisted mostly on that grain. There were now many thousands of acres of cleared land in Virginia, and about one hundred and fifty ploughs at work. Captain Brocas of the council, a great traveller, had planted a vineyard, and made excellent wine.

At Christmas, 1647, there were in the James River ten vessels from London, two from Bristol, twelve from Holland, and seven from New England. Mr. Richard Bennet expressed twenty butts of excellent cider from apples of his own orchard. They began now to engraft on the crab-apple tree, which was found indigenous. Another planter had for several years made, from pears of his own raising, forty or fifty butts of perry. The governor, Sir William Berkley, in his new orchard, had fifteen hundred fruit trees, besides his apricots, peaches, mellicotons, quinces, wardens, and the like.

Captain Matthews, an old planter, of above thirty years' standing, one of the council, and "a most deserving commonwealth man," had a fine house, sowed much hemp and flax, and had it spun; he kept weavers, and had a tannery, where leather was dressed; and had eight shoemakers at work; had forty negro servants, whom he brought up to mechanical trades; he sowed large crops of wheat and barley. The wheat he sold at four shillings (about a dollar) a bushel. He also supplied vessels trading in Virginia, with beef. He had a plenty of cows, a fine dairy, a large number of hogs and poultry. Captain Matthews married a daughter of Sir Thomas Hinton, and "kept a good house, lived bravely, and was a true lover of Virginia."

There was a free school, with two hundred acres of land appurtenant, a good house, forty milch cows, and other accommodations. It was endowed by Mr. Benjamin Symms. There were, besides, some small schools in the colony, probably such as are now known as "old-field schools."*

---

* Hening, i. 252.

CHAPTER XXIII.

1648-1659.

Beauchamp Plantagenet visits Virginia—Settlement of other Colonies—Dissenters persecuted and banished from Virginia—Some take refuge in Carolina; some in Maryland—Charles the First executed—Commonwealth of England—Virginia Assembly denounces the Authors of the King's Death—Colonel Norwood's Voyage to Virginia—The Virginia Dissenters in Maryland—The Long Parliament prohibits Trade with Virginia—A Naval Force sent to reduce the Colony, Bennet and Clayborne being two of the Commissioners—Captain Dennis demands surrender of Virginia—Sir William Berkley constrained to yield—Articles of Capitulation.

DURING the year 1648 Beauchamp Plantagenet, a royalist with a high-flown name, flying from the fury of the grand rebellion, visited America in behalf of a company of adventurers, in quest of a place of settlement, and in the course of his explorations came to Virginia. At Newport's News he was hospitably entertained by Captain Matthews, Mr. Fantleroy, and others, finding free quarter everywhere. The Indian war was now ended by the courage of Captain Marshall and the valiant Stillwell, and by the resolute march of Sir William Berkley, who had made the veteran Opechancanough prisoner. The explorer went to Chicaoen, on the Potomac, and found Maryland involved in war with the Sasquesahannocks and other Indians, and at the same time in a civil war. Kent Island appeared to be too wet, and the water was bad.*

In the month of March, 1648, Nickotowance, the Indian chief, visited Governor Berkley, at Jamestown, accompanied by five other chiefs, and presented twenty beaver skins to be sent to King Charles as tribute. About this time the Indians reported to Sir William Berkley that within five days' journey to the southwest there was a high mountain, and at the foot of it great rivers that run into a great sea; that men came hither in ships, (but not the same as the English;) that they wore apparel, and had red caps

---

* Description of New Albion, in Force's Hist. Tracts, ii.

on their heads, and rode on beasts like horses, but with much longer ears. These people were probably the Spaniards. Sir William Berkley prepared to make an exploration with fifty horse and as many foot,* but he was disappointed in this enterprise.

At this period the settlement of all the New England States had been commenced; the Dutch possessed the present States of New York, New Jersey, and part of Connecticut, and they had already pushed their settlements above Albany; the Swedes occupied the shores of Pennsylvania and Delaware; Maryland was still in her infancy; Virginia was prosperous; the country now known as the Carolinas belonged to the assignees of Sir Robert Heath, but as yet no advances had been made toward the occupation of it.†

Upon complaint of the necessities of the people, occasioned by barren and over-wrought land, and want of range for cattle and hogs, permission was granted them to remove during the following year to the north side of Charles (York) and Rappahannock rivers.‡

The congregation of dissenters collected by the three missionaries before mentioned from Massachusetts, amounted in 1648 to one hundred and eighteen members. They encountered the continual opposition of the colonial authorities. Mr. Durand, their elder, had already been banished by the governor; and in the course of this year their pastor, Harrison, being ordered to depart, retired to New England. On his arrival there he represented that many of the Virginia council were favorably disposed toward the introduction of Puritanism, and that "one thousand of the people, by conjecture, were of a similar mind."§ The members of the council at that time were Captain John West, Richard Kempe, secretary, Captain William Brocas, Captain Thomas Pettus, Captain William Bernard, Captain Henry Browne, and Mr. George Ludlow. When the pre-

---

* Hening, i. 353.

† Martin's History of North Carolina, i. 105–6. This is a valuable work, but marred, especially in the first volume, by the unparalleled misprinting, the engagements of the author not permitting him to correct the proofs.

‡ Force's Hist. Tracts, ii., "A New Description of Va."

§ Hawks' Narrative, 57, citing Savage's Winthrop, ii. 334.

valence of Puritanism in the mother country is considered, and the numerous ties of interest and consanguinity that connected it with the colony, the estimate of the number favorably disposed toward Puritanism does not appear improbable. John Hammond afterwards gave an account of the proceedings against the Puritans in Virginia.* According to him, during the reign of Charles the First, Virginia "was wholly for monarchy." A congregation of people calling themselves Independents having organized a church, (probably in Nansemond County,) and daily increasing, several consultations were held by the authorities of the colony how to suppress and extinguish them. At first their pastor was banished, next their other teachers, then many were confined in prison; next they were generally disarmed, which was a very harsh measure in such a country, where they were surrounded by the Indian savages; lastly, the non-conformists were put in a condition of banishment, so that they knew not how in those straits to dispose of themselves. The leader in this persecution, according to Hammond, was Colonel Samuel Matthews, member of the council in 1643, and subsequently agent for Virginia to the parliament. A number of these dissenters having gained the consent of Lord Baltimore and his deputy governor of Maryland, retired to that colony, and settled there. Among these, one of the principal was Richard Bennet, a merchant and a Roundhead. For a time these refugees prospered and remained apparently content with their new place of abode; and others, induced by their example, likewise removed thither.

King Charles the First, after having been a prisoner for several years, was beheaded in front of Whitehall Palace, on the 30th day of January, 1648. He died with heroic firmness and dignity.† The Commonwealth of England now commenced, and continued till the restoration of Charles the Second, in 1660. Upon the dissolution of the monarchy in England, there were not wanting those in Virginia who held that the colonial govern-

---

* Leah and Rachel, in Force's Hist. Tracts, iii., Leah and Rachel representing the two sisters, Virginia and Maryland.

† In the same year the Netherlands became independent.

ment, being derived from the crown, was itself now extinct; but the assembly, by an act of October of the same year, declared that whoever should defend the late traitorous proceedings against the king, should be adjudged an accessory after the fact, to his death, and be proceeded against accordingly; to asperse the late most pious king's memory was made an offence punishable at the discretion of the governor and council; to express a doubt of the right of succession of Charles the Second, or to propose a change of government, or to derogate from the full power of the government of the colony, was declared to be high treason.* The principle, however, that the authority of the colonial government ceased with the king's death, was expressly recognized at the surrender of the colony to the parliamentary naval force in 1651.

Colonel Norwood, a loyal refugee in Holland, having formed a plan with two comrades, Major Francis Morrison and Major Richard Fox, to seek their fortunes in Virginia, they met in London, August, 1649, for the purpose of embarking. At the time when they had first concerted their scheme, Charles the First was a prisoner at Carisbrook Castle, in the Isle of Wight. He had since been executed; the royalists, thunderstruck at this catastrophe, saw their last gleam of hope extinguished; and Norwood and his friends were eager to escape from the scene of their disasters. At the Royal Exchange, whose name was now for a time to be altered to the "Great Exchange," the three forlorn cavaliers engaged a passage to Virginia in the "Virginia Merchant," burden three hundred tons, mounting thirty guns or more. The charge for the passage was six pounds a head, for themselves and servants. The colony of Virginia they deemed preferable for them in their straitened pecuniary circumstances; and they brought over some goods with them for the purpose of mercantile adventure. September the 23d, 1649, they embarked in the "Virginia Merchant," having on board three hundred and thirty souls. Touching at Fayal, Norwood and his companions met with a Portuguese lady of rank with her family returning, in an English ship, the "John," from the Brazils to her own country. With her they drank the healths of their kings, amid

---

* Hening, i 360.

thundering peals of cannon. The English gentlemen discovered a striking resemblance between the lady's son and their own prince, Charles, which filled them with fond admiration, and flattered the vanity of the beautiful Portuguese. Passing within view of the charming Bermuda, the "Virginia Merchant" sailing for Virginia, struck upon a breaker early in November, near the stormy Cape Hatteras. Narrowly escaping from that peril, she was soon overtaken by a storm, and tossed by mountainous towering northwest seas. Amid the horrors of the evening prospect, Norwood observed innumerable ill-omened porpoises that seemed to cover the surface of the sea as far as the eye could reach. The ship at length losing forecastle and mainmast, became a mere hulk, drifting at the mercy of the winds and waves. Some of the passengers were swept overboard by the billows that broke over her; the rest suffered the tortures of terror and famine. At last the tempest subsiding, the ship drifted near the coast of the Eastern Shore. Here Norwood and a party landing on an island, were abandoned by the Virginia Merchant. After enduring the extremities of cold and hunger, of which some died, Norwood and the survivors in the midst of the snow were rescued by a party of friendly Indians. In the mean while the ship having arrived in the James River, a messenger was dispatched by Governor Berkley in quest of Norwood and his party. Conducted to the nearest plantation, they were everywhere entertained with the utmost kindness. Stephen Charlton (afterwards, in 1652, burgess from Northampton County,) would have the Colonel to put on a good farmer-like suit of his own. After visiting Captain Yeardley, (son of Sir George Yeardley, the former governor,) the principal person in that quarter of the colony, Norwood crossed the Chesapeake Bay in a sloop, and landed at 'Squire Ludlow's plantation on York River. Next he proceeded to the neighboring plantation of Captain Ralph Wormley, at that time burgess from York County, and member of his majesty's council. At Captain Wormley's he found some of his friends, who had likewise recently arrived from England, feasting and carousing. The cavaliers had changed their clime but not their habits. These guests were Sir Thomas Lundsford, Sir Henry Chicheley, (pronounced Chickley,) Sir Philip Honeywood, and Colonel Hammond. Sir Thomas Lundsford lies buried in the churchyard of Williamsburg. At Jamestown Norwood was cordially welcomed by Sir William Berkley, who took him to his house at Greenspring, where he remained for some months. Sir William, on many occasions, showed great respect to all the royal party who made that colony their refuge; and his house and purse were open to all such. To Major Fox, who had no other friend in the colony to look to for aid, he exhibited signal kindness; to Major Morrison he gave command of the fort at Point Comfort, and by his interest afterwards advanced him to be governor of the colony. In 1650 Governor Berkley dispatched Norwood to Holland to find the fugitive king, and to solicit for the place of treasurer of Virginia, which Sir William took to be void by "the delinquency" of William Clayborne, the incumbent, who had long held that place. The governor furnished Norwood with money to defray the charge of the solicitation, which was effectual, although Prince Charles was not found in Holland, he having gone to Scotland. Charles the Second was crowned by the Scotch at Scone, in 1651.*

Bennet and other dissenting Virginians, who had settled in Maryland, were not long there before they became dissatisfied with the proprietary government. The authority of Papists was irksome to Puritans, and they began to avow their aversion to the oath of allegiance imposed upon them; for by the terms of it Lord Baltimore affected to usurp almost royal authority, concluding his commissions and writs with "We," "us," and "given under our hand and greater seal of arms, in such a year of our dominion." The Protestants of Maryland, no doubt saw, in the political character of the Commonwealth of England, a fair prospect of the speedy subversion of Baltimore's power; nor were they disappointed in this hope.

In October, 1650, the Long Parliament passed an ordinance prohibiting trade with Barbadoes, Virginia, Bermuda, and Antigua. The act recited that these colonies were, and of right ought to be, subject to the authority of Parliament; that divers

---

* Force's Hist. Tracts, iii.; Churchill's Voyages. A Major Norwood is mentioned in Pepys' Diary, i. 46.

acts of rebellion had been committed by many persons inhabiting Virginia, whereby they have most traitorously usurped a power of government, and set themselves in opposition to this commonwealth. It therefore declared such persons notorious robbers and traitors; forbade all correspondence or commerce with them, and appointed commissioners, and dispatched Sir George Ayscue, with a powerful fleet and army, to reduce Barbadoes, Bermuda, and Antigua to submission.

Charles the Second having invaded England at the head of a Scottish army, was utterly defeated and overthrown by Cromwell, at Worcester, September the 3d, 1651. Charles himself, not long after, with difficulty and in disguise, escaped to France. In September of the same year the council of state, of which Bradshaw was president, issued instructions for Captain Robert Dennis, Mr. Richard Bennet, Mr. Thomas Steg,* and Captain William Clayborne, appointed commissioners, for the reducement of Virginia and the inhabitants thereof, to their due obedience to the Commonwealth of Virginia. A fleet was put under command of Captain Dennis, and the commissioners embarked in the Guinea frigate. They were empowered to assure pardon and indemnity to all the inhabitants of the said plantations that shall submit unto the present government and authority, as it is established in the Commonwealth of England. In case they shall not submit by fair ways and means, the commissioners were to use all acts of hostility that lay in their power to enforce them; and if they should find the people so to stand out as that they could by no other ways or means reduce them to their due obedience, they, or any two or more of them, whereof Captain Robert Dennis was to be one, had the power to appoint captains and other officers, and to raise forces within each of the aforesaid plantations, for the furtherance of the service; and such persons as should come in and serve as soldiers, if their masters should stand in opposition to the government of the English Commonwealth, might be discharged and set free from their masters, by the commissioners. A similar measure was adopted by Lord Dunmore in 1776. In

---

* A Mr. Thomas Stagg was a resident planter of Virginia in 1652. Hening, i. 375.

case of the death of Captain Dennis, his place was to be filled by Captain Edmund Curtis, commander of the Guinea frigate.* It is a mistake to suppose that the members of the Long Parliament were all of them, or a majority of them, Puritans, in the religious sense of the term; but they were so in political principles.

In March, 1652, Captain Dennis arrived at Jamestown, and demanded a surrender of the colony. It is said by some historians that Sir William Berkley, either with a hope of repelling them, or of commanding better terms, prepared for a gallant resistance, and undertook to strengthen himself by making use of several Dutch ships,† which happened to be there engaged in a contraband trade, and which he hired for the occasion; that there chanced to be on board of the parliament's fleet some goods belonging to two members of the Virginia council, and that Dennis sent them word that their goods should be forfeited if the colony was not immediately surrendered; and that the threat kindled dissensions in the council, and the governor found himself constrained to yield on condition of a general amnesty.‡

Such is the account of several chroniclers, but it appears to be based only on a loose and erroneous tradition. It would have been a mere empty gasconade for Sir William Berkley to oppose the English naval force, and the truth appears to be, that as soon as the parliamentary squadron entered the Chesapeake Bay, all thoughts of resistance were laid aside. If the story of the preparation for resistance were credited, it must at the same time be believed that this chivalry and loyalty suddenly evaporated under the more potent influence of pecuniary interest.§

The capitulation was ratified on the 12th of March, 1652, by which it was agreed that the Colony of Virginia should be subject

---

* Virginia and Maryland, 18; Force's Hist. Tracts, ii.
† Only one ship appears to have been confiscated. Hening, i. 382.
‡ Chalmers' Annals, 123; Beverley, B. i. 54.
§ Bancroft, Hist. of U. S., i. 223, citing Clarendon, B. xiii. 466, and other authorities, says that the fleet was sent over by Cromwell, and came to Virginia after having reduced the West India Islands. Cromwell, however, although at this time the master-spirit of England, had not yet assumed dictatorial powers.

to the Commonwealth of England; that the submission should be considered voluntary, not forced nor constrained by a conquest upon the country; and that "they shall have and enjoy such freedoms and privileges as belong to the free-born people of England;" the assembly to meet as formerly, and transact the affairs of the colony, but nothing to be done contrary to the government of the Commonwealth of England; full indemnity granted for all offences against the Parliament of England; Virginia to have and enjoy the ancient bounds and limits granted by the charters of former kings; "and that we shall seek a new charter from the Parliament to that purpose, against any that have entrenched upon the rights thereof," alluding no doubt to Lord Baltimore's intrusion into Maryland; that the privilege of having fifty acres of land for every person transported to the colony, shall continue as formerly granted; that the people of Virginia shall have free trade, as the people of England do enjoy, to all places, and with all nations, according to the laws of that Commonwealth; and that Virginia shall enjoy all privileges equally with any English plantation in America.

The navigation act had been passed in the preceding October, forbidding any goods, wares, or merchandise, to be imported into England, except either in English ships, or in ships of the country where the commodities were produced—a blow aimed at the carrying-trade of the Dutch. It was further agreed by the articles of surrender, that Virginia was to be free from all taxes, customs, and impositions whatsoever, and none to be imposed on them without consent of the grand assembly; and so that neither forts nor castles be erected, or garrisons maintained, without their consent: no charge to be made upon Virginia on account of this present fleet; the engagement or oath of allegiance to be tendered to all the inhabitants of Virginia; recusants to have a year's time to remove themselves and their effects out of Virginia, and in the mean time, during the said year, to have equal justice as formerly; the use of the Book of Common Prayer to be permitted for one year, with the consent of a majority of a parish, provided that those things which relate to kingship, or that government, be not used publicly; and ministers to be continued in their places, they not misdemeaning themselves; public ammunition, powder and arms, to be given up, security being given to make satisfaction for them; goods already brought hither by the Dutch to remain unmolested; the quit-rents granted by the late king to the planters of Virginia for seven years, to be confirmed; finally, the parliamentary commissioners engage themselves and the honor of the Parliament for the full performance of the articles, the governor and council and burgesses making the same pledge for the colony.*

On the same day some other articles were ratified by the commissioners and the governor and council, exempting the governor and council from taking the oath of allegiance for a year, and providing that they should not be censured for praying for, or speaking well of the king, for one whole year in their private houses, or "neighboring conference;" Sir William Berkley was permitted to send an agent to give an account to his majesty of the surrender of the country; Sir William and the members of the council were permitted to dispose of their estates, and transport themselves "whither they please." Protection of liberty and property were guaranteed to Sir William Berkley.

Major Fox, (comrade of Norwood,) commander of the fort, at Point Comfort, was allowed compensation for the building of his house on Fort Island. A general amnesty was granted to the inhabitants, and it was agreed that in case Sir William or his councillors should go to London, or any other place in England, that they should be free from trouble or hindrance of arrests, or such like, and that they may prosecute their business there for six months. It would seem that some important articles of surrender were not ratified by the Long Parliament.

The Fourth Article was, "That Virginia shall have and enjoy the ancient bounds and limits granted by the charters of the former kings, and that we shall seek a new charter from the Parliament to that purpose, against any that entrenched against the rights thereof." This article was referred in August, 1652, to the committee of the navy, to consider what patent was fit to be granted to the inhabitants of Virginia.

---

* Hening, i. 363.

The Seventh Article was, "That the people of Virginia have free trade, as the people of England do enjoy, to all places and with all nations, according to the laws of that commonwealth; and that Virginia shall enjoy all privileges equal with any English plantations in America." The latter clause was referred to the same committee.

The Eighth Article was, "That Virginia shall be free from all taxes, customs, and impositions, whatsoever, and none to be imposed on them without consent of the grand assembly, and so that neither forts nor castles be erected, or garrisons maintained, without their consent." This was also referred to the navy committee, together with several papers relative to the disputes between Virginia and Maryland. The committee made a report in December, which seems merely confined to the Fourth Article, relative to the question of boundary and the contest with Lord Baltimore. In the ensuing July the Long Parliament was dissolved.*

The articles of surrender were subscribed by Richard Bennet, William Clayborne, and Edmund Curtis, commissioners in behalf of the Parliament. Bennet, a merchant and Roundhead, driven from Virginia by the persecution of Sir William Berkley's administration, had taken refuge in Maryland. Having gone thence to England, his Puritanical principles and his knowledge of the colonies of Virginia and Maryland, had recommended him for the place of commissioner. Clayborne, too, who had formerly been obliged to fly to England, and whose office of treasurer of Virginia Sir William Berkley had held to be forfeited by delinquency, and which the fugitive Charles had bestowed on Colonel Norwood—this impetuous and indomitable Clayborne was another of

---

* "Virginia and Maryland," Force's Hist. Tracts, ii. 20, in note. Mr. Force, whose researches have brought to light such a magazine of curious and instructive historical materials, appears to have been the first to mention the non-ratification of some of the articles of surrender. He says: "Three of the articles were not confirmed," and therefore did not receive the last formal and final and definitive ratification which Burk [Hist. of Va., ii. 92,] supposes they did. But it appears that Burk referred only to the ratification by the parties at Jamestown, and had no reference to the ulterior confirmation by the Parliament.

the commissioners sent to reduce the colonies within the Chesapeake Bay.

A new era was now opening in these two colonies; and the prominent parts which Bennet and Clayborne were destined to perform in this novel scene, exhibit a signal example of the vicissitudes of human fortune. The drama that was enacted in the mother country was repeated on a miniature theatre in the colonies.

CHAPTER XXIV.

1652-1656.

Bennet and Clayborne reduce Maryland—Cromwell's Letter—Provisional Government organized in Virginia—Bennet made Governor—William Clayborne Secretary of State—The Assembly—Counties represented—Cromwell dissolves the Long Parliament, and becomes Lord Protector—Sir William Berkley—Francis Yeardley's Letter to John Ferrar—Discovery in Carolina—Roanoke Indians visit Yeardley—He purchases a large Territory—William Hatcher—Stone, Deputy Governor of Maryland, defies the Authority of the Commissioners Bennet and Clayborne—They seize the Government and entrust it to Commissioners—Battle ensues—The Adherents of Baltimore defeated—Several prisoners executed—Cromwell's Letters—The Protestants attack the Papists on the Birth-day of St. Ignatius.

NOT long after the surrender of the Ancient Dominion of Virginia, Bennet and Clayborne, commissioners, embarking in the Guinea frigate, proceeded to reduce Maryland. After effecting a reduction of the infant province, they, with singular moderation, agreed to a compromise with those who held the proprietary government under Lord Baltimore. Stone, the governor, and the council, part of them Papists, none well affected to the Commonwealth of England, were allowed, until further instructions should be received, to retain their places, on condition of issuing all writs in the name of the Keepers of the Liberty of England.* Sir William Berkley, upon the surrender of the colony, betook himself into retirement in Virginia, where he remained free from molestation; and his house continued to be a hospitable place of resort for refugee cavaliers. There was, no doubt, before the surrender, a considerable party in Virginia, who either secretly or openly sympathized with the parliamentary party in England; and upon the reduction of the colony these adherents of the Commonwealth found their influence much augmented.

---

* "Virginia and Maryland," 11, 34; Force's Hist. Tracts, ii.; Chalmers' Annals, 221.

On the 30th of April, 1652, Bennet and Clayborne, commissioners, together with the burgesses of Virginia, organized a provisional government, subject to the control of the Commonwealth of England. Richard Bennet, who had been member of the council in 1646, nephew of an eminent London merchant largely engaged in the Virginia trade,* was made governor, April 30, 1652; and William Clayborne, secretary of state for the colony. The council appointed consisted of Captain John West, Colonel Samuel Matthews, Colonel Nathaniel Littleton, Colonel Argal Yeardley, Colonel Thomas Pettus, Colonel Humphrey Higginson, Colonel George Ludlow, Colonel William Barnett,† Captain Bridges Freeman, Captain Thomas Harwood, Major William Taylor, Captain Francis Eppes, and Lieutenant-Colonel John Cheesman. The governor, secretary, and council were to have such power and authorities to act from time to time as should be appointed and granted by the grand assembly.‡ The government of the mother country was entitled "the States," as the United States are now styled in Canada. The act organizing the provisional government concludes with: "God save the Commonwealth of England, and this country of Virginia." The governor and councillors were allowed to be, ex-officio, members of the assembly. On the fifth day of May, this body, while claiming the right to appoint all officers for the colony, yet for the present, in token of their implicit confidence in the commissioners, referred all the appointments not already made to the governor and them. The administration of Virginia was now, for the first time, Puritan and Republican. The act authorizing the governor and council to appoint the colonial officers was renewed in the following year. The oath administered to the burgesses was: "You and every of you shall swear upon the holy Evangelist, and in the sight of God, to deliver your opinions faithfully and honestly, according to your best understanding and conscience, for the general good and prosperity of the country, and every particular member thereof, and to do your utmost endeavor to prosecute that without mingling with it any particular interest of any person or persons whatsoever."

---

* Stith's Hist. of Va., 199.   † Properly Bernard: see Hening, i. 408.
‡ Hening, i. 372.

The governor and members of the council were declared to be entitled to seats in the assembly, and were required to take the same oath. This assembly, which met on the 26th of April, 1652, appears to have sat about ten days. There were thirty-five burgesses present from twelve counties, namely: Henrico, Charles City, James City, Isle of Wight, Nansemond, (originally called Nansimum,) Lower Norfolk, Elizabeth City, Warwick, York, Northampton, Northumberland, and Gloucester—Lancaster not being represented.* Rappahannock County was formed from the upper part of Lancaster in 1656.

At the commencement of the ensuing session of the assembly, which met in October, 1652, Mr. John Hammond, returned a burgess from Isle of Wight County, was expelled from the assembly as being notoriously a scandalous person, and a frequent disturber of the peace of the country by libel and other illegal practices. He had passed nineteen years in Virginia, and now retired to Maryland; he was the author of the pamphlet entitled "Leah and Rachel."† Mr. James Pyland, another burgess, returned from the same county, was expelled, and committed to answer such charges as should be brought against him as an abettor of Mr. Thomas Woodward, in his mutinous and rebellious declaration, and concerning his the said Mr. Pyland's blasphemous catechism. These offenders appear to have been of the royalist party.

In the year 1653 there were fourteen counties in Virginia, Surry being now mentioned for the first time, and the number of burgesses was thirty-four. The people living on the borders of the Appomattox River were authorized to hold courts,

---

* Gloucester and Lancaster Counties are now named for the first time; when or how they were formed, does not appear. Sir William Berkley was of Gloucestershire, England. The name of Warrasqueake was changed to Isle of Wight in 1637, and first represented in 1642. In that year Charles River was changed to York, and Warwick River to Warwick. The boundaries of Upper and Lower Norfolk were fixed in 1642; and Upper Norfolk was changed to Nansimum (afterwards Nansemond) in 1646. Northumberland is first mentioned in 1645; Westmoreland in 1653; Surry, Gloucester, and Lancaster in 1652. New Kent was first represented in 1654, being taken from the upper part of York County. (*McSherry's Hist. of Maryland.*)

† Force's Hist. Tracts, iii.

and to treat with the Indians. Colonel William Clayborne, Captain Henry Fleet, and Major Abram Wood were empowered to make discoveries to the west and south. In July, some difference occurred between the governor and council on the one side, and the house of burgesses on the other, relative to the election of speaker. The affair was amicably arranged, the governor's views being assented to. Bennet appears to have enjoyed the confidence of the Virginians. He was too generous to retaliate upon Sir William Berkley and the royalists who had formerly persecuted him. Some malecontents were punished for speaking disrespectfully of him, and refusing to pay the castle duties. From the charges brought against one of these, it appears that the Virginians considered themselves, under the articles of surrender, entitled to free trade with all the world, the navigation act to the contrary notwithstanding; and that act does not appear to have been enforced against Virginia during the Commonwealth of England.* By the articles of surrender the use of the prayer-book was permitted, with the consent of a majority of the people of the parish, for one year; so that it would seem that its use was prohibited after March 12th, 1653; but the prohibition was not enforced, and public worship continued as before without interruption.† In April, 1653, Oliver Cromwell dissolved the Long Parliament, and in December, in the same year, assumed the office of Lord Protector of the Commonwealth of England, Scotland, and Ireland. Owing to the war with Holland, Sir William Berkley's departure from Virginia was delayed, and, in conformity with the articles of convention of 1651, he now became subject to arrest. But the assembly passed an act, stating that as the war between England and Holland had prevented the confirmation of the convention of 1651, in England, or the coming of a ship out of Holland, and Sir William Berkley desiring a longer time, namely, eight months further, to procure a ship out of Flanders, in respect of the war with Holland, and that he should be exempted from impost duty on such tobacco as he should lade in her; "it is condescended that his request shall be granted." Some seditious disturbances having taken place in Northampton County, on the Eastern

---

* Burk, ii. 97   † Virginia's Cure, p. 19, in Force's Hist. Tracts, iii.

Shore, in which Edmund Scarburgh was a ringleader, it was found necessary for Governor Bennet, Secretary Clayborne, and a party of gentlemen, to repair thither for the purpose of restoring order. Roger Green, and others, living on the Nansemond River, received a grant of land on condition of their settling the country bordering on the Moratuck or Roanoke River,* and on the south side of the Chowan. Divers gentlemen requesting permission, were authorized, in 1653, to explore the mountains. The ship Leopoldus, of Dunkirk, was confiscated for the use of the Commonwealth of England, for violating the navigation act; and the proceeds, amounting to four hundred pounds sterling, were given to Colonel Samuel Matthews, agent for Virginia at the court of the Protector, Colonel William Clayborne, secretary, and other officers, in return for their services in the matter of the forfeited ship.

Captain Francis Yeardley, who has been mentioned before, was a son of Sir George Yeardley, some time governor of Virginia, and Lady Temperance, his wife, and was born in Virginia. A letter dated in May, 1654, was addressed by him to John Ferrar, at Little Gidding, in Huntingdonshire, brother to Nicholas Ferrar, whose name is so honorably connected with the early annals of Virginia. The younger Yeardley describes the country as very fertile, flourishing in all the exuberance of nature, abounding especially in the rich mulberry and vine, with a serene air and temperate clime, and rich in precious minerals. A young man engaged in the beaver trade having been accidentally separated from his own sloop, had obtained a small boat and provisions from Yeardley, and had gone with his party to Roanoke, at which island he hoped to find his vessel. He there fell in with a hunting party of Indians, and persuaded them and some of the other tribes, both in the island and on the mainland, to go back with him and make peace with the English. He brought some of these Indians with the great man, or chief of Roanoke, to Yeardley's house, which was probably on the Eastern Shore, where his

---

* Called Moratuck or Moratoc above the falls, and Roanoke below. Roanoke signifies "shell:" Roanoke and Wampumpeake were terms for Indian shell-money.

father had lived before him. The Indians passed a week at Yeardley's. While there, the "great man" observing Yeardley's children reading and writing, inquired of him whether he would take his only son, and teach him "to speak out of the book, and make a writing." Yeardley assured him that he would willingly do so; and the chief at his departure expressing his strong desire to serve the God of the Englishmen, and his hope that his child might be brought up in the knowledge of the same, promised to bring him back again in four months. In the mean time Yeardley had been called away to Maryland; and the planters of the Eastern Shore suspecting, from the frequent visits and inquiries of the Indian, that Yeardley was carrying on some scheme for his own private advantage, were disposed to maltreat the chief. Upon one occasion, when Yeardley's wife had brought him to church with her, some over-busy justices of the peace, after sermon, threatened to whip him, and send him away. The "great man" being terrified, the lady taking him by the hand, resolutely stood forth in his defence, and pledged her whole property, as a guarantee, that no harm to the settlement was intended, or was likely to arise from the Indian's alliance. Upon Yeardley's return from Maryland, he dispatched, with his brother's assistance, a boat with six men, one being a carpenter, to build the great man an English house; and two hundred pounds for the purchase of Indian territory. The terms of the purchase were soon agreed upon, and Yeardley's people "paid for three great rivers and also all such others as they should like of, southerly." In due form they took possession of the country in the name of the Commonwealth of England, receiving as a symbol of its surrender, a turf of earth with an arrow shot into it. The territory thus given up by the Indians was a considerable part of what afterwards became the province of North Carolina. As soon as the natives had withdrawn from it to a region farther south, Yeardley built the great commander a handsome house, which he promised to fit up with English utensils and furniture.

Yeardley's people were introduced to the chief of the Tuscaroras, who received them courteously, and invited them to visit his country, of which he gave an attractive account; but his offer could not be accepted, owing to the illness of their interpreter.

Upon the completion of his house, the Roanoke chief came, with the Tuscarora chief and forty-five others, to Yeardley's house, presented his wife and son and himself for baptism, and offered again the same symbol of the surrender of his whole country to Yeardley: and he in his turn tendering the same to the Commonwealth of England, prayed only "that his own property and pains might not be forgotten." The Indian child was presented to the minister before the congregation, and having been baptized in their presence, was left with Yeardley to be bred a Christian, "which God grant him grace (he prays) to become." The charges incurred by Yeardley in purchasing and taking possession of the country, had already amounted to three hundred pounds.*

At the meeting of the assembly in November, 1654, William Hatcher being convicted of having stigmatized Colonel Edward Hill, speaker of the house, as an atheist and blasphemer, (from which charges he had been before acquitted by the quarterly court,) was compelled to make acknowledgment of his offence, upon his knees, before Colonel Hill and the assembly. This Hatcher appears to have been a burgess of Henrico County in 1652. More than twenty years afterwards, in his old age, he was fined eight thousand pounds of pork, for the use of the king's soldiers, on account of alleged mutinous words uttered shortly after Bacon's rebellion.

Upon the dissolution of the Long Parliament and the establishment of the Protectorate, Lord Baltimore took measures to recover the absolute control of Maryland; and Stone, (who since June, 1652, had continued in the place of governor of Maryland,) in obedience to instructions received from his lordship, violated the terms of the agreement, which had been arranged with Bennet and Clayborne, acting in behalf of the Parliament, and set them at defiance. These commissioners having addressed a letter to Stone proposing an interview, he refused to accede to it, and gave it as his opinion, that they were "wolves in sheep's clothing." Bennet and Clayborne, claiming authority derived from his High-

---

* Anderson's Hist. of Col. Church, ii. 506. The letter is preserved in Thurloe's State Papers, xi. 273.

ness the Lord Protector, seized the government of the province, and entrusted it to a board of ten commissioners.*

When Lord Baltimore received intelligence of this proceeding, he wrote to his deputy, (Stone,) reproaching him with cowardice, and peremptorily commanded him to recover the colony by force of arms. Stone and the Marylanders now accordingly fell to arms, and disarmed and plundered those that would not accept the oath of allegiance to Baltimore. The province contained, as has been mentioned before, among its inhabitants a good many emigrants from Virginia of Puritan principles, and these dwelt mainly on the banks of the Severn and the Patuxent, and on the Isle of Kent. They were disaffected to the proprietary government, and protested that they had removed to Maryland, under the express engagement with Governor Stone, that they should enjoy freedom of conscience, and be exempt from the obnoxious oath. These recusants now took up arms to defend themselves, and civil war raged in infant Maryland. Stone, to reduce the malecontents, embarking for Providence with his men, landed on the neck, at the mouth of the Severn. Here, on the 25th of March, 1654, he was attacked by the Protestant adherents of Bennet and Clayborne, and utterly defeated; the prisoners being nearly double of the number of the victors, twenty killed, many wounded, and "all the place strewed with Papist beads where they fled."

During the action, a New England vessel seized the boats, provision, and ammunition of the governor and his party. Among the prisoners was this functionary, who had been "shot in many places." Several of the prisoners were condemned to death by a court-martial; and four of the principal, one of them a councillor, were executed on the spot. Captain William Stone, likewise sentenced, owed his escape to the intercession of some women, and of some of Bennet and Clayborne's people.† John Hammond, (the same who had been, two years before, expelled from the Virginia Assembly,) also one of the condemned, fled in disguise, and escaped to England in the ship Crescent. The master

---

* "Virginia and Maryland," Force's Hist. Tracts, ii.
† "Leah and Rachel," Force's Hist. Tracts, iii.; Chalmer's Annals, 222.

of this vessel was afterwards heavily fined by the Virginia assembly for carrying off Hammond without a pass. Of the four that were shot, three were Romanists; and the Jesuit fathers, hotly pursued, escaped to Virginia, where they inhabited a mean low hut.*

Thus Maryland became subject to the Protectorate. The administration of the Puritan commissioners was rigorous, and the Maryland assembly excluded Papists from the pale of religious freedom. Such were even Milton's views of toleration;† but Cromwell, the master-spirit of his age, soared higher, and commanded the commissioners "not to busy themselves about religion, but to settle the civil government." He addressed the following letter, dated at Whitehall, in January, 1654, to Richard Bennet, Esq., Governor of Virginia:—

"SIR:—Whereas, the differences between the Lord Baltimore and the inhabitants of Virginia, concerning the bounds by them respectively claimed, are depending before our council and yet undetermined; and whereas, we are credibly informed you have, notwithstanding, gone into his plantation in Maryland, and countenanced some people there in opposing the Lord Baltimore's officers; whereby and with other forces from Virginia, you have much disturbed that colony and people, to the engendering of tumults and much bloodshed there, if not timely prevented:

"We, therefore, at the request of the Lord Baltimore and divers other persons of quality here, who are engaged by great adventures in his interest, do, for preventing of disturbances or tumults there, will and require you, and all others deriving any authority from you, to forbear disturbing the Lord Baltimore, or his officers, or people in Maryland, and to permit all things to remain as they were before any disturbance or alteration made by you, or by any other, upon pretence of authority from you, till the said differences, above mentioned, be determined by us here, and we give farther order herein.

"We rest, your loving friend,
"OLIVER, P."

---

* White's Relation, 44, in Force's Hist. Tracts, iv.
† Milton's Prose Works, ii. 346.

Cromwell was now endeavoring to heal the wounds of civil war, to allay animosities, and to strengthen his power by a generous and conciliatory policy, blended with irresistible energy of action. In return for Lord Baltimore's ready submission to his authority, the Protector apparently recognized his proprietary rights in Maryland, yet at the same time, he sustained and protected his commissioners, only curbing the violent contest that had arisen between Virginia and Maryland respecting their boundary. His policy as to the internal government of these colonies was one of a masterly inactivity.

"*To the Commissioners of Maryland.*

"WHITEHALL, 26th September, 1655.

"SIRS:—It seems to us, by yours of the twenty-ninth of June, and by the relation we received by Colonel Bennet, that some mistake or scruple hath arisen concerning the sense of our letters of the twelfth of January last; as if by our letters we had intimated that we should have a stop put to the proceedings of those commissioners who were authorized to settle the civil government of Maryland. Which was not at all intended by us; nor so much as proposed to us by those who made addresses to us to obtain our said letter. But our intention (as our said letter doth plainly import) was only to prevent and forbid any force or violence to be offered by either of the plantations of Virginia or Maryland, from one to the other, upon the differences concerning their bounds, the said differences being then under the consideration of ourself and council here. Which, for your more full satisfaction, we have thought fit to signify to you, and rest

"Your loving friend,
"OLIVER, P."*

Remembering, however, Lord Baltimore's ready submission to his authority, he nominally, at the least, restored him to his control over the province.

It was the custom of the Maryland Romanists to celebrate, by a salute of cannon, the thirty-first of July, the birth-day of St.

---

* Carlyle's Cromwell, ii. 182.

Ignatius, (Loyola,) Maryland's patron saint. On the 1st of August, 1656, the day following the anniversary, a number of Protestant soldiers, aroused by the nocturnal report of the cannon, issued from their fort, five miles distant, rushed upon the habitations of the Papists, broke into them, and plundered whatever there was found of arms or powder.

CHAPTER XXV.

1655-1658.

Digges elected Governor—Bennet goes to England the Colony's Agent—Colonel Edward Hill defeated by the Ricahecrians—Totopotomoi, with many Warriors, slain—Miscellaneous matters—Matthews Elected Governor—Letter to the Protector—Acts of Assembly—Magna Charta recognized as in force—Governor and Council excluded from Assembly—Matthews declares a Dissolution—The House resists—Dispute referred to the Protector—Declaration of Sovereignty—Matthews re-elected—Council newly reorganized—Edward Hill elected Speaker—Rules of the House.

In March, 1655, Edward Digges was elected by the assembly governor of the colony of Virginia. He was of an ancient and distinguished family, and had been made a member of the council in November, 1654, "he having given a signal testimony of his fidelity to this colony and Commonwealth of England." He succeeded Bennet, who had held the office since April, 1652, and who was now appointed the colony's agent at London.

In the year 1656, six or seven hundred Ricahecrian Indians having come down from the mountains, and seated themselves near the falls of the James River, Colonel Edward Hill, the elder, was put in command of a body of men, and ordered to dislodge them. He was reinforced by Totopotomoi, chief of Pamunkey, with one hundred of his tribe. A creek enclosing a peninsula in Hanover County, retains the name of Totopotomoy; and Butler, in Hudibras, alludes to this chief:—

> "The mighty Tottipotimoy
> Sent to our elders an envoy,
> Complaining sorely of the breach
> Of league held forth by brother Patch."

Hill was disgracefully defeated, and the brave Totopotomoi, with the greater part of his warriors, slain. It appears probable that Bloody Run, near Richmond, derived its name from this sanguinary battle. The action in which so many Indians were afterwards massacred by Bacon and his men, and with which a loose tradition has identified Bloody Run, did not occur near the falls of the James River. Hill, in consequence of his bad conduct in this affair, was subsequently, by unanimous vote of the council and the house of burgesses, condemned to pay the expenses of effecting a peace with the Indians, and was disfranchised.* During this year an act was passed allowing all free men the right of voting for burgesses, on the ground that "it is something hard and unagreeable to reason that any persons shall pay equal taxes, and yet have no votes in elections." So republican was the elective franchise in Virginia, under the Protectorate of Oliver Cromwell two centuries ago! In this year, 1656, Colonel Thomas Dew, of Nansemond, sometime before speaker of the house of burgesses, and others, were authorized to explore the country between Cape Hatteras and Cape Fear. The County of Nansemond had long abounded with non-conformists.

The salary of the governor, as ordered at this time, consisted of twenty-five thousand pounds of tobacco, worth two hundred and fifty pounds sterling, together with certain duties levied from masters of vessels, called castle duties, and marriage license fees. A reward of twenty pounds was offered to any one who should import a minister; ministers, with six servants each, were exempted from taxes, it being provided that they should be examined by Mr. Philip Mallory and Mr. John Green, and should be recommended by them to the governor and council, who were invested with discretionary control of the matter.† Letters were sent to Matthews, Virginia's agent at the Protector's court, directing him to suspend for the present the further prosecution of the long and fruitless controversy with Lord Baltimore respecting the disputed boundary.‡ Matthews, returning from England, was elected by the assembly to succeed Digges in the office of governor, who was now employed as agent. Colonel Francis Morrison, speaker, was desired by the assembly to write a letter to the Protector, and another to the secretary of state, which was as follows:—

---

* Hening, i. 402, 422; Burk's Hist. of Va., ii. 107.   † Hening, i. 424.
‡ Burk's Hist. of Va., ii. 116. An Armenian was imported by Digges for the purpose of making silk.

"May it please your Highness,—

"We could not find a fitter means to represent the condition of this country to your highness, than this worthy person, Mr. Digges, our late governor, whose occasions calling him into England, we have instructed him with the state of this place as he left it; we shall beseech your highness to give credit to his relations, which we assure ourselves shall be faithful, having had many experiences of his candor in the time of his government, which he hath managed under your highness, with so much moderation, prudence, and justice, that we should be much larger in expressing this truth, but that we fear to have already too much trespassed, by interrupting your highness' most serious thoughts in greater affairs than what can concern your highness' most humble, most devoted servants.

"Dated from the Assembly of Virginia, 15th December, 1656."

Superscribed, for his "Highness, the Lord Protector."

The letter to the secretary of state was as follows:—

"Right Honorable,—

"Though we are persons so remote from you, we have heard so honorable a character of your worth, that we cannot make a second choice without erring, of one so fit and proper as yourself to make our addresses to his Highness, the Lord Protector. Our desires we have intrusted to that worthy gentleman, Mr. Digges, our late governor; we shall desire you would please to give him access to you and by your highness. And as we promise you will find nothing but worth in him, so we are confident he will undertake for us that we are a people not altogether ungrateful, but will find shortly a nearer way than by saying so, to express really how much we esteem the honor of your patronage, which is both the hopes and ambition of your very humble and then obliged servants.

"From the Assembly of Virginia, 15th December, 1656."

Superscribed, to the "Right Honorable John Thurlow, Secretary of State."

The allusion in the close of the letter appears to be to a douceur which it was intended to present to the secretary.

Digges was instructed to unite with Matthews and Bennet, in London, and to treat with the leading merchants in the Virginia trade, and to let them know how much the assembly had endeavored to diminish the quantity, and improve the quality of the tobacco; and to see what the merchants, on their part, would be willing to do in giving a better price; for if the planters should find that the bad brought as high a price as the good, they would of course raise that which could be raised the most easily.* It appears that Digges was appointed agent conjointly with Bennet. Matthews was elected by the assembly to succeed Digges as governor; but the latter was requested to hold the office as long as he should remain in Virginia. Digges departing for England toward the close of 1655, would appear to have co-operated for a short while with both Matthews and Bennet. By a singular coincidence, Digges, Matthews, and Bennet, who were the first three governors of Virginia under the Commonwealth of England, were transferred from the miniature metropolis, Jamestown, and found themselves together near the court of his Highness the Lord Protector, Oliver Cromwell.

Digges was succeeded as governor by Matthews, early in the year 1656. The laws of the colony were revised, and reduced into one volume, comprising one hundred and thirty-one acts, well adapted to the wants of the people and the condition of the country. Of the transactions from 1656 to 1660, the year of the restoration, Burk says there is an entire chasm in the records; Hening, on the contrary, declares that, "in no portion of the colonial records under the Commonwealth, are the materials so copious as from 1656 to 1660." The editor of the Statutes at Large is the better authority on this point.

The church government was settled by giving the people the entire control of the vestry; while the appointment of ministers and church wardens, the care of the poor, and parochial matters, were entrusted to the people of each parish. An act was passed for the keeping holy the Sabbath, and another against divulgers of false news. The ordinary weight of a hogshead of tobacco at this time did not exceed three hundred and fifty pounds, and its dimensions by law were forty-three inches long and twenty-six wide. Letters, superscribed "For the Public Service," were

---

* Burk's Hist. of Va., ii. 116.

ordered to be conveyed from one plantation to another, to the place of destination. A remedy was provided for servants complaining of harsh usage, or of insufficient food or raiment. The penalty for selling arms or ammunition to the Indians was the forfeiture of the offender's whole estate. It was enacted that no sheriff, or deputy sheriff, then called under-sheriff, should hold his office longer than one year in any one county. The penalty of being reduced to servitude was abolished. The twenty-second day of March and the eighteenth of April were still kept as holy days, in commemoration of the deliverance of the colonists from the bloody Indian massacres of 1622 and 1644. The planters were prohibited from encroaching upon the lands of the Indians. The vessels of all nations were admitted into the ports of Virginia; and an impost duty of ten shillings a hogshead was laid on all tobacco exported, except that laden in English vessels, and bound directly for England; from the payment of which duty vessels belonging to Virginians were afterwards exempted. An act was passed to prohibit the kidnapping of Indian children.

In the year 1656 all acts against mercenary attorneys were repealed; but two years afterwards attorneys were again expelled from the courts,* and no one was suffered to receive any compensation for serving in that capacity. The governor and council made serious opposition to this act, and the following communication was made to the house of burgesses: "The governor and council will consent to this proposition so far as shall be agreeable to Magna Charta. WM. CLAYBORNE." The burgesses replied, that they could not see any such prohibition contained in Magna Charta; that two former assemblies had passed such a law, and that it had stood in force upwards of ten years. It thus appears that Magna Charta was held to be in force in the colony.

The ground leaves of tobacco, or lugs, were declared to be not merchantable; and it was ordered that no tobacco should be planted after the tenth day of July, under the penalty of a fine of ten thousand pounds of that staple. The exportation of hides, wool, and old iron, was forbidden. The salary of the governor,

---

* Hening, i. 434, 482.

derived from the impost duty on tobacco exported, was fixed at sixteen hundred pounds sterling.

The burgesses having rescinded the order admitting the governor and council as members of the house, and having voted an adjournment, Matthews, on the 1st of April, 1658, declared a dissolution of the assembly. The house resisted, and declared that any burgess who should depart at this conjuncture, should be censured as betraying the trust reposed in him by his country; and an oath of secrecy was administered to the members. The governor, upon receiving an assurance that the business of the house would be speedily and satisfactorily concluded, revoked the order of dissolution, referring the question in dispute, as to the dissolving power, to his Highness the Lord Protector. The burgesses, still unsatisfied, appointed a committee, of which Colonel John Carter, of Lancaster County, was chairman, to draw up a resolution asserting their powers; and in consonance with their report the burgesses made a declaration of popular sovereignty: that they had in themselves the full power of appointing all officers, until they should receive an order to the contrary from England; that the house was not dissolvable by any power yet extant in Virginia but their own; that all former elections of governor and council should be void; that the power of governor for the future should be conferred on Colonel Samuel Matthews, who by them was invested with all the rights and privileges belonging to the governor and captain-general of Virginia; and that a council should be appointed by the burgesses then convened, with the advice of the governor.

The legislative records do not disclose the particular ground on which the previous elections of governor and appointments of councillors under the provisional government were annulled; but from the exclusion of the governor and council from the house, it might be inferred that it was owing to a jealousy of these functionaries being members of the body that elected them. Yet Bennet, the first of the three governors, and his council, were, in 1652, expressly allowed to be *ex officio* members of the assembly. An order was also made, April 2d, 1758, by the assembly, in the name of his Highness the Lord Protector, to the sheriff of James City, and sergeant-at-arms, to obey no warrant but those signed by the speaker of the house; and William Clayborne, secretary of state, (under Bennet, Digges, and Matthews,) was directed to deliver the records to the assembly. The oath of office was administered to Governor Matthews by the committee before mentioned, and the members of the council nominated by the governor and approved by the house, took the same oath.*

The number of burgesses present at the session commencing in March, 1659, was thirty. Colonel Edward Hill, who had been disfranchised, was now unanimously elected speaker. Colonel Moore Fantleroy, of Rappahannock County, not being present at the election, "moved against him, as if clandestinely elected, and taxed the house of unwarrantable proceedings therein." He was suspended until the next day, when, acknowledging his error, he was readmitted.

Any member absent from the house was subject to a penalty of twenty pounds of tobacco. A member "disguised with overmuch drink" forfeited one hundred pounds of tobacco. A burgess was required to rise from his seat, and to remain uncovered, while speaking. The oath was administered to the burgesses by a committee of three sent from the council.

---

* The governor and council were as follows: Colonel Samuel Matthews, Governor and Captain-general of Virginia, Richard Bennet, Colonel William Clayborne, Secretary of State, Colonel John West, Colonel Thomas Pettus, Colonel Edward Hill, Colonel Thomas Dew, Colonel William Bernard, Colonel Obedience Robins, Lieutenant-Colonel John Walker, Colonel George Reade, Colonel Abraham Wood, Colonel John Carter, Mr. Warham Horsmenden, Lieutenant-Colonel Anthony Elliott.

CHAPTER XXVI.

1659-1661.

Death of Oliver Cromwell—Succeeded by his Son Richard—Assembly acknowledge his Authority—Character of Government of Virginia under the Commonwealth of England—Matthews dies—Richard Cromwell resigns the Protectorate—Supreme Power claimed now by the Assembly—Sir William Berkley elected Governor—Act for suppressing Quakers—Free Trade established—Stuyvesant's Letter—Charles the Second restored—Sends a new Commissioner to Berkley—His Reply—Grant of Northern Neck—The Navigation Act.

On the 8th of March, 1660, the house of burgesses having sent a committee to notify the governor that they attended his pleasure, he presented the following letter:—

"Gentlemen,—His late Highness, the Lord Protector, from that general respect which he had to the good and safety of all the people of his dominion, whether in these nations, or in the English plantations abroad, did extend his care to his colony in Virginia, the present condition and affairs whereof appearing under some unsettledness through the looseness of the government, the supplying of that defect hath been taken into serious consideration, and some resolutions passed in order thereunto, which we suppose would have been brought into act by this time, if the Lord had continued life and health to his said highness. But it hath pleased the Lord, on Friday, the third of this month, to take him out of the world, his said highness having in his lifetime, according to the humble petition and advice, appointed and declared the most noble and illustrious lord, the Lord Richard, eldest son to his late highness, to be his successor, who hath been accordingly, with general consent and applause of all, proclaimed Protector of this Commonwealth of England, Scotland, and Ireland, and the dominions and territories thereunto belonging. And, therefore, we have thought fit to signify the same unto you, whom we require, according to your duty, that you cause his said Highness, Richard, Lord Protector, forthwith to be proclaimed in all parts of your colony. And his highness' council have thought fit hereby to assure you, that the settlement of that colony is not neglected; and to let you know, that you may expect shortly to receive a more express testimony of his highness' care in that behalf; till the further perfecting whereof, their lordships do, will, and require you, the present governor and council there, to apply yourselves with all seriousness, faithfulness, and circumspection, to the peaceable and orderly management of the affairs of that colony, according to such good laws and customs (not repugnant to the laws of England) as have been heretofore used and exercised among you, improving your best endeavors as for maintaining the civil peace, so for promoting the interest of religion, wherein you will receive from hence all just countenance and encouragement. And if any person shall presume, by any undue ways, to interrupt the quiet or hazard the safety of his highness' people there, order will be taken, upon the representation of such proceedings, to make further provision for securing of your peace in such a way as shall be found meet and necessary, and for calling those to a strict account who shall endeavor to disturb it.

"Signed in the name and by the order of the council.

"H. LAWRENCE, *President.*

"Whitehall, 7th September, 1658."

Superscription, to the "Governor and Council of his Highness' Colony of Virginia."

Upon the reading of this letter, the governor and council withdrew from the assembly; and the house of burgesses unanimously acknowledged their obedience to his Highness, Richard, Lord Protector, and fully recognized his power.* So much truth is there in Mr. Jefferson's remark,† that in the contest with the house of Stuart, Virginia accompanied the footsteps of the mother country. The government of Virginia under the Commonwealth of England was wholly provisional. By the convention of March the 12th, 1652, Virginia secured to herself her ancient limits, and was entitled to reclaim that part of her chartered territory

---

* Hening, i. 509.

† Preface to T. M.'s Account of Bacon's Rebellion, in Kercheval's History of Valley of Va., 21. The clause quoted from Mr. Jefferson is omitted in the copy of the same introduction found in Force's Hist. Tracts, i.

which had been unjustly and illegally given away to Lord Baltimore. In this, however, owing to the perplexed condition of affairs in England, Virginia was disappointed; but she secured, by the articles of convention, free trade, exemption from taxation, save by her own assembly, and exclusion of military force from her borders. Yet all these rights were violated by subsequent kings and parliaments.*

The administration of the colonial government, under the Commonwealth of England, was judicious and beneficent; the people were free, harmonious, and prosperous; and while Cromwell's sceptre commanded the respect of the world, he exhibited toward the infant and loyal colony a generous and politic lenity; and during this interval she enjoyed free trade, legislative independence, civil and religious freedom, republican institutions, and internal peace. The Governors Bennet, Digges, and Matthews, by their patriotic virtues, enjoyed the confidence, and affection, and respect of the people; no extravagance, rapacity, corruption, or extortion was charged against their administration; intolerance and persecution were unknown. But rapine, corruption, extortion, intolerance, and persecution were all soon to be revived under the restored dynasty of the Stuarts.

Richard Cromwell resigned the Protectorate on the 22d day of April, 1659. Matthews, the governor, had died in the preceding January. England was without a monarch; Virginia without a governor. It was during this interval that public opinion in England was in suspense, the result of affairs depending upon the line of conduct which might be pursued by General Monk. The Virginia assembly, convening on the 13th day of March, 1660, declared by their first act that as there was then in England no resident, absolute, and generally acknowledged power, therefore the supreme government of the colony should rest in the assembly; and writs previously issued in the name of his Highness, the Lord Protector, now issued in the name of the Grand Assembly of Virginia. By the second act, Sir William Berkley was elected governor; he was required to call a grand assembly once in two years at the least, and was restricted from dissolving the assembly

---

* Jefferson's Notes, 125.

without its consent. The circumstances of this reappointment of Sir William Berkley have been frequently misrepresented; historians from age to age following each other in fabulous tradition, erroneous conjecture, or wilful perversion, have asserted that Sir William was hurried from retirement by a torrent of popular enthusiasm, and made governor by acclamation, and that Charles the Second was boldly proclaimed in Virginia, and his standard reared several months, some say sixteen, before the restoration; and thus the Virginians, as they had been the last of the king's subjects who renounced their allegiance, so they were the first who returned to it!*

Error in history is like a flock of sheep jumping over a bridge; if one goes, the rest all follow. Sir William Berkley, as has been before mentioned, was not elected by a tumultuary assemblage of the people, but by the assembly; the royal standard was not raised upon the occasion, nor was the king proclaimed. The bulk of the Virginia planters undoubtedly retained their habitual attachment to monarchy and to the Established Church; and some royalist refugees had been driven hither by the civil war. Yet, as the colonists had formerly been greatly dissatisfied with some acts of the government during the reign of Charles the First, they certainly had much reason to approve of the wise, and liberal, and magnanimous policy of Cromwell. Besides this, a good many republicans and Puritans had found their way to Virginia. The predominant feeling, however, in Virginia as in England, was in favor of the restoration of Charles the Second. Sir William Berkley, in his speech addressed to the assembly on their proffer of the place of governor, said: "I do, therefore, in the presence of God and you, make this safe protestation for us all, that if any supreme settled power appears, I will immediately lay down my commission, but will live most submissively obedient to any power God shall set over me, as the experience of eight years has shewed I have done." In his address to the house of burgesses, he alludes to the late king, as "my most gracious master,

---

* Robertson's Hist. of America, iv. 230; Beverley's Hist. of Va., B. i. 55; Chalmers' Annals, 124; Burk's Hist. of Va., ii. 120; Grahame's Colonial Hist. of U. S., i. 89; Hawks' Prot. Episcopal Church in Va., 63. See, also, Hening's Statutes at Large of Va., i. 126. Hening first corrected these errors.

King Charles, of ever blessed memory," and as "my ever honored master, who was put to a violent death." The Berkleys were staunch adherents of Charles the First, and extreme royalists. Referring in his address to the surrender of the colony, Sir William said, that the parliament "sent a small power to force my submission, which, finding me defenceless, was quietly (God pardon me) effected." Of the several parliaments and the protectorate he remarked: "And I believe, Mr. Speaker, (Theodorick Bland,) you think, if my voice had been prevalent in most of their elections, I would not voluntarily have made choice of them for my supremes. But, Mr. Speaker, all this I have said, is only to make this truth apparent to you, that in and under all these mutable governments of divers natures and constitutions, I have lived most resignedly submissive. But, Mr. Speaker, it is one duty to live obedient to a government, and another of a very different nature, to command under it." It thus appears that Sir William accepted the place hoping for the restoration of Charles the Second; but with an explicit pledge, that he would resign in case that event should not occur.* This speech was made March the nineteenth, and on the twenty-first the council unanimously concurred in his election. The members were Richard Bennet, (late Puritan Governor,) William Bernard, John Walker, George Reade, Thomas Pettus, William Clayborne, Edward Hill, Thomas Dew, Edward Carter, Thomas Swan, and Augustine Warner. Nearly all of these were colonels. The title of colonel and member of the council appears to have been a sort of order of nobility in Virginia. Sir William Berkley was elected two months before the restoration of Charles the Second, which took place on the 20th of May, 1660, that being his birth-day. Yet the word "king" or "majesty" nowhere occurs in the legislative records, from the commencement of the Commonwealth of England until the 11th day of October, 1660, more than four months after the restoration.† Virginia was indeed loyal, but she was too feeble to avow her loyalty.

An act was passed, entitled an act for the suppressing the Quakers; the preamble of which describes them as an unreason-

---

* Southern Lit. Messenger for January, 1845. † Hening, ii. 9, in note.

able and turbulent sort of people, who daily gather together unlawful assemblies of people, teaching lies, miracles, false visions, prophecies, and doctrines tending to disturb the peace, disorganize society, and destroy all law, and government, and religion. Masters of vessels were prohibited from bringing in any of that sect, under the penalty of one hundred pounds of tobacco; all of them to be apprehended and committed, until they should give security that they would leave the colony; if they should return, they should be punished, and returning the third time should be proceeded against as felons. No person should entertain any Quakers that had been questioned by the governor and council; nor permit any assembly of them in or near his house, under the penalty of one hundred pounds sterling; and no person to publish their books, pamphlets, and libels.* This act was passed in March, 1660, shortly after the election of Sir William Berkley.

Of late years, certain masters of vessels trading to Virginia, in violation of the laws and of the articles of surrender granting the privilege of free trade, had "molested, troubled, and seized divers ships, sloops, and vessels, coming to trade with us." The assembly therefore required every master to give bond not to molest any person trading under the protection of the laws.

Act XVI. establishes free trade: "Whereas, the restriction of trade hath appeared to be the greatest impediment to the advance of the estimation and value of our present only commodity, tobacco, *be it enacted and confirmed*, That the Dutch, and all strangers of what Christian nation soever, in amity with the people of England, shall have free liberty to trade with us for all allowable commodities." And it was provided, "That if the said Dutch, or other foreigners, shall import any negro slaves, they, the said Dutch, or others, shall, for the tobacco really produced by the sale of the said negro, pay only the impost of two shillings per hogshead, the like being paid by our own nation." The regular impost being ten shillings, this exemption was a bounty of eight shillings per hogshead for the encouragement of the importation of negroes.†

When Argall, in 1614, returning from his half-piratical excur-

---

* Hening, i. 532. † Hening, i. 535.

sion against the French at Port Royal, entered what is now New York Bay, he found three or four huts erected there by Dutch mariners and fishermen, on the Island of Manhattan. Near half a century had since elapsed, and the colony planted there had grown to an importance that justified something of diplomatic correspondence. In the spring of 1660 Nicholas Varleth and Brian Newton were sent by Governor Stuyvesant, celebrated by Knickerbocker, from Fort Amsterdam to Virginia, for the purpose of forming a league acknowledging the Dutch title to New York. Sir William Berkley evaded the proposition in the following letter:—

"SIR,—I have received the letter you were pleased to send me by Mr. Mills his vessel, and shall be ever ready to comply with you in all acts of neighborly friendship and amity; but truly, sir, you desire me to do that concerning your letter and claims to land in the northern part of America which I am incapable to do, for I am but a servant of the assembly's; neither do they arrogate any power to themselves further than the miserable distractions of England force them to. For when God shall be pleased in His mercy to take away and dissipate the unnatural divisions of their native country, they will immediately return to their own professed obedience. What then they should do in matters of contract, donation, and confession of right, would have little strength or signification; much more presumptive and impertinent would it be in me to do it, without their knowledge or assent. We shall very shortly meet again, and then, if to them you signify your desires, I shall labor all I can to get you a satisfactory answer.

"I am, sir, your humble servant,
"WILLIAM BERKLEY.

"Virginia, August 20th, 1660."

Peter Stuyvesant, the last of the Dutch governors of New Amsterdam, within a few years was dispossessed by a small English squadron, and 'the captured colony was retained. Sir William Berkley's letter was written nearly three months after the actual restoration, and yet, not having received intelligence of it, he alludes to the English government as in a state of interregnum, and writes not one word in present recognition of his majesty Charles the Second; on the contrary, he expressly avows himself a servant of the assembly.

Tea was introduced into England about this time; the East India Company made the king a formal present of two pounds and two ounces.*

The address of the Parliament and General Monk to Charles the Second, then at Breda, in Holland, was carried over by Lord Berkley, of Berkley Castle. On the eighth of May Charles was proclaimed in England king, and he returned in triumph to London on the twenty-ninth of that month, being his birth-day. The restored monarch transmitted a new commission, dated July the 31st, 1660, at Westminster, to his faithful adherent Sir William Berkley. He had remained in Virginia during the Commonwealth of England under various pretexts, and it is probable that he kept up a secret correspondence with refugee royalists, and it is said that he even invited Charles to come over to Virginia. This tradition, however, is without proof or plausibility; had the exiled Charles sought refuge in Virginia, an English frigate would have found it easy to make him a prisoner. Virginia would have presented few attractions to the royal profligate; and it could have hardly been a matter of regret to the Virginians that he never came here. Sir William Berkley's letter of acknowledgment, written in March, 1661, is extravagantly loyal. He apologizes for having accepted office from the assembly thus: "It was no more, may it please your majesty, than to leap over the fold to save your majesty's flock, when your majesty's enemies of that fold had barred up the lawful entrance into it, and enclosed the wolves of schism and rebellion, ready to devour all within it," etc. By "the wolves of schism and rebellion" he probably meant the Puritan and Republican party in Virginia, and he appears to have looked upon them as formidable enemies.

Charles the Second, in the first year of his reign, that is, in the first year after the death of his father, for he was considered or imagined to have reigned all the while, had granted all the tract of land lying between the Rappahannock and the Potomac,

---

* Pepys' Diary, i. 110. Pepys was pronounced *Peeps*.

known as the Northern Neck, to Lord Hopton, the Earl of St. Albans, Lord Culpepper, and others, to hold the same forever, paying yearly six pounds thirteen shillings and four pence to the crown.

The Anglo-American colonies now established, Virginia, New England, and Maryland, contained eighty-five thousand inhabitants. The navigation act had not been recognized by Virginia as obligatory on her; had been opposed by Massachusetts as an invasion of her rights; and had been evaded by Maryland. James the First, Charles the First, and the Commonwealth, had expressly exempted the colonies from direct taxation, but the Restoration parliament extended the customs of tonnage and poundage to every part of the dominion of the crown; and the colonists did not for years resist the collection of those imposts.*

---

* Chalmers' Revolt of Amer. Colonies, 99.

CHAPTER XXVII.

1661-1663.

Settlements of Virginia—The Church—Laws for establishment of Towns—Intelligence received of Restoration—Assembly sends Address to the King—Demonstrations of Loyalty—Berkley visits England—Morrison elected by the Council in his stead—Assembly's tone altered—Act for ducking "Brabbling Women"—Power of Taxation vested in Governor and Council for three years—Miscellaneous Affairs—Act relating to Indians—Persons trespassing on the Indians, punished—Sir William Berkley returns from England—Instructions relative to the Church—Acts against Schismatics and Separatists—Berkley superintends establishment of a Colony on Albemarle Sound.

THE settlements of Virginia now included the territory lying between the Potomac and the Chowan, and embraced, besides, the isolated Accomac. There were fifty parishes. The plantations lay dispersed along the banks of rivers and creeks, those on the James stretching westward, above a hundred miles into the interior. Each parish extended many miles in length along the river-side, but in breadth ran back only a mile. This was the average breadth of the plantations, their length varying from half a mile to three miles or more. The fifty parishes comprehending an area supposed to be equal to one-half of England, it was inevitable that many of the inhabitants lived very remote from the parish church. Many parishes, indeed, were as yet destitute of churches and glebes; and not more than ten parishes were supplied with ministers. Hammond* says: "They then began to provide, and send home for gospel ministers, and largely contributed for their maintenance; but Virginia savoring not handsomely in England, very few of good conversation would adventure thither, (as thinking it a place wherein surely the fear of God was not,) yet many came, such as wore black coats, and could babble in a pulpit, roar in a tavern, exact from their pa-

---

* "Leah and Rachel," published at London in 1656, in Force's Historical Tracts, iii.

rishioners, and rather by their dissoluteness destroy than feed their flocks." Hammond's statements are not to be unreservedly received. Where there were ministers, worship was usually held once on Sunday; but the remote parishioners seldom attended. The planters, either from indifference or from the want of means, were remiss in the building of churches and the maintenance of ministers. Through the licentious lives of many of them, the Christian religion was dishonored, and the name of God blasphemed among the heathen natives, (who were near them and often among them,) and thus their conversion hindered.*

In 1661 the Rev. Philip Mallory was sent over to England as Virginia's agent to solicit the cause of the church. The general want of schools, likewise owing to the sparseness of the population, was most of all bewailed by parents. The children of Virginia, naturally of beautiful persons, and generally of more genius than those in England, were doomed to grow up unserviceable for any great employments in church or state. As a principal remedy for these ills, the establishment of towns in each county was recommended. It was further proposed to erect schools in the colony, and for the supply of ministers to establish, by act of parliament, Virginia fellowships at Oxford and Cambridge, with an engagement to serve the church in Virginia for seven years. To raise the funds necessary for this purpose, it was proposed to take up a collection in the churches of Great Britain; and the assembly ordered a petition to the king to that end, to be drawn up.† Another feature of this plan was to send over a bishop, so soon as there should be a city for his see. These recommendations, although urged upon the attention of the bishop of London, seem, from whatever cause, to have proved fruitless. The Virginia assembly, in no instance, expressed any

---

* Virginia's Cure, (*Force's Hist. Tracts*, iii.,) printed at London, 1662, and composed by a minister. The initials on the title-page, R. G. He appears to have taken refuge in Virginia during the Commonwealth of England; and it is evident that he had resided in the colony for a considerable time. "Virginia's Cure" is addressed to the Bishop of London: it is a clear and vigorous document, acrimonious toward the late government, but earnest in behalf of the spiritual welfare of Virginia.

† Hening, ii. 33.

desire for the appointment of a bishop; they remembered with abhorrence the cruelties that had been exercised by the prelates in England.

Mr. Jefferson remarked that the legislature of Virginia has frequently declared that there should be towns in places where nature had declared that they should not be. The scheme of compelling the planters to abandon their plantations, and to congregate in towns, built by legislation, was indeed chimerical. The failure of the schemes proposed in the Virginia assembly for the establishment of towns, is attributed by the author of "Virginia's Cure" to the majority of the house of burgesses, who are said to have come over at first as servants, and who, although they may have accumulated by their industry competent estates, yet, owing to their mean education, were incompetent to judge of public matters, either in church or state. Yet many of the early laws appear to have been judicious, practical, and well adapted to the circumstances of a newly settled country. The legislature, eventually finding the scheme of establishing towns by legal enactments impracticable, declared it expedient to leave trade to regulate itself.

The assembly of March, 1661, consisted in the main of new members. At another session held in October of the same year, there appeared still fewer of the members who had held seats during the Commonwealth; and it may be reasonably inferred that the bulk of the retiring members were well affected to the Commonwealth of England. Intelligence of the restoration of Charles the Second had already reached Virginia, and was joyfully received. The word "king," or "majesty," was used in the public acts now for the first time, since the commencement of the Commonwealth of England—an interval of twelve years.

An address was sent to the king, praying him to pardon the inhabitants of Virginia for having yielded to a force—which they could not resist. Forty-four thousand pounds of tobacco, worth two thousand and two hundred dollars, were appropriated to Major-General Hammond and Colonel Guy Molesworth, for "being employed in the address." Sir Henry Moody was dispatched on an embassy "to the Manados," or Manhattan. Colonel Carter was required to declare what passed between him and Colonel William Clayborne at the assembly of 1653 or 1654, relative to the making an act of non-address to the Right Honorable Sir William Berkley; but the particulars of this affair have not been handed down. The rent paid for the use of the house where the assembly met, was three thousand five hundred pounds of tobacco, equivalent to one hundred and seventy-five dollars. Four thousand pounds of tobacco, worth two hundred dollars, were paid for the rent of the room where the governor and council held their meetings. The name of Monroe occurs at this early day in the County of Westmoreland as one of the commissioners, or justices of the peace.

The assembly strove to display its loyalty by bountiful appropriations to the governor and the leading royalists; the restoration in England was reflected by the restoration in Virginia. The necessity of the case had made the government of the colony republican; she was as free and almost as independent during the Commonwealth of England as after the revolution of 1776. For a short time even Sir William Berkley appears to have been identified with this system. He and the new assembly were now eagerly running in an opposite tack, and were impatient to wipe out all traces of their late forced disobedience and involuntary recognition of the popular sovereignty.

Sir William continued as governor till the 30th of April, 1661, when being about to visit England, Colonel Francis Morrison was elected by the council in his place. Sir William, it is said, was dispatched to England as agent to defend the colony against the monopoly of the navigation act, which threatened to violate their "freedoms," as is declared by the first act of the assembly held at James City, on the 23d of March, 1661. Sir William was heartily opposed to the restrictions on the commerce of Virginia; but any efforts that he may have used in opposition to them were fruitless.

He embarked in May for England, and returned in the fall of the following year, 1662. His pay on account of this mission was two hundred thousand pounds of tobacco, or five hundred and seventy-one hogsheads, the average weight of a hogshead at this period being three hundred and fifty pounds.* This quantity of

---

* Hening, i. 435.

tobacco was worth two thousand pounds sterling, or ten thousand dollars.* The ordinary salary of the governor consisted of castle duties, license fees, tobacco, corn, and customs, and probably amounted to not less than twelve thousand dollars per annum.†

The assembly's tone was now altered; during the Commonwealth of England, Oliver Cromwell had been addressed as "His Highness," and the burgesses had subscribed themselves his "most humble, most devoted servants;" nor had Richard Cromwell been treated with a less obsequious and respectful submission. But now the following language was employed: "Whereas, our late surrender and submission to that execrable power, that so bloodily massacred the late King Charles the First of ever blessed and glorious memory, hath made us, by acknowledging them, guilty of their crimes; to show our serious and hearty repentance and detestation of that barbarous act, be it enacted, That the thirtieth of January, the day the said king was beheaded, be annually solemnized with fasting and prayers, that our sorrows may expiate our crime, and our tears wash away our guilt."‡ Their compulsory acknowledgment of the sovereign power of the Commonwealth of England, if they all the while remained in their hearts loyal, could not have implicated them in the execution of the king.

Colonel Francis Morrison continued to fill the place of Sir William Berkley until his return, which took place some time between September and the 21st of November, 1662.

An act was passed, entitled "Women causing scandalous suits, to be ducked:" "Whereas, oftentimes many brabbling women often slander and scandalize their neighbors, for which their poor husbands are often brought into chargeable and vexatious suits, and cast in great damages; be it therefore enacted by the authority aforesaid, That in actions of slander occasioned by the wife, as aforesaid, after judgment passed for the damages, the woman shall be punished by ducking; and if the slander be so enormous as to be adjudged at a greater damage than five hundred pounds of tobacco, then the woman to suffer a ducking for each five

---

* Hening, i. 398, 418. † Ibid., i. 545, and ii. 9.
‡ Ibid., ii. 24.

hundred pounds of tobacco against the husband adjudged, if he refuse to pay the tobacco." A ducking-stool had been already established in each county.

The anniversary both of the birth and the restoration of Charles the Second was established as a holiday. The navigation act was now enforced in Virginia, and in consequence the price of tobacco fell very low, while the cost of imported goods was also augmented. An act prohibiting the importation of luxuries seems to have been negatived by the governor. It was ordered that "no person shall trade with the Indians for any beaver, otter, or any other furs, unless he first obtain a commission from the governor." This act gave great offence to the people; it was in effect conferring on the governor an indirect monopoly of the fur-trade. By a still more high-handed measure the governor and council were empowered to lay taxes for the ensuing three years, unless in the mean time some urgent occasion should necessitate the calling together of the assembly. Thus taxation was dissevered from representation; the main safeguard of freedom was given to the executive. Major John Bond, a magistrate in Isle of Wight County, was disfranchised for "factious and schismatical demeanors." He had repeatedly been returned as one of the burgesses of his county during the Commonwealth of England. An act making provision for a college, appears to have remained a dead letter; other acts equally futile, passed at ensuing sessions, frequently recur. The assembly ventured to declare that the king's pardon did not extend to a penalty incurred for planting tobacco contrary to law.

Colonel William Clayborne, secretary of state, was displaced by Thomas Ludwell, commissioned by the king. Colonel Francis Morrison and Henry Randolph, clerk of the assembly, were appointed revisers of the laws. Beverley* says that Morrison made an abridgement of the laws. In this revised code the common law of England is, for the first time, expressly adopted, being spoken of as "those excellent and oft-refined laws of England.† But it has been seen that Magna Charta had been previously

---

* Hist. of Virginia, second edition.
† Beverley, B. i. 43; Chalmers' Revolt, i. 101.

recognized as of force in Virginia. In making a revision of the laws it was ordered that all acts which "might keep in memory our forced deviation from his majesty's obedience," should be repealed "and expunged." In the absence of ministers it was enacted that readers should be appointed, where they could be found, with the advice and consent of the nearest ministers, to read the prayers and homilies, and catechise children and servants, as had been practised in the time of Queen Elizabeth. Although not more than one-fifth of the parishes were supplied with ministers, yet the laws demanded a strict conformity, and required all to contribute to the support of the established church. But the right of presentation still remained in the people. The number of the vestry was limited to twelve, elected by the people, but they were now invested with the power of perpetuating their own body by filling vacancies themselves.* Vestries were ordered to procure subscriptions for the support of the ministry. The number of burgesses to represent each county was limited to two; the number of magistrates to twelve. The assembly confirmed an order of the quarter court prohibiting "Roger Partridge and Elizabeth, his wife, from keeping any maid-servant for the term of three years."

The assembly say, that "they have set down certain rules to be observed in the government of the church, until God shall please to turn his majesty's pious thoughts" toward them, and "provide a better supply of ministers." "The pious thoughts" of Charles the Second were never turned to this remote corner of his empire. Magistrates, heretofore called commissioners, were now styled "justices of the peace," and their courts "county courts."† A duty was laid on rum, because "it had, by experience, been found to bring diseases and death to divers people." An impost, first established during the Commonwealth of England, was still levied on every hogshead of tobacco exported; this became a permanent source of revenue, and rendered the executive independent of the legislature.

The numerous acts relating to the Indians were reduced into one: prohibiting the English from purchasing Indian lands; securing their persons and property; preventing encroachments

---

* Ibid., 44. † Hening, ii. 69.

on their territory; ordering the English seated near to assist them in fencing their corn-fields; licensing them to oyster, fish, hunt, and gather the natural fruits of the country; prohibiting trade with them without license, or imprisonment of an Indian chief without special warrant; bounds to be annually defined; badges of silver and copper plate to be furnished to Indian chiefs; no Indian to enter the English confines without a badge, under penalty of imprisonment, till ransomed by one hundred arms'-length of roanoke; Indian chiefs tributary to the English, to give alarm of approach of hostile Indians; Indians not to be sold as slaves.*

It was ordered that a copy of the revised laws should be sent to Sir William Berkley in England, that he might procure the king's confirmation of them. Beverley mentions a tradition that the king, in compliment to Virginia, wore, at his coronation, a robe made of Virginia silk, and adds, that this was all the country received in return for their loyalty, the parliament having re-enacted the navigation act, (first enacted during the Commonwealth,) with still severer restrictions and prohibitions. Even the traditional compliment of the king's wearing a robe of Virginia silk appears to be unfounded.

Wahanganoche, chief of Potomac, charged with treason and murder by Captain Charles Brent, before the assembly, was acquitted; and Brent, together with Captain George Mason and others, were ordered to pay that chief a certain sum in roanoke, or in matchcoats, (from matchkore, a deerskin,) in satisfaction of the injuries. Brent, Mason, and others were afterwards punished by fines, suspension from office, and disfranchisement, for offences committed against the Indians, and for showing contempt to the governor's warrant in relation to the chief of Potomac. The counties of Westmoreland and Northumberland were especially exposed to Indian disturbances at this time. Colonel Moore Fantleroy was disfranchised for maltreating the Rappahannock Indians; Mrs. Mary Ludlow was restrained from encroaching on the lands of the Chesquiack Indians at Pyanketanke; Colonel Goodrich was charged with burning the English house of the chief of the Matapony Indians. George Harwood was ordered to ask

---

* Hening, ii. 138.

forgiveness in open court on his knees, for speaking disrespectfully of the right honorable governor, Francis Morrison; and, at the next court held in Warwick County, to ask forgiveness of Captain John Ashton for defaming him, and to pay two thousand pounds of tobacco.

It was during this year, 1662, that Charles the Second married Catherine, the Portuguese Infanta.

The court of Boston, in New England, having discharged a servant belonging to William Drummond, an inhabitant of Virginia, the assembly ordered reprisal to be made on the property belonging to inhabitants of the Northern colony to the amount of forty pounds sterling.*

Sir William Berkley returned in the fall of 1662 from England, having accomplished nothing for the colony, but having secured for himself an interest in a part of the Virginia territory, now North Carolina, granted to himself and other courtiers and court favorites. He brought out with him instructions from the crown, comprising directions relative to church matters; that the Book of Common Prayer should be read, and the sacrament administered according to the rites of the Church of England; that the churches should be well and orderly kept; that the number of them should be increased as the means might justify; that a competent maintenance should be assigned to each minister, and a house built for him, and a glebe of one hundred acres attached. It was further directed that no minister should be preferred by the governor to any benefice, without a certificate from the Lord Bishop of London; and that ministers should be admitted into their respective vestries; that the oaths of obedience and supremacy should be administered to all persons bearing any part of the government, and to all persons whatsoever of age in the colony. The last of these instructions is in the following words: "And because we are willing to give all possible encouragement to persons of different persuasions in matters of religion, to transport themselves thither with their stocks, you are not to suffer any man to be molested or disquieted in the exercise of his religion, so he be content with a quiet and peaceable enjoying it, not giving therein offence or scandal to the government; but we oblige

---

* Hening, ii. 158.

you in your own house and family to the profession of the Protestant religion, according as it is now established in our kingdom of England, and the recommending it to all others under your government, as far as it may consist with the peace and quiet of our said colony. You are to take care that drunkenness and debauchery, swearing, and blasphemy, be discountenanced and punished; and that none be admitted to publick trust and employment whose ill fame and conversation may bring scandal thereupon."*

The spirit of toleration expressed in these instructions was insincere and hypocritical, and dictated by the apprehensions of a government yet unstable, and by a temporizing policy. In December, 1662, the assembly declared that "many schismatical persons, out of their averseness to the orthodox established religion, or out of the new-fangled conceits of their own heretical inventions, refuse to have their children baptized," and imposed on such offenders a fine of two thousand pounds of tobacco.

The act for the suppression of the sect of Quakers was now extended to all separatists, and made still more rigorous. Persons attending their meetings were fined, for the first offence, two hundred pounds of tobacco; for the second, five hundred; and for the third, banished. In case the party convicted should be too poor to pay the fine, it was to be levied from such of his sect as might be possessed of ampler means.

A Mr. Durand, elder in a Puritan "very orthodox church," in Nansemond County, had been banished from Virginia in 1648. In 1662, the Yeopim Indians granted to "George Durant" the neck of land in North Carolina which still bears his name. He was probably the exile. In April, 1663, George Cathmaid claimed from Governor Berkley a large tract of land on the borders of Albemarle Sound, in reward of having colonized a number of settlers in that province. In the same year Sir William Berkley was commissioned to organize a government over this newly settled region, which, in honor of the perfidious General Monk, now made Duke of Albemarle, received the name which time has transferred to the Sound.

---

* MS. (Virginia) in State Paper office, (London,) cited in Anderson's Hist of Colonial Church, ii. 548–9.

CHAPTER XXVIII.

1663.

Report of Edmund Scarburgh, Surveyor-General, of his Proceedings in establishing the Boundary Line between Virginia and Maryland on the Eastern Shore—The Bear and the Cub—Extracts from Records of Accomac.

A CONTROVERSY existed between Virginia and Lord Baltimore relative to the boundary line on the Eastern Shore of the Chesapeake Bay. The dispute turned on the true site of Watkins' Point, which was admitted to be the southern limit of Maryland on that shore. The Virginia assembly, in 1663, declared the true site of Watkins' Point to be on the north side of Wicocomoco River, at its mouth, and ordered publication thereof to be made by Colonel Edmund Scarburgh, his majesty's surveyor-general, commanding, in his majesty's name, all the inhabitants south of that Point, "to render obedience to his majesty's government of Virginia." A conference with Lord Baltimore's commissioners was proposed in case he should be dissatisfied, and Colonel Scarburgh, Mr. John Catlett, and Mr. Richard Lawrence were appointed commissioners on the part of Virginia. Lawrence will reappear in Bacon's Rebellion. The surveyor-general was further directed "to improve his best abilities in all other his majesty's concerns of land relating to Virginia, especially that to the northward of forty degrees of latitude, being the utmost bounds of the said Lord Baltimore's grant, and to give an account of his proceedings therein to the right honorable governor and council of Virginia."*

Colonel Scarburgh's report of his proceedings on this occasion is preserved.† He set out with "some of the commission, and about forty horsemen," an escort which he deemed necessary "to

---

* Hening, ii. 183.

† This document, entitled "The Account of Proceedings in his Majt's Affairs at Anamessecks and Manokin, on the Eastern Shore of Virginia," is preserved in the records of Accomac County Court, and a copy, furnished by Thomas R.

repel the contempt" which, as he was informed, "some Quakers and a fool in office has threatened to obtrude." The party reached Anamessecks on Sunday night, the eleventh of October. On the next day, at the house of an officer of the Lord Baltimore, the surveyor-general began to publish the assembly's commands by repeatedly reading the act to the officer, who labored under the disadvantage of being unable to read. He declared that he would not be false to the trust put in him by the Lord-Lieutenant of Maryland. To this Colonel Scarburgh replied, "that there could be no trust where there was no intrust," (interest.) The officer declining to subscribe his obedience, lest he might be hanged by the Governor of Maryland, was arrested and held to security (given by some of Scarburgh's party) to appear before the governor and council of Virginia, and "the broad arrow" was set on his door. This matter being so satisfactorily adjusted, the colonel and his company proceeded to the house of a Quaker, where the act was published "with a becoming reverence;" but the Quakers scoffing and deriding it, and refusing their obedience, were arrested, to answer "their contempt and rebellion," and it being found impracticable to obtain any security, "the broad arrow was set on the door." At Manokin the housekeepers and freemen, except two of Lord Baltimore's officers, subscribed. "One Hollinsworth, merchant, of a northern vessel," at this juncture, "came and presented his request for liberty of trade;" which, Scarburgh suspecting to be "some plan of the Quakers," to defeat their design, "presumed, in their infant plantation, to give freedom of trade without impositions." Scarburgh gives a descriptive list of those who stood out against submitting to the jurisdiction of Virginia: one was "the ignorant yet insolent officer, a cooper by profession, who lived long in the lower parts of Accomac; once elected a burgess by the common crowd, and thrown out of the assembly for a factious and tumultuous person." George Johnson was "the Proteus of heresy," notorious for "shifting schismatical pranks." "He stands arrested," and "bids

---

Joynes, Esq., the clerk, (himself a descendant of Colonel Edmund Scarburgh,) was published in 1833, by order of the legislature of Maryland. I am indebted to William T. Joynes, Esq., of Petersburg, for the use of this report, and for some other interesting particulars relating to the Eastern Shore.

defiance." "Thomas Price, a creeping Quaker, by trade a leather-dresser," and "saith nothing else but that he would not obey government, for which he also stands arrested." "Ambrose Dixon, a caulker by profession," "often in question for his Quaking profession," "a prater of nonsense," "stands arrested, and the broad arrow at his door, but bids defiance." "Henry Boston, an unmannerly fellow, that stands condemned on the records for fighting and contemning the laws of the country; a rebel to government, and disobedient to authority, for which he received a late reward with a rattan, and hath not subscribed; hides himself, so scapes arrest." "These are all, except two or three loose fellows that follow the Quakers for scraps, whom a good whip is fittest to reform."

On the 10th day of November, 1663, the county court of Accomac authorized Captain William Thorn and others to summon the good subjects of Manokin and other parts of the county, so far as Pocomoke River, to come together and arm themselves for defence against any that might invade them, in consequence "of the rumors that the Quakers and factious fools have spread, to the disturbance of the peace and terror of the less knowing."

The following extracts, from the records of the county court of Accomac, exemplify the simplicity of the times, and the quaint orthography, and the verbosity of the records of courts; while the final decision of the case is not less equitable than those of Sancho Panza, sometime Governor of the Island of Barataria, or those celebrated in Knickerbocker's History of New York.

"At a Court held in Accomack County, y⁶ 16th of November, by his ma^ties Justices of y⁶ Peace for y⁶ s^d County, in y⁶ Seaventeenth yeare of y⁶ Reigne of o^r Sovraigne Lord Charles y⁶ Second, By y⁶ Grace of God, of Great Britaine, France, and Ireland, King, Defender of y⁶ Faith, &c.: And in y⁶ Yeare of o^r Lord God 1665.

"Whereas, Cornelius Watkinson, Philip Howard, and William Darby, were this Day accused by Mr. Jno. Fawsett, his ma^ties Attory for Accomack County, for acting a play by them called y⁶ Bare & y⁶ Cubb, on y⁶ 27th of August last past; upon examination of the same, The Court have thought fitt to suspend the Cause till y⁶ next Court, & doe order y^t the said Cornelius Watkinson, Phillip Howard, & W^m. Darby, appeare ye next Court, in those habilemts that they then acted in, and give a draught of such verses, or other speeches and passages, which were then acted by them; & that ye Sherr detaine Cornelius Watkinson & Philip Howard in His Custody untill they put in Security to performe this order. It is ordered y^t the Sherr. arrest ye Body of William Darby, for his appearance ye next Court, to answere at his ma^ties suit, for being actour of a play commonly called ye Beare and ye Cubb.

"At a Court held in Accomack County, ye 18th of December, by his ma^ties Justices of ye Peace for ye s^d County, in ye Seaventeenth yeare of ye Raigne of o^r Sovraigne Lord Charles ye Second, By ye Grace of God, of Great Britain, France, & Ireland, King, Defend^r of ye Faith, &c.: And in ye yeare of o^r Lord God 1665.

"Its ordered y^t ye Sherr sumons Edward Martin to ye next Court, to show cause why hee should not pay ye charges wch accrued upon ye Information given by him against Cornelius Watkinson, Philip Howard, & William Darby.

"At a Court held in Accomack County, ye 17th of January, by his ma^ties Justices of ye Peace for ye s^d County, in the Seaventeenth year of ye Reigne of o^r Sovraigne Lord Charles ye Second, By ye Grace of God, of Great Britain, France, and Ireland, King, Defender of the Faith, &c.: And in the year of o^r Lord God 1665.

"Whereas, Edward Martin was this day examined concerning his information given to Mr. Fawset, his ma^ties Attory for Accomack County, about a play called the bare & ye Cubb, whereby severall persons were brought to Court & charges thereon arise, but the Court finding the said p'sons not guilty of fault, suspended ye payment of Court charges; & forasmuch as it appeareth upon ye Oath of ye said Mr. Fawsett, that upon ye s^d Edward Martin's information, the Charge & trouble of that suit did accrew, It's therefore ordered that ye said Edward Martin pay all ye Charges in ye suit Els. Exon."*

---

* "The foregoing are true transcripts from the Records of the Court of the County of Accomack, in the State of Virginia."—Test: *J. W. Gillett, C. A. C.*

CHAPTER XXIX.

1666-1675.

Plot discovered—Miscellaneous Matters—England at war with the Dutch—The Plague in London—Tobacco—Forts—Cessation of planting Tobacco for one year—Drummond's Petition rejected—Baptism of Slaves—Tributary Indians—Batt's Expedition—The Algonquin Tribes—The Powhatan Confederacy—Convicts sent to Virginia—Legislative Acts.

THE Northern colonies appear at this time to have been styled the "Dutch Plantations."* The persecution of the dissenters, the restrictions imposed upon commerce by the navigation act, the low price of tobacco, and high price of imported goods, so inflamed the discontents of the poor people as to give rise to a plot, which was well-nigh resulting in tragical effects in 1663. The conspiracy was attributed to certain Cromwellian soldiers, who had been sent out to Virginia as servants; but the real grounds and true character of it can now hardly be ascertained. The plot was discovered only the night before that appointed for its execution, (the assembly being then in session,) by one of the conspirators named Birkenhead, a servant to Mr. Smith, of Purton, in Gloucester County. Poplar Spring, near that place, was the appointed rendezvous. As soon as the information reached Sir William Berkley, who was then at his residence, Green Spring, he issued secret orders to a party of militia, to meet at Poplar Spring, and anticipate the outbreak. Only a few were taken, of whom four were hanged. Birkenhead was rewarded† with his freedom and five thousand pounds of tobacco; Beverley‡ makes the reward two hundred pounds sterling. The thirteenth of September, the day fixed for the execution of the plot, was set apart by the assembly as an anniversary thanksgiving. The news of this affair being transmitted to the king, he sent orders for the building of a fort

---

* Hening, ii. 188. † Ibid., ii. 204. ‡ Beverley, B. i. 61.

at Jamestown; but the Virginians thinking that the danger had blown over, only erected a battery of some small pieces of cannon.

The Indian chief of Potomac, and other northern werowances and mangais, were required to give hostages of their children and others, who were to be kindly treated and instructed in English, as far as practicable. Measures were taken to bring Indian murderers to justice, especially the hostile Doeggs. The chief of Potomac was inhibited from holding any matchacomico, or council, with any strange tribe, before the delivery of hostages.

John Bland, a London merchant, and brother of Theodoric Bland, a leading man in Virginia, received the thanks of the assembly for goods advanced for the use of the colony. In this year, 1663, a conference was held, by royal command, at Mr. Aleston's, at Wicocomico, in Virginia, in May, by commissioners appointed by Governor Berkley, and Charles Calvert, Governor of Maryland, for the purpose of devising means of improving the staple of tobacco. The Virginia commissioners were Thomas Ludwell, secretary, Richard Lee, John Carter, Robert Smith, and Henry Corbin. The Maryland commissioners were Philip Calvert, Henry Sewall, secretary, Edward Koydes, and Henry Coursey. They recommended that in the year 1664 no tobacco should be planted after the twentieth day of June.

In 1665 further acts were passed to prevent the depredations of Indians. If a white should be murdered, the nearest Indian town was held responsible; the Indian werowances to be in future appointed by the governor; colonists to go armed to church, court, and other public meetings; Indians south of the James River, not to cross a line extending from the head of Blackwater River to the Appomattox Indian town, (probably where Petersburg now stands,) and thence across to the Mannakin town.

In the year 1665 Charles the Second, instigated by France, engaged in an unprovoked war with Holland, the object being mainly to strike a blow at the Protestant interest.* During the same year the plague raged in London, the victims for some time

---

* Evelyn's Diary, i. 391.

perishing at the rate of ten thousand weekly. In this fatal year Secretary Bennet, a plausible man, of good address, but mediocre capacity, was made Lord Arlington. The English monopolizing laws now reduced the condition of the planters of Virginia so low, that they proposed to discontinue the planting of tobacco for one year, so as to enhance the price of it; and an act was passed preparatory to a "stint or cessation." To render this remedy effectual, it appeared necessary to obtain the co-operation of the colonies of Maryland and North Carolina. For some years it was found impracticable to effect this object, and in the mean time, in order to prevent Virginia from receiving any supplies, save those sent from England, and also for defence against the Dutch, the king sent directions that forts should be built on the rivers, and that ships should lie under them, and that those places alone should be ports of trade. These instructions were obeyed for a year; breast-works were erected at places appointed by the assembly, and the shipping lay at them for a time; but the great fire and plague occurring in London at this juncture, rendered their supplies very uncertain, and the fear of the plague being brought over with the goods imported, prevented the people from living at those ports, and thus all were again at liberty.*

The Virginia planters supposed that by lessening the quantity of tobacco, called a "stint," they would improve the quality and enhance the price of it. The merchants, to whom the planters were indebted, were favorable to a stint; but although they would certainly be benefited by its operation, yet they were apparently not willing to abate any part of their claims against their debtors. The nett proceeds derived from the sale of the staple were barely enough to furnish the planters with clothing. As some remedy for this state of things, the legislature ordered looms and work-houses to be set in operation at the charge of each county. Bounties were again offered for encouragement of the raising of silk, and measures were adopted to foster the culture of flax and hemp.

In the year 1666, while London was desolated by fire and depopulated by the plague, war added her horrors. A government

---

* Beverley, B. i. 63.

imbecile and corrupt, a court frivolous and debauched, darkened the shadows of the gloomy picture. The English colonies shared in the miseries of the mother country. It is remarkable that a book published in England many years before contained a prediction that the year 1666 would be the very climax of public disaster.* It was not unreasonable to conclude, that the wickedness of men had been directly avenged by a visitation of Heaven. Evelyn† says: "These judgments we highly deserved for our prodigious ingratitude, burning lusts, dissolute court, profane and abominable lives."

The assembly met in September, 1664, by prorogation from the preceding September—a compendious mode of dispensing with the popular election. However, in act vi., the assembly, declaring that the principal end of their coming together was to provide for the people's safety, and to redress their grievances, ordered that in future due notice of the convening of the burgesses should be given to the people by publication in the parish churches, so that they may then make known their grievances. The act for a "cessation" passed in June, 1666, commanded that no tobacco should be planted between the 1st of February, 1667, and the 1st of February, 1668.‡ The governor of Carolina at this time, and the first governor of that province, was William Drummond, a native of Scotland.

Similar acts were passed by Maryland and Carolina, but the latter province, owing to trouble with the Indians, not having given formal notice by the day agreed upon, Maryland availed herself of the informality to decline enforcing the cessation. Thus, as has been before mentioned, action was long delayed. Virginia, nevertheless, adhering to the scheme, again, at the session of October of the same year, confirmed her former act, and by dint of negotiation it was finally consummated.

---

* Pepy's Diary, ii. † Diary, ii. 17.

‡ The commissioners appointed to treat with Maryland and Carolina on this subject were, of the council, Thomas Ludwell, Esq., secretary of Virginia, Major-General Robert Smith, and Major-General Richard Bennet; and of the burgesses, Robert Wynne, speaker, Colonel Nich. Spencer, Captain Daniel Parke, Captain Joseph Bridger, Captain Peter Jennings, and Mr. Thomas Ballard.

The County of Stafford is mentioned in this year for the first time, and it was now represented by a burgess, Colonel Henry Mees.

The petition of William Drum, probably a misprint for Drummond, concerning a grant of land in what was commonly called "the governor's land," in the main reserve, was rejected, the house being of opinion that such grants appertained only to the governor and council. The assembly asserted their right to assess the levy without the interposition of the governor and council; and Sir William Berkley assented to this decision; the sincerity of the terms in which he expressed his willing acquiescence may well be doubted.

The Dutch about this time appear to have surprised several vessels, laden with tobacco, in the James River; and it was determined to erect several forts: one on James River, one on Nansemond River, one on York River at Tindall's Point, (now Gloucester Point,) one on the Rappahannock at Corotoman, and one on the Potomac at Yeohocomico.

It was declared that baptism did not exempt slaves from bondage. As the reducing of negroes to slavery was justified on the ground that they were heathens, so the opinion prevailed among some that when they ceased to be heathens they were, by the very fact, released from slavery.

In 1668, peace being restored, vessels were relieved from the necessity of anchoring under the forts. The war with the Dutch, unjustly commenced by the English, ended very disgracefully to them. A day of humiliation was appointed, and all persons were required to attend the parish churches, "with fasting and prayers, to implore God's mercy, and deprecate the evils justly impending over us."

It was ordered that work-houses should be built in each county, for the instruction of poor children in spinning, weaving, and other useful occupations and trades. An act was passed for the "suppressing and restraint of the exhorbitant number of ordinaries and tippling houses."

The Indians were required to bring in one hundred and forty-five wolves' heads annually, the reward for each head being one hundred pounds of tobacco and cask. To prevent fraud, the ears were cut off from the heads of the wolves.*

The elective franchise was restricted, in 1670, to freeholders and housekeepers.

Sir William Berkley sent out a company of fourteen English and as many Indians, under Captain Henry Batt, to explore the country to the west. Setting out from the Appomattox River, in seven days they reached the foot of the mountains. The first ridge was not found very high or steep, but after crossing that they encountered others that seemed to touch the clouds, and so steep that in a day's march they could not advance more than three miles. They came upon extensive valleys of luxuriant verdure, abounding with turkeys, deer, elk, and buffalo, gentle and, as yet, undisturbed by the fear of man. Grapes were seen of the size of plums. After crossing the mountains they discovered a charming level country, and a rivulet that flowed westward. Following this for some days, they reached old fields and cabins recently occupied by the natives; in these Batt left toys. Not far from the cabins, at some marshes, the Indian guides halted and refused to go any farther, saying that not far off dwelt a powerful

---

* The tributary Indians of Virginia at this period were, in

		Bowmen, or Hunters.
Nansemond County		45
Surrey County	Powchay-icks	30
	Weyenoakes	15
Charles City County	Men Heyricks	50
	Nottoways, two towns	90
	Appamattox	50
Henrico County	Manachees	30
	Powhites	10
New Kent County	Pamunkeys	50
	Chickahominies	60
	Mattaponeys	20
	Rappahannocks	30
	Totas-Chees	40
Gloucester	Chiskoyackes	15
Rappahanock	Portobaccoes	60
	Nanzcattico } Mattehatique	50
Northumberland Co.	Wickacomico	70
Westmoreland County	Appomattox	10
Total		725

tribe, that never suffered strangers, who discovered their towns, to escape. Batt was therefore reluctantly compelled to return. Upon receiving his report, Sir William Berkley resolved to make an exploration himself, but his intention was frustrated by the troubles that shortly after fell upon the country.* Beverley alone gives an account of Batt's explorations, leaving the date of it uncertain between 1666 and 1676. Burk dates it in 1667.

The Algonquin tribes are said to have been included within lines extending from Cape Hatteras to the head of the Mississippi, and thence eastward to the coast north of Newfoundland, and thence along the Atlantic shore to the cape first mentioned.† The bulk of the Indians within this triangle spoke various dialects of the same generic language.

The thirty tribes of Indians comprised within the Powhatan confederacy, south of the Potomac, at the time of the landing at Jamestown, are conjecturally estimated at about eight thousand souls, being one to the square mile.‡ The population of the mountain country was probably sparser than that of the country east of the mountains. The number of square miles in Virginia at the present day is upwards of sixty-five thousand. The number of warriors belonging to the tribes tributary to Virginia in 1669, as has been before mentioned, was seven hundred and twenty-five, and their proportion to the entire population being reckoned as three to ten, their aggregate number was about twenty-four hundred. Thus in about sixty years the diminution of their numbers amounted to about five thousand six hundred; of these, part had perished from disease, exposure, famine, and war; the rest were driven back into the wilderness.

In the year 1670 complaints were made to the general court by members of the council and others, being gentlemen, of the counties of York, Gloucester, and Middlesex, representing their apprehensions of danger from the great number of felons, and other desperate villains, sent hither from the prisons of England. Masters of vessels were prohibited from landing any such convicts or jail-birds. In 1671 Captain Bristow and Captain Walker

---

* Beverley, B. i. 64.   † P. W. Leland, in Hist. Mag., iii. 41.
‡ Jefferson's Notes on Virginia, 97; Hening, ii. 274.

were required to give security in the sum of one million pounds of tobacco and cask, that Mr. Nevett should send out the Newgate-birds within two months. Mr. Jefferson* has made the following remark: "The malefactors sent to America were not sufficient in number to merit enumeration as one class out of three which peopled America. It was at a late period of their history that the practice began. I have no book by me which enables me to point out the date of its commencement; but I do not think the whole number sent would amount to two thousand." And he supposed that they and their descendants did not, in 1786, exceed four thousand, "which is little more than one-thousandth part of the whole inhabitants." Mr. Jefferson appears to have been mistaken in his opinion, that malefactors were not sent over until a late period in the annals of Virginia; and he probably underrated the number of their descendants.

The acts prohibiting the exportation of wool, hides, and iron, were repealed, and every one was "permitted to make the best he can of his own commodity." The preamble to the act for the naturalization of foreigners declares, that "nothing can tend more to the advancement of a new plantation, either to its defence or prosperity, nor nothing more add to the glory of a prince, than being a gracious master of many subjects; nor any better way to produce those effects than the inviting of people of other nations to reside among us by communication of privileges."†

In 1672 the assembly provided for the defence of the country by rebuilding and repairing of forts. Repeated and vigorous laws were enacted providing for the apprehension of runaways; rewards were offered the Indians for apprehending them. A negro slave was valued at four thousand five hundred pounds of tobacco; an Indian slave at three thousand pounds of tobacco.

---

* Writings of Jefferson, i. 405. † Hening, ii. 289.

CHAPTER XXX.

1670-1671.

Governor Berkley's Reply to Inquiries of the Lords Commissioners of Plantations—Government of Virginia—Militia—Forts—Indians—Boundary—Commodities—Population—Health—Trade—Restrictions on it—Governor's Salary—Quit-rents—Parishes—Free Schools, and Printing.

THE lords commissioners of foreign plantations, in 1670, were Arlington, Ashley, Richard George W. Alington, T. Clifford, S. Trevor, Orlando Bridgeman, C. S. Sandwich, president, Thomas Grey, —— Titus, A. Broucher, H. Slingsby, secretary, Hum. Winch, and Edmund Waller. These, during this year, propounded inquiries to Sir William Berkley, governor, respecting the state and condition of Virginia; and his answers made in the year following present a satisfactory statistical account of the colony. The executive consisted of a governor and sixteen councillors, commissioned by the king, to determine all causes above fifteen pounds; causes of less amount were tried by county courts, of which there were twenty. The assembly met every year, composed of two burgesses from each county. Appeals lay to the assembly; and this body levied the taxes. (This power was delegated for some years to the executive.) The legislative and executive powers rested in the governor, council, assembly, and subordinate officers. The secretary of the colony sent the acts of the assembly to the lord chancellor, or one of the principal secretaries of state. All freemen were bound to muster monthly in their own counties; the force of the colony amounted to upwards of eight thousand horsemen. There were five forts: two on the James, and one on each of the three rivers, Rappahannock, York, and Potomac; the number of cannon was thirty. His majesty, during the late Dutch war, had sent over thirty more, but the most of them were lost at sea. The Indians were in perfect subjection. The eastern boundary of Virginia, on the sea-coast, had been reduced from ten degrees to half of one degree. Tobacco was the only commodity of any great value; exotic mulberry-trees had been planted, and attempts made to manufacture silk. There was plenty of timber; of iron ore but little discovered. The whole population was forty thousand; of which two thousand were negro slaves, and six thousand white servants. (The negroes had increased one hundredfold in fifty years, since 1619, when the first were imported.) The average annual importation of servants was about fifteen hundred; most of them English, a few Scotch, fewer Irish; and not more than two or three ships with negroes in seven years. New plantations were found sickly, and in such four-fifths of the new settlers died. Eighty vessels arrived yearly from England and Ireland for tobacco; a few small coasters came from New England. Virginia had not more than two vessels of her own, and those not over twenty tons. Sir William Berkley complains bitterly of the act of parliament restricting the commerce of Virginia to the British kingdom—a policy injurious to both parties; and he adds that "this is the cause why no small or great vessels are built here; for we are most obedient to all laws, while the New England men break through and trade to any place that their interest leads them to." Sir William gave it as his opinion, that nothing could improve the trade of Virginia, unless she was allowed to export her staves, timber, and corn to other places besides the king's dominions. The only duty levied was that of two shillings on every hogshead of tobacco exported; the exportation of the year 1671 amounting to fifteen thousand hogsheads. Out of this revenue the king allowed the governor one thousand pounds, to which the assembly added two hundred more, making twelve hundred pounds, which was four-fifths of the entire customs revenue for that year. Yet he complains: "I can knowingly affirm, that there is no government of ten years' settlement but has thrice as much allowed him. But I am supported by my hopes, that his gracious majesty will one day consider me."

The king had no revenue in the colony except quit-rents; these were not of much value, and the king gave them to Colonel Henry Norwood. Every man instructed his children at home according to his ability. "There were forty-eight parishes, and our ministers are well paid; by my consent should be better, if they would pray oftener, and preach less. But as of all other commodities, so of this, the worst are sent us; and we have had few that we could boast of, since Cromwell's tyranny drove divers men hither. But I thank God there are no free schools, nor printing, and I hope we shall not have these hundred years; for learning has brought disobedience into the world, and printing has divulged them and libels against the best governments. God keep us from both!"*

---

* Hening, ii. 511.

CHAPTER XXXI.

1673-1675.

Acts of Assembly—The Northern Neck—Earl of Arlington—Threatened Revolt in 1674—Agents sent to England to solicit a Revocation of the Grants of Territory and to obtain a Charter—The effort fruitless.

The acts of a session were headed as follows: "At a Grand Assembly holden at James City, by prorogation from the 24th day of September, 1672, to the 20th of October, Annoque Regni Regis Caroli Secundi Dei Gratia Angliæ, Scotiæ, Franciæ et Hiberniæ, Regis, fidei Defensoris, &c., Anno Domini 1673. To the glory of Almighty God and public weal, of this his majesty's colony of Virginia, were enacted as followeth."

Provision was made during this year for a supply of arms and ammunition. The commissioners appointed for determining the boundaries of the Counties of Northumberland and Lancaster were Colonel John Washington, Captain John Lee, Captain William Traverse, William Mosely, and Robert Beverley.

The restoration, that worst of all governments, re-established an arbitrary and oppressive administration in Virginia in church and state; and as soon as reinstated, tyranny, confident of its power, rioted in wanton and unbridled license.

The grant which had been made by Charles the Second in the first year of his reign, dated at St. Germain en Laye, of the Northern Neck, including four counties and a half, to Lord Hopton, the Earl of St. Albans, Lord Culpepper, etc., was surrendered, in May, 1671, to the crown, and new letters-patent were issued, with some alterations, to the Earl of St. Albans, Lord Berkley, Sir William Morton, and others,—to hold the same forever, paying annually the quit-rent of six pounds thirteen shillings and four pence to his majesty and his successors. In February, 1673, the king granted to the Earl of Arlington and Thomas, Lord Culpepper, the entire territory of Virginia, not merely the wild lands, but private plantations long settled and

(274)

improved, for the term of thirty-one years, at the yearly rent of forty shillings. The patents entitled them to all rents and escheats, with power to convey all vacant lands, nominate sheriffs, escheators, surveyors, etc., present to all churches and endow them with lands, to form counties, parishes, etc. Although the grants to these noblemen were limited to a term of years, yet they were preposterously and illegally authorized to make conveyances in fee simple.*

Henry Bennet, Earl of Arlington, said to have been the best bred person at court, like his master, as far as he had any pretension whatever to religion, was a disguised Papist. He became allied to the monarch as father-in-law to the first Duke of Grafton, the king's son by Lady Castlemaine. Arlington had received, while fighting on the royal side in the civil war, a wound on the nose, the scar of which was covered with a black patch. Barbara Villiers, only daughter of William, Viscount Grandison, and wife of Roger Palmer, created Earl of Castlemaine in 1661, distinguished for her beauty and her profligacy, becoming mistress to Charles at his restoration, was made, in 1670, Duchess of Cleveland. Henry Bennet was created Baron of Arlington in 1663, and Viscount Hetford and Earl of Arlington in 1672. He was also Knight of the Garter and chamberlain to the king, his chief favorite, companion in profligate pleasure, and political adviser. He and Culpepper were members of the commission of trade and plantations.

The Virginians grew so impatient under their accumulated grievances that a revolt was near bursting forth in 1674, but no person of note taking the lead, it was suppressed by the advice of "some discreet persons," and the insurgents were persuaded to disperse in compliance with the governor's proclamation. The movement was not entirely ineffectual, for justices of the peace were prohibited from levying any more taxes for their own emolument.† The assembly determined to make an humble address "to his sacred majesty," praying for a revocation of the forementioned grants of her territory, and for a confirmation of the rights and privileges of the colony. Francis Morrison, Thomas

---

* Hening, ii. 519.   † Ibid., ii. 315.

Ludwell, and Robert Smith were appointed agents to visit England and lay their complaints before the king; and their expenses were provided for by onerous taxes, which fell heaviest on the poorer class of people. These expenses included douceurs to be given to courtiers; for without money nothing could be effected at the venal court of Charles the Second.* Besides the revocation of the patents, the Virginia agents were instructed to endeavor to obtain a new charter for the colony. They prayed "that Virginia shall no more be transferred in parcels to individuals, but may remain forever dependent on the crown of England; that the public officers should be obliged to reside within the colony; that no tax shall be laid on the inhabitants except by the assembly." This petition affords a curious commentary on the panegyrics then but recently lavished by "his majesty's most loyal colony" upon his "most sacred majesty," who repaid their fervid loyalty by an unrelenting system of oppression. The negotiations were long, and display evidence of signal diplomatic ability, together with elevated and patriotic views of colonial rights and constitutional freedom. After many evasions and much delay, the mission eventually proved fruitless.† Application was also made to Secretary Coventry to secure the place of governor to Sir William Berkley for life.

---

* Account of Bacon's Rebellion in Va. Gazette, 1766.
† Hening, ii. 518, 531.

CHAPTER XXXII.

1675.

The Reverend Morgan Godwyn's Letter describing Condition of the Church in Virginia.

THE Bishop of Winchester, during the whole negotiation, lent his assistance to the agents; he also brought to their notice a libel which had been published against all the Anglo-American plantations, especially Virginia. It was written by the Rev. Morgan Godwyn, who had served some time in Virginia; and he had given a copy of it to each of the bishops. The agents make mention of him as "the fellow," and "the inconsiderable wretch." They sent a copy of it to Virginia, thinking it necessary that a reply should be prepared, and addressed to the Bishop of Winchester and the Archbishop of Canterbury. It is probable that this pamphlet is no longer extant; but the character of its contents may be inferred from a letter addressed by the author to Sir William Berkley, and appended to a pamphlet published by him in 1680, entitled the "Negro's and Indian's Advocate." Indeed this letter may have been itself the libellous pamphlet circulated in England in 1674, and referred to by the Virginia agents. In this letter Godwyn gives the following account of the state of religion, as it was in that province some time before the late rebellion, *i.e.* Bacon's, which occurred in 1676. Godwyn acknowledges that Berkley had, "as a tender father, nourished and preserved Virginia in her infancy and nonage. But as our blessed Lord," he reminds him, "once said to the young man in the gospel, 'Yet lackest thou one thing;' so," he adds, "may we, and I fear too truly, say of Virginia, that there is one thing, the propagation and establishing of religion in her, wanting." And this he essays to prove in various ways: saying that "the ministers are most miserably handled by their plebeian juntos, the vestries, to whom the hiring (that is the usual word there) and admission of ministers is solely left. And there being no law obliging them to any more than to procure a lay reader, (to be obtained at a very moderate rate,) they either resolve to have none at all, or reduce them to their own terms; that is, to use them how they please, pay them what they list, and to discard them whensoever they have a mind to it. And this is the recompense of their leaving their hopes in England, (far more considerable to the meanest curate than what can possibly be apprehended there,) together with the friends and relations and their native soil, to venture their lives into those parts among strangers and enemies to their profession, who look upon them as a burden; as being with their families (where they have any) to be supported out of their labor. So that I dare boldly aver that our discouragements there are much greater than ever they were here in England under the usurper." After citing various evidences in support of these statements, among which he specifies the hiring of the clergy from year to year, and compelling them to accept of parishes at under-rates, Godwyn thus proceeds: "I would not be thought to reflect herein upon your excellency, who have always professed great tenderness for churchmen. For, alas! these things are kept from your ears; nor dare they, had they opportunity, acquaint you with them, for fear of being used worse. And there being no superior clergyman, neither in council nor any place of authority, for them to address their complaints to, and by his means have their grievances brought to your excellency's knowledge, they are left without remedy. Again, two-thirds of the preachers are made up of leaden lay priests of the vestry's ordination; and are both the shame and grief of the rightly ordained clergy there. Nothing of this ever reaches your excellency's ear; these hungry patrons knowing better how to benefit by their vices than by the virtues of the other." And here Godwyn cites an instance of a writing-master, who came into Virginia, professing to be a doctor in divinity, showing feigned letters of orders, and under different names continuing in various places to carry on his work of fraud. He states also that owing to a law of the colony, which enacted that four years' servitude should be the penalty exacted of any one who permitted himself to be sent thither free of charge, some of the clergy, through ignorance of the law, were left thereby under the mastery of persons who had given them the means of gratuitous transport; and that they could only escape from such bondage by paying a ransom four or five times as large as that to which the expenses of their passage would have amounted. Moreover, he describes the parishes as extending, some of them, sixty or seventy miles in length, and lying void for many years together, to save charges. Jamestown, he distinctly states, had been left, with short intervals, in this destitute condition for twenty years. "Laymen," he adds, "were allowed to usurp the office of ministers, and deacons to undermine and thrust out presbyters; in a word, all things concerning the church and religion were left to the mercy of the people." And, last of all: "To propagate Christianity among the heathen—whether natives or slaves brought from other parts—although (as must piously be supposed) it were the only end of God's discovering those countries to us, yet is that looked upon by our new race of Christians, so idle and ridiculous, so utterly needless and unnecessary, that no man can forfeit his judgment more than by any proposal looking or tending that way." Such is the Rev. Mr. Godwyn's account of the state of religion and the condition of the clergy in Virginia during Sir William Berkley's administration.*

---

* Anderson's Hist. of Col. Church, first edition, ii. 558, 561.

CHAPTER XXXIII.

1675.

Lands at Greenspring settled on Sir William Berkley—Indian Incursions—Force put under command of Sir Henry Chicheley—Disbanded by Governor's Order—The Long Parliament of Virginia—Colonial Grievances—Spirit of the Virginians—Elements of Disaffection.

The lands at Greenspring, near Jamestown, were settled during this year on Sir William Berkley, the preamble to the act reciting among his merits, "the great pains he hath taken and hazards he has run, even of his life, in the government and preservation of the country from many attempts of the Indians, and also in preserving us in our due allegiance to his majesty's royal father of blessed memory, and his now most sacred majesty, against all attempts, long after all his majesty's other dominions were subjected to the tyranny of the late usurpers; and also seriously considering that the said Sir William Berkley hath in all time of his government, under his most sacred majesty and his royal father, made it his only care to keep his majesty's country in a due obedience to our rightful and lawful sovereign," etc. The Rev. John Clayton, (supposed to be father of the Virginia naturalist,) writing in 1688, says: "There is a spring at my Lady Berkley's called Green Spring, whereof I have been often told, so very cold, that 'tis dangerous drinking thereof in summer time, it having proved of fatal consequence to several. I never tried anything of what nature it is of."

The Indians having renewed their incursions upon the frontier, the people petitioned the governor for protection. Upon the meeting of the assembly, war was declared against them in March, 1676; five hundred men enlisted, and the forts garrisoned. The force raised was put under command of Sir Henry Chicheley, who was ordered to disarm the neighboring Indians. The forts were on the Potomac, at the falls of the Rappahannock, (now Fredericksburg,) on the Matapony, on the Pamunkey, at the falls of the Appomattox, (now Petersburg,) either at Major-General Wood's, or at Fleets', on the opposite side of the river, on the Blackwater, and at the head of the Nansemond. Provision was made for employing Indians; articles of martial law were adopted; arms to be carried to church; the governor authorized to disband the troops when expedient; days of fasting appointed. The Indians having been emboldened to commit depredations and murders by the arms and ammunition which they had received, contrary to law, from traders, a rigorous act was passed to restrain such. When Sir Henry Chicheley was about to march against the Indians he was ordered by Sir William Berkley to disband his forces, to the general surprise and dissatisfaction of the colony.

There had now been no election of burgesses since the restoration, in 1660, the same legislature since that time having continued to hold its sessions by prorogation. It may be called the Long Parliament of Virginia in respect to its duration. Among its members may be mentioned Colonel William Clayborne, Captain William Berkley, Captain Daniel Parke, Adjutant-General Jennings, Colonel John Washington, Colonel Edward Scarburgh. Robert Wynne was made speaker shortly after the restoration, and so continued until 1676, when he was succeeded by Augustine Warner, of Gloucester. James Minge, of Charles City, was now the clerk, and had been for several years.

The price of tobacco was depressed by the monopoly of the English navigation act, and the cost of imported goods, enhanced. Duties were laid on the commerce between one colony and another, and the revenue thence derived was absorbed by the collecting officers. The planters, it is said,* had been driven to seek a remedy by destroying the crop in the fields, called "plant cutting." The endeavors of the agents in England to obtain a release from the grants to the lords and a new charter, appeared abortive. The Indian incursions occurring at this conjuncture, filled the measure of panic and exasperation. Groaning under exactions and grievances, and tortured by apprehensions, the Virginians began to meditate violent measures of relief. Many of the feudal institutions of England, the hoary buttresses of mediæ-

---

* Account of Bacon's Rebellion, in Va. Gazette, 1766.

val power, could have no existence in America; a new position gradually moulded a new system; and men transplanted to another hemisphere changed opinions as well as clime. Thus, in Virginia, the most Anglican, oldest, and most loyal of the colonies, a spirit of freedom and independence infused itself into the minds of the planters. The ocean that separated them from England lessened the terror of a distant sceptre. The supremacy of law being less firmly established, especially in the frontier, a wild spirit of justice had arisen which was apt to decline into contempt of authority. Added to this, the colony contained malecontent Cromwellian soldiers reduced to bondage, perhaps some of them men of heroic soul, victims of civil war, ripe for revolt. The Indian massacres of former years made the colonists sensitive to alarms, and impatient of indifference to their cruel apprehensions, which can hardly be realized by those who have never been subjected to such dangers. The fatigues, privations, hardships, perils of a pioneer life, imparted energy; the wild magnificence of nature, the fresh luxuriance of a virgin soil, unpruned forests, great rivers and hoary mountains, these contributed to kindle a love of liberty and independence. Moreover, the disaffection of the colonists was somewhat emboldened by the civil dissensions of England, which appeared now again to threaten the stability of the throne.

CHAPTER XXXIV.

1675-1676.

Three Ominous Presages—Siege of Piscataway—Colonel John Washington—Indian Chiefs put to death—Fort evacuated—Indians murder Inhabitants of Frontier—Servant and Overseer of Nathaniel Bacon, Jr., slain—The People take up Arms—Bacon chosen Leader—His Character—Solicits Commission from Berkley—He proclaims the Insurgents Rebels—Pursues them—Planters of Lower Country revolt—Forts dismantled—Rebellion not the Result of Bacon's Pique or Ambition—He marches into the Wilderness—Massacre of friendly Indians—Bacon returns—Elected a Burgess—Arrested—Released on Parole—Assembly meets—Bacon sues for Pardon—Restored to the Council—Nathaniel Bacon, Sr.—Berkley issues secret Warrants for arrest of the younger Bacon.

"ABOUT the year 1675," says an old writer, "appeared three prodigies in that country, which, from the attending disasters, were looked upon as ominous presages. The one was a large comet, every evening for a week or more at southwest, thirty-five degrees high, streaming like a horse-tail westward, until it reached (almost) the horizon, and setting toward the northwest. Another was flights of wild pigeons, in breadth nigh a quarter of the mid-hemisphere, and of their length was no visible end; whose weights broke down the limbs of large trees whereon these rested at nights, of which the fowlers shot abundance, and ate them; this sight put the old planters under the more portentous apprehensions because the like was seen (as they said) in the year 1644, when the Indians committed the last massacre; but not after, until that present year, 1675. The third strange phenomenon was swarms of flies about an inch long, and big as the top of a man's little finger, rising out of spigot holes in the earth, which ate the new-sprouted leaves from the tops of the trees, without other harm, and in a month left us."*

The author of this account, whose initials are T. M., says of himself, that he lived in Northumberland County, on the lower

---

* T. M.'s Account of Bacon's Rebellion, in Force's Hist. Tracts, i.

part of the Potomac, where he was a merchant; but he had a plantation, servants, cattle, etc., in Stafford County, on the upper part of that river; and that he was elected a burgess from Stafford in 1676, Colonel Mason being his colleague. T. M., perhaps, was Thomas Matthews, son of Colonel Samuel Matthews, some time governor. He owned lands acquired from the Wicocomoco Indians in Northumberland, and it is probable that his son, Thomas Matthews, came into possession of them.* He appears to have lived at a place called Cherry Point, probably on the Potomac, in 1681.†

On a Sunday morning, in the summer of 1675, a herdsman, named Robert Hen, together with an Indian, was slain in Stafford County, by a party of the hostile tribe of Doegs, and the victims were found by the people on their way to church.‡ Colonel Mason and Captain Brent, with some militia, pursued the offenders about twenty miles up the river, and then across into Maryland, and, coming upon two parties of armed warriors, slaughtered indiscriminately a number of them and of the Susquehannocks, a friendly tribe. These latter, recently expelled from their own country, at the head of the Chesapeake Bay, by the Senecas, a tribe of the Five Nations, now sought refuge in a fort of the Piscataways, a friendly tribe near the head of the Potomac, supposed to be near the spot where now stands the City of Washington. In a short time several Marylanders were murdered by the savages, and some Virginians in the County of Stafford. The fort on the north bank of the Piscataway consisted of high earth-works having flankers pierced with loop-holes, and surrounded by a ditch. This again was encircled by a row of tall trees from five to eight inches in diameter, set three feet in the earth and six inches apart, and wattled in such a manner as to protect those within, and, at the same time, to afford them apertures for shooting through. It was probably an old fort erected by Maryland as a protection to the frontier, but latterly

---

* Hening, i. 515, and ii. 14. † Va. Hist. Reg., i. 167.

‡ For the following details, see T. M.'s Account; Hening, ii. 341, 543; Beverley, B. i. 65; Keith's Hist. of Va., 156; Breviarie and Conclusion, Burk, ii. 250; Account of Bacon's Rebellion, in Va. Gazette, 1766, and Bacon's Proceedings, in Force's Hist. Tracts, i.

unoccupied. The Susquehannocks, to the number of one hundred warriors, with their old men, women, and children, entrenched themselves in this stronghold. Toward the end of September they were besieged by a thousand men from Virginia and Maryland, united in a joint expedition, at the instance of the latter. The Marylanders were commanded by Major Thomas Truman, the Virginians by Colonel John Washington.* John Washington had emigrated from Yorkshire, England, to Virginia in 1657, and purchased lands in Westmoreland. Not long after, being, as has been conjectured, a surveyor, he made a location of lands, which, however, was set aside until the Indians, to whom these lands had been assigned, should vacate them. In the year 1667 he was a member of the house of burgesses.†

To return to the siege: six of the Indian chiefs were sent out from the fort on a parley proposed by Major Truman. These chiefs, on being interrogated, laid the blame of the recent outrages perpetrated in Virginia and Maryland upon the Senecas. Colonel Washington, Colonel Mason, and Major Adderton now came over from the Virginia encampment, and charged the chiefs with the murders that had been committed on the south side of the Potomac. On the next day the Virginia officers renewed the charges against the Susquehannock chiefs; at this juncture a detachment of rangers arrived, bringing with them the mangled bodies of some recent victims of Indian cruelty. Five of the chiefs were instantly bound, and put to death—"knocked on the head." The savages now made a desperate resistance; but their sorties were repelled, and they had to subsist partly on horses captured from the whites. At the end of six weeks, seventy-five warriors, with their women and children, (leaving only a few decrepid old men behind,) evacuated the fort during the night, marching off by the light of the moon, killing ten of the militia found asleep, as they retired, and making the welkin ring with

---

* Chalmers' Annals, 332, 335, 348; The Fall of the Susquehannocks, by S. F. Streeter, in Hist. Mag., i. 65.

† Burk, ii. 144; Account of our Late Troubles in Virginia, written in 1676, by Mrs. Ann Cotton, of Queen's Creek, 3 in Force's Hist. Tracts, i. This curious narrative was published from the original MS. in the *Richmond Enquirer* of September 12th, 1804. T. M.'s Account was republished in the same paper.

the war-whoop and yells of defiance. They pursued their way by the head-waters of the Potomac, the Rappahannock, the York, and the James, joining with them the neighboring Indians, slaying such of the inhabitants as they met with on the frontier, to the number of sixty—sacrificing ten ordinary victims for each one of the chiefs they had lost. The Susquehannocks now sent a message to Governor Berkley, complaining of the war waged upon them, and of the murder of their chiefs, and proposing, if the Virginians, their old friends, would make them reparation for the damages which they had suffered, and dissolve their alliance with the Marylanders, they would renew their ancient friendship; otherwise they were ready for war.*

At the falls of the James the savages had slain a servant of Nathaniel Bacon, Jr., and his overseer, to whom he was much attached. This was not the place of Bacon's residence; Bacon Quarter Branch, in the suburbs of Richmond, probably indicates the scene of the murder. Bacon himself resided at Curles, in Henrico county, on the lower James River.† It is said that when he heard of the catastrophe he vowed vengeance. In that time of panic, the more exposed and defenceless families, abandoning their homes, took shelter together in houses, where they fortified themselves with palisades and redoubts. Neighbors banding together, passed in co-operating parties, from plantation to plantation, taking arms with them into the fields where they labored, and posting sentinels, to give warning of the approach of the insidious foe. No man ventured out of doors unarmed. Even Jamestown was in danger. The red men, stealing with furtive glance through the shade of the forest, the noiseless tread of the moccasin scarce stirring a leaf, prowled around like panthers in quest of prey. At length the people at the head of the James and the York, having in vain petitioned the governor for protection, alarmed at the slaughter of their neighbors, often murdered with every circumstance of barbarity, rose tumultuously in self-

---

* Narrative of the Indian and Civil Wars in Va., in the years 1675 and 1676, 1, in Force's Hist. Tracts, i. This account is evidently in the main, if not altogether, by the same hand with the letter bearing the signature of Mrs. Ann Cotton. Several passages are identical.

† Account of Bacon's Rebellion, in Va. Gazette, 1766.

defence, to the number of three hundred men, including most, if not all the officers, civil and military, and chose Nathaniel Bacon, Jr., for their leader. According to another authority, Bacon, before the murder of his overseer and servant, had been refused the commission, and had sworn that upon the next murder he should hear of, he would march against the Indians, "commission or no commission." And when one of his own family was butchered, "he got together about seventy or ninety persons, most good housekeepers, well armed," etc. Burk* makes their number "near six hundred men," and refers to ancient (MS.) records.

Bacon had been living in the colony somewhat less than three years, having settled at Curles, on the lower James, in the midst of those people who were the greatest sufferers from the depredations of the Indians, and he himself had frequently felt the effects of their inroads. In the records of the county court of Henrico there is a deed from Randolph to Randolph, dated November 1st, 1706, conveying a tract of land called Curles, lately belonging to Nathaniel Bacon, Esq., and since found to escheat to his majesty. At the breaking out of these disturbances he was a member of the council. He was gifted with a graceful person, great abilities, and a powerful elocution, and was the most accomplished man in Virginia; his courage and resolution were not to be daunted, and his affability, hospitality, and benevolence, commanded a wide popularity throughout the colony.

The men who had put themselves under Bacon's command made preparations for marching against the Indians, but in the mean time sent again to obtain from the governor a commission of general for Bacon, with authority to lead out his followers, at their own expense, against the enemy. He then stood so high in the council, and the exigency of the case was so pressing, that Sir William Berkley, thinking it imprudent to return an absolute refusal, concluded to temporize. Some of the leading men about him, it was believed, took occasion to foment the difference between him and Bacon, envying a rising luminary that threatened to eclipse them. This conduct is like that of some of the leading

---

* In Hist. of Va., ii. 164.

men in Virginia who, one hundred years later, compelled Patrick Henry to resign his post in the army.

Sir William Berkley sent his evasive reply to the application for a commission, by some of his friends, and instructed them to persuade Bacon to disband his forces. He refused to comply with this request, and having in twenty days mustered five hundred men, marched to the falls of the James. Thereupon the governor, on the 29th day of May, 1676, issued a proclamation, declaring all such as should fail to return within a certain time, rebels. Bacon likewise issued a declaration, setting forth the public dangers and grievances, but taking no notice of the governor's proclamation.* Upon this the men of property, fearful of a confiscation, deserted Bacon and returned home; but he proceeded with fifty-seven men. Sir William Berkley, with a troop of horse from Middle Plantation, pursued Bacon as far as the falls, some forty miles, but not overtaking him, returned to Jamestown, where the assembly was soon to meet. During his absence the planters of the lower country rose in revolt, and declared against the frontier forts as a useless and intolerable burden; and to restore quiet they were dismantled, and the assembly, the odious Long Parliament of Virginia, was at last dissolved, and writs for a new election issued. This revolt in the lower country, with which Bacon had no immediate connection, demonstrates how widely the leaven of rebellion, as it was styled, pervaded the body of the people, and how unfounded is the notion, that it was the result merely of personal pique and ambition in Bacon. Had he never set his foot on the soil of Virginia there can be little doubt but that an outbreak would have occurred at this time. There was no man in the colony with a brighter prospect before him than Bacon, and he could hardly have engaged in this popular movement without a sacrifice of selfish considerations, nor without incurring imminent risk. The movement was revolutionary—a miniature prototype of the revolution of 1688 in England, and of 1776 in America. But Bacon, as before mentioned, with a small body of men proceeded into the wilderness, up the river, his provisions being nearly exhausted before he discovered the

---

* Burk, ii. 247

Indians. At length a tribe of friendly Mannakins were found entrenched within a palisaded fort on the further side of a branch of the James. Bacon endeavoring to procure provisions from them and offering compensation, they put him off with delusive promises till the third day, when the whites had eaten their last morsel. They now waded up to the shoulder across the branch to the fort, again soliciting provisions and tendering payment. In the evening one of Bacon's men was killed by a shot from that side of the branch which they had left, and this giving rise to a suspicion of collusion with Sir William Berkley and treachery, Bacon stormed the fort, burnt it and the cabins, blew up their magazine of arms and gunpowder, and with a loss of only three of his own party, put to death one hundred and fifty Indians. It is difficult to credit, impossible to justify, this massacre. The Virginians, a hundred years afterwards, suspected Governor Dunmore of colluding with Indians. Bacon with his followers returned to their homes, and he was shortly after elected one of the burgesses for the County of Henrico. Brewse or Bruce, his colleague and a captain of the insurgents, was not less odious to the governor. It was subsequently charged by the king's commissioners that the malecontent voters on this occasion illegally returned freemen, not being freeholders, for burgesses.* The charge was well founded. It is probable also that others were allowed to vote besides freeholders and housekeepers. Bacon, upon being elected, going down the James River with a party of his friends, was met by an armed vessel, ordered on board of her, and arrested by Major Howe, High Sheriff of James City, who conveyed him to the governor at that place, by whom he was accosted thus: "Mr. Bacon, you have forgot to be a gentleman." He replied, "No, may it please your honor." The governor said, "Then I'll take your parole;" which he accordingly did, and gave him his liberty; but a number of his companions, who had been arrested with him, were still kept in irons.

On the 5th day of June, 1676, the members of the new assembly, whose names are not recorded, met in the chamber over the general court, and having chosen a speaker, the governor sent for

---

* Breviarie and Conclusion, Burk, ii. 251.

them down, and addressed them in a brief abrupt speech on the Indian disturbances, and in allusion to the chiefs who had been slain, exclaimed: "If they had killed my grandfather and my grandmother, my father and mother, and all my friends, yet if they had come to treat of peace, they ought to have gone in peace." After a short interval, he again rose and said: "If there be joy in the presence of the angels over one sinner that repenteth, there is joy now, for we have a penitent sinner come before us. Call Mr. Bacon." Bacon appearing, was compelled upon one knee, at the bar of the house, to confess his offence, and beg pardon of God, the king, and governor, in the following words:* "I, Nathaniel Bacon, Jr., Esq., of Henrico County, in Virginia, do hereby most readily, freely, and most humbly acknowledge that I am, and have been guilty of divers late unlawful, mutinous, and rebellious practices, contrary to my duty to his most sacred majesty's governor, and this country, by beating up of drums; raising of men in arms; marching with them into several parts of his most sacred majesty's colony, not only without order and commission, but contrary to the express orders and commands of the Right Honorable Sir William Berkley, Knt., his majesty's most worthy governor and captain-general of Virginia. And I do further acknowledge that the said honorable governor hath been very favorable to me, by his several reiterated gracious offers of pardon, thereby to reclaim me from the persecution of those my unjust proceedings, (whose noble and generous mercy and clemency I can never sufficiently acknowledge,) and for the re-settlement of this whole country in peace and quietness. And I do hereby, upon my knees, most humbly beg of Almighty God and of his majesty's said governor, that upon this my most hearty and unfeigned acknowledgment of my said miscarriages and unwarrantable practices, he will please to grant me his gracious pardon and indemnity, humbly desiring also the honorable council of state, by whose goodness I am also much obliged, and the honorable burgesses of the present grand assembly to intercede, and mediate with his honor, to grant me such pardon. And I do hereby promise, upon the word and faith of a Christian and a gentleman, that upon such pardon granted me,

---

* Hening, ii. 543.

as I shall ever acknowledge so great a favor, so I will always bear true faith and allegiance to his most sacred majesty, and demean myself dutifully, faithfully, and peaceably to the government, and the laws of this country, and am most ready and willing to enter into bond of two thousand pounds sterling, and for security thereof bind my whole estate in Virginia to the country for my good and quiet behavior for one whole year from this date, and do promise and oblige myself to continue my said duty and allegiance at all times afterwards. In testimony of this, my free and hearty recognition, I have hereunto subscribed my name, this 9th day of June, 1676.

"NATH. BACON."

The intercession of the council was in the following terms: "We, of his majesty's council of state of Virginia, do hereby desire, according to Mr. Bacon's request, the right honorable the governor, to grant the said Mr. Bacon his freedom.

PHIL. LUDWELL,	HEN. CHICHELEY,
JAMES BRAY,	NATHL. BACON,
WM. COLE,	THOS. BEALE,
RA. WORMELEY,	THO. BALLARD,

JO. BRIDGER.

"Dated the 9th of June, 1676."

When Bacon had made his acknowledgment, the governor exclaimed: "God forgive you, I forgive you;" repeating the words thrice. Colonel Cole, of the council, added, "and all that were with him." "Yea," echoed the governor, "and all that were with him." Sir William Berkley, starting up from his chair for the third time, exclaimed: "Mr. Bacon, if you will live civilly but till next quarter court, I'll promise to restore you again to your place there," (pointing with his hand to Mr. Bacon's seat,) he having, as has been already mentioned, been of the council before those troubles, and having been deposed by the governor's proclamation. But instead of being obliged to wait till the quarter court, Bacon was restored to his seat on that very day; and intelligence of it was hailed with joyful acclamations by the people in Jamestown. This took place on Saturday. Bacon was also promised a commission to go out against the Indians, to be delivered to him on the Monday following. But being delayed or disappointed, a few days after (the assembly being engaged in devising measures against the Indians) he escaped from Jamestown. He conceived the governor's pretended generosity to be only a lure to keep him out of his seat in the house of burgesses, and to quiet the people of the upper country, who were hastening down to Jamestown to avenge all wrongs done him or his friends. According to another account, he obtained leave of absence to visit his wife, "sick, as he pretended;" but from T. M.'s Account, and others, this version appears to be unfounded.

There was in the council at this time one Colonel Nathaniel Bacon, a near relative of Nathaniel Bacon, Jr., who was not yet thirty years of age. The elder Bacon was a wealthy politic old man, childless, and intending to make his namesake and cousin his heir. It was by the pressing solicitations of this old gentleman, as was believed, that young Bacon was reluctantly prevailed upon to repeat at the bar of the house the recantation written by the old gentleman. It was he also, as was supposed, who gave timely warning to the young Bacon to fly for his life. Three or four days after his first arrest, many country people, from the heads of the rivers, appeared in Jamestown; but finding him restored to his place in the council, and his companions at liberty, they returned home satisfied. But in a short time the governor, seeing all quiet, issued secret warrants to seize him again, intending probably to raise the militia, and thus prevent a rescue.

CHAPTER XXXV.

1676.

Bacon, with an armed Force, enters Jamestown—Extorts a Commission from the Governor—Proceedings of Assembly—Bacon marches against the Pamunkies—Berkley summons Gloucester Militia—Bacon countermarches upon the Governor—He escapes to Accomac—Bacon encamps at Middle Plantation—Calls a Convention—Oath prescribed—Sarah Drummond—Giles Bland seizes an armed Vessel and sails for Accomac—His Capture—Berkley returns to Jamestown—Bacon exterminates the Indians.

WITHIN three or four days after Bacon's escape, news reached James City that he was some thirty miles above, on the James River, at the head of four hundred men. Sir William Berkley summoned the York train-bands to defend Jamestown, but only one hundred obeyed the summons, and they arrived too late, and one-half of them were favorable to Bacon. Expresses almost hourly brought tidings of his approach, and in less than four days he marched into Jamestown unresisted, at two o'clock P.M., and drew up his force, (now amounting to six hundred men,) horse and foot, in battle array on the green in front of the state-house, and within gunshot. In half an hour the drum beat, as was the custom, for the assembly to meet, and in less than thirty minutes Bacon advanced, with a file of fusileers on either hand, near to the corner of the state-house, where he was met by the governor and council. Sir William Berkley, dramatically baring his breast, cried out, "Here! shoot me—fore God, fair mark; shoot!" frequently repeating the words. Bacon replied, "No, may it please your honor, we will not hurt a hair of your head, nor of any other man's; we are come for a commission to save our lives from the Indians, which you have so often promised, and now we will have it before we go." Bacon was walking to and fro between the files of his men, holding his left arm akimbo, and gesticulating violently with his right, he and the governor both like men distracted. In a few moments Sir William withdrew to his private apartment at the other end of the state-house, the council accompanying him. Bacon followed, frequently hurrying his hand from his sword-hilt to his hat; and after him came a detachment of fusileers, who, with their guns cocked and presented at a window of the assembly chamber, filled with faces, repeating in menacing tone, "We will have it, we will have it," for half a minute, when a well-known burgess, waving his handkerchief out at the window, exclaimed, three or four times, "You shall have it, you shall have it;" when, uncocking their guns, they rested them on the ground, and stood still, till Bacon returning, they rejoined the main body. It was said that Bacon had beforehand directed his men to fire in case he should draw his sword. In about an hour after Bacon re-entered the assembly chamber, and demanded a commission, authorizing him to march out against the Indians. Godwyn, the speaker,* who was himself a Baconian, as were a majority of the house, remaining silent in the chair, Brewse, (or Bruce,)† the colleague of Bacon, alone found courage to answer: "'Twas not in our province, or power, nor of any other, save the king's vicegerent, our governor." Bacon, nevertheless, still warmly urged his demand, and harangued the assembly for nearly half an hour on the Indian disturbances, the condition of the public revenues, the exorbitant taxes, abuses and corruptions of the administration, and all the grievances of their miserable country. Having concluded, and finding "no other answer, he went away dissatisfied."

On the following day the governor directed the house to take measures to defend the country against the Indians, and advised them to beware of two rogues among them, meaning Lawrence and Drummond, who both lived at Jamestown. But some of the burgesses, in order to effect a redress of some of the grievances that the country labored under, made motions for inspecting the public revenues, the collector's accounts, etc., when they received pressing messages from the governor to meddle with nothing else till the Indian business was disposed of. The debate on this matter rose high, but the governor's orders were finally acquiesced in.

---

* Hening, ii. 606.
† Breviarie and Conclusion, in Burk, ii. 250. T. M. calls him Blayton.

While the committee on Indian affairs was sitting, the Queen of Pamunkey, a descendant of Opechancanough, was introduced into their room. Accompanied by an interpreter and her son, a youth of twenty years, she entered with graceful dignity. Around her head she wore a plait of black and white wampum-peake, a drilled purple bead of shell, three inches wide, after the manner of a crown. There is preserved at Fredericksburg a silver frontlet, purchased from some Indians, with a coat of arms, and inscribed "The Queen of Pamunkey," "Charles the Second, King of England, Scotland, France, Ireland, and Virginia," and "Honi soit qui mal y pense." She was clothed in a mantle of dressed buckskin, with the fur outward, and bordered with a deep fringe from head to foot. Being seated, the chairman asked her "How many men she would lend the English for guides and allies?" She referred him to her son, who understood English, being the reputed son of an English colonel. But he declining to answer, she burst forth in an impassioned speech of a quarter of an hour's length, often repeating the words, "Totopotomoi dead," referring to her husband, who, as has been seen, had fallen while fighting under Colonel Hill, the elder. The chairman, untouched by this appeal, roughly repeated the inquiry, how many men she would contribute. Averting her head with a disdainful look she sate silent, till the question being pressed a third time, she replied in a low tone, "Six." When still further importuned she said "Twelve," although she had then one hundred and fifty warriors in her town. She retired silent and displeased.

The assembly went on to provide for the Indian war, and made Nathaniel Bacon, Jr., general and commander-in-chief, which was ratified by the governor and council. An act was also passed indemnifying Bacon and his party for their violent acts; and a highly applausive letter was prepared, justifying Bacon's designs and proceedings, addressed to the king and subscribed by the governor, council, and assembly. Sir William Berkley at the same time communicated to the house a letter addressed to his majesty, saying: "I have above thirty years governed the most flourishing country the sun ever shone over, but am now encompassed with rebellion like waters, in every respect like that of Massaniello, except their leader." Massaniello, or Thomas Anello, a fisherman of Naples, born 1623, exasperated by the oppressive taxes imposed by Austria upon his countrymen, at the head of two thousand young men, armed with canes, overthrew the viceroy, seized upon the supreme power, and after holding it for some years, fell by the hands of assassins in 1647. Some of the burgesses also wrote to the king, setting forth the circumstances of the outbreak. The amnesty extended from the 1st day of March to the 25th day of June, 1676, and excepted only offences against the law concerning the Indian trade.* The assembly did not restrict itself to measures favorable to Bacon. According to the letter of the law, at least, he had been guilty of rebellion in assuming a military command and marching against the savages without a commission, and he had so acknowledged. Yet he was not more guilty than the bulk of the people of the colony, and probably not more so than a majority of the assembly itself; and the popular movement seemed justified by an urgent necessity of self-defence, and an intolerable accumulation of public grievances. On the other hand, Sir William Berkley had violated his solemn engagement to grant the commission. Besides, it did not escape the notice of the assembly that the term of ten years for which, it was believed, he had been appointed, had expired; and this circumstance, although it might not be held absolutely to terminate his authority, served at the least to attenuate it. The assembly adopted measures with a view at once to vindicate the supremacy of the law; to heal the wounded pride of the aged governor; to protect the country; to screen Bacon and his confederates from punishment, and to reform the abuses of the government.

It is remarkable that the resolutions, instructing the Virginia delegates in Congress to declare the colonies free and independent, were passed in June, 1776, and that the assembly, under Bacon's influence, met in June, 1676. The first act of this session declared war against the hostile Indians, ordering a levy of one thousand men, and authorizing General Bacon to receive volunteers; and if their number should prove sufficient, to dispense with the regular force; Indians taken in war to be made

---

* Hening, ii. 363.

slaves; the forces divided into southern and northern, and such officers to be appointed to command these divisions as the governor should commission. An act was then passed for the suppressing of tumults, the preamble reciting that there had of late "been many unlawful tumults, routs, and riots, in divers parts of this country, and that certain ill-disposed and disaffected people of late gathered, and may again gather themselves together, by beat of drum and otherwise, in a most apparent rebellious manner, without any authority or legal commission, which may prove of very dangerous consequences," etc. The act for regulating of officers and offices, shows how many abuses and how much rapacity had crept into the administration. By this act it was declared that no person, not being a native or minister, could hold any office until he had resided in the colony for three years. The democratic spirit of this assembly displayed itself in a law "enabling freemen to vote for burgesses;" and another making the church vestries eligible by the freemen of the parish, once in three years. Representatives were to be chosen by the people in each parish to vote with the justices in laying the county levy, and in making by-laws. The county courts were authorized to appoint their own collectors; and members of the council were prohibited from voting with the justices. An act for suppressing of ordinaries, or country taverns, suppressed all except three, one at James City, and one at each side of York River, at the great ferries; and these were prohibited from retailing any liquors, except beer and cider. Lieutenant-Colonel Hill, and Lieutenant John Stith, both of the parish of Westover, and County of Charles City, were disabled from holding office in that county, for having fomented misunderstandings between the honorable governor and his majesty's good and loyal subjects, the inhabitants of the Counties of Charles City and Henrico, and having been instrumental in levying unjust and exorbitant taxes.* In evidence of the excitement and suspicion then prevailing, it was observed that some of the burgesses wore distinctive badges; a hundred years afterwards the opposite parties walked on opposite sides of the street.

---

* Hening, ii. 341, 365.

In a few days the assembly was dissolved by the governor, who, seeing how great Bacon's influence was, apprehended only further mischief from their proceedings. A number of the burgesses, intending to depart on the morrow, having met in the evening to take leave of each other, General Bacon, as he now came to be styled, entered the room with a handful of papers, and, looking around, inquired, "Which of these gentlemen shall I interest to write a few words for me?" All present looking aside, being unwilling to act, Lawrence, Bacon's friend, pointing to one of the company, (the author of T. M.'s Account,) said: "That gentleman writes very well," and he, undertaking to excuse himself, Bacon, bowing low, said: "Pray, sir, do me the honor to write a line for me;" and he now consenting, was detained during the whole night, filling up commissions obtained from the governor, and signed by him. These commissions Bacon filled almost altogether with the names of the militia officers of the country, the first men in the colony in fortune, rank, and influence.

His vigorous measures at once restored confidence to the planters, and they resumed their occupations. Bacon, at the head of a thousand men, marched against the Pamunkies, killing many and destroying their towns. Meanwhile the people of Gloucester, the most populous and loyal county, having been disarmed by Bacon, petitioned the governor for protection against the savages. Reanimated by this petition, he again proclaimed Bacon a rebel and a traitor, and hastened over to Gloucester. Summoning the train-bands of that county and Middlesex, to the number of twelve hundred men, he proposed to them to pursue and put down the rebel Bacon—when the whole assembly unanimously shouted, "Bacon! Bacon! Bacon!" and withdrew from the field, still repeating the name of that popular leader, the Patrick Henry of his day, and leaving the aged cavalier governor and his attendants to themselves. The issue was now fairly joined between the people and the governor. Francis Morryson, afterwards one of the king's commissioners, in a letter dated at London, November 28th, 1677, and addressed to Secretary Ludwell, says: "I fear when that part of the narrative comes to be read that mentions the Gloucester petitions, your brother may be prejudiced, for there are two or three that will be summoned, will lay the contrivance at your brother's door and Beverley's, but more upon your brother, who, they say, was the drawer of it. For at the first sight, all the lords judged that that was the unhappy accident that made the Indian war recoil into a civil war; for the reason you alleged that bond and oath were proffered the governor, intended not against Bacon but the Indians, confirmed the people that Bacon's commission was good, it never being before disavowed by proclamation, but by letters writ to his majesty in commendation of Bacon's acting, copies thereof dispersed among the people."* According to another authority† the people of Gloucester refused to march against Bacon, but pledged themselves to defend the governor against him, if he should turn against Sir William Berkley and his government, which they hoped would never happen. From the result of this affair of the Gloucester petitions, we may conclude that either they contained nothing unfavorable to Bacon, or if they did, that they were gotten up by designing leaders without the consent of the people. It is certain that now, when Bacon's violent proceedings at Jamestown were known, the great body of the people espoused his cause and approved his designs.

Bacon, before he reached the head of York River, hearing from Lawrence and Drummond of the governor's movements, exclaimed, that "it vexed him to the heart, that while he was hunting wolves which were destroying innocent lambs, the governor and those with him should pursue him in the rear with full cry; and that he was like corn between two mill-stones, which would grind him to powder if he didn't look to it." He marched immediately back against the governor, who finding himself abandoned, again, on the twenty-ninth of July, proclaimed Bacon a rebel, and made his escape, with a few friends, down York River and across the Chesapeake Bay to Accomac, on the Eastern Shore. A vindication of Sir William, afterwards published, says: "Nor is it to be wondered at that he did not immediately put forth proclamations to undeceive the people, because he had then no means of securing himself, nor forces to have maintained such a proclamation by; but he took the first opportunity he could of

---

* Burk, ii. 268.   † Narrative of Indian and Civil Wars, 14.

doing all this, when Gloucester County, having been plundered by Bacon before his going out against the Indians, made an address."*

Bacon, upon reaching Gloucester, sent out parties of horse to patrol the country, and made prisoners such as were suspected of disaffection to his Indian expedition; releasing on parole those who took an oath to return home and remain quiet. This oath was strict in form but practically little regarded.

About this time there was detected in Bacon's camp a spy, who pretended to be a deserter from the opposite party, and who had repeatedly changed sides. Upon his being sentenced to death by a court-martial, Bacon declared that "if any one in the army would speak a word to save him, he should not suffer;" but no one interceding, he was put to death. Bacon's clemency won the admiration of the army, and this was the only instance of capital punishment under his orders, nor did he plunder any private house.

Having now acquired the command of a province of forty-five thousand inhabitants, and from which the crown derived a revenue of a hundred thousand pounds, he sate down with his army at Middle Plantation, and sent out an invitation, subscribed by himself and four of the council, to all the principal gentlemen of the country, to meet him in a convention at his headquarters, to consult how the Indians were to be proceeded against, and himself and the army protected against the designs of Sir William Berkley.† Bacon also put forth a reply to the governor's proclamations, demanding whether those who are entirely devoted to the king and country, can deserve the name of rebels and traitors? In vindication of their loyalty, he points to the peaceable conduct of his soldiers, and calls upon the whole country to witness against him if they can. He reproaches some of the men in power with the meanness of their capacity; others with their ill-gotten wealth; he inquires what arts, sciences, schools of learning or manufactures they had promoted; he justifies his warring against the In-

---

* Burk, ii. 261.

† T. M. says: "Bacon calls a convention at Middle Plantation, fifteen miles from Jamestown."

dians, and inveighs against Sir William Berkley for siding with them; insisting that he had no right to interfere with the fur-trade, since it was a monopoly of the crown, and asserting that the governor's factors on the frontier trafficked in the blood of their countrymen, by supplying the savages with arms and ammunition, contrary to law. He concludes by appealing to the king and parliament.

In compliance with Bacon's invitation, a great convention, including many of the principal men of the colony, assembled at his quarters in August, 1676, at Middle Plantation. In preparing an oath to be administered to the people, the three articles proposed were read by James Minge, clerk of the house of burgesses: First, that they should aid General Bacon in the Indian war; second, that they would oppose Sir William Berkley's endeavors to hinder the same; third, that they would oppose any power sent out from England, till terms were agreed to, granting that the country's complaint should be heard against Sir William before the king and parliament. A "bloody debate" ensued, especially on this last article, and it lasted from noon till midnight, Bacon and some of the principal men supporting it, and he protested that unless it should be adopted he would surrender his commission to the assembly. Some report[*] that Bacon contended in this debate single-handed against "a great many counted the wisest in the country." With what interest would we read a report of his speech! But his eloquence, like Henry's, lives only in tradition. In this critical conjuncture, when the scales of self-defence and of loyalty hung in equipoise, "the gunner of York Fort brought sudden news of fresh murders perpetrated by the Indians in Gloucester County, near Carter's Creek, adding that a great number of poor people had taken refuge in the fort. Bacon demanded, "How it could be possible that the chief fort in Virginia should be threatened by the Indians?" The gunner replied, "That the governor on the day before had conveyed all arms and ammunition out of the fort into his own vessel." This probably took place on the twenty-ninth of July. Dunmore removed the gunpowder a century afterwards. The dis-

---

[*] Narrative of Indian and Civil Wars, 18.

closure produced a deep sensation, and the convention now became reconciled to the oath. Among the subscribers on this occasion were Colonel Ballard, Colonel Beale, Colonel Swan, and 'Squire Bray, of the council; Colonels Jordan, Smith, of Purton, Scarburgh, Miller, Lawrence, and William Drummond. He had been recently governor of North Carolina. It has been supposed that he was a Presbyterian. He was a Scotchman; but the command of a colony would hardly at that time have been intrusted to a Presbyterian.* Writs were issued in his majesty's name for an assembly to meet on the fourth day of September; they were signed by the four members of the council. The oath was administered to the people of every rank, except servants, and it was as follows: "Whereas, the country hath raised an army against our common enemy, the Indians, and the same, under the command of General Bacon, being upon the point to march forth against the said common enemy, hath been diverted and necessitated to move to the suppressing of forces by evil-disposed persons raised against the said General Bacon purposely to foment and stir up civil war among us, to the ruin of this, his majesty's country. And whereas, it is notoriously manifest that Sir William Berkley, Knight, governor of the country, assisted counselled, and abetted by those evil-disposed persons aforesaid, hath not only commanded, fomented, and stirred up the people to the said civil war, but failing therein hath withdrawn himself, to the great astonishment of the people and the unsettlement of the country. And whereas, the said army raised by the country for the causes aforesaid remain full of dissatisfaction in the middle of the country, expecting attempts from the said governor and the evil counsellors aforesaid. And since no proper means have been found out for the settlement of the distractions, and preventing the horrid outrages and murders daily committed in many places of the country by the barbarous enemy; it hath been thought fit by the said general to call unto him all such sober and discreet gentlemen as the present circumstances of the country will admit, to the Middle Plantation, to consult and advise of re-establishing the peace of the country. So we, the said

---

* Bancroft, ii. 136; Anderson's Hist. of Col. Church, ii. 519, in note.

gentlemen, being, this 3d of August, 1676, accordingly met, do advise, resolve, declare, and conclude, and for ourselves do swear in manner following: First, That we will at all times join with the said General Bacon, and his army, against the common enemy in all points whatsoever. Secondly, That, whereas, certain persons have lately contrived, and designed the raising forces against the said general and the army under his command, thereby to beget a civil war, we will endeavor the discovery and apprehending all and every of those evil-disposed persons, and them secure until further order from the general. Thirdly, And whereas, it is credibly reported, that the governor hath informed the king's majesty that the said general and the people of the country in arms under his command, their aiders and abettors, are rebellious and removed from their allegiance, and that upon such like information, he, the said governor, hath advised and petitioned the king to send forces to reduce them: we do further declare, and believe in our consciences, that it consists with the welfare of this country, and with our allegiance to his most sacred majesty, that we, the inhabitants of Virginia, to the utmost of our power, do oppose and suppress all forces whatsoever of that nature, until such time as the king be fully informed of the state of the case by such person or persons as shall be sent from the said Nathaniel Bacon, in the behalf of the people, and the determination thereof be remitted hither. And we do swear that we will him, the said general, and the army under his command, aid and assist accordingly."*

Drummond advised that Sir William Berkley should be deposed, and Sir Henry Chicheley substituted in his place; his counsel not being approved of, he said: "Do not make so strange of it, for I can show from ancient records, that such things have been done in Virginia," referring probably to the case of Sir John Harvey But it was agreed that the governor's withdrawal should be taken for an abdication. Sarah Drummond, a patriot heroine, was no less enthusiastic in Bacon's favor than her husband. She exclaimed, "The child that is unborn shall have cause to rejoice for the good that will come by the rising of the coun-

---

* Beverley, B. i. 74.

try." Ralph Weldinge said: "We must expect a greater power from England that would certainly be our ruin." But Sarah Drummond remembered that England was divided into two hostile factions between the Duke of York and the Duke of Monmouth. Picking up from the ground a small stick and breaking it, she added: "I fear the power of England no more than a broken straw." Looking for relief from the odious navigation act, she declared: "Now we can build ships, and, like New England, trade to any part of the world;" for New England evaded that act, which her people considered an invasion of their rights, they not being represented in parliament.

Bacon also issued proclamations, commanding all men in the land, in case of the arrival of the forces expected from England, to join his standard and to retire into the wilderness, and resist the troops, until they should agree to treat of an accommodation of the dispute.

There was a gentleman in Virginia, Giles Bland, only son of John Bland, an eminent London merchant, who was personally known to the king, and had a considerable interest at court. He was, as has been seen, also a generous friend of Virginia. His brother, Theodorick Bland, sometime a merchant at Luars, in Spain, came over to Virginia in 1654, where, settling at Westover, upon James River, in Charles City County, he died, in April, 1671, aged forty-five years, and was buried in the chancel of the church, which he built, and gave, together with ten acres of land, a court-house and prison for the county and parish. He lies buried in the Westover churchyard between two of his friends, the church having long since fallen down. He was of the king's council and speaker of the house of burgesses, and was, in fortune and understanding, inferior to no man of his time in the country. He married Ann, daughter of Richard Bennet, sometime governor of the colony.* When John Bland sent out his son Giles Bland to Virginia to take possession of the estate of his uncle Theodorick, he got him appointed collector-general of the customs. The governors had hitherto held this office, and it was in 1676 that a collector of the revenue was first sent over

---

* Bland Papers, i. 148.

from England under parliamentary sanction, and it is therefore probable that the appointment of Bland diminished the perquisites of Governor Berkley. Giles Bland, in his capacity of collector, had a right to board any vessel whenever he might think it proper. He was a man of talents, education, courage, and haughty bearing, and having before quarrelled with the governor, now sided warmly with Bacon. There happened to be lying in York River a vessel of sixteen guns, commanded by a Captain Laramore, and Bland went on board of her with a party of armed men, under pretence of searching for contraband goods, and seizing the captain, confined him in the cabin. Laramore, discovering Bland's designs, resolved to deceive him in his turn, and entered into his measures with such apparent sincerity that he was restored to the command of his vessel. With her, another vessel of four guns, under Captain Carver, and a sloop, Bland, now appointed Bacon's lieutenant-general, sailed with two hundred and fifty men for Accomac, and after capturing another vessel, appeared off Accomac with four sail.

This peninsula, separated from the main land of Virginia by the wide Chesapeake Bay, was then hardly accessible by land, owing to the great distance and the danger of Indians. The position was therefore geographically advantageous for the fugitive governor; but as yet few of the inhabitants had rallied to his standard. They indeed shared in the general disaffection, and availed themselves of this occasion to lay their grievances before Sir William Berkley, who found himself unable to redress his own. Some of the inhabitants of the Eastern Shore at this time were engaged in committing depredations on the estates of the planters on the other side of the bay, just as the adherents of Lord Dunmore acted a century afterwards. Upon the appearance of Bland and his little squadron, Sir William Berkley, having not a single vessel to defend him, was overwhelmed with despair; but at this juncture he received a note from Laramore, offering, if he would send him some assistance, to deliver Bland, with all his men, prisoners into his hands. The governor, having no high opinion of Laramore, suspected that his note might be only a bait to entrap him; but upon advising with his friend Colonel Philip Ludwell, he knowing Laramore and having a good opinion of him, counselled the governor to accept the offer as the best alternative now left him, and gallantly undertook to engage in the enterprise at the hazard of his life. Sir William consenting, Ludwell, with twenty-six well-armed men, appeared at the appointed time alongside of Laramore's vessel. Laramore was prepared to receive the loyalists, and Ludwell boarded her without the loss of a man, and soon after captured the other vessels. According to T. M.'s Account, Captain Carver was at this time, upon Sir William's invitation, holding an interview with him on shore. Bland, Carver, and the other chiefs were sent to the governor, and the rest of the prisoners secured on board of the vessels. Bland's expedition appears to have been very badly managed, and the drunkenness of his men probably rendered his party so easy a prey.* The greater part of the prisoners screened themselves from punishment by entering into the governor's service. When Laramore waited on the governor, he clasped him in his arms, called him his deliverer, and gave him a large share of his favor. In a few days the brave old Carver was hanged on the Accomac shore. Sir William Berkley afterwards described him as "a valiant man and stout seaman, miraculously delivered into my hand." Sir Henry Chicheley, the chief of the council, who, with several other gentlemen, was a prisoner in Bacon's hands, afterwards exclaimed against this act of the governor as most rash and cruel, and he expected, at the time, to be executed in the same manner by way of retaliation. Bland was put in irons and badly treated, as it was reported.

Captain Gardner, sailing from the James River, went to the governor's relief with his own vessel, the Adam and Eve, and ten or twelve sloops, which he had collected upon hearing of Bland's expedition. Sir William Berkley, by this unexpected turn of affairs, raised from the abyss of despair to the pinnacle of hope, resolved to push his success still further. With Laramore's vessel and Gardner's, and sixteen or seventeen sloops, and a motley band of six hundred, or, according to another account, one thousand men in arms, "rogues and royalists," the governor returned in triumph to Jamestown, September 7th, 1676, where, falling

---

* Bacon's Proceedings, 20; Force's Hist. Tracts, i.

on his knees, he returned thanks to God, and again proclaimed Bacon and his adherents rebels and traitors. There were now in Jamestown nine hundred Baconites, as they had come to be styled, under command of Colonel Hansford, commissioned by Bacon. Berkley sent in a summons for surrender of the town, with offer of pardon to all except Drummond and Lawrence. Upon this, all of them retired to their homes except Hansford, Lawrence, Drummond, and a few others, who made for the head of York River, in quest of Bacon, who had returned to that quarter.

During these events Bacon was executing his designs against the Indians. As soon as he had dispatched Bland to Accomac, he crossed the James River at his own house, at Curles, and surprising the Appomattox Indians, who lived on both sides of the river of that name, a little below the falls, (now Petersburg,) he burnt their town, killed a large number of the tribe, and dispersed the rest.* Burk† places this battle or massacre on Bloody Run, a small stream emptying into the James at Richmond, but he refers to no authority, and probably had none better than a loose tradition. The Appomattox Indians, it appears, occupied both sides of the river in question, and it is altogether improbable that Indians still inhabited the north bank of the James River near Curles. Besides, if they had still inhabited that side, it would have been unnecessary to cross the James before commencing the attack. Curles was a proper point for crossing the James with a view of attacking the Indians on the Appomattox.

From the falls of the Appomattox, Bacon traversed the country to the southward, destroying many towns on the banks of the Nottoway, the Meherrin, and the Roanoke. His name had become so formidable, that the natives fled everywhere before him, and having nothing to subsist upon, save the spontaneous productions of the country, several tribes perished, and they who survived were so reduced as to be never afterwards able to make any firm stand against the Long-knives, and gradually became tributary to them.

---

* History of Bacon's Rebellion, in Va. Gazette for 1769.
† Burk, ii. 176.

CHAPTER XXXVI.

1676.

Bacon Marches back upon Jamestown—Singular Stratagem—Berkley's Second Flight—Jamestown Burnt—Bacon proceeds to Gloucester to oppose Brent—Bacon dies—Circumstances of his Death and Burial—His Father an Author—Marriage and Fortune of Nathaniel Bacon, Jr.—His Widow.

BACON, having exhausted his provisions, had dismissed the greater part of his forces before Lawrence, Drummond, Hansford, and the other fugitives from Jamestown joined him. Upon receiving intelligence of the governor's return, Bacon, collecting a force variously estimated at one hundred and fifty, three hundred, and eight hundred, harangued them on the situation of affairs, and marched back upon Jamestown, leading his Indian captives in triumph before him. The contending parties came now to be distinguished by the names of Rebels and Royalists. Finding the town defended by a palisade ten paces in width, running across the neck of the peninsula, he rode along the work, and reconnoitred the governor's position. Then, dismounting from his horse, he animated his fatigued men to advance at once, and, leading them close to the palisade, sounded a defiance with the trumpet, and fired upon the garrison. The governor remained quiet, hoping that want of provisions would soon force Bacon to retire; but he supplied his troops from Sir William Berkley's seat, at Greenspring, three miles distant. He afterwards complained that "his dwelling-house at Greenspring was almost ruined; his household goods, and others of great value, totally plundered; that he had not a bed to lie on; two great beasts, three hundred sheep, seventy horses and mares, all his corn and provisions, taken away."

Bacon adopted a singular stratagem, and one hardly compatible with the rules of chivalry. Sending out small parties of horse, he captured the wives of several of the principal loyalists then with the governor, and among them the lady of Colonel Bacon, Sr., Madame Bray, Madame Page, and Madame Ballard. Upon their being brought into the camp, Bacon sends one of them into Jamestown to carry word to their husbands that his purpose was to place their wives in front of his men in case of a sally.* Colonel Ludwell† reproaches the rebels with "ravishing of women from their homes, and hurrying them about the country in their rude camps, often threatening them with death." But, according to another and more impartial authority,‡ Bacon made use of the ladies only to complete his battery, and removed them out of harm's way at the time of the sortie. He raised by moonlight a circumvallation of trees, earth, and brush-wood, around the governor's outworks. At daybreak next morning the governor's troops, being fired upon, made a sortie; but they were driven back, leaving their drum and their dead behind them. Upon the top of the work which he had thrown up, and where alone a sally could be made, Bacon exhibited the captive ladies to the views of their husbands and friends in the town, and kept them there until he completed his works. The peninsula of Jamestown is formed by the James River on the south, and a deep creek on the north encircling it within ten paces of the river. This island, for it is so styled, is about two miles long, east and west, and one mile broad. It is low, consisting mainly of marshes and swamps, and in consequence very unhealthy. There are no springs, and the water of the wells is brackish. Jamestown stood along the river bank about three-quarters of a mile, containing a church, and some sixteen or eighteen well-built brick houses. The population of this diminutive metropolis consisted of about a dozen families, (for all of the houses were not inhabited,) "getting their living by keeping of ordinaries at extraordinary rates."

Bacon, after completing his works, in which he was much assisted by the conspicuous white aprons of the ladies, now mounted a small battery of two or three cannon, according to some commanding the shipping, but not the town, according to others

---

* Mrs. Cotton's Letter. † Letter in Chalmers' Annals, 349.
‡ Narrative of Indian and Civil Wars.

commanding both. Sir William Berkley had three great guns planted at the distance of about one hundred and fifty paces. But such was the cowardice of his motley crowd of followers, the bulk of them mere spoilsmen, "rogues and royalists," intent only on the plunder of forfeited estates promised them by "his honor," that although superior to Bacon's force in time, place, and numbers, yet out of six hundred of them, only twenty gentlemen were found willing to stand by him. So great was their fear, that in two or three days after the sortie they embarked in the night with all the town people and their goods, and leaving the guns spiked, weighing anchor secretly, and dropping silently down the river; retreating from a force inferior in number, and which, during a rainy week of the sickliest season, had been exposed, lying in open trenches, to far more hardship and privation than themselves. At the dawn of the following day, Bacon entered, where he found empty houses, a few horses, two or three cellars of wine, a small quantity of Indian-corn, "and many tanned hides." It being determined that it should be burned, so that the "rogues should harbor there no more," Lawrence and Drummond, who owned two of the best houses, set fire to them in the evening with their own hands, and the soldiers, following their example, laid in ashes Jamestown, including the church, the first brick one erected in the colony. Sir William Berkley and his people beheld the flames of the conflagration from the vessels riding at anchor, about twenty miles below.

Bacon now marched to York River, and crossed at Tindall's (Gloucester) Point, in order to encounter Colonel Brent, who was marching against him from the Potomac, with twelve hundred men. But the greater part of his men, hearing of Bacon's success, deserting their colors declared for him, "resolving with the Persians, to go and worship the rising sun."* Bacon, making his headquarters at Colonel Warmer's, called a convention in Gloucester, and administered the oath to the people of that county, and began to plan another expedition against the Indians, or, as some report, against Accomac, when he fell sick of a dysentery brought on by exposure. Retiring to the house of a Dr.

---

* Mrs. Cotton's Letter.

Pate, and, lingering for some weeks, he died. Some of the loyalists afterwards reported that he died of a loathsome disease, and by a visitation of God; which is disproven by T. M.'s Account, by that published in the Virginia Gazette, and by the Report of the King's Commissioners. Some of Bacon's friends suspected that he was taken off by poison; but of this there is no proof. In his last hours he requested the assistance of a minister named Wading, whom he had arrested not long before for his opposition to the taking of the oath in Gloucester, telling him that "it was his place to preach in the church, and not in the camp."

The place of Bacon's interment has never been discovered, it having been concealed by his friends, lest his remains should be insulted by the vindictive Berkley, in whom old age appears not to have mitigated the fury of the passions. According to one tradition, in order to screen Bacon's body from indignity, stones were laid on his coffin by his friend Lawrence, as was supposed; according to others, it was conjectured that his body had been buried in the bosom of the majestic York where the winds and the waves might still repeat his requiem:—

> "While none shall dare his obsequies to sing
> In deserved measures; until time shall bring
> Truth crowned with freedom, and from danger free,
> To sound his praises to posterity."*

Lord Chatham, in his letters addressed to his nephew, the Earl of Camelford, advises him to read "Nathaniel Bacon's Historical and Political Observations, which is, without exception, the best and most instructive book we have on matters of that kind." This book, though at present little known, formerly enjoyed a high reputation. It is written with a very evident bias to the principles of the parliamentary party, to which Bacon adhered. It was published in 1647, again in 1651, secretly reprinted in 1672, and again in 1682, for which edition the publisher was indicted and outlawed. The author was probably related to the

---

* Extract from verses on his death, attributed to a servant, or attendant, who was with him in his last moments, and entitled "Bacon's Epitaph made by his Man." (*Force's Hist. Tracts*, i.)

great Lord Bacon.* Nathaniel Bacon, Jr., came over to Virginia about the year 1672, when the third edition of that work was secretly reprinted in England. In the quarto edition the author, Nathaniel Bacon, is said to have been of Gray's Inn. It was published during the Protectorate. He appears probably to have been, in Oliver Cromwell's time, recorder of the borough of Ipswich, and to have lived at Freston, near Saxmundham, in Suffolk. His son, Nathaniel Bacon, Jr., styled the Rebel, married, against the consent of his father, who violently exhibited his disapprobation, Elizabeth, eldest daughter of Sir Edward Duke, and sister to Sir John Duke, of Benhill-lodge, near Saxmundham. Ray, who set out upon his travels into foreign parts in 1663, says he was accompanied by Mr. Willoughby, Sir Philip Skippon, and Mr. Nathaniel Bacon, "a hopeful young gentleman."† He owned lands in England of the yearly value of one hundred and fifty pounds; and after his marriage, being straitened for money, he applied to Sir Robert Jason for assistance, conveyed the lands to him for twelve hundred pounds sterling,‡ and removed with his wife to Virginia. Dying, he left Elizabeth a widow, and children. She afterwards married in Virginia Thomas Jervis, a merchant, who lived in Elizabeth City County, on the west side of Hampton River,§ and upon his death she became his executrix, and in 1684 claimed her jointure out of the lands sold to Jason, under a settlement thereof made by Bacon on his marriage, in consideration of her portion.‖ Nathaniel Bacon, Jr., was cousin to Thomas, Lord Culpepper,¶ subsequently governor of Virginia. Jervis appears to have been owner of a vessel, the "Betty," (so called after his wife,) in which Culpepper sailed from Virginia for Boston, August 10th, 1680. Elizabeth, relict of Jervis, married third a Mr. Mole. There are, at the present day, persons in Virginia of the name of Bacon, who claim to be lineal descendants of the rebel.

---

* Hist. Magazine, i. 216. † Ibid., i. 125.
‡ Hening, ii. 374. § Ibid., ii. 472.
‖ Vernon's Reports, i. 284. ¶ Va. Hist. Reg., iii. 190.

CHAPTER XXXVII.

1676.

Bacon succeeded by Ingram—Hansford and others executed—Ingram and others hold West Point—They surrender—Close of Rebellion—Proceedings of Court-Martial—Execution of Drummond—His Character—Mrs. Afra Behn—Richard Lawrence—His Character.

UPON Bacon's death, toward the end of 1676, the exact date of which can hardly be ascertained, he was succeeded by his lieutenant-general, Joseph Ingram, (whose real name was said to be Johnson,) who had lately arrived in Virginia. Ingram, supported by George Wakelet, or Walklett, his major-general, who was very young, Langston, Richard Lawrence, and their adherents, took possession of West Point, at the head of York River, fortified it, and made it their place of arms. West Point, or West's Point, so called from the family name of Lord Delaware, was at one time known as "De la War," and is so laid down on John Henry's Map, dated 1770. There is still extant there* a ruinous house of stone-marl, which was probably occupied by Ingram and his confederates. A bake-oven serves to strengthen the conjecture.

As soon as Berkley heard of Bacon's death, he sent over Robert Beverley, with a party, in a sloop to York River, where they captured Colonel Hansford and some twenty soldiers, at the house where Colonel Reade had lived, which appears to have been at or near where Yorktown now stands. Hansford was taken to Accomac, tried, and condemned to be hanged, and was the first native of Virginia that perished in that ignominious form, and in America the first martyr that fell in defending the rights of the people. He was described by Sir William Berkley as "one Hansford, a valiant stout man, and a most resolved rebel." When he came to the place of execution, distant about

---

* 1847.

a mile from the place of his confinement, he appeared well resolved to bear his fate, complaining only of the manner of his death. Neither during his trial before the court-martial, nor afterwards, did he supplicate any favor, save that "he might be shot like a soldier, and not hanged like a dog;" but he was told that he was condemned not as a soldier, but as a rebel. During the short respite allowed him after his sentence, he professed repentance and contrition for all the sins of his past life, but refused to acknowledge what was charged against him as rebellion, to be one of them; desiring the people present to take notice that "he died a loyal subject and lover of his country, and that he had never taken up arms but for the destruction of the Indians, who had murdered so many Christians." His execution took place on the 13th of November, 1676.*

Captain Wilford, Captain Farloe, and several others of less note, were put to death in Accomac. Wilford, younger son of a knight who had lost his estate and life in defence of Charles the First, had taken refuge in Virginia, where he became an Indian interpreter, in which capacity he was very serviceable to Bacon. Farloe had been made an officer by Bacon, upon the recommendation of Sir William Berkley, or some of the council. He was a mathematical scholar, and of a peaceable disposition, and his untimely end excited much commiseration. Major Cheesman died in prison, probably from ill usage. His wife took to herself the entire blame for his having joined Bacon, and on her bended knees implored Sir William Berkley to put her to death in his stead. The governor answered by applying to her an epithet of infamy. Several other prisoners came to their death in prison in the same way with Cheesman.

Sir William Berkley now repaired to York River with four merchant-ships, two or three sloops, and one hundred and fifty men.† According to another account,‡ he sent Colonel Ludwell with part of his forces to York River, while he himself with the rest repaired to Jamestown; but this appears to be erroneous. Sir William proclaimed a general pardon, excepting certain per-

---

* Ingram's Proceedings, 33; Force's Hist. Tracts, i.
† T. M. and Mrs. Cotton. ‡ In Va. Gazette.

sons named, especially Lawrence and Drummond. Greenspring, the governor's residence, still held out, being garrisoned with a hundred men under a captain Drew, previously a miller, the approaches barricaded, and three pieces of cannon planted. A party of one hundred and twenty, dispatched by the governor to surprise at night a guard of about thirty men and boys, under Major Whaley, at Colonel Bacon's house on Queen's Creek, were defeated, with the loss of their commander, named Farrel. Colonel Bacon and Colonel Ludwell were present at this affair. Major Lawrence Smith, with six hundred Gloucester men, was likewise defeated by Ingram at Colonel Pate's house, Smith saving himself by flight, and his men being all made prisoners. The officer next in command under Smith was a minister. Captain Couset with a party being sent against Raines, who headed the insurgents on the south side of James River, Raines was killed, and his men captured.

Meanwhile Ingram, Wakelet, and their companions in arms, foraged with impunity on the estates of the loyalists, and bade defiance to the aged governor. They defended themselves against the assaults of Ludwell and others with such resolution and gallantry, that Berkley, fatigued and exhausted, at length sent, by Captain Grantham, a complaisant letter to Wakelet—or, as some say, to Ingram—offering an amnesty, on condition of surrender. This was agreed to, and in reward for his submission, Berkley presented to Wakelet all the Indian plunder deposited at West Point. Greenspring was also surrendered by Drew upon terms offered by Sir William Berkley. A court-martial was held on board of a vessel in York River, January the 11th, 1676-7.[*] Four of the insurgents were condemned by this court: one of them, by name Young, had, according to Sir William Berkley, held a commission under General Monk long before he declared for the king; another, a carpenter, who had formerly

---

[*] Consisting of the Right Honorable Sir William Berkley, Knight, Governor and Captain-General of Virginia; Colonel Nathaniel Bacon, Colonel William Clayborne, Colonel Thomas Ballard, Colonel Southy Littleton, Colonel Philip Ludwell, Lieutenant-Colonel John West, Colonel Augustine Warner, Major Lawrence Smith, Major Robert Beverley, Captain Anthony Armistead, Colonel Matthew Kemp, and Captain Daniel Jenifer.

been a servant of the governor, but had been made a colonel in Bacon's army; one, Hall, was a clerk of a county court, but, by his writings, "more useful to the rebels than forty armed men."

When West Point was surrendered, Lawrence and Drummond were at the Brick-house in New Kent, on the opposite side of the river. On the nineteenth day of January, Drummond was taken in the Chickahominy Swamp, half famished, and on the following day was brought in a prisoner to Sir William Berkley, who was then on board of a vessel at Colonel Bacon's, on Queen's Creek. The governor, who, through personal hostility, had vowed that Drummond should not live an hour after he fell into his power, upon hearing of his arrival, immediately went on shore and saluted him with a courtly bow, saying, "Mr. Drummond, you are very *un*welcome; I am more glad to see you than any man in Virginia. Mr. Drummond, you shall be hanged in half an hour." He replied, "What your honor pleases." A court-martial was immediately held, in time of peace, at the house of James Bray, Esq., whither the prisoner was conveyed in irons. He was stripped; and a ring—a pledge of domestic affection—was torn from his finger before his conviction; he was condemned without any charge being alleged, and although he had never borne arms; and he was not permitted to defend himself. Condemned at one o'clock, he was hurried away to execution on a gibbet at four o'clock, at Middle Plantation, with one John Baptista, "a common Frenchman, that had been very bloody." Drummond was a sedate Scotch gentleman, who had been governor of the infant colony of North Carolina, of estimable character, unsullied integrity, and signal ability. He had rendered himself extremely obnoxious to the governor's hatred by the lively concern which he had always evinced in the public grievances. Sir William Berkley mentions him as "one Drummond, a Scotchman, that we all suppose was the original cause of the whole rebellion." When afterwards the petition of his widow, Sarah Drummond, depicting the cruel treatment of her husband, was read in the king's council in England, the lord chancellor, Finch, said: "I know not whether it be lawful to wish a person alive, otherwise I could wish Sir William

Berkley so, to see what could be answered to such barbarity; but he has answered it before this."*

Mrs. Afra Behn celebrated Bacon's Rebellion in a tragi-comedy, entitled "The Widow Ranter, or the History of Bacon in Virginia." Dryden honored it with a prologue. The play failed on the stage, and was published in 1690; there is a copy of it in the British Museum.† It sets historical truth at defiance, and is replete with coarse humor and indelicate wit. It is probable that Sarah Drummond may have been intended by "The Widow Ranter." It appears that one or two expressions in the Declaration of Independence occur in this old play.

On the 24th of January, 1677, six other insurgents were condemned to death at Greenspring, and executed. Henry West was banished for seven years, and his estate confiscated, save five pounds allowed him to pay his passage. William West and John Turner, sentenced to death at the same time, escaped from prison. William Rookings, likewise sentenced, died in prison. Richard Lawrence, with four companions, disappeared from the frontier, proceeding on horseback and armed, through a deep snow, preferring to perish in the wilderness rather than to share Drummond's fate. Lawrence was educated at Oxford, and for wit, learning, and sobriety, was equalled by few there. He had been one of the commissioners for adjusting the boundary line between Maryland and Virginia in 1663. He had been defrauded of a handsome estate by Berkley's corrupt partiality in behalf of a favorite. The rebellion, as it was called, was by most people mainly attributed to Lawrence; and it is said that he had before thrown out intimations that he hoped to find means by which he not only should be able to repair his own losses, but also see the country relieved from the governor's "avarice and French despotic modes." Lawrence had married a rich widow, who kept a large house of entertainment at Jamestown, which gave him an extensive influence. Nathaniel Bacon, Jr., probably had lodged

---

* Morrison's Letter, in Burk, ii. 268.

† Thomas H. Wynne, Esq., of Richmond, who is laudably curious in matters connected with Virginia history, has a copy of this play, and I have been indebted to him for the use of that and several other rare books.

at his house when search was made for him on the morning of his escape. The author of T. M.'s Account says: "But Mr. Bacon was too young, too much a stranger there, and of a disposition too precipitate, to manage things to that length those were carried, had not thoughtful Mr. Lawrence been at the bottom."

CHAPTER XXXVIII.

1677.

Arrival of an English Regiment—The Royal Commissioners—Punishment of Rebels—Execution of Giles Bland—Commissioners investigate the Causes of the Rebellion—Seize the Assembly's Journals—Number of Persons executed—Cruel Treatment of Prisoners—Bacon's Laws repealed—Act of Pardon—Exceptions—Singular Penalties—Evaded by the Courts—Many of Bacon's Laws re-enacted—Berkley recalled—Succeeded by Jeffreys—Sir William Berkley's Death—Notice of his Life and Writings—His Widow.

On the 29th day of January, 1677, a fleet arrived within the capes, from England, under command of Admiral Sir John Berry, or Barry, with a regiment of soldiers commanded by Colonel Herbert Jeffreys and Colonel Morrison. Sir William Berkley held an interview with them at Kiquotan, on board of the Bristol; and these three were associated in a commission to investigate the causes of the late commotions and to restore order. They were instructed to offer a reward of three hundred pounds to any one who should arrest Bacon, who was to be taken by "all ways of force, or design." And the other colonies were commanded by the king not to aid or conceal him; and it was ordered, in case of his capture, that he should be brought to trial here; or, if his popularity should render it expedient, be sent to England for trial and punishment. They were authorized to pardon all who would duly take the oath of obedience, and give security for their good behavior. Freedom was to be offered to servants and slaves who would aid in suppressing the revolt.* The same measure had been before adopted by the Long Parliament, and was resorted to a century afterwards by Governor Dunmore. It is the phenomenon of historical pre-existence. The general court and the assembly having now met, several more of

---

* Chalmers' Annals, 336.

Bacon's adherents were convicted by a civil tribunal held at Greenspring, and put to death—most of them men of competent fortune and respectable character. Among them was Giles Bland, whose friends in England, it was reported, had procured his pardon to be sent over with the fleet; but if so, it availed him nothing. It was indeed whispered that he was executed under private orders brought from England, the Duke of York having declared, with an oath, that "Bacon and Bland shall die." Bland was convicted March eighth, and executed on the fifteenth, at Bacon's Trench, near Jamestown, with another prisoner, Robert Jones. Three others were put to death on another day at the same place. Anthony Arnold was hung on the fifteenth of March, in chains, at West Point. Two others suffered capitally on the same day, but at what place does not appear, probably in their own counties.*

In the month of April, Secretary Ludwell wrote to Coventry, the English secretary of state, "that the grounds of this rebellion have not proceeded from any real fault in the government, but rather from the lewd disposition of desperate fortunes lately sprung up among them, which easily seduced the willing minds of the people from their allegiance, in the vain hopes of taking the country wholly out of his majesty's hands into their own. Bacon never intended more by the prosecution of the Indian war than as a covert to his villanies."

The commissioners, who assisted in the trial of these prisoners, now proceeded to inquire into the causes of the late distractions; they sat at Swan's Point. The insurgents, who comprised the great body of the people of Virginia, had found powerful friends among the people of England, and in parliament; and the commissioners discountenanced the excesses of Sir William Berkley, and the loyalists, and invited the planters in every quarter to bring in their grievances without fear. Jeffreys, one of the commissioners, was about to succeed Governor Berkley. In their zeal for investigation the commissioners seized the journals of the assembly; and the burgesses in October, 1677, demanded satisfaction for this indignity, declaring that such a seizure could not

---

* Burk, ii. 255.

have been authorized even by an order under the great seal, because "they found that such a power had never been exercised by the king of England"—an explicit declaration of the legislative independence of the colony. Their language was stigmatized by Charles the Second as seditious.*

The number of persons executed was twenty-three,[†] of whom twelve were condemned by court-martial. The jails were crowded with prisoners, and in the general consternation many of the inhabitants were preparing to leave the country. During eight months Virginia had suffered civil war, devastation, executions, and the loss of one hundred thousand pounds,—so violent was the effort of nature to throw off the malady of despotism and misrule. Charles the Second, in October, issued two proclamations, authorizing Berkley to pardon all except Nathaniel Bacon, Jr.; and afterwards another, declaring Sir William's of February, 1677, not conformable to his instructions, in excepting others besides Bacon from pardon, and abrogating it. Yet the king's commissioners assisted in the condemnation of several of the prisoners. An act of pardon, under the great seal, brought over by Lord Culpepper, was afterwards unanimously passed by the assembly in June, 1680, and several persons are excepted in it who were included in Sir William's "bloody bill" in February, 1677.[‡]

The people complained to the commissioners of the illegal seizing of their estates by the governor and his royalist supporters; and of their being imprisoned after submitting themselves upon the governor's proclamation of pardon and indemnity; and of being compelled to pay heavy fines and compositions by threats of being brought to trial, which was in every instance tantamount to conviction. Berkley and some of the royalists that sat on the trial of the prisoners, were forward in impeaching, accusing, and reviling them—accusing and condemning, both at once. Sir William Berkley caused Drummond's small plantation to be seized upon and given to himself by his council, removing and embezzling the personal property, and thus compelling his widow, with her children, to fly from her home, and

---

* Chalmers' Revolt, i. 163, and Annals, 337.   † Hening, ii. 370.
‡ Hening, ii. 366, 428, 458.

wander in the wilderness and woods until they were well-nigh reduced to starvation, when relieved by the arrival of the commissioners. At length the assembly, in an address to the governor, deprecated any further sanguinary punishments, and he was prevailed upon, reluctantly, to desist. All the acts of the assembly of June, 1676, called "Bacon's Laws," were repealed, as well by the order and proclamation of King Charles, as also by act of the assembly held at Greenspring, in February, 1677.*

The assembly granted indemnity and pardon for all acts committed since the 1st of April, 1676, excepting Nathaniel Bacon, Jr., and about fifty others, including certain persons deceased, executed, escaped, and banished. The principal persons excepted were Cheesman, Hunt, Hansford, Wilford, Carver, Drummond, Crewes, Farloe, Hall, William and Henry West, Lawrence, Bland, Whaley, Arnold, Ingram, Wakelet, Scarburgh, and Sarah, wife of Thomas Grindon. Twenty were attainted of high treason, and their estates confiscated. The provisoes of the act virtually left the whole power of punishment still in the hands of the governor and council. Minor punishments were inflicted on others; some were compelled to sue for pardon on their knees, with a rope about the neck; others fined, disfranchised, or banished. These penalties did not meet with the approbation of the people, and were in several instances evaded by the connivance of the courts. John Bagwell and Thomas Gordon, adjudged to appear at Rappahannock Court with halters about their necks, were allowed to appear with "small tape;" in the same county William Potts wore "a Manchester binding," instead of a halter.

The assembly, in accordance with one of Bacon's laws, declared Indian prisoners slaves, and their property lawful prize. An order was made for building a new state-house at Tindall's (Gloucester) Point, on the north side of York River, but it was never carried into effect. Many of the acts of this session are almost exact copies of "Bacon's Laws," the titles only being altered—a conclusive proof of the abuses and usurpations of those in power, and of the merits of acts passed by those stigmatized and punished as rebels and traitors. Such likewise was the conduct of

---

* Hening, ii. 365.

the British Parliament in relation to the legislation of the Commonwealth of England. The fourth of May was appointed a fast-day, and August the twenty-second a day of thanksgiving.

Sir William Berkley, worn down with agitations which his age was unequal to, and in feeble health, being recalled by the king, ceased to be governor on the 27th of April, 1677, and returned in the fleet to London, leaving Colonel Herbert Jeffreys in his place, who was sworn into office on the same day. His commission was dated November the 11th, 1676—the twenty-eighth year of Charles the Second. In July, 1675, Lord Culpepper had been appointed governor-in-chief of Virginia, but he did not arrive till the beginning of 1680; had he come over when first appointed, it might have prevented Bacon's Rebellion.

Sir William Berkley died on the thirteenth of July, 1677, of a broken heart, as some relate,* without ever seeing the king, having been confined to his chamber from the day of his arrival. According to others, King Charles expressed his approbation of his conduct, and the kindest regard for him, and made frequent inquiry respecting his health.† Others again, on the contrary, report that the king said of him: "That old fool has hanged more men in that naked country than I have done for the murder of my father."‡ Sir William Berkley was a native of London, and educated at Merton College, Oxford, of which he was afterwards a fellow, and in 1629 was made Master of Arts. He made the tour of Europe in the year 1630. He held the place of governor of Virginia from 1639 to 1651, and from 1659 to 1677—a period of thirty years, a term equalled by no other governor of the colony. He published a tragi-comedy, "The Lost Lady," in 1639, the year in which he came first to Virginia. Pepys, in his Diary, mentions seeing it acted. Sir William published also, in 1663, "A Discourse and View of Virginia." He was buried at Twickenham, since illustrated by the genius of Pope. Sir William Berkley left no children. By a will, dated May the 2d, 1676, he bequeathed his estate to his widow. He declares himself to have been under no obligation whatever to any of his

---

* Chalmers' Introduction, i. 164. † Beverley, B. i. 79.
‡ T. M.'s Account.

kindred except his sister, Mrs. Jane Davies, (of whom he appears to have been fond,) and his brother, Lord Berkley. Sir William married the widow of Samuel Stephens, of Warwick County, Virginia. She, after Sir William's death, was sued by William Drummond's widow for trespass, in taking from her land a quantity of corn, and in spite of a strenuous defence, a verdict was found against the defendant. In 1680 she intermarried with Colonel Philip Ludwell, of Rich Neck, but still retained the title of "Dame (or Lady) Frances Berkley."

Samuel Stephens was the son of Dame Elizabeth Harvey (widow of Sir John Harvey) by a former marriage.*

It does not appear when Colonel William Clayborne, first of the name in Virginia, died, or where he was buried, but probably in the County of New Kent. There is a novel entitled "Clayborne the Rebel."†

Colonel William Clayborne, Jr., eldest son of the above mentioned, was probably the one appointed (1676) to command a fort at Indiantown Landing, in New Kent, together with Major Lyddal,‡ as the father was probably then too old for that post. Some suppose also that it was the son that sat on the trial of the rebels. A certificate of the valor of William Clayborne, Jr., is recorded in King William County Court-house, signed by Sir William Berkley, dated in March, 1677, attested by Nathaniel Bacon, Sir Philip Ludwell, Ralph Wormley, and Richard Lee.

Lieutenant-Colonel Thomas Clayborne, only brother of William Clayborne, Jr., lies buried not far from West Point, in King William County. He was killed by an Indian arrow which wounded him in the foot. It appears that each of the sons of Secretary Clayborne had a son named Thomas. Colonel Thomas Clayborne, son of Captain Thomas Clayborne, is said to have married three times, and to have been father of twenty-seven children. One of his daughters married a General Phillips of the British army, and is said to have been the mother of Colonel Ralph Phillips, of the British army, who fell at Waterloo, and of the

---

* Mass. Gen. and Antiq. Register for 1847, p. 348.
† By William H. Carpenter, Esq., of Maryland. Published in 1846.
‡ Hening, ii. 526.

distinguished Irish orator who died recently. Another son, William Clayborne, married a Miss Leigh, of Virginia, and was father of William Charles Cole Clayborne, Governor of Louisiana, and of General Ferdinand Leigh Clayborne, late of Mississippi. He assisted General Jackson in planning the battle of New Orleans. The widow of this Governor Clayborne married John R. Grymes, Esq., the eminent New Orleans lawyer. And a daughter of the governor married John H. B. Latrobe, Esq., of Baltimore.

Colonel Augustine Clayborne, son of Colonel Thomas Clayborne, was appointed clerk of Sussex County Court in the year 1754, by William Adair, secretary of the colony. His son, Buller Clayborne, was aid-de-camp to General Lincoln, and is said to have received a wound while interposing himself between the general and a party of British soldiers. Mary Herbert, a sister of Buller Clayborne, married an uncle of General William Henry Harrison. Herbert Clayborne, eldest son of Colonel Augustine Clayborne, married Mary, daughter of Buller Herbert, of Puddledock, near Petersburg. Puddledock is the name of a street in London. Herbert Augustine Clayborne was second son of Herbert Clayborne, of Elson Green, King William County, and Mary Burnet, eldest daughter of William Burnet Browne, of Elson Green, and before of Salem, Massachusetts.

The Honorable William Browne, of Massachusetts, married Mary Burnet, daughter of William Burnet, (Governor of New York and of Massachusetts,) and Mary, daughter of Dean Stanhope, of Canterbury. William Burnet was eldest son of Gilbert Burnet, Bishop of Salisbury, and Mrs. Mary Scott, his second wife. Thus it appears that Herbert Clayborne married a descendant of Bishop Burnet.

CHAPTER XXXIX.

1677-1681.

Failure of the Charter—Sir William Berkley's Proclamation revoked—Ludwell's Quarrel with Jeffreys—Jeffreys dying is succeeded by Sir Henry Chicheley—Culpepper, Governor-in-Chief, arrives—His Administration—He returns to England by way of Boston.

THE agents of Virginia, in 1675, had strenuously solicited the grant of a new charter, and their efforts, though long fruitless, seemed at length about to be crowned with success, when the news of Bacon's rebellion furnished the government with a new pretext for violating its engagements. By the report of the committee for plantations, adopted by the king in council, and twice ordered to be passed into a new charter under the great seal, it was provided, "that no imposition or taxes shall be laid or imposed upon the inhabitants and proprietors there, but by the common consent of the governor, council, and burgesses, as hath been heretofore used," reserving, however, to parliament the right to lay duties upon commodities shipped from the colony. The news of the rebellion frustrated this scheme; the promised charter slept in the Hamper* office; and the one actually sent afterwards was meagre and unsatisfactory. Colonel Jeffreys, successor to Berkley, effected a treaty of peace with the Indians, each town agreeing to pay three arrows for their land, and twenty beaver skins for protection, every year. He convened an assembly at the house of Captain Otho Thorpe, at Middle Plantation, in October, 1677, being the twenty-ninth year of Charles the Second. William Traverse was speaker, and Robert Beverley clerk. The session lasted for one month. According to instructions given to Sir William Berkley, dated in November, 1676, the governor was no longer obliged to call an assembly yearly, but only once in two years, and the session was limited

---

* Hening, ii. 531; Hamper, *i.e.* Hanaper.

to fourteen days, unless the governor should see good cause to continue it beyond that time; and the members of the assembly were to be elected only by freeholders. During this session regulations were adopted for the Indian trade, and fairs appointed for the sale of Indian commodities; but the natives being suspicious of innovations, these provisions soon became obsolete.

In 1677 Colonel Nathaniel Bacon, Sr., by a warrant from the treasury in England, was appointed auditor of the public accounts. At this time Colonel Norwood was treasurer, but the governor and council, from motives of economy, united his office with that of auditor.

It has before been mentioned that the king, by proclamation in 1677, revoked and abrogated Sir William Berkley's proclamation of February of the same year, as containing "an exception and exclusion from pardon of divers and sundry persons in his said proclamation named, for which he hath no ground or authority from our foresaid proclamation, the same being free and without exception of any person besides the said Nathaniel Bacon, who should submit themselves according to the tenor of our said proclamation."*

This appears to be unjust to the governor; for the words of the king's proclamation of October are: "And we do by these presents give and grant full power and authority to you, our said governor, for us and in our name to pardon, release, and forgive unto all such our subjects (other than the said Nathaniel Bacon) as you shall think fit and convenient for our service, all treasons, felonies," etc., evidently investing the governor with discretionary powers. The capitulation agreed upon with Ingram and Walklet, at West Point, appears to have been violated by Governor Berkley and the assembly. Colonel Philip Ludwell, alleging that he had suffered loss by Walklet's incursions, sued him in New Kent for damages. The defendant appealing to Jeffreys, he granted him a protection. Whereupon, Ludwell declared that "the governor, Jeffreys, was a worse rebel than Bacon, for he had broke

---

* The direction of this proclamation is as follows: "To our trusty and well-beloved Herbert Jeffreys, Esq., Lieutenant-Governor, and the council of our colony and plantation of Virginia in the West Indies."

the laws of the country, which Bacon never did; that he was perjured in delaying or preventing the execution of the laws, contrary to his oath of governor; that he was not worth a groat in England; and that if every pitiful little fellow with a periwig that came in governor to this country had liberty to make the laws, as this had done, his children, nor no man's else, could be safe in the title or estate left them." Jeffreys having laid these charges and criminations before the council, they submitted the case to a jury who found Ludwell guilty. The matter was referred to the king in council; and in the mean while the accused was compelled to give security in the penalty of a thousand pounds, to abide the determination of the case, and five hundred for his good behavior to the governor.

Westmoreland was the only county that declared that it had no grievances to complain of, and the sincerity of this declaration may well be doubted. Accomac claimed as a reward for her loyalty an exemption from taxation for a period of twenty years. A letter, bearing date December the 27th, 1677, addressed by the king to Jeffreys, informed him that Lord Culpepper had been appointed governor, but that while he (Jeffreys) continued to perform the duties of the office, he should be no loser, and stating the arrangement which had been made as to the payment of their salaries. Jeffreys dying in December, 1678, was succeeded by the aged Sir Henry Chicheley, deputy governor, who entered upon the duties on the thirteenth of that month, his commission being dated February 28th, 1674.

Thomas, Lord Culpepper, Baron of Thorsway, had been appointed in July, 1675, governor of Virginia for life—an able, but artful and covetous man.* He had been one of the commissioners for plantations some years before. He was disposed to look upon his office as a sinecure, but being reproved in December, 1679, by the king for remaining so long in England, he came over to the colony in 1680, and was sworn into office on the tenth of May. He found Virginia tranquil. He brought over several bills ready draughted in England to be passed by the assembly,

---

* Account of Va. in Mass. Hist. Coll., first series, v. 142.

it being "intended to introduce here the modes of Ireland."*
His lordship being invested with full powers of pardon, found it the more easy to obtain from the people whatever he asked. After procuring the enactment of several popular acts, including one of indemnity and oblivion, he managed to have the impost of two shillings on every hogshead of tobacco made perpetual, and instead of being accounted for to the assembly, as formerly, to be disposed of as his majesty might think fit. Culpepper, notwithstanding the impoverished condition of the colony, contrived to enlarge his salary from one thousand pounds to upwards of two thousand, besides perquisites amounting to eight hundred more. After the rebellion, the governor was empowered to suspend a councillor from his place. It was also ordered, that in case of the death or removal of the governor, the president, or oldest member of the council, with the assistance of five members of that body, should administer the government until another appointment should be made by the crown.†

In the year 1680 Charles the Second granted to William Blathwayt the place of surveyor and auditor-general of all his revenues in America, with a salary of five hundred pounds to be paid out of the same, Virginia's share of the salary being one hundred pounds.

In August of this year, Lord Culpepper returned to England, by way of Boston, in the ship "Betty," belonging to Jervis, who married the widow of Nathaniel Bacon, Jr., (a cousin of Culpepper,) Jervis being also a passenger. Elizabeth, or Betty, was the Christian name of Bacon's widow. The vessel having run aground in the night, his lordship landed on the wild New England shore, one hundred and thirty miles from Boston, with two servants, each carrying a gun, and made his way twenty miles to Sandwich, where he was furnished with horses and a guide, and so reached Boston, where the Betty arrived ten days thereafter. In a letter, dated September the twentieth, addressed to his sister, he mentions that he has with him, "John Polyn, the cook, the

---

* Chalmers' Introduction, i. 164.
† In 1678 the vestry at Middle Plantation determined to erect a brick church, the former one being of wood.

page, the great footman, and the little one that embroiders." The Betty conveyed soldiers, servants, plate, goods, and furniture. Culpepper was received at Boston by twelve companies of militia; and was well pleased with the place, "finding no difference between it and Old England, but only want of company."*

Virginia now enjoyed repose, and large crops of tobacco were raised, and the price again fell to a low ebb. The discontents of the planters were aggravated by the act "for cohabitation and encouragement of trade and manufacture," restricting vessels to certain prescribed ports where the government desired to establish towns.

In the year 1680 Charleston was founded, the metropolis of the infant colony of South Carolina. By the grant of Pennsylvania, made by Charles the Second to William Penn, dated in March, 1681, Virginia lost another large portion of her territory.

---

* Va. Hist. Reg., iii. 189.

CHAPTER XL.

1681-1683.

Statistics of Virginia—Colonial Revenue—Courts of Law—Ecclesiastical Affairs—Militia—Indians—Negroes—Riotous cutting up of Tobacco-plants—Culpepper returns—Declaration of Assembly expunged—The Governor alters the Value of Coin by Proclamation.

From a statistical account of Virginia, as reported by Culpepper to the committee of the colonies, in 1681, it appears that there were at that time forty-one burgesses, being two from each of twenty counties, and one from Jamestown. The colonial revenue consisted—First, of parish levies, "commonly managed by sly cheating fellows, that combine to cheat the public." Secondly, public levies raised by act of assembly, both derived from tithables or working hands, of which there were about fourteen thousand. The cost of collecting this part of the revenue was estimated at not less than twenty per centum. Thirdly, two shillings per hogshead on tobacco exported, which, together with some tonnage duties, amounted to three thousand pounds a year. The county courts held three sessions in the year, an appeal lying to the governor and council, and from them, in actions of three hundred pounds sterling value, to his majesty; in causes of less consequence, to the assembly.

The ecclesiastical affairs of the colony were subject to the control of the governor, who granted probates of wills, and had the right of presentation to all livings, the ordinary value of which was sixty pounds per annum; but at that particular time, owing to the impoverishment of the country and the low price of tobacco, not worth half that sum. The number of livings was seventy-six. Lord Culpepper adds: "And the parishes paying the ministers themselves, have used to claim the right of presentation, (or rather of not paying,) whether the governor will or not, which must not be allowed, and yet must be managed with great caution." There was no fort in Virginia defensible against a European enemy, nor any security for ships against a superior sea force. There were perhaps fifteen thousand fighting men in the country.*

His lordship describes the north part of Carolina as "the refuge of our renegades, and till in better order, dangerous to us." Yet it is certain that some of the early settlers of this part of North Carolina were of exemplary character, and were driven from Virginia by intolerance and persecution. According to his lordship, "Maryland is now in a ferment, and not only troubled with our disease, poverty, but in a great danger of falling to pieces." The colony of Virginia was at peace with the Indians; but long experience had taught, in regard to that treacherous race, that when there was the least suspicion then was there the greatest danger. But the most ruinous evil that afflicted the colony was the extreme low price of the sole commodity, tobacco. "For the market is overstocked, and every crop overstocks it more. Our thriving is our undoing, and our buying of blacks hath extremely contributed thereto by making more tobacco."†

Emancipated Indian or negro slaves were prohibited from buying Christian servants, but were allowed to buy those of their own nation. Negro children imported had their ages recorded by the court, and became tithable at the age of twelve years. In June, 1680, an act was passed for preventing an insurrection of the negro slaves, and it was ordered that it should be published twice a year at the county courts of the parish churches.‡ Negroes were not allowed to remain on another plantation more than four hours without leave of the owner or overseer.

After "his excellency," Lord Culpepper, went away from Virginia in August, 1680, leaving Sir Henry Chicheley deputy governor, tranquillity prevailed until the time for shipping tobacco in the following year, when the trade was greatly obstructed by the act for establishing towns, which required vessels to be laden at certain specified places. The act being found impracticable, was disobeyed, and much disturbance ensued. In compli-

---

* The number of half-armed train-bands, in 1680, were 7268 foot and 1300 horse—total, 8568.—*Chalmers' Annals*, 357.

† Chalmers' Annals, 355.   ‡ Hening, ii. 481, 492.

ance with the petitions of several dissatisfied counties, an assembly was called together in April, 1682, by Sir Henry Chicheley, without the consent of the council. The session being occupied in agitating debates, the body was dissolved, and another summoned, according to an order just received from the crown, to meet in November, 1682, by which time Culpepper was commanded to return to Virginia. The disaffected in the petitioning counties, Gloucester, New Kent, and Middlesex, in May proceeded riotously to cut up the tobacco-plants in the beds, especially the sweet-scented, which was produced nowhere else. To put a stop to this outbreak, the deputy governor issued sundry proclamations.*

Lord Culpepper having arrived, the assembly met shortly afterwards. He demanded of the council an account of their administration during his absence, and it was rendered. In his address to the assembly, he enlarged upon the king's generous and undeserved concessions to the colony; he announced the king's high displeasure at the declaration made by them that the seizing of their records by the king's commissioners was an unwarrantable violation of their privileges, and, in the king's name, ordered the same to be expunged from the journal of the house, and proposed to them a bill asserting the right of the king and his officers to call for all their records and journals whenever they should think it necessary for the public service.

The governor claiming authority to raise the value of the coin, the assembly warmly opposed it, as a dangerous encroachment on their constitutional rights; and a bill was brought in for regulating the value of coins, which was interrupted by the governor, who claimed that power as belonging to the royal prerogative. He issued a proclamation, in 1683, raising the value of crowns, rix dollars, and pieces of eight, from five to six shillings, half pieces to three shillings, quarter pieces to eighteen pence, and the New England coin to one shilling, declaring money at this rate a lawful tender, except for the duty of two shillings a hogshead on tobacco, the quit-rents, and other duties payable to his majesty, and for debts contracted for bills of exchange. His own salary

---

* Hening, ii. 561.

and the king's revenues were, in this way, in a period of distress, exempted from the operation of the act, a proceeding characteristic of the reign of Charles the Second, in which official energy was mainly exhibited in measures of injustice and extortion.

The ringleaders in the plant cutting were arrested, and some of them hanged upon a charge of treason; and this, together with the enactment of a riot act, and making the offence high treason, put a stop to the practice.*

---

* Chalmers' Annals, 340; Hening, iii. 10.

CHAPTER XLI.

1683-1688.

Persecution of Robert Beverley—Plots and Executions in England—Culpepper returns to England—Spencer, President—Culpepper is displaced—Succeeded by Effingham—Beverley, found guilty, asks Pardon, and is released—Miscellaneous Affairs—Death of Charles the Second—Succeeded by James the Second—Beverley again Clerk—Duke of Monmouth beheaded—Adherents of Monmouth sent Prisoners to Virginia—Instructions respecting them—Death of Robert Beverley—Despotism of James the Second—Servile Insurrection prevented—Virginia refuses to contribute to the erection of Forts in New York—Commotions in Virginia—Effingham's Corruption and Tyranny—He embarks for England—Ludwell dispatched to lay Virginia's Grievances before the Government—Abdication of James the Second.

THE vengeance of the government fell heavily upon Major Robert Beverley, clerk of the house of burgesses, as the chief instigator of these disturbances. He had incurred the displeasure of the governor and council by refusing to deliver up to them copies of the legislative journals, without permission of the house. Beverley had rendered important services in suppressing Bacon's rebellion, and had won the special favor of Sir William Berkley; but as circumstances change, men change with them, and now by a steady adherence to his duty to the assembly, he drew down upon his head unrelenting persecution. In the month of May, 1682, he was committed a close prisoner on board the ship Duke of York, lying in the Rappahannock.* Ralph Wormley, Matthew Kemp, and Christopher Wormley, were directed to seize the records in Beverley's possession, and to break open doors if necessary. He complained, in a note addressed to the captain, and claimed the rights of a freeborn Englishman. He was transferred from the Duke of York to Captain Jeffries, commander of the Concord, and a guard set over him. He was next sent on board of Colonel Custis's sloop, to be taken

---

* Hening, iii. 540.

(335)

to Northampton. Escaping from the custody of the sheriff of York, the prisoner was retaken at his own house in Middlesex, and sent to Northampton, on the Eastern Shore. Some months after, he applied for a writ of *habeas corpus*, which was refused; and in a short time, being again found at large, he was remanded to Northampton. In January, 1683, new charges were brought against him: First, that he had broken open letters addressed to the secretary's office; Secondly, that he had made up the journal, and inserted his majesty's letter therein, notwithstanding it had first been presented at the time of the prorogation; Thirdly, that in 1682 he had refused copies of the journal to the governor and council, saying "he might not do it without leave of his masters."

In the year 1680, England was agitated and alarmed with the "Popish plot;" and the Earl of Stafford and divers others were executed on the information of Oates and other witnesses. In July, 1683, Lord Russell was beheaded on a charge of treason, and others suffered the same fate as being implicated in what was styled the "Protestant plot."

Culpepper, after staying about a year in Virginia, returned to England, leaving his kinsman, secretary Nicholas Spencer, president. Thus, again, quitting the colony in violation of his orders, he was arrested immediately on his arrival; and having received presents from the assembly, contrary to his instructions, a jury of Middlesex found that he had forfeited his commission. This example having shown that he who acts under independent authority will seldom obey even reasonable commands, no more governors were appointed for life.* Beverley† gives a different account: "The next year, being 1684, upon the Lord Culpepper refusing to return, Francis, Lord Howard of Effingham, was sent over governor." But Chalmers, having access to the records of the English government, appears to be the better authority.

Lord Culpepper having it in view, as was said, to purchase the propriety of the Northern Neck, lying between the Rappahannock and the Potomac, in order to further his design, had fomented a dispute between the house of burgesses and the coun-

---

* Chalmers' Annals, 345. † Beverley, B. i. 89.

cil; and the quarrel running high, his lordship procured from the king instructions to abolish appeals from the general court to the assembly, and transfer them to the crown. However, Culpepper being a man of strong judgment, introduced some salutary amendments to the laws. During his time, instead of fixed garrisons, rangers were employed in guarding the frontier. In October died Lieutenant-Colonel Thomas Clayborne, (son of Colonel William Clayborne,) mortally wounded in an engagement with the Indians, which took place near West Point, at the head of York River; he lies buried on the same spot, in compliance with his dying request. The son appears to have inherited the spirit of his father.

Lord Culpepper was succeeded by Francis, Lord Howard of Effingham, whose appointment was the last act of Charles the Second in relation to the colony of Virginia. Lord Effingham was appointed in August, 1683, the thirty-fifth year of the king's reign, commissioned in September, and arriving in Virginia during February, 1684, entered upon the duties of the office in April. The assembly met on the following day. Acts were passed to prevent plant cutting, and preserve the peace; to supply the inhabitants with arms and ammunition; to repeal the act for encouragement of domestic manufactures; to provide for the better defence of the colony; laying for the first time an impost on liquors imported from other English plantations; exempting such as were imported by Virginians for their own use, and in their own vessels. The burgesses, in behalf of the inhabitants of the Northern Neck, then called Potomac Neck, prayed the governor to secure them by patent in their titles to their lands, which had been invaded by Culpepper's charter. The governor replied that he was expecting a favorable decision on the matter from the king.

About this time the name of Zach. Taylor, a surveyor, is mentioned, an ancestor of General Zachary Taylor, some time President of the United States.*

In May, 1684, Robert Beverley was found guilty of high mis-

---

* One of the James River merchant-vessels mentioned by the first William Byrd, was called the "Zach. Taylor."

demeanors, but judgment being respited, and the prisoner asking pardon on his bended knees, was released, upon giving security for his good behavior. His counsel was William Fitzhugh, of Stafford County, a lawyer of reputation, and a planter. Beverley was charged with having led the people to believe that there would be a "cessation" of the tobacco crop in 1680, and such appears to have been the general impression in the summer of that year.* The abject terms in which he now sued for pardon form a singular contrast to his former constancy; and it is curious to find the loyal Beverley, the strenuous partizan of Berkley, now the victim of the tyranny which he had formerly defended with so much energy and success.

On the twentieth day of May, of this year, Lord Baltimore was at Jamestown on a visit to the governor, with a view of embarking there for England.

Owing to the incursions of the Five Nations upon the frontiers of Virginia, it was deemed expedient to treat with them through the governor of New York; and for this purpose Lord Effingham, Governor of Virginia, leaving the administration in the hands of Colonel Bacon, of the council, and accompanied by two councillors, sailed, June the twenty-third, in the "Quaker Ketch," to New York, and thence repaired to Albany, in July. There he met Governor Dongan, of New York, the agent of Massachusetts, the magistrates of Albany, and the chiefs of the warlike Mohawks, Oneidas, Onondagos, and Cayugas. The tomahawk was buried, the chain of friendship brightened, and the tree of peace planted. It was during this year that the charter of Massachusetts was dissolved by a writ of *quo warranto*. In the same year Talbot, a kinsman of the Calverts, and a member of the Maryland Council, killed, in a private rencontre, Rousby, the collector of the customs for that province; he was tried in Virginia, and convicted, but subsequently pardoned by James the Second.

Evelyn† says: "I can never forget the inexpressible luxury, and profaneness, gaming, and all dissoluteness, and, as it were, total forgetfulness of God, (it being Sunday evening,) which this

---

* Va. Hist. Reg., i. 166. † Diary, ii. 211.

day se'nnight I was witness of, the king sitting and toying with his concubines, Portsmouth, Cleveland, and Mazarine, etc., a French boy singing love-songs in that glorious gallery, while about twenty of the great courtiers, and other dissolute persons, were at basset round a large table, a bank of at least two thousand pounds in gold before them; upon which two gentlemen, who were with me, made reflections with astonishment. Six days after, all was in the dust."

Rochester, in his epigram, described Charles the Second as one

> Who never said a foolish thing, and never did a wise one.

But it is much easier to discover the foolish things that he did, than the wise things that he said. He was good-natured, free from vindictiveness, and had some appreciation of science.

The succession of James the Second to the throne was proclaimed in the Ancient Dominion of Virginia "with extraordinary joy." The enthusiasm of their loyalty was soon lowered, for the assembly meeting on the 1st day of October, 1685, and warmly resisting the negative power claimed by the governor, was prorogued on the same day to the second of November following. Robert Beverley was again clerk. Strong resolutions, complaining of the governor's veto, were passed. After sitting for some time this and other bills were presented to him for his signature, which he refused to give, and appearing suddenly in the house prorogued it again to the 20th of October, 1686.

The Duke of Monmouth, an illegitimate son of Charles the Second, failing in a rash insurrection, was beheaded, July the fourteenth of this year.

The first parliament of the new reign laid an impost on tobacco; the planters, in abject terms, supplicated James to suspend the duty imposed on their staple; but he refused to comply. They also took measures to encourage domestic manufactures, which were disapproved of by the lords of the committee of colonies, as contrary to the acts of navigation. Nevertheless, on the reception of the news of the defeat of the Duke of Monmouth, the Virginians sent a congratulatory address to the king.

A number of the prisoners taken with Monmouth, and who had escaped the cruelty of Jeffreys, were sent to Virginia; and King

James instructed Effingham on this occasion in the following letter:*

"RIGHT TRUSTY AND WELL-BELOVED,—We greet you well. As it has pleased God to deliver into our hands such of our rebellious subjects as have taken up arms against us, for which traitorous practices some of them have suffered death according to law; so we have been graciously pleased to extend our mercy to many others by ordering their transportation to several parts of our dominions in America, where they are to be kept as servants to the inhabitants of the same; and to the end their punishment may in some measure answer their crimes, we do think fit hereby to signify our pleasure unto you, our governor and council of Virginia, that you take all necessary care that such convicted persons as were guilty of the late rebellion, that shall arrive within that our colony, whose names are hereunto annexed,† be kept there, and continue to serve their masters for the space of ten years at least. And that they be not permitted in any manner to redeem themselves by money or otherwise until that term be fully expired. And for the better effecting hereof, you are to frame and propose a bill to the assembly of that our colony, with such provisions and clauses as shall be requisite for this purpose, to which you, our governor, are to give your assent, and to transmit the same unto us for our royal confirmation. Wherein expecting a ready compliance, we bid you heartily farewell. Given at our court at Whitehall, the 4th of October, 1685, in the first year of our reign.

"SUNDERLAND."

Virginia made no law conformable to the requisitions of the king.

James the Second, strongly resenting the too democratical proceedings of the Virginia assembly, ordered their dissolution, and that Robert Beverley, as chief promoter of these disputes, should be disfranchised and prosecuted,‡ and directed that in future the appointment of the clerk of the house of burgesses should be

---

* Chalmers' Annals, 358
† The list is still preserved in the London state-paper office.
‡ Hening, iii. 40.

made by the governor. Several persons were punished about this time for seditious and treasonable conduct. In May, 1687, the assembly was dissolved. In the spring of this year Robert Beverley died—the victim of tyranny and martyr of constitutional liberty: long a distinguished loyalist, he lived to become still more distinguished as a patriot. It is thus in human inconsistency that extremes meet.

The English merchants engaged in the tobacco trade, in August, 1687, complained to the committee of the colonies of the mischiefs consequent upon the exportation of tobacco in bulk; and the committee advised the assembly to prohibit this practice. The assembly refused compliance; but the regulation was subsequently established by parliament. A meditated insurrection of the blacks was discovered in the Northern Neck just in time to prevent its explosion. In November a message had been received from the Governor of New York, communicating the king's instructions to him to build forts for the defence of that colony, and the king's desire that Virginia should contribute to that object, as being for the common defence of the colonies. This project of James, it was suspected, had its origin in his own proprietary interest in New York. The Virginians replied, that the Indians might invade Virginia without passing within a hundred miles of those forts, and the contribution was refused. In December, William Byrd succeeded Colonel Nathaniel Bacon, Sr., as auditor of the accounts of his majesty's revenue in Virginia; he continued to hold that place for seventeen years. His MS. accounts are still preserved.

James the Second, influenced by the counsels and the gold of France, and in violation of the most solemn pledges made to the parliament when he ascended the throne, showed himself incorrigibly bent upon introducing absolute government and establishing the Roman Catholic religion in England. In Virginia the council displayed, as usual, servility to power. Upon the dissolution of the assembly, the colony was agitated with apprehensions and alarm. Rumors were circulated of terrible plots, now of the Papists, then of the Indians. The County of Stafford was inflamed by the bold harangues of John Waugh, a preacher of the established church, and three councillors were dispatched to allay the commotions. Part of Rappahannock County was in arms. Colonel John Scarburgh, of the Eastern Shore, was prosecuted for saying to the governor that "his majesty King James would wear out the Church of England, for that when there were any vacant offices he supplied them with men of a different persuasion." Scarburgh was discharged by the council. Others were prosecuted and imprisoned; and James Collins was put in irons for treasonable words uttered against the king.

Effingham, no less avaricious and unscrupulous than his predecessor Culpepper, by his extortions and usurpations aroused a general spirit of indignation. He prorogued and dissolved the assembly; he erected a new court of chancery, making himself a petty lord chancellor; he multiplied fees, and stooped to share them with the clerks, and silenced the victims of his extortions by arbitrary imprisonment. The house of burgesses, preparing to petition the king against the new invention of a seal, by which his lordship extracted from the country one hundred thousand pounds of tobacco per annum of extraordinary fees and perquisites, and the governor getting wind of it, sent for them, and they, knowing that his object was to dissolve them, completed the petition, signed it, and ordered their clerk and one of their members to transmit it to Whitehall for the king. But instead of being delivered to his majesty, the original petition was sent back from England to the governor, with an account of the manner in which it had been transmitted. In consequence whereof, Colonel Thomas Milner, being a surveyor and clerk of the house, was removed from those offices, and the burgess being a lawyer, was prohibited from practising at the bar.*

At length, the complaints of the Virginians having reached England, Effingham embarked, in 1688, for that country, and the assembly dispatched Colonel Ludwell to lay their grievances before the government; but before they reached the mother country, the revolution had taken place, and James the Second† had closed a short and inglorious reign, spent in preposterous invasions of civil and religious liberty, by abdicating the crown.

---

* Account of Virginia, in Mass. Hist. Coll., first series.
† Chalmers' Annals, 347.

CHAPTER XLII.

1688-1696.

Accession of William and Mary—Proclaimed in Virginia—The House of Stuart—President Bacon—Colonel Francis Nicholson, Lieutenant-Governor—The Rev. James Blair, Commissary—College of William and Mary chartered—Its Endowment, Objects, Professorships—Death of John Page—Nicholson succeeded by Andros—Post-office—Death of Queen Mary—William the Third—Board of Trade.

WILLIAM, PRINCE OF ORANGE, landed at Torbay in November, 1688, and he and Mary were proclaimed king and queen on the 13th day of February, 1689. The coronation took place on the eleventh day of April. They had been for several months seated on the throne before they were proclaimed in Virginia. The delay was owing to the reiterated pledges of fealty made by the council to James, and from an apprehension that he might be restored to the kingdom. Some of the Virginians insisted that, as there was no king in England, so there was also an interregnum in the government of the colony. At length, in compliance with the repeated commands of the privy council, William and Mary were proclaimed, at James City, in April, 1689, Lord and Lady of Virginia. This glorious event, with the circumstances connected with it, was duly announced to the lords commissioners of plantations, in a letter, dated on the twenty-ninth of that month, by Nicholas Spencer, secretary of state.

The accession of the Prince of Orange dispelled the clouds of discontent and alarm, and inspired the people of the colony with sincere joy. For about seventy years Virginia had been subject to the house of Stuart, and there was little in the retrospect to awaken regret at their downfall. They had cramped trade by monopolies and restrictions, lavished vast bodies of land on their profligate minions, and often entrusted the reigns of power to incompetent, corrupt, and tyrannical governors. The dynasty of the Stuarts fell buried in the ruins of misused power.

When the last of the Stuart governors, Lord Howard of Effingham, returned to England, he had left the administration in the hands of Colonel Nathaniel Bacon, Sr., president of the council. Upon the accession of William and Mary, England being on the eve of a war with France, the president and council of Virginia were directed by the Duke of Shrewsbury to put the colony in a posture of defence.

Colonel Philip Ludwell, who had been sent out as an agent of the colony to prefer complaints against Lord Howard of Effingham before the privy council, now at length obtained a decision in some points rather favorable to the colony, but the question of prerogative was determined in favor of the crown, and it was declared that an act of 1680 *was* revived by the king's disallowing the act of repeal.

Bacon's administration was short; he had now obtained an advanced age. In his time the project of a college was renewed, but not carried into effect. President Bacon resided in York County. He married Elizabeth, daughter of Richard Kingsmill, Esq., of James City County. Leaving no issue, by his will he bequeathed his estates to his niece, Abigail Burwell, and his "riding horse, Watt, to Lady Berkley," at that time wife of Colonel Philip Ludwell. President Bacon died on the 16th of March, 1692, in the seventy-third year of his age, and lies buries on King's Creek,* as does also Elizabeth, his wife, who died in the year 1691, aged sixty-seven.† The name of the wife of Nathaniel Bacon, Jr., was likewise Elizabeth.

In the year 1690 Lord Effingham, reluctant to revisit a province where he was so unacceptable, being still absent from Virginia on the plea of ill health, Francis Nicholson, who had been driven from New York by a popular outbreak, came over as lieutenant-governor. He found the colony ready for revolt. The people were indignant at seeing Effingham still retained in the office of governor-in-chief, believing that Nicholson would become his tool. The revolution in England seemed as yet productive of no amendment in the colonial administration. Nicholson, however, now

---

* James City Records, cited in "Farmer's Register" for 1839, p. 407.

† Dr. Williamson, of Williamsburg, obligingly sent me the inscription and the coat of arms, as copied by him from her tombstone, which was ploughed up on the banks of Queen's Creek.

courted popularity; he instituted athletic games, and offered prizes to those who should excel in riding, running, shooting, wrestling, and fencing. The last alone could need any encouragement in such a country as Virginia. He proposed the establishment of a post-office, and recommended the erection of a college, but refused to call an assembly to further the scheme, being under obligations to Effingham to stave off assemblies as long as possible, for fear of complaints being renewed against his arbitrary administration.* Nevertheless, Nicholson and the council headed a private subscription, and twenty-five hundred pounds were raised, part of this sum being contributed by some London merchants. The new governor made a progress through the colony, mingling freely with the people, and he carried his indulgence to the common people so far as frequently to suffer them to enter the room where he was entertaining company at dinner, and diverted himself with their scrambling among one another and carrying off the viands from the table—like Sancho Panza's on the Island of Barataria. There is but one step from the courtier to the demagogue.

Virginia felt the embarrassments which war had brought upon England, and acts were passed for encouraging domestic manufactures, for which Nicholson found an apology in the scanty supplies imported. The assembly congratulated the Prince of Orange on his accession, and thanking him for his present of warlike stores, begged for further favors of the royal bounty.

When Colonel Nicholson entered on the duties of governor, the Rev. James Blair, a native of Scotland, newly appointed commissary of Virginia, assumed the supervision of the churches of the colony. He came over to this country in 1685, and settled in the County of Henrico, where he remained till 1694, when he removed to Jamestown. The functions of commissary, who was a deputy of the Bishop of London, had been previously discharged by the Rev. Mr. Temple, but he was not regularly commissioned.

At the instance of the Rev. Mr. Blair, in 1691 the assembly entered heartily into the scheme of a college, and in the same year he was dispatched with an address to their majesties, King William and Queen Mary, soliciting a charter.

---

* Beverley, B. i. 92.

The first assembly under the new dynasty met at James City, in April, 1691, being the third year of their reign. Acts were passed for putting the colony in a better state of defence, for reducing the poll tax, and laying a duty on liquors, and for appointing a treasurer. Colonel Edward Hill was appointed to that office. The same assembly met again by prorogation, in April of the ensuing year.

Commissary Blair was graciously received at court, and in February, 1692, their majesties granted the charter.* The college was named in honor of their majesties. The king gave about two thousand pounds toward the building, out of the quit-rents. Seymour, the English attorney-general, having received the royal commands to prepare the charter of the college, which was to be accompanied with a grant of money, remonstrated against this liberality, urging that the nation was engaged in an expensive war; that the money was wanted for better purposes, and that he did not see the slightest occasion for a college in Virginia. The Rev. Mr. Blair, in reply, represented to him that its intention was to educate and qualify young men to be ministers of the gospel; and begged Mr. Attorney would consider that the people of Virginia had souls to be saved as well as the people of England. "Souls!" exclaimed the imperious Seymour; "damn your souls!—make tobacco."†

The site selected for the college was in the Middle Plantation Old Fields, near the church. The college was endowed by the crown with twenty thousand acres of land in Pamunkey Neck, and on the south side of Blackwater Swamp; the patronage of the office of surveyor-general; together with the revenue arising from a duty of one penny a pound on all tobacco exported from Virginia and Maryland to the other plantations, the nett pro-

---

* The following gentlemen, nominated by the assembly, were constituted a senate, or board of trustees: Francis Nicholson, lieutenant-governor of the colony; William Cole, Ralph Wormley, William Byrd, Esquires, of the council; John Leare, James Blair, John Farnifold, Stephen Fauce, and Samuel Gray, clerks (clergymen;) Thomas Milner, Christopher Robinson, Charles Scarburgh, John Smith, Benjamin Harrison, Miles Cary, Henry Hartwell, William Randolph, and Matthew Page, gentlemen and burgesses.

† Franklin's Correspondence.

ceeds being two hundred pounds. The college was also allowed to return a burgess to the assembly. The assembly afterwards added to the revenue a duty on skins and furs.* Dr. Blair was the first president of the college, being appointed under the charter to hold the office for life. The plan of the building was the composition of Sir Christopher Wren. The objects proposed by the establishment of the college were declared to be the furnishing of a seminary for the ministers of the gospel, and that the youth may be piously educated in good letters and manners, and that the Christian faith should be propagated among the Western Indians.† In addition to the five professorships of Greek and Latin, the mathematics, moral philosophy, and two of divinity provided for by the charter, a sixth, called the Brafferton, from an estate in England which secured the endowment, had been annexed by the celebrated Robert Boyle, for the instruction and conversion of the Indians.

The trustees met with many difficulties in their undertaking during the administration of Governor Andros, and were involved in a troublesome controversy concerning the lands appropriated to the institution, with Secretary Wormley, the most influential man in the colony, next to the governor.

In January, 1692, died John Page, of Rosewell, of the king's council in the colony, aged sixty—a learned and pious man; first of the name in Virginia, and father of the Honorable Colonel Matthew Page, who was also of the council. A religious work, entitled "A Deed of Gift for my Son," by this John Page, has been published.

During the same year Governor Nicholson was succeeded by Sir Edmund Andros, whose high-handed course had rendered him so odious to the people of New England that they had lately imprisoned him. He was, nevertheless, kindly received by the Virginians, whose solicitations to King William for warlike stores he had promoted. He soon gave offence by ordering ships to cruise against vessels engaged in contraband trade. In the year 1693 an act was passed for the organizing of a post-office esta-

---

* Hening, iii. 123, 241, 356: Catalogue of William and Mary College.

† Anderson's Hist. of Church of England in the Colonies, second ed., iii. 108.

blishment in Virginia, to consist of a central office, and a sub-office in each county, fixing the rates of postage to be paid to Thomas Neale, Esq., who was authorized by an act of parliament to establish post-offices in the colonies. The postage on a letter consisting of one sheet, for a distance not exceeding eighty miles, was three pence. Four companies of rangers protected the frontiers, while English frigates guarded the coast; and the colony enjoyed a long repose.

The amiable and excellent Queen Mary died on the 28th day of December, 1694; and the king now assumed the title of William the Third. Since the dissolution of the Virginia Company, the superintendence of the colonies had been entrusted to a committee of the privy council; in 1696 the board of trade was established for that purpose.

CHAPTER XLIII.

1696-1698.

State and Condition of Virginia—Exhausting Agriculture—Depression of Mechanic Art—Merchants—Current Coin—Grants of Land—Powers of Governor—The Council—Court of Claims—County Courts—General Court—Secretary, Sheriffs, Collectors, and Vestries—Revenue—The Church.

THE following statistical account of Virginia appears to have been reported by Lord Culpepper, in 1781, to the Committee of the colonies. It is to be found in the Historical Collections of Massachusetts,* the manuscript having been communicated by Carter B. Harrison, Esq., of Virginia, by the hands of the Rev. John Jones Spooner, corresponding member. The picture is harsh, but drawn by a vigorous hand, without fear, favor, or affection.

In point of natural advantages Virginia was surpassed by few countries on the globe, but in commerce, manufactures, education, government in church and state, was one of the poorest and most miserable. The staple tobacco swallowed up every thing, so that the markets were often glutted with bad tobacco, which became a mere drug, and would not pay freight and customs. Perhaps not one hundredth part of the land was yet cleared, and none of the marsh or swamp drained. As fast as the soil was worn out by exhausting crops of tobacco and corn, it was left to grow up again in woods. The plough was not much used, in the first clearing the roots and stumps being left, and the ground tilled only with hoes, and by the time the stumps were decayed the ground was worn out. Manure was neglected. Of grain the planters usually raised only enough for home consumption, there being no market for it, and scarce any money. But their main labor in this crop being in the summer, they fell into habits of

---

* First Series, v. 124.

indolence for the rest of the year. The circumstances of the country, destitute of towns, and consisting of dispersed plantations, were unfavorable for mechanics, then called tradesmen. The depression of this useful and important class although lessened, continues in the present day, and appears to be inevitably connected with the system of negro slavery. It is a tax paid by the whites for the elevation of the black race. The merchants were the most prosperous class in the colony, but they labored under great disadvantages, being obliged to sell on credit, and to carry on "a pitiful retail trade," and to depend on the receivers who went about among the planters to receive the tobacco due, and this mode of collecting was subject to great delays and losses. The native-born Virginians, who for the most part had never been out of the colony, were averse to town life, and felt dissatisfied, like Daniel Boone in more modern times, whenever "the settlements became too thick." The scarcity of money was aggravated by the governor, who found it to his interest to be paid in tobacco. The current coin of the dominion of Virginia consisted of pieces of eight, the value of which was fixed by law at five shillings; and the value being made greater in Pennsylvania money, they were consequently drained from Virginia, as at the present day gold and silver are ostracised by a depreciated paper currency.

The method of settling the colonial territory was by the king's grant of fifty acres to every actual settler, but this rule was evaded and perverted in various ways, and rights for that quantity of land could easily be purchased from the clerks in the secretary's office at from one to five shillings each. The powers of the governor were extensive; he was a sort of viceroy, being commander-in-chief and vice-admiral, lord treasurer in issuing warrants for the paying of moneys, lord chancellor or lord keeper as passing grants under the colony's seal, president of the council, chief justice of the courts, with some powers of a bishop or ordinary. The governors managed to evade the king's instructions, and by official patronage to silence the opposition of the council, and even to hold the burgesses in check. The governor and councillors were all colonels and honorable, and their adherents monopolized the offices. The governor's salary was for many years one thousand pounds per annum, to which the assembly added perquisites, amounting to five hundred more, and a further addition of two hundred pounds was made to Sir William Berkley's salary, making the whole salary seventeen hundred pounds. The council, in effect the creatures and clients of the governor, being appointed at his nomination, and receiving office and place from him, had the powers of council of state, (in case of vacancy of the governor the oldest of them *ex officio* acting as president *ad interim*,) of upper house of assembly or house of lords, in the general court of supreme judges, and as colonels, answering to the English lord-lieutenants of counties. The councillors were also naval officers in the customs department, collectors of the revenue, farmers of the king's quit-rents; out of the council were chosen the secretary, auditor, and escheators; the councillors were exempt from arrests, and had a compensation of three hundred and fifty pounds divided among them, according to their attendance. They met together after the manner of the king and council. Their clerk received fifty pounds per annum salary, besides perquisites. The office of collector, held by members of the council, was indeed incompatible with their office of judge, and their office of councillor unfitted them for auditing their own accounts as collectors, and in different capacities they both bought and sold the royal quit-rents.*

Upon the election of burgesses there was commonly held a court, called a court of claims, where all who had any claims

---

* The council, in the time of Governor Andros, consisted of Ralph Wormley, collector and naval officer of Rappahannock River; Colonel Richard Lee, collector and naval officer of upper district of Potomac River—these two having been appointed while Sir William Berkley was governor; Colonel William Byrd, who was appointed auditor during Lord Culpepper's administration; Colonel Christopher Wormley, collector and naval officer of the lower district of the Potomac River, appointed while Lord Effingham was governor; Colonel Edward Hill, collector and naval officer of upper district of James River; Colonel Edmund Jennings, collector and naval officer of York River—these two being appointed in Lord Effingham's time; Colonel Daniel Parke, collector and naval officer of the lower district of James River, and escheator between York and Rappahannock Rivers; Colonel Charles Scarburgh, collector and naval officer on the Eastern Shore, and Mr. John Lightfoot, who had lately arrived in the country—these last four appointed while Sir Edmund Andros was governor.

against the public might present them to the burgesses, together with any propositions or grievances, "all which the burgesses carry to the assembly." There was at that early day much confusion in the laws, and it was difficult to know what laws were in force and what were not. All causes were decided in the county court or in the general court. The county court consisted of eight or ten gentlemen, receiving their commission from the governor, who renewed it annually. They met once a month, or once in two months, and had cognizance of all causes exceeding in value twenty shillings, or two hundred pounds of tobacco. These country gentlemen, having no education in law, not unfrequently fell into mistakes in substance and in form. The insufficiency of these courts was now growing more apparent than formerly, since the old stock of gentry, who were educated in England, were better acquainted with law and with the business of the world than their sons and grandsons, who were brought up in Virginia, and commonly knew only reading, writing, and arithmetic, and were not very proficient in them.

The general court, so called because it had jurisdiction of causes from all parts of the colony, was held twice a year, in April and October, by the governor and council as judges, at Jamestown. This court was never commissioned, but grew up by custom or usurpation; from it there was no appeal, except in cases of over three hundred pounds sterling value, to the king, which was for most persons impracticable, on account of the distance and the expensiveness. Virginia appears to have been the only colony where the executive constituted the supreme court. The general court tried all causes of above sixteen pounds sterling, or sixteen hundred pounds of tobacco in value, and all appeals from the county courts, and it had cognizance of all causes in chancery, in king's bench, the common pleas, the exchequer, the admiralty, and spirituality. The forms of proceeding in the general court were quite irregular. The duties of the secretary were as multifarious as those of the governor; it was, however, for the most part a sinecure, the business being performed by a clerk, styled the clerk of the general court, who also employed one or two clerks under him. The secretary, who was properly the clerk of the court, yet sate as judge of that court.

The governor signed all patents or deeds of land, and there was a recital in them that he granted the land "by and with the consent of the council," yet the patents were never read by the governor, nor did the council take any notice of them. He likewise countersigned the patents after the words "compared, and agrees with the original," yet the secretary never read or compared them, and indeed the patent which he signed was itself the original. "Men make laws, but we live by custom." The sheriffs collected all money duties. The auditor audited the accounts of the collectors, and was receiver-general of all public moneys. The parish levy, for the support of the church and of the poor, was assessed by the vestry, about the month of October, when tobacco was ready; the whole amount assessed was divided by the number of tithables of the parish, and collected from the heads of families. The county levy for county expenses was assessed by the justices of the peace, and the sum divided by the number of tithables in the county. The public levy was assessed by the assembly for the general expenses of the colony, and the sum was divided by the number of tithables in the colony, amounting in the year 1690 to about twenty thousand. The three levies were all collected by the sheriffs; they averaged about one hundred pounds of tobacco for each tithable, the aggregate amounting to two millions of pounds per annum.

The revenues and customs that came into the auditor's hands were of four kinds: First, the quit-rents, being one shilling per annum on every fifty acres of land, payable in tobacco, at one penny per pound, or twenty-four pounds of tobacco for every hundred acres. In the Northern Neck, lying between the Potomac and Rappahannock, the quit-rents were paid by the heirs of Lord Culpepper. The tobacco due for quit-rents was sold by the auditor to the several members of the council, who paid for it in money, or bills of exchange, according to the quantity. The quit-rent revenue amounted to about eight hundred pounds sterling per annum. The second source of revenue consisted of two shillings per hogshead, export duty, on tobacco, and fort duties, being fifteen pence per ton on all vessels arriving. These amounted to three thousand pounds sterling per annum. Ten per cent. of this amount was paid to masters of vessels, to induce them to give a true account. The collectors received ten per cent. for collecting, and the auditor seven per cent. The third source of revenue was one penny per pound upon tobacco exported from Virginia to any other English plantation in America. This, as has been mentioned, was, in 1692, granted to the college of William and Mary. The college paid for collecting it no less than twenty per cent., and to the auditor five per cent. The nett proceeds were worth one hundred pounds annually. The fourth source of revenue was any money duty that might be raised by the assembly.

The governor was lieutenant-general, the councillors lieutenants of counties, with the title of colonel, and in counties where no councillor resided, some other person was appointed, with the rank of major. The people in general professed to be of the Church of England. The only dissenters were three or four meetings of Quakers and one of Presbyterians. There were fifty parishes, and in each two, and sometimes three, churches and chapels. The division of the parishes was unequal and inconvenient. The governor had always held the government of the church, as of everything else, in his hands. Ministers were obliged to produce their orders to him, and show that they had been episcopally ordained. The power of presentation was, by a colonial law, in the vestry, but by a custom of hiring preachers by the year, it came to pass that presentation rarely took place. The consequence was that a good minister either would not come to Virginia, or if he did, was soon driven away by the highhanded proceedings of the vestry. The minister was obliged to be careful how he preached against the vices that any great man of the vestry was guilty of, else he would be in danger of losing his living at the end of the year. They held them by a precarious tenure, like that of chaplains; they were mere tenants at sufferance. There were not half as many ministers in Virginia as parishes. The governor connived at this state of things. The minister's salary was sixteen thousand pounds of tobacco per annum. King Charles the Second gave the Bishop of London jurisdiction over the church in the plantations, in all matters except three, viz.: marriage licenses, probates of wills, and induction of ministers, which were reserved to the governor. The bishop's commissary made visitation of the churches and inspection of the clergy. He received no salary, but was allowed, by the king, one hundred pounds per annum out of the quit-rents.*

---

* Account of Va., in Mass. Hist. Coll., first series.

CHAPTER XLIV.

1698-1702.

Administration of Andros—Controversy with Blair—The Rev. Hugo Jones' Account of Maryland—Andros succeeded by Nicholson—Alteration in his Conduct—Supposed Cause—Williamsburg made the Seat of Government—His tyrannical Proceedings—Prejudice of Beverley, the Historian—Act against Pirates—Offices of Speaker and Treasurer combined—Capture of a piratical Vessel—Death of Edward Hill—Commencement at William and Mary—Demise of William the Third—Succeeded by Anne—Nicholson's Description of the People of Virginia.

GOVERNOR ANDROS took singular pains in arranging and preserving the public records; and when, in 1698, the State-house was burned, he caused the papers that survived to be arranged with more exactness than before. He ordered that all the English statutes should be law in Virginia; this preposterous rule gave great dissatisfaction. He was a patron of manufactures; but the acts for establishing fulling-mills were rejected by the board of trade. He encouraged the culture of cotton, which, however, fell into disuse.

By royal instructions, Andros was invested with the powers of ordinary, or representative of the king and the bishop of London, in the affairs of the church. This brought him into collision with Commissary Blair, and in 1694 the governor arbitrarily suspended him from his place in the council, to which he had been appointed in the preceding year. While in England on the business of the college, in 1695, the doctor preferred charges against Andros as an enemy to religion, to the church, the clergy, and the college. The charges and the proofs covered thirty-two folio pages of manuscript, and were drawn up with ability. But Blair had to contend with formidable opposition, for Governor Andros sent over to London, in his defence, Colonel Byrd, of Westover, Mr. Harrison, of Surry County, Mr. Povey, who was high in office in the colony, and a Mr. Marshall, to arraign the Rev.

Commissary himself before the Bishop of London and the Archbishop of Canterbury. Two days were spent at Lambeth Palace, in the examination, the charges and answers filling fifty-seven folio pages of manuscript, and Dr. Blair's accusers were signally discomfited. Much of the prejudice against him was owing to his being a Scotchman—a prejudice at that time running very high in England. The result was that Blair returned after successfully accomplishing the object of his mission, and having been reinstated in the council by the king. He was, nevertheless, again removed upon a pretence equally frivolous.* Andros was sent back to England to answer in person the charges alleged against him, and eventually, they being substantiated, he was removed from his office of deputy governor of Virginia.†

William the Third, by the treaty of Ryswick, in 1697, obtained an acknowledgment of his right to the crown, and vindicated the principles of constitutional freedom.

The Rev. Hugo Jones, author of a work entitled "Present State of Virginia," writing from Maryland in this year, says of the people there: "They are, generally speaking, crafty, knavish, litigious, dissemblers, and debauched. A gentleman (I mean one of a generous Cambro-Briton temper) is *rara avis in terris*. A man must be circumspect and prudent if he will maintain his reputation among them. Of dealing, it is very true what was told me by a man at London, that none is fit to deal with a Virginian but a Virginian; however, I having made it my business both in London and at sea to inquire into the nature of the people, that I might know the better how to behave myself among them, have gained as good a reputation as in modesty I could expect; neither have I been much imposed upon in my bargains. As to the people's disposition in matters of religion, they will follow none out of the path of interest, and they heartily embrace none but such as will fill the barn and the basket. Most sects are here professed, but in general they are practical atheists."‡

---

* Account of Va. in Mass. Hist. Coll., first series, v. 144.
† Old Churches, Ministers, and Families of Virginia, i. 157.
‡ European Magazine, 1796.

The uncharitable judgments of this narrow-minded writer are not entitled to much weight. Among a people requiring so much ministerial care, he found ample time to devote to the study of natural history, and was curious in the examination of "fishes' bones" and "petrified mushrooms."

In the year 1698 died Thomas Ludwell, Esq., some time secretary of Virginia. He was born at Bruton, County Somerset, England. Sir Edmund Andros was succeeded in November, 1698, by Colonel Nicholson, transferred from the government of Maryland. He entertained a plan of confederating the colonies together, and aspired to become himself the viceroy of the contemplated union. Finding himself thwarted in these projects, his conduct became self-willed and overbearing. In a memorial sent to England, he stated that tobacco bore so low a price as not to yield even clothes to the planters; yet, in the same paper, advised parliament to prohibit the plantations from making their own clothing; in other words, proposing that they should be left to go naked.* Indeed, he appeared to be quite altered from what he had been during his former administration in Virginia; and the change was thought to be not a little owing to a disappointment in love. He had become passionately attached to a daughter of Lewis Burwell, Jr., and failing to win her favor or that of her parents, in his suit, he became infuriated, and persisted, Quixotically, for years in his fruitless purpose. The young lady's father, and her brothers, and Commissary Blair, and the Rev. Mr. Fouace, minister of the parish, were especial objects of his vengeance. To the young lady he threatened the death of her father and her brothers, if she did not yield to his suit. He committed other outrages no less extraordinary.

For the sake of a healthier situation, Governor Nicholson removed the seat of government from Jamestown, now containing only three or four good inhabited houses, to Middle Plantation, so called from its lying midway between James and York Rivers. Here he projected a large town, laying out the streets in the form of a W and M, in honor of King William and Queen Mary. This plan, however, appears to have been abandoned, or only

---

* Beverley, B. i. 98.

partially carried out.* According to the contemporary historian Beverley, Nicholson declared openly to the lower order of people "that the gentlemen imposed upon them; that the servants had all been kidnapped, and had a lawful action against their masters." In the year 1700 Mr. Fowler, the king's attorney-general for the colony, declaring some piece of service against law, the governor seized him by the collar, and swore "that he knew no laws they had, and that his commands should be obeyed without hesitation or reserve." He committed gentlemen who offended him to prison without any complaint, and refused to allow bail; and some of them having intimated to him that such proceedings were illegal, he replied, "that they had no right at all to the liberties of English subjects, and that he would hang up those that should presume to oppose him, with magna charta about their necks." He often extolled the governments of Fez and Morocco, and at a meeting of the governors of the college, told them "that he knew how to govern the Moors, and would beat them into better manners." At another time he avowed that he knew how to govern the country without assemblies, and if they should deny him anything after he had obtained a standing army, "he would bring them to reason with halters about their necks." His outrages made him jealous, and to prevent complaints being sent to England against him, he is said to have intercepted letters, employed spies, and even played the eavesdropper himself. He sometimes held inquisitorial courts to find grounds of accusation against such as incurred his displeasure.†

Robert Beverley, author of a "History of Virginia," published the first edition of it in 1705. He was a son of Robert Beverley, the persecuted clerk, who died in 1687. This may account somewhat for his extreme acrimony against Culpepper and Effingham, who had persecuted his father, and against Nicholson, who was Effingham's deputy. In his second edition, when time had, perhaps, mitigated his animosities, Beverley

---

* Hugh Jones' Present State of Virginia; Beverley, B. i. 99; Va. Hist. Reg., vi. 15.
† Beverley, B. i. 97.

omitted many of his accusations against these governors. In favor of Nicholson, it is also to be observed, that his administration in Maryland and in South Carolina was more satisfactory. But it is certain that he was an erratic, Quixotic, irascible man, who could not bear opposition, and an extreme high churchman.

In the eleventh year of William the Third an act was passed for the restraining and punishing of pirates and privateers, the preamble reciting that "nothing can more conduce to the honor of his most sacred majesty than that such articles of peace as are concluded in all treaties should be kept and preserved inviolable by his majesty's subjects in and over all his majesty's territories and dominions, and that great mischief and depredations are daily done upon the high seas by pirates, privateers, and sea-robbers, in not only taking and pillaging several ships and vessels belonging to his majesty's subjects, but also in taking, destroying, and robbing several ships belonging to the subjects of foreign princes, in league and amity with his majesty;" and they prayed that crimes committed on the high seas should be punished as if committed on land, in Virginia.* A committee was appointed during the same session "to revise the laws of this his majesty's ancient and great colony and dominion of Virginia."†

Among the subjects upon which a tax was laid for the building of a capitol, were servants imported, not being natives of England or Wales, fifteen shillings per poll, and twenty shillings on every negro or other slave. Colonel Robert Carter, speaker of the house, was elected to fill the office of treasurer; and it came to be the custom for the two offices of speaker and treasurer to be held by the same person. The establishment of the office of a treasurer appointed by the assembly, giving that body control of the colonial purse, added much to the independence of its legislative power.

---

* Hening, iii. 177.

† The members of it were Edward Hill, Matthew Page, and Benjamin Harrison, Esquires, members of the council; and Miles Cary, John Taylor, Robert Beverley, Anthony Armistead, Henry Duke, and William Buckner, gentlemen of the house of burgesses.

In the second year of Nicholson's administration a piratical vessel was captured within the capes of Virginia. She had taken some merchant-vessels in Lynhaven Bay, and a small vessel happening to witness an engagement between her and a merchantman, conveyed intelligence of it to the Shoram, a fifth-rate man-of-war, commanded by Captain Passenger, and newly arrived. Nicholson chanced to be at Kiquotan sealing up his letters, and, going on board the Shoram, was present in the engagement that followed. The Shoram, by daybreak, having got in between the capes and the pirate, intercepted her, and an action took place on the 29th of April, 1700, when the pirate surrendered upon condition of being referred to the king's mercy. In this affair fell Peter Heyman, grandson of Sir Peter Heyman, of Summerfield, in the County of Kent, England. Being collector of the customs in the lower district of James River, he volunteered to go on board the Shoram, and after behaving with undaunted courage, standing on the quarter-deck near the governor, was killed by a small shot.

During this year died the Honorable Colonel Edward Hill, of Shirley, on the James River, in the sixty-third year of his age; he was of the council, colonel and commander-in-chief of the Counties of Charles City and Surry, judge of his majesty's high court of admiralty, and some time treasurer of Virginia. He lies buried at Shirley, and a portrait of him and his wife is preserved there.

In the year preceding this, Protestant dissenters, qualified according to the toleration act of the first year of William and Mary, were exempted from penalties for not repairing to the parish church, if they attended some legal place of worship once in two months.* The press was not yet free in Virginia, and the writ of *habeas corpus* was still withheld.

There was a commencement at William and Mary College in the year 1700, at which there was a great concourse of people; several planters came thither in coaches, and others in sloops from New York, Pennsylvania, and Maryland, it being a new thing in that part of America to hear graduates perform their

---

* Hening, iii. 171.

exercises. The Indians themselves had the curiosity, some of them, to visit Williamsburg upon that occasion; and the whole country rejoiced as if they had some relish of learning. Fifty-eight years before this there had been celebrated a commencement at Harvard College, in Massachusetts.*

In the year 1701 Colonel Quarry, surveyor-general of the customs, wrote to the board of trade: "This malignant humor is not confined to Virginia, formerly the most remarkable for loyalty, but is universally diffused."

During the month of March of this year died William the Third. His manner was taciturn, reserved, haughty; his genius military; his decision inflexible. In his fondness of prerogative he showed himself a grandson of the first Charles; as the defender of the Protestant religion, and Prince of Orange, he displayed toleration toward all except Papists. The government of Virginia under him was not materially improved. He was succeeded by Anne, daughter of James the Second. Louis the Fourteenth having recognized the Pretender as lawful heir to the British crown, Anne, shortly after she succeeded to the throne, in 1702, declared war against France, and its ally Spain; but Virginia was not directly affected by the long conflict that ensued. In compliance with the requests of the assembly, the queen granted the colony warlike stores, to the value of three thousand and three hundred pounds, which the governor was directed to pay from the revenue of quit-rents. Her majesty, at the same time, renewed the requisition formerly made by the crown for an appropriation in aid of the defences of New York; but the burgesses still steadily refused.

During the reign of William the Third the commerce of Vir-

---

* In 1701 the population of the colonies was as follows:—

Connecticut	30,000	Pennsylvania	20,000
Maryland	25,000	Rhode Island	10,000
Massachusetts	70,000	South Carolina	7,000
New Hampshire	10,000	Virginia	40,000
New Jersey	15,000		
New York	30,000	Total	262,000
North Carolina	5,000		

(*Compendium of United States Census.*)

ginia had been seriously interrupted, and her customary supplies withheld; she, therefore, encouraged the domestic manufacture of linen and wool; but an act for the establishment of fulling-mills was rejected by the board of trade, as also was one for "the better securing the liberty of the subject." Governor Nicholson, in a memorial to the council of trade, described the people of Virginia as numerous, rich, and of republican principles, such as ought to be lowered in time; that then or never was the time to maintain the queen's prerogative, and put a stop to those pernicious notions, which were increasing daily, not only in Virginia, but in all her majesty's other governments, and that a frown from her majesty now would do more than an army thereafter; and he insisted on the necessity of a standing army.*

---

* Beverley, B. i. 104.

CHAPTER LXV.

1703.

Assembly held in the College—Ceremony of opening the Session—The Governor's Speech.

A MEETING of the general assembly was held at her majesty's Royal College of William and Mary, in March, 1703, being the second year of Queen Anne's reign, and, by prorogation, again in April, 1704.* The clerk of the general assembly was ordered to wait upon the house of burgesses and inform them that his excellency commanded their immediate attendance on him in the council chamber. The burgesses having complied with this order, his excellency was pleased to let them know that her most sacred majesty having been pleased to renew his commission to be her majesty's lieutenant and governor-general of this her majesty's most ancient and great colony and dominion of Virginia, he would cause the said commission to be read to them. This being done, he read them that part of his instructions wherein the council are nominated, and informed the house that upon the death of Colonel Page, the number of councillors having fallen under nine, he had appointed one to supply that vacancy. The governor next mentioned to the house that he had commissioned some of her majesty's honorable council to administer the oath to the burgesses. Whereupon they withdrew, and the oath was administered by the Honorable William Byrd, John Lightfoot, and Benjamin Harrison. These gentlemen returning to the council chamber, the clerk of the assembly was ordered to wait again upon the house of burgesses, and acquaint them that his excellency commanded their immediate attendance on him. The

---

* A meeting of the council was held, consisting of his Excellency Francis Nicholson, Esq., lieutenant and governor-general, and William Byrd, John Lightfoot, Benjamin Harrison, Robert Carter, John Custis, Philip Ludwell, William Basset, Henry Duke, Robert Quarry, and John Smith, Esquires.

house of burgesses complying with this order, the governor made the following speech:—

"HONORABLE GENTLEMEN,—

"God Almighty, I hope, will be graciously pleased so to direct, guide, and enable us, as that we may, to all intents and purposes, answer her majesty's writ by which this assembly was called, and by prorogation is now met in this her majesty Queen Anne her royal capitol; which being appointed by law for holding general assemblies and general courts, my hopes likewise are that they may continue to be held in this place for the promoting of God's glory, her majesty, and her successors' interest and service with that of the inhabitants of this her majesty's most ancient and great colony and dominion of Virginia, so long as the sun and moon endure. Gentlemen, her most sacred majesty having been graciously pleased to send me her royal picture and arms for this her colony and dominion, I think the properest place to have them kept in, will be this council chamber; but it not being as yet quite finished, I cannot have them so placed as I would.

"By private accounts which I have from England, I understand her majesty hath lately thought fit to appoint a day of public fasting and humiliation there; but I have not yet seen her majesty's royal proclamation for it, which makes me not willing to appoint one here till I have. And had it not been for this, I designed that her majesty's royal picture and arms should have been first seen by you on St. George his day, and to have kept it as a day of public thanksgiving, it being the day on which her majesty was crowned, and bearing the name of his royal highness the Prince of Denmark, and likewise of the patron of our mother kingdom of England.

"Honorable gentlemen, I don't in the least doubt but that you will join with me in paying our most humble and dutiful acknowledgments and thanks to her most sacred majesty for this great honor and favor which she hath been pleased to bestow upon your country, and in praying that she may have a long, prosperous, successful, and victorious reign, as also that she may in all respects not only equal, but even outdo her royal predecessor,

Queen Elizabeth, of ever-glorious memory, in the latter end of whose reign this country was discovered, and in honor of her called Virginia.

"It is now within two years of a century since its being first seated, at which time, if God Almighty and her majesty shall be so pleased, I design to celebrate a jubilee, and that the inhabitants thereof may increase exceedingly, and also abound with riches and honors, and have extraordinary good success in all their undertakings, but chiefly that they may be exemplary in their lives and conversations, continue in their religion of the Church of England as by law established, loyal to the crown thereof, and that all these things may come to pass, I question not but you will most cordially join with me in our most unfeigned and hearty prayers to God Almighty for them."

At the close of this verbose speech, the burgesses returned to their house, and the council adjourned.*

---

* Documents in S. Literary Messenger, communicated by Wyndham Robertson, Esq., having been copied by his father, while he was clerk of the council, from old papers in the council chamber.

CHAPTER XLVI.

1703-1705.

Quit-rents—Northy's Opinion against the Custom of the Vestry's employing a Minister by the Year—The Free Church Disruption in Scotland—Controversy between Blair and Nicholson—Convocation—Nicholson recalled—Notice of his Career—Huguenots.

By the account of Colonel William Byrd, receiver-general, the nett proceeds of her majesty's revenue of quit-rents for the year 1703 amounted to five thousand seven hundred and forty-five pounds.

In the Church of England the people have no part in the choice of their minister; a patron appoints him, and a living supports him. In Virginia, on the contrary, the salary being levied directly from the people by the vestries, they fell upon the expedient, as has been repeatedly mentioned, of employing a minister for a year. Governor Nicholson, an extreme high-churchman, procured from the attorney-general, Northy, an opinion against this custom, and it was sent to all the vestries, with directions to put it on record. The vestries, nevertheless, pertinaciously resisted this construction of the law. In two important points the church establishment in Virginia differed from that in England—in the appointment of the minister by the vestry, according to the act of 1642, and in the absence of a bishop.

In recent times the disruption of the Scottish general assembly resulted in the Free Church of Scotland, which thus, by sacrificing the temporalities, vindicated its independence of the government in things spiritual. In Virginia the vestries virtually maintained a like independence. In Scotland the contest arrayed against each other schismatic parties in the established kirk, known as the Evangelical and the Moderates, whereas in Virginia it was a mere contest for power between the vestries and the government. The Free Church of Scotland, at the time of the disruption, was still in theory in favor of an establishment in which the clergy should be chosen by the people and paid by the government.* Even in England, under the constitution of the established church, the ministers of certain exceptional chapels were formerly elected by the freeholders of the parish, subject to the approval of the vicar, and the violation of their rights in this particular was sometimes resented in the ruder districts of Yorkshire, by outrageous insults offered to the new incumbent during the time of service, and by brutal personal assaults upon the minister.†

Before the beginning of the eighteenth century the proprietary government, granted by Charles the First to Lord Baltimore, had at length been abolished, and the Church of England established there. There was less tolerance under this establishment than before. In Maryland as in Virginia, the discipline of the church was loose, the clergy by no means exemplary, and their condition precarious and dependent.

The differences between Dr. Blair and Governor Nicholson led to a tedious controversy, in which charges of malfeasance in official duty and private misconduct, especially in the affair of his attachment for Miss Burwell, and his maltreatment of the Rev. Mr. Fouace, were transmitted to the government in England, covering forty-four pages folio of manuscript. The controversy produced no little excitement and disturbance in the colony; a number of the clergy adhered to the governor, being those with whom Commissary Blair was unpopular, and whom the governor had ingratiated by siding with them against the vestries, and by representing the commissary as less favorable to their cause. Governor Nicholson ordered a convocation to be assembled, and during its session held private interviews with his adherents among the clergy, who signed a paper denying the charges made by the commissary and the council. A public entertainment given to them was satirized in a ballad, setting forth their unclerical hilarity, and depicting some of them in unfavorable colors. This ballad soon appeared in London. In this convocation seventeen of the clergy were opposed to the commissary,

---

* Memoirs of Dr. Chalmers, iv. 287, 316.
† Mrs. Gaskell's Life of Charlotte Brontë.

and only six in his favor. Nevertheless his integrity and indomitable perseverance and energy triumphed; and at length, upon the complaint made by him, together with six members of the council and some of the clergy, particularly the Rev. Mr. Fouace, Colonel Nicholson was recalled.* He ceased to be governor in August, 1705. Before entering on the government of Virginia he had been lieutenant-governor of New York under Andros, and afterwards at the head of administration from 1687 to 1689, when he was expelled by a popular tumult. From 1690 to 1692 he was lieutenant-governor of Virginia. From 1694 to 1699 he held the government of Maryland, where, with the zealous assistance of Commissary Bray, he busied himself in establishing Episcopacy. Returning to the government of Virginia, Governor Nicholson remained until 1705. In the year 1710 he was appointed general and commander-in-chief of the forces sent against Fort Royal, in Acadia, which was surrendered to him. During the following year he headed the land force of another expedition directed against the French in Canada. The naval force on this occasion was commanded by the imbecile Brigadier Hill. The enterprise was corrupt in purpose, feeble in execution, and abortive in result. This failure was attributable to the mismanagement and inefficiency of the fleet. In 1713 Colonel Nicholson was governor of Nova Scotia. Having received the honor of knighthood in 1720, Sir Francis Nicholson was appointed governor of South Carolina, where during four years, it is said, he conducted himself with a judicious and spirited attention to the public welfare, and this threw a lustre over the closing scene of his long and active career in America. Returning to England, June, 1725, he died at London in March, 1728. He is described as an adept in colonial governments, trained by long experience in New York, Virginia, and Maryland; brave, and not penurious, but narrow and irascible; of loose morality, yet a fervent supporter of the church.†

Upon the revocation of the edict of Nantes, by Louis the Fourteenth, in 1685, more than half a million of French Protestants, called Huguenots, fled from the jaws of persecution to foreign

---

* Old Churches, etc., i. 158; ii. 291. † Bancroft, ii. 82.

countries. About forty thousand took refuge in England. In 1690 William the Third sent over a number of them to Virginia, and lands were allotted to them on James River. During the year 1699 another body came over, conducted by their clergyman, Claude Philippe de Richebourg. He and others were naturalized some years afterwards. Others followed in succeeding years; the larger part of them settled at Manakintown, on the south bank of the James River, about twenty miles above the falls, on rich lands formerly occupied by the Monacan Indians. The rest dispersed themselves over the country, some on the James, some on the Rappahannock. The settlement at Manakintown was erected into the parish of King William, in the County of Henrico, and exempted from taxation for many years. The refugees received from the king and the assembly large donations of money and provisions; and they found in Colonel William Byrd, of Westover, a generous benefactor. Each settler was allowed a strip of land running back from the river to the foot of the hill. Here they raised cattle, undertook to domesticate the buffalo, manufactured cloth, and made claret wine from wild grapes. Their settlement extended about four miles along the river. In the centre they built a church; they conducted their public worship after the German manner, and repeated family worship three times a day. Manakintown was then on the frontier of Virginia, and there was no other settlement nearer than the falls of the James River, yet the Indians do not appear to have ever molested these pious refugees. There was no mill nearer than the mouth of Falling Creek, twenty miles distant, and the Huguenots, having no horses, were obliged to carry their corn on their backs to the mill.

Many worthy families of Virginia are descended from the Huguenots, among them the Maurys, Fontaines, Lacys, Munfords, Flournoys, Dupuys, Duvalls, Bondurants, Trents, Moncures, Ligons, and Le Grands. In the year 1714 the aggregate population of the Manakintown settlement was three hundred. The parish register of a subsequent date, in French, is preserved.

CHAPTER XLVII.

1702-1708.

Parishes—The Rev. Francis Makemie—Dissenters—Toleration Act—Ministers—Commissary.

In the year 1702 there were twenty-nine counties in Virginia, and forty-nine parishes, of which thirty-four were supplied with ministers, fifteen vacant. In each parish there was a church, of timber, brick, or stone; in the larger parishes, one or two Chapels of Ease; so that the whole number of places of worship, for a population of sixty thousand, was about seventy. In every parish a dwelling-house was provided for the minister, with a glebe of two hundred and fifty acres of land, and sometimes a few negroes, or a small stock of cattle. The salary of sixteen thousand pounds of tobacco was, in ordinary quality, equivalent to £80; in sweet-scented, to £160. It required the labor of twelve negroes to produce this amount. There were in Virginia, at this time, three Quaker congregations, and as many Presbyterian; two in Accomac under the care of Rev. Francis Makemie; the other on Elizabeth River.

The Rev. Francis Makemie, who is styled the father of the American Presbyterian Church, was settled in Accomac County before the year 1690, when his name first appears upon the county records. He appears to have been a native of the north of Ireland, being of Scotch extraction, and one of those called Scotch-Irish. Licensed by the presbytery of Lagan in 1680, and in two or three years ordained as an evangelist for America, he came over, and labored in Barbadoes, Maryland, and Virginia. The first mention of his name on the records of the county court of Accomac bears date in 1690, by which he appears to have brought suits for debts due him in the business of merchandise. He married Naomi, eldest daughter of William Anderson, a wealthy merchant of Accomac, and thus acquired an independent estate. In the year 1699 he obtained from the court of that county a certificate of qualification as a preacher under the toleration act, the first of the kind known to be on record in Virginia. At the same time, upon his petition, two houses belonging to him were licensed as places of public worship.* In a letter written in 1710 by the presbytery of Philadelphia to that of Dublin, it is said: "In all Virginia we have one small congregation on Elizabeth River, and some few families favoring our way in Rappahannock and York." Two years after, the Rev. John Macky was the pastor of the Elizabeth River congregation. It is probable that the congregations organized by Mr. Makemie, in 1690, were not able to give him a very ample support; but, prosperous in his worldly affairs, he appears to have contributed liberally from his own means to the promotion of the religious interests in which he was engaged. According to tradition, he suffered frequent annoyances from the intolerant spirit of the times in Virginia; but he declared that "he durst not deny preaching, and hoped he never should, while it was wanting and desired." Beverley, in his "History of Virginia," published in 1705, says: "They have no more than five conventicles among them, namely, three small meetings of Quakers, and two of Presbyterians. 'Tis observed that those counties where the Presbyterian meetings are produce very mean tobacco, and for that reason can't get an orthodox minister to stay among them; but whenever they could, the people very orderly went to church."

---

* It appears from his will, dated in 1708, that he also owned a house and lot in the new town in Princess Anne County, on the eastern branch of Elizabeth River, and a house and lot in the new town on Wormley's Creek, called Urbanna. Whether he used these houses for merchandise, or for public worship, is not known. It appears from Commissary Blair's report on the state of the church in Virginia, that the congregation on Elizabeth River existed before the year 1700. From the fact of Mr. Makemie's directing, in his will, that his dwelling-house and lot on that river should be sold, it has been inferred that he had resided there before he moved to the opposite shore of the Chesapeake, and that the church in question was gathered by him; if so, it must have been formed before 1690; for in that year he was residing on the Eastern Shore. Others have supposed that the congregation on Elizabeth River was composed of a small company of Scotch emigrants, whose descendants are still to be found in the neighborhood of Norfolk.

From this it may be inferred that the Eastern Shore, where Makemie was settled, produced poor tobacco, and that in consequence of it there was no minister of the established church in his neighborhood. He is supposed to have had four places of preaching; his labors proved acceptable; his hearers and congregations increased in number, and there was a demand for other ministers of the same denomination. Mr. Makemie, about the year 1704, returned to the mother country and remained there about a year. During the following year two ministers, styled his associates, were licensed, by authority of Governor Seymour, to preach in Somerset County, in Maryland, notwithstanding the opposition of the neighboring Episcopal minister. Makemie's imprisonment in New York (by Lord Cornbury) for preaching in that city, and his able defence upon his trial, are well known. He died in 1708, leaving a large estate. His library was much larger than was usually possessed by Virginia clergymen in that day, and included a number of law books. He appointed the Honorable Francis Jenkins, of Somerset County, Maryland, and Mary Jenkins, his lady, executors of his last will and testament, and guardians of his children.*

In 1699 a penalty of five shillings was imposed on such persons in Virginia as should not attend the parish church once in two months; but dissenters, qualified according to the toleration act of the first year of William and Mary, were exempted from this penalty, provided they should attend at "any congregation, or place of religious worship, permitted and allowed by the said act of parliament, once in two months."† Hening remarks of this law: "It is surely an abuse of terms to call a law a toleration act which imposes a religious test on the conscience, in order to avoid the penalties of another law equally violating every principle of religious freedom. The provisions of this act may be seen in the fourth volume of Blackstone's Commentaries, page 53. Nothing could be more intolerant than to impose the penalties by this act prescribed for not repairing to church, and then to hold

---

* Foote's Sketches of Va., first series, 40, 58, 63, 84; and Force's Historical Tracts, iv.
† Hening, iii. 171.

out the idea of exemption, by a compliance with the provisions of such a law as the statute of 1 William and Mary, adopted by a mere general reference, when not one person in a thousand could possibly know its contents." It was an age when the state of religion was low in England, and of those ministers sent over to Virginia not a few were incompetent, some openly profligate; and religion slumbered in the languor of moral lectures, the maxims of Socrates and Seneca, and the stereotyped routine of accustomed forms. Altercations between minister and people were not unfrequent; the parson was a favorite butt for aristocratic ridicule. Sometimes a pastor more exemplary than the rest was removed from mercenary motives, or on account of a faithful discharge of his duties. More frequently the unfit were retained by popular indifference. The clergy, in effect, did not enjoy that permanent independency of the people which properly belongs to a hierarchy. The vestry, a self-perpetuated body of twelve gentlemen, thought themselves "the parson's master," and the clergy in vain deplored the precarious tenure of their livings. The commissary's powers were few, limited, and disputed; he was but the shadow of a bishop; he could not ordain nor confirm; he could not depose a minister. Yet the people, jealous of prelatical tyranny, watched his feeble movements with a vigilant and suspicious eye. The church in Virginia was destitute of an effective discipline.*

---

* Hawks; Bancroft; Beverley, B. iv. 26.

CHAPTER XLVIII.

1704-1710.

Edward Nott, Lieutenant-Governor—Earl of Orkney, Titular Governor-in-chief—Nott's Administration—Robert Hunter appointed Lieutenant-Governor—Captured by the French—The Rev. Samuel Sandford endows a Free School—Lord Baltimore.

On the 13th day of August, 1704, the Duke of Marlborough gained a celebrated victory over the French and Bavarians at Blenheim.* During the same month Edward Nott came over to Virginia, lieutenant-governor under George Hamilton, Earl of Orkney, who had been appointed governor-in-chief, and from this time the office became a pensionary sinecure, enjoyed by one residing in England, and who, out of a salary of two thousand pounds a year, received twelve hundred. The Earl of Orkney, who enjoyed this sinecure for forty years, having entered the army in his youth, was made a colonel in 1689-90, and in 1695-6 was created Earl of Orkney, in consideration of his merit and gallantry. He was present at the battles of the Boyne, Athlone, Limerick, Aghrim, Steinkirk, Lauden, Namur, and Blenheim, and was a great favorite of William the Third. In the first year of Queen Anne's reign he was made a major-general, and shortly after a Knight of the Thistle, and served with distinction in all the wars of her reign. As one of the sixteen peers of Scotland he was a member of the house of lords for many years. He married, in 1695, Elizabeth, daughter to Sir Edward Villiers, Knight, (Maid of Honor to Queen Mary,) sister to Edward, Earl of Jersey, by whom he had three daughters, Lady Anne, who married the Earl of Inchequin, Lady Frances, who married Sir Thomas Sanderson, Knight of the Bath, Knight of the Shire of Lincoln, and brother to the Earl of Scarborough, and Lady Harriet, married to the Earl of Orrery.

---

* In the following year appeared the first American newspaper, "The Boston News-Letter."

Nott, a mild, benevolent man, did not survive long enough to realize what the people hoped from his administration. In the fall after his arrival he called an assembly, which concluded a general revisal of the laws that had been long in hand. Some salutary acts went into operation, but those relating to the church and clergy proving unacceptable to the commissary, as encroaching on the confines of prerogative, were suspended by the governor, and thus fell through. Governor Nott procured the passage of an act providing for the building of a palace for the governor, and appropriating three thousand pounds to that object, and he dissented to an act infringing on the governor's right of appointing justices of the peace, by making the concurrence of five of the council necessary. An act establishing the general court was afterwards disallowed by the board of trade, because it did not recognize the appellate rights of the crown. This assembly passed a new act for the establishment of ports and towns, "grounding it only upon encouragements according to her majesty's letter;" but the Virginia merchants complaining against it, this measure also failed.

During the first year of Nott's administration the College of William and Mary was destroyed by fire.* The assembly had held their sessions in it for several years. Governor Nott died in August, 1706, aged forty-nine years. The assembly erected a monument to his memory in the graveyard of the church at Williamsburg. In the inscription he is styled, "His Excellency, Edward Nott, the late Governor of this Colony." It appears that he and his successors were allowed to retain the chief title, as giving them more authority with the people, the Earl of Orkney being quite content with a part of the salary.

England having now adopted the French policy of appointing military men for the colonial governments, in 1708 Robert Hunter, a brigadier-general, a scholar, and a wit—a friend of Addison and Swift—was appointed lieutenant-governor of Virginia; but he was captured on the voyage by the French. Dean Swift, in

---

* The same disaster has recently befallen this venerable institution, on the 8th of February, 1859. The library, comprising many rare and valuable works, shared the fate of the building The walls are rising again on the same spot.

January, 1708–9, writes to him, then a prisoner in Paris, that unless he makes haste to return to England and get him appointed Bishop of Virginia, he will be persuaded by Addison, newly appointed secretary of state for Ireland, to accompany him.* Two months later he writes to him: "All my hopes now terminate in being made Bishop of Virginia." In the year 1710 Hunter became Governor of New York and the Jerseys, and his administration was happily conducted.

Samuel Sandford, who had been some time resident in Accomac County: by his will, dated at London in this year, he leaves a large tract of land, the rents and profits to be appropriated to the education of the children of the poor. It appears probable that he had served as a minister in Accomac, and at the time of the making of his will was a minister in the County of Gloucester, England.

About the year 1709, Benedict Calvert, Lord Baltimore, abandoned the Church of Rome and embraced Protestantism. To Charles Calvert, his son, likewise a Protestant, the full privileges of the Maryland charter were subsequently restored by George the First.†

---

* Anderson's Hist. Col. Church, iii. 127.   † Ibid., iii. 183.

CHAPTER XLIX.

1710-1714.

Spotswood, Lieutenant-Governor—His Lineage and Early Career—Dissolves the Assembly—Assists North Carolina—Sends Cary and others Prisoners to England—Death of Queen Anne—Accession of George the First—German Settlement—Virginia's Economy—Church Establishment—Statistics.

IN the year 1710 Colonel Alexander Spotswood was sent over as lieutenant-governor, under the Earl of Orkney. He was descended from the ancient Scottish family of Spottiswoode. The surname is local, and was assumed by the proprietors of the lands and Barony of Spottiswoode, in the Parish of Gordon, and County of Berwick, as soon as surnames became hereditary in Scotland. The immediate ancestor of the family was Robert de Spotswood, born during the reign of King Alexander the Third, who succeeded to the crown of Scotland in 1249. Colonel Alexander Spotswood was born in 1676, the year of Bacon's Rebellion, at Tangier, then an English colony, in Africa, his father, Robert Spotswood, being physician to the governor, the Earl of Middleton, and the garrison there. The grandfather of Alexander was Sir Robert Spotswood, Lord President of the College of Justice, and Secretary of Scotland in the time of Charles the First, and author of "The Practicks of the Laws of Scotland." He was the second son of John Spotswood, or Spottiswoode, Archbishop of St. Andrews, and author of "The History of the Church of Scotland." The mother of Colonel Alexander Spotswood was a widow, Catharine Elliott; his father died at Tangier in 1688, leaving this his only child.* Colonel Alexander Spotswood was bred in the army from his childhood, and uniting genius with energy, served with distinction under the Duke of Marlborough.

---

* Douglas's Peerage of Scotland; Burke's Landed Gentry of Great Britain and Ireland, ii., Art. SPOTTISWOODE; Chalmers' Introduction, i. 394; Keith's Hist. of Va., 173.

He was dangerously wounded in the breast by the first fire which the French made on the Confederates at the battle of Blenheim. He served during the heat of that sanguinary war as deputy quartermaster-general. In after-life, while governor of Virginia, he sometimes showed to his guests a four-pound ball that struck his coat. Blenheim Castle is represented in the background of a portrait of him, preserved at Chelsea, in the County of King William.

The arrival of Governor Spotswood in Virginia was hailed with joy, because he brought with him the right of Habeas Corpus—a right guaranteed to every Englishman by Magna Charta, but hitherto denied to Virginians. He entered upon the duties of his office in June, 1710. The two houses of the assembly severally returned thanks for an act affording them "relief from long imprisonments," and appropriated upwards of two thousand pounds for completing the governor's palace. In the following year Spotswood wrote back to England: "This government is in perfect peace and tranquillity, under a due obedience to the royal authority and a gentlemanly conformity to the Church of England." The assembly was continued by several prorogations to November, 1711. During the summer of this year, upon an alarm of an intended French invasion of Virginia, the governor exerted himself to put the colony in the best posture of defence. Upon the convening of the assembly their jealousy of prerogative power revived, and they refused to pay the expense of collecting the militia, or to discharge the colonial debt, because, as Spotswood informed the ministry, "they hoped by their frugality to recommend themselves to the populace." The assembly would only consent to levy twenty thousand pounds, by duties laid chiefly on British manufactures; and notwithstanding the governor's message, they insisted on giving discriminating privileges to Virginia owners of vessels in preference to British subjects proper, saying that the same exemption had always existed. The governor declined the proffered levy, and finding that nothing further could be obtained, dissolved the assembly, and in anticipation of an Indian war was obliged to solicit supplies from England.

About this time, the feuds that raged in the adjoining province of North Carolina, threatening to subvert all regular government there, Hyde, the governor, called upon Spotswood for aid. He at first sent Clayton, a man of singular prudence, to endeavor to reconcile the hostile factions. But Cary, the ringleader of the insurgents, having refused to make terms, Spotswood ordered a detachment of militia toward the frontier of North Carolina, while he sent a body of marines, from the coast-guard ships, to destroy Cary's naval force. In a dispatch, Spotswood complained to Lord Dartmouth of the reluctance that he found in the inhabitants of the counties bordering on North Carolina, to march to the relief of Governor Hyde. No blood was shed upon the occasion, and Cary, Porter, and other leaders in those disturbances retiring to Virginia, were apprehended by Spotswood in July, 1711, and sent prisoners to England, charged with treason. In the ensuing year Lord Dartmouth addressed letters to the colonies, directing the governors to send over no more prisoners for crimes or misdemeanors, without proof of their guilt.

In the Tuscarora war, commenced by a massacre on the frontier of North Carolina in September of this year, Spotswood again made an effort to relieve that colony, and prevented the tributary Indians from joining the enemy. He felt that little honor was to be derived from a contest with those who fought like wild beasts, and he rather endeavored to work upon their hopes and fears by treaty. To allay the clamors of the public creditors the governor convened the assembly in 1712, and demonstrated to them that during the last twenty-two years the permanent revenue had been so deficient as to require seven thousand pounds from the monarch's private purse to supply it. In the month of January, 1714, he at length concluded a peace with these ferocious tribes, who had been drawn into the contest, and, blending humanity with vigor, he taught them that while he could chastise their insolence he commiserated their fate.

On the seventeenth day of November the governor, in his address to the assembly, announced the death of Queen Anne, the last of the Stuart monarchs, and the succession of George the First, the first of the Guelfs, but maternally a grandson of James the First.

The frontier of the colony of Virginia was now undisturbed by

Indian incursions, so that the expenditure was reduced to one-third of what had been previously required. A settlement of German Protestants had recently been effected under the governor's auspices, in a region hitherto unpeopled, on the Rapidan.* The place settled by these Germans was called Germanna, afterwards the residence of Spotswood. These immigrants, being countrymen of the new sovereign, could claim an additional title to the royal favor on that account. Spotswood was at the time endeavoring to extend the blessings of a Christian education to the children of the Indians, and although the beneficial result of this scheme might to some appear too remote, he declared that for him it was a sufficient encouragement to think that posterity might reap the benefit of it. The Indian troubles, by which the frontier of Virginia had of late years suffered so much, the governor attributed mainly to the clandestine trade carried on with them by unprincipled men. The same evil has continued down to the present day. In the before-mentioned address to the assembly, Spotswood informed them that since their preceding session he had received a supply of ammunition, arms, and other necessaries of war, sent out by the late Queen Anne.

During eleven years, from 1707 to 1718, while other colonies were burdened with taxation for extrinsic purposes, Virginia steadily adhered to a system of rigid economy, and during that interval eighty-three pounds of tobacco per poll was the sum-total levied by all acts of assembly.† The Virginians now began to scrutinize, with a jealous eye, the circumstances of the government, and the assembly "held itself entitled to all the rights and privileges of an English parliament."

The act of 1642, reserving the right of presentation to the parish, the license of the Bishop of London, and the recommendation of the governor, availed but little against the popular will, and there were not more than four inducted ministers in the colony. Republicanism was thus finding its way even into the

---

* There are several rivers in Virginia called after Queen Anne: the North Anna, South Anna, Rivanna, and Rapidan; and the word Fluvanna appears to be derived from the same source.

† Va. Hist. Reg., iv. 11.

church, and vestries were growing independent. The parish sometimes neglected to receive the minister; sometimes received but did not present him, the custom being to employ a minister by the year. In 1703 it was decided that the minister was an incumbent for life, and could not be displaced by the parish, but the vestries, by preventing his induction, excluded him from acquiring a freehold in his living, and he might be removed at pleasure. The ministers were not always men who could win the esteem of the people or command their respect. The Virginia parishes were so extensive that parishioners sometimes lived at the distance of fifty miles from the parish church, and the assembly would not augment the taxes by narrowing the bounds of the parishes, even to avoid the dangers of "paganism, atheism, or sectaries." Schism was threatening "to creep into the church, and to generate faction in the civil government."* "In Virginia," says the Rev. Hugh Jones,[†] "there is no ecclesiastical court, so that vice, profaneness, and immorality are not suppressed. The people hate the very name of bishop's court." "All which things," he adds, "make it absolutely necessary for a bishop to be settled there, to pave the way for mitres in English America."

There is preserved the record of the trial of Grace Sherwood, in the County of Princess Anne, for witchcraft. Being put in the water, with her hands bound, she was found to swim. A jury of old women having examined her, reported that "she was not like them." She was ordered by the court to be secured "by irons, or otherwise," in jail for further trial. The picturesque inlet where she was put in the water is still known as "Witch Duck." The custom of nailing horse-shoes to the doors to keep out witches is not yet entirely obsolete.

The Virginians at this time were deterred from sending their children across the Atlantic to be educated, through fear of the smallpox.[‡]

From the statistics of the year 1715, it appears that Virginia

---

* Bancroft, iii. 27, 28, citing Spotswood MS., an account of Virginia during his administration, composed by the governor; Hawks, p. 88.
† The Present State of Virginia ‡ Bishop Meade's "Old Churches."

was, in population second only to Massachusetts,* which exceeded her in total number by one thousand, and in the number of whites by twenty-two thousand. All the colonies were at this time slaveholding; the seven Northern ones comprising an aggregate of 12,150 slaves, and the four Southern ones 46,700. The proportion of whites to negroes in Virginia was upwards of four to one. Their condition was one of rather rigorous servitude. The number of Africans imported into Virginia during the reign of George the First was upwards of ten thousand. In addition to the slaves, the Virginians had three kinds of white servants,—some hired in the ordinary way; others, called kids, bound by indenture for four or five years; the third class consisted of convicts. The two colonies, Virginia and Maryland, supplied the mother country, in exchange for her manufactures, with upwards of twenty-five millions of pounds of tobacco, of which there were afterwards exported more than seventeen millions, leaving for internal consumption more than eight millions. Besides the revenue which Great Britain derived from this source, in a commercial point of view, Virginia and Maryland were at this period of more consequence to the fatherland than all the other nine colonies combined. Virginia exchanged her corn, lumber, and salted provisions, for the sugar, rum, and wine of the West Indies and the Azores.

---

* The comparative population of the eleven Anglo-American colonies in 1715 was as follows:—

	White Men.	Negroes.	Total.
New Hampshire	9,500	150	9,650
Massachusetts	94,000	2,000	96,000
Rhode Island	8,500	500	9,000
Connecticut	46,000	1,500	47,500
New York	27,000	4,000	31,000
New Jersey	21,000	1,500	22,500
Pennsylvania	43,300	2,500	45,800
Maryland	40,700	9,500	50,200
Virginia	72,000	23,000	95,000
North Carolina	7,500	3,700	11,200
South Carolina	6,250	10,500	16,750
	375,750	58,850	434,600

(*Chalmers' Amer. Colonies*, ii. 7.)

CHAPTER L.

1714-1716.

Indian School at Fort Christanna—The Rev. Mr. Griffin, Teacher—Governor Spotswood visits Christanna—Description of the School and of the Saponey Indians.

GOVERNOR SPOTSWOOD, who was a proficient in the mathematics, built the Octagon Magazine, rebuilt the College, and made improvements in the governor's house and gardens. He was an excellent judge on the bench. At his instance a grant of £1000 was made by the governors and visitors of William and Mary College in 1718, and a fund was established for instructing Indian children in Christianity,* and he erected a school for that purpose on the southern frontier, at fort Christanna, established on the south side of the Meherrin River, in what is now Southampton County.† This fort, built on a rising ground, was a pentagon enclosure of palisades, and instead of bastions, there were five houses, which defended each other; each side of the fort being about one hundred yards long. It was mounted with five cannon, and had a garrison of twelve men. The Rev. Charles Griffin had charge of the school here, being employed, in 1715, by Governor Spotswood to teach the Indian children, and to bring them to Christianity. The Rev. Hugh Jones‡ says that he had seen there "seventy-seven Indian children at school at a time, at the governor's sole expense, I think." This appears to be a mistake. The school-house was built at the expense of the Indian Company.§ They were taught the English tongue, and to repeat the catechism, and to read the Bible and Common Prayers, and to write. These some of them learned tolerably well. The ma-

---

* Keith's Hist. of Va., 173.

† Huguenot Family, 271, and map opposite page 357. The names on this little map, taken from a letter by Peter Fontaine, are reversed, by mistake of the engraver.

‡ State and Condition of Virginia.

§ Rev. C. Griffin's Letter, in Bishop Meade's Old Churches, etc., i. 287.

jority of them could repeat the Creed, the Lord's Prayer, and Ten Commandments, behaved reverently at prayers, and made the responses. The Indians became so fond of this worthy missionary, that they would sometimes lift him up in their arms; and they would have chosen him chief of their tribe, the Saponeys. They alone remained steadfastly at peace with the whites. They numbered about two hundred persons, and lived within musket-shot of Fort Christanna. They had recently been governed by a queen, but she dying they were now governed by twelve old men. When Governor Spotswood visited them in April, 1716, these old men waited on him at the Fort, and laid several skins at his feet, all bowing to him simultaneously. They complained through their interpreter of fifteeen of their young men having been surprised, and murdered, by the Genitoes, and desired the governor's assistance in warring against them until they killed as many of them. They governor agreed that they might revenge themselves, and that he would furnish them with ammunition. He also made restitution to them for losses which they complained they had suffered by being cheated by the English. Sixty young men next made their appearance with feathers in their hair and run through their ears, their faces painted with blue and vermilion, their hair cut in fantastic forms, some looking like a cock's-comb; and they had blue and red blankets wrapped around them. This was their war-dress, and it made them look like furies. They made no speech. Next came the young women with long, straight, black hair reaching down to the waist, with a blanket tied round them, and hanging down like a petticoat. Most of them had nothing to cover them from the waist upwards; but some wore a mantle over the shoulders, made of two deer-skins sewed together. These Indians greased their bodies and heads with bear's oil, which, with the smoke of their cabins, gave them a disagreeable odor. They were very modest and faithful to their husbands. "They are straight and well-limbed, of good shape and extraordinary good features, as well the men as the women. They look wild, and are mighty shy of an Englishman, and will not let you touch them."*

---

* Huguenot Family, 272.

The Saponey town was situated on the bank of the Meherrin, the houses all joining one another and making a circle. This circle could be entered by three passages, each about six feet wide. All the doors are on the inside of the circle, and the level area within was common for the diversion of the people. In the centre was a large stump of a tree, on which the head men stood when making a speech. The women bound their infants to a board cut in the shape of the child; the top of the board was round, and there was a hole for a string, by which it is hung to the limb of a tree, or to a pin in a post, and there swings and diverts himself out of harm's way. The Saponeys lived as lazily and as miserably as any people in the world. The boys with their bows shot at the eye of an axe, set up at twenty yards distance, and the governor rewarded their skill with knives and looking-glasses. They also danced the war-dance; after which the governor treated them to a luncheon, which they devoured with animal avidity.

CHAPTER LI.

1716.

Spotswood's Tramontane Expedition—His Companions—Details of the Exploration—They cross the Blue Ridge—The Tramontane Order—The Golden Horseshoe.

It was in the year 1716 that Spotswood made the first complete discovery of a passage over the Blue Ridge of mountains. Robert Beverley, in the preface to the second edition of his "History of Virginia," published at London in 1722, says: "I was with the present governor* at the head-spring of both those rivers,† and their fountains are in the highest ridge of mountains." The governor, accompanied by John Fontaine, who had been an ensign in the British army, and who had recently come over to Virginia, started from Williamsburg, on his expedition over the Appalachian Mountains, as they were then called. Having crossed the York River at the Brick-house, they lodged that night at the seat of Austin Moore, now Chelsea, on the Matapony River, a few miles above its junction with the Pamunkey. On the following night they were hospitably entertained by Robert Beverley, the historian, at his residence in Middlesex. The governor left his chaise there, and mounted his horse for the rest of the journey; and Beverley accompanied him in the exploration. Proceeding along the Rappahannock they came to the Germantown, ten miles below the falls, where they halted for some days. On the twenty-sixth of August Spotswood was joined here by several gentlemen, two small companies of rangers, and four Meherrin Indians. The gentlemen of the party appear to have been Spotswood, Fontaine, Beverley, Colonel Robertson, Austin Smith, who returned home owing to a fever, Todd, Dr. Robinson, Taylor, Mason, Brooke, and Captains Clouder and Smith. The whole number of the party, including gentlemen, rangers,

---

* Spotswood.   † York and Rappahannock.

pioneers, Indians, and servants, was probably about fifty. They had with them a large number of riding and pack-horses, an abundant supply of provisions, and an extraordinary variety of liquors. Having had their horses shod, they left Germantown on the twenty-ninth of August, and encamped that night three miles from Germanna. The camps were named respectively after the gentlemen of the expedition, the first one being called "Camp Beverley," where "they made great fires, supped, and drank good punch."

Aroused in the morning by the trumpet, they proceeded westward, each day being diversified by the incidents and adventures of exploration. Some of the party encountered hornets; others were thrown from their horses; others killed rattlesnakes. Deer and bears were shot, and the venison and bear-meat were roasted before the fire upon wooden forks. At night they lay on the boughs of trees under tents. At the head of the Rappahannock they admired the rich virgin soil, the luxuriant grass, and the heavy timber of primitive forests. Thirty-six days after Spotswood had set out from Williamsburg, and on the fifth day of September, 1716, a clear day, at about one o'clock, he and his party, after a toilsome ascent, reached the top of the mountain. It is difficult to ascertain at what point they ascended, but probably it was Swift Run Gap.

As the company wound along, in perspective caravan line, through the shadowy defiles, the trumpet for the first time awoke the echoes of the mountains, and from the summit Spotswood and his companions beheld with rapture the boundless panorama that lay spread out before them, far as the eye could reach, robed in misty splendor. Here they drank the health of King George the First, and all the royal family. The highest summit was named by Spotswood Mount George, in honor of his majesty, and the gentlemen of the expedition, in honor of the governor, named the next in height, Mount Spotswood, according to Fontaine, and Mount Alexander, according to the Rev. Hugh Jones.[*] The explorers were on the water-shed, two streams

---

[*] He says that Spotswood graved the king's name on a rock on Mount George; but, according to Fontaine, "the governor had graving-irons, but could not grave anything, the stones were so hard."

rising there, the one flowing eastward and the other westward. Several of the company were desirous of returning, but the governor persuaded them to continue on. Descending the western side of the mountain, and proceeding about seven miles farther, they reached the Shenandoah, which they called the Euphrates, and encamped by the side of it. They observed trees blazed by the Indians, and the tracks of elks and buffaloes, and their lairs. They noticed a vine bearing a sort of wild cucumber, and a shrub with a fruit like the currant, and ate very good wild grapes. This place was called Spotswood Camp. The river was found fordable at one place, eighty yards wide in the narrowest part, and running north. It was here that the governor undertook to engrave the king's name on a rock, and not on Mount George.

Finding a ford they crossed the river, and this was the extreme point which the governor reached westward. Recrossing the river, some of the party using grasshoppers for bait, caught perch and chub fish; others went a hunting and killed deer and turkeys. Fontaine carved his name on a tree by the river-side; and the governor buried a bottle with a paper inclosed, on which he wrote that he took possession for King George the First of England. Dining here they fired volleys, and drank healths, they having on this occasion a variety of liquors—Virginia red wine and white wine, Irish usquebaugh, brandy, shrub, two kinds of rum, champagne, canary, cherry punch, cider, etc. On the seventh the rangers proceeded on a farther exploration, and the rest of the company set out on their return homeward. Governor Spotswood arrived at Williamsburg on the seventeenth of September, after an absence of about six weeks. The distance which they had gone was reckoned two hundred and nineteen miles, and the whole, going and returning, four hundred and thirty-eight. "For this expedition," says the Rev. Hugh Jones, they were obliged to provide a great quantity of horseshoes, things seldom used in the eastern parts of Virginia, where there are no stones. Upon which account the governor upon his return presented each of his companions with a golden horseshoe, some of which I have seen covered with valuable stones resembling heads of nails, with the inscription on one side, 'Sic juvat transcendere montes.' This he instituted to encourage gentlemen to venture backward and make discoveries and settlements, any gentleman being entitled to wear this golden horseshoe on the breast who could prove that he had drank his majesty's health on Mount George." Spotswood instituted the Tramontane Order for this purpose; but it appears to have soon fallen through. According to Chalmers, the British government penuriously refused to pay the cost of the golden horseshoes. A novel called the "Knight of the Horseshoe," by Dr. William A. Caruthers, derives its name and subject from Spotswood's exploit.*

---

* Memoirs of a Huguenot Family, 281, 292; Introduction to Randolph's edition of Beverley's Hist. of Va., 5; Rev. Hugh Jones' Present State of Virginia. The miniature horseshoe that had belonged to Spotswood, according to a descendant of his, the late Mrs. Susan Bott, of Petersburg, who had seen it, was small enough to be worn on a watch-chain. Some of them were set with jewels. One of these horseshoes is said to be still preserved in the family of Brooke. A bit of colored glass, apparently the stopper of a small bottle, with a horseshoe stamped on it, was dug up some years ago in the yard at Chelsea, in King William County, the residence of Governor Spotswood's eldest daughter.

CHAPTER LII.

1715-1718.

Condition of the Colonies—South Carolina appeals to Virginia for Succor against the Indians—Proceedings of the Council and the Assembly—Disputes between them—Dissensions of Governor and Burgesses—He dissolves them—Blackbeard, the Pirate—Maynard's Engagement with him—His Death.

THE twenty-five counties of the Ancient Dominion were under a government consisting of a governor and twelve councillors appointed by the king, and fifty burgesses elected by the freeholders. The permanent revenue, established at the restoration, now amounted to four thousand pounds sterling, and this sum proving inadequate to the public expenditure, the deficit was eked out by three hundred pounds drawn from the quit-rents—private property of the king. Relieved from the dangers of Indian border warfare, and blessed with the able administration of Governor Spotswood, Virginia, under the tranquil reign of the first George, advanced in commerce, population, wealth, and power, more rapidly than any of her sister colonies.

A few of the principal families affected to establish an aristocracy or oligarchy, and Spotswood, at his first arrival, discovered that it was necessary "to have a balance on the Bench and the Board." He subsequently warned the ministers, "that a party was so encouraged by their success in removing former governors, that they are resolved no one shall sit easy who doth not entirely submit to their dictates; this is the case at present, and will continue, unless a stop is put to their growing power, to whom not any one particular governor, but government itself, is equally disagreeable."

At a council held at Williamsburg on the 26tn day of May, 1715, the governor presented a letter, received by express, from Governor Craven, of South Carolina, representing the deplorable condition of that colony from the murderous inroads of the Indians, the several tribes having confederated together and threatened the total destruction of the inhabitants, and requesting a supply of arms and ammunition. The council unanimously agreed to the request, and, conceiving that Virginia was also in imminent danger of invasion, desired the Indian Company to take from the magazine so much ammunition as was necessary for South Carolina, and to return the same "by the first conveniency, that so this colony may not be unprovided for its necessary defence." It was further ordered, that the governors of Maryland, New York, and New England, be exhorted to send ships of war to Charleston, and that the governor of South Carolina be invited to send hither their women and children, and such other persons as are useless in the war. Three pieces of cannon were sent to Christanna, and ammunition to Germanna, these being the two frontier settlements. Colonel Nathaniel Harrison was empowered to disarm the Nottoway Indians.

In June, upon the application of the governor of North Carolina for preventing the inhabitants of that province from deserting it in that time of danger, a proclamation was issued by Governor Spotswood ordering all persons coming thence, without a passport, to be arrested and sent back.

A letter from the governor of South Carolina, brought by Arthur Middleton, Esq., requested assistance of men from Virginia. South Carolina proposed, in order to pay the men, to send to Virginia slaves to the number of the volunteers, to work on the plantations for their benefit. The council unanimously resolved to comply with the request, and to defray the charges incurred until the men should arrive in South Carolina, and for this purpose the governor and council agreed to postpone the payment of their own salaries. It was ordered that a party of Nottoway and Meherrin Indians should be sent to the assistance of the South Carolinians. An assembly was summoned to meet on the third of August. The duty of five pounds on slaves imported was suspended for the benefit of planters sending their slaves from South Carolina to Virginia as a place of safety. The contract entered into on this occasion between the two provinces, for the raising of forces, was styled "A treaty made between this government and the Province of South Carolina." Early in July, Spotswood dispatched a number of men and arms.

The king of the Saran Indians visited Williamsburg, and agreed to bring chiefs of the Catawbas and Cherokees to treat of peace, and to aid in cutting off the Yamasees and other enemies of South Carolina.

The assembly met on the 3d of August, 1715, being the first year of the reign of George the First. The members of the council were Robert Carter, James Blair, Philip Ludwell, John Smith, John Lewis, William Cocke, Nathaniel Harrison, Mann Page, and Robert Porteus, Esquires. Daniel McCarty, Esq., of Westmoreland, was elected speaker of the house of burgesses. The governor announced in his speech that the object of the session was to secure Virginia against the murders, massacres, and tortures of Indian invasion, and to succor South Carolina in her distress, and he made known his desire to treat with the Indian chiefs who were expected, at the head of a body of men, on the frontiers. The burgesses expressed their hope that as the people of Virginia were so unable to afford supplies, the king would supply the deficiency out of his quit-rents, and requested further information as to the treaty made with South Carolina, and the aid required. A bill was introduced in the house for amending an act for preventing frauds in tobacco payments, and improving the staple. The burgesses requested the governor's assistance in arresting Richard Littlepage and Thomas Butts, who defied their authority. It appears that these gentlemen, being justices of the peace, sitting in the court of claims, in which the people presented their grievances, had refused to certify some such as being false and seditious. The governor refused to aid in enforcing the warrant. The house sent up a bill making a small appropriation for the succor of South Carolina, but clogged with the repeal of parts of the tobacco act, and the council rejected it, "the tacking things of a different nature to a money bill" being "an encroachment on the privileges of the council."

A controversy next ensued between the council and the house as to the power of redressing the grievances of the people. A dispute also occurred between the governor and the burgesses relative to the removal of the court of James City County from Jamestown to Williamsburg. The governor said: "After five years' residence upon the borders of James City County, I think it hard I may not be allowed to be as good a judge as Mr. Marable's rabble, of a proper place for the court-house."

The burgesses declared their sympathy with the suffering Carolinians, but insisted upon the extreme poverty of the people of Virginia, and so excused themselves for clogging the appropriation bill with the repeal of parts of the tobacco act, their object being by one act to relieve Virginia and succor Carolina. Governor Spotswood, in his reply, remarked: "When you speak of poverty and engagements, you argue as if you knew the state of your own country no better than you do that of others, for as I, that have had the honor to preside for some years past over this government, do positively deny that any public engagements have drawn any more wealth out of this colony than what many a single person in it has on his own account expended in the time, so I do assert that there is scarce a country of its figure in the Christian world less burdened with public taxes. If yourselves sincerely believe that it is reduced to the last degree of poverty, I wonder the more that you should reject propositions for lessening the charges of assemblies; that you should expel gentlemen out of your house for only offering to serve their counties upon their own expense, and that while each day of your sitting is so costly to your country, you should spend time so fruitlessly, for now, after a session of twenty-five days, three bills only have come from your house, and even some of these framed as if you did not expect they should pass into acts."

On the seventh day of September the council sent to the burgesses a review of some of their resolutions reflecting upon them, and the governor, and the preceding assembly. This review is able and severe. On this day the governor dissolved the assembly, after a speech no less able, and still more severe. After animadverting upon the proceedings of the house at length, and paying a high tribute to the merit of the council, the governor concludes thus:—*

"But to be plain with you, the true interest of your country is

---

* Extracts from Journal of the Council of Virginia, sitting as the upper house of assembly, preserved in the office of the Secretary of the Commonwealth, in *S. Lit. Messr.*, xvii. 585.

not what you have troubled your heads about. All your proceedings have been calculated to answer the notions of the ignorant populace, and if you can excuse yourselves to them, you matter not how you stand before God, your prince, and all judicious men, or before any others to whom you think you owe not your elections. The new short method you have fallen upon to clear your conduct by your own resolves, will prove the censure to be just, for I appeal to all rational men who shall read the assembly journals, as well of the last session as of this, whether some of your resolves of your house of the second instant are not as wide from truth and fair reasoning as others are from good manners. In fine, I cannot but attribute these miscarriages to the people's mistaken choice of a set of representatives, whom Heaven has not generally endowed with the ordinary qualifications requisite to legislators, for I observe that the grand ruling party in your house has not furnished chairmen for two of your standing committees* who can spell English or write common sense, as the grievances under their own handwriting will manifest. And to keep such an assembly on foot would be the discrediting a country that has many able and worthy gentlemen in it. And therefore I now dissolve you."

These proceedings throw light on the practical working of the colonial government, of the vigorous and haughty spirit of Spotswood, who was not surpassed in ability or in character by any of the colonial governors, and of the liberty-loving but factious house of burgesses. They also exhibit the critical condition of South Carolina, and the imminent danger of Virginia at that period. On this last point Chalmers fell into an error, in stating that the Indians then had ceased to be objects of dread in Virginia.

The assembly, as has been seen, expelled two burgesses for serving without compensation, which they stigmatized as tantamount to bribery—thus seeming indirectly to charge bribery upon the members of the British house of commons, who receive no per diem compensation. After five weeks spent in fruitless altercations, Spotswood, conceiving the assembly to be actuated by factious motives, dissolved them with harsh and contemptuous

---

* Privileges and Claims.

expressions, offending the spirit of the burgesses. He had previously wounded the pride of the council, long the oligarchy of the Old Dominion, when "colonel, and member of his majesty's council of Virginia," was a sort of provincial title of nobility. Frequent anonymous letters were now transmitted to England, inveighing against Spotswood. While the board of trade commended his general conduct, they reproved him for the offensive language which he had used in his speech to the burgesses, "who, though mean, ignorant people, and did not comply with his desires, ought not to have been irritated by sharp expressions, which may not only incense them, but even their electors." In other points, Spotswood vindicated himself with vigor and success, and he insisted "that some men are always dissatisfied, like the tories, if they are not allowed to govern; men who look upon every one not born in the country as a foreigner."

When, in 1717, the ancient laws of the colony were revised, the acts of 1663, for preventing the recovery of foreign debts, and prohibiting the assemblage of Quakers, and that of 1676, (one of Bacon's laws,) excluding from office all persons who had not resided for three years in Virginia, were repealed by the king.

John Teach, a pirate, commonly called Blackbeard, in the year 1718 established his rendezvous at the mouth of Pamlico River, in North Carolina. He surrendered himself to Governor Eden, (who was suspected of being in collusion with him,) and took the oath of allegiance, in order to avail himself of a proclamation of pardon offered by the king. Wasting the fruits of sea-robbery in gambling and debauchery, Blackbeard again embarked in piracy; and having captured and brought in a valuable cargo, the Carolinians gave notice of it to the government of Virginia. Spotswood and the assembly immediately proclaimed a large reward for his apprehension, and Lieutenant Maynard, attached to a ship-of-war stationed in the Chesapeake Bay, was sent with two small vessels and a chosen crew in quest of him. An action ensued in Pamlico Bay on the 21st of November, 1718. Blackbeard, it is said, had posted one of his men with a lighted match over the powder-magazine, to prevent a capture by blowing up his vessel, but if so, this order failed to be executed. Blackbeard, surrounded by the slain, and bleeding from his wounds, in the act of cocking a pistol, fell on the bloody deck and expired. His surviving comrades surrendered, and Maynard returned with his prisoners to James River, with Blackbeard's head hanging from the bowsprit. The captured pirates were tried in the admiralty court at Williamsburg, March, 1718, and thirteen of them were hung. Benjamin Franklin, then an apprentice in a printing-office, composed a ballad on the death of Teach, which was sung through the streets of Boston.*

---

* Grahame's Col. Hist. U. S., ii. 56, citing Williamson's Hist. of N. C. See, also, A General History of the Pyrates, published at London, (1726,) and "Lives and Exploits of Banditti and Robbers," by C. Macfarlane.

CHAPTER LIII.

1718-1739.

Complaints against Spotswood—The Governor and the Council—Dissension between Spotswood and the Assembly—Convocation of the Clergy—Controversy between Blair and Spotswood—Clergy address the Bishop of London—The Clergy side with Spotswood—Miscellaneous Matters—Governor Spotswood displaced—Succeeded by Drysdale—Spotswood's Administration reviewed—Germanna—Spotswood Deputy Postmaster General—Engaged in Iron Manufacture—His Account of it—Advertisement—Knighted—Appointed Commander-in-chief of the Carthagena Expedition—His Death—Indian Boys at William and Mary College—Change in Spotswood's Political Views—His Marriage—His Children—His Widow—Spottiswoode, the Family Seat in Scotland—Portraits of Sir Alexander Spotswood and his Lady.

AT length eight members of the council, headed by Commissary Blair, complained to the government in London, that Governor Spotswood had infringed the charter of the colony by associating inferior men with them in criminal trials. It was unfortunate that the Commissary's position involved him in these political squabbles: he would have been, doubtless, more usefully employed in those spiritual functions which were his proper sphere, and which he adorned. The governor lamented to the board of trade "how much anonymous obloquy had been cast upon his character, in order to accomplish the designs of a party, which, by their success in removing other governors, are so far encouraged, that they are resolved no one shall sit easy who doth not resign his duty, his reason, and his honor to the government of their maxims and interests." The domineering ambition of the council was long the fruitful source of mischiefs to Virginia; and it is on this account that many of the complaints and accusations against the governors are to be received with many grains of allowance. The twelve members of the council had a negative upon the governor's acts; they were members of the assembly, judges of the highest court, and held command of the militia as county lieutenants. Stith, in his "History of Virginia," complains of their overweening power, and expresses his apprehensions of its evil consequences.

As early as the year 1692, William the Third had appointed Neal postmaster for the Northern Colonies, with authority to establish posts. The rates being afterwards fixed by act of parliament, the system was introduced into Virginia in the year 1718, and Spotswood wrote to the board of trade, that "the people were made to believe that the parliament could not lay any tax (for so they call the rates of postage) on them without the consent of the general assembly. This gave a handle for framing some grievance against the new office; and thereupon a bill was passed by both council and burgesses, which, though it acknowledged the act of parliament to be in force in Virginia, doth effectually prevent its ever being put in execution; whence your lordships may judge how well affected the major part of the assemblymen are toward the collection of this branch of the revenue." The act, nevertheless, was enforced.

The assembly refused to pass measures recommended by the governor; invaded his powers by investing the county courts with the appointment of their own clerks; endeavored, as has been seen, to render inoperative the new post-office system, and transmitted an address to the king, praying that the instruction which required that no acts should be passed affecting the British commerce or navigation without a clause of suspension, might be recalled, and that the governor's power of appointing judges of oyer and terminer should be limited; and they complained that the governor's attempts went to the subversion of the constitution, since he made daily encroachments on their ancient rights. The governor, perceiving that it was the design of his opponents to provoke him, and then make a handle of the ebullitions of his resentment, displayed moderation as well as ability in these disputes, and when the assembly had completed their charges, prorogued them. This effervescence of ill humor excited a reaction in favor of Spotswood, and in a short time addresses poured in from the clergy, the college, and most of the counties, reprobating the factious conduct of the legislature, and expressing the public happiness under an administration which had raised the colony from penury to prosperity. Meantime Colonel Byrd, who had been sent out to London as colonial agent, having rather failed in his efforts against Spotswood, begged the board of trade "to recommend forgiveness and moderation to both parties." The recommendation, enforced by the advice of Lord Orkney, the governor-in-chief, the Duke of Argyle, and other great men who patronized Spotswood, quieted these discords; and the governor, the council, and the burgesses now united harmoniously in promoting the public welfare.

The chief apple of discord between the governor and the Virginians was the old question relating to the powers of the vestry. About this time Governor Spotswood was engaged in a warm dispute with the vestry of St. Anne's Parish, Essex, in which he took very high ground. The Rev. Hugh Jones subsequently, while on a visit in England, reported to the Bishop of London some things against the rubrical exactness of Commissary Blair. Evil reports had also reached the mother country as to the moral character of some of the clergy. A convention of the Virginia clergy was, therefore, held in compliance with the direction of the Bishop of London, at the College of William and Mary, in April, 1719. The governor, in a letter addressed to this body, assails the commissary as denying "that the king's government has the right to collate ministers to ecclesiastical benefices within this colony," "deserting the cause of the church," and countenancing disorders in divine worship "destructive to the establishment of the church." To all this, Commissary Blair made a reply, vindicating himself triumphantly.* He appears to have sympathized on these matters with the vestries and the people. Governor Spotswood, on the contrary, was an extreme high churchman and supporter of royal prerogative, as might have been expected from the descendant of a long line of ancestors always found arrayed on the side of the crown, and the church as established, and never with the people. The journal of this convocation throws much light on the condition of the church and the clergy of Virginia at that time. The powers exercised by the vestries, indeed, often made the position of the clergy precarious; but it would, perhaps, have engendered far greater evils

---

* Bishop Meade's Old Churches, etc., i. 160, ii. Appendix, 393.

if the governor had been allowed to be the patron of all the livings. Governor Spotswood's letter to the vestry of St. Anne's presents an elaborate argument against the right of the vestry to appoint or remove the minister; but, notwithstanding the opposition of the governor, bishop, clergy, and crown, the vestries and the people still steadfastly maintained this right. This question was the embryo of the revolution; political freedom is the offspring of religious freedom; it takes its rise in the church.

In answer to an inquiry made by the Bishop of London, the convention voted "that no member had any personal knowledge of the irregularity of any clergyman's life in this colony," a manifest equivocation.* In their address to the Bishop of London, the convention state that all the ministers in Virginia are episcopally ordained, except Mr. Commissary, of whose ordination a major part doubt;† that the circumstances of the country will not permit them to conform to the established liturgy as they would desire; that owing to the extent of the parishes they have service but once on Sunday, and but one sermon; that for the same reason the dead are not buried in churchyards, and the burial-service is usually performed by a layman; that the people observe no holidays except Christmas-day and Good Friday, being unwilling to leave their daily labor; and that of necessity the sacrament of the Lord's Supper is administered to persons who are not confirmed; that the ministers are obliged to baptize, and church women, marry, and bury at private houses, administer the Lord's Supper to a single sick person, perform in church the office of both sacraments without the habits, ornaments, and vessels required by the liturgy. The convention press upon his lordship's attention the precarious tenure of their livings, to which many of these deviations from the liturgy were attributable; they declare that the people are adverse to the induction of the clergy, which exposes them to the great oppression of the vestries. The clergy refer to Governor Spotswood as, under God, their chief support, whose efforts in their behalf were, as alleged by the governor, opposed by some of the council and Commissary Blair, who was himself accused of some irregulari-

---

* Bishop Meade's Old Churches, etc., i. 162. † A majority of one only.

ties. The convention also stated that the commissary found great difficulty in making visitations, owing to the refusal of church wardens to take the official oath, or to make presentments, and from "the general aversion of the people to everything that looks like a spiritual court." The commissary refused to subscribe to it. The contending parties in these disputes were the governor and the clergy on the one side, and the commissary with the people on the other. According to the opinion of the attorney-general, Sir Edward Northey, given in 1703, "the right of presentation by the laws of Virginia was in the parishioners, and the right of lapse in the governor;" that is, if the vestry failed to choose a minister within six months, the governor had the right of appointing him; but it was a right which the governors, although reinforced by royal authority, could not enforce. Of the twenty-five members of this clerical convention only eight appear to have sided with the commissary. He held that the difference between him and the governor as to the right of collation was this: the governor claimed the right in the first instance, like that of the king of England, to bestow livings of which he himself is patron; the commissary was of opinion that the governor's power corresponded to that of the bishop, not being original, but only consequent upon a lapse; that is, a failure of the vestry to present within the time limited by law. Commissary Blair, throughout these angry controversies, in the course of which he was very badly treated by the governor and the clergy, bore himself with singular ability and excellent temper, and proved himself more than a match for his opponents.*

Predatory parties of the Five Nations were repelled by force, and conciliated by presents. The frontier of Virginia was extended to the foot of the Blue Ridge, and two new Piedmont counties, Spotsylvania and Brunswick, were established in 1720—the seventh year of George the First.† Spotsylvania included the northern pass through the mountains. At the special solicitation of the governor, the two counties were exempted from

---

* Bishop Meade's Old Churches, etc., i. 160, ii. Appendix, 1.

† Spotsylvania, named from the first syllable of the governor's name, compounded with a Latinized termination answering to the other syllable—a sort of conceit.

taxation for ten years. An act was passed imposing penalties on "whosoever shall weed, top, hill, succor, house, cure, strip or pack any seconds, suckers, or slips of tobacco." Two hundred pounds of tobacco were offered in reward for every wolf killed. Warehouses for storing tobacco and other merchandize, when first established in 1712, were denominated rolling-houses, from the mode of rolling the tobacco to market, before wagons came into general use or the navigation of the rivers improved. This mode of transporting tobacco prevailed generally in 1820, and later.* Tobacco warehouses in Virginia are now devoted exclusively to that commodity. In 1720, King George County was carved off from Richmond County, and Hanover from New Kent. A house for the governor was completed about this time. An act was passed to encourage the making of tar and hemp, and another to oblige ships coming from places infected with the plague to perform quarantine. The Indians of the Five Nations, warring with the Southern Indians for many years, had been in the habit of marching along the frontier of Virginia and committing depredations. To prevent this, a treaty was effected with them, whereby they bound themselves not to cross Potomac River, nor to pass to the eastward of the great ridge of mountains, without a passport from the Governor of New York; and, on the other hand, the Indians tributary to this government engaged not to pass over the Potomac, or go westward of the mountains, without a passport from the Governor of Virginia. This treaty was ratified at Albany, September, 1722. An act concerning servants and slaves was repealed by proclamation.

Spotswood urged upon the British government the policy of establishing a chain of posts beyond the Alleghanies, from the lakes to the Mississippi, to restrain the encroachments of the French. The ministry did not enter into his views on this subject, and it was not till after the treaty of Aix-la-Chapelle that his wise, prophetic admonitions were heeded, and his plans adopted. He also failed in an effort to obtain from the government compensation for his companions in the Tramontane exploration. At length, owing, as his friends allege, to the in-

---

* Hening, iv. 32, 91.

trigues and envious whispers of men far inferior to him in capacity and honesty, but according to others, on account of his high-handed encroachments on the rights of the colony, Spotswood was displaced in 1722, and succeeded by Hugh Drysdale. Chalmers,* also a native of Scotland, and as extreme a supporter of prerogative, thus eulogizes Spotswood: "Having reviewed the uninteresting conduct of the frivolous men who had ruled before him, the historian will dwell with pleasure on the merits of Spotswood. There was an utility in his designs, a vigor in his conduct, and an attachment to the true interest of the kingdom and the colony, which merit the greatest praise. Had he attended more to the courtly maxim of Charles the Second, 'to quarrel with no man, however great might be the provocation, since he knew not how soon he should be obliged to act with him,' that able officer might be recommended as the model of a provincial governor. The fabled heroes who had discovered the uses of the anvil and the axe, who introduced the labors of the plough, with the arts of the fisher, have been immortalized as the greatest benefactors of mankind; had Spotswood even invaded the privileges, while he only mortified the pride of the Virginians, they ought to have erected a statue to the memory of a ruler who gave them the manufacture of iron, and showed them by his active example that it is diligence and attention which can alone make a people great."

Governor Spotswood was the author of an act for improving the staple of tobacco, and making tobacco-notes the medium of ordinary circulation. Being a master of the military art, he kept the militia of Virginia under admirable discipline. In Spotsylvania, Spotswood, previous to the year 1724, had founded, on a horseshoe peninsula of four hundred acres, on the Rapidan, the little town of Germanna, so called after the Germans sent over by Queen Anne, and settled in that quarter, and at this place he resided. A church was built there mainly at his expense. In the year 1730 he was made deputy postmaster-general for the colonies, and held that office till 1739; and it was he who promoted Benjamin Franklin to the office of postmaster for the

---

* Introduction, ii. 78.

Province of Pennsylvania. Owning an extensive tract of forty-five thousand acres of land, and finding it to abound in iron ore, he engaged largely in partnership with Mr. Robert Cary, of England, and others in Virginia, in the manufacture of it. He is styled by Colonel Byrd the "Tubal Cain of Virginia;" he was, indeed, the first person that ever established a regular furnace in North America, leading the way and setting the example to New England and Pennsylvania. Pennsylvania, at this period, was unable to export iron, owing to the scarcity of ships, and made it only for domestic use. Spotswood expressed the hope that "he had done the country very great service by setting so good an example;" and stated "that the four furnaces now at work in Virginia circulated a great sum of money for provisions and all other necessaries in the adjacent counties; that they took off a great number of hands from planting tobacco, and employed them in works that produced a large sum of money in England to the persons concerned, whereby the country is so much the richer; that they are besides a considerable advantage to Great Britain, because it lessens the quantity of bar iron imported from Spain, Holland, Sweden, Denmark, and Muscovy, which used to be no less than twenty thousand tons yearly, though, at the same time, no sow iron is imported thither from any country, but only from the plantations. For most of this bar iron they do not only pay silver, but our friends in the Baltic are so nice they even expect to be paid all in crown pieces. On the contrary, all the iron they receive from the plantations, they pay for it in their own manufactures and send for it in their own shipping."*

There was as yet no forge set up in Virginia for the manufacture of bar iron. The duty in England upon it was twenty-four shillings a ton, and it sold there for from ten to sixteen pounds per ton, which paid the cost of forging it abundantly; but Spotswood "doubted; the parliament of England would soon forbid us that improvement, lest after that we should go farther, and manufacture our bars into all sorts of ironware, as they already do in New England and Pennsylvania. Nay, he questioned whether

---

* Westover MSS., 132.

we should be suffered to cast any iron which they can do themselves at their furnaces."

The whole expense was computed at two pounds per ton of sow, (or pig iron,) and it sold for five or six pounds in England, leaving a nett profit of three pounds or more on a ton. It was estimated that a furnace would cost seven hundred pounds. One hundred negroes were requisite, but on good land these, besides the furnace-work, would raise corn and provisions sufficient for themselves and the cattle. The people to be hired were a founder, a mine-raiser, a collier, a stock-taker, a clerk, a smith, a carpenter, a wheelwright, and some carters, these altogether involving an annual charge of five hundred pounds.

At Massaponux, a plantation on the Rappahannock, belonging to Governor Spotswood, he had in operation an air-furnace for casting chimney-backs, andirons, fenders, plates for hearths, pots, mortars, rollers for gardeners, skillets, boxes for cart-wheels. These were sold at twenty shillings a ton and delivered at the purchaser's home, and being cast from the sow iron were much better than the English, which were made, for the most part, immediately from the ore.

In 1732, besides Colonel Willis, the principal person of the place, there were at Fredericksburg only one merchant, a tailor, a blacksmith, and an ordinary keeper.

The following advertisement is found in the "Virginia Gazette" for 1739: "Colonel Spotswood, intending next year to leave Virginia with his family, hereby gives notice that he shall, in April next, dispose of a quantity of choice household furniture, together with a coach, chariot, chaise, coach-horses, house-slaves, etc. And that the rich lands in Orange County, which he has hitherto reserved for his own seating, he now leases out for lives renewable till Christmas, 1775, admitting every tenant to the choice of his tenement, according to the priority of entry. He further gives notice that he is ready to treat with any person of good credit for farming out, for twenty-one years, Germanna and its contiguous lands, with the stock thereon, and some slaves. As also for farming out, for the like term of years, an extraordinary grist-mill and bolting-mill, lately built by one of the best millwrights in America, and both going by water taken by a long race out of the Rapidan, together with six hundred acres of seated land adjoining the said mill.

"N. B.—The chariot (which has been looked upon as one of the best made, handsomest, and easiest chariots in London,) is to be disposed of at any time, together with some other goods. No one will be received as a tenant who has not the character of an industrious man."

Major-General Sir Alexander Spotswood, when on the eve of embarking with the troops destined for Carthagena, died at Annapolis, on the 7th day of June, 1740. There is reason to believe that he lies buried at Temple Farm, his country residence near Yorktown, and so called from a sepulchral building erected by him in the garden there. It was in the dwelling-house at Temple Farm (called the Moore House) that Lord Cornwallis signed the capitulation. This spot, so associated with historical recollections, is also highly picturesque in its situation.*

Governor Spotswood left a historical account of Virginia during the period of his administration, and Mr. Bancroft had access to this valuable document, and refers to it in his history.†

During the sanguinary war with the Indians in which North Carolina had been engaged, Governor Spotswood demanded of the tribes tributary to Virginia a number of the sons of their chiefs, to be sent to the College of William and Mary, where they served as hostages to preserve peace, and enjoyed the advantage of learning to read and write English, and were instructed in the Christian religion. But on returning to their own people they relapsed into idolatry and barbarism.‡

Governor Spotswood's long residence in Virginia, and the identity of his interests with those of the people of the colony, appear to have greatly changed his views of governmental prerogative and popular rights, for during this year he gave it as his opinion that "if the assembly in New England would stand bluff,

---

* Bishop Meade's Old Churches, etc., 227.

† This MS., after remaining long in the Spotswood family of Virginia, was at length communicated to an English gentleman then in this country, and it is supposed to be still in his possession in Europe. It is much to be regretted that there is no copy of it in Virginia.

‡ Westover MSS., 36.

he did not see how they could be forced to raise money against their will, for if they should direct it to be done by act of parliament, which they have threatened to do, (though it be against the right of Englishmen to be taxed but by their representatives,) yet they would find it no easy matter to put such an act in execution."*

Governor Spotswood married, in 1724, Miss Butler Bryan, (pronounced Brain,) daughter of Richard Bryan, Esq., of Westminster, an English lady, whose Christian name was taken from James Butler, Duke of Ormond, her godfather. Their children were John and Robert, Anne Catherine and Dorothea. John Spotswood married, in 1745, Mary Dandridge, daughter of William Dandridge, of the British navy, Commander of the Ludlow Castle ship-of-war, and their children were two sons, General Alexander Spotswood and Captain John Spotswood of the army of the Revolution, and two daughters, Mary and Anne. Robert, the younger son of the governor, an officer under Washington in the French and Indian war, being detached with a scouting party from Fort Cumberland, (1756,) was supposed to have been killed by the Indians. He died without issue.† His remains were found near Fort Du Quesne; and in an elegiac poem published in "Martin's Miscellany," in London, the writer assumes that young Spotswood was slain by the savages.

> "Courageous youth! were now thine honored sire
> To breathe again, and rouse his wonted ire,
> Nor French nor Shawnee dare his rage provoke,
> From great Potomac's spring to Roanoke.
>
> "May Forbes yet live the cruel debt to pay,
> And wash the blood of Braddock's field away;
> The fair Ohio's blushing waves may tell
> How Britons fought, and how each hero fell."‡

Anne Catherine, the elder daughter of Governor Spotswood, married Bernard Moore, Esq., of Chelsea, in the County of

---

* Westover MSS., 135.
† Washington's Writings, ii. 239, 252.
‡ Lossing's Field-Book of the Revolution, ii. 471. This work is a reservoir of valuable information.

King William. Dorothea, the other daughter, married Captain Nathaniel West Dandridge, of the British navy, son of Captain William Dandridge, of Elson Green.*

The governor's lady surviving him, and continuing to live at Germanna, November the 9th, 1742, married second the Rev. John Thompson, of Culpepper County, a minister of exemplary character. From this union was descended the late Commodore Thompson of the United States navy. Lady Spotswood's children objected to the match on the ground of his inferior rank, so that after an engagement she requested to be released; but he appears to have overcome her scruples by a curious letter addressed to her on the subject.†

The present representative of the family‡ is John Spottiswoode, Esq., M.P., Laird of Spottiswoode.§ His brothers are George Spottiswoode, of Gladswood, County Berwick, lieutenant-colonel in the army, and Andrew Spottiswoode, of Broom Hall, County Surrey. The representative of the family resides during the greater portion of the year at Spottiswoode, on his extensive hereditary estate, the modern mansion being one of the finest in Southern Scotland. The old mansion still remains. Thirty miles of underground drains have been made on this estate, reclaiming hundreds of acres of land lying between the Blackadder and the Leader.‖

Governor Spotswood¶ was half-brother to a General Elliott. The governor had a country-seat near Williamsburg, called Porto-Bello. Besides the portrait of him preserved at Chelsea,

---

* Douglas's Peerage of Scotland; Burke's Landed Gentry, ii., art. SPOTTISWOOD.

† See Hist. of St. George's Parish, by Rev. Philip Slaughter, 55, and Bishop Meade's Old Churches, etc., ii. 77.

‡ 1852.

§ Letter of Andrew Spottiswoode, Esq., written in 1852, to Rev. John B. Spotswood, of New Castle, Delaware.

‖ Beattie's Scotland Illustrated, i. 31.

¶ *Arms of Governor Spotswood.*—Argent, a cheveron gules, between three oak-trees eradicate, vert. Supporters, two satyrs proper. Crest: an eagle displayed gules, looking to the sun in his splendor, proper. Motto: "Patior ut potiar." Chief seat: at the old Castle of Spotswood, in Berwickshire.—(*Burke's Landed Gentry.*)

in the County of King William, there is another at the residence of William Spotswood, Esq., in Orange County, where there is also a portrait of Lady Spotswood, and one of General Elliott, half-brother of the governor, in complete armor. The descendants of Governor Spotswood in Virginia are numerous, and his memory is held in great respect.

CHAPTER LIV.

1722-1726.

Drysdale, Governor—Intemperance among the Clergy—The Rev. Mr. Lang's Testimony—Acts of Assembly—Death of Governor Drysdale—Colonel Robert Carter, President—Called King Carter—Notice of his Family.

In the month of September, 1722, Hugh Drysdale assumed the administration of Virginia, amid the prosperity bequeathed him by his predecessor, and being a man of mediocre calibre, yielded to the current of the day, solicitous only to retain his place. Commissary Blair wished the governor, when a vacancy of more than six months occurred, to send and induct a minister as by law directed; but what Spotswood had not been bold enough to do, Drysdale feared to undertake without the authority of a royal order. Opinion is queen of the world.

There were frequent complaints of the scandalous lives of some of the clergy; but it was difficult to obtain positive proof, there being many who would cry out against such, and yet would not appear as witnesses to convict them. Intemperance appears to have been the predominant evil among the clergy, as it was also among the laity.

The Rev. Mr. Lang, who was highly recommended by the governor and commissary, wrote, in 1726, to the Bishop of London: "I observe the people here are very zealous for our holy church, as it is established in England, so that (except some few inconsiderable Quakers) there are scarce any dissenters from our communion; and yet, at the same time, the people are supinely ignorant in the very principles of religion, and very debauched in morals. This, I apprehend, is owing to the general neglect of the clergy in not taking pains to instruct youth in the fundamentals of religion, or to examine people come to years of discretion, before they are permitted to come to church privileges." Referring to the prevailing evils he says: "The great cause of all which I humbly conceive to be in the clergy, the sober part being slothful and negligent, and others so debauched that they are the foremost and most bent on all manner of vices. Drunkenness is the common vice." Mr. Lang was minister of the parish of St. Peters, in New Kent County.* The religious instruction of the negroes was for the most part neglected. There were no schools for the education of the children of the common people; no parish libraries.

The assembly was held from time to time, according to long established custom, by writ of prorogation; the people being thus deprived of the right of frequent elections. An act regulating the importation of convicts was rejected by the board of trade. To relieve the people from a poll-tax a duty was laid on the importation of liquors and slaves, but owing to the opposition of the African Company and interested traders, the measure was repealed as an encroachment on the trade of England.

Acts prohibiting the importation of negro slaves were repeatedly passed by New York, Maryland, and South Carolina, and were invariably rejected in England. Governor Drysdale congratulated the Duke of Newcastle "that the benign influence of his auspicious sovereign was conspicuous here in a general harmony and contentment among all ranks of persons." Hugh Drysdale dying in July, 1726, and Colonel Edmund Jennings, next in order of succession, being suspended, (for what cause does not appear,) Colonel Robert Carter succeeded as president of the council. This gentleman, owing to the extent of his landed possessions, and to his being agent of Lord Fairfax, proprietary of a vast territory in the Northern Neck, between the Potomac and the Rappahannock, acquired the sobriquet of "King Carter." He was speaker of the house of burgesses for six years, treasurer of the colony, and for many years member of the council, and as president of that body he was at the head of the government upwards of a year. He lived at Corotoman, on the Rappahannock, in Lancaster County. Here a church was completed in the year 1670, under the direction of John Carter, first of the family in Virginia, who came over from England, 1649. A fine old church was built about 1732 by Robert Carter, on the site of the

---

* Old Churches, i. 385.

former one, and is still in good preservation. He married first Judith Armistead, second a widow, whose maiden name was Betty Landon, of the ancient family of that name, of Grednal, in Hereford County, England, by whom he left many children. His portrait and that of one of his wives, are preserved at Shirley, on James River, seat of Hill Carter, Esq.* The first John Carter was a member of the house of burgesses for Upper Norfolk County, now Nansemond, in 1649 and in 1654, and subsequently for Lancaster County. Colonel Edward Carter was, in 1658, burgess for Upper Norfolk, and in 1660 member of the council.

---

* The Carter arms bear cart-wheels, vert.

CHAPTER LV.

1727-1740.

William Gooch, Governor—The Dividing Line—Miscellaneous—Colonel Byrd's Opinion of New England—John Holloway—William Hopkins—Earl of Orkney—Expedition against Carthagena—Gooch commands the Virginia Regiment—Lawrence Washington—Failure of attack on Carthagena—Georgia recruits Soldiers in Virginia to resist the Spaniards—Acts of Assembly—Printing in Virginia—In other Colonies—The Williamsburg Gazette—Miscellaneous Items—Proceedings at opening of General Assembly—Sir John Randolph, Speaker—Governor Gooch's Speech—Richmond laid off—Captain William Byrd—Bacon Quarter—Colonel Byrd and others plan Richmond and Petersburg in 1733—Virginia Gazette—The Mails.

In June, 1727, George the Second succeeded his father in the throne of England. About the middle of October, William Gooch, a native of Scotland, who had been an officer in the British army, became Governor of Virginia. The council, without authority, allowed him three hundred pounds out of the royal quit-rents, and he in return resigned, in a great measure, the helm of government to them. Owing partly to this coalition, partly to a well-established revenue and a rigid economy, Virginia enjoyed prosperous repose during his long administration. There was at this time one Presbyterian congregation in Virginia, and preachers from the Philadelphia Synod visited the colony.

During the year 1728 the boundary line between Virginia and North Carolina was run by Colonel Byrd and Messrs. Fitzwilliam and Dandridge, commissioners in behalf of Virginia, and others in behalf of North Carolina. "A History of the Dividing Line," by Colonel Byrd, has been published in a work entitled the "Westover MSS.;"* it contains graphic descriptions of the country passed through, its productions, and natural history. The author was a learned man and accurate observer.

There remained in their native seat two hundred Nottoway Indians, the only tribe of any consequence surviving in Virginia.

---

* By Edmund and Julian C. Ruffin, at Petersburg, 1841.

There were also still remains of the Pamunkey tribe, but reduced to a small number, and intermixed in blood. The rest of the native tribes had either removed beyond the limits of the colony, or dwindled to a mere handful by war, disease, and intemperance. An act of parliament prohibiting the exportation of stripped or stemmed tobacco was complained of by the planters as causing a decline of the trade. They undertook to enhance the value by improving its quality, and in July, 1732, sent John Randolph to lay their complaint before the crown.

With this accomplished and able man, afterwards knighted, and made attorney-general, Governor Spotswood was engaged in an angry personal controversy in the *Williamsburg Gazette*. The merits of the dispute cannot now be ascertained. Spotswood claims to have been Randolph's benefactor, and to have been the first to promote him in the world.

Virginia, notwithstanding some obstacles in the way of her trade, continued to prosper, and from the year 1700 her population doubled in twenty-five years. The New England Colonies improved still more. Colonel Byrd said of them: "Though these people may be ridiculed for some Pharisaical particularities in their worship and behavior, yet they were very useful subjects, as being frugal and industrious, giving no scandal or bad example, at least by any open and public vices. By which excellent qualities they had much the advantage of the Southern Colony, who thought their being members of the established church sufficient to sanctify very loose and profligate morals. For this reason New England improved much faster than Virginia, and in seven or eight years New Plymouth, like Switzerland, seemed too narrow a territory for its inhabitants."*

Boston, the principal town in the Anglo-American Colonies, founded in 1630, contained, in 1733, eight thousand houses and forty thousand inhabitants; and its shipping and trade were already extensive.

In 1734 died John Holloway, Esq., who for thirty years had practised the law with great reputation and success. He was for fourteen years speaker of the house of burgesses, and eleven

---

* Westover MSS., 4.

years treasurer. A native of England, he had first served as a clerk, then went into the army in Ireland early in the reign of King William the Third; next came to be one of the attorneys of the Marshalsea Court; afterwards turned projector, and being unfortunate, came over to Maryland, and thence removed to Virginia. He is described by Sir John Randolph as more distinguished for industry than for learning, and as relying more upon the subtle artifice of an attorney, than the solid reasoning of a lawyer. His opinions, however, were looked upon as authoritative; and clients thought themselves fortunate if they could engage his services upon any terms, and his fees were often exorbitant. He is portrayed by Sir John as haughty, passionate, and inhospitable; yet it seems difficult to reconcile this with his acknowledged popularity and predominant influence. In friendship he was sincere but inconstant. His management of the treasury contributed to the ruin of his fortune, and involved him in disgrace. But this account of him must be taken with allowance.

About the same time died, in London, William Hopkins, Esq., another lawyer, who had practised in Virginia about twelve years. He was well educated, understanding Latin and French well, and gifted with a retentive memory, quick penetration, sound judgment, and a handsome person. In spite of some defects of manner, he acquired a large practice, which he neglected, owing to the versatility of a mind fond of various knowledge. In fees he was moderate, in argument candid and fair, never disputing plain points. He is taxed by Sir John Randolph with an overweening vanity, which made him jealous of any other standing on a level with him; but as there had been a personal falling out between them, his testimony in regard to this particular is entitled to the less weight. Mr. Hopkins appears to have been a man of high order; and his premature death, in the flower of his age, was a loss to be deplored by Virginia.*

The Earl of Orkney died at his house in Albemarle Street, London, January, 1737, in the seventy-first year of his age. His titles were Earl of Orkney, one of the Sixteen Scottish Peers, Governor of Virginia, Constable, Governor and Captain of

---

* Va. Hist. Reg., i. 119.

Edinburgh Castle, Knight of the most ancient and most honorable order of the Thistle, one of his Majesty's Field Marshals, and Colonel of a regiment of foot. By his death his title became extinct. He left a very large fortune.

During the administration of Governor Gooch, troops for the first time were transported from the colonies to co-operate with the forces of the mother country in offensive war. An attack upon Carthagena being determined on, Gooch raised four hundred men as Virginia's quota, and the assembly appropriated five thousand pounds for their support. Major-General Sir Alexander Spotswood, who had been appointed to the command of the troops raised in the colonies, consisting of a regiment of four battalions, dying at Annapolis, when on the eve of embarcation, Governor Gooch assumed command of the expedition. The colonial troops joined those sent out from England, at Jamaica. The amount of Virginia's appropriation on this occasion exceeding the sum in the treasury, the remainder was borrowed from wealthy men, with a view to avoid the frauds of depreciation, and to secure the benefits of circulation. Lawrence Washington, half-brother of George, and fourteen years older, obtained a captain's commission in the newly-raised regiment, and, being now twenty years of age, embarked with it for the West Indies in 1740.* An accomplished gentleman, educated in England, he acquired the esteem of General Wentworth and Admiral Vernon, the commanders of the British forces, and after the latter named his seat on the Potomac. The attack upon Carthagena was unsuccessful; the ships not getting near enough to throw their shells into the town, and the scaling-ladders of the soldiers proving to be too short. That part of the attack in which Lawrence Washington was present, sustained, unflinching, a destructive fire for several hours. The small land force engaged on this occasion lost no less than six hundred killed and wounded.

Shortly after the failure at Carthagena, an express from South

---

* He took with him a number of his neighbors, who had thus an opportunity of seeing something of war. Some of these men, on their return, soon emigrated to the Valley of Virginia, and afterwards were engaged in the Revolution. Among them was John Grigsby, of Stafford, progenitor of the family of that name in Western Virginia.

Carolina brought tidings that the Spaniards had made a descent upon Georgia; and Captain Dandridge, commander of the South Sea Castle, together with the "snows" Hawk and Swift, was dispatched to the assistance of General Oglethorpe. The Spaniards were repulsed. Georgia being still threatened by a Spanish force concentrated at St. Augustine, in Florida, Oglethorpe sent Lieutenant-Colonel Heron to recruit a regiment in Virginia. Captain Lawrence Washington, with a number of officers and soldiers of Gooch's Carthagena Regiment, recently discharged, just now arriving at Hampton, and meeting with Heron, many of them enlisted again under him.

About this time apprehensions were felt of foreign invasion by sea, of Indian incursions, and of servile insurrections. An act was passed to prevent excessive and deceitful gaming, making all gaming obligations void, imposing heavy penalties upon persons cheating at games, and declaring them infamous, authorizing justices of the peace to bind common gamblers over to their good behavior. Means were adopted for encouraging adventurers in iron works. The towns of Fredericksburg and Falmouth were established at the head of tide-water, on the Rappahannock. Caroline County was formed, and Goochland carved out from Henrico. Long and elaborate acts were passed for amending the staple of tobacco. The tending of seconds was prohibited; all tobacco exported to be inspected; to be exported from warehouses only; the planter to receive from the inspectors a promissory note specifying the quantity of tobacco deposited, and the quality, whether sweet-scented or Oronoko, stemmed or leaf; these tobacco-notes were made current within the county or other adjacent county. This salutary measure of making tobacco the basis of a currency was devised by Governor Spotswood.* Tobacco-notes were still in use in Virginia at the beginning of the present century. In the year 1730 Prince William County was established.

Sir William Berkley (1671) "thanked God that there were no free schools nor printing in Virginia." In 1682 John Buckner was called before the Lord Culpepper and his council for printing

---

* Keith, 173.

the laws of 1680 without his excellency's license, and he and the printer ordered to enter into bond in one hundred pounds, not to print anything thereafter, until his majesty's pleasure should be known.* The earliest surviving evidence of printing done in Virginia is the edition of "The Revised Laws," published in 1733. In 1719 two newspapers were issued at Boston; in 1725 one at New York, and in the following year a printing-press was introduced into Maryland. One had been established at Cambridge, in Massachusetts, before 1647. A printing-press was first established in South Carolina, and a newspaper published in 1734. The first Virginia newspaper, "The Virginia Gazette," appeared at Williamsburg, in August, 1736, published by William Parks, weekly, at fifteen shillings per annum. It was a small sheet, on dingy paper, but well printed. It was in the interest of the government, and for a long time the only journal of the colony. Parks printed "Stith's History of Virginia" and "The Laws of Virginia."

In 1732, in accordance with royal instructions, a duty was laid of five per centum on the purchase-money of slaves, to be paid by the purchaser. The difference between sterling money and the ordinary currency was twenty per centum. Stealing of slaves was made felony, without benefit of clergy.

The Nottoway Indians (1734) still possessed a large tract of land on the river of that name, in Isle of Wight County. They were much reduced by wars and disease, and were allowed to sell part of their lands for their better support. The tributary Indians now speaking the English language, the use of interpreters was dispensed with.

An act for regulating the fees of "the practisers in physic," recites that the practice is commonly in the hands of surgeons, apothecaries, or such as have only served apprenticeships to those trades, who often prove very unskilful, and yet demand excessive fees and prices for their medicines.

The general assembly met at Williamsburg, in August, 1736, and sixty burgesses appearing, and it being the first session of this assembly, they were qualified by taking the oaths and sub-

---

* Hening, ii. 518.

scribing the test. The burgesses having attended the governor in the council-chamber, and having returned, in compliance with the governor's commands, a speaker was elected, and the choice fell upon Sir John Randolph. He being conducted to the chair by two members, made a speech to the house. On the next day the burgesses waited on the governor in the council-chamber again, and presented their new speaker to his honor, and the speaker made an address to the governor, giving a concise history of the constitution of Virginia, from the first period of arbitrary government and martial law to the charter granted by the Virginia Company, establishing an assembly, consisting of a council of state and a house of burgesses, which legislative constitution was confirmed by James the First, Charles the First, and their successors. Under it the house of burgesses claimed, as undoubted rights, freedom of speech, exemption from arrests, protection of their estates, jurisdiction over their own body, and the sole right of determining all questions concerning elections. The speaker next eulogized the administration of Governor Gooch.

The governor then addressed the gentlemen of the council, Mr. Speaker, and the gentlemen of the house of burgesses. He recommended the better regulation of the militia for the preventing of servile insurrections, the danger of which was increased by the large importation of negroes; mentions that his majesty had been graciously pleased to confirm an act for the better support and encouragement of the College of William and Mary, and another facilitating the barring of entails of small value, to perpetuate which, in a new country like Virginia, could serve only to impoverish the present possessor. Governor Gooch's reply closed this long series of addresses.*

The borough of Norfolk was incorporated in 1736. Sir John Randolph, Knight, was made recorder, although not a resident.†

In the year 1737 the town of Richmond was laid off near the falls of James River, by Colonel William Byrd, of Westover, who

---

* Va. Hist. Register, iv. 121, where a list of the members may be seen.

† In the colony, *residence* was not necessary to render a candidate eligible to a seat in the house of burgesses The same practice continues to this day in England.

was proprietor of an extensive tract of land there. Shoccoe Warehouse had been already established there for a good many years. Fort Charles, called after the prince royal, afterwards Charles the Second, was erected (1645) at the falls of James River. A tract of land there, extending five miles in length and three in breadth, and lying on both sides of the river, was claimed (1679) by Captain William Byrd, father of the first Colonel William Byrd, of Westover.* This Captain Byrd was born in London about the year 1653, and came over to Virginia probably about 1674. He was a merchant and planter. His residence, appropriately named Belvidere, was on the north side of the river, opposite the falls. A large part of this land had, a few years before, belonged to Nathaniel Bacon, Jr. The names "Bacon Quarter" and "Bacon Quarter Branch," are still preserved there. The word Quarter thus used, means land owned and cultivated, but not resided on—a place where servants are quartered, and is still in common use in the tobacco-growing counties. Captain Byrd had been active in bringing some of the rebels to punishment. Bacon's confiscated land at the falls, perhaps, may have been given to him in reward for his loyal services on that occasion. He was a burgess from Henrico.† His letter-book, containing letters from 1683 to 1691, is preserved in the library of the Virginia Historical Society.

Colonel Byrd, second of the name, made a visit to his plantations on the Roanoke River, (1733,) accompanied by Major Mayo, Major Munford, Mr. Banister, and Mr. Peter Jones. While here, he says: "We laid the foundation of two large cities, one at Shoccoe's, to be called Richmond, and the other at the Point of Appomattox, to be called Petersburg. These Major Mayo offered to lay out in lots without fee or reward. The truth of it is these two places, being the uppermost landing of James and Appomattox Rivers, are naturally intended for marts where the traffic of the outer inhabitants must centre. Thus we did not build castles only, but cities in the air."‡ The following advertisement appeared in April, 1737, in "The Virginia Gazette:"

---

* Hening, ii. 453. † Va. Hist. Register, i. 61.
‡ Westover MSS., 107.

"This is to give notice that on the north side of James River, near the uppermost landing, and a little below the falls, is lately laid off by Major Mayo, a town called Richmond, with streets sixty-five feet wide, in a pleasant and healthy situation, and well supplied with springs and good water. It lies near the public warehouse at Shoccoe's, and in the midst of great quantities of grain and all kinds of provisions. The lots will be granted in fee simple on condition only of building a house in three years' time, of twenty-four by sixteen feet, fronting within five feet of the street. The lots to be rated according to the convenience of their situation, and to be sold after this April general court by me, William Byrd." Richmond is said to be named from Richmond, near London, or, as others think, from the Duke of Richmond, whom Byrd may have known in England; but this is less probable.

Among the arrivals about this time is mentioned the ship Carter, with forty-four pipes of wine, "for gentlemen in this country;" and a ship arrived in the Potomac with a load of convicts. The Hector man-of-war, Sir Yelverton Peyton commander, arrived in the James River from England, by way of Georgia, whither he had accompanied the Blandford man-of-war, and the transport-ships which conveyed General Oglethorpe and his regiment. Captain Dandridge is mentioned as commanding his majesty's ship Wolf. "Warner's Almanac" was advertised for sale. According to a new regulation adopted by the deputy postmaster-general, Spotswood, the mail from the north arrived at Williamsburg weekly, and William Parks, printer of "The Virginia Gazette," was commissioned to convey the mail monthly from Williamsburg, by way of Nansemond Court-house and Norfolktown, to Edenton, in North Carolina. The general post-office was then at New Post, a few miles below Fredericksburg.

CHAPTER LIV.

1733-1749.

Scotch-Irish Settlers—Death of Sir John Randolph—Settlement of the Valley of Shenandoah—Physical Geography of Virginia—John Lewis, a Pioneer in Augusta—Burden's Grant—First Settlers of Rockbridge—Character of the Scotch-Irish—German Settlers of Valley of Shenandoah.

DURING the reign of Queen Elizabeth, the disaffected and turbulent Province of Ulster, in Ireland, suffered pre-eminently the ravages of civil war. Quieted for a time by the sword, insurrection again burst forth in the second year of James the First, and repeated rebellions crushed in 1605, left a large tract of country desolate, and fast declining into barbarism. Almost the whole of six counties of Ulster thus, by forfeiture, fell into the hands of the king. A London company, under his auspices, colonized this unhappy district with settlers, partly English, principally Scotch—one of the few wise and salutary measures of his feeble reign. The descendants of these colonists of the plantation of Ulster, as it was now called, came to be distinguished by the name of Scotch-Irish. Archbishop Usher, who was disposed to reconcile the differences between the Presbyterians and Episcopalians, consented to a compromise of them, in consequence of which there was no formal separation from the established church. But it was not long before the persecutions of the house of Stuart, inflicted by the hands of Strafford and Laud, augmented the numbers of the non-conformists, riveted them more closely to their own political and religious principles, and compelled them to turn their eyes to America as a place of refuge for the oppressed. The civil war of England ensuing, they were for a time relieved from this necessity. Their unbending opposition to the proceedings of Cromwell drew down upon them (1649) the sarcastic denunciation of Milton.*

---

* Milton's Prose Works, i. 422, 430, 437.

The persecutions that followed the restoration (1679) and afterwards, at length compelled the Scotch-Irish to seek refuge in the New World, and many of them came over from the north of Ireland, and settled in several of the colonies, especially in Pennsylvania. From thence a portion of them gradually migrated to the western parts of Virginia and North Carolina, inhabiting the frontier of civilization, and forming a barrier between the red men and the whites of the older settlements. The Scotch-Irish enjoyed entire freedom of religion, for which they were indebted to their remote situation.* The people of eastern, or old Virginia, were distinguished by the name of Tuckahoes, said to be derived from the name of a small stream; while the hardy mountaineers, west of the Blue Ridge, were styled Cohees, according to tradition, from their frequent use of the term "Quoth he," or "Quo-he."

In the month of March, 1737, died the Honorable Sir John Randolph, Knight, speaker of the house of burgesses, treasurer of the colony, and representative for William and Mary College. He was interred in the chapel of the college, his body being borne there at his own request, by six honest, industrious, poor housekeepers, of Bruton Parish, who had twenty pounds divided among them. His funeral oration in Latin was pronounced by the Rev. Mr. Dawson, a professor in the college. Sir John was, at the time of his death, in his forty-fourth year. His father, William Randolph, a native of Warwickshire, England, came over to seek his fortunes in Virginia some time subsequent to the year 1760. He was poor, and it is said, for a time "made his living by building barns." By industry, integrity, and good fortune, he acquired a large landed estate, and became a burgess for the County of Henrico.† On the maternal side, Sir John Randolph was descended from the Ishams, an ancient family of Northamptonshire, in England, which had emigrated to the colony. A

---

* Foote's Sketches of North Carolina; Grahame, ii. 57; Davidson's Hist. of Presbyterian Church in Kentucky, 16.

† Va. Convention of '76, by Hugh Blair Grigsby, 77, citing Carrington Memoranda. Mr. Grigsby has given an interesting account of several of the distinguished Randolphs in a newspaper article, entitled "The Dead of the Chapel of William and Mary."

love of learning which he early evinced was improved by the tuition of a Protestant clergyman, a French refugee. His education was completed at William and Mary College, for which he retained a grateful attachment. He studied the law at Gray's Inn and the Temple; and, after assuming the barrister's gown, returned to Virginia, where he soon became distinguished at the bar. He was gifted with a handsome person, and a senatorial dignity. With extraordinary talents he united extensive learning; in his writings he indulged rather too much the native luxuriance of his genius. In his domestic relations he is described as exemplary; his income was ample, and his hospitality proportionate. Blessed with an excellent judgment, he filled his public stations with signal ability. He was buried in the chapel of William and Mary; and his elegant marble tablet, graced with a Latin inscription, after having endured one hundred and twenty-three years, was recently destroyed by the fire which consumed the college. Sir John Randolph was succeeded in the office of treasurer by John Robinson, Jr.

From the preamble to the act for the better preservation of deer, it appears that in the upper country they were so numerous that they were killed (as buffalo often are in the far West) for their skins. They were shot while feeding on the moss growing on the rocks in the rivers; and their carcases attracted wolves and other wild beasts to the destruction of cattle, hogs, and sheep. Many deer were also killed by hounds running at large, and by fire-hunting, that is, by setting on fire, in large circles, the coverts where the deer lodged, which likewise destroyed the young timber, and the food for cattle.

From the settlement of Jamestown a century elapsed before Virginia began to extend her settlements to the foot of the Blue Ridge. Governor Spotswood (1716) explored those mountains beyond the head-springs of the confluents of the Rappahannock. After a good many years, Joist Hite, of Pennsylvania, obtained from the original patentees a warrant for forty thousand acres of land lying among the beautiful prairies at the northern or lower end of the valley of the Shenandoah. Hite, with his own and a number of other families, removed (1632) from Pennsylvania, and seated themselves on the banks of the Opeckon, a few miles south of the site of Winchester. This handful of settlers could venture more securely into this remote country, as coming from Pennsylvania, a province endeared to the Indians by the gentle and humane policy of its first founder, William Penn. Toward the Virginians—the "Long Knives"—the Indians bore an implacable hostility, and warmly opposed their settling in the valley.*

In her physical geography Virginia is divided into four sections: the first, the alluvial section, from the sea-coast to the head of tide-water; the second, the hilly, or undulating section, from the head of tide-water to the Blue Ridge; the third, the valley section, lying between the Blue Ridge and the Alleghanies; and the fourth, the Trans-Alleghany or western section, the waters of which empty into the Ohio. The mountains of Virginia are arranged in ridges, one behind another, nearly parallel to the sea-coast, rather bending toward it to the northeast. The name Apalachian, borrowed from the country bordering on the Gulf of Mexico to the southwest, was applied to the mountains of Virginia in different ways, by the European maps; but none of these ridges was in fact ever known to the inhabitants of Virginia by that name. These mountains extend from northeast to southwest, as also do the limestone, coal, and other geological strata. So also range the falls of the principal rivers, the courses of which are at right angles with the line of the mountains, the James and the Potomac making their way through all the ridges of mountains eastward of the Alleghany range. The Alleghanies are broken by no water-course, being the spine of the country between the Atlantic and the Mississippi River. The spectacle presented at Harper's Ferry—so called after the first settler—impresses the beholder with the opinion that the mountains were first upraised, the very signification of the word in the Greek, and the rivers began to flow afterwards; that here they were dammed up by the Blue Ridge, and thus formed a sea, or lake, filling the whole valley lying between that ridge and the Alleghanies. The waters continuing to rise, they at length burst their way through the mountain, the shattered fragments of this

---

* De Hass's Hist. of Western Va., 37; Kercheval, 70.

disruption still remaining to attest the fact. As the observer lifts his eye from this scene of grandeur, he catches through the fissure of the mountain a glimpse of the placid blue horizon in the distant perspective, inviting him, as it were, from the riot and tumult roaring around to pass through the breach and participate in the calm below.*

A settlement was effected (1734) on the north branch of the Shenandoah, about twelve miles south of the present town of Woodstock. Other adventurers gradually extended the settlements, until they reached the tributaries of the Monongahela. Two cabins erected (1738) near the Shawnee Springs, formed the embryo of the town of Winchester, long the frontier out-post of the colony in that quarter. The glowing reports of the charms of the tramontane country induced other pioneers to plant themselves in that wild, picturesque region. For the want of towns and roads the first settlers were supplied by pedlars who went from house to house. Shortly after the first settlement of Winchester, John Marlin, a pedlar, who traded from Williamsburg to this new country, and John Salling, a weaver, two adventurous spirits, set out from that place to explore the "upper country," then almost unknown. Proceeding up the valley of the Shenandoah they crossed the James River, and had reached the Roanoke River, when a party of Cherokees surprised them, and took Salling prisoner, while Marlin escaped. Carried captive into Tennessee, Salling remained with those Indians for several years, and became domesticated among them. While on a buffalo-hunting excursion to the Salt Licks of Kentucky, a middle or debateable ground of hunting and war, the Flanders of the Northern and Southern Indians, with a party of them, he was at length captured by a band of Illinois Indians. They carried him to Kaskaskia, where an old squaw adopted him for a son. Hence he accompanied the tribe on many distant expeditions, once as far as the Gulf of Mexico. But after two years the squaw sold him to some Spaniards from the Lower Mississippi, who wanted him as an interpreter. He was taken by them northward, and finally, after six years of captivity and wanderings through

---

* Jefferson's Notes, 16.

strange tribes and distant countries, he was ransomed by the Governor of Canada, and transferred to New York. Thence he made his way to Williamsburg, in Virginia. About the same time a considerable number of immigrants had arrived there—among them John Lewis and John Mackey. Lewis was a native of Ireland. In an affray that occurred in the County of Dublin, with an oppressive landlord and his retainers, seeing a brother, an officer in the king's army, who lay sick at his house, slain before his eyes, he slew one or two of the assailants. Escaping, he found refuge in Portugal, and after some years came over to Virginia with his family, consisting of Margaret Lynn, daughter of the Laird of Loch Lynn, in Scotland, his wife, four sons, Thomas, William, Andrew, and Charles, and one daughter. Pleased with Salling's glowing picture of the country beyond the mountains, Lewis and Mackey visited it under his guidance. Crossing the Blue Ridge and descending into the lovely valley beyond, where virgin nature reposes in all her native charms, the three determined to fix their abode in that delightful region. Lewis selected a residence near the Middle River, on the border of a creek which yet bears his name, in what was denominated Beverley Manor; Mackey chose a spot farther up that river, near the Buffalo Gap; and Salling built his log cabin fifty miles beyond, on a beautiful tract overshadowed by mountains in the forks of the James River.* John Lewis erected on the spot selected for his home a stone-house, still standing, and it came to be known as Lewis's Fort. It is a few miles from Staunton, of which town he was the founder. It is the oldest town in the valley. He obtained patents for a hundred thousand acres of land in different parts of the circumjacent country, and left an ample inheritance to his children.

In the spring of 1736 John Lewis, the pioneer of Augusta, visiting Williamsburg, met there with Burden, who had recently come to Virginia as agent for Lord Fairfax, proprietor of the Northern Neck. Burden, in compliance with Lewis's invitation, visited him at his sequestered home in the backwoods; and the visit of several months was occupied in exploring the teeming

---

* Ruffner, in Howe's Hist. Coll. of Va., 451.

beauties of the Eden-like valley, and in hunting, in company with Lewis and his sons, Samuel and Andrew. A captured buffalo calf was given to Burden, and he, on returning to Lower Virginia, where that animal was not found, presented it to Governor Gooch, who, thus propitiated, authorized him to locate five hundred thousand acres of land in the vast Counties of Frederick and Augusta, (formed two years thereafter,) on condition that within ten years he should settle one hundred families there, in which case he should be entitled to one thousand acres adjacent to every house, with the privilege of entering as much more at one shilling per acre. This grant covered one-half of what is now Rockbridge County, from the North Mountain to the Blue Ridge. The grantee was required to import and place on the land one settler for every thousand acres. For this purpose he brought over from England (1737) upwards of one hundred families from the north of Ireland, Scotland, and the border counties of England, and it is said that he resorted to stratagem to comply apparently with the conditions.* The first settlers of this Rockbridge tract were Ephraim McDowell (ancestor of Governor James McDowell) and James Greenlee, in 1737. Mary Greenlee, his sister, attained the age of one hundred years and upwards, and was known to two or three generations. The Scotch-Irish retained much of the superstitious nature of the Highlanders of Scotland, and Mary Greenlee was by many believed to be a witch. At a very advanced age she rode erect on horseback. Robert and Archibald Alexander also settled in the Rockbridge region. Robert, a graduate of Trinity College, Dublin, taught the first classical school west of the Blue Ridge. Archibald, who was agent of Burden and drew up all his complex conveyances, was grandfather of the Rev. Dr. Archibald Alexander. Besides these, among the early settlers of this part of Virginia, were the families of Moore, Paxton, Telford, Lyle, Stuart, Crawford, Matthews, Brown, Wilson, Cummins, Caruthers, Campbell, McCampbell, McClung, McKee, McCue, Grigsby, and others.†

---

* Ruffner, ubi supra.

† The Grigsbys, from whom is descended Hugh Blair Grigsby, removed into the valley from Eastern Virginia, having originally come into the colony at the time of the restoration.

An austere, thoughtful race, they constituted a manly, virtuous population. Their remote situation secured to them religious freedom, but little interrupted by the ruling powers. Of the stern school of Calvin and Knox, so much derided for their Puritanical tenets, they were more distinguished for their simplicity and integrity, their religious education, and their uniform attendance on the exercises and ordinances of religion, than for the graceful and courteous manners which lend a charm to the intercourse of a more aristocratic society. Trained in a severe discipline, they expressed less than they felt; and keeping their feelings under habitual restraint, they could call forth exertions equal to whatever exigencies might arise. In the wilderness they devoted themselves to agriculture, domestic pursuits, and the arts of peace; they were content to live at home. Pascal says that the cause of most of the trouble in the world is that people are not content to live at home. As soon as practicable they erected churches; and all within ten or twelve miles, young and old, repaired on horseback to the place of worship. Their social intercourse was chiefly at religious meetings. The gay and fashionable amusements of Eastern Virginia were unknown among them.*
Other colonies, emanating from the same quarters, followed the first, and settled that portion of the valley intervening between the German settlements and the borders of the James River. The first Presbyterian minister settled west of the Blue Ridge was the Rev. John Craig, a native of the north of Ireland. His congregation was that of the church then known as the Stone Meeting House, since Augusta Church, near Staunton, in the County of Augusta. He became pastor there in the year 1740. Augusta was then a wilderness with a handful of Christian settlers in it; the Indians travelling through the country among them in small parties, unless supplied with whatever victuals they called for, became their own purveyors and cooks, and spared nothing that they chose to eat or drink. In general they were harmless; sometimes they committed murders. Such was the school in which the tramontane population were to be moulded and trained, civilizing the wilderness, and defending

---

* Ruffner.

themselves against the savages. In the month of December, 1743, Captain John McDowell, surveyor of the lands in Burden's grant, falling into an ambush, was slain, together with eight comrades, in a skirmish with a party of Shawnee Indians. This occurred at the junction of the North River with the James. The alarmed inhabitants of Timber-ridge* hastened to the spot, and, removing the dead bodies, sorrowfully performed the rites of burial, while the savages, frightened at their own success, escaped beyond the mountains.

So rapid was the settlement of the valley about this time, that in this year it was found necessary to lay off the whole country west of the Blue Ridge into the two new counties, Frederick and Augusta. The picturesque and verdant valleys embosomed among the mountains were gradually dotted with farms. The fertile County of Frederick was first settled by Germans, Quakers, and Irish Presbyterians, from the adjoining province of Pennsylvania. A great part of the country lying between the North Mountain and the Shenandoah River, for one hundred and fifty miles, and embracing ten counties, now adorned with fine forest trees, was then an extensive open prairie—a sea of herbage—the pasture ground of buffalo, elk, and deer. It was a favorite hunting-ground, or middle ground of the Indians.† The rich lands bordering the Shenandoah, and its north and south branches, were settled by a German population which long retained its language, its simplicity of manners and dress. Augusta County was settled by Scotch-Irish from Pennsylvania, (descendants of the Covenanters,) a race respectable for intelligence, energy, morality, and piety.

In compliance with the petition of John Caldwell and others, the synod of Philadelphia (1738) addressed a letter to Governor Gooch, soliciting his favor in behalf of such persons as should remove to Western Virginia, in allowing them "the free enjoyment of their civil and religious liberties;" and the governor gave a favorable answer. This John Caldwell, who was grandfather of

---

* So called, being a high strip of timber in an open prairie, at the first settlement.

† Kercheval's Hist. of the Valley of Virginia, 69; Foote's Sketches, second series, 14.

John Caldwell Calhoun, of South Carolina, led the way in colonizing Prince Edward, Charlotte, and Campbell Counties.

Colonel James Patton, of Donegal, a man of property, commander and owner of a ship, emigrating to Virginia about this time, obtained from the governor, for himself and his associates, a grant of one hundred and twenty thousand acres of land in the valley. He settled on the south fork of the Shenandoah. John Preston, a shipmaster in Dublin, a brother-in-law of Patton, came over with him, and subsequently established himself near Staunton—the progenitor of a distinguished race of his own name, and of the Browns and Breckenridges.* While the first settlement of the valley took place in Hite's patent, nearer to Pennsylvania, the filling up of that region was somewhat retarded by a claim which Lord Fairfax set up for a region westward of the Blue Ridge, comprehending ten counties. This claim was grounded upon the terms of the conveyance which included all the country between the head of the Rappahannock and the head of the Potomac; and this river was found to have its source in the Alleghanies. Although the claim was not admitted by the Governor of Virginia, yet, as it involved settlers in the danger of a lawsuit, they preferred moving farther on to the tract of country in Augusta County, included in the grants to Beverley and to Burden.

---

* Foote's Sketches, ii. 36.

CHAPTER LVII.

1744-1747.

Treaty with the Six Nations—Death and Character of Rev. James Blair—Colonel William Byrd—The Pretender's Rebellion—Governor Gooch—Dissent in Virginia—Whitefield—Origin of Presbyterianism in Hanover—Morris—Missionaries—Rev. Samuel Davies—Gooch's Measures against Moravians, New Lights, and Methodists.

In 1742 an act was passed to prevent lawyers from exacting or receiving exorbitant fees. In this year the town of Richmond was established by law, and the County of Louisa formed from a part of Hanover.

Governor Spotswood had effected a treaty (1722) with the Six Nations, by which they stipulated never to appear to the east of the Blue Ridge, nor south of the Potomac. As the Anglo-Saxon race gradually extended itself, like a vapor, beyond the western base of that range, collisions with the native tribes began to ensue. A treaty was concluded (July, 1744,) at Lancaster, in Pennsylvania, by which the Six Nations unwillingly relinquished, for four hundred pounds paid, and a further sum promised, the country lying westward of the frontier of Virginia to the River Ohio. The tomahawk was again buried, and the wampum belts of peace again delivered, to brighten the silver chain of friendship. The Virginia commissioners were men of high character, but they negotiated with the red men according to the custom of that day, and regaled them with punch, wine, and bumbo—that is, rum and water. The consideration apparently so inadequate, was yet perhaps equivalent to the value of their title and the fidelity of their pledge. The expense of this treaty was paid out of the royal quit-rents.

The Rev. Anthony Gavin, a zealous minister of St. James's Parish, Goochland, (1738,) complains to the Bishop of London of difficulties with Quakers, who were countenanced by men in high station, and of the disregard of Episcopal control in Virginia, the cognizance of spiritual affairs, by the laws of the colony, being in the hands of the governor and council, and that the greatest part of the ministers "are taken up in farming, and buying slaves." The ministers were compelled either to hire or buy slaves to cultivate their glebes, on which they depended for a livelihood.* The Rev. Mr. Gavin, besides his regular duties, appears to have performed a sort of missionary service, making distant journeys as far as to the country near the Blue Ridge.

Robert Dinwiddie having been appointed (1741) surveyor-general of the customs, was named, as his predecessors had been, a member of the several councils of the colonies. Gooch readily complied with the royal order, but the council, prompted both by jealousy of Dinwiddie's functions and by an aristocratic exclusiveness, refused to allow him to act with them, and sent the king a remonstrance against it. The board of trade decided the case in Dinwiddie's favor. We may see in this affair the germ of that mutual jealousy which afterwards grew up between him and some of the leading characters in Virginia.

In the year 1743 died Edward Barradall, Esq., an eminent lawyer; he held the office of attorney-general, judge of the admiralty court, and other high posts. He married Sarah, daughter of the Honorable William Fitzhugh. He was buried in the churchyard in Williamsburg, where a Latin epitaph records his worth.

In the same year died the Rev. James Blair, Commissary to the Bishop of London. Finding his ministry in Scotland obstructed by popular prejudice, he retired to London, whence he was sent over to Virginia as a missionary, (1685.) He was minister for Henrico Parish nine years; in 1689 was appointed commissary. From Henrico he removed to Jamestown, in order to be near the college, which he was raising up. He became (1710) the minister of Bruton Parish, and resided at Williamsburg. He was a minister in Virginia for about fifty-eight years, commissary for fifty-four years, and president of the college fifty years. His sermons, one hundred and seventeen in number, expository of the Sermon on the Mount, were published in England, (1722,) and passed through two editions. They are highly commended

---

* Bishop Meade's Old Churches, etc., i. 456.

by Dr. Waterland and Dr. Doddridge. Dr. Blair appears to have been a plain-spoken preacher, who had the courage to speak the truth to an aristocratic congregation. Alluding in one of these sermons to the custom of swearing, he says: "I know of no vice that brings more scandal to our Church of England. The church may be in danger from many enemies, but perhaps she is not so much in danger from any as from the great number of profane persons that pretend to be of her, enough to make all serious people afraid of our society, and to bring down the judgments of God upon us: 'by reason of swearing the land mourneth.' But be not deceived: our church has no principles that lead to swearing more than the Dissenters; but whatever church is uppermost, there are always a great many who, having no religion at all, crowd into it, and bring it into disgrace and disreputation." Commissary Blair left his library and five hundred pounds to the college of which he was the founder, and ten thousand pounds to his nephew, John Blair, and his children.* Commissary Blair was alike eminent for energy, learning, talents, piety, and a catholic spirit; he was a sincere lover of Virginia and her benefactor; his name is identified with her history, and his memory deserves to be held in enduring respect and veneration.

In November, 1743, William Fairfax, son of Lord Fairfax, proprietor of the Northern Neck, was appointed one of the council in the place of Dr. Blair. The Rev. William Dawson succeeded him as president of the College of William and Mary, and as commissary.

About this time also died Colonel William Byrd, of Westover, second of the name, one of the council. A vast fortune enabled him to live in a style of hospitable splendor before unknown in Virginia. His extensive learning was improved by a keen observation, and refined by an acquaintance and correspondence with the wits and noblemen of his day in England. His writings display a thorough knowledge of the natural and civil history of the colony, and abound in photographic sketches of the manners of his age. His diffuse style is relieved by frequent ebullitions of humor, which, according to the spirit of his times, is often coarse

---

* Old Churches, i. 154, 165; Evang. and Lit. Mag., ii. 341.

and indelicate. His sarcasm is sometimes unjust, and his ridicule frequently misplaced, yet his writings are among the most valuable that have descended from his era, and to him is due the honor of having contributed more perhaps to the preservation of the historical materials of Virginia than any other of her sons, by the purchase of the Records of the Virginia Company. He lies buried in the garden at Westover, where a marble monument bears the following inscription: "Here lieth the Honorable William Byrd, Esq. Being born to one of the amplest fortunes in this country, he was sent early to England for his education, where, under the care and direction of Sir Robert Southwell, and ever favored with his particular instructions, he made a happy proficiency in polite and various learning. By the means of the same noble friend he was introduced to the acquaintance of many of the first persons of that age for knowledge, wit, virtue, birth, or high station, and particularly contracted a most intimate and bosom friendship with the learned and illustrious Charles Boyle, Earl of Orrery. He was called to the bar in the Middle Temple; studied for some time in the Low Countries; visited the court of France, and was chosen Fellow of the Royal Society. Thus eminently fitted for the service and ornament of his country, he was made receiver-general of his majesty's revenues here; was thrice appointed public agent to the court and ministry of England; and being thirty-seven years a member, at last became president of the council of this colony. To all this were added a great elegancy of taste and life, the well-bred gentleman and polite companion, the splendid economist, and prudent father of a family, withal the constant enemy of all exorbitant power, and hearty friend to the liberties of his country. Nat. Mar. 28, 1674. Mort. Aug. 26, 1744. An. Ætat. 70." His portrait, a fine face, is preserved. Colonel Byrd amassed the finest private library which had then been seen in the New World, a catalogue of which, in quarto, is preserved in the Franklin Library, Philadelphia. Sir Robert Southwell was envoy extraordinary to Portugal in 1665, and to Brussels in 1671; was subsequently clerk of the privy council, and was repeatedly chosen president of the Royal Society. He died in 1702.

France, endeavoring to impose a popish pretender of the house of Stuart upon the people of England, the colonies were advised to put themselves in readiness against the threatened blow. Accordingly in the following year the assembly met, but still adhering to a rigid economy, the burgesses refused to make any appropriation of money for that purpose. About this time Edward Trelawney, governor of Jamaica, was authorized to recruit a regiment in Virginia. In 1745 a rebellion burst forth in Scotland in favor of the Pretender, Charles Edward Stuart, grandson of James the Second. When intelligence of this event reached Virginia, the assembly was again called together, and the college, the clergy, and the assembly, unanimously pledged their private resources and those of the colony to support the house of Hanover. A proclamation was also issued against Romish priests, sent, it was alleged, as emissaries from Maryland, to seduce the people of Virginia from their allegiance. The tidings of the overthrow of the Pretender by the Duke of Cumberland, at Culloden, on the 16th of April, 1746, were joyfully received in the Ancient Dominion, and celebrated by burning the effigies of the unfortunate prince, and by bonfires, processions, and illuminations.

About this time the Rev. William Stith was engaged in composing his "History of Virginia," at Varina, on the James River. It is much to be regretted that this accurate, judicious, and faithful writer did not receive encouragement to complete the work down to his own times.

In May, 1746, the assembly appropriated four thousand pounds to the raising of Virginia's quota of troops for the invasion of Canada. They sailed from Hampton in June, under convoy of the Fowey man-of-war; the expedition proved abortive. Governor Gooch, who had been appointed commander, but had declined the appointment, was knighted during this year. Not long afterwards the capitol at Williamsburg was burnt, and the burgesses availed themselves of this conjuncture to propose the establishment of the metropolis at a point more favorable to commerce; but this scheme was rejected by the council. Governor Gooch, on this occasion, appears to have exhibited some duplicity: in his communications to the board of trade he extolled the enlarged views of the burgesses, while he censured the selfishness of the council; yet in public he blamed the burgesses, "as he thought this the best method to stifle the flame of contention." In this case he would seem not to have reckoned "honesty the best policy;" and it often is not, else there would perhaps be more of it in the world; but it is certainly always better than policy.

In the year 1748 Petersburg and Blandford were incorporated. In the same year the town of Staunton, in Augusta County, was laid off, and it was incorporated in the following year. This happened to be one of the acts repealed by the crown under subsequent protest of the house of burgesses; and another act of incorporation was not applied for until about 1762-63. Hence originated a mistake in all the histories as to the date of the charter.* Staunton thus appears to be the oldest town in the valley.

The assembly appointed a committee to revise the laws of Virginia; it consisted of Peyton Randolph, Philip Ludwell, Beverley Whiting, Carter Burwell, and Benjamin Waller. During this year the vestries were authorized to make presentation to benefices, an act which Bishop Sherlock complained of as a serious encroachment on the rights of the crown.

Dissent from the established church began to develope itself in Virginia. In 1740 the celebrated Whitefield, then about twenty-six years of age, preached at Williamsburg, by the invitation of Commissary Blair. The extraordinary religious excitement which took place at this time in America, and which was increased by the impassioned eloquence of Whitefield, was styled "the New Light Stir." It produced a temporary schism in the American Presbyterian Church, and the two parties were known as Old Side and New Side. The Synod of Philadelphia was Old Side; the Presbyteries of New Castle, New Brunswick, and New York, New Side. The preachers of the New Side were often styled "New Lights." A hundred years before, the Presbyterians of Ireland denounced the sectarian (or Cromwell) party of England, as those who "vilify public ordinances, speak evil of church government,

---

* Letter from Bolivar Christian, Esq., of Staunton, referring to the records of Augusta.

and invent damnable errors, under the specious pretence of a gospel-way and new light."*

Between the years 1740 and 1743 a few families of Hanover County, in Lower Virginia, withdrawing themselves from attendance at the services of the established church, were accustomed to meet for worship at the house of Samuel Morris, the zealous leader of this little company of dissenters. One of these, a planter, had been first aroused by a few leaves of "Boston's Fourfold State," that fell into his hands. Morris, an obscure man, a bricklayer, of singular simplicity of character, sincere, devout, earnest, was in the habit of reading to his neighbors from a few favorite religious works, particularly "Luther on the Galatians," and his "Table-Talk," with the view of communicating to others impressions that had been made on himself. Having (1743) come into possession of a volume of Whitefield's Sermons, preached at Glasgow, he commenced reading them to his audience, who met to hear them on Sunday and on other days. The concern of some of the hearers on these occasions was such that they cried out and wept bitterly. Morris's dwelling-house being too small to contain his increasing congregation, it was determined to build a meeting-house merely for reading, and it came to be called "Morris's Reading-Room." None of them being in the habit of extemporaneous prayer no one dared to undertake it. Morris was soon invited to read these sermons in other parts of the country, and thus other reading-houses were established. Those who frequented them were fined for absenting themselves from church, and Morris himself often incurred this penalty. When called on by the general court to declare to what denomination they belonged, these unsophisticated dissenters, knowing little of any such except the Quakers, and not knowing what else to call themselves, assumed for the present the name of Lutherans, (unaware that this appellation had been appropriated by any others,) but shortly afterwards they relinquished that name.†

---

* Milton's Prose Works, i. 423.

† Memoir of Samuel Davies, in Evang. and Lit. Mag., (edited by Rev. Dr. John H. Rice,) ii. 113, 186, 201, 330, 353, 474. "Origin of Presbyterianism," ib., 346. "Sketch of Hist. of the Church in Va," (by Rev. Moses Hoge, President of Hampden Sidney College,) appended to J. W. Campbell's Hist. of Va.,

Partaking in the religious excitement which then pervaded the colonies, limited in information and in the means of obtaining it, these unorganized dissenters became bewildered by discordant opinions. Some of them seemed to be verging toward antinomianism; and it came to be a question among them whether it was right to pray, since prayer could not alter the Divine purposes, and it might be impious to desire that it should. At length, Morris and some of his associates were summoned to appear before the governor and council at Williamsburg. Having discarded the name of Lutherans, and not knowing what to call themselves, they were filled with apprehensions in the prospect of the interview. One of them making the journey to Williamsburg alone, met with, at a house on the way, an old Scotch Presbyterian "Confession of Faith," which he recognized as embodying his own creed. The book being given to him, upon rejoining his friends at Williamsburg they examined it together, and they determined to adopt it as their confession of faith. When called before the governor and council and interrogated, they exhibited the book as containing their creed. Gooch, being a Scotchman, and, as is said, having been educated a Presbyterian, immediately remarked, on seeing the book, "These men are Presbyterians," and recognized their right to the privileges of the toleration act. The interview between the governor and council and Morris and his friends, was interrupted by a thunder-storm of extraordinary fury; the council was softened; and this was one of a series of incidents which Morris and his companions looked upon as providentially instrumental in bringing about the favorable issue of this affair.

The Rev. William Robinson, a Presbyterian, was the first minister, not of the Church of England, that preached in Hanover. The son of a Quaker physician near Carlyle, in England, he emigrated to America, and (1743) sent out by the Presbytery of New Brunswick, visited the frontier settlements of Virginia and North Carolina. Near Winchester he was apprehended by

---

290; Hawks, chap. 6; Burk, iij. 119: Hodge's Hist. of Presbyterian Church, part ii. 42, 284; Foote's Sketches of Va., 119.

the sheriff, to be sent to the governor to answer for preaching without license, but the sheriff soon released him. He preached among the Scotch-Irish settlers of Charlotte, Prince Edward, Campbell, and Albemarle, and in Charlotte established a congregation. Overtaken at Rockfish Gap by a deputation from Hanover, he was induced to return and visit that county, and he preached for some days to large congregations, some of his hearers publicly giving utterance to their emotions, and many being converted. Before his departure he corrected some of the errors into which the dissenters had fallen, and taught them to conduct public worship with better order, prayer and singing being now introduced, so that "he brought them into some kind of church order on the Presbyterian model."* He was followed shortly afterwards by the Rev. John Blair, whose preaching was equally impressive. Another missionary, the Rev. John Roan, from the New Castle Presbytery, preached to crowded congregations there and in the neighboring counties. The consequent excitement, and his speaking freely in public and in private of the delinquency of the parish ministers, and his denouncing them with unsparing invective, in spite of reproaches, ridicule, and threats, gave alarm to them and their supporters, and measures were concerted to arrest the inroads of these offensive innovations. To aggravate the indignation of the government a witness swore "that he heard Mr. Roan utter blasphemous expressions in his sermons," preached at the house of Joshua Morris, in James City County.

At the meeting of the general court in April, Governor Gooch, in his charge to the grand jury, denounced, in strong terms, "certain false teachers lately crept into this government, who, without order or license, or producing any testimonial of their education or sect, professing themselves ministers under the pretended influence of new light, extraordinary impulse, and such like satirical [sic] and enthusiastic knowledge, lead the innocent and ignorant people into all kinds of delusion." He even suspected them to be Romish emissaries, saying, "their religious professions are very justly suspected to be the result of jesuiti-

---

* Evang. and Lit. Mag., ii. 351.

cal policy, which also is an iniquity to be punished by the judges." He calls upon the jury to present and indict these offenders. On the next day the jury presented John Roan for "reflecting upon and vilifying the established religion," and Thomas Watkins, of Henrico County, for saying "your churches and chapels are no better than the synagogues of Satan," and Joshua Morris, "for permitting John Roan, the aforementioned preacher, and very many people, to assemble in an unlawful manner at his house on the seventh, eighth, and ninth of January last past."

The intolerant spirit of the government continuing unabated, the Conjunct Presbyteries of New Castle and New Brunswick, at the instance of Morris and some of his friends, who were apprehensive of severe measures being adopted against them, sent an address in their behalf to Governor Gooch, by two clergymen, Gilbert Tennent and Samuel Finley. They were respectfully received, and allowed to preach in Hanover, where they remained for a week.

The Synod of Philadelphia being now apprehensive that their congregations in the valley of Virginia might also be involved in the penalties threatened by the governor, in May, 1745, in an address to him, disclaimed all connection with the Presbytery of New Castle, which had commissioned Mr. Roan, and expressed their deep regret that any who assume the name of Presbyterians should be guilty of conduct so uncharitable and so unchristian as that mentioned in his honor's charge to the grand jury; and they assure him that these persons never belonged to their body, but were missionaries sent out by some who, in May, 1741, had been excluded from the Synod of Philadelphia by reason of their divisive and uncharitable doctrines and practices, and whose object was, in a spirit of rivalry, "to divide and trouble the churches." To this address Gooch made a very kind and respectful reply.

In the summer of the ensuing year he issued a proclamation against the Moravians. New Lights, and Methodists, prohibiting their meetings under severe penalties. There would seem to be some inconsistency in bringing such harsh and sweeping charges against those ministers whom he had recently received so courteously, and had permitted to preach. Perhaps when he at first reckoned the visits of these missionaries transient, and their influence inconsiderable, he was willing to indulge his courtesy and obliging disposition toward them; but when dissent was found spreading with such unexpected rapidity, Gooch, together with the clergy and other friends of the establishment, became alarmed, and had recourse to measures of intolerance, which they would rather have avoided. Besides this, the address of the Synod of Philadelphia could not but confirm the unfavorable opinion at first formed of the missionaries.

CHAPTER LVIII.

1747-1752.

Statistics of Virginia—Whitefield—Davies—Conduct of the Government toward Dissenters—Resignation of Governor Gooch—His Character—The People of the Valley and of Eastern Virginia—John Robinson, Sr., President—Richard Lee, President—Earl of Albemarle, Governor-in-Chief—Lewis Burwell, President—Population of the Colonies.

From Bowen's Geography, published at London in 1747, the following particulars are gathered: in 1710 the total population of Virginia was estimated to be 70,000, and in 1747 at between 100,000 and 140,000. The number of burgesses was 52. Of the fifty-four parishes, thirty or forty were supplied. The twelve vestrymen having the presentation of ministers were styled "the patrons of the church." The governor's salary, together with perquisites, amounted to three thousand pounds per annum. The president of the council acting as governor received a salary of five hundred pounds, and also a small amount paid him as a councillor. The professors of William and Mary College, when they began with experiments on plants and minerals, were assisted by the French refugees at Manakintown. Dr. Bray procured contributions of books for the library.*

Sweet-scented tobacco, the most valuable in the world, was found in the strip of country between the York and the James. The number of hogsheads of tobacco shipped from Virginia and Maryland together annually was 70,000, of which half was consumed in England, and half exported to other countries.

---

* The value of coins in Virginia was:—

	£	s.	d.		£	s.	d.
Spanish double doubloons..	3	10	00	Pieces of eight...............	0	5	00
Doubloons......................	1	15	00	French crowns................	0	5	00
Pistole..........................	0	17	06	Dutch dollars..................	0	5	00
Arabian Chequin.............	0	10	00				

All English coins at the same value as in England.

This trade employed two hundred ships, and yielded his majesty's treasury a revenue of upwards of £300,000, in time of peace. Jamestown at this time contained several brick houses, with sundry taverns and eating-houses,—sixty or seventy houses in all. Williamsburg or Williamstadt contained twenty or thirty houses. There was a fort or battery erected there mounting ten or twelve guns. Governor Nicholson caused several streets to be laid out in the form of a W, in honor of King William the Third, but a V or one angle of it was not as yet completed, and the plan appears to have been given up. The main street was three-quarters of a mile long, and very wide; at one end of it was the college, and at the other the capitol. The college was thought to be something like Chelsea Hospital. The capitol, in the shape of an H, is described as "a noble pile." The church was "adorned and convenient as the best churches in London." Besides these there were an octagon magazine for arms and ammunition, a bowling-green, and a play-house. There were several private houses of brick, with many rooms on a floor, but not high. It was observed that wherever the water was brackish, it was sickly; but Williamsburg was on a healthy site.* Gloucester was at this time the most populous county; Essex or Rappahannock "overrun with briars, thorns, and wild beasts." The Atlantic Ocean is denominated the "Virginian Sea."†

Whitefield, while at Charleston, in South Carolina, during the spring of 1747, being presented with a sum of money, expended it in the purchase of a plantation and negroes for the support of the orphan-house.‡ Having come on to Virginia, in a letter written from Williamsburg in April of that year, he says to a friend in Philadelphia: "Men in power here seem to be alarmed; but truth is great and will prevail. I am to preach this morning." By a remarkable coincidence, Samuel Davies, so preeminently instrumental in organizing and extending Presbyterianism in Middle Virginia, happened to come to Virginia about the same time. He was born in the County of New Castle, Penn-

---

* Williamsburg is said to be now a very healthy place, except during the months of vacation.
† Bowen's Geography, ii. 649, 652.   ‡ Port Folio for 1812, p. 152.

sylvania, now Delaware, November 3d, 1723, of Welsh extraction, on both paternal and maternal side. He was educated principally in Pennsylvania, under the care of the Rev. Samuel Blair, at Fagg's Manor, where he was thoroughly instructed in the classics, sciences, and theology. By close study his slender frame was enfeebled. He married Sarah Kirkpatrick in October, 1746. Deputed to perform a mission in so perplexing a field, without experience, and in delicate health, he started with hesitation and reluctance. Passing down the Eastern Shore associated with the labors of Makemie, Davies came to Williamsburg. Here he applied to the general court for license to preach at three meeting-houses in Hanover, and one in Henrico. The council hesitated to comply; but, by the governor's influence, the license was obtained on the fourteenth of April. The members of the court present on this occasion were William Gooch, Governor; John Robinson, John Grymes, John Custis, Philip Lightfoot, Thomas Lee, Lewis Burwell, William Fairfax, John Blair, William Nelson, Esqs.; William Dawson, Clerk. This was only two days after Whitefield had preached in Williamsburg, and he and Davies were probably there at the same time. Davies, proceeding at once to Hanover, was received with joy, since, on the preceding Sunday, a proclamation had been attached to the door of Morris's Reading-house, requiring magistrates to suppress itinerant preachers, and warning the people against gathering to hear them. After a brief sojourn, returning home, he languished under ill health, aggravated by the sudden death of his wife, and threatening to cut him off prematurely. He, however, recovered sufficient strength to return to Hanover in May, 1748, and settled at a place about twelve miles from the falls of the James River. In this second visit he was accompanied by the Rev. John Rodgers, who, finding it impossible to obtain permission to settle in Virginia, returned to the North. Governor Gooch favored the application, but a majority of the council stood out against it, saying: "We have Mr. Rodgers out, and we are determined to keep him out." Some of the clergy of the established church were vehement in their opposition to Davies and Rodgers. A majority of the council lent their countenance to this opposition, but Gooch took occasion to rebuke it in severe terms. John Blair, nephew of the commissary, Commissary Dawson, and another member of the council, whose name is forgotten, united with the governor on this occasion in treating the strangers kindly, and endeavored to procure a reconsideration of the case, but in vain. According to Burk,* most of the intelligent men of that day, including Edmund Pendleton, appear in the character of persecutors. It must be remembered, however, that the council and its friends had no right to proclaim religious freedom, and that the controversy depended on the true interpretation of the act of parliament and the Virginia statutes. These made the law, and the council was but the executive of the law, without authority to repeal or amend it.

Davies was now left to labor alone in Virginia. In April the court decided the long-pending suits against Isaac Winston, Sr., and Samuel Morris, by fining them each twenty shillings and the costs of prosecution. Severe laws had been passed in Virginia in accordance with the English act of uniformity, and enforcing attendance at the parish church. The toleration act was little understood in Virginia; Davies examined it carefully, and satisfied himself that it was in force in the colony, not, indeed, by virtue of its original enactment in England, but because it had been expressly recognized and adopted by an act of the Virginia assembly.

In October, 1748, licenses were with difficulty obtained upon the petitions of the dissenters for three other meeting-houses lying in Caroline, Louisa, and Goochland. Davies was only about twenty-three years of age; yet his fervid eloquence attracted large congregations, including many churchmen. On several occasions he found it necessary to defend the cause of the dissenters at the bar of the general court. When on one occasion, by permission, he rose to reply to the argument of Peyton Randolph, the king's attorney-general, a titter at first ran through the court; but it ceased at the utterance of the very first sentence, and his masterly argument extorted admiration; and during his stay in Williamsburg he received many civilities, especially from the Honorable John Blair, of the council, and Sir William Gooch. Samuel Davies happening to be in London at

---

* Hist. of Va., iii. 121.

the same time with Peyton Randolph, some years afterwards, mentions him in his Diary as "my old adversary," and adds, "he will, no doubt, oppose whatever is done in favor of the dissenters in Hanover." Davies, who was a man of exquisite sensibility, repeatedly alludes to the torture to which his feelings had been subjected by the mortifications that he suffered when appearing before the general court.

There was eventually obtained from Sir Dudley Rider, the king's attorney-general in England, a decision confirming the view which Davies had taken of the toleration act. He expressed himself in regard to the governor and council as follows: "The Honorable Sir William Gooch, our late governor, discovered a ready disposition to allow us all claimable privileges, and the greatest aversion to persecuting measures; but considering the shocking reports spread abroad concerning us by officious malignants, it was no great wonder the council discovered a considerable reluctance to tolerate us. Had it not been for this, I persuade myself they would have shown themselves the guardians of our legal privileges, as well as generous patriots to their country, which is the character generally given them."

In his "State of Religion among the Dissenters," Davies remarks: "There are and have been in this colony a great number of Scotch merchants, who were educated Presbyterians, but (I speak what their conduct more loudly proclaims) they generally, upon their arrival here, prove scandals to their religion and country by their loose principles and immoral practices, and either fall into indifferency about religion in general, or affect to be polite by turning deists, or fashionable by conforming to the church." Of the dissenters in Virginia he says, that at the first they were not properly dissenters from the orginal constitution of the Church of England, but rather dissented from those who had forsaken it.

Sir William Gooch, who had now been governor of Virginia for twenty-two years, left the colony, with his family, in August, 1749, amid the regrets of the people. Notwithstanding some flexibility of principle, he appears to have been estimable in public and private character. His capacity and intelligence were of a high order, and were adorned by uniform courtesy and dignity, and singular amenity of manners. If he exhibited something of intolerance toward the close of his administration, he seems, nevertheless, to have commanded the esteem and respect of the dissenters. After his departure from Virginia he continued to be the steady friend of the colony. A county was named after him.* During Sir William Gooch's administration, from 1728 to 1749, the population of Virginia had nearly doubled, and there had been added one-third to the extent of her settlements.† The taxes were light, industry revived, foreign commerce increased, and Virginia enjoyed a prosperity hitherto unknown. The frugal and industrious Germans were filling up one portion of the valley and the Piedmont country; the hardy, well-disciplined, and energetic Scotch-Irish were peopling the other portion of the valley, and planting colonies eastward of the Blue Ridge. Like the strawberry, the population continually sent out "runners" to possess the land. The contact and commingling of the English, the French, the German, the Scotch, the Irish, while it brought about some collision, yet produced an excitement which was salutary and beneficial to all. So the meeting of the opposite currents of electricity, although accompanied by a shock, results in the renovation of the atmosphere. The people of Eastern Virginia and the inhabitants of the valley have each been benefited by the other; each section has its virtues and its faults, its advantages and its disadvantages, and Virginia does not derive its character from either one, but the elements of both are mixed up in her. This is not the result of chance, or the mere work of man, but the order of a superintending Providence that presides in human affairs.

The government of Virginia now devolved upon John Robinson, Sr., president of the council, but he dying in a few days, Thomas Lee succeeded as president. Had Lee lived longer, it was believed his influence and connexions in England would have secured for him the appointment of deputy governor. He was father of Philip Ludwell, Richard Henry, Thomas L., Arthur,

---

* His son married a Miss Bowles, of Maryland, who, after his death, married Colonel William Lewis.
† Chalmers' Introduction, ii. 202.

Francis Lightfoot, and William. As Westmoreland, their native county, is distinguished above all others in Virginia as the birth-place of great men, so perhaps no other Virginian was the father of so many distinguished sons as President Lee.

The Earl of Albemarle, after whom the county of that name was called, was still titular governor-in-chief. Of this nobleman, when ambassador at Paris, Horace Walpole says: "It was convenient to him to be anywhere but in England. His debts were excessive, though ambassador, groom of the stole, governor of Virginia, and colonel of a regiment of guards. His figure was genteel, his manner noble and agreeable. The rest of his merit was the interest Lady Albemarle had with the king through Lady Yarmouth. He had all his life imitated the French manners till he came to Paris, where he never conversed with a Frenchman. If good breeding is not different from good sense, Lord Albemarle, at least, knew how to distinguish it from good nature. He would bow to his postillion while he was ruining his tailor."

Lee was succeeded by Lewis Burwell, of Gloucester County, also president of the council. During his brief administration, some Cherokee chiefs, with a party of warriors, visited Williamsburg for the purpose, as they professed, of opening a direct trade with Virginia. A party of the Nottoways, animated by inveterate hostility, approached to attack them; and the Cherokees raised the war song; but President Burwell effected a reconciliation, and they sat down and smoked together the pipe of peace. A New York company of players were permitted to erect a theatre in Williamsburg. President Burwell, who was educated in England, was distinguished for his scholarship; he is said to have embraced almost every branch of human knowledge within the circle of his studies. The Burwells are descended from an ancient family of that name of the Counties of Bedford and Northampton, England. The first of the family, Major Lewis Burwell, came over to Virginia at an early date, and settled in Gloucester. He died in 1658, two hundred years ago. He appears to have married Lucy, daughter of Captain Robert Higginson, one of the first commanders that "subdued the country of Virginia from the power of the heathen." She survived till the year 1675.

Matthew Burwell married Abigail Smith, descended from the celebrated family of Bacon, and heiress of the Honorable Nathaniel Bacon, President of Virginia. Nathaniel Burwell, who died in 1721, married Elizabeth, eldest daughter of Robert Carter, Esq. Carter's Creek, the old seat of the Burwells, is situated in Gloucester, on a creek of that name, and not far back from the York River. The stacks of antique diamond-shaped chimneys, and the old-fashioned panelling of the interior, remind the visitor that Virginia is truly the "Ancient Dominion." There is the family graveyard shaded with locusts, and overrun with parasites and grape-vines. The family arms are carved on some of the tomb-stones; and hogs show that the Bacon arms are quartered upon those of the Burwells.*

---

* The population of the colonies at this time was as follows:—

COLONIES.		Increase per cent. per annum.
Connecticut	100,000	4·65
Georgia	6,000	.....
Maryland	85,000	5·00
Massachusetts	220,000	4·46
New Hampshire	30,000	4·17
New Jersey	60,000	6·25
New York	100,000	4·86
North Carolina	45,000	16·67
Pennsylvania*	250,000	23·96
Rhode Island	35,000	5·21
South Carolina	30,000	6·84
Virginia	85,000	2·34
All classes	1,046,000	6·23

By this table it appears that the greatest advance in population took place in Pennsylvania and North Carolina; the least in Virginia. The average increase of all the colonies was a little more than six per cent. in forty-eight years, from 1701 to 1749.

Delaware included in Pennsylvania.

CHAPTER LIX.

1752.

Dinwiddie, Governor—Ohio Company—Lawrence Washington—His Views on Religious Freedom—Davies and the Dissenters—Dissensions between Dinwiddie and the Assembly—George Washington—His Lineage—Early Education—William Fairfax—Washington a Surveyor—Lord Fairfax—Washington Adjutant-General.

A NEW epoch dawns with the administration of Robert Dinwiddie, who arrived in Virginia as lieutenant-governor early in 1752, with the purpose of repressing the encroachments of the French, of extending the confines of Virginia, and of enlarging the Indian trade. A vast tract of land, mostly lying west of the mountains and south of the Ohio, was granted by the king about the year 1749, to a company of planters and merchants. This scheme appears to have been brought forward in the preceding year by Thomas Lee of the council, and he became associated with twelve persons in Virginia and Maryland, and with Mr. Hanbury, a London Quaker merchant, and they were incorporated as "The Ohio Company." Lawrence and Augustine Washington were early and prominent members of this company. The company sent out Mr. Christopher Gist to explore the country on the Ohio as far as the falls. He was, like Boone, from the banks of the Yadkin, an expert pioneer, at home in the wilderness and among the Indians, adventurous, hardy, and intrepid. Crossing the Ohio, he found the country well watered and wooded, with here and there plains covered with wild rye, or meadows of blue grass and clover. He observed numerous buffaloes, deer, elk, and wild turkeys. Returning to the Ohio and recrossing it, Gist proceeded toward the Cuttawa or Kentucky River. Ascending to the summit of a mountain, he beheld that magnificent region long before it was seen by Daniel Boone.*

On the 13th of June, 1752, a treaty was effected with the western Indians at Logstown, on the Ohio, by which they agreed not to molest any settlements that might be made on the southeast side of the Ohio. Colonel Fry and two other commissioners represented Virginia on this occasion, while Gist appeared as agent of the Ohio Company.

Thomas Lee, the projector of this company, having not survived long after its incorporation, the chief conduct of it fell into the hands of Lawrence Washington. Governor Dinwiddie and George Mason were also members. There were twenty shares and as many members. Lawrence Washington, being desirous of colonizing Germans on the company's lands, wrote to Mr. Hanbury as follows: "While the unhappy state of my health called me back to our springs,† I conversed with all the Pennsylvanian Dutch whom I met with, either there or elsewhere, and much recommended their settling on the Ohio. The chief reason against it was, the paying of an English clergyman, when few understood and none made use of him. It has been my opinion, and I hope ever will be, that restraints on conscience are cruel in regard to those on whom they are imposed, and injurious to the country imposing them. England, Holland, and Prussia, I may quote as examples, and much more, Pennsylvania, which has flourished under that delightful liberty so as to become the admiration of every man who considers the short time it has been settled. As the ministry have thus far shown the true spirit of patriotism, by encouraging the extending of our dominions in America, I doubt not by an application they would still go farther, and complete what they have begun, by procuring some kind of charter to prevent the residents on the Ohio and its branches from being subject to parish taxes. They all assured me that they might have from Germany any number of settlers, could they but obtain their favorite exemption. I have promised to endeavor for it, and now do my utmost by this letter. I am well

---

* Sparks' Writings of Washington, ii. 478; Irving's Washington, i. 59.
† At Bath, in Virginia.

assured we shall never obtain it by a law here. This colony was greatly settled, in the latter part of Charles the First's time and during the usurpation, by the zealous churchmen, and that spirit which was then brought in has ever since continued, so that, except a few Quakers, we have no dissenters. But what has been the consequence? We have increased by slow degrees, except negroes and convicts, while our neighboring colonies, whose natural advantages are greatly inferior to ours, have become populous."* He also wrote to Governor Dinwiddie, then in England, to the same effect. He replied that it would be difficult to obtain the desired exemption for the Dutch settlers, but promised to use his utmost endeavors to effect it. It does not appear whether the ministry ever came to a decision on this subject. The nonconformists augured favorably of Dinwiddie's administration. The Rev. Jonathan Edwards, in a letter addressed to Rev. John Erskine, of the Kirk of Scotland, says: "What you write of the appointment of a gentleman to the office of lieutenant-governor of Virginia, who is a friend to religion, is an event that the friends of religion in America have great reason to rejoice in, by reason of the late revival of religion in that province, and the opposition that has been made against it, and the great endeavors to crush it by many of the chief men of the province. Mr. Davies, in a letter I lately received from him, dated March 2d, 1752, mentions the same thing. His words are, 'We have a new governor who is a candid, condescending gentleman. And as he has been educated in the Church of Scotland, he has a respect for the Presbyterians, which I hope is a happy omen.'" Jonathan Edwards was invited in the summer of 1751 to come and settle in Virginia, and a handsome sum was subscribed for his support; but he was installed at Stockbridge, in Massachusetts, before the messenger from Virginia reached him.†

Dinwiddie, the new governor, an able man, had been a clerk to a collector in a West India custom-house, whose enormous defalcation he exposed to the government; and for this service, it is said, he was promoted, in 1741, to the office of surveyor of the

---

* Sparks' Writings of Washington, ii. 481.
† Foote's Sketches, 219.

customs for the colonies, and now to the post of governor of Virginia. She was at this time one of the most populous and the most wealthy of all the Anglo-American colonies. Dinwiddie, upon his arrival, gave offence by declaring the king's dissent to certain acts which Gooch had approved; and in June, 1752, the assembly remonstrated against this exercise of the royal prerogative; but their remonstrance proved unavailing. The Virginians were in the habit of acquiring lands without expense, by means of a warrant of a survey without a patent. Dinwiddie found a million of unpatented acres thus possessed, and he established, with the advice of the council, a fee of a pistole (equivalent to three dollars and sixty cents) for every seal annexed to a grant. Against this measure the assembly, in December, 1753, passed strong resolutions, and declared that whoever should pay that fee should be considered a betrayer of the rights of the people; and they sent the attorney-general, Peyton Randolph, as their agent, to England, with a salary of two thousand pounds, to procure redress. The board of trade, after virtually deciding in favor of Dinwiddie, recommended a compromise of the dispute, and advised him to reinstate Randolph in the office of attorney-general, as the times required harmony and mutual confidence. The assembly appear to have been much disturbed upon a small occasion. During Randolph's absence Dinwiddie wrote to a correspondent in England: "I have had a great deal of trouble and uneasiness from the factious disputes and violent heats of a most impudent, troublesome party here, in regard to that silly fee of a pistole; they are very full of the success of their party, which I give small notice to."

The natural prejudice felt by the aristocracy of Virginia against Dinwiddie, as an untitled Scotchman, was increased by a former altercation with him. When, in 1741, he was made surveyor-general of the customs, he was appointed, as his predecessors had been, a member of the several councils of the colonies. Gooch obeyed the order; but the council, prompted by their old jealousy of the surveyor-general's interfering with their municipal laws, and still more by their overweening exclusiveness, refused to permit him to act with them, either in the council or on the bench. The board of trade decided the controversy in favor of Dinwiddie.*

It was during Dinwiddie's administration that the name of George Washington began to attract public attention. The curiosity of his admirers has traced the family back to the Conquest. Sir William Washington, of Packington, in the County of Kent, married a sister of George Villiers, Duke of Buckingham, and favorite of Charles the First. Lieutenant-Colonel James Washington, taking up arms in the royal cause, lost his life at the siege of Pontefract Castle. Sir Henry Washington, son and heir of Sir William, distinguished himself while serving under Prince Rupert, at the storming of Bristol, in 1643, and again a few years after, while in command of Worcester. His uncles, John and Lawrence Washington, in the year 1657, emigrated to Virginia, and settled in Westmoreland. John married a Miss Anne Pope, and resided at Bridge's or Bridge Creek, in that county. It is he who has been before mentioned as commanding the Virginia troops against the Indians not long before the breaking out of Bacon's rebellion. He and his brother Lawrence both died in 1677; their wills are preserved; they both appear to have had estates in England as well as in Virginia. His grandson, Augustine, father of George, born in 1694, married first in April, 1715, Jane Butler; and their two sons, Lawrence and Augustine, survived their childhood. In March, 1730, Augustine Washington, Sr., married secondly, Mary Ball. The issue of this union were four sons, George, Samuel, John Augustine, and Charles, and two daughters, Elizabeth or Betty, and Mildred, who died an infant. George Washington was born on the twenty-second day of February, N. S., 1732. The birthplace is sometimes called Bridge's Creek, and sometimes Pope's Creek; the house stood about a mile apart between the two creeks, but nearer to Pope's. Of the steep-roofed house which overlooked the Potomac, a brick chimney and some scattered bricks alone remain. George, it is seen, was the eldest child of a second marriage.

Not long after his birth his father removed to a seat opposite

---

* Chalmers' Hist. of Revolt of Amer. Colonies, ii. 199.

Fredericksburg; and this was the scene of George's boyhood; but the house has disappeared. He received only a plain English education, having obtained his first instruction at an old field school, under a teacher named Hobby—the parish sexton. The military spirit pervading the colony reached the school; in these military amusements George Washington was predominant; but he found a competitor in William Bustle.

Augustine Washington, the father of George, died in April, 1743, aged forty-nine years. He left a large estate. Not long afterwards Lawrence Washington married Anne, eldest daughter of the Honorable William Fairfax, and took up his residence at Mount Vernon, in Fairfax County. Augustine resided at Bridge's Creek, and married Anne, daughter of William Aylett, Esq., of Westmoreland County. George remained under the care of his mother, and was sent to stay for a time with his brother Augustine, to go to a school under charge of a teacher named Williams. It is probable that, as he taught him his daily lesson, he little anticipated the figure which his pupil was destined to make in the world. While he became thorough in what he learned he became expert in manly and athletic exercises. As he advanced in years he was a frequent guest at Mount Vernon, and became familiar with the Fairfax family at Belvoir, (called in England Beaver,) a few miles below, on the Potomac.

In the year 1747, when George was in his fourteenth year, a midshipman's warrant was obtained for him by his brother Lawrence. His father-in-law, William Fairfax, in September of the preceding year, had written to him: "George has been with us, and says he will be steady, and thankfully follow your advice as his best friend." From his promise to be steady, it may be inferred that he was then not so. And from his consenting to follow thankfully his brother's advice, it would appear that the plan of his going to sea originated with Lawrence, and not from George's strong bent that way, as has been commonly stated.

While the matter was still undetermined, his uncle, Joseph Ball, who, having married an English lady, had settled as a lawyer in London, wrote as follows to his sister Mary, the mother of Washington, in a letter dated at Strafford-by-Bow, May the 19th, 1747: "I understand that you are advised, and have some thoughts of putting your son George to sea. I think he had better be put apprentice to a tinker; for a common sailor before the mast has by no means the liberty of the subject; for they will press him from a ship where he has fifty shillings a month, and make him take twenty-three, and cut, and slash, and use him like a negro, or rather like a dog. And as to any considerable preferment in the navy, it is not to be expected, as there are always so many gaping for it here who have interest, and he has none. And if he should get to be master of a Virginia ship, (which it is very difficult to do,) a planter that has three or four hundred acres of land, and three or four slaves, if he be industrious, may live more comfortably and have his family in better bread, than such a master of a ship can. He must not be too hasty to be rich, but go on gently and with patience as things will naturally go. This method without aiming at being a fine gentleman before his time, will carry a man more comfortably and surely through the world than going to sea, unless it be a great chance indeed. I pray God keep you and yours.

"Your loving brother,

"JOSEPH BALL."*

At length the mother's affectionate opposition prevented the execution of this scheme. George Washington now devoted himself to his studies, especially the mathematics and surveying.

The marriage of his brother, Lawrence Washington, with Miss Fairfax, introduced George to the favor of Thomas Lord Fairfax, proprietor of the Northern Neck, who gave him an appointment as surveyor. He was now little more than sixteen years of age. After crossing the Blue Ridge, the surveying party, including George Fairfax, entered a wilderness where they were exposed to the inclemency of the season, and subjected to hardship and fatigue. It was in the month of March, in the eventful year 1748; snow yet lingered on the mountain-tops, and the streams were swollen into torrents. The survey-lands lay on the Shenandoah, near the site of Winchester, and beyond the first range of the Alleghanies, on the south branch of the Potomac,

---

* Bishop Meade's Old Churches, etc.

about seventy miles above Harper's Ferry. This kind of life was well fitted to train young Washington for his future career: a knowledge of topography taught him how to select a ground for encampment or for battle; while hardy exercise and exposure invigorated a frame naturally athletic, and fitted him to endure the privations and encounter the dangers of military life. He now became acquainted with the temper and habits of the people of the frontier, and the Indians; and grew familiar with the wild country which was to be the scene of his early military operations. His regular pay was a doubloon (seven dollars and twenty cents) a day, and occasionally six pistoles (twenty-one dollars and sixty cents.)

Appointed by the president of William and Mary College, in July, 1749, a public surveyor, he continued to engage in this pursuit for three years, except during the rigor of the winter months. Lord Fairfax had taken up his residence at Greenway Court, thirteen miles southeast of the site of Winchester. A graduate of Oxford, accustomed to that society in England to which his rank entitled him, fond of literature, and having contributed some numbers to the *Spectator*, this nobleman, owing to a disappointment in love, had come to superintend his vast landed possessions, embracing twenty-one large counties, and live in the secluded Valley of the Shenandoah. Here Washington, the youthful surveyor, was a frequent inmate; and here he indulged his taste for hunting, and improved himself by reading and conversing with Lord Fairfax.

CHAPTER LX.

French Encroachments—Mission of Washington—Virginia resists the French—First Engagement — Death of Jumonville — Lieutenant-Colonel Washington retreats—Surrenders at Fort Necessity.

At the age of nineteen, in 1751, Washington was appointed one of the adjutants-general of Virginia, with the rank of major. In the autumn of that year he accompanied his brother Lawrence, then in declining health, to Barbadoes, in the West Indies, who returned to Virginia, and after lingering for awhile died at Mount Vernon, aged thirty-four.

In the same year also died the Rev. William Dawson, Commissary and President of William and Mary College. Davies expresses veneration for his memory.

After the arrival of Governor Dinwiddie, the colony was divided into four military districts, and the northern one was allotted to Major Washington. France was now undertaking to stretch a chain of posts from Canada to Louisiana, in order to secure a control over the boundless and magnificent regions west of the Alleghanies, which she claimed by a vague title of La Salle's discovery. The French deposited, (1749,) under ground, at the mouth of the Kenhawa and other places, leaden plates, on which was inscribed the claim of Louis the Fifteenth to the whole country watered by the Ohio and its tributaries. England claimed the same territory upon a ground equally slender—the cession made by the Iroquois at the treaty of Lancaster. A more tenable ground was, that from the first discovery of Virginia, England had claimed the territory to the north and northwest from ocean to ocean, and that the region in question was the contiguous back country of her settlements. The title of the native tribes actually inhabiting the country commanded no consideration from the contending powers. The French troops had now commenced establishing posts in the territory on the Ohio claimed by Virginia. Dinwiddie having communicated information of these encroachments to his government, had been instructed to repel force by force if necessary, after he had remonstrated with them; he had also received a supply of cannon and warlike stores. A treaty with the Ohio tribes was held September, 1753, at Winchester, when, in exchange for presents of arms and ammunition, they promised their aid, and consented that a fortlet should be erected by the governor of Virginia on the Monongahela.

Dinwiddie, deeming it necessary to remonstrate against the French encroachments, found in Major Washington a trusty messenger, who cheerfully undertook the hazardous mission. Starting from Williamsburg on the last day of October, he reached Fredericksburg on the next day, and there engaged as French interpreter Jacob Van Braam, who had served in the Carthagena expedition under Lawrence Washington. At Alexandria they provided necessaries, and at Winchester baggage and horses, and reached Will's Creek, now Cumberland River, on the fourteenth of November. Thence, accompanied by Van Braam, Gist, and four other attendants, he traversed a savage wilderness, over rugged mountains covered with snow, and across rapid swollen rivers. He reconnoitred the face of the country with a sagacious eye, and selected the confluence of the Alleghany and Monongahela Rivers, where they form the beautiful Ohio, as an eligible site for a fort. Fort Du Quesne was afterwards erected there by the French. After conferring, through an Indian interpreter, with Tanacharisson, called the half-king, (as his authority was somewhat subordinate to that of the Iroquois,) Washington provided himself with Indian guides, and, accompanied by the half-king and some other chiefs, set out for the French post. Ascending the Alleghany River by way of Venango, he at length delivered Dinwiddie's letter to the French commander, Monsieur Le Gardeur de St. Pierre, a courteous Knight of the Order of St. Louis. Detained there some days, young Washington examined the fort, and prepared a plan and description of it. It was situated on a branch of French Creek, about fifteen miles south of Lake Erie, and about seven hundred and fifty from Williamsburg. When he departed with a sealed reply, a canoe was hospitably stocked with liquors and provisions, but the French gave him no little anxiety by their intrigues to win the half-king over to their interests, and to retain him at the fort. Getting away at last with much difficulty, after a perilous voyage of six days they reached Venango, where they met their horses. They growing weak, and being given up for packs, Washington put on an Indian dress and proceeded with the party for three days, when, committing the conduct of them to Van Braam, he determined to return in advance. With an Indian match-coat tied around, taking his papers with him, and a pack on his back and a gun in his hand, he proceeded on foot, accompanied by Gist. At a place of ill-omened name, Murderingtown, on the southeast fork of Beaver Creek, they met with a band of French Indians lying in wait for them, and one of them, being employed as a guide, fired at either Gist or the major, at the distance of fifteen steps, but missed. Gist would have killed the Indian at once, but he was prevented by the prudence of Washington. They, however, captured and detained him till nine o'clock at night, when releasing him, they pursued their course during the whole night. Upon reaching the Alleghany River they employed a whole day in making a raft with the aid only of a hatchet. Just as the sun was sinking behind the mountains they launched the raft and undertook to cross: the river was covered with ice, driving down the impetuous stream, by which, before they were half way over, they were blocked up and near being sunk. Washington, putting out his setting-pole to stop the raft, was thrown by the revulsion into the water, but recovered himself by catching hold of one of the logs. He and his companion, forced to abandon it, betook themselves to an island near at hand, where they passed the night, December the twenty-ninth, in wet clothes and without fire: Gist's hands and feet were frozen. In the morning they were able to cross on the ice, and they passed two or three days at a trading-post near the spot where the battle of the Monongahela was afterwards fought. Here they heard of the recent massacre of a white family on the banks of the Great Kenhawa. Washington visited Queen Aliquippa at the mouth of the Youghiogeny. At Gist's house, on the Monongahela, he purchased a horse, and, separating from this faithful companion, proceeded to Belvoir, where he rested one day, and arrived at Williamsburg on the 16th day of January, 1754, after an absence of eleven weeks, and a journey of fifteen hundred miles, one-half of it being through an untrodden wilderness. A journal which he kept was published in the colonial newspapers and in England. For this hazardous and painful journey he received no compensation save the bare amount of his expenses.

The governor and council resolved to raise two companies, of one hundred men each, the one to be enlisted by him at Alexandria, and the other by Captain Trent on the frontier, the command of both being given to Washington. He received orders to march as soon as practicable to the fork of the Ohio, and complete a fort, supposed to have been already commenced there by the Ohio Company. The assembly which met December, 1753, refused Dinwiddie supplies for resisting the French encroachments, "because they thought their privileges in danger," and they did not apprehend much danger from the French. The governor called the assembly together again in January, 1754, when at length, after much persuasion, they appropriated ten thousand pounds of the colonial currency for protecting the frontier against the hostile attempts of the French. The bill, however, was clogged with provisoes against the encroachments of prerogative. Dinwiddie increased the military force to a regiment of three hundred men, and the command was given to Colonel Joshua Fry, and Major Washington was made lieutenant-colonel. Cannon and other military equipments were sent to Alexandria. The English minister, the Earl of Holdernesse, also ordered the governor of New York to furnish two independent companies, and the governor of South Carolina one, to co-operate in this enterprise.

Early in April, 1754, Washington, with two companies, proceeded to the Great Meadows. At Will's Creek, on the twenty-fifth, he learned that an ensign, in command of Trent's company, had surrendered, on the seventeenth, the unfinished fort at the fork of the Ohio, (now Pittsburg,) to a large French force, which had come down under Contrecœur from Venango, with many pieces of cannon, batteaux, canoes, and a large body of men. This was regarded as the first open act of hostility between

France and England in North America. In the war which ensued Great Britain indeed triumphed gloriously, yet that triumph served only to bring on in its train the revolt of the colonies and the dismemberment of the empire.

Washington, upon hearing of the surrender of the fort, marched slowly for the mouth of Red Stone Creek, preparing the roads for the passage of cannon which were to follow. Governor Dinwiddie, about the same time, repaired to Winchester for the purpose of holding a treaty with the Indians, which, however, failed, only two or three chiefs of inferior note attending.

Virginia refused to send delegates to the Albany Convention; and the assembly and governor united in disapproving of Franklin's Plan of Union, adopted on that occasion. Dinwiddie during the previous year had proposed to Lord Halifax a plan of colonial government, dividing the colonies into two districts, northern and southern, in each of which there should be a congress, or general council, for the regulation of their respective interests.

The money appropriated by the assembly for the support of the troops was expended under the care of a committee of the assembly, associated with the governor, and the niggardly economy of this committee gave great disgust to Washington and the officers under him. He declared that he would prefer serving as a volunteer to "slaving dangerously for the shadow of pay through woods, rocks, mountains." Expecting a collision with the enemy, he wrote to Governor Dinwiddie, "We have prepared a charming field for an encounter." Ascertaining that a French reconnoitering detachment was near his camp, and believing their intentions hostile, he determined to anticipate them. Guided by friendly Indians, in a dark and rainy night he approached the French encampment, and early on the twenty-eighth of May, with forty of his own men and a few Indians, surrounded the French. A skirmish ensued; M. De Jumonville, the officer in command, and ten of his party were killed, and twenty-two made prisoners. Several of them appeared to have a mixture of Indian blood in them. The death of Jumonville created no little indignation in France, and became the subject of a French poem. It is said that Washington, in referring to this affair, remarked that "he knew of no music so pleasing as the whistling of bullets."

This being mentioned in the presence of George the Second, he observed, "He would not say so if he had been used to hear many." The king had himself fought at the battle of Dettingen. Inquiry being many years afterwards made of Washington as to the expression, he replied, "If I said so, it was when I was young." Charles the Twelfth, of Sweden, expressed delight when he first heard the whistling of bullets. Of Washington's men one was killed and two or three were wounded. While the regiment was on its march to join the detachment in advance, the command devolved, at the end of May, on Lieutenant-Colonel Washington by the death of Colonel Fry. This officer, a native of England, was educated at Oxford. Coming over to Virginia, he appears to have resided for a time in the County of Essex. He was some time professor of mathematics in the College of William and Mary, and afterwards a member of the house of burgesses, and engaged in running a boundary line between Virginia and North Carolina to the westward. In concert with Peter Jefferson, father of Thomas, he made a map of Virginia, and he was, as has been mentioned before, a commissioner at the treaty of Logstown, in June, 1752. He died universally lamented.

Washington, in a letter addressed to Governor Dinwiddie about this time, said: "For my own part, I can answer that I have a constitution hardy enough to encounter and undergo the most severe trials, and I flatter myself, resolution to face what any man dares, as shall be proved when it comes to the test, which I believe we are upon the borders of." The provisions of the detachment being nearly exhausted, and the ground occupied disadvantageous, and the French at the fork of the Ohio, now called Fort Du Quesne, having been reinforced, and being about to march against the English, a council of war, held June the twenty-eighth, at Gist's house, thirteen miles beyond the Great Meadows, advised a retreat, and Colonel Washington fell back to the post at the Great Meadows, now styled Fort Necessity, which he reached on the first of July. His force, amounting, with the addition of an independent company of South Carolinians, to about four hundred men, were at once set to work to raise a breastwork and to strengthen the fortification as far as possible. Forty or fifty Indian families took shelter in the fort, and among them

Tanacharisson, or the half-king, and Queen Aliquippa. They proved to be of more trouble than advantage, being as spies and scouts of some service when rewarded, but in the fort useless. Before the completion of the ditch, M. De Villiers, a brother of De Jumonville, appeared on the 3d of July, 1754, in front of the fort with nine hundred men, and at eleven o'clock A.M., commenced an attack by firing at the distance of six hundred yards, but without effect. The assailants fought, under cover of the trees and high grass, on rising ground near the fort. They were received with intrepidity by the Americans. Some of the Indians climbed up trees overlooking the fort, and fired on Washington's men, who returned the compliment in such style that the red men slipped down the trees with the celerity of monkeys, which excited a loud laugh among the Virginians.

The rain fell heavily during the day; the trenches were filled with water; and many of the arms of Washington's men were out of order. The desultory engagement lasted till eight o'clock in the evening, when the French commander, having twice sounded a parley, and the stock of provisions and ammunition in the fort being much reduced, it was accepted. About midnight, during a heavy rain, one half of the garrison being drunk, a capitulation took place, after the articles had been modified in some points at Washington's instance. The French at first demanded a surrender of the cannon; but this being resisted it was agreed that they should be destroyed, except one small piece reserved by the garrison upon the point of honor; but which they were eventually unable to remove.

These guns, probably only spiked and abandoned, were subsequently restored, and lay for a long time on the Great Meadows. After the Revolution it was an amusement of settlers moving westward, to discharge them. They were at last removed to Kentucky.

The troops were to retain their other arms and baggage; to march out with drums beating and colors flying, and return home unmolested. The terms of the surrender, as published at the time from the duplicate copy retained by Colonel Washington, implied ("by the too great condescension of Van Braam," the interpreter) an acknowledgment on his part that M. de Jumonville had been "assassinated." It appears that Washington was misled by the inaccuracy of Van Braam in translating the word, he being a Dutchman, and the only officer in the garrison who was acquainted with the French language. It was so stormy at the time that he could not give a written translation of the articles, and they could scarcely keep a candle lighted to read them by, so that it became necessary to rely upon the interpreter's word. The American officers present afterwards averred that the word "assassination" was not mentioned, and that the terms employed were, "the death of Jumonville." The affair is involved in obscurity: for why should the French require Washington to acknowledge himself the author of "his death," unless the killing was unjustifiable? On the other hand, with what consistency could Villiers allow such honorable terms in the same articles in which it was demanded of Washington that he should sign a confession of his own disgrace?

Of the Virginia regiment, three hundred and five in number, twelve were killed, and forty-three wounded. The loss sustained by Captain Mackay's Independent Company was not ascertained. Villiers' loss was three killed, and seventeen dangerously wounded. The horses and cattle having been captured or killed by the enemy, it was found necessary to abandon a large part of the baggage and stores, and to convey the remainder, with the wounded, on the backs of the soldiers. Washington had agreed to restore the prisoners taken at the skirmish with Jumonville; and to insure this, two captains, Van Braam and Stobo, were given up as hostages.

Washington, early on the 4th of July, 1754, perhaps the most humiliating of his life, marched out according to the terms; but in the confusion the Virginia standard, which was very large, was left behind, and was carried off in triumph by the enemy. But the regimental colors were preserved. In a short time the Virginians met a body of Indians who plundered the baggage, and were with difficulty restrained from attacking the men. Washington hastened back to Will's Creek, whence he proceeded to Williamsburg. The assembly voted him and his officers thanks, and gave him three hundred pistoles to be distributed among his men; but dissatisfaction was expressed at some of the articles of capitulation when they came to be made public.* Among the prisoners taken at the time when Jumonville was killed, was La Force, who, on account of his influence among the Indians, was looked upon as a dangerous character, and was imprisoned at Williamsburg. He managed to escape from prison in the summer of 1756, but was recaptured near West Point; and he was now kept in irons. This severe usage, and his being detained by Dinwiddie a prisoner, in violation of the treaty of Fort Necessity, cannot be justified, and was unjust to Stobo and Van Braam, who were, consequently, long retained as prisoners of war, and for some time confined in prison at Quebec. It is true that the French suffered the Indians to violate the article of the treaty securing the troops from molestation; but an excuse might be found in the difficulty of restraining savages.

Much blame was laid on poor Van Braam at the time, and in the thanks voted by the assembly his name was excepted, as having acted treacherously in interpreting the treaty. Washington, who had shortly before the surrender pronounced him "an experienced, good officer, and very worthy of the command he has enjoyed," appears to have been at a loss whether to attribute his misinterpretation to "evil intentions or negligence," but was rather disposed to believe that it was owing to his being but little acquainted with the English language. Van Braam appears to have been rather hardly judged in this affair.† Stobo, a native of Scotland, who emigrated early to Virginia, was brave, energetic, and a man of genius, but eccentric; his fidelity was never doubted. He was an acquaintance of David Hume, and a friend of Smollett, and was, it is said, the original of the character of Lismahago.

---

* Washington's Writings, ii. 456.

† Ibid., ii. 365, 456; Va. Hist. Register, v. 194; Hist. of Expedition against Fort Du Quesne, edited by Winthrop Sargent, Esq., and published by the Pennsylvania Hist. Society, 51.

CHAPTER LXI.

1754-1755.

Dinwiddie's injudicious Orders—Washington resigns—Statistics—Braddock's arrival—Washington joins him as aid-de-camp—Braddock's Expedition—His Defeat—Washington's Bravery—His account of the Defeat.

THE Virginia regiment quartered at Winchester being re-enforced by some companies from Maryland and North Carolina, Dinwiddie injudiciously ordered this force to march at once again over the Alleghanies, and expel the French from Fort Du Quesne, or build another near it. This little army was under command of Colonel Innes, of North Carolina, who, having brought three hundred and fifty men with him from that colony, had been appointed, upon Colonel Fry's death, commander-in-chief. Innes had been with Lawrence Washington at Carthagena. The force under Innes did not exceed half the number of the enemy, and was unprovided for a winter campaign. The assembly making no appropriation for the expedition, it was fortunately abandoned.

Two independent companies, ordered from New York by Dinwiddie, arrived in Hampton Roads, in his majesty's ship Centaur, Captain Dudley Digges, in June, 1754. They were marched to Will's Creek, where they were joined by an independent company from South Carolina; and these troops, under command of Colonel Innes, during the autumn, built Fort Cumberland in the fork between Will's Creek and the north branch of the Potomac, on the Maryland side, about fifty-five miles northwest of Winchester. It was called after the Duke of Cumberland, captain-general of the British army. The fort was mounted with ten four-pounders, and some swivels; and contained magazines and barracks. A prosperous town has arisen on the spot.

The North Carolina troops at Winchester, not duly receiving their pay, disbanded themselves in a disorderly way, and returned home. Dinwiddie wrote to the board of trade that "the progress of the French would never be effectually opposed, but by means of an act of parliament compelling the colonies to contribute to the common cause independently of assemblies;" and to the secretary of state: "I know of no method to compel them to their duty to the king, but by an act of parliament for a general poll-tax of two shillings and six pence a head, from all the colonies on this continent." This scheme had been suggested a long time before.

In 1738 the assembly of Virginia, which had long exercised the right of choosing a treasurer, had placed their speaker, John Robinson, in that office; and he continuing to hold both places for many years, exerted an undue influence over the assembly by lending the public money to the members. Dinwiddie ruled on ordinary occasions, but Robinson was dictator in all extraordinary emergencies.*

When the assembly met in October, 1754, they granted twenty thousand pounds for the public exigencies; Maryland and New York also contributed their quotas to the common cause; and Dinwiddie received ten thousand pounds from England. He now enlarged the Virginia forces to ten companies, under the pretext of peremptory orders from England, and made each of them independent, with a view, as was alleged, of terminating the disputes between the regular and provincial officers respecting command. The effect of this upon Washington would have been to reduce him to the grade of captain, and to subject him to officers whom he had commanded; officers of the same rank, but holding the king's commission, would rank before him. This would have been the more mortifying to him, after the catastrophe of the Great Meadows. He, therefore, although his inclinations were still strongly bent to arms, resigned, and passed the winter at Mount Vernon. He was now twenty-two years of age.

In the meanwhile Horatio Sharpe, professionally a military man, and Lord Baltimore's lieutenant-governor of Maryland, was appointed by the crown commander-in-chief of the forces against the French. Colonel William Fitzhugh, of Virginia,

---

* Chalmers' Revolt, ii. 353.

who was to command in the absence of Sharpe, had endeavored to persuade Washington to continue in the service, retaining for the present his commission of colonel. Replying in November, 1754, he said: "If you think me capable of holding a commission that has neither rank nor emolument annexed to it, you must entertain a very contemptible opinion of my weakness, and believe me to be more empty than the commission itself." Washington was dissatisfied with Dinwiddie's action in this matter.

The population of the American colonies at this period was estimated at 1,485,000, of whom 292,000 were blacks, and the number of fighting men 240,000; while the French population in Canada was not over 90,000. Virginia was reckoned the first of the colonies in power, Massachusetts the second, Pennsylvania the third, and Maryland the fourth; and either one of these had greater resources than Canada. Yet the power of the French was more concentrated; they were better fitted for the emergencies of the war, and they had more regular troops.* The colonies were not united in purpose; and the Virginians were described by Dinwiddie as "an indolent people, and without military ardor."

Sharpe's appointment was sent over by Arthur Dobbs, Governor of North Carolina, who arrived in Hampton Roads on the first of October. Sharpe, proceeding to Williamsburg, concerted with Dinwiddie and Dobbs a plan of operations against Fort Du Quesne. This plan was abandoned, owing to intelligence of the French being re-enforced by numerous Indian allies.

In February, 1755, General Edward Braddock, newly appointed commander-in-chief of all the military forces in America, arrived in Virginia with a small part of the troops of the intended expedition, the remainder arriving afterwards, being two British regiments, each consisting of five hundred men, the forty-fourth commanded by Sir Peter Halket, the forty-eighth by Colonel Dunbar. Braddock went immediately to Williamsburg to confer with Dinwiddie. Sir John St. Clair, who had come over to

---

* Chalmers' Revolt, ii. 273.

America some time before, was already there awaiting the general's arrival.

In compliance with Braddock's invitation, dated the second of March, Washington entered his military family as a volunteer, retaining his former rank. This proceeding aroused his mother's tender solicitude, and she hastened to Mount Vernon to give expression to it.

From Williamsburg Braddock proceeded to Alexandria, then sometimes called Belhaven, the original name, where he made his headquarters, the troops being quartered in that place and the neighborhood until they marched for Will's Creek. On the thirteenth of April the governors of Massachusetts, New York, Pennsylvania, Maryland, and Virginia, met General Braddock at Alexandria, to concert a plan of operations. Washington was courteously received by the governors, especially by Shirley, with whose manners and character he was quite fascinated. Overtaking Braddock (who marched from Alexandria on the twentieth) at Fredericktown, Maryland, he accompanied him to Winchester, and thence to Fort Cumberland. Early in May Washington was made an aid-de-camp to the general. Being dispatched to Williamsburg to convey money for the army-chest, he returned to the camp with it on the thirtieth.

The army consisted of the two regiments of British regulars, together originally one thousand men, and augmented by Virginia and Maryland levies to fourteen hundred. The Virginia captains were Waggener, Cock, Hogg, Stephen, Poulson, Peyrouny, Mercer, and Stuart. The provincials included the fragments of two independent companies from New York, one of which was commanded by Captain Horatio Gates, afterwards a major-general in the revolutionary war. Of the remaining provincials one hundred were pioneers and guides, called Hatchetmen: there were besides a troop of Virginia light-horse, and a few Indians. Thirty sailors were detached by Commodore Keppel, commander of the fleet that brought over the forces. The total effective force was about two thousand one hundred and fifty, and they were accompanied by the usual number of noncombatants. The army was detained by the difficulty of procuring provisions and conveyances. The apathy of the legislatures and the bad faith of the contractors, so irritated Braddock that he indulged in sweeping denunciations against the colonies. These led to frequent disputes between him and Washington, who found the exasperated general deaf to his arguments on that subject. The plan suggested by him of employing pack-horses for transportation, instead of wagons, was afterwards in some measure adopted.

Benjamin Franklin, deputy postmaster-general of the colonies, who, at Governor Shirley's instance, had accompanied him to the congress at Alexandria, visited Braddock at Frederictown, for the purpose of opening a post-route between Will's Creek and Philadelphia. Learning the general's embarrassment, he undertook to procure the requisite number of wagons and horses from the Pennsylvania farmers. Issuing a handbill addressed to their interests and their fears, and exciting among the Germans an apprehension of an arbitrary impressment to be enforced by Sir John St. Clair, "the Hussar," he was soon able to provide the general with the means of transportation.* It was a long time before Franklin recovered compensation for the farmers; Governor Shirley at length paid the greater part of the amount, twenty thousand pounds; but it is said that owing to the neglect of Lord Loudoun, Franklin was never wholly repaid. Washington and Franklin were both held in high estimation by Braddock, and they were unconsciously co-operating with him in a war destined in its unforeseen consequences to dismember the British empire.

Braddock's army, with its baggage extending (along a road twelve feet wide) sometimes four miles in length, moved from Fort Cumberland, at the mouth of Will's Creek, early in June, and advanced slowly and with difficulty, five miles being considered a good day's march. There was much sickness among the soldiers: Washington was seized with a fever, and obliged to travel in a covered wagon. Braddock, however, continued to consult him, and he advised the general to disencumber himself of his heavy guns and unnecessary baggage, to leave them with a rear division, and to press forward expeditiously to Fort Du Quesne. In a council of war it was determined that Braddock

---

* Gordon's Hist. of Pa.; Braddock's Expedition, 163.

should advance as rapidly as possible with twelve hundred select men, and Colonel Dunbar follow on slowly with a rear-guard of about six hundred,—a number of the soldiers being disabled by sickness. The advance corps proceeded only nineteen miles in four days, losing occasionally a straggler, cut off by the French and Indian scouts. Trees were found near the road stripped of their barks and painted, and on them the French had written many of their names and the number of scalps recently taken, with many insolent threats and scurrilous bravados.

Washington was now (by the general's order) compelled to stop, his physician declaring that his life would be jeoparded by a continuance with the army, and Braddock promising that he should be brought up with it before it reached Fort Du Quesne. On the day before the battle of the Monongahela, Washington, in a wagon, rejoined the army, at the mouth of the Youghiogany River, and fifteen miles from Fort Du Quesne. On the morning of Wednesday, the 9th of July, 1755, the troops, in high spirits, confident of entering the gates of Fort Du Quesne triumphantly in a few hours, crossed the Monongahela, and advanced along the southern margin. Washington, in after-life, was heard to declare it the most beautiful spectacle that he had ever witnessed—the brilliant uniform of the soldiers, arranged in columns and marching in exact order; the sun gleaming on their burnished arms; the Monongahela flowing tranquilly by on the one hand, on the other, the primeval forest projecting its shadows in sombre magnificence. At one o'clock the army again crossed the river at a second ford ten miles from Fort Du Quesne. From the river a level plain extends northward nearly half a mile, thence the ground, gradually ascending, terminates in hills. The road from the fording-place to the fort led across this plain, up this ascent, and through an uneven country covered with woods.* Beyond the plain on both sides of the road were ravines unnoticed by the English. Three hundred men, under Lieutenant-Colonel Gage, subsequently commander of the British troops at Boston, made the advanced party, and it was immediately followed by another of two hundred. Next came Braddock with the artil-

---

* A plan of the ground is given in Washington's Writings, ii. 90.

lery, the main body, and the baggage. Brigadier-General Sir Peter Halket was second in command. No sooner had the army crossed the river, at the second ford, than a sharp firing was heard upon the advanced parties, who were now ascending the hill about a hundred yards beyond the edge of the plain.*

At an early hour De Beaujeu had been detached from Fort Du Quesne, at the head of about two hundred and thirty French and Canadians, and six hundred and thirty Indian savages, with the design of attacking the English at an advantageous ground selected on the preceding evening. Before reaching it he came upon the English. The greater part of Gage's command was advanced beyond the spot where the main battle was fought, when Mr. Gordon, one of the engineers in front marking out the road, perceived the enemy bounding forward. Before them with long leaps came Beaujeu, the gay hunting-shirt and silver gorget denoting him as the chief. Halting he waved his hat above his head, and at this signal the Indians dispersed themselves to the right and left, throwing themselves flat on the ground, or gliding behind rocks and trees into the ravines. The French occupied the centre of the Indian semicircle, and a fierce attack was commenced. Gage's troops, recovering from their first surprise, opened a fire of grape and musketry. Beaujeu and twelve others fell dead upon the spot; the Indians, astonished by the report of the

---

* The surprise of the Roman army under Titurius Sabinus on his march, by the Gauls (as described by Cæsar) resembles Braddock's defeat in several particulars.

"At hostes, posteaquam ex nocturno fremitu vigiliis que de profectione eorum senserunt, collocatis insidiis bipartito in silvis opportuno atque occulto loco, a millibus passuum circiter duobus, Romanorum adventum expectabant: et cum se major pars agminis in magnam convallem demisisset, ex utraque parte ejus vallis subito se ostenderunt, novissimosque premere et primos prohibere ascensu atque iniquissimo nostris loco prœlium committere cœperunt." Lucius Cotta was the Washington of that defeat; but he fell in the general massacre. "At Cotta qui cogitasset hæc posse in itinere accidere, atque ob eam causam profectionis auctor non fuisset, nulla in re communi saluti deerat, et in appellandis cohortandisque militibus, imperatoris, et in pugna, militis officia præstabat."

The following sentence describes the war-whoop: "Tum vero suo more victoriam conclamant, atque ululatum tollunt, impetuque in nostros facto, ordines perturbant."

cannon, began to fly. Rallied by Dumas, who succeeded Beaujeu, they resumed the combat: the French in front, the Indians on the flank. For a time the issue was doubtful: cries of "Vive le Roi" were answered by the cheers of the English. But while the officers of the Forty-fourth led on their men with waving swords, the enemy, concealed in the woods and ravines, secure and invisible, kept up a steady, well-aimed, and fatal fire. Their position was only discovered by the smoke of their muskets. Gage, not reinforcing his flanking parties, they were driven in, and the English, instead of advancing upon the hidden enemy, returned a random and ineffectual fire in full column.

In the mean time Braddock sent forward Lieutenant-Colonel Burton with the vanguard. And while he was forming his men to face a rising ground on the right, the advanced detachment, overwhelmed with consternation by the savage war-whoop and the mysterious danger, fell back upon him in great confusion, communicating a panic from which they could not be recovered. Braddock now came up and endeavored to form the two regiments under their colors, but neither entreaties nor threats could prevail. The baggage in the rear was attacked, and many horses killed; some of the drivers fell, the rest escaped by flight. Two of the cannon flanking the baggage for some time protected it from the Indians; the others fired away most of their ammunition, and were of some service in awing the enemy, but could do but little execution against a concealed foe. The enemy extended from front to rear, and fired upon every part at once. The general finding it impossible to persuade his men to advance, many officers falling, and no enemy appearing in sight, endeavored to effect a retreat in good order, but such was the panic that he could not succeed. They were loading as fast as possible and firing in the air.

Braddock and his officers made every effort to rally them, but in vain; in this confusion and dismay they remained in a road twelve feet wide, enclosed by woods, for three hours, huddled together, exposed to the insidious fire, doing the enemy little hurt, and shooting one another. None of the survivors could afterwards say that they saw one hundred of the enemy, and many of the officers that were in the heat of the action would not assert that they saw one.*

The Virginia troops preserved their presence of mind, and behaved with the utmost bravery, adopting the Indian mode of combat, and fighting each man for himself behind a tree. This was done in spite of the orders of Braddock, who still endeavored to form his men into platoons and columns, as if they had been manœuvring in the plains of Flanders or parading in Hyde Park. Washington and Sir Peter Halket in vain advised him to allow the men to shelter themselves: he stormed at such as attempted to take to the trees, calling them cowards, and striking them with his sword. Captain Waggener, of the Virginia troops, resolved to take advantage of the trunk of a tree five feet in diameter, lying athwart the brow of a hill. With shouldered firelocks he marched a party of eighty men toward it, and losing but three men on the way, the remainder throwing themselves behind it, opened a hot fire upon the enemy. But no sooner were the flash and report of their muskets perceived by the mob behind, than a general discharge was poured upon them, by which fifty were killed and the rest compelled to fly.†

The French and Indians, concealed in deep ravines, and behind trees, and logs, and high grass, and tangled undergrowth, kept up a deadly fire, singling out their victims. The mounted officers were especially aimed at, and shortly after the commencement of the engagement, Washington was the only aid not wounded. Although still feeble from the effects of his illness, on him now was devolved the whole duty of carrying the general's orders, and he rode a conspicuous mark in every direction. Two horses were killed under him, four bullets penetrated his coat, but he escaped unhurt, while every other officer on horseback was either killed or wounded. Dr. Craik afterwards said: "I expected every moment to see him fall. His duty and situation exposed him to every danger. Nothing but the superintending care of Providence could have saved him from the fate of all around him." Washington, writing to his brother, said: "By the all-powerful dispensations of Providence I have been pro-

---

* Bancroft, iv. 189. † Braddock's Expedition, 231.

tected beyond all human probability or expectation, for I had four bullets through my coat and two horses shot under me, yet escaped unhurt, although death was levelling my companions on every side."

More than half of the army were killed or wounded, two-thirds of them, according to Washington's conjecture, by their own bullets; Sir Peter Halket was killed on the field; Shirley, Braddock's secretary, was shot through the head; Colonels Burton, Gage, and Orme, Major Sparks, Brigade-Major Halket, Captain Morris, etc., were wounded. Out of eighty-six officers, twenty-six were killed and thirty-seven wounded. The whole number of killed was estimated at four hundred and fifty-six, wounded four hundred and twenty one, the greater part of whom were brought off; the aggregate loss, eight hundred and seventy-seven. The enemy's force, variously estimated, did not exceed eight hundred and fifty men, of whom six hundred, it was conjectured, were Indians. The French loss was twenty-eight killed, including three officers, one of whom, Beaujeu, was chief in command; and twenty-nine badly wounded, including two officers. The French and Indians being covered by ravines, the balls of the English passed harmless over their heads; while a charge with the bayonet, or raking the ravines with cannon, would have at once driven them from their lurking places, and put them to flight, or, at the least, dispersed them in the woods. Any movement would have been better than standing still.

During the action, or massacre, of three hours, Braddock had three horses killed under him, and two disabled. At five o'clock in the afternoon, while beneath a large tree standing between the heads of two ravines, and in the act of giving an order, he received a mortal wound. Falling from his horse, he lay helpless on the ground, surrounded by the dead. His army having fired away all their ammunition, now fled in disorder back to the Monongahela. Pursued to the water's edge by a party of savages, the regulars threw away arms, accoutrements, and even clothing, that they might run the faster. Many were tomahawked at the fording-place; but those who crossed were not pursued, as the Indians returned to the harvest of plunder. The provincials, better acquainted with Indian warfare were less disconcerted, and retreated with more composure.

Not one of his British soldiers could be prevailed upon to stay and aid in bearing off the wounded general. In vain Orme offered them a purse of sixty guineas. Braddock begged his faithful friends to provide for their own safety, and declared his resolution to die on the field. Orme disregarded these desperate injunctions; and Captain Stewart, of the Virginia Light-horse, (attached to the general's person,) and his servant, together with another American officer, hastening to Orme's relief, brought off Braddock, at first on a small tumbrel, then on a horse, lastly by the soldiers.

According to Washington's account, in a letter written to Dinwiddie: "They were struck with such an inconceivable panic, that nothing but confusion and disobedience of orders prevailed among them. The officers in general behaved with incomparable bravery, for which they greatly suffered, there being upwards of sixty killed and wounded, a large proportion out of what we had. The Virginia companies behaved like men and died like soldiers; for, I believe, out of three companies on the ground that day, scarcely thirty men were left alive. Captain Peyrouny, a Frenchman by birth, and all his officers down to a corporal, were killed. Captain Poulson had almost as hard a fate, for only one of his escaped. In short, the dastardly behavior of the regular troops (so called) exposed those who were inclined to do their duty to almost certain death; and, at length, in spite of every effort to the contrary, they broke and ran like sheep before hounds, leaving the artillery, ammunition, provisions, baggage, and, in short, everything a prey to the enemy, and when we endeavored to rally them in hopes of regaining the ground and what we had left upon it, it was with as little success as if we had attempted to have stopped the wild bears of the mountains, or the rivulets with our feet; for they would break by in spite of every effort to prevent it."

Braddock was brave and accomplished in European tactics; but not an officer of that comprehensive genius which knows how to bend and accommodate himself to circumstances. Burke says that a wise statesman knows how to be governed by circumstances: the maxim applies as well to a military commander. Braddock, headstrong, passionate, irritated, not without just grounds, against the provinces, and pursuing the policy of the

British government to rely mainly on the forces sent over, and to treat the colonial troops as inferior and only secondary, rejected the proposal of Washington to lead in advance the provincials, who, accustomed to border warfare, knew better how to cope with a savage foe.* Braddock, however, showed that although he could not retrieve these errors, nor reclaim a degenerate soldiery, he could at any rate fall like a soldier.†

Although no further pursued, the remainder of the army continued their flight during the night and the next day. Braddock continued for two days to give orders; and it was in compliance with them that the greater part of the artillery, ammunition, and other stores were destroyed. It was not until the thirteenth that the general uttered a word, except for military directions. He then bestowed the warmest praise on his gallant officers, and bequeathed, as is said, his charger, and his body-servant, Bishop, to Washington.‡ The dying Braddock ejaculated in reference to the defeat, "Who would have thought it?" Turning to Orme he remarked, "We shall better know how to deal with them another time;" and in a few moments expired, at eight o'clock, in the evening of Sunday, the 13th of July, 1755, at the Great Meadows. On the next morning he was buried in the road, near Fort Necessity, Washington, in the absence of the chaplain, who was wounded, reading the funeral service. Washington retired to Mount Vernon, oppressed with the sad retrospect of the recent disaster. But his reputation was greatly elevated by his signal gallantry on this occasion. Such dreary portals open the road of fame.

The green and bosky scene of battle was strewn with the wounded and the dead. Toward evening the forest resounded

---

* Chalmers' Hist. of Revolt, ii. 276. True to his unvarying prejudice against the colonies, he justifies the conduct of Braddock.

† The History of Braddock's Expedition, by Winthrop Sargent, Esq., is full, elaborate, and authentic. The volume, a beautiful specimen of typography, was printed, 1856, by Messrs. J. B. Lippincott & Co., for the Pennsylvania Historical Society. I am indebted to Townsend Ward, Esq., Librarian, for a copy of it.

‡ Gilbert, a slave, is said to have been with Washington at the battle of the Monongahela, and at the siege of York. John Alton is likewise mentioned as a servant attending him during Braddock's expedition.

with the exulting cries and war-whoop of the returning French and Indians, the firing of small arms, and the responsive roar of the cannon at the fort. A lonely American prisoner confined there listened during this anxious day to the various sounds, and with peering eye explored the scene. Presently he saw the greater part of the savages, painted and blood-stained, bringing scalps, and rejoicing in the possession of grenadiers' caps, and the laced hats and splendid regimentals of the English officers. Next succeeded the French, escorting a long train of pack-horses laden with plunder. Last of all, just before sunset, appeared a party of Indians conducting twelve British regulars, naked, their faces blackened, their hands tied behind them. In a short while they were burned to death on the opposite bank of the Ohio, with every circumstance of studied barbarity and inhuman torture, the French garrison crowding the ramparts of the fort to witness the spectacle.

The remains of the defeated detachment retreated to the rear division in precipitate disorder, leaving the road behind them strewed with signs of the disaster. Shortly after, Colonel Dunbar marched with the remaining regulars to Philadelphia. Colonel Washington returned home, mortified and indignant at the conduct of the regular troops.

CHAPTER LXII.

1755-1756.

Stith—Davies visits England and Scotland—Patriotic Discourse—Waddel, the Blind Preacher—Washington made Colonel of Virginia Regiment—Indian Incursions—Washington visits Boston.

During the year 1755 died the Rev. William Stith, president of the College of William and Mary, and author of an excellent "History of Virginia," from the first settlement to the dissolution of the London Company. He was of exemplary character and catholic spirit, a friend of well-regulated liberty, and a true patriot.

The Rev. Samuel Davies, during the year 1754, went on a mission to England and Scotland for the purpose of raising a fund for the endowment of a college at Princeton, New Jersey. His eloquence commanded admiration in the mother country. The English Presbyterians he found sadly fallen away from the doctrines of the Reformation, and their clergy, although learned and able, deeply infected with the "modish divinity"—Socinianism and Arminianism. In Scotland, where he met a warm welcome, he found the young clergy no less imbued with the "modish divinity," and the cause of religion and the spiritual independence of the kirk lamentably impaired by the overweening influence of secular patronage. Davies was of opinion that in genuine piety the Methodists, who commenced their reform in the Church of England, ranked the highest. He returned to Virginia early in 1755, and during the French and Indian wars he often employed his eloquence in arousing the patriotism of the Virginians.

After Braddock's defeat, such was the general consternation that many seemed ready to desert the country. On the 20th of July, 1755, Davies delivered a discourse, in which he declared: "Christians should be patriots. What is that religion good for that leaves men cowards upon the appearance of danger? And permit me to say, that I am particularly solicitous that you, my brethren of the dissenters, should act with honor and spirit in this juncture, as it becomes loyal subjects, lovers of your country, and courageous Christians. That is a mean, sordid, cowardly soul that would abandon his country and shift for his own little self, when there is any probability of defending it. To give the greater weight to what I say, I may take the liberty to tell you, I have as little personal interest, as little to lose in the colony, as most of you. If I consulted either my safety or my temporal interest, I should soon remove with my family to Great Britain, or the Northern colonies, where I have had very inviting offers. Nature has not formed me for a military life, nor furnished me with any great degree of fortitude and courage; yet I must declare, that after the most calm and impartial deliberation, I am determined not to leave my country while there is any prospect of defending it."*

Dejection and alarm vanished under his eloquence, and at the conclusion of his address every man seemed to say, "Let us march against the enemy!" A patriotic discourse was delivered by him on the 17th of August, 1755, before Captain Overton's company of Independent Volunteers, the first volunteer company raised in Virginia after Braddock's defeat. In a note appended to this discourse, Davies said: "As a remarkable instance of this, I may point out to the public that heroic youth, Colonel Washington, whom I cannot but hope Providence has hitherto preserved in so signal a manner for some important service to his country."†

It is probable that Patrick Henry caught the spark of eloquence from Davies, as in his early youth, and in after years, he often heard him preach. They were alike gifted with a profound sensibility. Henry always remarked that Mr. Davies was "the

---

* Davies' Sermons, iii. 169; Sermon on the defeat of General Braddock going to Fort Du Quesne; Memoir of Davies in Evan. and Lit. Mag.

† Davies' Sermons, iii. 38. "Who is Mr. Washington?" inquired Lord Halifax. "I know nothing of him," he added; "but they say he behaved in Braddock's action as bravely as if he really loved the whistling of bullets."

greatest orator he had ever heard." Presbyterianism steadily advanced in Virginia under the auspices of Davies and his successors, particularly Graham, Smith, Waddell, "the blind preacher" of Wirt's "British Spy," and Brown.

The Rev. James Waddell, a Presbyterian minister, was born in the North of Ireland, in July, 1739, as is believed. He was brought over in his infancy by his parents to America; they settled in the southeastern part of Pennsylvania, on White-clay Creek. James was sent to school at Nottingham to Dr. Finley, afterwards president of the College of New Jersey. In the school young Waddell made such proficiency in his studies as to become an assistant teacher; and Dr. Benjamin Rush, the signer of the Declaration of Independence, recited lessons to him there. He devoted his attention chiefly to the classics, in which he became very well versed. He was afterwards an assistant to the elder Smith, father of the Rev. John Blair Smith, president of Hampden Sidney College, Virginia, and of the Rev. Samuel Stanhope Smith, president of the College of New Jersey. Waddell, intending to pursue the vocation of a teacher, and to settle with that view at Charleston, in South Carolina, set out for the South. In passing through Virginia he met with the celebrated preacher, Davies, and that incident gave a different turn to his life. Shortly after, he became an assistant to the Rev. Mr. Todd in his school in the County of Louisa, with whom he studied theology. He was licensed to preach in 1761, and ordained in the following year, when he settled as pastor in Lancaster County. Here, about the year 1768, he married Mary, daughter of Colonel James Gordon, of that county,* a wealthy and influential man. In the division of the Presbyterian Church Mr. Waddell was of the "New Side," as it was termed. The Rev. Samuel Davies often preached to Mr. Waddell's congregation; as also did Whitefield several times.

In the year 1776 Mr. Waddell removed from Lower Virginia, in very feeble health, to Augusta County. His salary was now only forty-five pounds, Virginia currency, per annum. In 1783

---

* Ancestor of the late General Gordon, of Albemarle.

he came to reside at an estate purchased by him, and called Hopewell, at the junction of Louisa, Orange, and Albemarle—the dwelling-house being in Louisa. Here he again became a classical teacher, receiving pupils in his own house. James Barbour, afterwards governor of Virginia, was one of these, and Merriwether Lewis, the companion of Clarke in the exploration beyond the Rocky Mountains, another. Mr. Waddell resided in Louisa County about twenty years, and died there, and was buried, according to his request, in his garden. During his residence here he was, for a part of the time, deprived of his sight; but he continued to preach. In person he was tall and erect; his complexion fair, with a light blue eye. His deportment was dignified; his manners elegant and graceful. He is represented by Mr. Wirt, in the "British Spy," as preaching in a white linen cap; this was, indeed, a part of his domestic costume, but when he went abroad he always wore a large full-bottomed wig, perfectly white. Mr. Wirt held him as equal to Patrick Henry, in a different species of oratory. In regard to place, time, costume, and lesser particulars, Mr. Wirt used an allowable liberty in grouping together incidents which had occurred apart, and perhaps imagining, as in a sermon, expressions which had been uttered at the fire-side. Patrick Henry's opinion of Mr. Waddell's eloquence has been before mentioned. It was the remark of another cotemporary, that when he preached, "whole congregations were bathed in tears." It might also be said by his grave, as at that of John Knox,—

"Here lies one who never feared the face of man."

The late Rev. Dr. Archibald Alexander married a daughter of Dr. Waddell, and the late Rev. Dr. James Waddell Alexander thus derived his middle name.

August, 1755, the assembly voted forty thousand pounds for the public service, and the governor and council immediately resolved to augment the Virginia Regiment to sixteen companies, numbering fifteen hundred men. To Washington was granted the sum of three hundred pounds in reward for his gallant behavior and in compensation for his losses at the battle of Monongahela. Colonel Washington was, during this month, commissioned commander-in-chief of the forces, and allowed to appoint his own officers. The officers next in rank to him were Lieutenant-Colonel Adam Stephen and Major Andrew Lewis. Washington's military reputation was now high, not only in Virginia, but in the other colonies. Peyton Randolph raised a volunteer company of one hundred gentlemen, who, however, proved quite unfit for the frontier service.

After organizing the regiment and providing the commissariat, Washington repaired early in October to Winchester, and took such measures as lay in his power to repel the cruel outrages of a savage irruption. Alarm, confusion, and disorder prevailed, so that he found no orders obeyed but such as a party of soldiers, or his own drawn sword, enforced. He beheld with emotion calamities which he could not avert, and he strenuously urged the necessity of an act to enforce the military law, to remedy the insolence of the soldiers and the indolence of the officers. He even intimated a purpose of resigning, unless his authority should be re-enforced by the laws, since he found himself thwarted in his exertions at every step by a general perverseness and insubordination, aggravated by the hardships of the service and the want of system. At length, by persevering solicitations, he prevailed on the assembly to adopt more energetic military regulations. The discipline thus introduced was extremely rigorous, severe flogging being in ordinary use. The penalty for fighting was five hundred lashes; for drunkenness, one hundred. The troops were daily drilled and practised in bush-fighting. A Captain Dagworthy, stationed at Fort Cumberland, commissioned by General Sharpe, governor of Maryland, refusing, as holding a king's commission, to obey Washington's orders, the dispute was referred by Governor Dinwiddie to General Shirley, commander-in-chief of his majesty's armies in America, who was then at Boston. He was also requested to grant royal commissions to Colonel Washington and his field-officers, such commissions to imply rank but to give no claim to pay.

The Indians, after committing murders and barbarities upon the unhappy people of the border country, retired beyond the mountains. Colonel Byrd and Colonel Randolph were sent out with presents to the Cherokees, Catawbas, and other Southern

Indians, in order to conciliate their good-will and counteract the intrigues of the French.

Colonel Washington obtained leave to visit General Shirley, so as to deliver in person a memorial from the officers of the Virginia Regiment, requesting him to grant them king's commissions; and also in order to make himself better acquainted with the military plans of the North. He set out from Alexandria early in February, 1756, accompanied by his aid-de-camp, Colonel George Mercer, and on his route passed through Philadelphia, New York, New London, Newport, and Providence. He visited the governors of Pennsylvania and New York, and spent several days in each of the principal cities. He was well received by General Shirley, with whom he continued ten days, mingling with the society of Boston, attending the sessions of the legislature, and visiting Castle William. During the tour he was everywhere looked upon with interest as the hero of the Monongahela. Shirley decided the contested point between Dagworthy and him in his favor.

While in New York he was a guest of his friend Beverley Robinson (brother of the speaker.) Miss Mary Philipse, a sister of Mrs. Robinson, and heiress of a vast estate, was an inmate of the family, and Washington became enamored of her. The flame was transient; he probably having soon discovered that another suitor was preferred to him. She eventually married Captain Roger Morris, his former associate in arms, and one of Braddock's aids. She and her sister, Mrs. Robinson, and Mrs. Inglis, were the only females who were attainted of high treason during the Revolution. Imagination dwells on the outlawry of a lady who had won the admiration of Washington. Humanity is shocked that a woman should have been attainted of treason for clinging to the fortunes of her husband.* Mary Philipse is the original of one of the characters in Cooper's "Spy."

---

* Sabine's Loyalists, 476.

CHAPTER LXIII.

1756-1758.

First Settlers of the Valley—Sandy Creek Expedition—Indian Irruption—Measures of Defence—Habits of Virginians—Washington and Dinwiddie—Congress of Governors—Dinwiddie succeeded by Blair—Davies' Patriotic Discourse.

THE inhabitants of tramontane Virginia are very imperfectly acquainted with its history. This remark applies particularly to that section commonly called the Valley of Virginia, which, lying along the Blue Ridge, stretches from the Potomac to the Alleghany Mountains. Of this many of the inhabitants know little more than what they see. They see a country possessing salubrity and fertility, yielding plentifully, in great variety, most of the necessaries of life, a country which has advantages, conveniences, and blessings, in abundance, in profusion, it may almost be said in superfluity. But they know not how it came into the hands of the present occupants; they know not who were the first settlers, whence they came, at what time, in what numbers, nor what difficulties they had to encounter, nor what was the progress of population. One who would become acquainted with these matters must travel back a century or more; he must witness the early adventurers leaving the abodes of civilization, and singly, or in families, or in groups composed of several families, like pioneers on a forlorn hope, entering the dark, dreary, trackless forest, which had been for ages the nursery of wild beasts and the pathway of the Indian. After traversing this inhospitable solitude for days or weeks, and having become weary of their pilgrimage, they determined to separate, and each family taking its own course in quest of a place where they may rest, they find a spot such as choice, chance, or necessity points out; here they sit down; this they call their home—a cheerless, houseless home. If they have a tent, they stretch it, and in it they all nestle; otherwise the umbrage of a wide-spreading oak, or mayhap the canopy of heaven, is their only covering. In this new-found home, while they are not exempt from the common frailties and ills of humanity, many peculiar to their present condition thicken around them. Here they must endure excessive labor, fatigue, and exposure to inclement seasons; here innumerable perils and privations await them; here they are exposed to alarms from wild beasts and from Indians. Sometimes driven from home, they take shelter in the breaks and recesses of the mountains, where they continue for a time in a state of anxious suspense; venturing at length to reconnoitrè their home, they perhaps find it a heap of ruins, the whole of their little *peculium* destroyed. This frequently happened. The inhabitants of the country being few, and in most cases widely separated from each other, each group, fully occupied with its own difficulties and distresses, seldom could have the consolation of hoping for the advice, assistance, or even sympathy of each other. Many of them, worn out by the hardships inseparable from their new condition, found premature graves; many hundreds, probably thousands, were massacred by the hands of the Indians; and peace and tranquillity, if they came at all, came at a late day to the few survivors.

"Tantæ erat molis—condere gentem."

Here have been stated a few items of the first cost of this country, but the half has not been told, nor can we calculate in money the worth of the sufferings of these people, especially we cannot estimate in dollars and cents the value of the lives that were lost.*

In the year 1756 took place the "Sandy Creek Expedition" against the Shawnees on the Ohio River. With the exception of a few Cherokees, it consisted exclusively of Virginia troops, under the conduct of Major Andrew Lewis.† Although this expedition proved in the event abortive, yet its incidents, as far as known, are interesting. Nor are such abortive enterprises without their useful effects: they are the schools of discipline, the rehearsals of future success. The rendezvous from which the expedition

---

* Memoir of Battle of Point Pleasant, by Samuel L. Campbell, M.D., of Rockbridge County, Va.

† Washington's Writings, ii. 125; Va. Hist. Reg.

started was Fort Frederick, on New River, in what was then Augusta County. Under Major Andrew Lewis were Captains William Preston, Peter Hogg, John Smith, Archibald Alexander, father of Rev. Dr. Archibald Alexander, Breckenridge, Woodson, and Overton. Their companies appear to have been already guarding the frontier when called upon for this new service. There were also the volunteer companies of Captains Montgomery and Dunlap, and a party of Cherokees under Captain Paris. A party of this tribe had come to the assistance of the Virginians in the latter part of 1755, and they were ordered by Governor Dinwiddie to join the Sandy Creek Expedition; but whether they all actually joined it is not known. The war leaders of these savages were old Outacité, the Round O, and the Yellow Bird. Captain David Stewart,* of Augusta, seems to have acted as commissary to the expedition. The whole force that marched from Fort Frederick amounted to three hundred and forty. While waiting to procure horses and pack-saddles, the soldiers were preached to by the pioneer Presbyterian clergymen of the valley, Craig and Brown. Major Lewis marched on the eighteenth of February, and passing by the Holston River and the head of the Clinch, they reached the head of Sandy Creek on the twenty-eighth. This stream was found exceedingly tortuous; on the twenty-ninth, they crossed it sixty-six times in the distance of fifteen miles. Although some bears, deer, and buffaloes were killed, yet their provisions began to run low early in March, when they were reduced to half a pound of flour per man, and no meat except what they could kill, which was very little. There being no provender for the horses, they strayed away. The march was fatiguing, the men having frequently to wade laboriously across the deepening water of the river; they suffered with hunger, and starvation began to stare them in the face. The Cherokees undertook to make bark canoes to convey themselves down the creek, and Lewis ordered a large canoe to be made to transport the ammunition and the remaining flour. The

---

* Father of the late Judge Archibald Stewart, of Augusta County, and grandfather of the Honorable A. H. H. Stewart, Secretary of the Interior under President Taylor.

men murmured, and many threatened to return home. Lewis ordered a cask of butter to be divided among them. An advance party of one hundred and thirty, with nearly all of the horses, proceeded down the creek, Lewis with the rest remaining to complete the canoes. No game was met with by the party proceeding down the stream, and the mountains were found difficult to cross. Hunger and want increased, and the men became almost mutinous. Captain Preston proposed to kill the horses for food, but this offer was rejected. About this time some elks and buffaloes were killed, and this relief rescued some of the men from the jaws of starvation. The advance party had now, as they supposed, reached the distance of fifteen miles below the forks of the Sandy. Captain Preston, who commanded it, was greatly perplexed at the discontents which prevailed, and which threatened the ruin of the expedition. The men laid no little blame on the commissaries, who had furnished only fifteen days' provision for what they supposed to be a march of three hundred miles. Major Lewis preserved his equanimity, and remarked that "he had often seen the like mutiny among soldiers." On the eleventh of March ten men deserted; others preparing to follow them, were disarmed and forcibly detained, but some of them soon escaped. They were pursued and brought back. When Major Lewis rejoined the advance party, one of his men brought in a little bear, which he took to Captain Preston's tent, where the major lodged that night, "by which," says Preston, "I had a good supper and breakfast—a rarity." Major Lewis addressed the men, encouraging them to believe that they would soon reach the hunting-ground and find game, and reminded them that the horses would support them for some time. The men, nevertheless, appeared obstinately bent upon returning home, for they said that if they went forward they must either perish or eat horses—neither of which they were willing to do. The major then, stepping off a few yards, called upon all those who would serve their country and share his fate, to go with him. All the officers and some twenty or thirty privates joined him; the rest marched off. In this conjuncture, when deserted by his own people, Lewis found old Outacité, the Cherokee chief, willing to stand by him. Outacité remarked, that "the white men could not bear hunger like Indians." The expedition was now, of necessity, abandoned when they had arrived near the Ohio River, and all made the best of their way home.

It appears to have required two weeks for them to reach the nearest settlements, and during this interval they endured great sufferings from cold and hunger, and some who separated from the main body, and undertook to support themselves on the way back by hunting, perished. When the main body reached the Burning Spring, in what is now Logan County, they cut some buffalo hides, which they had left there on the way down, into tuggs or long thongs, and ate them, after exposing them to the flame of the Burning Spring. Hence Tugg River, separating Virginia from Kentucky, derives its name. During the last two or three days, it is said that they ate the strings of their moccasins, belts of their hunting-shirts, and shot-pouch flaps. The art of extracting nutriment from such articles is now lost.

"The Sandy Creek Voyage," as it was sometimes styled, appears to have been directed against the Shawnee town near the junction of the Kanawha and the Ohio, and perhaps to erect a fort there. The conduct of the expedition was left almost entirely to the discretion of Major Lewis.* Washington predicted the failure of the expedition, on account of the length of the march, and even if it reached the Ohio, "as we are told that those Indians are removed up the river into the neighborhood of Fort Du Quesne."†

Old Outacité, or the Man-killer, was in distinction among the Cherokee chiefs, second only to Attacullaculla, or the Little Carpenter. Outacité attained a venerable age, and continued to be a steadfast friend of the whites. At the massacre committed near Fort Loudoun, by his interposition he rescued many from destruction.

Early in April, 1756, another Indian irruption, led on by the French, spread consternation in the tramontane country, and threatened to exterminate the inhabitants. Washington, now

---

* Lyman C. Draper, in Va. Hist. Register, 61; Howe's Hist. Collections of Va., 352.
† Washington's Writings, ii. 125, 135.

aged twenty-four, gave it as his opinion that "five hundred Indians have it more in their power to annoy the inhabitants than ten times their number of regulars." While the unhappy people were flying from the barbarous foe, Washington, in view of the inadequate means of protection, wrote to Governor Dinwiddie: "The supplicating tears of the women and moving petitions of the men melt me into such deadly sorrow, that I solemnly declare, if I know my own mind, I could offer myself a willing sacrifice to the butchering enemy, provided that would contribute to the people's ease." In this sentence we find the key to his whole character and history.

The governor immediately gave orders for a re-enforcement of militia to assist him. The "Virginia Gazette," however, cast discredit and blame on Washington and the force under his command. Virginia continued to be too parsimonious and too indifferent to the sufferings of her people beyond the mountains. The woods appeared to be alive with French and Indians; each day brought fresh disasters and alarms. Washington found no language expressive enough to portray the miseries of the country. Affording all the succor in his power, he called upon the governor for arms, ammunition, and provisions, and gave it as his opinion that a re-enforcement of Indian allies was indispensable, as Indians alone could be effectually opposed to Indians. Winchester, incorporated in 1752, was now almost the only settlement west of the Blue Ridge that was not almost entirely deserted, the few families that remained being sheltered in forts. West of the North Mountain the country was depopulated, save a few families on the South Branch of the Potomac and on the Cacapehon. About the close of April the French and Indians returned to Fort Du Quesne laden with plunder, prisoners, and scalps.

Governor Dinwiddie recommended to the board of trade an extensive cordon of forts, to cover the entire frontier of the colonies from Crown Point to the country of the Creek Indians. His project was to pay for these forts and support their garrisons by a land and poll tax, levied on all the colonies by an act of parliament. Washington advised that Virginia should guard her frontier by additional forts about fifteen miles apart. Fort Loudoun was erected at Winchester, the key of that region, under his superintendence. It was a square with four bastions; the batteries mounted twenty-four guns; a well was sunk, mostly through a bed of limestone; the barracks were sufficient for four hundred and fifty men. Vestiges of this fortification still remain. Winchester, after the erection of Fort Loudoun, increased rapidly, owing to its being the rendezvous of the Virginia troops: in 1759 it contained two hundred houses.

It is remarkable that as late as the year 1756, when the colony was a century and a half old, the Blue Ridge of mountains was virtually the western boundary of Virginia, and great difficulty was found in completing a single regiment for the protection of the inhabitants of the border country from the cruel irruptions of the Indians. Yet at this time the population of the colony was estimated at two hundred and ninety-three thousand, of whom one hundred and seventy-three thousand were white, and one hundred and twenty thousand black, and the militia were computed at thirty-five thousand fit to bear arms.

Dinwiddie wrote to Fox, (father of Charles James,) one of the secretaries of state: "We dare not venture to part with any of our white men any distance, as we must have a watchful eye over our negro slaves, who are upwards of one hundred thousand." Some estimated them at one hundred and fifty thousand, equal in number to the whites, but the smaller estimate is probably more correct. The increase of the blacks was rapid, and many lamented that the mother country should suffer such multitudes to be brought from Africa to gratify the African Company, "and overrun a dutiful colony." As to the question whether enslaving the negroes is consistent with Christianity the Rev. Peter Fontaine remarks: "Like Adam, we are all apt to shift off the blame from ourselves and lay it upon others; how justly, in our case, you may judge. The negroes are enslaved by the negroes themselves before they are purchased by the masters of the ships who bring them here. It is, to be sure, at our choice whether we buy them or not; so this, then, is our crime, folly, or whatever you will please to call it. But our assembly, foreseeing the ill consequences of importing such numbers among us, hath often attempted to lay a duty upon them which would amount to a prohibition, such as ten or twenty pounds a head; but no governor dare pass such a law, having instructions to the contrary from the board of trade at home. By this means they are forced upon us whether we will or will not. This plainly shows the African Company hath the advantage of the colonies, and may do as it pleases with the ministry." "To live in Virginia without slaves is morally impossible," and it was a hard task for the planter to perform his duty toward them; for, on the one hand, if they were not compelled to work hard, he would endanger his temporal ruin; on the other hand, was the danger of not being able, in a better world, to render a good account of his humane stewardship of them.*

A long interval of tranquillity had enervated the planters of Virginia; luxury had introduced effeminate manners and dissolute habits. "To eat and drink delicately and freely; to feast, and dance, and riot; to pamper cocks and horses; to observe the anxious, important, interesting event, which of two horses can run fastest, or which of two cocks can flutter and spur most dexterously; these are the grand affairs that almost engross the attention of some of our great men. And little low-lived sinners imitate them to the utmost of their power. The low-born sinner can leave a needy family to starve at home, and add one to the rabble at a horse-race or a cock-fight. He can get drunk and turn himself into a beast with the lowest as well as his betters with more delicate liquors." Burk, the historian of Virginia, who was by no means a rigid censor, noticing the manners of the Virginians during the half century preceding the Revolution, says: "The character of the people for hospitality and expense was now decided, and the wealth of the land proprietors, particularly on the banks of the rivers, enabled them to indulge their passions even to profusion and excess. Drinking parties were then fashionable, in which the strongest head or stomach gained the victory. The moments that could be spared from the bottle were devoted to cards. Cock-fighting was also fashionable."†
On the same pages he adds: "I find, in 1747, a main of cocks advertised to be fought between Gloucester and James River.

---

* Huguenot Family, 348, 351.
† Burk's Hist. of Va., iii. 402.

The cocks on one side were called '*Bacon's Thunderbolts*,' after the celebrated rebel of 1676."

The pay of the soldiers in 1756 was but eight pence a day, of which two pence was reserved for supplying them with clothes. The meagre pay, and the practice of impressing vagrants into the military service, increased much the difficulty of recruiting and of enforcing obedience and subordination. Even Indians calling themselves friendly did not scruple to insult and annoy the inhabitants of the country through which they passed. One hundred and twenty Cherokees, passing through Lunenburg County, insulted people of all ranks, and a party of Catawbas behaved so outrageously at Williamsburg that it was necessary to call out the militia.

Although Governor Dinwiddie was an able man, his zeal in military affairs sometimes outstripped his knowledge, and Washington was at times distracted by inconsistent and impracticable orders, and harassed by undeserved complaints. It was indeed alleged by some, that if he could have withstood the strong interest arrayed in favor of Washington, the governor would rather have given the command to Colonel Innes, although far less competent, and an inhabitant of another colony, North Carolina. Dinwiddie's partiality to Innes was attributed, by those unfriendly to the governor, to national prejudice, for they were both natives of Scotland.[*] Yet it appears by Dinwiddie's letters that he urgently pressed the rank of colonel on Washington.[†] Washington, in his letters to Speaker Robinson, complains heavily of the governor's line of conduct, and Robinson's replies were such as would widen the breach.[‡] The tenor of the governor's correspondence with Washington, in 1757, became so ungracious, peremptory, and even offensive, that he could not but attribute the change in his conduct toward him to some secret detraction, and he gave utterance to a noble burst of eloquent self-defence. Dinwiddie's position was indeed trying, his measures being thwarted by a rather disaffected legislature and an arrogant aristocracy, and the censures thrown upon him, coming to us

---

[*] Bancroft, iv. 223.   [†] Sparks' Writings of Washington, ii. 262.
[‡] Washington's Writings, ii. 217, in note.

through a discolored medium of prejudice, ought to be taken with much allowance. However this may be, harsh and rather overbearing treatment from a British governor, together with the invidious distinctions drawn between colonial and British officers in regard to rank, naturally tended to abate Washington's loyalty, and thus gradually to fit him for the great part which he was destined to perform in the war of Independence.

Lord Loudoun, the newly-appointed governor of Virginia, and commander-in-chief of the colonies, now arrived in America, and called a conference of governors and military officers to meet him at Philadelphia. Washington, by the rather ungracious and reluctant leave of Dinwiddie, attended the conference. Yet Dinwiddie, in his letters to Loudoun, said of him: "He is a very deserving gentleman, and has from the beginning commanded the forces of this Dominion. He is much beloved, has gone through many hardships in the service, has great merit, and can raise more men here than any one." He therefore urged his promotion to the British establishment.* Washington had previously transmitted to the incompetent Loudoun an elaborate statement of the posture of affairs in Virginia, exhibiting the insufficiency of the militia and the necessity of an offensive system of operations. But Loudoun determined to direct his main efforts against Canada, and to leave only twelve hundred men in the middle and southern provinces. Instead of receiving aid, Virginia was required to send four hundred men to South Carolina. The Virginia Regiment was now reduced to a thousand men. Colonel Washington, nevertheless, insisted that a favorable conjuncture was presented for capturing Fort Du Quesne, since the French, when attacked in Canada, would be unable to re-enforce that remote post. This wise advice, although approved by Dinwiddie, was unheeded; and the campaign of the North proved inglorious, that of the South ineffectual. Toward the close of the year, Washington, owing to multiplied cares, vexations, and consequent ill health, relinquished his post, and retired to Mount Vernon, where he remained for several months.

In January, 1758, Robert Dinwiddie, after an arduous and

---

* Bancroft, iv. 236.

disturbed administration of five years, worn out with vexation and age, sailed from Virginia not much regretted, except by his particular friends. A scholar, a wit, and an amiable companion, in private life he deservedly won esteem. The charge alleged against him of avarice and extortion in the exaction of illegal fees, appears to have originated in political prejudice, and that of failing to account for sums of money transmitted by the British government, rests on the unsupported assertions of those who were inimical to him. His place was filled for a short time by John Blair, president of the council.

The Rev. Samuel Davies, by invitation, preached to the militia of Hanover County, in Virginia, at a general muster, on the 8th of May, 1758, with a view to the raising a company for Captain Samuel Meredith. In this discourse Davies said: "Need I inform you what barbarities and depredations a mongrel race of Indian savages and French Papists have perpetrated upon our frontiers? How many deserted or demolished houses and plantations? How wide an extent of country abandoned? How many poor families obliged to fly in consternation and leave their all behind them? What breaches and separations between the nearest relations? What painful ruptures of heart from heart? What shocking dispersions of those once united by the strongest and most endearing ties? Some lie dead, mangled with savage wounds, consumed to ashes with outrageous flames, or torn and devoured by the beasts of the wilderness, while their bones lie whitening in the sun, and serve as tragical memorials of the fatal spot where they fell. Others have been dragged away captives, and made the slaves of imperious and cruel savages: others have made their escape, and live to lament their butchered or captivated friends and relations. In short, our frontiers have been drenched with the blood of our fellow-subjects through the length of a thousand miles, and new wounds are still opening. We, in these inland parts of the country are as yet unmolested, through the unmerited mercy of Heaven. But let us only glance a thought to the western extremities of our body politic, and what melancholy scenes open to our view! Now perhaps while I am speaking, now while you are secure and unmolested, our fellow-subjects there may be feeling the calamities I am now describing. Now, perhaps, the savage shouts and whoops of Indians, and the screams and groans of some butchered family, may be mingling their horrors and circulating their tremendous echoes through the wilderness of rocks and mountains."* There appears to be some resemblance between this closing sentence and the following, in Fisher Ames' speech on the western posts: "I can fancy that I listen to the yells of savage vengeance and the shrieks of torture. Already they seem to sigh in the western wind; already they mingle with every echo from the mountains."†

---

* Davies' Sermons, iii. 68.
† These eloquent words may have been suggested by those of Davies.

CHAPTER LXIV.

1758-1762.

Earl of Loudoun—General Forbes—Pamunkey Indians—Fauquier, Governor—Forbes' Expedition against Fort Du Quesne—Its Capture—Burnaby's Account of Virginia—Washington, member of Assembly—His Marriage—Speaker Robinson's Compliment—Stobo—Germans on the Shenandoah—Miscellaneous.

THE Earl of Loudoun had been commissioned to fill Dinwiddie's place, but his military avocations prevented him from entering on the duties of the gubernatorial office, and it is believed that he never visited the colony of Virginia. Pitt, now minister, had resolved on a vigorous prosecution of the war in America, and it was quickly felt in every part of the British empire that there was a man at the helm. The department of the Middle and Southern Colonies was entrusted to General Forbes, and he was ordered to undertake an expedition against Fort Du Quesne. Washington rejoined the army. Forbes having deferred the campaign too late, the French and Indians renewed their merciless warfare. In the County of Augusta sixty persons were murdered. The Virginia troops were augmented to two thousand men, divided into two regiments: one under Washington, who was still commander-in-chief; the other, the new regiment, under Colonel William Byrd, of Westover. The strength of Colonel Byrd's regiment at Fort Cumberland (August 3d, 1758,) was eight hundred and fifty nine.*

As late as 1758 there were some descendants of the Pamunkey Indians still residing on their original seat. The Rev. Andrew Burnaby makes mention of them in his Travels. A few words of their language were found surviving as late as 1844.

Francis Fauquier, appointed governor, now reached Virginia.

---

* The officers were Lieutenant-Colonel George Mercer, Major William Peachy, Captains S. Munford, Thomas Cocke, Hancock Eustace, John Field, John Posey, Thomas Fleming, John Roote, and Samuel Meredith.

Late in June, 1758, the Virginia troops left Winchester, and early in July halted at Fort Cumberland.* At Washington's suggestion the light Indian dress, hunting-shirt and blanket, were adopted by the army. Contrary to his advice, Forbes, instead of marching immediately upon the Ohio, by Braddock's road, undertook to construct another from Raystown, in Pennsylvania. The general, it was supposed, was influenced by the Pennsylvanians to open for them a more direct avenue of intercourse with the west. The new road caused great delay. In disregard of Washington's advice, Major Grant had been detached from the Loyal Hanna, with eight hundred men, to reconnoitre the country about Fort Du Quesne. Presumptuous temerity involved the detachment in a surprise and defeat similar to Braddock's; Grant and Major Andrew Lewis were made prisoners. Of the eight Virginia officers present five were slain, a sixth wounded, and a seventh captured. Captain Thomas Bullit, and fifty Virginians, defended the baggage with great resolution, and contributed to save the remnant of the detachment. He was the only officer who escaped unhurt. Of one hundred and sixty-two Virginians, sixty-two were killed, and two wounded. Grant's total loss was two hundred and seventy-three killed, and forty-two wounded.

When the main army was set in motion Washington requested to be put in advance, and Forbes, profiting by Braddock's fatal error, complied with his wish. Washington was called to headquarters, attended the councils of war, and, in compliance with the general's desire, drew up a line of march and order of battle. Forbes' army consisted of twelve hundred Highlanders, three hundred and fifty Royal Americans, twenty-seven hundred provincials from Pennsylvania, sixteen hundred from Virginia, two or three hundred from Maryland, and two companies from North Carolina, making in all, including the wagoners, between six and seven thousand men. This army was five months in reaching the Ohio. The main body left Raystown on the 8th of October,

---

* See in Bland Papers, i. 9, Robert Munford's letter, dated at the Camp near Fort Cumberland. He was father of the translator of Homer, and grandfather to George W. Munford, Esq., Secretary of the Commonwealth.

1758, and reached the camp at Loyal Hanna early in November. The troops were worn out with fatigue and exposure; winter had set in, and more than fifty miles of rugged country yet intervened between them and Fort Du Quesne. A council of war declared it unadvisable to proceed further in that campaign. Just at this juncture, three prisoners were brought in, and they gave such a report of the feeble state of the garrison at the fort, that it was determined to push forward at once. Washington, with his provincials, opened the way. The French, reduced to five hundred men, and deserted by the Indians, set fire to the fort, and retired down the Ohio. Forbes took possession of the post on the next day, (November 25th, 1758.) The works were repaired, and the fort was now named Fort Pitt. An important city, called after the same illustrious statesman, has been reared near the spot. General Forbes, whose health had been declining during the campaign, died shortly afterwards at Philadelphia. He was a native of Scotland, and was educated as a physician; was an estimable and brave man, and of fine military talents.

Burnaby, who visited Virginia about this time, in describing Williamsburg, mentions the governor's palace as the only tolerably good public building. The streets being unpaved are dusty, the soil being sandy. The miniature capital had the rare advantage of being free from mosquitoes; and it was, all things considered, a pleasant place of residence. During the session of the assembly and of the general court, it was crowded with the gentry of the country. On these occasions there were balls, and other amusements; but as soon as the public business was dispatched the visitors returned to their homes, and Williamsburg appeared to be deserted. Lightning-rods were now generally used in Virginia, and proved efficacious. At Spotswood's iron mines, on the banks of the Rappahannock, there were smelted, annually, upwards of six hundred tons of metal. Coal mines had been opened with good success on the James River near the falls. Not a tenth of the land in Virginia was cultivated; yet, besides tobacco, she produced considerable quantities of fruit, cattle, and grain. The bacon was held to be superior in flavor to any in the world; but the mutton and beef inferior to that of

Great Britain. The horses were fleet and beautiful; and the breed was improved by frequent importations from England. Delicious fruits abounded, and in the early spring the eye of the traveller was charmed with the appearance of the orchards in full blossom. There were fifty-two counties and seventy-seven parishes, and on the pages of the statute-book forty-four towns; but one-half of these had not more than five houses, and the other half, for the most part, were inconsiderable villages. The exports of tobacco were between fifty and sixty thousand hogsheads, each weighing eight hundred or a thousand pounds. Their other exports were, to the Madeiras and the West Indies, cider, pork, lumber, and grain; to Great Britain, bar-iron, indigo, and a little ginseng. The only domestic manufacture of any consequence was Virginia cloth, which was commonly worn. There were between sixty and seventy clergymen, "men in general of sober and exemplary lives." Burnaby describes the Virginians as indolent, easy, good-natured, fond of society, and much given to convivial pleasures. They were devoid of enterprise and incapable of enduring fatigue. Their authority over their slaves rendered them vain, imperious, and destitute of refinement. Negroes and Indians they looked upon as scarcely of the human species; so that in case of violence, or even murder committed upon them, it was almost impossible to bring them to justice. Such was Burnaby's report on this subject. During the reign of James the Second, John Page, in a religious work composed by him, thought it necessary to combat, in an elaborate argument, the opinion that a master had the power of life and death over his slave.

Washington, after furnishing a detachment from his regiment as a garrison for Fort Pitt, then considered as within the jurisdiction of Virginia, marched back to Winchester. Thence he proceeded to Williamsburg to take his seat in the assembly, having been elected by the County of Frederick. He resigned his military commission in December, after having been engaged in the service for more than five years. His health had been impaired, and domestic affairs demanded his attention. On the 6th day of January, 1759, he was married to Martha, widow of

John Parke Custis, and daughter of John Dandridge, a lady in whom were united wealth, beauty, and an amiable temper.

By an order of the assembly, Speaker Robinson was directed to return their thanks to Colonel Washington, on behalf of the colony, for the distinguished military services which he had rendered to the country. As soon as he took his seat in the house, the speaker performed this duty in such glowing terms as quite overwhelmed him. Washington rose to express his acknowledgments for the honor, but was so disconcerted as to be unable to articulate a word distinctly. He blushed and faltered for a moment, when the speaker relieved him from his embarrassment by saying, "Sit down, Mr. Washington, your modesty equals your valor, and that surpasses the power of any language that I possess."

Captain Stobo, a hostage in the hands of the French, was detained for years at Quebec, enduring frequently the hardships of actual imprisonment, and for a time being under condemnation of death. At length he was released from this apprehension and from close confinement, and in May, 1759, in company of several others, effected his escape. Eluding the enemy by prudence and gallantry, he and his associates made their way to Louisburg. Here Stobo was gladly welcomed, and he joined General Wolfe, to whom his information proved serviceable; and he appears to have been present at the capture of Quebec. Shortly afterwards he returned to Virginia, (November, 1759.) The assembly granted him a thousand pounds, requested the governor to promote him, and presented their thanks to him for his fidelity, fortitude, and courage, by Mr. R. C. Nicholas, Mr. Richard Bland, and Mr. George Washington. Stobo returned to England, where his memoirs were published. In 1760 he was made a captain in Amherst's Regiment, then serving in America; and he held that position in 1765.

Van Braam, who had been kept prisoner at Montreal, was not released until the surrender of that city to the British in the ensuing year. He returned to Williamsburg shortly afterwards. In 1770 he obtained his share of the Virginia bounty lands; and in 1777 was made major in the Royal Americans, then in the West Indies.

During this year (1759) Rev. Andrew Burnaby visited Mount Vernon, of which he remarks: "This place is the property of Colonel Washington, and truly deserving of its owner. The house is most beautifully situated upon a very high hill on the banks of the Potomac, and commands a noble prospect of water, of cliffs, of woods, and plantations. The river is near two miles broad though two hundred from the mouth; and divides the dominions of Virginia from Maryland."

Burnaby, in his Travels, describes the condition of the Germans on the Shenandoah as follows: "I could not but reflect with pleasure on the situation of these people, and think, if there is such a thing as happiness in this life, that they enjoy it. Far from the bustle of the world, they live in the most delightful climate and richest soil imaginable; they are everywhere surrounded with beautiful prospects and sylvan scenes, lofty mountains, transparent streams, falls of water, rich valleys, and majestic woods; the whole, interspersed with an infinite variety of flowering shrubs, constitute the landscape surrounding them; they are subject to few diseases; are generally robust, and live in perfect liberty; they are ignorant of want, and acquainted with but few vices; their inexperience of the elegancies of life precludes any regret that they possess not the means of enjoying them; but they possess what many princes would give their dominions for— health, content, and tranquillity of mind."

In the year 1761 died the Rev. Thomas Dawson, President of the College of William and Mary; he was succeeded by the Rev. William Yates. During the same year died the Rev. Samuel Davies.* He accepted the presidency of the College of New Jersey in 1759, and died on the 4th of February, 1761. In this year was incorporated the town of Staunton, in Augusta County, and in the following year Romney, in the County of Hampshire.

During the tragic scenes of the French and Indian war, the

---

* John Rodgers Davies, his third son, was at Princeton College at the same time with Mr. Madison, and leaving it, at the commencement of the revolutionary war, became an officer in the army, and as such enjoyed the esteem of Washington. He is said to have been engaged in the auditor's office at Richmond. He removed to Sussex County, and died there.

persecutions of the dissenting Presbyterians, whose aid was so necessary in defending the frontiers, were essentially lessened. They were indebted to the confusion and dangers of the times for a freedom in matters of religion which was denied them in a period of tranquillity. Their ministers now enjoyed the privilege of preaching where they pleased, and were no longer restrained by the Virginia intolerant construction of the toleration act. The Baptists began to multiply their number in Virginia, and their new enthusiasm became the object of persecution. But events were about to turn the tide of popular prejudice, and direct it against the clergy of the established church, and to give to the dissenters a stronger foothold and a higher vantage ground. Those ministers of the establishment who had been vainly endeavoring to repress the progress of dissent by ridicule, detraction, and insult, some of them combining with and leading on a mob of "lewd fellows of the baser sort" in these persecuting indignities, now began to find it necessary to defend themselves against the rising storm of public indignation.

CHAPTER LXV.

1763.

The Parsons' Cause—Patrick Henry's Speech.

In the year 1763 occurred the famous "Parsons' Cause," in which the genius of Patrick Henry first shone forth. The emoluments of the clergy of the established church for a long time had consisted of sixteen thousand pounds of tobacco, contributed by each parish. The tobacco crop of 1755 failing, in consequence of a drought, and the exigencies of the colony being greatly augmented by the French and Indian war, the assembly passed an act, to endure for ten months, authorizing all debts due in tobacco to be paid either in kind or in money, at the rate ot sixteen shillings and eight pence for every hundred pounds of tobacco. This was equivalent to two pence per pound, and hence the act was styled by the clergy the "Two Penny Act." As the price of tobacco now rose to six pence per pound, the reduction amounted to sixty-six and two-thirds per cent. At two pence the salary of a minister clergy was about one hundred and thirty-three pounds; at six pence, about four hundred pounds. Yet the act must have operated in relief of the indebted clergy equally with other debtors, and many of the ministers were in debt. It was by no means the intention of the assembly to abridge the maintenance of the clergy, or to bear harder upon them than upon all other public creditors; and as they, under the new act, in fact, received in general a larger salary than they had received in any year since it was first regulated by law, they, above all men, ought to have been content with it in a year of so much distress.* The taxes were enormous, and fell most heavily upon planters of limited means; and the tobacco-crop was greatly fallen off. The Rev. James Maury, in whose behalf the suit was

---

* Colonel Richard Bland's Letter to the Clergy.

afterwards brought, had himself at the time expressly approved of the Two Penny Act, and said: "In my own case, who am entitled to upwards of seventeen thousand weight of tobacco per annum, the difference amounts to a considerable sum. However, each individual must expect to share in the misfortunes of the community to which he belongs."* The law was universal in its operation, embracing private debts, public, county, and parish levies, and the fees of all civil officers. Its effect upon the clergy was to reduce their salary to a moderate amount in money, far less, indeed, than the sixteen thousand pounds which they were ordinarily entitled to, yet still rather more than what they had usually received. The act did not contain the usual clause, by which acts altering previous acts approved by the crown were suspended until they should receive the royal sanction, since it might require the entire ten months, the term of its operation, to learn the determination of the crown. The king had a few years before expressly refused to allow the assembly to dispense with the suspending clause in any such act. The regal authority was thus apparently abnegated; necessity discarding forms, and the safety of the people being the supreme law. Up to the time of the Revolution the king freely exercised his authority in vetoing acts of the assembly when they had been approved by large majorities of the house of burgesses and of the council. The practice was to print all the acts at the close of each session, and when an act was negatived by the king, that fact was written against the act with a pen.†

No open resistance was offered to the Two Penny Act; but the greater number of clergy petitioned the house of burgesses to grant them a more liberal provision for their maintenance. Their petition set forth: "That the salary appointed by law for the clergy is so scanty that it is with difficulty they support themselves and families, and can by no means make any provision for their widows and children, who are generally left to the charity of their friends; that the small encouragement given to clergy-

---

* Memoirs of Huguenot Family, 402.

† Journals of the house of burgesses thus marked are in the possession of Mr. Grigsby.

men is a reason why so few come into this colony from the two universities; and that so many, who are a disgrace to the ministry, find opportunities to fill the parishes; that the raising the salary would prove of great service to the colony, as a decent subsistence would be a great encouragement to the youth to take orders, for want of which few gentlemen have hitherto thought it worth their while to bring up their children in the study of divinity; that they generally spent many years of their lives at great expense in study, when their patrimony is pretty well exhausted; and when in holy orders they cannot follow any secular employment for the advancement of their fortunes, and may on that account expect a more liberal provision."* Another relief act, similar to that of 1755, fixing the value of tobacco at eighteen shillings a hundred, was passed in 1758† upon a mere anticipation of another scanty crop.‡ Burk§ attributes the rise in the price of tobacco to the arts of an extravagant speculator; but he cites no authority for the statement, and the acts themselves expressly attribute the scarcity, in 1755, to "drought," and in 1757 to "unseasonableness of the weather."|| The crop did fall short, and the price rose extremely high; and contention ensued between the planters and the clergy. The Rev. John Camm, rector of York Hampton Parish, assailed the "Two Penny Act" in a pamphlet of that title, which was replied to severally by Colonel Richard Bland and Colonel Landon Carter. An acrimonious controversy took place in the *Virginia Gazette;* but the cause of the clergy became at length so unpopular, that a printer could not be found in Virginia willing to publish Camm's rejoinder to Bland and Carter, styled the "Colonels Dismounted," and he was obliged to resort to Maryland for that purpose. The colonels retorted, and this angry dispute threw the colony into great excitement. At last the clergy appealed to the king in council. By an act of assembly passed as early as the year 1662, a salary of eighty pounds per annum was set-

---

* Colonel Bland's Letter to the Clergy, 6.   † Hening, vii. 240.
‡ Ibid., vi. 568.   § Hist. of Va., iii. 302.
|| See also A. H. Everett's Life of Patrick Henry, in Sparks' American Biog., (second series,) i. 230.

tled upon every minister, "to be paid in the valuable commodities of the country—if in tobacco, at twelve shillings the hundred; if in corn, at ten shillings the barrel." In 1696 the salary of the clergy was fixed at sixteen thousand pounds of tobacco, worth at that time about eighty pounds. This continued to be the amount of their stipends until 1731, when, the value of tobacco being raised, they increased to about one hundred or one hundred and twenty pounds, exclusive of their glebes and other perquisites. In Virginia, besides the salaries of the clergy, the people had to bear parochial, county, and public levies, and fees of clerks, sheriffs, surveyors, and other officers, all of which were payable in tobacco, the paper currency of the colony having banished gold and silver from the colony.* The consequence of this state of things was that a failure in the crop involved the people in general distress; for by law if the salaries of the clergy and the fees of officers were not paid in tobacco by the tenth day of April, the property of delinquents was liable to be distrained, and if not replevied within five days, to be sold at auction. Were they to be exposed to cruel imposition and exactions; to have their estates seized and sacrificed, "for not complying with laws which Providence had made it impossible to comply with? Common sense, as well as common humanity, will tell you that they are not, and that it is impossible any instruction to a governor can be construed so contrary to the first principles of justice and equity, as to prevent his assent to a law for relieving a colony in a case of such general distress and calamity."† Sherlock, Bishop of London, in his letter to the lords of trade and plantations, denounced the act of 1758, as binding the king's hands, and manifestly tending to draw the people of the plantations from their allegiance to the king. It was replied, on the other hand, that if the Virginians could ever entertain the thought of withdrawing from their dependency on England, nothing could be more apt to bring about such a result than the denying them the right to protect themselves from distress and calamity in so trying an emergency. In the year when this relief act was passed, many thousands of the colonists did not make one pound of to-

---

* Burnaby's Travels. † Bland's Letter to the Clergy, 14.

bacco, and if all of it raised in the colony had been divided among the tithables, "they would not have had two hundred pounds a man to pay the taxes, for the support of the war, their levies and other public dues, and to provide a scanty subsistence for themselves and families;" and "the general assembly were obliged to issue money from the public funds to keep the people from starving." The act had been denounced as treasonable; but were the legislature to sit with folded arms, silent and inactive, amid the miseries of the people? "This would have been treason indeed,—treason against the state,—against the clemency of the royal majesty." Many landlords and civil officers were members of the assembly in 1758, and their fees and rents were payable in tobacco; nevertheless, they cheerfully promoted the enactment of a measure by which they were to suffer great losses. The royal prerogative in the hands of a benign sovereign could only be exerted for "the good of the people, and not for their destruction." "When, therefore, the governor and council (to whom this power is in part delegated) find, from the uncertainty and variableness of human affairs, that any accident happens which general instructions can by no means provide for, or which, by a rigid construction of them, would destroy a people so far distant from the royal presence, before they can apply to the throne for relief, it is their duty as good magistrates to exercise this power as the exigency of the state requires; and though they should deviate from the strict letter of an instruction, or, perhaps in a small degree from the fixed rule of the constitution, yet such a deviation cannot possibly be treason, when it is intended to produce the most salutary end—the preservation of the people."

The Rev. Andrew Burnaby, who passed some months in Virginia about the time of this dispute, travelling through the colony and conversing freely with all ranks of people, expresses himself on the subject in the following manner: "Upon the whole, however, as on the one hand I disapprove of the proceedings of the assembly in this affair, so on the other I cannot approve of the steps which were taken by the clergy; that violence of temper, that disrespectful behavior toward the governor, that unworthy treatment of their commissary, and, to mention nothing else, that confusion of proceeding in the convention,* of which some, though not the majority, as has been invidiously represented, were guilty; these things were surely unbecoming the sacred character they are invested with, and the moderation of those persons who ought in all things to imitate the conduct of their Divine Master. If instead of flying out in invectives against the legislature, of accusing the governor of having given up the cause of religion by passing the bill, when, in fact, had he rejected it, he would never have been able to have got any supplies during the course of the war, though ever so much wanted; if instead of charging the commissary† with want of zeal, for having exhorted them to moderate measures, they had followed the prudent counsels of that excellent man, and had acted with more temper and moderation, they might, I am persuaded, in a very short time have obtained any redress they could reasonably have desired. The people in general were extremely well affected toward the clergy."‡

The following paper exhibits the view maintained by Richard Henry Lee on this mooted topic:—

"*Reasons and Objections to Mr. Camm's Appeal.*

"OBJECTED, on the part of Mr. Camm: That the law of 1758, as it tended to suspend the act of 1748, which had obtained the royal approbation, and as it was contrary to his majesty's instructions to his governor, was void *ab initio*, and was so declared by his majesty's order of disapprobation of 10th of August, 1759.

"ANSWER.—Whatever might be allowed to be the effect of these objections, and however they might affect those who made the law, it would be very hard that they should subject to a heavy penalty two innocent subjects,§ who have been guilty of no offence but that of obeying a law passed regularly in appearance through the several branches of the legislature of the colony while it had

---

* The record of this convention of the clergy, which is probably in the archives of the See of London, would be extremely interesting at the present day.

† Robinson.

‡ Travels through the Middle Settlements in North America in the year 1759 and 1760, with Observations upon the state of the Colonies, by the Rev Andrew Burnaby, A.M., Vicar of Greenwich. Second edition. London, 1775.

§ The collectors.

the force of a law upon the spot. It would be to punish them for a mistake of the assembly. But the objections do not prove either that the law was a nullity from the beginning by its tending to suspend the act of 1748, or by being assented to by the governor, contrary to his majesty's instructions to him, or that it became void by relation, *ab initio*, from any retrospective declarations of his majesty. As to the law in question tending to suspend the act of 1748, which had received the royal approbation, a power given by the crown to make laws implies a power to suspend or even repeal former laws which are become inconvenient or mischievous, as the law of 1748 was; otherwise a country at the distance of three thousand miles might be subject to great calamities, before relief could be obtained, for which reason such power is lodged in the legislature of the country.

"As to the governor's consent being contrary to his majesty's instructions to him, it is imagined that his majesty's instructions to the governor are private directions for his conduct in his government, liable to be sometimes dispensed with upon extraordinary emergencies, the propriety of which he may be called to explain. The instructions are not addressed to the people nor promulgated among them; they are not public instruments, nor lodged among the public records of the province. The people know the governor's authority by his commission; his assent is virtually that of the crown, and by his assent the law is in force till his majesty's disapprobation arrives and is ratified, consequently everything done in the colony till then conformably thereto is legal.

"As to the order in council having declared the act void *ab initio*, it seems to have been a mistake, the order being as usual generally expressed that the act be disallowed, declared void, and of none effect, which purposely left the effect of the law, during the interval, open to its legal consequences.

"The king's commission to his governor directs him that he shall transmit all laws in three months after their passage. That when the laws are so signified, then such and so many of the said laws as shall be disallowed and signified to the governor should from thenceforth cease, etc. Upon appeal from the Cockpit to the privy council, the cause was put off *sine die*."

When the clergy appealed to the king, they sent over the Rev. John Camm to plead their cause in England, and agents were employed by the assembly to resist it. Mr. Camm remained eighteen months in England in prosecution of the appeal. The king at length, by the unanimous advice of the lords of trade, denounced the Two Penny Act as an usurpation, and declared it null and void: and the governor, by express instructions, issued a proclamation to that effect. Fauquier was reprimanded for not having negatived the bill, and was threatened with recall; and he pleaded in excuse that he had subscribed the law in conformity with the advice of the council, and contrary to his own judgment. The board of trade deemed the apology unsatisfactory.*

But the king's decision not being retrospective, the repeal of the act not rendering it void from the beginning, was in effect futile, the act having been passed to be in force for only one year.

At Mr. Camm's instance a suit was brought against the vestry of his parish of York Hampton, for the recovery of the salary in tobacco, the assembly having, in the mean while, determined to support the vestries in their defence. The case was decided against the plaintiff, Mr. Camm, who, in accordance with the advice of the board of trade, thereupon appealed to the king in council. The appeal was dismissed upon some informality. Camm experienced the perfidy of courtiers, and it being the policy of the government to avoid a collision with the assembly, the clergy were left in the lurch, to take their chances in the Virginia courts of law. The Rev. Mr. Warrington, grandfather of Commodore Lewis Warrington, endeavored to bring a suit for his salary, payable in tobacco, in the general court, but it was not permitted to be tried, the court awaiting the determination of Camm's case in England, which was in effect an indefinite postponement. Mr. Warrington then brought suit in the county court of Elizabeth City, and the jury brought in a special verdict, allowing him some damages, but declaring the law valid, notwithstanding the king's decision to the contrary. The Rev. Alexander White, of King William County, brought a similar

---

* Old Churches of Va., i. 217.

suit, and the court referring both the law and the fact to the jury, they gave the plaintiff trivial damages. The County of Hanover was selected as the scene of the most important trial of this question, and as all the causes stood on the same foot, the decision of this would determine all. This was the suit brought by the Rev. James Maury, of an adjoining parish. The county court of Hanover (November, 1763,) decided the point of law in favor of the minister, thus declaring the "Two Penny Act" to be no law, as having been annulled by the crown, and it was ordered that at the next court a jury, on a writ of inquiry, should determine whether the plaintiff was entitled to damages, and if so, how much? Maury's success before the jury seemed now inevitable, since there could be no dispute relative to the facts of the case. Mr. John Lewis, who had defended the popular side, retired from the cause as virtually decided, and as being now only a question of damages. The defendants, the collectors of that court, as a dernier resort, employed Patrick Henry, Jr., to appear in their behalf at the next hearing. The suit came to trial again on the first of December, a select jury being ordered to be summoned. On an occasion of such universal interest, an extraordinary concourse of people assembled at Hanover Court-house, not only from that county, but also from the counties adjoining. The court-house (which is still standing, but somewhat altered,) and yard were thronged, and twenty clergymen sat on the bench to witness a contest in which they had so much at stake. The Rev. Patrick Henry, uncle to the youthful attorney, retired from the court and returned home, at his request, he saying that he should have to utter some harsh things toward the clergy, which he would not like to do in his presence. The presiding magistrate was the father of young Henry. The sheriff, according to Mr. Maury's own account, finding some gentlemen unwilling to serve on the jury, summoned men of the common people. Mr. Maury objected to them, but Patrick Henry insisting that "they were honest men," they were immediately called to the book and sworn. Three or four of them, it was said, were dissenters "of that denomination called 'New Lights.'" On the plaintiff's side the only evidence was that of Messrs. Gist and McDowall, tobacco-buyers, who testified that fifty shillings per hundred weight was the current price of tobacco at that time. On the defendant's side was produced the Rev. James Maury's receipt for one hundred and forty-four pounds paid him by Thomas Johnson, Jr. The case was opened for the plaintiff by Peter Lyons. When Patrick Henry rose to reply, his commencement was awkward, unpromising, embarrassed. In a few moments he began to warm with his subject, and catching inspiration from the surrounding scene, his attitude grew more erect, his gesture bolder, his eye kindled and dilated with the radiance of genius, his voice ceased to falter, and the witchery of its tones made the blood run cold and the hair stand on end. The people, charmed by the enchanter's magnetic influence, hung with rapture upon his accents; in every part of the house, on every bench, in every window, they stooped forward from their stands in breathless silence, astonished, delighted, riveted upon the youthful orator, whose eloquence blended the beauty of the rainbow with the terror of the cataract. He contended that the act of 1758 had every characteristic of a good law, and could not be annulled consistently with the original compact between king and people, and he declared that a king who disallowed laws so salutary, from being the father of his people degenerated into a tyrant, and forfeited all right to obedience. Some part of the audience were struck with horror at this declaration, and the opposing advocate, Mr. Lyons, exclaimed, in impassioned tones, "The gentleman has spoken treason!" and from some gentlemen in the crowd arose a confused murmur of "Treason! Treason!" Yet Henry, without any interruption from the court, proceeded in his bold philippic; and one of the jury was so carried away by his feelings as every now and then to give the speaker a nod of approbation. He urged that the clergy of the established church by thus refusing acquiescence in the law of the land counteracted the great object of their institution, and, therefore, instead of being regarded as useful members of the State, ought to be considered as enemies of the community. In the close of his speech of an hour's length, he called upon the jury, unless they were disposed to rivet the chains of bondage on their own necks, to teach the defendant such a lesson, by their decision of this case, as would be a warning to him and his brethren not to have the temerity in future to dispute the validity of laws authenticated by the only authority which, in his opinion, could give force to laws for the government of this colony.* Amid the storm of his invective the discomfited and indignant clergy, feeling that the day was lost, retired. Young Henry's father sat on the bench bedewed with tears of conflicting emotions and fond surprise. The jury, in less than five minutes, returned a verdict of one penny damages. Mr. Lyons insisted that as the verdict was contrary to the evidence, the jury ought to be sent out again, but the court admitted the verdict without hesitation. The plaintiff's counsel then in vain endeavored to have the evidence in behalf of the plaintiff recorded. His motion for a new trial met with the same fate. He then moved, "that it might be admitted to record, that he had made a motion for a new trial because he considered the verdict contrary to evidence, and that the motion had been rejected," which, after much altercation, was agreed to. He lastly moved for an appeal, which too was granted. Acclamations resounded within the house and without, and in spite of cries of "Order! Order!" Patrick Henry was reluctantly lifted up and borne in criumph on the shoulders of his excited admirers. He was now the man of the people. In after-years, aged men who had been present at the trial of this cause reckoned it the highest encomium that they could bestow upon an orator to say of him: "He is almost equal to Patrick when he plead† against the parsons."‡

This speech of Henry's was looked upon by the clergy and their supporters as pleading for the assumption of a power to bind the king's hands, as asserting such a supremacy in provincial legisla-

---

* Letter of Rev. James Maury, in Memoirs of Huguenot Family, 421, 422.

† In Virginia to this day the preterite of "plead" is pronounced "pled." Wirt actually prints the word "pled," and has raised a smile at his expense. It is proper, however, to observe that "plead" and "read" followed the same analogies even in England in the seventeenth century. Many of the quaint words used by the common people, obsolete among the well educated, and usually set down as illiterate mistakes, are really grounded in traditional authority. Thus the word "gardein," for guardian, is the old law term: and the verb "learn," still often used actively, was, according to Trench, originally employed indifferently in a transitive sense as well as intransitive. The common people are often right without being able to prove it.

‡ Wirt's Life of Patrick Henry; Hawks, 124; Old Churches, etc., i. 219.

tures as was incompatible with the dignity of the Church of England, and as manifestly tending to draw the people of the colonies away from their allegiance to the king. Mr. Cootes, merchant on James River, on coming out of the court, said that he would have given a considerable sum out of his own pocket rather than his friend Patrick should have been guilty of treason, but little, if any, less criminal than that which had brought Simon Lord Lovat to the block. The clergy and their adherents deemed Henry's speech as exceeding the most inflammatory and seditious harangues of the Roman tribunes of the common people. The Rev. Mr. Boucher, rector of Hanover Parish, in the County of King George, accounted one of the best preachers of his time, said: "The assembly was found to have done and the clergy to have suffered wrong. The aggrieved may, and we hope often do, forgive, but it has been observed that aggressors rarely forgive. Ever since this controversy, your clergy have experienced every kind of discourtesy and discouragement."*

It was evident that the municipal affairs of Virginia could not be rightly managed, or safely interfered with, by a slow-moving government three thousand miles distant. The act of 1758 appears to have been grounded on humanity, the law of nature, and necessity.

Henry's speech in "the Parsons' Cause," and the verdict of the jury, may be said in a certain sense to have been the commencement of the Revolution in Virginia; and Hanover, where dissent had appeared, was the starting-point. Wirt's description of the scene has rendered it classic, and notwithstanding the faults of a style sometimes too florid and extravagant, there is a charm in the biography of Henry which stamps it as one of those works of genius which "men will not willingly let die."

---

* Anderson's Hist. Col. Church, iii. 158.

CHAPTER LXVI.

PATRICK HENRY.

PATRICK HENRY, the second of nine children, was born on the 29th day of May, 1736, at Studley, in Hanover County. The dwelling-house is no longer standing; antique hedges of box and an avenue of aged trees recall recollections of the past. Studley farm, devoid of any picturesque scenery, is surrounded by woods; so that Henry was actually,—

> "The forest-born Demosthenes,
> Whose thunder shook the Philip of the seas."*

His parents were in moderate but easy circumstances. The father, John Henry, was a native of Aberdeen, in Scotland; he was a cousin of David Henry, who was a brother-in-law of Edward Cave, and co-editor with him of the *Gentleman's Magazine*, and his successor. Some say that John Henry married Jane, sister of Dr. William Robertson, the historian, and that in this way Patrick Henry and Lord Brougham came to be related. John Henry, who emigrated to Virginia some time before 1730, enjoyed the friendship and patronage of Governor Dinwiddie, who introduced him to the acquaintance of Colonel John Syme, of Hanover, in whose family he became domesticated, and with whose widow he intermarried. Her maiden name was Sarah Winston, of a good old family. Colonel Byrd describes her as "a portly, handsome dame," "of a lively, cheerful conversation, with much less reserve than most of her countrywomen. It becomes her very well, and sets off her other agreeable qualities to advantage." "The courteous widow invited me to rest myself there that good day, and to go to church with her; but I excused myself by telling her she would certainly spoil my devotion.

---

* Lord Byron so calls him, in the Age of Bronze.

Then she civilly entreated me to make her house my home whenever I visited my plantations, which made me bow low, and thank her very kindly." She possessed a mild and benevolent disposition, undeviating probity, correct understanding, and easy elocution. Colonel Syme had represented the County of Hanover in the house of burgesses. He left a son who, according to Colonel Byrd, inherited all the strong features of his sire, not softened in the least by those of his mother.*

John Henry, father of Patrick Henry, Jr., was colonel of his regiment, county surveyor, and, for many years, presiding magistrate of Hanover County. He was a loyal subject, and took pleasure in drinking the king's health at the head of his regiment. He enjoyed the advantage of a liberal education; his understanding was plain but solid. He was a member of the established church, but was supposed to be more conversant with

---

* Several persons of the name of Winston came over from Yorkshire, England, and settled in Hanover. Isaac Winston, one of these, or a son of one of them, had children: 1. William, father of Judge Edmund Winston. 2. Sarah, mother of Patrick Henry, Jr., the orator. 3. Geddes. 4. Mary, who married John Coles. 5. A daughter who married —— Cole. She was grandmother to Dorothea or Dolly Payne, who married James Madison, President of the United States. Of these five children, William, the eldest, called Langaloo William, married Alice Taylor, of Caroline. He was a great hunter; had a quarter in Bedford or Albemarle, where he spent much time in hunting deer. He was fond of the Indians, dressed in their costume, and was a favorite with them. He was also distinguished as an Indian-fighter. He is said to have been endowed with that rare kind of magnetic eloquence which rendered his nephew, Patrick Henry, so famous. Indeed it was the opinion of some that he alone excelled him in eloquence. During the French and Indian war, shortly after Braddock's defeat, when the militia were marched to the frontier, this William Winston was a lieutenant of a company, which, being poorly clothed, without tents, and exposed to the rigors of an inclement season, became very much dissatisfied, and were clamorous to return to their homes. At this juncture, Lieutenant Winston, mounting a stump, made to them an appeal so patriotic and overpowering that when he concluded, the general cry was, "Let us march on; lead us against the enemy!" This maternal uncle of Patrick Henry, Jr., being so gifted with native eloquence, it may be inferred that he derived his genius from his mother. William Winston's children were: 1. Elizabeth, who married Rev. Peter Fontaine. 2. Fanny, who married Dr. Walker. 3. Edmund, the judge, who married, first, Sarah, daughter of Isaac Winston; second, the widow of Patrick Henry, the orator, (Dolly Dandridge that was.)

Livy and Horace than with the Bible. He appears to have made a map of Virginia which was published in London in 1770.*

When James Waddel first came to Virginia he visited the Rev. Samuel Davies in Hanover, near where Colonel John Henry lived, and being introduced to him, on a Sunday, he accepted an invitation to accompany him home. At parting, Mr. Davies remarked to young Waddel, that he would not find the Sabbath observed in Virginia as in Pennsylvania; and he would have to bear with many things which he would wish to be otherwise. Soon after the settlement of Colonel John Henry in Virginia, Patrick, his brother, followed him, and after some interval became, by his brother's interest, (April, 1733,) rector of St. George's Parish, in the new County of Spotsylvania, where he remained only one year. He afterwards became rector of St. Paul's Church in Hanover. John Henry, in a few years after the birth of his son Patrick, removed from Studley to Mount Brilliant, now the Retreat, in the same county; and it was here that the future orator was principally educated. The father, a good classical scholar, had opened a grammar-school in his own house, and Patrick, after learning the first rudiments at an "old field school" in the neighborhood, at ten years of age commenced his studies under his father, with whom he acquired an English education, and at the age of fifteen had advanced in Latin so far as to read Virgil and Livy; had learned to read the Greek characters, and attained some proficiency in the mathematics. At this age his scholastic education appears to have ended, and, as he mentioned to John Adams in 1774, he never read a Latin book after that. His attainments, however, evince that he could not have been so deficient in application to study as has been commonly supposed. With a taste so prevalent, and for which his kinsmen, the Winstons, were peculiarly distinguished, he was fond of hunting and angling. He would, it is said, recline under the shade of a tree overhanging the sequestered stream, watching in indolent repose the motionless cork of his fishing-

---

* A copy of this rare map is in possession of Joseph Horner, Esq., of Warrenton, Virginia. Appended to it is an epitome of the state and condition of Virginia. The marginal illustration is profuse, and, like the map, well executed.

line. He loved solitude, and in hunting chose not to accompany the noisy set that drove the deer, but preferred to occupy the silent "stand," where for hours he might muse alone and indulge "the pleasing solitariness of thought." The glowing fancy of Wirt has, perhaps, thrown over these particulars some prismatic coloring. Young Henry, probably, after all, fished and hunted pretty much like other lads in his neighborhood. It would, perhaps, not be easy to prove that he was fonder of fishing and hunting than George Mason, George Washington, and many other of his cotemporaries. From his eleventh to his twenty-second year he lived in the neighborhood where Davies preached, and occasionally accompanied his mother to hear him. His eloquence made a deep impression on young Henry, and he always spoke of Davies and Waddel as the greatest orators that he had ever heard. Whether he ever heard Whitefield does not appear.

Isaac Winston was one of the persons informed against in 1748 for allowing the Rev. John Roan to preach in his house. Two of the sisters of Patrick Henry—Lucy, who married Valentine Wood, and Jane, who married Colonel Samuel Meredith—were members of Davies' congregations.

At the age of fifteen Patrick Henry was placed, about the year 1751, in a store, to learn the mercantile business, and after a year so passed the father set up William, an elder brother, and Patrick together in trade. There is reason to believe that his alleged aversion to books and his indolence, have been exaggerated by Wirt's artistic romancing. There is no royal road to learning; men do not acquire knowledge by intuition. Aversion to study is by no means unusual among the young; nor is it probable that Patrick Henry was much more averse to it than the generality of youth; indeed, his domestic educational advantages were uncommonly good, and the early development of his mind proves that he did not neglect them. The mercantile adventure, after the experiment of a year, proving a failure, William, who, it would appear, had less energy than Patrick, retired from the concern, and the management was devolved upon the younger brother. Patrick, disgusted with an unpromising business, listened impatiently to the hunter's horn, and the cry of hounds echoing in the neighboring woods. Debarred from these congenial sports, he sought a resource in music, and learned to play not unskilfully on the flute and the violin, the latter being the favorite instrument in Virginia. He found another source of entertainment in the conversation of the country people who met at his store, particularly on Saturday; and was fond of starting debates among them, and observed the workings of their minds; and by stories, real or fictitious, studied how to move the passions at his will. Many country storekeepers have done the same thing, but they were not Patrick Henrys. That he employed part of his leisure in storing his mind with information from books, cannot be doubted. Behind the counter he could con the news furnished by the *Virginia Gazette*, and he probably dipped sometimes into the *Gentleman's Magazine*. At the end of two or three years, a too generous indulgence to his customers, and negligence in business, together perhaps with the insuperable difficulties of the enterprise itself, in a period of war, disaster, and public distress, forced him to abandon his store almost in a state of insolvency. William Henry, the older brother, was then wild and dissipated; but became in after-life a member of the assembly from the County of Fluvanna, enjoyed the title of colonel, and had a competent estate. In the mean time Patrick had married the daughter of a poor but honest farmer of the neighborhood, named Shelton; and now by the joint assistance of his father and his father-in-law, furnished with a small farm and one or two slaves, he undertook to support himself by agriculture. Yet, although he tilled the ground with his own hands, whether owing to his negligent, unsystematic habits, much insisted on by Wirt and others, or to the sterility of the soil, or to both, or to neither, after an experiment of two years he failed in this enterprise, as utterly as in the former. It was a period of unexampled scarcity and distress in Virginia; and young Henry was suffering a reverse of fortune which befell many others at the same time; and it would be, perhaps, unjust to attribute his failure exclusively or even mainly to his neglect or incompetency. However that may be, selling his scanty property at a sacrifice for cash, for lack of more profitable occupation he returned to merchandise. Still displaying indifference to the business of his store, he resumed his violin, his flute, his books, and his curious inspection of human nature; and occasionally shut up his store to indulge his favorite sports. He studied geography, and became a proficient in it; he examined the charters and perused the history of the colony, and pored over the translated annals of Greece and Rome. Livy became his favorite, and in his early life he read it at least once in every year. Such a taste would hardly have developed itself in one who had wasted his schoolboy days in the torpor of indolence. It is true that Mr. Jefferson said of him in after years, "He was the hardest man to get to read a book that he ever knew." Henry himself perhaps somewhat affected a distaste for book-learning, in compliance with the vulgar prejudice; but he probably read much more than he got credit for. He did not, indeed, read a large number of books, as very few in Virginia did then; but he appears to have read solid books, and to have read them thoroughly. He was fond of British history. Having himself a native touch of Cervantic humor, he was not unacquainted with the inimitable romance of Don Quixote. But he did not read books to talk about them. Soame Jenyns was a favorite. He often read Puffendorf, and Butler's Analogy was his standard volume through life.

His second mercantile experiment turned out more unfortunate than the first, and left him again stranded on the shoals of bankruptcy. It was probably an adventure which no attention or energy could have made successful under the circumstances. These disappointments, made the more trying by an early marriage, did not visibly depress his spirit: his mind rose superior to the vicissitudes of fortune. The golden ore was passing through the alembic of adversity. He lived now for some years with his father-in-law, who was then keeping the tavern at Hanover Court-house. When Mr. Shelton was occasionally absent, Mr. Henry supplied his place and attended to the guests.

In the winter of the year 1760 Thomas Jefferson, then in his seventeenth year, on his way to the College of William and Mary, spent the Christmas holidays at the seat of Colonel Dandridge, in Hanover County. Patrick Henry, now twenty-four years of age. being a near neighbor, young Jefferson met with him there for the first time, and observed that his manners had something of coarseness in them; that his passion was music, dancing, and pleasantry; and that in the last he excelled, and it attached everybody to him. But it is likely that the music of his voice was more attractive than even that of his violin. Henry displayed on that occasion, which was one of festivity, no uncommon calibre of intellect or extent of information; but his misfortunes were not to be traced in his countenance or his conduct: self-possessed repose is the characteristic of native power; complaint is the language of weakness. A secret consciousness of superior genius and a reliance upon Providence buoyed him up in the reverses of fortune. While young Jefferson and Henry were enjoying together the Christmas holidays of 1760, how little did either anticipate the parts which they were destined to perform on the theatre of public life! Young Henry embraced the study of the law, and after a short course of reading, was, in consideration of his genius and general information, and in spite of his meagre knowledge of law, and his ungainly appearance, admitted to the bar in the spring of 1760. His license was subscribed by Peyton and John Randolph and Robert C. Nicholas. Mr. Wythe refused to sign it.

In the "Parsons' Cause" Henry emerged from the horizon, and thenceforth became the star of the ascendant.

CHAPTER LXVII.
1763.
Rev. Jonathan Boucher's Opinions on Slavery—Remarks.

THE Rev. Jonathan Boucher, a minister of the established church, in a sermon preached at Bray's, in Leedstown, Hanover Parish, on occasion of the general peace proclaimed in 1763, expressed himself on the subject of slavery as follows: "The united motives of interest and humanity call on us to bestow some consideration on the case of those sad outcasts of society, our negro slaves; for my heart would smite me were I not in this hour of prosperity to entreat you (it being their unparalleled hard lot not to have the power of entreating for themselves) to permit them to participate in the general joy. Even those who are the sufferers can hardly be sorry when they see wrong measures carrying their punishment along with them. Were an impartial and competent observer of the state of society in these middle colonies asked whence it happens that Virginia and Maryland—which were the first planted, and which are superior to many colonies, and inferior to none in point of natural advantages—are still so exceedingly behind most of the other British transatlantic possessions in all those improvements which bring credit and consequence to a country, he would answer, 'They are so because they are cultivated by slaves.' I believe it is capable of demonstration, that except the immediate interest he has in the property of his slaves, it would be for every man's interest that there were no slaves, and for this plain reason, because the free labor of a free man, who is regularly hired and paid for the work he does, and only for what he does, is in the end cheaper than the eye-service of a slave. Some loss and inconvenience would no doubt arise from the general abolition of slavery in these colonies, but were it done gradually, with judgment and with good temper, I have never yet seen it satisfactorily proved that such inconvenience would be either great or lasting. North American or West Indian planters might possibly for a few years make less tobacco, or less rice, or less sugar, the raising of which might also cost them more; but that disadvantage would probably soon be amply compensated to them by an advanced price, or (what is the same thing) by the reduced expense of cultivation. * * * * * * *

"I do you no more than justice in bearing witness that in no part of the world were slaves ever better treated than, in general, they are in these colonies. That there are exceptions needs not to be concealed: in all countries there are bad men. And shame be to those men who, though themselves blessed with freedom, have minds less liberal than the poor creatures over whom they so meanly tyrannize! Even your humanity, however, falls short of their exigencies. In one essential point I fear we are all deficient: they are nowhere sufficiently instructed. I am far from recommending it to you at once to set them all free, because to do so would be a heavy loss to you and probably no gain to them; but I do entreat you to make them some amends for the drudgery of their bodies by cultivating their minds. By such means only can we hope to fulfil the ends which we may be permitted to believe Providence had in view in suffering them to be brought among us. You may unfetter them from the chains of ignorance, you may emancipate them from the bondage of sin—the worst slavery to which they can be subjected—and by thus setting at liberty those that are bruised, though they still continue to be your slaves, they shall be delivered from the bondage of corruption into the glorious liberty of the children of God."*

The Rev. Jonathan Boucher, was born in Cumberland County, England, in 1738, and brought up at Wigton Grammar School. He came over to Virginia at the age of sixteen, and was nominated by the vestry of Hanover Parish, in the County of King George, before he was in orders. Returning to England for ordination, he recrossed the Atlantic, and entered upon the duties of that parish on the banks of the Rappahannock. He removed soon afterwards to St. Mary's Parish, in Caroline County, upon the same river. After remaining here a good many years and enjoying the esteem

---

* Anderson's Hist. of Church of England in the Colonies, second ed., iii. 159.

of his people, he removed to Maryland, and was there ejected from his rectory at the breaking out of the Revolution, when he returned to England. His Discourses, preached between 1763 and 1775, were published by him when he was Vicar of Epsom, in Surrey, in 1797.

Abraham, the father of the faithful, was a slaveholder; upon his death his servants passed by descent to his son Isaac, as in like manner those of Isaac descended to Jacob. They were hereditary bondsmen, and, like chattels, bought and sold. Job, a pattern of piety, was a slaveholder, and, like Abraham, Isaac, and Jacob, won no small portion of his claims to a character of high and exemplary virtue from the manner in which he discharged his duty to his slaves.

The master who faithfully performs his duties toward his slaves is a high example of virtue, and the slave who renders his service faithfully is worthy of equal commendation. If the rights of the slave are narrow, his duties are proportionally limited.

The institution of slavery, divinely appointed, was maintained for five hundred years in Abraham's family. When the patriarchal dispensation came to an end, the right of property in slaves was recognized in the decalogue. The system was incorporated into the Mosaic law, and so continued to the end of the Jewish dispensation, and was nowhere denounced as a moral evil, nor was any reproof uttered by the prophets against the system on account of the evils connected with it.

The primitive Christian church consisted largely of slaveholders and slaves, and the slavery of the Roman empire, in which the early churches were planted, corresponded with that of Virginia, and where it differed, it was worse. The relation of master and servant is placed by the apostles upon the same footing as that of parent and child, and of husband and wife.* It is enjoined upon servants to be obedient to their masters, whether "good and gentle, or froward." Christian servants were commanded to obey their masters, whether heathens or believers; and Christians, to withdraw themselves from any, who, rejecting divine authority, should teach a contrary doctrine.†

---

* Ephesians, vi.; Colossians, iii., iv. † 1 Timothy, vi.

In the New Testament no censure is cast upon the institution of slavery, no master is denounced for holding slaves, nor advised to emancipate them. The evils incidental to the relation of master and slave are, in kind, like those incidental to the other domestic relations, and do not render the one unlawful or sinful any more than the others. The evils of slavery are not in the relation, but in the parties to it; therefore the abolition of the relation (the whites and the blacks still continuing together) would not extinguish the evils, but only change them, and a new relation would be substituted, fraught with still greater evils. The two races, separated by a barrier of natural incompatibility, cannot coalesce, nor can they coexist on equal terms.

The evils connected with slavery are, like others, to be remedied by the reforming influence of Christianity. Slavery originated in a curse, but out of it Providence has mysteriously educed a blessing, as from poisonous flowers honey is extracted by the bee.*

The religious instruction of the slaves in Virginia was, with some honorable exceptions, too generally neglected by the ministers of the established church. The churches afforded but little room or accommodation for the negroes, and the difficulties in the way of imparting instruction to them were no doubt great, yet by no means insuperable. The Rev. Samuel Davies appears to have labored more successfully for their benefit than any other minister in Virginia, either before his time or since. The Rev. Mr. Wright, co-operating with him in this work, established Sunday-schools, for the instruction of negroes, in the County of Cumberland, in the year 1756.†

---

* Brief Examination of Scripture Testimony on the Institution of Slavery, by the Rev. Thornton Stringfellow; Essay on Abolition of Slavery, by the Rev. Dr. George A. Baxter; Rights and Duties of Masters, by the Rev. Dr. J. H. Thornwell; The Christian Doctrine of Slavery, by the Rev. George D. Armstrong, D.D.

† Foote's Sketches, first series, 291.

CHAPTER LXVIII.

1764.

Disputes between Colonies and Mother Country—Stamp Act—Patrick Henry—Contested Election — Speaker Robinson — Randolph — Bland — Pendleton — Wythe—Lee.

THE successful termination of the war with France paved the way for American independence. Hitherto, from the first settlement of the colonies, Great Britain, without seeking a direct revenue from them, with perhaps some inconsiderable exceptions, had been satisfied with the appointment of their principal officers, and a monopoly of their trade. Now, when the colonies had grown more capable of resisting impositions, the mother country rose in her demands. Thus it was that disputes between Great Britain and the colonies, commencing in 1764 and lasting about twelve years, brought on the war of the Revolution, and ended in a disruption of the empire. This result, inevitable sooner or later in the natural course of events, was only precipitated by the impolitic and arbitrary measures of the British government. In the general loyalty of the colonies, new commercial restrictions, although involving a heavy indirect taxation, would probably have been submitted to for many years longer; but the novel scheme of direct taxation, without their consent, was reprobated as contrary to their natural and chartered rights; and a flame of discontent, bursting forth here and there, finally overspread the whole country.

There appears, indeed, to have been no essential difference between internal and external taxation; for it was still taxation; and taxation without representation. But the internal or direct taxation was new, obvious, and more offensive. The restrictions of the navigation act, vehemently resisted at their first enactment, and not less so in Virginia and other Southern colonies than in the North, had never been acquiesced in, but only submitted to from necessity; and long eluded not only by New England, but also by other colonies, by a trade originally contraband, indeed, but which had lost much of its illegitimate character by immemorial usage, and had acquired a sort of prescriptive right by that consent on the part of the British government which was to be inferred from its apparent acquiescence in the violation. For a hundred years preceding the Revolution the commerce of the colonies may be said to have been in the main practically free, as Great Britain was able to furnish the manufactures which the colony needed. But now the mother country undertook to enforce the obsolete navigation act and her revenue laws with a new vigor, which was not confined to the American colonies, but embraced the whole British empire. As applied to the colonies the measure was equally impolitic and unjust: impolitic, because by breaking up the colonial trade with the West Indies, England crippled her own customer; unjust, because this trade had grown up by the tacit consent of the government, and a dissolution of it would be ruinous to the commercial colonies. Besides these new restraints upon commerce, parliament had long endeavored to restrict colonial industry; and although these restrictions fell most heavily on the Northern colonies, their injurious effects were felt by all of them. As far back as the time of Bacon's rebellion, a patriotic woman of the colony congratulated her friends that now "Virginia can build ships, and, like New England, trade to any part of the world." And the parenthesis of religious liberty and free trade enjoyed by Virginia under Cromwell was never forgotten. But, inasmuch as these restrictions fell more heavily on the North than on the South, so the co-operation of the South was the more meritorious as being more disinterested. And the oppressions of Great Britain must have been intolerable, when, notwithstanding all the differences of opinion and of institutions, the thirteen colonies became united in a compact phalanx of resistance.*

The recent war had inspired the provincial troops with more confidence in themselves, and had rendered the British regulars less formidable in their eyes. Everything unknown is magnifi-

---

* Sabine's Loyalists, 36.

cent. The success of the allied arms had put an end to the dependency of the colonies upon the mother country for protection against the French. In several of the provinces Germans, Dutch, Swedes, and Frenchmen were found commingled with the Anglican population. Great Britain, by long wars ably conducted during Pitt's administration, had acquired glory and an extension of empire; but, in the mean time, she had incurred an enormous debt. The British officers, entertained with a hospitality in America, carried back to England exaggerated reports of the wealth of the colonies. The colonial governors and the British ministry had often been thwarted and annoyed by the republican and independent, and sometimes factious spirit, of the colonial assemblies, and longed to see them curbed. The British merchants complained to the government of the heavy losses entailed upon them by the depreciated colonial paper currency. The Church of England was indignant at the violent opposition to the introduction of bishops into the colonies, at the decision of the "Parsons' Cause," and other provocations and indignities. The advice of many governors and military officers had deeply impressed the government with the necessity of laying direct taxes as the only means of retaining the control of the colonies. The British administration, in the first years of the reign of George the Third, was in the hands of a corrupt oligarchy, and the ministers determined to lessen the burden at home by levying a direct tax upon the colonies. The loyalty of the Americans had never been warmer than at the close of the war. They had expended their treasure and their blood freely; and the recollection of mutual sufferings and a common glory strengthened their attachment to the mother country; but these loyal sentiments were destined soon to wither and expire. The colonies, too, had involved themselves in a heavy debt. Within three years, intervening between 1756 and 1759, parliament had granted them a large amount of money to encourage their efforts; yet, notwithstanding that and the extraordinary supplies appropriated by the assemblies, a heavy debt still remained unliquidated. When, therefore, parliament in a few years thereafter undertook to extort money by a direct tax from provinces to which she had recently granted incomparably larger sums, it was conceived that the object of the minister, in this innovation, was not simply to raise the inconsiderable amount of the tax, but to establish gradually a new and absolute system of "taxation without representation." It was easy to foresee that it would be made the instrument of unlimited extortions, and would extinguish the practical legislative independence of the Anglo-American colonies. Neither the English parliament, nor those who were represented by the lords and commons, would pay a farthing of the tax which they imposed on the colonies. On the contrary, their property would have been exempted in exact proportion to the burdens laid on the colonies. Taxes without reason or necessity, and oppressions without end, would have ensued from submitting to the usurpation.*

After war had raged for nearly eight years, peace was concluded at Paris, in February, 1763, by which France ceded Canada, and Spain the Floridas, to Great Britain. On this occasion the territory of Virginia was again reduced in extent. The conquests, and the culminating power, and the arrogant pretensions of the proud island of Great Britain excited the jealousy and the fears of Europe; while in England the administration had engendered a formidable opposition at home. In the year 1763 the national debt had accumulated to an enormous amount; for which an annual interest of twenty-two millions of dollars was paid. The minister proposed to levy upon the colonies part of this sum, alleging that as the recent war had been waged partly on their account, it was but fair that they should contribute a share of the expense; and the right was claimed for parliament, according to the British constitution, to tax every portion of the empire. The absolute right of legislating for the colonies had long, if not always, been claimed, theoretically, by England; but she had never exerted it in practice to any sensible extent in the essential article of taxation. The inhabitants of the colonies admitted their obligation to share the expense of the war, but insisted that the necessary revenue could be legitimately levied only by their own legislatures; that taxation and

---

* Letter from R. H. Lee to his sister, Mrs. Corbin, written in 1778. *Hist. Mag.*, i. 360.

representation were inseparable; and that remote colonies not represented in parliament were entitled to tax themselves. The justice of parliament would prove a feeble barrier against the demands of avarice; and as in England the privilege of granting money was the palladium of the people's liberty against the encroachment of the crown, so the same right was the proper safeguard of the colonies against the tyranny of the imperial government. Such were the views of American patriots; yet it was a subject on which wise and good men might differ in Great Britain and in America.

Upon the death of the Rev. William Yates, in 1764, the Rev. James Horrocks succeeded him as President of the College of William and Mary. About the same time the Rev. William Robinson, commissary, dying, Mr. Horrocks succeeded him in that place. Rev. John Camm, who aspired to the office, was disappointed in it owing to some difficulty with Governor Dinwiddie.

In March, 1764, parliament passed resolutions declaratory of an intention to impose a stamp-duty in America, and avowing the right and expediency of taxing the colonies. This was the immediate fountain-head of the Revolution. These resolutions gave great dissatisfaction in America; but were popular in England, where the prospect of lightening their own burdens at the expense of the colonists recommended them to the English taxpayers. The resolutions met with no overt opposition, but the public discontents were increased when it came to be known that large bodies of British soldiers were to be sent over and quartered in the colonies.

Patrick Henry, during the year, removed from Hanover to Louisa, where he soon endeared himself to the people, although he never courted their favor by flattery. He sometimes hunted deer for several days together, carrying his provision with him, and at night camping out in the woods. He was known to enter Louisa court in a coarse cloth coat, stained with the blood of the deer, greasy leather breeches, with leggings for boots, and a pair of saddle-bags on his arm.*

In the fall of 1764 there occurred in the house of burgesses a

---

* Wirt's Life of Patrick Henry, 37.

case of contested election, the parties being James Littlepage, the member returned for the County of Hanover, and the other candidate, Nathaniel West Dandridge. Mr. Littlepage was charged with bribery and corruption. The case was tried before the committee of privileges and elections, and Mr. Henry appeared as attorney for Mr. Dandridge. Mr. Henry was coarsely dressed and quite unknown, yet retained his self-possession in spite of the supercilious smiles of aristocracy. The right of suffrage and the purity of the elective franchise afforded him a theme for a speech which astonished the audience; and Judge Winston pronounced the argument "superior to anything he had ever heard."

The speaker of the house, John Robinson, had held that post for a quarter of a century, and combining with it the office of treasurer, his influence was wide and well established. His personal popularity was great, and embraced men of all classes. His strong and cultivated mind was set off by polished manners; his presence, imposing and commanding.

Peyton Randolph, the king's attorney-general, in influence second only to the speaker, was discreet and dignified; thoroughly versed in legislative proceedings; of excellent judgment, yet without extraordinary genius; a sound lawyer; in politics conservative; intolerant to dissenters.

Richard Bland was enlightened and laborious, a profound reasoner, an ungraceful speaker, but an excellent writer; a wise but over-cautious statesman, like Dickinson, of Pennsylvania, marching up with fearless logic to his conclusions, but pausing there, unwilling to carry them into effect.

Edmund Pendleton was the grandson of Philip Pendleton, a teacher, who came over to Virginia about the year 1674 with his brother, Nathaniel, a minister. Philip Pendleton's eldest son, at the age of eighteen, married Mary Taylor, aged only thirteen, and Edmund was the fourth son of this union. From a sister was descended General Edmund Pendleton Gaines, of the United States army. Edmund Pendleton was born (his father dying before his birth) in 1721, in Caroline County. Left poor and without any classical education, it is said that after ploughing all day he pursued his studies at night. Placed in his fourteenth year in the office of Colonel Benjamin Robinson, (brother of the speaker,) clerk of the county court of Caroline, he became acquainted with legal forms. He could hardly have spent much time in ploughing before his fourteenth year. At the age of sixteen he was appointed clerk to the vestry of St. Mary's Parish; and the salary derived from that petty office he expended in the purchase of books, which he diligently read. In his twentieth year he was licensed to practise the law, after having been strictly examined by the eminent lawyer Barradall. About the same time young Pendleton was made clerk of the county court martial. Before he was of age he married, in opposition to the advice of his friends, Betty Roy, remarkable for her beauty. Upon being licensed he soon acquired a large practice. His wife dying in less than two years after the marriage, in his twenty-fourth year he married Sarah Pollard. He now began to practise in the general court. In the year 1752 he was elected one of the representatives of Caroline, and so continued down to the time of the Revolution. Mr. Wirt says that he was a protégé of Speaker Robinson, who introduced him into the circle of refined society. Mr. Grigsby thinks that the term protégé was inapplicable to him, as he was the architect of his own fortune. It is certain that Speaker Robinson found in him his ablest supporter in the question of separating the offices of speaker and treasurer. Mr. Pendleton became the leader of the conservative party, who, while they wished to effect a redress of grievances, were opposed to a revolution of the government, and who stood out against it until opposition became unavailing. Nevertheless, by his integrity, the charm of his manners, and his great abilities, he attained and filled with honor several of the highest posts. As a lawyer, debater, statesman, he was of the highest order in the colony; yet he read little besides law, and was without taste for literature. The report of a law case had for him the charm which a novel has for others. As a writer he was unskilled, and quite devoid of the graces of style and rhythm. His voice was melodious, and his articulation distinct; his elocution graceful and effective; with a serene self-possession that nothing could disturb, he was ever ready to seize every advantage that occurred in debate; but he could lay no claim to the lofty powers which "shake the human soul." Although a new man, he was, as often happens, behind none in his extreme conservative views in church and state. In a brief autobiography, he says of himself: "Without any classical education, without patrimony, without what is called the influence of family connection, and without solicitation, I have attained the highest offices of my country. I have often contemplated it as a rare and extraordinary instance, and pathetically exclaimed, 'Not unto me, not unto me, O Lord, but unto thy name be the praise!'"*

George Wythe was born in Elizabeth City, (1726,) his father having been a burgess from that county. George, on the side of his mother's family, named Keith, inherited a taste for letters. After studying the law, having come into possession of a competent estate, he wasted several years in indolence and dissipation; but he afterwards became a close student, having imbibed a taste for learning from the society of Governor Fauquier and Professor Small. He became accomplished in classic literature, and profoundly versed in the law. He is described as having been simple and artless, incapable of the little crooked wisdom of cunning, and his integrity was incorruptible.

Richard Henry Lee was distinguished by a face of the Roman order: his forehead high but not wide, his head leaning gracefully forward; his person and face fine. He was an accomplished scholar, of wide reading. His voice was musical. He had lost the use of one hand by an accident, and kept it covered with a bandage of black silk; but his gesture was graceful. His style of eloquence was chaste, classic, electric, and delightful. As Mr. Jefferson has said that Patrick Henry spoke as Homer wrote, so Mr. Lee may be, perhaps, compared to Virgil. Henry and Lee coincided in political views, co-operated in public life, and were confidential correspondents and warm and constant friends.

---

* Wirt's Life of Henry, 47; Old Churches, Ministers, etc., 298; Grigsby's Convention of '76, p. 16.

CHAPTER LXIX.

1765-1766.

The Stamp Act—Virginia opposes it—Loan-office Scheme—Members of Council and Burgesses—Repeal of Stamp Act—Treasurer Robinson's Defalcation—Offices of Speaker and Treasurer separated—Lee's Speech—Miscellaneous—Family of Robinson.

ON the 7th day of February, 1765, Grenville introduced in the house of commons the stamp act, declaring null and void instruments of writing in daily use in the colonies, unless executed on stamped paper or parchment, charged with a duty imposed by parliament. The bill, warmly debated in that house, but carried by a vote of five to one, met with no opposition in the house of lords, and on the twenty-second of March received the royal sanction. At first it was taken for granted that the act would be enforced. It was not to take effect till the first day of November, more than seven months from its passage. The Virginians were a proud race, the more jealous of their liberties, having, like the Spartans, the degradation of slavery continually in their view, impatient of restraint, and unwilling to succumb to the control of any superior power, "snuffing the tainted breeze of tyranny afar." Many of them even affected to consider the colonies as independent states, only linked to Great Britain as owing allegiance to a common crown, and as bound to her by natural affection.

The assembly met on the 1st day of May, 1765. Patrick Henry took his seat in it on the twentieth. Notwithstanding the opposition of the people to the stamp act, yet the place-men, the large landed proprietors, who were the professed adherents of government, still held the control of the legislature. Disgusted by the delays and sophistries of this class during the preceding session, one of the Johnsons, two brothers that represented

Louisa County, declared his intention to bring into the house Patrick Henry, who was equally distinguished by his eloquence and by an opposition to the claims of parliament, verging on sedition. Johnson accordingly, by accepting the office of coroner, vacated his seat in favor of Henry, who thus came to be one of the representatives of that frontier county in the assembly of 1765—an incident connected with events of transcendent importance.

On the twenty-fourth, Peyton Randolph reported to the house, from the committee of the whole, a scheme for the establishment of a loan-office or bank. The plan was to borrow £240,000 sterling from British merchants, at an interest of five per cent.; a fund for paying the interest and sinking the principal to be raised by an impost duty on tobacco; bills of exchange to be drawn for £100,000, with which the paper money in circulation was to be redeemed, the remaining £140,000 to be imported in specie, and deposited here for a stock whereon to circulate bank notes, to be lent out on permanent security, at an interest of five per cent., to be paid yearly, a proportion of the principal at the end of four years, another proportion at the end of five years, and afterwards by equal payments once in four years, until the whole should be repaid.

When it was urged in favor of this scheme, that from the distressed condition of the colony, men of fortune had contracted debts, which, if exacted suddenly, must ruin them, but which, with a little indulgence, might be liquidated, Mr. Henry exclaimed: "What, sir! is it proposed then to reclaim the spendthrift from his dissipation and extravagance by filling his pockets with money?" Thomas Jefferson, then a law-student at Williamsburg, was present during this debate, and the manner in which Henry uttered this sentence was indelibly impressed on his memory.

The resolutions embodying this scheme were passed by the house, and a committee of conference was appointed at the same time, and before the vote upon them was taken in the council. In this conference the managers on the part of the house were Edmund Pendleton, Mr. Archibald Cary, Mr. Benjamin Harrison, Mr. Burwell, Mr. Braxton, and Mr. Fleming. The council* refused to concur in the scheme. Had it been carried into effect, the indebtedness of Virginia at the eve of the Revolution would have probably been greatly augmented.

Virginia led the way in opposing the stamp act. On the 30th of May, 1765, near the close of the session, Patrick Henry offered the following resolutions:—

"Resolved, That the first adventurers and settlers of this his majesty's colony and dominion, brought with them, and transmitted to their posterity and all other his majesty's subjects since inhabiting in this his majesty's said colony, all the privileges, franchises, and immunities that have at any time been held, enjoyed, and possessed by the people of Great Britain.

"Resolved, That by two royal charters granted by King James the First, the colonists aforesaid are declared entitled to all the privileges, liberties, and immunities of denizens and natural-born subjects, to all intents and purposes as if they had been abiding and born within the realm of England.

"Resolved, That the taxation of the people by themselves, or by persons chosen by themselves to represent them, who can only know what taxes the people are able to bear, and the easiest mode of raising them, and are equally affected by such taxes themselves, is the distinguishing characteristic of British freedom, and without which the ancient constitution cannot subsist.

"Resolved, That his majesty's liege people of this most ancient colony have uninterruptedly enjoyed the right of being thus governed by their own assembly in the article of their taxes and internal police, and that the same hath never been forfeited, or

---

* The following is a list of the council in 1764:—
The Honorable JOHN BLAIR, President.

William Nelson,	Philip Ludwell Lee,
Thomas Nelson,	John Tayloe,
Peter Randolph,	Robert Carter,
Richard Corbin,	Presley Thornton,
William Byrd,	Robert Barwell, Esquires.

Of the members of the house at this time may be mentioned the names of Cabell, Cary, Wythe, Pendleton, Harrison, Marshall, Washington, Carter, Robinson, Lee, Bland, Mercer, Page, Braxton, Henry, Nelson, and Randolph.

any other way given up, but hath been constantly recognized by the king and people of Great Britain.

"Resolved, Therefore, that the general assembly of this colony have the sole right and power to lay taxes and impositions upon the inhabitants of this colony, and that every attempt to vest such power in any person or persons whatsoever other than the general assembly aforesaid, has a manifest tendency to destroy British as well as American freedom."*

Mr. Henry was young, being about twenty-eight years of age, and a new member; but finding the men of weight in the house averse to opposition, and the stamp act about to take effect, and no person likely to step forth, alone, unadvised, and unassisted, he wrote these resolutions on a blank leaf of an old law book, "Coke upon Littleton." Before offering them, he showed them to two members, John Fleming, of Goochland, and George Johnson, of Fairfax. Mr. Johnson seconded the resolutions. Speaker Robinson objected to them as inflammatory. The first three appear to have passed by small majorities, without alteration. The fourth was passed amended, so as to read as follows: "Resolved, That his majesty's liege people of this his most ancient and loyal colony have, without interruption, enjoyed the inestimable right of being governed by such laws respecting their internal polity and taxation as are derived from their own consent, with the approbation of their sovereign or his substitute, and that the same hath never been forfeited or yielded up, but hath been constantly recognized by the king and people of Great Britain."

The last of the five resolutions was carried by a majority of only one vote, being twenty to nineteen, and the debate on it, in the language of Mr. Jefferson, was "most bloody." Speaker Robinson, Peyton Randolph, attorney-general, Richard Bland, Edmund Pendleton, George Wythe, and all the old leaders of the house and proprietors of large estates, made a strenuous resistance. Mr. Jefferson says the resolutions of Henry "were

---

* Two other resolutions were offered, but not by Henry, to the effect that the people of Virginia were not under any obligation to obey any laws not enacted by their own assembly, and that any one who should maintain the contrary should be deemed an enemy to the colony. These two did not pass.

opposed by Robinson and all the cyphers of the aristocracy." John Randolph resisted them with all his might. How Washington voted is not known, the yeas and nays never being recorded on the journal in that age. He considered the stamp act ill-judged and unconstitutional, and was of opinion that it could not be enforced. Mr. Henry was ably supported in a logical argument by Mr. George Johnson, a lawyer of Alexandria.

In the course of this stormy debate many threats were uttered by the party for submission, and much abuse heaped upon Mr. Henry, but he carried the young members with him. Jefferson, then a student of William and Mary, standing at the door of the house, overheard the debate. After Speaker Robinson had declared the result of the vote, Peyton Randolph, as he entered the lobby near Jefferson, exclaimed with an oath, "I would have given five hundred guineas for a single vote!" One more vote would have defeated the last resolution.*

Scarce a vestige of this speech of Henry survives. Mr. Jefferson declared that he never heard such eloquence from any other man. While Mr. Henry was inveighing against the stamp act, he exclaimed: "Tarquin and Cæsar had each his Brutus, Charles the First his Cromwell, and George the Third"—("Treason!" cried the speaker; "Treason! Treason!" resounded from every part of the house. Henry, rising to a loftier attitude, with unfaltering voice, and unwavering eye fixed on the speaker, finished the sentence,)—"may profit by the example. If this be treason, make the most of it." Henry was now the leading man in Virginia, and his resolutions gave the impulse to the other colonies, and the spirit of resistance spread rapidly through them, gathering strength as it proceeded. On the afternoon of the same day Mr. Henry left Williamsburg, passing along Duke of Gloucester Street, on his way to his home in Louisa, wearing buckskin breeches, his saddle-bags on his arm, leading a lean horse, and chatting with Paul Carrington, who walked by his side.

Young Jefferson happened on the following morning to be in the hall of the burgesses before the meeting of the house, and he

---

* Paul Carrington, in after years, distinctly remembered seeing Thomas Jefferson among the auditors in this debate.

observed Colonel Peter Randolph, one of the council, sitting at the clerk's table examining the journals, to find a precedent for expunging a vote of the house. Part of the burgesses having gone home, and some of the more timid of those who had voted for the strongest resolution having become alarmed, as soon as the house met, a motion was made and carried to expunge the last resolution from the journals. The manuscript journal of that day disappeared shortly after and has never been found.* The four remaining on the journal and the two additional ones offered in committee, but not reported, were published in the *Gazette*. On the first of June the governor dissolved the assembly.

At the instance of Massachusetts, guided by the advice of James Otis, a congress met in October, 1765, at New York. The assemblies of Virginia, North Carolina, and Georgia were prevented by their governors from sending deputies. The congress made a declaration denying the right of parliament to tax the colonies, and concurred in petitions to the king and the commons and a memorial to the lords. Virginia and the other two colonies not represented forwarded petitions accordant with those adopted by the congress. The committee appointed by the Virginia assembly to draught the petitions consisted of Peyton Randolph, Richard Henry Lee, Landon Carter, George Wythe, Edmund Pendleton, Benjamin Harrison, Richard Bland, Archibald Cary, and Mr. Fleming. The address to the king was written by Peyton Randolph, the address to the commons by George Wythe, and the memorial to the lords was attributed to Richard Bland.

Opposition to the stamp act now blazed forth everywhere; and it was disregarded and defied. In the last week of October, George Mercer, distributor of stamps for Virginia, landed at Hampton, and was rudely treated by the mob, who, by the interposition of some influential gentlemen, were prevailed on to disperse without offering him any personal injury. At Williamsburg, as he was walking toward the capitol, on his way to the governor's palace, he was required by several gentlemen from different counties, the general court being in session, to say

---

* Wirt's Henry, 56—61.

whether he intended to enter on the duties of the office. At his request he was allowed to wait on the governor before replying, and he was accompanied to the coffee-house where the governor, most of the council, and many gentlemen were assembled. The crowd increasing and growing impatient in their demands, Mr. Mercer came forward and promised to give a categorical answer at five o'clock the next evening. At that time he met a large concourse of people, including the principal merchants of the colony. He then engaged not to undertake the execution of the stamp act until he received further orders from England, nor then, without the assent of the assembly of Virginia. He was immediately borne out of the capitol gate, amid loud acclamations, and carried to the coffee-house, where an elegant entertainment was prepared for him, and was welcomed there by renewed acclamations, drums beating, and French-horns and other musical instruments sounding. At night the bells were set a-ringing, and the town was illuminated. Mr. Mercer was, in 1769, appointed lieutenant-governor of North Carolina.*

The colonists began to betake themselves to domestic manufactures; and foreign luxuries were laid aside. In the mean while a change had taken place in the British ministry; the stamp act was reconsidered in parliament; Dr. Franklin was examined at the bar of the house of commons. Lord Camden, in the house of lords, and Mr. Pitt, in the commons, favored a repeal of the act; and, after providing for the dependence of America on Great Britain, parliament repealed the stamp act in March, 1766. On the second day of May news of the repeal reached Williamsburg by the ship Lord Baltimore, arrived in York River, from London. The joyful intelligence was celebrated at Norfolk; and at Williamsburg by a ball and illumination.

At the session of November, 1766, Mr. John Robinson, who had for many years held the offices of speaker and treasurer, being now dead, an investigation of his accounts exposed an enormous defalcation. A motion to separate the offices, brought forward by Richard Henry Lee, and supported by Mr. Henry,

---

* Martin's Hist. of N. C., ii. 203, 250.

proved successful. Edmund Pendleton was at the head of the party that resisted it.*

Mr. Lee on this occasion pursued his course in opposition to the confederacy of the great in place, the influence of family connections, and that still more dangerous foe to public virtue, private friendship. The contest appears to have been bitter, and it engendered animosities which survived the lapse of years and the absorbing scenes of the outbreaking Revolution.

A fragment of the speech delivered by Mr. Lee on this occasion has been preserved.† After supporting his views by historical examples, he remarks: "If, then, wise and good men in all ages have deemed it for the security of liberty to divide places of power and profit; if this maxim has not been departed from without either injury or destroying freedom—as happened to Rome with her decemvirs and her dictator—why should Virginia so early quit the paths of wisdom, and seal her own ruin, as far as she can do it, by uniting in one person the only two great places in the power of her assembly to bestow?" The fragment of this speech ends just where Mr. Lee was about to combat the arguments in support of the union of the two offices. Among

---

* This affair formed the subject of some crude verses, entitled "The Contest." The following is an extract:—

> "And Curtius, too, who, from clear Chellowe's height,
> Secrets deep lying in the dark recess
> Of ——'s clouded brain, can well explore,
> Demands my thanks sincere; freed from the froth
> Of Metriotes'* hyperbolic style,
> Or wine burgessian, potent to deceive,
> And to produce a vote of huge expense.
> The tribute due to genius and to sense
> Is yours, judicious Burke! without compeer;
> The reverend priest the bayic crown presents;
> Accept it, then; nor Grymes of mighty bone,
> And fist, sledge-hammer like; nor grimful face
> Of Ampthill's rustic chief,† nor the abuse
> By him in senatorial consult used,
> Eulogies to true merit shall prevent."

† Lee Papers in *S. Lit. Messenger*, 1858, p. 119.

---

* John Randolph, afterwards attorney-general. † Archibald Cary.

these arguments were, that innovation is dangerous; that the additional office of treasurer was necessary to give the speaker that pre-eminence that is befitting his station; that the parliamentary powers of the speaker give the chair no influence, as in the exercise thereof in pleasing one he may offend a dozen; that a separation of the offices might induce the government at home to take the appointment out of their hands altogether; and that the support of the dignity of the chair necessarily involved a great expense.

It could not have been difficult to refute these arguments. The combination of the offices of speaker and treasurer was itself an innovation of as recent date as 1738. The speaker of the English house of commons did not find the office of treasurer necessary to maintain his dignity. If the office of speaker of itself gave no influence, why had it been always sought for? Nor could the separation of the offices induce the home government to take the appointments from the assembly, for that separation was itself virtually a government measure. Chalmers, who was well versed in the documentary history of the colonies, says: "Too attentive to overlook the dangerous pre-eminence of Robinson, the board of trade took this opportunity to enjoin [1758] the new governor* to use every rational endeavor to procure a separation of the conjoined offices which he improperly held."† Lee, Henry, and others, who voted for the separation, were in effect carrying out the wishes of the English government. Nor does it appear probable that the government was any more favorable to the loan-office scheme than to the union of the offices of speaker and treasurer.

Upon the death of Speaker Robinson, Richard Bland was a candidate for the chair, and was in favor of a separation of the offices of speaker and treasurer. He, in the latter part of May, entertained no suspicion of any malversation in office on the part of the late treasurer, although he was aware that such suspicions prevailed much among the people. He was at this time maturing a scheme for a loan-office, or government bank, which he thought would be of signal advantage, and would in a few years enable

---

* Fauquier.   † Hist. of Amer. Colonies, ii. 354.

Virginia to discharge her debts without any tax for the future. It is singular that he should have been preparing to renew a scheme so recently defeated. Whether he ever again revived it in the assembly, does not appear. Robert Carter Nicholas, at the same time a candidate for the place of treasurer, was likewise in favor of a disjunction of the two offices. To this position he and Bland were brought, as well by the inducements of personal promotion as by a regard for the public good.

Peyton Randolph was made speaker; and Mr. Nicholas, who had been already appointed in May treasurer *ad interim*, by Governor Fauquier, was elected to that post by the assembly.

Lewis Burwell, George Wythe, John Blair, Jr., John Randolph, and Benjamin Waller were appointed to examine the state of the treasury. The deficit of the late treasurer exceeded one hundred thousand pounds. Mr. Robinson, amiable, liberal, and wealthy, had long been at the head of the aristocracy, and exerted an extraordinary influence in political affairs. He had lent large sums of the public money to friends involved in debt, especially to members of the assembly, confiding for its replacement upon his own ample fortune, and the securities taken on the loans. Mr. Wirt says that at length, apprehensive of a discovery of the deficit, he, with his friends in the assembly, devised the scheme of the loan-office the better to conceal it. The entire amount of the defalcation was eventually recovered from the estate of Robinson, which was sold in 1770 by Edmund Pendleton and Peter Lyons, surviving administrators.[*] Burk attributes Robinson's death to the mortification that he suffered on account of his defalcation. Bland and Nicholas, in their letters addressed to Richard Henry Lee, allude to it in terms of exquisite delicacy.

The first of the family of Speaker Robinson of whom we have any account was John Robinson, of Cleasby, Yorkshire, England. His son John was Bishop of Bristol, and British envoy at the court of Sweden; he was also British plenipotentiary at the treaty of Utrecht, being, it is said, the last divine employed in a service of that kind. He was afterwards Bishop of London, in which office he continued until his death in 1723. Leaving no

---

[*] Hening, viii. 349.

issue he devised his real estate to his nephew, Christopher Robinson, who had settled on the Rappahannock. His eldest son, John Robinson, born in 1682, was president of the council. He married Catherine, daughter of Robert Beverley, the historian. John Robinson, Jr., their eldest son, was treasurer and speaker, and is commonly known as "Speaker Robinson."* He resided at Mount Pleasant, on the Matapony, in King and Queen, the house there having been built for him, it is said, by Augustine Moore, of Chelsea, in King William, father of Lucy Moore, one of his wives. Her portrait is preserved at Chelsea; his is preserved by his descendants. His other wife was Lucy Chiswell. He lies buried in the garden at Mount Pleasant.

---

* Old Churches of Virginia, i. 378, in note.

CHAPTER LXX.

1766-1768.

Bland's Inquiry—Duties imposed by Parliament—Death of Fauquier—Succeeded by Blair—Baptists persecuted—Blair's Letter.

In the year 1766 there was published at Williamsburg "An Inquiry into the Rights of the British Colonies," from the pen of Richard Bland.* In discussing the question, "Whether the colonies are represented in the British Parliament?" he traces the English constitution to its Saxon origin, when every freeholder was a member of the Wittenagemote or Parliament. This appears from the statutes 1st Henry the Fifth, and 8th Henry the Sixth, limiting the elective franchise, that is, depriving many of the right of representation in parliament. How could they have been thus deprived, if, as was contended, all the people of England were still virtually represented? He acknowledged that a very large portion of the people of Great Britain were not entitled to representation, and were, nevertheless, bound to obey the laws of the realm, but then the obligation of these laws does not arise from their being virtually represented. The American colonies, excepting the few planted in the eighteenth century, were founded by private adventurers, who established themselves, without any expense to the nation, in this uncultivated and almost uninhabited country, so that they stand on a different foot from the Roman or any ancient colonies. Men have a natural right to quit their own country and retire to another, and set up there an independent government for themselves. But if they have

---

* The title-page is as follows: "An Inquiry into the Rights of the British Colonies, intended as an Answer to 'The Regulations lately made concerning the Colonies, and the Taxes imposed upon them, considered.' In a Letter addressed to the Author of that Pamphlet, by Richard Bland, of Virginia. Dedit omnibus Deus pro virili portione sapientiam, ut et inaudita investigare possent et audita perpendere. Lactantius." Williamsburg: printed by Alexander Purdie & Co., MDCCLXVI.

this so absolute a right, they must have the lesser right to remove, by compact with their sovereign, to a new country, and to form a civil establishment upon the terms of the compact. The first Virginia charter was granted to Raleigh by Queen Elizabeth, in 1584, and by it the new country was granted to him, his heirs and assigns, in perpetual sovereignty, as fully as the crown could grant, with full power of legislation and the establishment of a government. The country was to be united to the realm of England in perfect league and amity; was to be within the allegiance of the crown, and to be held by homage and the payment of one-fifth of all gold and silver ore. In the thirty-first year of Elizabeth's reign, Raleigh assigned the plantation of Virginia to a company, who afterwards associating other adventurers with them, procured new charters from James the First, in whom Raleigh's rights became vested upon his attainder. The charter of James was of the same character with that of Elizabeth, with an express clause of exemption forever from all taxation or impost upon their imports or exports. Under this charter, and the auspices of the company, the colony of Virginia was settled, after struggling through immense difficulties, and without receiving the least aid from the British government. In 1621 a government was established, consisting of a governor, council, and house of burgesses, elected by the freeholders. In 1624 James the First dissolved the company, and assumed the control of the colony, which, upon his demise, devolved upon Charles the First, who, in 1625, asserted his royal claim of authority over it. To quiet the dissatisfaction of the colonists at the loss of their chartered rights, the privy council afterwards, in the year 1634, communicated the king's assurance that "all their estates and trade, freedom and privileges, should be enjoyed by them in as extensive a manner as they enjoyed them before the recalling of the company's patent." Moreover, Charles the First, in 1644, assured the Virginians that they should always be immediately dependent upon the crown. After the king's death Virginia displayed her loyalty by resisting the parliamentary forces sent out to reduce the colony, and by exacting the most honorable terms of surrender. Here the author of "the Inquiry," although exceedingly well informed in general as to the history of the colony, falls into the common error that Charles the Second was proclaimed in Virginia some time before he was restored to the throne in England.

Thus Virginia was, as to her internal affairs, a distinct, independent state, but united with the parent state by the closest league and amity, and under the same allegiance. If the crown had indeed no prerogative to form such a compact, then the royal engagements wherein "the freedom and other benefits of the British constitution" were secured to them, could not be made good; and a people who are liable to taxation without representation, cannot be held to enjoy "the freedom and benefits of the British constitution." Even in the arbitrary reign of Charles the First, when it was thought necessary to establish a permanent revenue for the support of the government in Virginia, the king did not apply to the British parliament, but to the assembly of Virginia, and sent over an act under the great seal, by which it was enacted, "By the king's most excellent majesty, by and with the consent of the general assembly," etc. After the restoration, indeed, the colonies lost the freedom of trade which they had before enjoyed, and the navigation act of 25th Charles the Second not only circumscribed the trade of the colonies with foreign nations within very narrow limits, but imposed duties on goods manufactured in the colonies and exported from one to another. The right to impose these duties was disputed by Virginia; and her agents, in April, 1676, procured from Charles the Second a declaration, under his privy seal, that "taxes ought not to be laid upon the inhabitants and proprietors of the colony but by the common consent of the general assembly, except such impositions as the parliament should lay on the commodities imported into England from the colony." But if no protest had been made against the navigation act, that forbearance could in no way justify an additional act of injustice. If the people of the colonies had in patience endured the oppressions of the English commercial restrictions, could that endurance afford any ground for new oppressions in the shape of direct taxes? If the people of England and of the colonies stood, as was contended, on the same foot, being both equally and alike subjects of the British government, why was the trade of the colonies subject to restrictions not imposed on the mother country? If parliament had a right to lay taxes of every kind on the colonies, the commerce of the colonies ought to be as free as that of England, "otherwise it will be loading them with burdens, at the same time that they are deprived of strength to sustain them; it will be forcing them to make bricks without straw." When colonies are deprived of their natural rights, resistance is at once justifiable; but when deprived of their civil rights, when great oppressions are imposed upon them, their remedy is "to lay their complaints at the foot of the throne, and to suffer patiently rather than disturb the public peace, which nothing but a denial of justice can excuse them in breaking." But a colony "treated with injury and violence is become an alien. They were not sent out to be slaves, but to be the equals of those that remain behind." It was a great error in the supporters of the British ministry to count upon the sectional jealousies and clashing interests of the colonies. Their real interests were the same, and they would not allow minor differences to divide them, when union was become necessary to maintain in a constitutional way their rights. How was England to prevent this union? Was it by quartering armed soldiers in their families? by depriving the colonists of legal trials in the courts of common law? or by harassing them by tax-gatherers, and prerogative judges, and inquisitorial courts? A petty people united in the cause of liberty is capable of glorious actions—such as adorn the annals of Switzerland and Holland.

The news of the repeal of the stamp act was joyfully welcomed in America, but the joy was premature; for, simultaneously with the repeal, parliament had declared that "it had, and of right ought to have, power to bind the colonies in all cases whatsoever." Townshend,* afterwards chancellor of the exchequer, brought into parliament a bill to levy duties in the colonies on glass, paper, painters' colors, and tea, and it became a law. The duties were external, and did not exceed in amount twenty thousand pounds; but the colonies suspected the mildness of the measure to be only a lure to inveigle them into the net. The new act was to take effect in November, 1767. The flame of resistance,

---

* 1767.

smothered for awhile by the repeal of the stamp act, now burst forth afresh: associations were everywhere organized to defeat the duties; altercations between the people and the king's officers grew frequent; the passions of the conflicting parties were exasperated. Two British regiments and some armed vessels arrived at Boston.

In Virginia, the assembly, encountering no opposition from the mild and patriotic Blair, remonstrated loudly against the new oppressions. Opposition to the arbitrary measures of the British administration broke forth in England, and in London the fury of civil discord shook the pillars of the government.

Francis Fauquier, lieutenant-governor, died early in 1768, at the age of sixty-five years, ten of which he had passed in Virginia. He brought with him the frivolous tastes and dissipated habits of a man of fashion and a courtier; he was addicted to gaming, and by his example diffused a rage for play. He was generous and elegant, an accomplished scholar, and, in Mr. Jefferson's opinion, the ablest of the governors of Virginia. A county is named after him. His death devolved the duties of government upon John Blair, president of the council. He was a nephew of Commissary Blair, whom he had succeeded in the council. He had long represented Williamsburg in the house of burgesses, having been a member as early as 1736. During the trying period of his presidency, his vigilance and discretion were displayed in protecting the frontier from Indian invasion.[*]

In 1714 some English emigrant Baptists settled in southeast Virginia, and in 1743 another party settled in the northwest; but the most important accession came from New England, about the period of "the New Light stir." Those who had left the established church were called Separates, the rest Regulars. Their preachers, not unfrequently illiterate, were characterized by an impassioned manner, vehement gesticulation, and a singular tone of voice. The hearers often gave way to tears, trembling, screams, and acclamations. The number of converts increased rapidly in some counties. The preachers were imprisoned and

---

[*] Hugh Blair Grigsby's Discourse on Convention of 1776, pp. 69, 70; Old Churches, i. 160.

maltreated by magistrates and mobs; but persecution stimulated their zeal and redoubled their influence: they sang hymns while on the way to the prison, and addressed crowds congregated before the windows of the jails. At this time Deputy-Governor Blair addressed the following letter to the king's attorney in Spotsylvania:—

"SIR:—I lately received a letter, signed by a good number of worthy gentlemen, who are not here, complaining of the Baptists; the particulars of their misbehavior are not told, any further than their running into private houses and making dissensions. Mr. Craig and Mr. Benjamin Waller are now with me, and deny the charge; they tell me they are willing to take the oaths as others have: I told them I had consulted the attorney-general, who is of opinion that the general court only have a right to grant licenses, and therefore I referred them to the court; but on their application to the attorney-general,* they brought me his letter, advising me to write to you that their petition was a matter of right, and that you may not molest these conscientious people, so long as they behave themselves in a manner becoming pious Christians and in obedience to the laws, till the court, when they intend to apply for license, and when the gentlemen who complain may make their objections and be heard. The act of toleration (it being found by experience that persecuting dissenters increases their numbers) has given them a right to apply in a proper manner for licensed houses for the worship of God, according to their consciences, and I persuade myself the gentlemen will quietly overlook their meetings till the court. I am told they administer the sacrament of the Lord's Supper near the manner we do, and differ in nothing from our church but in that of baptism and their renewing the ancient discipline, by which they have reformed some sinners and brought them to be truly penitent; nay, if a man of theirs is idle and neglects to labor and provide for his family as he ought, he incurs their censures, which have had good effects. If this be their behavior, it were to be wished we had some of it among us; but at least I hope all may

---

* John Randolph.

remain quiet till the court." This letter was dated at Williamsburg, July the 16th, 1768.

The persecution of the Baptists commenced in Chesterfield, in 1770, and in no county was it carried farther. According to tradition, Colonel Archibald Cary, of Ampthill, was the archpersecutor. In few counties have the Baptists been more numerous than in Chesterfield.

While many of the preachers were men of exemplary character, yet by the facility of admission into their pulpits impostors sometimes brought scandal upon the name of religion. Schisms, too, interrupted the harmony of their associations. Nevertheless, by the striking earnestness and the pious example of many of them, the Baptists gained ground rapidly in Virginia. In their efforts to avail themselves of the toleration act, they found Patrick Henry ever ready to step forward in their behalf, and he remained through life their unwavering friend. They still cherish his memory with grateful affection.

The Baptists, having suffered persecution under the establishment, were, of all others, the most inimical to it, and the most active in its subversion.*

---

* Semple's Hist. of Va. Baptists, 16, 24; Hawks, 120.

CHAPTER LXXI.

1768-1771.

Botetourt, Governor—Resolutions against the encroachments of Parliament—Assembly dissolved—Non-importation Agreement—The Moderates—Assembly called—Botetourt's Address—Association—Death of Botetourt—His Character—William Nelson, President—Great Fresh—American Episcopate—Assembly opposes it—Controversy—Methodists.

In November, 1768, Norborne Berkeley, Baron de Botetourt, arrived in Virginia as governor-in-chief. The season was delightful, with its tinted foliage, serene sky, and bracing air. Botetourt, just relieved from the confinement of a sea-voyage, was charmed with his new place of abode; the palace appeared commodious; the grounds well planted and watered. While his new residence was fitting up for him he daily enjoyed the hospitalities of the people. He found that while they would never willingly submit to be taxed by the mother country, yet they were ardently desirous of giving assistance, as formerly, upon requisition. In the mean time the duties complained of were collected without any resistance whatever. Botetourt, solicitous to gratify the Virginians, pledged "his life and fortune" to extend the boundary of the State on the west to the Tennessee River, on the parallel of thirty-six and a half degrees. This boundary, Andrew Lewis and Thomas Walker wrote, would give some room to extend the settlements for ten or twelve years.*

On the 11th day of May, 1769, when the assembly was convened, the governor rode from the palace to the capitol in a state-coach drawn by six milk-white horses, a present from George the Third, and the insignia of royalty were displayed with unusual pomp. The pageant, supposed to be intended to dazzle, served rather to offend. On that day and the following he entertained fifty-two guests at dinner.

---

* Bancroft, vi. 228.

When, in Massachusetts, the custom-house officers had demanded* from the courts writs of assistance for enforcing the revenue act, the eloquent James Otis had resisted the application in a speech which gave a mighty impulse to the popular sentiment. The same question was now argued before Botetourt and the council, forming the general court, and he concurred in declaring them illegal. During this session, Mr. Jefferson made an unsuccessful effort for the enactment of a law authorizing owners to manumit their slaves.

In February, parliament, refusing to consider a redress of American grievances, had advised his majesty to take vigorous measures against Massachusetts, and to make inquisition there for treason, and, if sufficient ground should appear, to transport the accused to England for trial before a special commission; and George the Third, a king of exemplary character, but obstinate temper, heartily concurred in those views. Upon receiving intelligence of this fact, the burgesses of Virginia again† passed resolutions unanimously, vindicating the rights of the colonies, claiming the sole right to levy taxes, and asserting the right of bringing about a concert of the colonies in defence against the encroachments of parliament; exposing the injustice and tyranny of applying to America an obsolete act of the reign of Henry the Eighth, warning the king of the dangers that would ensue if any American should be transported to England for trial, and finally ordering the resolutions to be communicated to the legislatures of the other colonies, and requesting their concurrence. Even the merchants of peaceable Pennsylvania approved these resolutions; Delaware adopted them word for word; and the colonies south of Virginia eventually imitated her example. An address was also prepared to be laid before the king. Botetourt took alarm at what he termed, in his correspondence with the government, "the abominable measure," and having convoked the assembly, addressed them thus: "Mr. Speaker and Gentlemen of the house of burgesses,—I have heard of your resolves, and augur ill of their effects. You have made it my duty to dissolve you, and you are dissolved accordingly."

---

* 1769.   † May 16th.

The burgesses immediately repaired in a body to the Raleigh, and unanimously adopted a non-importation agreement, drawn by George Mason, and presented by George Washington. The resolutions included one not to import, or purchase any imported slaves, after the first day of November, until the objectionable acts of parliament should be repealed. Mr. Mason, not yet a member of the assembly, was not present at this meeting. The moderate party in the assembly, while they had opposed measures which appeared to them injudicious and premature, nevertheless avowed themselves as firmly riveted to the main principle in dispute. Their views, they averred, had been made public in the several memorials to government; and from the position so assumed they were resolved never to recede. They had not, indeed, expected that parliament would ever explicitly acknowledge itself in the wrong; but it had been their hope that the dispute would have been left to rest upon reciprocal protestations, and finally have died away. The late measures of the British government had extinguished such delusive hopes. That government claimed the right of subjecting America to every act of parliament as being part of the British dominions; and at the same time that Americans should be liable to punishment under an act of Henry the Eighth, made to punish offences committed *out of* the realm. The deportation of Americans for trial, depriving them of the right of trial by a jury of the vicinage, appeared to be fraught with worse mischiefs than the stamp act, in as much as life is more precious than property.*

On the 9th of May, 1769, the king had, in his speech to parliament, re-echoed their determination to enforce the laws in every part of his dominions. Nevertheless, on the thirteenth the Earl of Hillsborough, secretary of state for the colonies, wrote to Botetourt, assuring him that it was not the intention of ministers to propose any further taxes, and that they intended to propose a repeal of the duties on glass, paper, and paints, not on the question of right, but upon the ground that those duties had been imposed contrary to the true principles of commerce. Botetourt, calling the assembly together, communicated these assurances, adding: "It is my firm opinion that the plan I have stated to

---

* Letter of R. C. Nicholas to Arthur Lee, *S. Lit. Messenger*, 1858, p. 184.

you will certainly take place, and that it will never be departed from; and so determined am I to abide by it, that I will be content to be declared infamous, if I do not to the last hour of my life, at all times, in all places, and upon all occasions, exert every power with which I am, or ever shall be, legally invested, in order to obtain and maintain for the continent of America, that satisfaction which I have been authorized to promise this day by the confidential servant of our gracious sovereign, who, to my certain knowledge, rates his honor so high that he would rather part with his crown than preserve it by deceit." The council, in reply, advised the repeal of the existing parliamentary taxes; the burgesses expressed their gratitude for "information sanctified by the royal word," and considered the king's influence as pledged "toward protecting the happiness of all his people." Botetourt, pleased with the address, wished them "freedom and happiness till time should be no more." William Lee regarded this as mere bombastic rant. During this year appeared a pamphlet, asserting the rights of the colonies, entitled "The Monitor's Letters," by Arthur Lee.

Lord North succeeded the Duke of Grafton as prime minister, in January, 1770, and in the ensuing March all the duties on the American imports were repealed, except that on tea. Lord North, at the same time, however, avowed the absolute determination of the government not to yield the right of taxing the colonies.

The first association appears not to have been adhered to, and the English merchants declared that the exports to Virginia of the prohibited articles were never greater.

On the 22d day of June, 1770, a second association was entered into at Williamsburg, by the burgesses and the merchants of the colony appointing committees, to be chosen by the associators of each county, to enforce the non-importation agreement; resolving to promote industry and frugality; enumerating the articles not to be imported or purchased after a certain day, specially mentioning slaves and wine; engaging not to advance the price of goods, wares, and merchandise; binding themselves not to import or purchase any article which should be taxed by parliament for the purpose of raising a revenue in America.

The estimable Botetourt died in October, 1770, in his fifty-third year, and after an administration of two years. Promoted to the peerage in 1764, he had succeeded Sir Jeffrey Amherst as governor-in-chief in 1768, and was the first of that title since Lord Culpepper, who had condescended to come over to the colony. On his arrival it was his purpose to reduce the Virginians to submission, either by persuasion or by force; but when he became better acquainted with the people he changed his views, and entreated the ministry to repeal the offensive acts. Such a promise was, indeed, held out to him; but finding himself deceived, he demanded his recall, and died shortly afterwards of a bilious fever, exacerbated by chagrin and disappointment. He was a patron of learning and the arts, giving out of his own purse silver and gold medals as prizes to the students of William and Mary College. His death was deeply lamented by the colony, and the assembly erected a statue in honor of him, which is still standing, somewhat mutilated, in front of the college. At his death the administration devolved upon William Nelson, president of the council.

In May, 1771, a great fresh occurred in Virginia, the James in three days rising twenty feet higher than ever was known before. The low grounds were inundated, standing crops destroyed, corn, fences, chattels, merchandise, cattle, and houses carried off, and ships forced from their moorings. Many of the inhabitants, masters and slaves, in endeavoring to rescue property, or to escape from danger, were drowned. Houses were seen drifting down the current, and people clinging to them, uttering fruitless cries for succor. Fertile fields were covered with a thick deposit of sand; islands were torn to pieces, bars accumulated, the channel diverted, and the face of nature altered. At Turkey Island, on the James River, there is a monument bearing the following inscription: "The foundations of this pillar were laid in the calamitous year 1771, when all the great rivers of this country were swept by inundations never before experienced, which changed the face of nature and left traces of their violence that will remain for ages." One hundred and fifty persons were drowned by this rise in the rivers.

The assembly met in July, 1771. About this time the question of an American episcopate was agitated; and in some of the Northern colonies the measure was warmly contended for in the public papers. New York and New Jersey desired to secure the co-operation of Virginia in petitioning the king on this subject, and deputed the Rev. Dr. Cooper, President of King's College, New York, and the Rev. Mr. McKean, deputies to visit the South in this behalf; and at their urgent solicitation, Commissary Horrocks, himself aspiring to the mitre, as was supposed, called a convocation of the clergy to take the matter into consideration. Only a few attended; but after some vacillation they determined to join in the petition to the crown, the Rev. John Camm taking the lead in this proceeding. Four of the clergy in attendance, Henley and Gwatkin, professors in the College of William and Mary, and Hewitt and Bland, entered a protest against the scheme of introducing a bishop, as endangering the very existence of the British empire in America. The assembly having expressed its disapprobation of the project, and it being urged but by few, and resisted by some of the clergy, it fell to the ground; and the thanks of the house were presented, through Richard Henry Lee and Richard Bland, to the protesting clergymen for their "wise and well-timed opposition." Churchmen naturally sided with the English government, and the bench of bishops were arrayed in opposition to the rights of the colonies. The protest of the four ministers gave rise to a controversy between them and the United Episcopal Conventions of New York and New Jersey; and a war of pamphlets and newspapers ensued in the Northern and Middle States; and the stamp act itself, according to some writers, did not evoke more bitter denunciations, nor more violent threats, than the project of an episcopate: New England was in a flame against it. It was believed, that if bishops should be sent over they would unite with the governors in opposition to the rights of America. The laity of the Episcopal Church in America were, excepting a small minority, opposed to the measure. Neither the people of Virginia, nor any of the American colonies, were at any time willing to receive a bishop appointed by the English government. Among the advocates of the scheme the Rev. Jonathan Boucher took a prominent part, and he sustained it ably from the pulpit. He held that the refusal of Virginia to consent to the appointment of a bishop, was "to unchurch the church;" and his views on this subject were re-echoed by Lowth, Bishop of Oxford, in an anniversary sermon delivered before the Society for the Propagation of the Gospel in Foreign Parts. On this point of ecclesiastical government the members of the establishment in Virginia appear to have been looked upon as themselves dissenters. In one sense they were so; but their repugnance was to prelacy, not to the episcopate; a prelatical bishop was in their minds associated with ideas of expense beyond their means, and of opposition to the principles of civil liberty. Boucher, in a sermon that he preached in this year at St. Mary's Church, in Caroline County, of which he was then rector, says of the dissenters in Virginia: "I might almost as well pretend to count the gnats that buzz around us in a summer's evening."

The scheme of sending over a bishop had been entertained more than a hundred years before; and Dean Swift at one time entertained hopes of being made Bishop of Virginia, with power, as is said, to ordain priests and deacons for all the colonies, and to parcel them out into deaneries, parishes, chapels, etc., and to recommend and present thereto. The favorite sermons of many of the Virginia clergy were Sterne's.*

During this year died the Rev. James Horrocks, President of the College and Commissary. He had been at the head of William and Mary since the death of Rev. William Yates, in 1764. Mr. Horrocks was succeeded in both places by the Rev. John Camm.

John Murray, Earl of Dunmore, was transferred† from the government of New York to that of Virginia. The town of Fincastle, the title of one of his sons, in Botetourt County, was now incorporated. The Honorable William Nelson, president, died in this year. About this time the Methodists appeared in Virginia; they still avowed that attachment to the Church of England which Wesley and Whitefield both, in the early years of their career, had uniformly professed. Although they allowed laymen to preach, the communion was received by them at the hands of the clergy only; and they even affirmed that "whosoever left the church left the Methodists." They, therefore, now were visited with a share of the odium which fell upon the established church.

---

* Old Churches, i. 25. † 1772.

CHAPTER LXXII.

THE REV. DEVEREUX JARRATT.

The Rev. Devereux Jarratt was born in the County of New Kent, Virginia, in January, 1733, of obscure parentage. His grandfather, an Englishman, had served during the civil wars under Robert Devereux, Earl of Essex, and hence probably was derived the Christian name of the grandson. His grandmother was a native of Ireland. His father was a carpenter, and from the manner in which he and his family lived, some idea may be formed of the condition of the common people in that day. Their food consisted of the produce of the soil, except a little sugar, which was used only on rare occasions. Their clothes were all of maternal manufacture, except hats and shoes, and these last were worn only in the winter. They not only used no tea or coffee themselves, but they knew no family that did use them. Meat and bread and milk constituted the diet of that class. They looked upon the gentry as a superior caste. Jarratt, in his autobiography, describing his early days, says: "For my part, I was quite shy of them, and kept off at an humble distance. A periwig in those days was a distinguishing badge of gentle-folk, and when I saw a man riding the road near our house with a wig on, it would so alarm my fears and give me such a disagreeable feeling, that I dare say I would run off as for my life." He lived to see society reduced to the opposite, and, in his opinion, worse extreme of republican levelling, insubordination, and irreverence. His early education was confined to reading, writing, and elementary arithmetic, some short prayers, and the church catechism. Upon his father's death, Robert, the eldest son, inherited the land, and Devereux's share of the personal property was twenty-five pounds, Virginia currency, which he was to receive when he should reach the age of twenty-one. The relative value of money was four times greater then than it was fifty years afterwards. A good horse could be bought for five pounds, and a good cow and calf for a pistole, or three dollars and sixty cents. At eight or nine years of age young Jarratt was sent to school, and so continued, with great interruptions, for three or four years. By this time he had learned to read the Bible indifferently, to write a sorry hand, and had acquired some knowledge of arithmetic, and this closed his educational curriculum. Being placed now under the guardianship of his elder brother, his employments for some years were threefold: 1st, taking care of and training race-horses; 2d, taking care of game-cocks and preparing them for a match and main; 3d, ploughing, harrowing, and other plantation work. At the age of seventeen he undertook the business of a carpenter, under another brother, who often had recourse to "hard words and severe blows," which he "did not at all relish;" but he continued to labor in this way until about 1750. During the five or six years while he lived with his brothers, he never heard or saw anything of a religious nature, nor did he go to the parish church once a year. The parish minister was a poor preacher, very near-sighted, and, reading his sermons closely, he kept his eyes fixed on the paper, and so near that what he said "seemed rather addressed to the cushion than to the congregation." This parson was rarely observed to stand erect and face the audience, except when he denounced some individual in the congregation with whom he happened to have a quarrel. Cards, dancing, racing, etc., were then the favorite pastimes, and young Jarratt participated in them as far as his leisure and circumstances would permit, and this as well on Sundays as on other days. Not being content with his stock of learning, and skill in arithmetic being the chief desideratum among the common people, he borrowed a book, and while his plough-horse was grazing at noon applied himself to that study, and made rapid progress. He felt conscious at this time that the plough and the axe were not his element; and his skill in the division of crops, in the rule of three, and in practice, soon became so widely known that he was, unexpectedly, when at the age of nineteen, invited to set up a school in Albemarle County, one hundred miles distant from New Kent. His baggage appears to have constituted no considerable impediment to his journey, for he says: "I think I carried the whole on my back except one shirt." His entire wardrobe at this time consisted of a pair of coarse breeches, one or two Oznaburg shirts, a pair of shoes and stockings, an old felt hat, and a bear-skin coat, the first garment of that kind that had ever been made for him. To improve the gentility of his appearance he put on a cast-off wig, which he procured from a servant. On setting out for Albemarle, young Jarratt had not a farthing of money, and never had been master of as much as five shillings cash. The income of the school scarce afforded him clothing of the coarsest kind, but he gained the confidence of his employer, who was an overseer for a lowland gentleman, so far, that he trusted him with "as much checks as made him two new shirts." Albemarle was then a frontier county; there was no minister or public worship within many miles, and the Sabbath was spent in sports and amusements. Here he met with Whitefield's Eight Sermons, delivered at Glasgow, the first book of sermons that he ever saw. Jarratt went next to live with a wealthy gentleman, whose wife was a pious Presbyterian, spoken of as a New Light. It was while he was under Presbyterian influences that his conversion took place. When upwards of twenty-five years old he commenced the study of Latin under Alexander Martin, sent from Princeton College, a private tutor in the family of a gentleman in Cumberland. Martin was afterwards governor of North Carolina. Mr. Jarratt intended to become a Presbyterian minister, but in 1762 changed his mind, and began to prepare to take orders in the established church. Upon a further acquaintance with the subject his prejudices against that church and its liturgy were removed, and he came to be of opinion that the Prayer Book contained, at the least, as good a system of doctrine and public worship as the Presbyterian; the doctrinal articles he considered the same, in substance, in both churches, and the different modes of worship he held to be not essential. His mind hung in equilibrium between the Church of England and the Presbyterian Church as regarded their theory, and balancing the secular advantages, he decided in favor of the established church, mainly because "he saw the Presbyterian ministers dependent on annual subscriptions—a mode of support very precarious in itself, and which subjects the minister to the caprice of so many people, and tends to bind his hands and hinder his usefulness." To this he adds: "The general prejudice of the people at that time against dissenters and in favor of the church, gave me a full persuasion that I could do more good in the church than anywhere else." The fact is, however, that at that time the popular feeling was growing less friendly to the clergy of the established church and more friendly to dissenters. Embarking for England, in October, 1762, and being ordained deacon by the Bishop of London, and priest by the Bishop of Chester, he preached several times in London, and was "suspected of being a Methodist." While in that city he heard Whitefield and Wesley. He returned to Virginia in July. Shortly afterwards he was received as minister of Bath Parish, in Dinwiddie, he being then in his thirty-first year. He found his people as ignorant of true religion as if they had never frequented a church or heard a sermon. As regarded other Episcopal clergymen, he did not know of one in Virginia like-minded with himself. He was indeed opposed and reproached by them as a fanatic, a dissenter, a Presbyterian. His preaching, although at first unacceptable, proved, ere long, effective, and crowded congregations attended his ministrations. The interest extending widely beyond his parish, he spent part of his time in itinerant preaching, going several hundred miles and in every direction. The clergy in general being unwilling to open their churches for him, and they being not large enough to contain the crowds which he attracted, he was in the habit of preaching in the open air, under trees, arbors, or booths, and he had the advantage of a voice which was audible to his large congregations. The clergy frequently threatened him with writs and prosecutions for the violation of canonical order, but he retorted upon them successfully, and maintained his ground. At length he met with sympathy and co-operation from the Rev. Mr. McRoberts, and an intimacy continued between them for many years. But as Mr. Jarratt, who was at first in effect a Presbyterian, became a minister of the established church, so eventually, many years afterwards, during the revolutionary war, his friend and coadjutor, Mr. McRoberts, became a Presbyterian minister. Their friendship remained uninterrupted.

About the year 1769 the increase of the number of Baptists produced some divisions among Mr. Jarratt's people. The Methodists appearing in Virginia about the same time, and professing to be virtually members of the Church of England, Mr. Jarratt (in order to resist the encroachments of the Baptists) co-operated with them in building up their societies; but he found reason subsequently to repent of this step, and although often styled a Methodist himself, yet he finally broke off entirely from that denomination.*

---

* Life of Rev. Devereux Jarratt, 5, 107. His sermons were published in several volumes

CHAPTER LXXIII.

1773-1774.

Duty on Tea—Dunmore, Governor—Proceedings of Assembly—Private Meeting of Patriots—Committees of Correspondence—Washington—Dunmore visits the Frontier.

In the year 1770, all the duties on articles imported into America having been repealed, save that on tea, the American merchants refused to import that commodity from England. Consequently a large stock of it was accumulated in the warehouses of the East India Company; and the government in 1773 authorized the company to ship it to America free from any export duty. The light import duty payable in America being far less than that from which it was exempted in England, it was taken for granted that it would sell more readily in the colony than before it had been made a subject of taxation. It was, indeed, by some looked upon as now rather a question of commerce than of taxation; the main object of the British government appears to have been to put an end to the trade between the colonies and Holland, (a trade contraband according to the letter of the law, but the law had been practically long obsolete,) and to give to the East India Company a monopoly of the colonial markets. But it was in general regarded in America as a test question of revenue.

The tea-ships arrived in America, and measures were taken to prevent the landing of the tea; at Boston several cargoes were thrown overboard in the night of December the eighteenth, into the sea, by a party of men disguised as Indians, acting under the advice of Samuel Adams, and other leading patriots. Other colonies either compelled the masters of the tea-ships to return with their cargoes, or excluded them from sale; and thus not a chest of it was sold for the benefit of the company. Tea had hitherto been imported by Pennsylvania, New York, and Massachusetts into the colonies to the value of three hundred thousand pounds annually from Holland and her dependencies. In Virginia the use of this beverage was now generally abandoned.*

Intelligence of the occurrences at Boston having reached England, parliament ordered the port of that town to be closed on the fourth day of June; and other strong measures were adopted in order to reduce Massachusetts to submission. The colonies, like the captives in the cave of Polyphemus, were conscious of being involved in a common danger; and that if one should fall a victim, the destruction of the rest would be only a question of time.

When John Murray, Earl of Dunmore, the newly-appointed governor of Virginia, reached Williamsburg, early in 1772, he found that he had already incurred suspicion on account of the appointment of Captain Foy as his clerk, or private secretary, with a salary of five hundred pounds, to be derived from new-created fees. Foy had distinguished himself at the battle of Minden, and had been afterwards governor of New Hampshire. Dunmore summoned the assembly which met in February; and his apparent haughtiness at the first rather heightened the prejudice against him. He, however, relinquished the objectionable fees, and thus conciliated so good a feeling that the assembly expressed their gratitude in warm and affectionate terms. Some important acts were passed during this session, including several for the promotion of internal improvement—for improving the navigation of the Potomac; for making a road from the Warm Spring to Jenning's Gap; for clearing the Matapony; for circumventing the falls of James River by a canal from Westham; and for cutting a canal across from Archer's Hope Creek to Queen's Creek, through Williamsburg, to connect the James River with the York. The Counties of Berkley and Dunmore were carved out from Frederick.†

The assembly was prorogued to the tenth of June. Dunmore,

---

* Some of the loyal ladies adhered to the use of it. The wife of Bernard Moore, of Chelsea, in King William, daughter of a British governor, Spotswood, according to family tradition, continued to sip her tea in her closet after it was banished from the table.

† The name of Dunmore was, in 1777, changed to Shenandoah.

notwithstanding his recent complaisance, evinced his distaste for assemblies by proroguing them from time to time, until at length a forgery of the paper-currency of the colony compelled him to call the legislature together again, by proclamation, March 4th, 1773—the thirteenth year of the reign of George the Third. His lordship's measures in apprehending the counterfeiters had been more energetic than legal, and the assembly, not diverted by their care for the treasury from a regard to personal rights, requested that his proceedings might not be drawn into a precedent.

The horizon was again darkened by gathering clouds. A British armed revenue vessel having been burnt in Narraganset Bay, an act of parliament was passed making such offences punishable by death, and authorizing the accused to be transported to England for trial. Virginia had already, in 1769, remonstrated against this last measure. The conservatives, the *statu quo* party in the assembly, as usual, differed with the movement party as to the proper measure to be adopted. Patrick Henry, Mr. Jefferson, Richard Henry Lee, Francis L. Lee, Dabney Carr, and perhaps one or two others were at this gloomy period in the habit of meeting together in the evening in a private room of the Raleigh, to consult on the state of affairs. In conformity with their agreement, Dabney Carr, on the twelfth of March, moved a series of resolutions, recommending a committee of correspondence, and instructing them to inquire in regard to the newly-constituted court in Rhode Island. Richard Henry Lee and Patrick Henry made speeches of memorable eloquence on this occasion. Mr. Lee was the author of the plan of intercolonial committees of correspondence; and Virginia was the first colony that adopted it. The resolutions passed without opposition, and Dunmore immediately dissolved the house. These resolutions "struck a greater panic into the ministers" than anything that had taken place since the passage of the stamp act.*

The committee of correspondence appointed were Peyton Randolph, Robert C. Nicholas, Richard Bland, Richard Henry Lee, Benjamin Harrison, Edmund Pendleton, Patrick Henry, Dudley

---

* MS. letter of William Lee, dated at London, January 1st, 1774.

Digges, Dabney Carr, Archibald Cary, and Thomas Jefferson. On the day after the dissolution, this committee addressed a circular to the other colonies. Robert Carter Nicholas published, during this year, a pamphlet in defence of colonial rights.

Dabney Carr, although young, was, according to Mr. Jefferson, a formidable rival at the bar to Patrick Henry, and promised to become a distinguished statesman; but he died shortly after, in the thirtieth year of his age, greatly lamented. The judge of the same name was his son. Washington was a member of this assembly, and supported the patriotic measures, perhaps, however, as yet little dreaming that the colonies were on the verge of revolution and war. He was still on friendly terms with Governor Dunmore, who appreciated his abilities and character. He, indeed, intended about this time, in compliance with the governor's invitation, to accompany him in a tour of observation to the western frontier of Virginia, where both of them had an interest in lands; but this was prevented by the illness and death of Miss Custis, the daughter of Mrs. Washington by a former marriage.

Dunmore visited the frontier and remained some time at Pittsburg, and endeavored, by the help of Dr. Conolly, to extend the bounds of Virginia in that quarter; and this was attributed to a design to foment a quarrel between Virginia and Pennsylvania; but the suspicion was probably without sufficient foundation.

CHAPTER LXXIV.

1774.

Lady Dunmore and Children—Gayety of Williamsburg—Boston Port Bill—Fast-day appointed—Governor dissolves the Assembly—Resolutions of Burgesses—Convention called—The Raleigh—Mason's Opinion of Henry—Patriotic Measures—Convention—Jefferson's "Summary View."

LATE in April there arrived at the palace in Williamsburg, the Right Honorable the Countess of Dunmore, with George, Lord Fincastle, the Honorable Alexander and John Murray, and the Ladies Catherine, Augusta, and Susan Murray, accompanied by Captain Foy and his lady. On this occasion there was an illumination, and the people with acclamations welcomed her ladyship and family to Virginia. The three sons of Lord Dunmore were students in the College of William and Mary in that year.

When the assembly met in May, Williamsburg presented a scene of unwonted gayety, and a court-herald published a code of etiquette for the regulation of the society of the little metropolis. Washington, arriving there on the sixteenth, dined with Lord Dunmore. At the beginning of the session the burgesses made an address congratulating the governor on the arrival of his lady, and the members agreed to give a ball in her honor on the twenty-seventh; but the sky was again suddenly overcast by intelligence of the act of parliament shutting up the port of Boston. The assembly made an indignant protest against this act, and,* imitating the example of the Puritans in the civil wars of England, set apart the first of June, appointed for closing the port, as a day of fasting, prayer, and humiliation, in which the Divine interposition was to be implored to protect the rights of the colonies, and avert the horrors of civil war, and to unite the people of America in the common cause.

On the next day Dunmore, summoning the burgesses to attend

---

* May twenty-fourth.

him in the council chamber, dissolved them in the following words: "Mr. Speaker and Gentlemen of the house of burgesses, I have in my hand a paper published by order of your house, conceived in such terms as reflect highly upon his majesty and the parliament of Great Britain, which makes it necessary for me to dissolve you, and you are dissolved accordingly."

The burgesses repaired immediately to the Raleigh,* and in the room called "the Apollo" adopted resolutions against the use of tea and other East India commodities, and recommended the annual convening of a congress. In this measure, as in the appointment of committees of correspondence, Virginia took the lead. North Carolina promptly followed her example. Notwithstanding the untoward turn of events, Washington dined with the governor on the twenty-fifth, and passed the evening with him, rode with him to his farm, and breakfasted there on the following day, and attended the ball given on the twenty-seventh in honor of Lady Dunmore.

Further news being received from Boston, the members who remained in Williamsburg held a meeting on the twenty-ninth, at which Peyton Randolph presided, and they issued a circular, recommending a meeting of deputies in a convention to assemble there on the first of August.

A dissolution of the assembly had been expected, but it had been supposed that it would be deferred until the public business should be despatched—toward the latter part of June. Consultations and measures for the preservation of the public rights and liberties were conducted and matured very privately, and by very few members, of whom Patrick Henry was the leader. George Mason, who arrived in Williamsburg in the latter part of May, says, in a letter to a friend: "At the request of the gentlemen concerned, I have spent an evening with them upon the subject, where I had an opportunity of conversing with Mr. Henry and knowing his sentiments, as well as hearing him speak in the

---

* The Raleigh tavern, a wooden house, is upwards of a hundred years old. There was formerly a bust of Sir Walter Raleigh in front of the house. The ball-room in the Raleigh was styled "The Apollo." There was a tavern in London called "The Apollo" in 1690.

house since on different occasions. He is by far the most powerful speaker I ever heard. Every word he says not only engages, but commands the attention, and your passions are no longer your own when he addresses them. But his eloquence is the least part of his merit. He is, in my opinion, the first man upon this continent as well in abilities as public virtues, and had he lived in Rome about the time of the first Punic war, when the Roman people had arrived at their meridian glory, and their virtue not tarnished, Mr. Henry's talents must have put him at the head of that glorious commonwealth."

Mr. Mason found the minds of all at Williamsburg entirely absorbed in the news from Massachusetts. The burgesses, at their own expense, sent to their counties copies of the resolution adopted against the Boston port bill, in order that it should be ratified by the people. Mr. Mason, as other members probably did, directed that his elder children should attend church on the day of fasting, humiliation, and prayer, in mourning. The first of June was observed as set apart by the house of burgesses. The same day being the time fixed for the discontinuance of the use of tea, the ladies, before that day, sealed up their stock, with a determination not to use it until the duty should be repealed, and resolutions of sympathy and encouragement, and contributions of money and provisions, were sent from Virginia for the relief of "our distressed fellow-subjects of Boston."

In the midst of these excitements John Page, of Rosewell, was elected president of the Society for the Advancement of Useful Knowledge.

In the latter part of June, Washington presided as moderator at a meeting held in his own county, Fairfax, and he was made chairman of a committee appointed to draught resolutions on the alarming state of public affairs, to be reported at a future meeting. He about this time warmly supported the patriotic measures, in a correspondence with his neighbor and friend, Bryan Fairfax, who adhered to the Anglican side in the dispute. On the twenty-fourth of August he wrote to him: "I could wish, I own, that the dispute had been left to posterity to determine; but the crisis is arrived when we must assert our rights, or submit to every imposition that can be heaped upon us, till custom and use will make us as tame and abject slaves as the blacks we rule over with such arbitrary sway."

The Fairfax committee framed resolutions, intimating that a persistence of the government in its measures of coercion would result of necessity only in a resort to the arbitrament of arms. These resolutions were adopted by a county meeting held on the eighteenth of July, and Washington was elected a delegate to the convention which was about to convene. This body met on the first day of August, (although Dunmore had issued writs for a new assembly,) its object being to consider the state and condition of the colony, and to appoint delegates to congress. A new and more thorough non-importation association was organized. Peyton Randolph, Richard Henry Lee, Washington, Henry, Bland, Benjamin Harrison, Jr., of Berkley, and Pendleton, were appointed* delegates to congress. Patrick Henry and Richard Henry Lee were listened to with delight, and Washington said, "I will raise one thousand men, subsist them at my own expense, and march myself at their head for the relief of Boston."†

Mr. Jefferson was elected a member of this convention, but was prevented from attending by the state of his health. In the interval before the meeting he prepared instructions for the Virginia delegates in congress, in which he assumed the ground that the British parliament had no right whatever to exercise any authority over the colony of Virginia. These instructions being communicated through the president of the convention, Peyton Randolph, were generally read and approved of by many, though considered too bold for the present. But they printed them in a pamphlet, under the title of "A Summary View of the Rights of British America."‡ The following excerpts are taken from it: "History has informed us that bodies of men as well as individuals are susceptible of the spirit of tyranny." "Scarcely have our minds been able to emerge from the astonishment into which one stroke of parliamentary thunder has involved us before another more heavy and more alarming is fallen on us." "The

---

* August eleventh. † Life and Works of John Adams, ii. 360.

‡ To be found in Amer. Archives, published by Congress, fourth series, i. 690, and in the Congress edition of Mr. Jefferson's works. See also Memoir and Correspondence of Jefferson, 100, 116.

great principles of right and wrong are legible to every reader; to pursue them requires not the aid of many counsellors. The whole art of government consists in the art of being honest; only aim to do your duty, and mankind will give you credit where you fail. No longer persevere in sacrificing the rights of one part of the empire to the inordinate desires of another, but deal out to all equal and impartial right. Let no act be passed by any one legislature which may infringe on the rights and liberties of another." "Accept of every commercial preference it is in our power to give for such things as we can raise for their use, or they make for ours. But let them not think to exclude us from going to other markets to dispose of those commodities which they cannot use, or to supply those wants which they cannot supply."

On the subject of slavery Mr. Jefferson used the following language: "The abolition of domestic slavery is the great object of desire in these colonies, where it was unhappily introduced in their infant state. But previous to the enfranchisement of the slaves we have, it is necessary to exclude all further importations from Africa, yet our repeated attempts to effect this, by prohibitions, and by imposing duties which might amount to a prohibition, have been hitherto defeated by his majesty's negative; thus preferring the immediate advantage of a few British corsairs to the lasting interests of the American States and to the rights of human nature deeply wounded by this infamous practice."

In consonance with these opinions, the convention adopted the following resolution: "After the first day of November next we will neither ourselves import, nor purchase any slave or slaves imported by any other person, either from Africa, the West Indies, or any other place."

Mr. Jefferson's pamphlet displays a thorough knowledge of the history and constitutional rights of the colony; it breathes a fiery spirit of defiance and revolution, and the rhythmical splendor of elevated declamation in some of its passages is hardly inferior to Junius. If some of its statements and views are extravagant or erroneous, yet it is bold, acute, comprehensive, luminous, and impressive. This pamphlet, it is said, found its way to England, was taken hold of by the opposition, interpolated a little by Edmund Burke, so as to make it answer opposition purposes, and in that form it ran through several editions.

CHAPTER LXXV.

Richard Henry Lee—Congress at Philadelphia—Henry—Proceedings of Congress—Washington—Military Spirit in Virginia.

RICHARD HENRY LEE was born at Stratford, on the Potomac, January 20th, 1732, his father being Thomas Lee, and his mother, Hannah, daughter of Colonel Ludwell, of Greenspring, near Jamestown. Richard, second son of Richard Lee, was of the council, and an adherent of Sir William Berkley; and Thomas Lee, third son, was some time president of the council. He was one of the majority of that body who persecuted the dissenters. Richard Henry Lee's maternal relations were conspicuous for their wealth, influence, and public stations. Colonel Ludwell, the father of Mrs. Lee, was of the council, as also was a son of his. Her grandfather was a collector of the customs, (having succeeded in that office Giles Bland, who was executed during Bacon's rebellion,) and afterwards governor of North Carolina. The Ludwells were staunch supporters of Sir William Berkley and the Stuart dynasty. Richard Henry Lee's mother, one of the hightoned aristocracy of the colony, confined her care chiefly to her daughters and her eldest son, and left her younger sons pretty much to shift for themselves. After a course of private tuition in his father's house, Richard Henry was sent to Wakefield Academy, Yorkshire, England, where he distinguished himself by his proficiency in his studies, particularly in the Latin and Greek. Having completed his course at this school, he travelled through England, and visited London. He returned when about nineteen years of age to his native country, two years after his father's death, which occurred in 1750. Young Lee's patrimony rendering it unnecessary for him to devote himself to a profession, he now passed a life of ease, but not of idleness; for he indulged his taste for letters, and diligently stored his mind with knowledge. In 1755, being chosen captain of a company of volunteers raised in Westmoreland, he marched with them to Alexandria, and offered their services to General Braddock; but the offer was declined. In his twenty-fifth year Mr. Lee was appointed a justice of the peace, and shortly afterwards elected a burgess for his county. Naturally diffident, and finding himself surrounded by able men, for one or two sessions he took no part in the debates. One of his early efforts was in support of a resolution "to lay so heavy a tax on the importation of slaves as effectually to put an end to that iniquitous and disgraceful traffick within the colony of Virginia." On this question he argued against the institution of slavery as a portentous evil, moral and political.* When the defalcations of Treasurer Robinson came to be suspected, Mr. Lee insisted with firmness, in the face of a proud and embittered opposition, on an investigation of the treasury. In November, 1764, when the stamp act was first heard of in America, Mr. Lee, at the instance of a friend, wrote to England, making application for a collector's office under that act. He alleged that at that time neither he, nor, as he believed, his countrymen, had duly reflected on the real nature of that act. Observing soon, however, the growing dissatisfaction with that measure, and bestowing more deliberate reflection upon it, he became convinced of its pernicious character, and of the impropriety of his application; and from that time he became one of the most strenuous opponents of the stamp act. In the year 1766 he brought to the consideration of the assembly the act of parliament claiming a right to tax America; and he draughted the address to the king, and the memorial to the commons. His accomplishments, learning, courtesy, patriotism, republican principles, decision of character and eloquence, commanded the attention of the legislature. Although a member at the time of the introduction of Henry's resolutions, in 1765, Mr. Lee happened not to be present at the discussion; but he heartily concurred in their adoption. Shortly afterwards he organized an association in furtherance of them in Westmoreland. He vigorously opposed the act laying a duty on tea, and that for quartering British troops in the colonies. He was now residing at Chantilly, his seat on the Potomac, a few

---

* Life of Richard Henry Lee, 17.

miles below Stratford, in Westmoreland. The house at Chantilly is no longer standing. On the 25th of July, 1768, in a letter to John Dickinson, of Pennsylvania, Mr. Lee suggested "that not only select committees should be appointed by all the colonies, but that a private correspondence should be conducted between the lovers of liberty in every province." In the year 1773 the Virginia assembly, at the suggestion of Mr. Lee, appointed the first committee of intercolonial correspondence, consisting of six members, of whom he was one.

Washington was joined at Mount Vernon by Henry and Pendleton, and they proceeded together to Philadelphia. Here the old Continental Congress, consisting of fifty-five delegates, representing all the colonies except Georgia, assembled on the 5th day of September, 1774.*

Upon the motion of Mr. Lynch, of South Carolina, Peyton Randolph, of Virginia, was unanimously elected president, and Charles Thomson, secretary. At the opening of the session, on the second day, the prolonged silence was at length broken by Patrick Henry. Reciting the grievances of the colonies, he declared that all government was dissolved, and that they were reduced to a state of nature; that the congress which he was addressing was the first in a perpetual series of congresses. A few sentences roughly jotted down in John Adams' diary[†] are all that survive of this celebrated speech.

Patrick Henry and Richard Henry Lee towered supereminent in debate; yet it soon came to be remarked that in composition and the routine of actual business they were surpassed by many.[‡] But "the egotism of human nature will seldom allow us to credit a man for one excellence, without detracting from him in other respects; if he has genius, we imagine he has not common sense;

---

* Carpenter's Hall, instituted in 1721 by the Company of Carpenters, is in a court a little back from Chestnut Street. There is in the Hall the following inscription: "Within these walls Henry, Hancock, and Adams inspired the delegates of the colonies with nerve and sinew for the toils of war resulting in our national independence." Two high-backed arm-chairs are preserved, marked "Continental Congress, 1774."

† See his Life and Works, ii. 366.

‡ Wirt's Life of Patrick Henry.

if he is a poet, we suppose that he is not a logician."* It has been seen that George Mason considered Henry "the first man on this continent in ability as in public virtues." A great man only can adequately appreciate a great man. Henry was capable of being no less efficient in the committee-room than on the floor of debate.† There was no test of intellectual excellence too severe for him. The state-papers of Richard Henry Lee are sufficient proofs of his capacity.

The proceedings were conducted in secret session. Intelligence which was received from Boston riveted more closely the union of the North and South; minor differences were lost sight of in view of the portentous common danger. The congress made a declaration of rights. Dickinson composed the petition to the king, and the address to the inhabitants of Quebec; Jay an address to the people of Great Britain; and Richard Henry Lee a memorial to the inhabitants of the British colonies. The congress, after a session of fifty-one days, adjourned in October.

Mr. Henry, on his return home, being asked, "Who is the greatest man in congress?" replied, "If you speak of eloquence, Mr. Rutledge, of South Carolina, is by far the greatest orator; but if you speak of solid information and sound judgment, Colonel Washington is unquestionably the greatest man on that floor." John Adams, the eloquent and indomitable advocate of independence, mentions Lee, Henry, and Hooper as the orators of that body. Washington, in a letter addressed to Captain Mackenzie, who had formerly served under him, and was now among the British troops at Boston, gave it as his opinion, that it was neither the wish nor the interest of Massachusetts, nor of any of the colonies, to set up for independence; yet they never would submit to the loss of their constitutional rights. The same opinion was avowed by Jefferson, Franklin, and other leading men; yet there was undoubtedly then, and long had been, a strong undercurrent, a heavy ground-swell in the direction of independence, it being evident that England would never restore the colonies to their condition previous to 1763. A declaration of war is usually

---

* Lord Brougham. † Grigsby's Va. Convention of 1776, p. 150.

preceded by a hypothetical denial of hostile designs: it is the lull whose mysterious silence heralds in the approaching storm.

Patrick Henry stood foremost among the statesmen of Virginia, from the beginning of the contest, in favor of independence; he was on this point ten years in advance of them;* standing out in bold relief the prominent and pre-eminent figure on the canvas. Samuel Adams, in Massachusetts, was a patriot of the same stamp.

The danger of an outbreak of hostilities between the people of Boston and the British troops growing daily more imminent, the spirit of warlike preparation, by a sort of contagion, pervaded the colonies. It had long been a custom in Virginia to form independent military companies; and several of these now solicited Colonel Washington to review them and take command; and he consented; and in the apprehension of war, all eyes involuntarily turned to him as the first military character in the colony. At Mount Vernon he occasionally saw his former companions in arms, Dr. James Craik, and Captain Hugh Mercer, also a physician, both natives of Scotland, and with them talked over the recollections of former years, and discussed the prospects of the future. Washington was visited during the year also by General Charles Lee and Major Horatio Gates, natives of England, who had distinguished themselves in the British army, and destined to become conspicuous in the American war of revolution. They had recently purchased estates in Berkley County, Virginia.

---

* Grigsby's Va. Convention of 1776, p. 148.

CHAPTER LXXVI.

1774.

Indian Hostilities—Battle of Point Pleasant—General Andrew Lewis—Death of Colonel Charles Lewis—Cornstalk—Indignation against Dunmore—General Lewis and his Brothers.

IN April, 1774, some extraordinary hostilities occurred between the Indians and the whites on the frontier of Virginia. On which side these outrages commenced was a matter of dispute, but the whites appear to have been probably the aggressors. An Indian war being apprehended, Dunmore appointed General Andrew Lewis, of Botetourt County, then a member of the assembly, to the command of the southern division of the forces raised in Botetourt, Augusta, and the adjoining counties east of the Blue Ridge, while his lordship in person took command of those levied in the northern counties, Frederick, Dunmore, and those adjacent. According to the plan of campaign, as arranged at Williamsburg, Lewis was to march down the valley of the Kanawha* to Point Pleasant, where that river empties into the Ohio, there to be joined by the governor, who was to march by way of Fort Pitt, and thence descend the Ohio.

Late in August the *Virginia Gazette* announced news from the frontier that Lord Dunmore was to march in a few days for the mouth of New River, where he was to be joined by Lewis.

Early in September the troops under his command made their rendezvous at Camp Union,† now Lewisburg, in the County of Greenbrier. They consisted of two regiments, under Colonel William Fleming, of Botetourt, and Colonel Charles Lewis, of Augusta, comprising about four hundred men. At Camp Union they were joined by a company under Colonel Field, of Culpepper, one from Bedford, under Colonel Buford, and two from the Holston settlement, (now Washington County,) under Captains Shelby

---

* Or "River of the Woods," as the word signifies, or New River, as it was also sometimes called.

† Styled by Stuart, in his "Memoir of Indian Wars," Fort Savannah.

and Harbert. These were part of the forces to be led on by Colonel Christian, who was to join the troops at Point Pleasant as soon as his regiment should be completed.

On the eleventh of September General Lewis, with eleven hundred men, commenced his march through the wilderness, piloted by Captain Matthew Arbuckle; flour, ammunition, and camp equipage being transported on pack-horses and bullocks driven in the rear of the little army. After a march of one hundred and sixty miles, they reached, on the thirtieth of September, Point Pleasant, at the junction of the Great Kanawha with the beautiful Ohio. "This promontory was elevated considerably above the high-water mark, and afforded an extensive and variegated prospect of the surrounding country. Here were seen hills, mountains, valleys, cliffs, plains, and promontories, all covered with gigantic forests, the growth of centuries, standing in their native grandeur and integrity, unsubdued, unmutilated by the hand of man, wearing the livery of the season, and raising aloft in mid-air their venerable trunks and branches as if to defy the lightning of the sky and the fury of the whirlwind. This widely-extended prospect, though rudely magnificent and picturesque, wanted, nevertheless, some of those softer features which might embellish and beautify, or, if the expression were permitted, might civilize the savage wilderness of some of nature's noblest efforts. Here were to be seen no villages nor hamlets, not a farm-house nor cottage, no fields nor meadows with their appropriate furniture, shocks of corn, nor herds of domestic animals. In its widest range the eye would in vain seek to discover a cultivated spot of earth on which to repose. Here were no marks of industry, nor of the exercise of those arts which minister to the comfort and convenience of man; here nature had for ages on ages held undisputed empire. In the deep and dismal solitude of these woodlands the lone wanderer would have been startled by the barking of the watch-dog, or the shrill clarion of a chanticleer. Here the whistling of the plough-boy, or the milk-maid's song, sounds elsewhere heard with pleasing emotions, would have been incongruous and out of place."[*]

---

[*] Memoir of Battle of Point Pleasant, by Samuel L. Campbell, M.D.

Dunmore, who had marched across the country to the Shawnee towns, failing to join Lewis, runners were sent out by him toward Fort Pitt in quest of his lordship. October the sixth the *Williamsburg Gazette* announced advices from the frontier that the Earl of Dunmore had concluded a treaty of peace with the Delaware Indians. And before the return of the runners despatched from Point Pleasant, an express from the governor reached Point Pleasant on Sunday, the nineteenth of October, ordering General Lewis to march for the Chilicothe towns and there join him. Preparations were immediately made for crossing the Ohio.

In the mean time the Indians, headed by Cornstalk, had determined to cross the Ohio, some miles above Point Pleasant, and to march down during the night, so as to surprise the camp at daybreak. "Accordingly, on the evening of the ninth of October, soon after dark, they began to cross the river on rafts previously prepared. To ferry so many men over this wide river and on these clumsy transports must have required considerable time. But before morning they were all on the eastern bank, ready to proceed. Their route now lay down the margin of the river, through an extensive bottom. On this bottom was a heavy growth of timber, with a foliage so dense as in many places to intercept, in a great measure, the light of the moon and the stars. Beneath lay many trunks of fallen trees, strewed in different directions, and in various stages of decay. The whole surface of the ground was covered with a luxuriant growth of weeds, interspersed with entangling vines and creepers, and in some places with close-set thickets of spice-wood or other undergrowth. A journey through this in the night must have been tedious, tiresome, dark, and dreary. The Indians, however, entered on it promptly, and persevered until break of day, when, about a mile distant from the camp, one of those unforeseen incidents occurred which so often totally defeat or greatly mar the best concerted military enterprises."[*]

Two soldiers setting out very early from the camp on a hunting excursion, proceeded up the bank of the Ohio, and when they

---

[*] Dr. Campbell's Memoir of the Battle of Point Pleasant.

had gone about two miles they came suddenly upon a large body of Indians, who had crossed the river the evening before, and were now just rising from their encampment and preparing for battle. Espying the hunters they fired and killed one of them; the other escaping unhurt, ran back to the camp, where he arrived just before sunrise, and reported that "he had seen about five acres of ground covered with Indians as thick as they could stand one beside another." It was Cornstalk at the head of an army of Delawares, Mingoes, Cayugas, Iowas, Wyandots, and Shawnees, and but for the hunter's intelligence they would have surprised the camp. In a few moments two other men came in and confirmed the report, and then General Lewis lit his pipe, and sent forward the first division under his brother, Colonel Charles Lewis, and the second under Colonel Fleming; the first marching to the right at some distance from the Ohio, the bottom being a mile wide there; the second marching to the left along the bank of the river. General Andrew Lewis remained with the reserve to defend the camp. Colonel Lewis's division had not advanced along the river bottom quite half a mile from the camp when he was vigorously attacked in front, a little after sunrise, by the enemy, numbering between eight hundred and a thousand. Fleming's division was likewise attacked on the bank of the river. In a short time Colonel Charles Lewis was mortally wounded; this gallant and estimable officer, when struck by the bullet, fell at the foot of a tree, when he was, against his own wish, carried back to his tent by Captain Morrow and a private, and he died in a few hours, deeply lamented. Colonel Fleming also was severely wounded, two balls passing through his arm and one through his breast. After cheering on the officers and soldiers, he retired to the camp. The Augusta troops, upon the fall of their leader, Colonel Lewis, and several of the men, gave way, and retreated toward the camp, but being met by a re-enforcement of about two hundred and fifty, under Colonel Field, they rallied and drove back the enemy, and at this juncture this officer was killed. His place was taken by Captain Shelby. At length the Indians formed a line behind logs and trees, at right angles to the Ohio, through the woods to Crooked Creek, which empties into the Great Kanawha a little above its mouth. The engagement now became general, and was obstinately sustained in the bush-fighting manner on both sides. The Virginia troops being hemmed in between the two rivers, with the Indians in front, General Lewis employed the troops from the more eastern part of the colony (who were less experienced in Indian fighting) in throwing up a breastwork of the boughs and trunks of trees, across the delta between the Kanawha and Ohio. About twelve o'clock the Indian fire began to slacken, and the enemy slowly and reluctantly gave way, being driven back less than two miles during six or seven hours. A desultory fire was still kept up from behind trees, and the whites as they pressed on the savages were repeatedly ambuscaded. At length General Lewis detached three companies, commanded by Captains Shelby, Matthews, and Stuart, with orders to move secretly along the banks of the Kanawha and Crooked Creek, so as to gain the enemy's rear. This manœuvre being successfully executed, the Indians, as some report, at four o'clock P.M., fled; according to other accounts, the firing continued until sunset. During the night they recrossed the Ohio. The loss of the Virginians in this action has been variously estimated at from forty to seventy-five killed and one hundred and forty wounded—a large proportion of the number of the troops actually engaged, who did not exceed five hundred and fifty, as one hundred of General Lewis's men, including his best marksmen, were absent in the woods hunting, and knew nothing of the battle until it was all over. Among the killed were Colonel Charles Lewis, Colonel Field, who had served in Braddock's war, Captains Buford, Morrow, Murray, Ward, Cundiff, Wilson, and McClenachan, Lieutenants Allen, Goldsby, and Dillon. Of the officers present at the battle of Point Pleasant many became afterwards distinguished men.*

---

* There may be mentioned General Isaac Shelby, a native of Maryland, who distinguished himself at King's Mountain, and was subsequently the first governor of Kentucky; General William Campbell, the hero of King's Mountain, and Colonel John Campbell, who distinguished himself at Long Island; General Evan Shelby, who became an eminent citizen of Tennessee; Colonel William Fleming, a revolutionary patriot; Colonel John Stewart, of Greenbrier; Colonel William McKee, of Kentucky; Colonel John Steele, governor of the Mississippi Territory, and General George Matthews, who distinguished himself at

The loss of the savages was never ascertained; the bodies of thirty-three slain were found, but many had been thrown into the Ohio during the engagement. The number of the Indian army was not known certainly, but it comprised the flower of the northern confederated tribes, led on by Red Hawk, a Delaware chief; Scoppathus, a Mingo; Chiyawee, a Wyandot; Logan, a Cayuga; and Ellinipsico, and his father, Cornstalk, Shawnees. But some say that Logan was not present in the battle. The Shawnees were a formidable tribe, who had played a prominent part on many a bloody field. Cornstalk displayed great skill and courage at Point Pleasant. It is said that on the day before the battle he had proposed to his people to send messengers to General Lewis to see whether a treaty of peace could be effected, but his followers rejected the proposal. During the battle, when one of his warriors evinced a want of firmness, he slew him with one blow of his tomahawk; and during the day his sonorous voice was heard amid the din of arms exclaiming, in his native tongue, "Be strong, be strong."

On the morning after the battle General Lewis buried his dead. They were interred without the pomp of war, but the cheeks of hardy mountaineers were bedewed with tears at the fate of their brave comrades. "The dead bodies of the Indians who fell in battle were left to decay on the ground where they expired, or to be devoured by birds or beasts of prey. The mountain eagle, lord of the feathered race, while from his lofty cairn with piercing eye he surveyed the varied realms around and far beneath, would not fail to descry the sumptuous feast prepared for his use. Here he might whet his beak, and feast, and fatten, and exult. Over these the gaunt wolf, grim tyrant of the forest, might prolong his midnight revelry and howl their funeral dirge. While far remote in the deepest gloom of the wilderness, whither they had fled for safety, the surviving warriors might wail their fate, or chant a requiem to their departed spirits."*

General Lewis, after caring for the wounded, erected a small

Brandywine, Germantown, and Guilford, and was governor of Georgia, and United States senator from that State.—*Howe's Hist. Collections of Va.*, 363.

* Dr. Campbell's Memoir of Battle of Point Pleasant.

fort at Point Pleasant, and leaving a garrison there, marched to overtake Dunmore, who, with a thousand men, lay entrenched at Camp Charlotte, called after the queen, near the Shawnee town, (Chilicothe,) on the banks of the Scioto. The Indians having sued to him for peace, his lordship determined to make a treaty with them, and sent orders to Lewis to halt, or, according to others, to return to Point Pleasant. Lewis, suspecting the governor's good faith, and finding himself threatened by a superior force of Indians, who hovered in his rear, disregarded the order, and advanced to within three miles of his camp. His lordship, accompanied by the Indian chief, White Eyes, visited the camp of Lewis, who (as some report) with difficulty restrained his men from killing the governor and his Indian companion. Lewis, to his great chagrin, received orders to return home with his troops, and he obeyed reluctantly, as it seemed a golden opportunity to give the savage enemy a fatal blow.

General Andrew Lewis lived on the Roanoke, in the County of Botetourt. He was a native of Ireland, being one of five sons of John Lewis, who slew the Irish lord, settled Augusta County, founded the town of Staunton, and furnished several sons to fight the battles of their country. He was the son of Andrew Lewis and Mary Calhoun, his wife, and was born in Donegal County, Ireland, (1678,) and died in Virginia, (1762,) aged eighty-four: a brave man, and a firm friend of liberty. All his sons were born in Ireland except Charles, the youngest. Andrew Lewis was twice wounded at Fort Necessity; was appointed by Washington major of his regiment during the French and Indian war, and no officer more fully enjoyed his confidence. Major Lewis commanded the Sandy Creek expedition in 1756, and was made prisoner at Grant's defeat, where he exhibited signal prudence and bravery. His fortitude while a prisoner was equal to his courage in battle, and commanded the respect of the French officers. He was upwards of six feet in stature, of uncommon activity and strength, and of a form of exact symmetry. His countenance was stern and invincible, his deportment reserved and distant. When he was a commissioner on behalf of Virginia at the treaty of Fort Stanwix, in New York, in 1768, the governor of that colony remarked of him, that "the earth seemed to tremble under him as he walked along." At the commencement of the revolutionary war Washington considered him the foremost military man in America, and the one most worthy of the post of commander-in-chief of the American army. And it was to the country beyond the mountains that Washington looked as a place of refuge, in case he should be overpowered in the struggle, and there, defended by mountains and mountaineers, he hoped to defy the enemy. The statue of General Andrew Lewis is one of those to be placed on the monument in the capitol square, in Richmond.*

Dunmore remaining after the departure of Lewis, concluded a treaty with the Indians. Upon this occasion Cornstalk, in a long speech, charged the whites with having provoked the war, his tones of thunder resounding over a camp of twelve acres. The truth is that during the years which elapsed between Bouquet's treaty of 1764 and open war in 1774, a period of nominal peace was one of frequent actual collision and hostilities, and more lives were sacrificed on the frontier by the murderous Indians than during the whole of the year 1774, including the battle of Point Pleasant.†

---

* Thomas Lewis, eldest son of John Lewis, owing to a defective vision, was not actively engaged in the Indian wars. He was a man of learning, and representative of Augusta in the house of burgesses, and voted for Henry's resolutions of 1765; was a member of the conventions of 1776 and 1788. He married a Miss Strother, of Stafford. The second son, Samuel, died without issue. Andrew commanded at Point Pleasant. William, of the Sweet Springs, was distinguished in the frontier wars, and was an officer in the revolutionary army. He married first, Anne Montgomery, of Delaware, secondly, a Miss Thomson, a relative of the poet of "The Seasons." The fifth son, Colonel Charles Lewis, fell at Point Pleasant.

† Lyman C. Draper, in Va. Hist. Register.

CHAPTER LXXVII.

Logan—Kenton—Girty—Dunmore's ambiguous Conduct—His grandson, Murray.

LOGAN, the Cayuga chief, assented to the treaty, but, still indignant at the murder of his family, refused to attend with the other chiefs at the camp, and sent his speech in a wampum-belt by an interpreter: "I appeal to any white man to say, if ever he entered Logan's cabin hungry and he gave him not meat; if ever he came cold and naked, and he clothed him not? During the course of the last long and bloody war Logan remained idle in his cabin, an advocate for peace. Such was my love for the whites that my countrymen pointed as they passed, and said, 'Logan is the friend of white men.' I have even thought to have lived with you, but for the injuries of one man. Colonel Cresap, the last spring, in cold blood, and unprovoked, murdered all the relations of Lógan, not sparing even my women and children. There runs not a drop of my blood in the veins of any living creature. This called on me for revenge. I have sought it: I have killed many: I have fully glutted my vengeance. For my country I rejoice at the beams of peace. But do not harbor a thought that mine is the joy of fear. Logan never felt fear. He will not turn on his heel to save his life. Who is there to mourn for Logan? Not one." Tah-gah-jute, or Logan, so named after James Logan, the secretary of Pennsylvania, was the son of Shikellamy, a celebrated Cayuga chief, who dwelt at Shamokin, on the picturesque banks of the Susquehanna. When Logan grew to man's estate, living in the vicinity of the white settlers, he appears, about the year 1767, to have found the means of his livelihood in hunting deer, dressing their skins, and selling them. When the daughter of a neighboring gentleman was just beginning to walk, her mother one day happening to say that she was sorry that she could not get a pair of shoes for her, Logan, who stood by, said nothing then, but soon after requested that the little girl might be allowed to go and spend the day at his cabin, which stood on a sequestered spot near a beautiful spring (yet known as "Logan's Spring.") The mother's heart was at the first a little disconcerted at the singular proposal; but such was her confidence in the Indian that she consented. The day wore away; the sun had gone down behind the mountains in parting splendor, and evening was folding her thoughtful wing,— and the little one had not yet returned. Just at this moment the Indian was seen descending the path with his charge, and quickly she was in her mother's arms, and pointing proudly to a beautiful pair of moccasins on her tiny feet, the product of Logan's skilful manufacture.

Not long afterwards he removed to the far West, and he was remembered by an old pioneer as "the best specimen of humanity, white or red, that he had ever seen."* In 1772 the Rev. Mr. Heckwelder, Moravian missionary, met with Logan on the Beaver River, and took him to be an Indian of extraordinary capacity. He exclaimed against the whites for the introduction of ardent spirits among his people, and regretted that they had so few gentlemen among their neighbors; and declared his intention to settle on the Ohio, where he might live forever in peace with the whites; but confessed that he himself was too fond of the firewater. In the following year Heckwelder visited Logan's settlement, below the Big Beaver, and was kindly entertained by such members of his family as were at home. About the same time another missionary, the Rev. Dr. David McClure, met with Logan at Fort Pitt. "Tah-gah-jute, or 'Short-dress,' for such was his Indian name, stood several inches more than six feet in height; he was straight as an arrow; lithe, athletic, and symmetrical in figure; firm, resolute, and commanding in feature; but the brave, open, manly countenance he possessed in his earlier years was now changed for one of martial ferocity." He spoke the English language with fluency and correctness. The victim of intemperance, pointing to his breast, he exclaimed to the missionary, "I feel bad here. Wherever I go the evil Manethoes pursue me;" and he earnestly enquired, "What shall I do?" Logan's family were massacred by a party of whites in the spring of 1774, perhaps under the pretext of retaliation

---

* Tah-gah-jute, or Logan, and Captain Michael Cresap: a Discourse by Brantz Mayer. (Balt., 1851.)

for some Indian murders. But the charge against Cresap appears to have been unfounded. Logan's family being on a visit to a family of the name of Great-house, were murdered by them and their associates, under circumstances of extraordinary cowardice and brutality. The mistake is one into which Logan might, in view of some recent transactions that had happened under the command of Captain Cresap, naturally fall, and which does not at all impair the force of his speech. Mr. Jefferson meeting with a copy of it at Governor Dunmore's, in Williamsburg, transcribed it in his pocket-book, and afterwards immortalized it in his "Notes on Virginia." He gave implicit confidence to its authenticity. Doddridge is of the same opinion. Jacob, in his Life of Cresap,* insinuates that the speech was a counterfeit, and declares that Cresap was as humane as brave, and had no participation in the massacre. General George Rogers Clarke, who was well acquainted with Logan and Cresap both, vouches for the substantial truth of Mr. Jefferson's story of Logan. Devoting himself to the work of revenge, he, with others, butchered men, women, and children; knives, tomahawks, and axes were left in the breasts which had been cleft asunder; females were stripped, and outraged, too horrible to mention; brains of infants beaten out and the dead bodies left a prey to the beasts of the forest. The family of a settler on the north fork of the Holston was massacred, and a war-club was left in the house, and attached to it the following note, which had been previously, at Logan's dictation, written for him by one Robinson, a prisoner:—

"CAPTAIN CRESAP:

"What did you kill my people on Yellow Creek for? The white people killed my kin at Conestoga a great while ago, and I thought nothing of that. But you killed my kin again on Yellow Creek, and took my cousin prisoner. Then I thought I must kill too; and I have been three times to war since; but the Indians are not angry—only myself.
"CAPTAIN JOHN LOGAN.

"July 21st, 1774."

---

* Kercheval's Hist. of Valley of Va.

Thirty scalps it was known that he took in these murderous raids, but he joined not in open battle

Simon Kenton, a native of Fauquier County, a voyager of the woods, was employed by Dunmore as a spy (together with Simon Girty) during this campaign, in the course of which he traversed the country around Fort Pitt, and a large part of the present State of Ohio. His history is full of daring adventure, cruel sufferings, and extraordinary turns of fortune. He was eight times made to run the Indian gauntlet; three times bound to the stake. He was with Clarke in his expedition against Vincennes and Kaskaskia; and with Wayne in the campaign of 1794. He died in Ohio, in poverty and neglect, his once giant frame bowed down with age.* Girty, after playing for a time the spy on both sides in the revolutionary contest, became at length an adherent of the enemy, and proved, toward his countrymen, a cruel and barbarous miscreant, in whom every sentiment of humanity appears to have been extinct. Kenton and Girty are both good subjects for a novelist.

Suspicions were not wanting in the minds of many Virginians, especially the inhabitants of the west, that the frontier had been embroiled in the Indian war by Dunmore's machinations; and that his ultimate object was to secure an alliance with the savages to aid England in the expected contest with the colonies; and these suspicions were strengthened by his equivocal conduct during the campaign. He was also accused of fomenting, with the same sinister views, the boundary altercations between Pennsylvania and Virginia on the northwestern frontier. These charges and suspicions do not appear to be sustained by sufficient proof. It is probable that in these proceedings his lordship was prompted rather by motives of personal interest than of political manoeuvre. His agent, Dr. Conolly, was locating large tracts of land on the borders of the Ohio.

By the Quebec Act of 1774 Great Britain, with a view of holding the colonies in check, established the Roman Catholic religion in Canada, and enlarged its bounds so as to comprise all the territory northwest of the Ohio to the head of Lake Superior

---

* McClung's Sketches of Western Adventure, 92.

and the Mississippi. This attempt to extend the jurisdiction of Canada to the Ohio was especially offensive to Virginia. Richard Henry Lee, in congress, denounced it as the worst of all the acts complained of. In Virginia, Dunmore's avarice getting the better of his loyalty, he espoused her claims to western lands, and became a partner in enormous purchases in Southern Illinois. In 1773 Thomas and Cuthbert Bullet, his agents, made surveys of lands at the falls of the Ohio; and a part of Louisville and of towns opposite to Cincinnati are yet held under his warrant.

Murray, a grandson of the Earl of Dunmore, and page to Queen Victoria, visited the United States partly, it was said, for the purpose of making enquiry relative to western lands, the title of which was derived from his grandfather. Young Murray visited some of the old seats on the James, and makes mention of them in his entertaining "Travels in the United States."

The assembly, upon the return of Dunmore to Williamsburg, gave him a vote of thanks for his good conduct of the war—a compliment which it was afterwards doubted whether he had merited. His motives in that campaign were, to say the least, somewhat mysterious. There is a curious coincidence in several points between the administration of Dunmore and that of Berkley, one hundred years before.

CHAPTER LXXVIII.

DANIEL BOONE.

This famous explorer, a native of Pennsylvania, removed at an early age to North Carolina, and remained there till his fortieth year. In the year 1769 he left his home on the sequestered Yadkin, to wander through the wilderness in quest of the country of Kentucky, and to become the archetype of the race of pioneers. In this exploration of the unknown regions of Western Virginia, he was accompanied by five companions. Reaching Red River early in June, they beheld from an eminence the beautiful region of Kentucky. A pioneer named Finley is supposed by some to have been the first explorer of the interior of Kentucky, and it is said that he visited it alone; it is difficult to determine a matter of this kind, and the first exploration has been attributed to others. According to McClung,* it was Finley's glowing picture of the country, on his return home, in 1767, that allured Boone to venture into the wilderness. Kentucky, it appears, was not inhabited by the Indians, they having not a wigwam there; but the Southern and Northwestern Indians resorted there, as on a neutral ground, to hunt, and often came into collision and engaged in conflicts, which, according to some, gave it the name of Kentucky, or "the dark and bloody ground;" but the true signification of the word is a matter of doubt. Boone and his companions encamping, began to hunt and to reconnoitre the country. Innumerable buffaloes browsed on the leaves of the cane, or pastured on the herbage of the plains, or lingered on the border of the salt-lick. In December, Boone and a comrade, John Stuart, rambling in the magnificence of forests yet unscarred by the axe, were surprised by a party of Indians and captured. Boone met the catastrophe with a mien of stoical indifference. A week after

---

* Sketches of Western Adventure.

the capture the party encamped in the evening in a thick canebrake, and having built a large fire, lay down to rest. About midnight, Boone gently awaking his companion, they effected their escape, traversing the forest by the uncertain light of the stars, and by observing the mossy side of the trees. Returning to their camp they found it plundered and deserted; and the fate of its occupants could not be doubted. A brother of Boone, with another hardy adventurer, shortly after overtook the two forlorn survivors. It was not long before Stuart was slain by the savages and scalped, and the companion of Boone's brother devoured by wolves. The two brothers remained in a wilderness untrod by the white man, surrounded by perils, and far from the reach of succor. With unshaken fortitude they continued to hunt, and erected a rude cabin to shelter them from the storms of winter. When threatened by the approach of savages, they lay during the night concealed in swamps. In May, 1770, Boone's brother returned home for horses and ammunition, leaving him alone, without bread, salt, or sugar, or even a horse or a dog. Daniel Boone, in one of his solitary excursions made at this time, wandered during the whole day through a region whose native charms dispelled every gloomy thought. Just at the close of day, when the gales were lulled, not a breath of air stirring the leaves, he gained the summit of a commanding ridge, and, looking around, with delight beheld the ample regions mapped out beneath. On one hand he saw the beautiful Ohio delineating the western boundary of Kentucky; while at a distance the mountains lifted their peaks to the clouds. All nature was still. He kindled a fire near a fountain of sweet water, and feasted on the loin of a buck killed a few hours before. As night folded her mysterious wings he heard the distant yells of savages; but, worn out with fatigue, he fell asleep, and did not awake until the morning beams were glancing through the forest glades, and the birds warbling their matin songs. No populous city, with all its excitements and attractions, could have pleased him half so much as the charms of nature in Kentucky. Rejoined by his brother, in the summer of 1770, he explored the valley of the Cumberland River. In 1771 Daniel Boone, after an absence of three years, returned to his home on the Yadkin; sold such of his possessions as he could not carry with him, and started with his family to return and settle in Kentucky. Some cows, horses, and household utensils formed his baggage. His wife and children were mounted on horseback, their neighbors regarding them as doomed to certain destruction. On the route he was reenforced by five families, and forty armed men at Powell's Valley. In October the young men who had charge of the packhorses and cattle in the rear, were surprised by Indians, and of seven only one escaped; six were slain, and among them Boone's oldest son. This occurred near the gap of the Cumberland Mountains, whose dark gorges, rocky cliffs, and hoary summits strike the mind of the beholder with awe. The Indians were repulsed with heavy loss; but the whites retired forty miles to the settlement on the Clinch River, where Boone with his family remained for some time. Virginia in vain demanded of the Cherokees the surrender of the offenders. One of Boone's party, in retaliation, afterwards slew an Indian at a horse-race on the frontier, in spite of the interposition of the by-standers. In 1774, at the request of Governor Dunmore, Boone, leaving his family on the banks of the Clinch, went to assist in conveying a party of surveyors to the falls of the Ohio. He was next employed in the command of three garrisons during the campaign against the Shawnees. In March of the ensuing year, at the solicitation of some gentlemen of North Carolina, Boone, at the treaty of Watauga, purchased from the Cherokees of North Carolina the lands claimed by them, lying between the Kentucky River and the Tennessee. But Kentucky being within the chartered limits of Virginia, she* declared this treaty null and void, and proclaimed her own title. The North Carolina grantees, however, received in compensation a liberal grant of lands on Green River. Boone also undertook to mark out a road from the settlements to the wilderness of Kentucky; during this work several of his men were killed by the savages. In 1775 he erected a fort at Boonsborough, near the Kentucky River, and he removed his family there, and his wife and daughter were supposed to be the first white women that ever stood upon the banks

---

* See Journal of Convention of '76.

of the Kentucky River; and Boonsborough was long an outpost of civilization.

The remainder of Boone's career, full of stirring adventure, belongs rather to the early history of Kentucky. When the settlements around him began to grow too thick for his taste, he removed farther westward. This extraordinary man, who could neither read nor write, in 1792 dictated a brief account of his life to some youthful writer, whose attempt to enhance the interest of the narrative by rhetorical embellishments afforded no little satisfaction to the unsophisticated old voyager of the woods, and nothing pleased him better than to sit and listen to the reading of it. He would listen attentively, rub his hands together, smile complacently and ejaculate, "All true, every word true! not a lie in it." Solitary hunting, as it had been the charm of his earlier years, afforded him the solace of his old age; and when too old to walk through the woods, he would ride to the edge of the salt-licks and lie there in ambush for the sake of getting a shot at the deer. He was in person rough and robust; his countenance homely but kind; his manner cold, grave, taciturn; his conversation simple and unobtrusive; he never speaking of himself but when questioned. He was withal brave, humane, prudent, and modest.* He died in 1820, aged nearly ninety years.

---

* McClung's Sketches of Western Adventure, 92.

CHAPTER LXXIX.

1775.

Lord Dunmore—Second Convention—St. John's Church—Henry's Resolutions—
His Speech—Measures adopted.

IN the beginning of 1775 the people of Virginia were in a state of anxious suspense, expecting an outbreak of civil war. Dunmore remained in gloomy solicitude in his palace, tenacious of authority, but fearful of resisting the popular will. Intelligence was now continually received of commotions among the people; resolutions, essays, and speeches added new fuel to the excitement.

The second Virginia convention assembled at Richmond, on Monday, the twentieth day of March. St. John's Church, in which the sessions were held, stands on Richmond Hill, commanding a panorama of Richmond, (then a few straggling houses,) hills, and fields, and woods, and the James, with its rocks and islands, flashing rapids and murmuring falls, and poetic mists. The convention approved of the proceedings of congress, and of the conduct of the Virginia delegates. Resolutions were adopted thanking the assembly of Jamaica* for their petition and memorial to the king in behalf of the colonies; and expressing Virginia's ardent wish for "a speedy return of those halcyon days when they lived a free and happy people." The too abject tone of these resolutions aroused the patriotic indignation of Patrick Henry, and he introduced resolutions for putting the colony immediately into a state of defence against the encroachments of Great Britain, and for embodying, arming, and disciplining a force of well-regulated militia for that purpose. They were supported by Henry, the mover, Jefferson, the Lees, Pages, Mason, and others; but many of the members recoiled with horror from this startling measure; and it was strenuously resisted

---

* Jamaica and New York were acquired by conquest.

by Bland, Harrison, Pendleton, Nicholas, and Wythe, who held such a step premature, until the result of the last petition to the king should be more fully known. They still flattered themselves with the hope that the breach might yet be repaired in some way, either by the influence of the opposition in England, of the manufacturing interests, or the relenting of the king. They urged that Virginia was unmilitary, unprovided for war, weak, and defenceless, and insisted that desperate measures should not be resorted to, until hope herself had fled. Henry replied: "What has there been in the conduct of the British ministry for the last ten years to justify hope? Are fleets and armies necessary to a work of love and reconciliation? These are the implements of subjugation sent over to rivet upon us the chains which the British ministry have been so long forging. And what have we to oppose to them? Shall we try argument? We have been trying that for the last ten years. Have we anything new to offer? Shall we resort to entreaty and supplication? We have petitioned—we have remonstrated—we have supplicated; and we have been spurned from the foot of the throne. In vain may we indulge the fond hope of reconciliation. There is no longer room for hope. If we wish to be free we must fight! I repeat it, sir, we must fight! An appeal to arms, and to the God of hosts, is all that is left us!

"They tell me that we are weak; but shall we gather strength by irresolution? We are not weak. Three millions of people armed in the holy cause of liberty, and in such a country, are invincible by any force which our enemy can send against us. We shall not fight alone. A just God presides over the destinies of nations, and will raise up friends for us. The battle is not to the strong alone; it is to the vigilant, the active, the brave. Besides, we have no election. If we were base enough to desire it, it is too late to retire from the contest. There is no retreat but in submission and slavery. The war is inevitable—and let it come! let it come!

"Is life so dear, or peace so sweet, as to be purchased at the price of chains and slavery? Forbid it, Almighty God! I know not what course others may take; but as for me, give me liberty, or give me death."

Henry's voice, calm in his exordium, rose gradually to a higher and yet higher pitch, until the very walls of the church seemed to rock and tremble, as if conscious of the tremendous vibrations. The listeners, forgetful of order and of themselves, leaned forward in their seats, magnetized by the voice and look of the speaker, whose pale face and glaring eye assumed an appearance of preternatural emotion. His last exclamation, "Give me liberty, or give me death," sounded like the shout of the warrior in the tempest of battle.* When Mr. Henry sat down every eye remained still fixed on him, entranced and spell-bound.†

Richard Henry Lee supported Mr. Henry in a masterly review of the resources of the colonies and their means of resistance, exhorting the convention to remember that "the race is not to the swift, nor the battle to the strong, and that he is thrice armed whose cause is just." "But," says Wirt, "his melody was lost amid the agitations of that ocean which the master-spirit of the storm had lifted up on high." It would, however, be a wide mistake to believe that a melodious voice was Mr. Lee's highest qualification as a speaker. Plain, solid, common sense was the distinguishing characteristic of his mind as it was of Mr. Henry's.

The overweening caution of those who opposed Henry's resolutions perhaps served the purpose of the breaks in a train of railroad cars—while they endeavored to retard the movement, they made it eventually safer. The resolutions were carried, and a committee was appointed to prepare a plan of defence.‡

In conformity with a plan reported by the committee, the convention unanimously determined on the establishment of a well-regulated militia, by forming in every county one or more

---

* Randall's Life of Jefferson, i. 101.

† The expression, "after all, we must fight," had been used four months before by Joseph Hawley, of Massachusetts, in a letter to John Adams, which he showed to Patrick Henry while they were together in the first congress. Henry, upon reading the words, raised his hand, and with an oath exclaimed, "I am of that man's mind."

‡ The committee consisted of Patrick Henry, Richard Henry Lee, Robert C. Nicholas, Benjamin Harrison, Lemuel Riddick, George Washington, Adam Stephen, Andrew Lewis, William Christian, Edmund Pendleton, Thomas Jefferson, and Isaac Zane.

volunteer companies and troops of horse, to be in constant training and ready to act at a moment's warning, and hence called "minute-men." Mr. Nicholas, hitherto an extreme conservative, now proposed to raise an army of ten thousand regulars; the proposition evinced his enthusiasm in the cause; but the kind of force which he recommended still displayed his distrust in means of defence resting immediately on the body of the people. Measures were adopted by the convention to promote the raising of wool, cotton, flax, and hemp, and to encourage domestic manufactures of gunpowder, salt, iron, and steel; and the members agreed to make use of home-made fabrics, and recommended the practice to the people. The former delegates to congress were re-elected, with the substitution of Mr. Jefferson in lieu of Peyton Randolph, in case of his non-attendance. Mr. Randolph, being speaker of the house of burgesses, did not attend that congress, and Mr. Jefferson accordingly took his place.

CHAPTER LXXX.

JEFFERSON.

THOMAS JEFFERSON was born at Shadwell, in the County of Albemarle, on the 2d day of April, 1743.* According to family

---

* Randall's Life of Jefferson gives the following extract from Colonel Peter Jefferson's Book of Common Prayer:—

BIRTHS.

Jane Jefferson	1740, June	27.
Mary	1741, October	1.
Thomas	1743, April	2.
Elizabeth	1744, November	4.
Martha	1746, May	29.
Peterfield	1748, October	16.
A son	1750, March	9.
Lucy	1752, October	10.
Anna Scott Randolph	1755, October	1.

MARRIAGES.

Jane Jefferson		
Mary	1760, June	24.
Thomas	1772, January	1.
Elizabeth		
Martha	1765, June	20.
Peterfield		
A son		
Lucy	1769, September	12.
Anna Scott Randolph	1788, October.	

DEATHS.

Jane Jefferson	1765, October	1.
Mary		
Thomas		
Elizabeth	1773, January	1.
Martha		
Peterfield	1748, November	29.
A son	1750, March	9.
Lucy		
Anna Scott Randolph		

(603)

tradition his paternal ancestors, among the early settlers of Virginia, came from near Mount Snowden, in Wales, and one of them was a member of the first house of burgesses that met in 1619. The grandfather of Thomas lived at Osborne's, in Chesterfield. Peter, (father of Thomas,) a land surveyor, settled at Shadwell, where he had taken up a tract of land, including Monticello. Shadwell was called after the parish in London in which his wife was born. He was born in February, 1708, and married, in 1738, Jane, daughter of Isham Randolph, of Dungeness, in Goochland. "The Randolphs," says Mr. Jefferson, "trace their pedigree far back in England and Scotland, to which let every one ascribe the faith and merit he chooses." Peter Jefferson's early education had been neglected, but being a man of strong parts he read much, and so improved himself that he was chosen,[*] with Joshua Fry, professor of mathematics in William and Mary College, to continue the boundary line between Virginia and North Carolina, and was afterwards employed, with Mr. Fry, to make a map of the colony. This was the first regular map of Virginia ever made, that of Captain Smith, although remarkably well delineated, considering the circumstances under which it was made, being, of necessity, in large part conjectural.

Peter Jefferson was one of the first persons who settled in Goochland, since known as Albemarle, about the year 1737. That county was formed in 1744 out of a part of Goochland, which had been carved out of Henrico in 1727.

Thomas Jefferson's earliest recollection was of his being handed up and carried on a pillow on horseback by a servant when his father was removing, in 1745, from Shadwell to Tuckahoe. Peter Jefferson was a man of extraordinary physical strength; he could "head up," that is raise up from their sides to an upright position, at once, two hogsheads of tobacco weighing near a thousand pounds each. He was a favorite with the Indians, and they often made his house a stopping-place, and in this way Thomas imbibed an uncommon interest in that people.

Peter Jefferson dying in 1757, left a widow (who survived till 1776) with six daughters and two sons, of whom Thomas, then

---

[*] 1749.

fourteen years of age, was the elder. He inherited the lands on which he was born, and where he lived. When five years of age, he was placed at school at Tuckahoe, and when nine, upon the return of the family to Shadwell, at a Latin school, where he continued until his father's death. His teacher, the Rev. William Douglas, a native of Scotland, taught him the rudiments of Latin, Greek, and French. At his father's death he was put under the care of the Rev. James Maury, of Huguenot descent, a good classical scholar and thorough teacher, with whom he continued for two years at the parsonage, fourteen miles from Shadwell.* The student found recreation without in hunting on Peter's Mountain, within doors in playing on the violin. In the spring of 1760 he went to William and Mary College, and remained there for two years. Dr. William Small, a Scotchman, was then professor of mathematics there: a man of engaging manners, large views, and profound science. He shortly afterwards filled, for a time, the chair of ethics, rhetoric, and belles lettres. He formed a strong attachment to young Jefferson, and made him the daily companion of his leisure hours, and it was his conversation that first gave him a bent toward scientific pursuits. Small returned, in 1762, to Europe. Before his departure he had procured for Jefferson, from George Wythe, a reception as a student of law under his direction, and had also introduced him to the acquaintance of Governor Fauquier. At his table Jefferson met Dr. Small and Mr. Wythe, and from their conversation derived no little instruction. It was in 1765 that, while a law-student, he heard the "bloody debate" on Henry's resolutions. In May of the following year he made a northern trip, in a one-horse chair, by way of Annapolis, where he found the people rejoicing at the repeal of the stamp act. At Philadelphia he was inoculated for the small-pox by Dr. Shippen. At New York Mr. Jefferson became acquainted with Elbridge Gerry.

Jefferson, now twenty-four years old, entered upon the practice of the law in the general court, and continued in it until the Revolution closed the courts of justice. He was not fitted for the office of advocate, owing to a defective voice, and he never spoke

---

* Where now stands the mansion of the late William F. Gordon.

more than a few sentences at a time.* In 1769 he became a member of the assembly, and so continued, patriotic, active, and ardent, until the meetings were suspended by the war. He made an unsuccessful effort in that body for the emancipation of the slaves in Virginia. January the 1st, 1772, he married Martha, widow of Bathurst Skelton, and youngest daughter of John Wayles, born in Lancaster, England, a lawyer, who lived at "The Forest," in Charles City County. She was then twenty-three years old.† In 1773 Mr. Jefferson contributed to the formation of committees of correspondence between the colonial legislatures. In the year following he was elected member of the convention which met in August. Unable to attend, owing to sickness, he communicated his views in the form of written instructions, for the Virginia delegates in Congress.

---

* Randall's Jefferson, i. 50.

† Her father, who had married three times, dying in May, 1773, left issue three daughters, one of whom married Francis Eppes, (father of John W. Eppes, who married Maria, daughter of Thomas Jefferson,) and the other, Fulwar Skipwith, afterwards American consul in France. The portion that fell to Martha was encumbered with a debt, which ultimately, by the depreciation of paper money, resulted in a heavy loss.—*Randall's Jefferson, and Memoirs and Corr. of Jefferson,* i. 1, 3.

CHAPTER LXXXI.

1775.

Dunmore's Proclamation—Removal of Powder—Disturbances at Williamsburg—Military Movements—Volunteers at Fredericksburg—Governor and Council—Hanover Volunteers and Henry—He extorts compensation for Powder—Dunmore's Proclamation—Henry's popularity.

On the twenty-eighth of March Dunmore issued a proclamation, by command, as he said, of the king, for the prevention of the appointment of deputies from Virginia to the congress which was to assemble in May. And in compliance with instructions received from England, the governor ordered Captain Collins, with a party of marines and sailors from the Magdalen, lying at Burwell's Ferry, to remove the powder from the magazine at Williamsburg, and it was carried on board of that vessel secretly, between three and four o'clock A.M., of Thursday, April the twentieth, the day following the collision at Lexington and Concord. It had been rumored some days before in Williamsburg that Lord Dunmore had taken the locks off from most of the guns in the magazine, and that he intended to remove the powder. The people of the town were alarmed, and the volunteers for several nights kept guard over the magazine; at length growing negligent, and disbelieving the report, on Thursday night the guard was discharged at an early hour. Thus Collins with his party, who had been secreted in the palace, seized the powder without opposition. Dunmore, anticipating the resentment of the people, armed his servants and some Shawnee hostages, and muskets were laid on the floor, loaded and primed, and the captains of the ships of war lying at York were ordered to have in readiness an armed force for the defence of the palace. As soon as these proceedings became known, the Williamsburg volunteers flew to arms, and were with difficulty restrained by Peyton Randolph and Robert C. Nicholas from assaulting the palace and seizing the governor. The authorities of the town, in accordance with a resolution of a meeting of the people, solicited the governor to restore the powder immediately, urging among other reasons which demanded it, the apprehension of a servile war, instigated by "wicked and designing men." Dunmore, in his reply, pretended that he had removed the powder from the magazine as being an insecure place in case of such an insurrection;* declared that it should be returned as soon as it should appear that the precaution was unnecessary; that in case of an insurrection he would, upon his honor, return it in half an hour; but he expressed his surprise that the people were under arms, and said that he should not deem it prudent to put powder into their hands under such circumstances. The reply was considered evasive and false. When he had first heard that the people were in arms, he swore, "by the living God," that if any violence should be offered to him, or to the officers who had acted under his directions, he would proclaim freedom to the slaves, and lay the town in ashes. Some of the citizens, in consequence of this threat, sent their wives and children into the country.

The citizens of Williamsburg resolved unanimously to continue their contributions for the relief of the inhabitants of Boston. Intelligence of these occurrences at the capital soon spread through the country. More than six hundred volunteers met at Fredericksburg by the twenty-seventh of April, and were ready to march to Williamsburg. Gloucester and Henrico demanded the restitution of the powder, the Gloucester men threatening, in case of refusal, to seize the governor. Bedford offered a premium for the manufacture of gunpowder; the independent company of Dumfries and the Albemarle volunteers were ready for action. Dunmore renewed his threats, and was confident, as he wrote to Lord Dartmouth, the English minister, that "with a small re-enforcement of troops and arms he could raise such a body of Indians, negroes, and others as would reduce the refractory people of this colony to obedience."†

Three citizens, deputed by the troops assembled at Fredericksburg, repaired to Williamsburg for the purpose of ascertaining

---

* There had been an alarm of one from Surrey County.
† Bancroft, vii. 277.

the real state of affairs, and to offer military assistance if desired. Peyton Randolph, in behalf of the corporation, in replying to the committee, stated that: "Besides what has been said in his public answer, the governor has given private assurances to several gentlemen that the powder shall be returned to the magazine, though he has not condescended to fix the day for its return. So far as we can judge, from a comparison of all circumstances, the governor considers his honor at stake; he thinks that he acted for the best, and will not be compelled to what, we have abundant reason to believe, he would cheerfully do, if left to himself." "If we then may be permitted to advise, it is our opinion and most earnest request, that matters may be quieted for the present at least; we are firmly persuaded that perfect tranquillity will be speedily restored. By pursuing this course we foresee no hazard, or even inconvenience that can ensue. Whereas we are apprehensive, and this we think upon good grounds, that violent measures may produce effects which God only knows the consequence of."*

Upon this reply being reported to the volunteers at Fredericksburg, styled "The friends of constitutional liberty in America," they declared that it was dictated by fear, and resolved to march at all events to Williamsburg, under command of Captain Hugh Mercer, who was eager to redress the indignity which Virginia had suffered at the hands of the governor.

At this juncture Peyton Randolph happened to reach the house of Edmund Pendleton, one of his colleagues, on his route to Philadelphia, where the congress was about to meet. These two eminent men sent to Fredericksburg, on Saturday, the twenty-ninth, a letter advising that further action should be deferred until the congress should adopt a plan of resistance. Mercer, who had written to Washington for advice, received a reply to the same effect. One hundred and two deputies were appointed a council to consider this advice, and after a long and animated discussion it was assented to by a majority of one vote only.†

---

* Letter dated at Williamsburg April 27th, 1775, to Mann Page, Jr., Lewis Willis, and Benjamin Grymes, in S. Lit. Mess., 1858, 26.
† Burk's Hist. of Va., iii. 406.

The military, consisting of fourteen companies of light-horse, for several days were encamped in the fields near the town, armed and equipped, and they acquiesced reluctantly in the determination not to march at once to the capital. The Virginians were at the same time arming in other parts of the country to re-enforce, whenever necessary, those who had first taken up arms; troops were collected at the Bowling Green, and others on their march from Frederick, Berkley, Dunmore, and other counties, were arrested, by information that the affair of the gunpowder was about to be accommodated. The council of one hundred and two, before adjourning, adopted an address pledging themselves to re-assemble whenever necessary, and by force of arms to defend the laws, liberties, and rights of Virginia, or any sister colony, from unjust and wicked invasion. This address was read at the head of each company, and it concluded with the significant words, "God save the liberties of America!"

The council at this time consisted of President Nelson, Commissary Camm, Ralph Wormley, Colonel G. Corbin, G. Corbin, Jr., William Byrd, and John Page. Being summoned to hold a meeting, they assembled as usual in the council chamber, but Dunmore requested their attendance at the palace. He excused his removal of the powder as owing to his fear that the volunteers might have been tempted to seize upon the magazine; he complained that his life had been exposed to danger in the recent disturbances, and he recommended the issuing of a proclamation. John Page, the youngest member, boldly advised the governor to give up the powder and arms, as the measure necessary to restore public tranquillity. Dunmore, enraged, struck the table with his fist, exclaiming, "Mr. Page, I am astonished at you." The other councillors remained silent. Page, although he had been made a member of the council by Dunmore, had, nevertheless, opposed his nomination of John Randolph as one of the board of visiters of the college, declaring "that as he had been rejected on a former occasion as not possessing the disposition and character, moral and religious, which the charter and statutes of the college required, he ought not again to be nominated, till it could be proved that he had abandoned his former principles and practices, which no one could venture to say he had." Mr.

Page had then proposed Nathaniel Burwell in the place of the governor's nominee, and he was elected, the governor alone dissenting. This proceeding gave great offence to Dunmore and his secretary, Foy. Foy showed his resentment so offensively, that, says Page, "I was obliged to call him to account for it, and he, like a brave and candid man, made full reparation to me and my my friend, James Innes."

In Hanover the committee of safety for the county, and the members of the Independent Company, at the call of Patrick Henry, met at New Castle on the second day of May, and were addressed by him with such effect that they resolved either to recover the powder or make a reprisal for it.*

Burk† says: "The affair of the powder was decided before the battle of Lexington was ever talked of in Virginia." But as it appears that the express from Massachusetts reached Petersburg on Sunday, the first of May,‡ it is probable that Henry had already heard the news. Captain Meredith resigned in Henry's favor, and he was invested with the command, Meredith accepting the place of lieutenant. Having received orders from the committee consonant with his own suggestions, Captain Henry marched at once toward Williamsburg. Ensign Parke Goodall, with sixteen men, was detached into King and Queen County to Laneville, (on the Matapony,) the seat of Richard Corbin, the king's deputy receiver-general, to demand the estimated value of the powder, and in case of his refusal to make him a prisoner. The detachment reached Laneville about midnight, and a guard was stationed around the house. At daybreak Mrs. Corbin assured Goodall that the king's money was never kept there, but at Williamsburg, and that Colonel Corbin was then in that town. Henry had started from Hanovertown with only his own company, but the news of his march being speedily spread abroad, companies started up on all sides, and were in motion to join his standard, to the number, it was believed, of several, some say

---

* Wirt's Henry, 137; Burk's Hist. of Va., iv. 13. This volume is a continuation of Burk by Skelton Jones and Louis Hue Girardin, mainly by the latter, who enjoyed the advantage of Mr. Jefferson's assistance.

† Vol. iii. 416.

‡ Lossing's Field-Book of the Revolution, ii. 584. Wirt says that the news reached Virginia before the assembling of the volunteers at Fredericksburg.

five thousand men. The colony was governed by county committees. Lady Dunmore, with her children, retired in dismay to the Fowey, lying at Yorktown. Even the patriots at Williamsburg were alarmed at the approach of this tornado; message after message was despatched, and Captain Henry was implored to desist from entering Williamsburg. The messengers were detained, and he marched on. The scene resembled that presented by Bacon marching against Berkley a hundred years before. Dunmore, in the mean time, issued a proclamation calling upon the people to resist Henry, and planted cannon at his palace, and ordered up a detachment of marines from the Fowey. Before daybreak on the fourth of May, Captain Montague, of that ship, landed the detachment, and addressed a note to President Nelson, saying that he had received certain information that Lord Dunmore was threatened with an attack to be made at daybreak on that morning at the palace, and requesting him to endeavor to prevent any assault upon the marines, as in case of it he should be compelled to fire upon the town of York.

Henry, with one hundred and fifty men, halted at Doncastle's Ordinary, (sixteen miles from Williamsburg,) where Goodall had been ordered to rejoin him. In the meanwhile the authorities of the town were concerting measures to prevent the threatened collision. Dunmore denounced Henry as a rebel and the author of all the disturbances, and poured out a tirade of profane threats and abuse. Nevertheless, at his instance, Carter Braxton, son-in-law to Colonel Corbin, repaired to Henry's headquarters on the third, and interposed his efforts to prevent matters from coming to extremities. Finding that Henry would not disband without receiving the powder or its equivalent, he returned to Williamsburg, and procured from Colonel Corbin, the deputy receiver-general, a bill of exchange for the amount demanded, and delivering it to Henry at sunrise of Wednesday the fourth, succeeded in warding off the impending blow.* In this pacific

---

* The following is a copy of the receipt:—

"DONCASTLE'S ORDINARY, New Kent, May 4th, 1775.

"Received from the Hon. Richard Corbin, Esq., his majesty's receiver-general, £330, as a compensation for the gunpowder lately taken out of the public magazine by the governor's order, which money I promise to convey to the Virginia

course Mr. Braxton coincided with the moderate councils of the leading men at Williamsburg.

Yorktown and Williamsburg being in commotion at the landing of the marines, and an attack upon the public treasury being apprehended, Henry wrote to Nicholas, the treasurer, offering the services of his force to remove the public treasury to any place in the colony which might be deemed a safer place of deposite than Williamsburg. The treasurer replied that he did not apprehend any necessity for such a guard, and that the people of Williamsburg "were perfectly quiet;" which, however, could hardly have been the case, because at that time more than a hundred citizens patroled the streets and guarded the treasury.*

Henry, having attained the object of his march, returned with his volunteers to Hanover. The committee presented their thanks to the party for their good conduct, and also to the numerous volunteers who were marching to lend their co-operation.

Parke Goodall was a member of the convention of 1788, and afterwards kept a tavern called the "Indian Queen," in the City of Richmond.†

The contest between Henry and Dunmore concerning the powder, is like that between Colonel Hutchinson and Lord Newark on a similar occasion in 1642, at Nottingham, as related by Mrs. Hutchinson in her charming memoirs of her husband—‡ the most beautiful monument ever erected by female affection.

Two days after Henry had received compensation for the powder, Dunmore issued a proclamation denouncing "a certain

---

delegates at the general congress, to be, under their direction, laid out in gunpowder for the colony's use, and to be stored as they shall direct, until the next colony convention or general assembly, unless it shall be necessary in the mean time to use the same in the defence of the colony. It is agreed that in case the next convention shall determine that any part of the said money ought to be returned to his majesty's said receiver-general, that the same shall be done accordingly.

"PATRICK HENRY, JR.

"*Test:* SAMUEL MEREDITH,
  PARKE GOODALL."

* Burk, iv. 15.
† Richmond in By-gone Days, by Samuel Mordecai, 173.
‡ Page 102.

Patrick Henry, Jr., of Hanover," and a number of deluded followers, charging them with having unlawfully taken up arms, and by letters excited the people in divers parts of the country to join them in these outrageous and rebellious practices, extorting £330 from the king's receiver-general, and forbidding all persons to aid or abet "the said Patrick Henry, Jr.," or his confederates. The members of the council, with the exception of John Page, sided with the governor, and advised the issuing of the proclamation, and afterwards published an address, in which they expressed their "detestation and abhorrence for that licentious and ungovernable spirit that had gone forth and misled the once happy people of this country." The council now shared the public odium with Dunmore. There was a rumor that he intended to have Henry arrested on his way to the congress at Philadelphia; and it is also said that the governor denounced Henry as a coward for not having accompanied Randolph and Pendleton. Dunmore, writing to the ministry, described Henry as "a man of desperate circumstances, one who had been very active in encouraging disobedience and exciting a spirit of revolt among the people for many years past."* So in Massachusetts Samuel Adams, the model patriot of New England, was denounced by the British governor there. Henry set out for the congress May the eleventh, and was escorted in triumph by his admiring countrymen as far as Hooe's Ferry, on the Potomac, and was repeatedly stopped on the way to receive addresses full of thanks and applause.

---

* Bancroft, vii. 335.

CHAPTER LXXXII.

1775.

Mecklenburg Declaration.

THAT there was a Declaration of Independence made at Charlotte, by citizens of the County of Mecklenburg, North Carolina, on the 20th of May, 1775, is the commonly received opinion in that State, and has been often stated in print.* The closer scrutiny to which this declaration has been of late years subjected† appears to invalidate its authenticity. The patriotism, intelligence, and courage of the Scotch-Irish inhabitants of Mecklenburg—the Alexanders, Brevard, Polk, Balch, and others, are universally acknowledged; and that they "acted" independence as early as May, 1775, is admitted. But that they then made an absolute declaration of independence, (supposing them competent to do so,) does not appear to be substantiated by sufficient evidence. The original manuscript, it is alleged, was preserved by the secretary of the convention till the year 1800, when it was destroyed, with his dwelling-house, by fire.‡ It is said, however, that he had previously taken care to give copies of it to two or three persons; and mention is made of one of these transcripts as early as 1793. But they do not appear to have been any further multiplied. That a declaration of independence, made more than a year before that of July, 1776, should have been preserved by the secretary so long, and yet have remained unpublished and so little known, is extraordinary. It is remarkable, too, that such a paper should appear without date of time on the face of it. The meeting reported to have been held at Charlotte, on the twentieth of May, is styled "the convention;"

---

* Its authenticity was admitted in the former edition of this work.

† Especially by Mr. Grigsby, in his Discourse on the Virginia Convention of '76, p. 20.

‡ Foote's Sketches of North Carolina, 205.

but that of the thirty-first of the same kind, was simply a meeting of the committee of the county, and was so called at the time. It is asserted that the immediate exciting cause of the resolutions, or alleged declaration of the twentieth, was, that on that day a messenger arrived in hot haste with intelligence of the battle of Lexington. But it appears* that this intelligence reached Savannah, in Georgia, on the tenth; and it would appear hardly probable that it should have reached Charlotte ten days later.

Upon comparing one of the manuscript copies with the one published in Martin's History of North Carolina, there appears to be a remarkable difference between them. To explain this, it has, indeed, been conjectured, that Martin's copy contains the resolutions as at first draughted by Dr. Brevard, the author of them, and that the other contains them in their amended form. But the Martin copy, instead of being a rough draught, appears to be more formal and complete than the other. The Martin copy expresses the resolution in the present tense; the other in the imperfect, bearing upon its face the appearance of having been made up at a subsequent time by an effort of recollection.

The document styled a declaration, whatever may have been its origin, or terms, remained long in obscurity, public attention having been first drawn to it, in 1819, by the *Raleigh Register*, at the instance of Colonel Thomas Polk. But a declaration, to effect its object, must be published far and wide.

The Mecklenburg committee met at Charlotte on the thirtieth of May, and passed a series of resolutions, (making no reference whatever to a previous declaration of independence;) suspending the former civil constitution, and organizing a provisional republican government. The eighteenth resolution is in these words: "That these resolves be in full force and virtue, until instructions from the provincial congress regulating the jurisprudence of the province shall provide otherwise, or the legislative body of Great Britain resign its unjust and arbitrary pretentions with respect to America:" thus explicitly recognizing the right of eminent domain as belonging to Great Britain. It is not to be

---

* Bancroft, vii. 337.

credited that the Mecklenburg patriots made an absolute declaration of independence on the twentieth, and in ten days thereafter acknowledged the sovereignty of Great Britain. These admirable resolutions of the thirtieth were published in the *Mercury*, a North Carolina newspaper, (and others,) and a copy of it was transmitted by Governor Tryon to the British minister, and denounced as the boldest of all, "most traitorously declaring the entire dissolution of the laws and constitution, and setting up a system of rule and regulation subversive of his majesty's government." The alleged declaration of the twentieth, brief and absolute, was published in no newspaper, and was not denounced by the governor; while the resolutions of the thirty-first, recognizing the sovereignty of Great Britain, were so published and denounced. Mecklenburg, in North Carolina, was, nevertheless, then unquestionably in a condition of actual self-government and virtual independence; and the names of Brevard, the master-spirit of the Charlotte Convention, (afterwards a patriot-martyr,) and of his compatriots, stand on the page of history in characters of recorded honor which need no adventitious lustre.*

---

* Grigsby's Convention of Va. of '76; Martin's Hist. of N. C., ii. 372; Foote's Sketches of N. C.; Hawks' Lecture, in Revolut. Hist. of N. C. President Swain, in a lecture before the Historical Society of the University of North Carolina, referring to this subject, evidently considers the resolutions of the thirtieth of May as the Mecklenburg Declaration. (*Revolut. Hist. of N. C*, 101.) Mr. Bancroft takes the same view.

CHAPTER LXXXIII.
1775.

Congress—Dunmore offers the Olive Branch—New Commotions—Dunmore retires—Courts closed—Correspondence between Dunmore and Assembly—Washington, Commander-in-chief—Proceedings at Williamsburg—Proceedings in Congress—Washington at Cambridge—Lady Dunmore.

The second congress assembled on the 10th day of May, 1775, in the State House, Chestnut Street, Philadelphia. Peyton Randolph was again elected president, but finding it necessary to return to Virginia to perform the duties of speaker, was succeeded by the well-tried patriot, John Hancock. Many of the leading members, including Washington, still hoped for reconciliation with the mother country, and few as yet avowed themselves in favor of independence. But while the congress were pacific in theory, they were revolutionary in action. A second petition to the king was adopted; but, at the same time, a federal union was organized, and the executive power vested in a council of twelve. Measures were taken for enlisting troops, erecting forts, providing military stores, and issuing a paper currency. Massachusetts was advised to form an internal government for herself. Washington was chairman of the military committees, and the regulations of the army and defensive measures were mostly devised by him.

Shortly after the affair of the gunpowder, the public agitations were again quieted upon the reception of Lord North's conciliatory proposition, commonly called the "Olive Branch;" and Dunmore convened the burgesses, and Lady Dunmore and her family returned (to the great satisfaction of the people) from the Fowey, where they had taken refuge during these disturbances, to the palace. The assembly meeting on the first day of June, the governor presented Lord North's proposition. The council's answer was satisfactory; but before the burgesses could reply, a new explosion occurred. Upon Henry's recent approach toward Williamsburg some of the inhabitants, to the great offence of the graver citizens, had taken possession of a few of the guns remaining in the magazine. On the night of June the fifth a number of persons having assembled there to furnish themselves with arms, some of them were wounded by spring-guns placed there by order of the governor. Besides this, some barrels of powder were found buried in the magazine, to be used, it was suspected, as a mine when occasion should offer. Early on the next morning Lord Dunmore, with his family, escaped from Williamsburg to return no more, and took shelter on board of the Fowey, leaving behind him a message to the house, ascribing his departure to apprehensions of personal danger, and declaring his willingness to co-operate with the assembly in the public business. That body, by a deputation, requested him to return to the palace, assuring him that they would unite in whatever measures might be necessary for the protection of him and his family. Dunmore in reply complained of the inimical spirit of the burgesses toward him, of the countenance which they had given to the disorderly proceedings of the people, of his majesty's magazine having been broken open and rifled in the presence of members of the house; he further said that while some endeavors had been made by the committee of the house to prevail upon the people to restore the arms, no steps had been taken to bring the offenders to justice; that a body of men had assembled at Williamsburg for the purpose of attacking the king's troops, and that guards had been mounted under false pretences. He exhorted them to return to their constitutional duty; to open the courts of justice; to disband the independent companies; and to put an end to the persecutions of his majesty's loyal subjects.

The governor at the same time communicated papers containing terms upon which a reconciliation might take place—placing his return upon the condition of their acceptance of the "Olive Branch." The assembly in their reply, composed by Mr. Jefferson, declared that next to the preservation of liberty, a reconciliation would be the greatest of all human blessings; but that they could not consent to the proposed terms. Leaving the determination of these disputes to the wisdom of congress, for themselves they avowed that they had exhausted every means for obtaining redress; they had remonstrated to parliament, and parliament had only added new oppressions to the old; they had wearied the king with petitions which he had not deigned to answer; they had appealed to the native honor and justice of the British nation, but their efforts in favor of the colonies had as yet proved ineffectual. Nothing remained but to commit their cause to the even-handed justice of Him who doeth no wrong, "earnestly beseeching him to illuminate the counsels and prosper the endeavors of those to whom America hath confided her hopes, that through their wise direction we may again see re-united the blessings of liberty and property, and the most permanent harmony with Great Britain."

The courts of justice upon Dunmore's flight had been closed, the general court refusing to transact business, under the pretext that the fees of officers could not be legally taxed without an act of assembly—the real ground being, it is said, the desire of bringing about an independent meeting of that body, and of protecting debtors against suits, principally foreign.

In another correspondence with the governor, the assembly requested him to give an order for the return of the arms; but this he refused to do, alleging that they belonged to the king. They also complained of being compelled to communicate with his excellency on board of one of his majesty's armed ships, and at the distance of twelve miles from their usual place of meeting. His lordship laid the whole responsibility of these inconveniences upon the disorders that had driven him from the seat of government, and required the house to attend him on board the Fowey for the purpose of obtaining his signature to bills. Some of the burgesses were disposed to acquiesce in the proposed arrangement; but it was rejected upon a member's relating Æsop's fable of the sick lion and the fox. The assembly declared the governor's message a high breach of the rights and privileges of the house; they advised the people of Virginia to prepare for the preservation of their property, their rights, and their liberties. It was also resolved unanimously that "we do and will bear faith and true allegiance to our most gracious sovereign George the Third, our only lawful and rightful king; and that we will at all times, to the utmost of our power, and at the risk of our lives and property, maintain and defend his government in this colony, as founded on the established laws and principles of the constitution." They furthermore unanimously declared their earnest desire to preserve and strengthen the bands of amity with their fellow-subjects of Great Britain.

On the fourteenth day of June, George Washington, upon the nomination of Mr. Thomas Johnson, of Maryland, was unanimously elected by the congress, commander-in-chief of the armies of the United Colonies. John Adams, of Massachusetts, the eloquent and indomitable advocate of independence, had, on a previous occasion, recommended him for the post, as "a gentleman, whose skill and experience as an officer, whose independent fortune, great talents, and excellent universal character, would command the approbation of all America, and unite the cordial exertions of all the colonies better than any other person in the union." Mr. Adams had discovered that the preference of the Southern members for Washington was very strong. The pay of the commander-in-chief of the continental army was fixed at the sum of five hundred dollars a month. Washington, impressed with a profound sense of the arduous responsibility of the trust, while he gratefully accepted it, declared at the same time that he did not think himself equal to it. He declined all compensation for his services, and made known his intention to keep an account of his expenses, which he should rely on congress to discharge. A fac-simile copy of his account, published in recent times, attests the fidelity with which he performed this engagement. It is remarkable that while the Southern members in general preferred him, among those, who at the first suggestion of his name by Mr. Adams, were opposed to his appointment, were several of the Virginia delegates, and Mr. Pendleton, in particular, was absolutely against it; but upon further conference and reflection all objection was withdrawn. Four major-generals were appointed, Ward of Massachusetts, Charles Lee, an Englishman, Schuyler, of New York, and Putnam, of Connecticut. In compliance with General Washington's request, his old comrade, Major Horatio Gates, then on his estate in Virginia, was appointed adjutant-general. Washington was likewise warmly in favor of the appointment of General Charles Lee; yet not without misgivings as to his violent temper.

The Shawnee hostages had disappeared at the time with the governor; and George Washington, Thomas Walker, James Wood, Andrew Lewis, John Walker, and Adam Stephen were appointed commissioners to ratify a treaty with that tribe. It was determined that Lord Dunmore had voluntarily abdicated the post of governor, and that the president of the council should discharge the duties. The abdication was, no doubt, as "voluntary" as that of James the Second. The burgesses adjourned to the twelfth of October, and were summoned to meet in convention on the seventeenth of July.* It was on this occasion that Richard Henry Lee, standing on the 17th of June, 1775, with two other burgesses, in the portico of the capitol, inscribed with his pencil, on a pillar, these lines,—

> 'When shall we three meet again,
> In thunder, lightning, and in rain?
> When the hurlyburly's done,
> When the battle's lost and won."

On the twenty-fourth the arms were removed from the palace, and lodged in the magazine of which Dr. Bland had the charge. Among those engaged in removing them were Theodorick Bland, Jr., Richard Kidder Meade, Benjamin Harrison, of Berkley, George Nicholas, Harrison Randolph, and James Monroe.

On the twenty-sixth of June Mr. Jefferson was added to a committee of congress appointed to draw up a declaration of the grounds of taking up arms. He prepared one, but it proving too strong for Mr. Dickinson, of Pennsylvania, he was indulged in preparing a far tamer statement, which was accepted by congress. Yet disgust at its humility was general, and Mr. Dickinson's delight at its passage was the only circumstance which reconciled them to it. The vote being passed, although farther observation on it was out of order, Dickinson could not refrain from rising and expressing his satisfaction, and concluded by saying: "There is but one word, Mr. President, in the paper which I disapprove,

---

* Williamsburg invited the assistance of an additional volunteer force to guard the town.

and that is the word *congress*." On which Benjamin Harrison rose and said: "There is but one word, Mr. President, of which I approve, and that is the word *congress*."

The commander-in-chief received his commission from the president of congress on the twentieth of June, and on the following day set out for Boston on horseback, accompanied by General Lee, General Schuyler, and an escort of Philadelphia cavalry. They had proceeded about twenty miles, when they were met by an express bringing intelligence of the battle of Bunker's Hill. Amid cheers and the thunder of cannon he reached the headquarters of the army at Cambridge, on the second of July, and on the third assumed the command. The future was full of difficulty and of danger; but he confided in that Divine Providence which wisely orders human affairs.

Late in June the Magdalen sailed from York with Lady Dunmore, and the rest of the governor's family, bound for England. The Magdalen was convoyed down the York and across the bay, by the Fowey. This oft-mentioned old twenty-gun man-of-war was shortly afterwards relieved by the Mercury, and sailed with Captain Foy on board for Boston.

Dunmore issued a proclamation commanding all subjects on their allegiance, to repair to his standard.

CHAPTER LXXXIV.

1775.

Dunmore at Portsmouth—Convention—Committee of Safety—Carrington, Read, Cabell—Henry, Colonel and Commander-in-chief—George Mason—Miscellaneous Affairs—Death of Peyton Randolph—The Randolphs of Virginia.

DUNMORE'S domestics now abandoned the palace and removed to Porto Bello, his country-seat, about six miles below Williamsburg. The fugitive governor took up his station at Portsmouth.

On Monday, July the 17th, 1775, the convention met at Richmond. Measures were taken for raising two regiments of regular troops for one year, and two companies for the protection of the western frontier, and to divide the colony into sixteen districts, and to exercise the militia as minute-men, so as to be ready for service at a moment's warning. At the instance of Richard Bland an inquiry was made into certain charges reflecting on his patriotism; and his innocence was triumphantly vindicated. Although he had resisted extreme measures, yet when the crisis came, and the rupture took place, he was behind none in patriotic ardor and devotion to the common cause. A minister was implicated in propagating the charges against him.

A committee of safety was organized to take charge of the executive duties of the colony; it consisted of eleven gentlemen: Edmund Pendleton, George Mason, John Page, Richard Bland, Thomas Ludwell Lee, Paul Carrington, Dudley Digges, William Cabell, Carter Braxton, James Mercer, and John Tabb.

Paul Carrington, the ancestor of those bearing that name in Virginia, and his wife, of the Heningham family, emigrated from Ireland to Barbadoes. He died early in the eighteenth century, and left a widow and numerous children. The youngest, George, about the year 1727, came to Virginia with the family of Joseph Mayo, a Barbadoes merchant, who settled at Powhatan, the former seat of the chief of that name, and young Carrington lived with him in the capacity of storekeeper. About 1732 he married Anne, daughter of William Mayo, of Goochland, brother of Joseph, and went to reside on Willis's Creek, in what is now Cumberland County. Paul Carrington, eldest child of this marriage, married, in 1755, Margaret, daughter of Colonel Clement Read, of Bushy Forest, clerk of the court of Lunenburg, now Charlotte. Young Carrington, having attained a practical knowledge of the law in the clerk's office, soon acquired an extensive practice. He was a burgess from Charlotte in 1765, and appears to have voted against Henry's resolutions. He continued to be a member of the house down to the time of the Revolution; was a member of the association of 1670, and in 1774 of the first convention; and also of those of 1775 and 1776. In the latter he voted for the resolution instructing the delegates in congress to propose independence, and was a member of the committee which reported the bill of rights and the constitution. He was subsequently a judge of the general court and of the court of appeals, and a member of the convention of 1788. Three of his sons served in the army of Revolution: George, lieutenant in Lee's legion; Paul, who was at the battles of Guilford and Greenspring; and Clement, who was wounded in the battle of Eutaw Springs. Paul Carrington, member of the committee of safety, was upwards of six feet in stature, his features prominent, with bright blue eyes, and sandy hair. His seat was Mulberry Hill, on the banks of the Staunton.* He died at the age of eighty-five, having survived all the early Virginia patriots of the revolutionary era.

Edward Carrington, his younger brother, was a valued officer during the revolutionary war, and quartermaster-general for the Southern army under Greene.

Colonel Clement Read, father of Mrs. Paul Carrington, was born in Virginia, (1707,) his ancestors having, as is supposed, come over shortly after the Restoration, being probably of the Cromwellian party. Early bereft of his father, he was educated at William and Mary under the guardianship of John Robinson, of Spotsylvania, president of the council. In 1730 Mr. Read was married to Mary, only daughter of William Hill, an officer

---

* Foote's Sketches of Va., second series, 575; Grigsby's Convention of '76.

in the British navy, second son of the Marquis of Lansdowne. This William Hill had married the only daughter of Governor Jennings, and resided in what was then Isle of Wight County, now Brunswick.

Colonel Isaac Read, eldest son of Clement Read, was a member of the conventions of 1774 and 1775, co-operating with Henry and Jefferson. He received in June, 1776, a commission as lieutenant-colonel of the Fourth Virginia Regiment, but died not long after at Philadelphia, owing to exposure in the public service. Thomas Read, younger brother of Isaac, was a supporter of the views of Henry and Jefferson, and a member of the convention of 1776.* An accomplished gentleman, he retained the costume and manners of a former day.

Dr. William Cabell, head of the family of that name in Virginia, emigrated from Wiltshire, England, about 1720, and settled in what is now Nelson County. He had been a surgeon in the English navy; was a man of letters and science; in his profession well-skilled and successful; sagacious in business; of a humorous fancy; and fond of wild sports. He died in 1774 at an advanced age, leaving one daughter and four sons; of these, Joseph Cabell was a burgess in 1769 and 1770, and member of the convention in 1775. John Cabell was a member of the same, and of the convention of 1776. Nicholas Cabell served under La Fayette, and was also in political life. William Cabell, the eldest brother, was wise in council, energetic and fearless in action, and widely influential in his own region. He was fond of rural sports, and an expert horseman. His face was of the Roman cast. Tall, of a fine person, and commanding presence, he exhibited the dignified simplicity of the Virginia gentleman of the old school. He was a tobacco-planter, and his extensive and well-ordered plantations, besides the labors of agriculture, presented a scene of industry, where the various handicrafts were carried on by his own blacksmiths, carpenters, weavers, and shoemakers. Colonel Cabell was systematic in business, and of generous hospitality. He was a member of the assembly in 1769, and a signer of the association. He voted, in 1775,

---

* Foote's Sketches, second series, 573; Grigsby's Convention of '76.

against Henry's resolutions, preferring the scheme of a regular army presented by Colonel Nicholas.* Colonel Samuel J. Cabell, who was at the commencement of the Revolution a student of college, left it, and joined the first armed corps raised in Virginia, and soon attained the rank of lieutenant-colonel in the continental army. He was made a prisoner at the surrender of Charleston in 1780, and so remained till the close of the war. He was afterwards a member of congress, and died at his seat in Nelson County, in 1818, aged 61.

Patrick Henry was elected, in August, colonel of the first regiment and commander of all the forces raised and to be raised for the defence of the colony. William Woodford, of Caroline County, who had served meritoriously in the French and Indian war, was appointed to the command of the second regiment. A strong effort was made to elect Colonel Hugh Mercer, of Fredericksburg, to the command of the first regiment, and on the first ballot he received a plurality of one vote; but the question being narrowed down between him and Mr. Henry, the latter was elected.

The expense of the late Indian war was estimated at £150,000; Virginia's quota of the charge of the continental army £150,000; the charge of the two new regiments, and the minute-men, and other items of public expenditure, made a sum of upwards of £500,000. George Wythe was elected member of congress in the place of Washington, appointed commander-in-chief. When the delegates were chosen for the ensuing congress, Mr. Mason would have been elected but that he declared that he could not possibly attend. Upon the resignation of the aged Colonel Richard Bland, a day or two thereafter, a party headed by Colonel Henry, Mr. Jefferson, and Colonel Paul Carrington, appeared determined to elect Colonel Mason at all events. In consequence of this, just before the ballot was taken, he found himself constrained to make known the grounds of his refusal; "in doing which," he says, "I felt myself more distressed than ever I was in my life, especially when I saw tears run down the president's (Randolph's) cheeks." The cause of Mr. Mason's declining to

---

* Va. Hist. Reg., iii. 44 and 107; Grigsby's Convention of '76.

serve was the recent death of his wife, leaving a large family of children. Mr. Mason nominated Colonel Francis Lightfoot Lee, who was elected. Mr. Mason was, nevertheless, as has been seen, made a member of the committee of safety, which service was even more inconvenient to him than that of delegate to congress. But upon his begging permission to resign, he was answered by a unanimous "no." The staff officers of the First Regiment, under Colonel Henry, were Lieutenant-Colonel Christian and Major Eppes; and in the Second Regiment, under Colonel Woodford, Lieutenant-Colonel Charles Scott and Major Alexander Spotswood. The convention passed ordinances for raising money and imposing taxes, for furnishing arms and the procuring of saltpetre, lead, and sulphur, and for encouraging the manufacture of gunpowder; for regulating the elections of delegates; and for establishing a general test of fidelity to the country. The Maryland Convention not concurring in the resolution prohibiting the export of provisions, it was rescinded, and the ports were consequently kept open till the tenth of September. The merchants, natives of Great Britain, mostly Scotch, resident in Virginia, petitioned the convention to prescribe some rule of conduct in their business during the present crisis of affairs, and were allowed to remain neutral. The committee of safety met for the first time toward the end of August. At the beginning of the session of the convention, resolutions were passed by way of recommendations for the people; but afterwards ordinances were enacted on all matters of importance with the formalities of a bill, passing through three readings.

In September Colonel Henry selected an encampment in the rear of the College of William and Mary. The recruits, regular and minute-men, poured rapidly into Williamsburg. In October Matthew Phripp, a Virginian, in whom important trusts had been confided, proving a traitor, went on board of one of Dunmore's vessels. Phripp's son likewise deserted. Virginia contrived to import some powder at this juncture. The people became dissatisfied at the scarcity of salt, the importation of which was prohibited by the articles of association; but it would hardly have been possible to import it then, even if allowed by law, Virginia not having one armed vessel to protect her trade. Some persons began to manufacture it by evaporating sea-water in pans. The non-importation afforded a new incentive to industry and invention, threw the people upon their own resources, and taught them self-denial, and how to live within themselves. They made less tobacco, and applied themselves more to domestic manufactures.

On the 22d of this month, 1775, died suddenly of an apoplexy, at Philadelphia, the able and virtuous Peyton Randolph, president of congress, aged fifty-two years, descended from a family long noted in Virginia for its wealth, talents, and influence; he was the second son of Sir John Randolph, and Susan Beverley, his wife. Peyton Randolph, being bred to the law, was, in 1748, appointed king's attorney for the colony, being then but twenty-four years of age. He succeeded Speaker Robinson in the chair of the house of burgesses in 1766, and continued to preside over that body until it was superseded by the conventions. He was made, in 1773, a member of the committee of correspondence, and was at its head. In March, 1774, he was unanimously chosen president of the first convention of Virginia. In August he was appointed by the convention one of the delegates to the congress which assembled at Philadelphia in September, and was unanimously elected president of it. In person he was tall and stately; in manner grave and of senatorial dignity; at home generous and hospitable. As a lawyer sound and accurate; in public life of excellent judgment, large experience, and incorruptible integrity.* He lies buried in the chapel of William and Mary.

The progenitor of the Randolphs was William of Warwickshire, or as some say, of Yorkshire, England, who came over to Virginia probably between 1665 and 1675, poor, it is said. He accumulated a large estate, and became a member of the house of burgesses and of the council. He appears to have been intimate with the first Colonel William Byrd, and well acquainted with Lady Berkley. He settled at Turkey Island on the James River. He married Mary Isham, of Bermuda Hundred, who was descended from an ancient family in Northamptonshire. Several of their sons were men of distinction: William was

---

* Grigsby's Convention of Va. of '76.

member of the council, and treasurer; Isham a member of the house of burgesses from Goochland, (1740,) and adjutant-general; Richard was burgess for Henrico, and succeeded his brother as treasurer. Sir John, sixth son of the first William, was clerk, speaker, treasurer, and attorney-general. He died in March, 1737, aged forty-four, and lies buried in the chapel of William and Mary.* Peter, son of the second William Randolph, was clerk, and attorney-general. Peyton, son of Sir John, was attorney-general, speaker of the house of burgesses, and president of the first congress. John, brother of Peyton, was attorney-general, a votary of pleasure; of brilliant talents; he sided with Dunmore, withdrew from Virginia with him, and died in London, in January, 1784, aged fifty-six. He lies buried in the chapel of William and Mary. Thomas Mann Randolph, great grandson of the first William, was member of the Virginia convention of 1775, from Goochland. Beverley Randolph was member of assembly from Cumberland during the Revolution, and Governor of the State of Virginia. Edmund Randolph, (son of John, the attorney-general,) said to have been disinherited by his father for refusing to adhere to the royal cause, was aid-de-camp to General Washington, member of the convention of 1776, judge of the admiralty court, member of the congress of the confederation, and of the general convention that framed the constitution of the United States, and of the Virginia convention that ratified it, Governor of Virginia, Attorney-General of the United States, and Secretary of State. Robert Randolph, son of Peter, Richard Randolph, grandson of Peter, and David Meade Randolph, sons of the second Richard, were cavalry officers in the war of the Revolution. David Meade Randolph was United States Marshal for Virginia. John Randolph, of Roanoke, the orator, was grandson of the first Richard. Thomas Mann Randolph, Jr., was member of the legislature of Virginia, and of congress, and Governor of Virginia. Richard Bland, of the old congress, Thomas Jefferson, Theodorick Bland, Jr., Richard Henry Lee, Arthur Lee, and Francis Lightfoot Lee, William

---

* A small work on gardening, printed at Petersburg, in 1807, is attributed to him.

Stith, the historian, and Thomas Marshall, father of the chief justice, were all descended from William Randolph, of Turkey Island.

Jane Bolling, great granddaughter of Pocahontas, married Richard Randolph, of Curles. John Randolph, Sr., the seventh child of that marriage, married Frances Bland, and John Randolph, of Roanoke, the orator, was one of the children of this union.

The members of the numerous family of the Randolphs in several instances adopted the names of their seats for the purpose of distinction, as Thomas of Tuckahoe, Isham of Dungeness, Richard of Curles, John of Roanoke. The following were seats of the Randolphs on the James River: Tuckahoe, Chatsworth, Wilton, Varina, Curles, Bremo, and Turkey Island.

CHAPTER LXXXV.

1775.

Dunmore's War—Captain Squires—Woodford sent against Dunmore—Woodford and Henry—Affairs at Great Bridge—Battle of Great Bridge—Howe assumes Command—Indignity offered Henry—Committee of Safety—Pendleton—Howe occupies Norfolk.

DUNMORE in the meanwhile had rallied a band of tories, runaway negroes, and British soldiers, and collected a naval force, and was carrying on a petty warfare. Captain Squires, of his majesty's sloop Otter, during the summer cruised in the James and York, plundering the inhabitants and carrying off slaves. Early in September a tender laden with stores, being driven ashore near Hampton, Squires (who happened to be in her) and most of the crew escaped. The sloop was burnt by the inhabitants. Squires in retaliation threatening Hampton, Major Innes, with a hundred men, was sent down from Williamsburg to defend it. Squires in the latter part of October appeared near Hampton with several vessels, and threatened to land and burn the town. It was defended by a company of regulars under Captain George Nicholas, a company of minute-men, and some militia. Upon Squires attempting to land a skirmish ensued, and the enemy was driven off with some loss. Squires' party returning on the next day, burnt down a house belonging to a Mr. Cooper. Intelligence of this affair having reached Williamsburg, a company of riflemen was sent to Hampton, and Colonel Woodford was despatched to take command there. Upon their arrival on the next morning, Squires began to fire upon the town, but was again compelled to retire. These petty hostilities were the subject of humorous remark in the *Virginia Gazette*.*

---

* John Banister proposing to turn his saw-mill at Petersburg into a powder-mill, the convention ordered saltpetre and sulphur to be sent there for him.

Dunmore, on the 7th of November, 1775, proclaimed martial-law, summoned all persons capable of bearing arms to his standard, on penalty of being proclaimed traitors, and offered freedom to all servants and slaves who should join him. He had now the ascendency in the country around Norfolk, which abounded in tories. The committee of safety despatched Woodford with his regiment and two hundred minute-men, amounting in all to eight hundred men, with orders to cross the James River at Sandy Point and go in pursuit of Dunmore. Colonel Henry had been desirous to be employed in this service, and, it was said, solicited it, but the committee of safety refused, and amid such exciting events he found himself, eager as he was for action, and ardent and impetuous as was his nature, still compelled to sit down inactive in Williamsburg, where he had been quartered since September. At length after the lapse of nearly another month of tedious inaction, during which he received no regular communications from Colonel Woodford, Colonel Henry wrote to him thus: "Not hearing of any despatch from you for a long time, I can no longer forbear sending to know your situation and what has occurred?" Woodford on the next day replied from the Great Bridge, near Norfolk, and said: "When joined I shall always esteem myself immediately under your command, and will obey accordingly, but when sent to command a separate and distinct corps, under the immediate instructions of the committee of safety, whenever that body, or the honorable convention is sitting, I look upon it as my indispensable duty to address my intelligence to them as the supreme power in this colony." Thus Colonel Henry's chagrin at not being permitted to march himself against Dunmore was aggravated by Colonel Woodford's declining, while detached, to acknowledge his superiority in command. Woodford, upon approaching Dunmore, found that he had entrenched himself on the north side of the Elizabeth River, at the Great Bridge, about twenty miles from Norfolk. Judge Marshall says that it was necessary for the Provincials to cross it in order to reach

---

Richard Bland advised that saltpetre should be made at Appomattox warehouses, (Petersburg,) fearing that supineness possessed all ranks, and offering to contribute toward that useful work.

Norfolk, but Thomas Ludwell Lee, writing at the time, says that there were other ways by which to pass to Norfolk. "Our army has been for some time arrested in its march to Norfolk by a redoubt, or stockade, or hog-pen, as they call it here, by way of derision, at the end of this bridge. Though, by the way, this hog-pen seems filled with a parcel of wild boars, which we appear not overfond to meddle with." Some of the more eager patriots were apprehensive that Woodford would be amused at that post until Dunmore should finish his fortifications at Norfolk, where he was now entrenching and mounting cannon, some hundreds of negroes being employed in the work. Added to this the advanced season of the year and the hourly expectation of the enemy's receiving a re-enforcement from St. Augustine, as was known by intercepted intelligence, made a bold movement necessary, "while we walk too cautiously in the road of prudence."

Dunmore's power on land was confined to the counties of Norfolk and Princess Anne; his recent course had united the colony with few exceptions against him, and if the ministry had ransacked the whole world for the person of all others the best fitted to ruin their cause, they could not have found a fitter agent than Lord Dunmore. He had just now proclaimed liberty to the slaves, and declared martial-law.

It was believed that one frigate could capture the whole of his fleet, and other vessels laden with the floating property of tories, of enormous value. John Page wished earnestly for a few armed vessels to keep possession of the rivers, the arteries of commerce, at the least the upper parts of them. While five thousand men could not defend so exposed a coast against the depredations of Dunmore's fleet, yet five hundred in armed vessels could easily take the fleet. But a majority of the committee of safety and of the convention, held it in vain for Virginia then to attempt any thing by water.*

Dunmore had erected a small fort on an oasis surrounded by a morass, not far from the Dismal Swamp, accessible on either side only by a long causeway. Woodford encamped within cannon-

---

* Lee Papers, S. Lit. Messr., 1858, p. 254.

shot of this post, in mud and mire, in a village at the southern end of the causeway, across which he threw up a breast-work, but being destitute of artillery he did not attack the fort. After a few days Dunmore, hearing by a servant lad, who had deserted from Woodford's camp, that his force did not exceed three hundred men, mustered his whole strength and despatched them in the night to the fort, with orders to force the breast-works early next morning, or die in the attempt. On the 9th of December, 1775, a little before sunrise, Captain Fordyce, at the head of sixty grenadiers, who six abreast led the column, advanced along the causeway. Colonel Bullet first discovered the enemy, and the alarm being given in Woodford's camp, a small guard at the breast-works began the fire, others hastened from their tents, and regardless of order, kept up a fire on the head of the column. Fordyce, though received so warmly in front, and flanked by a party posted on a rising ground to his right, rallied his men, and marched up within twenty yards of the breast-work, when he fell pierced with bullets. His followers now retreated, and at this juncture Colonel Woodford arrived, and directed a pursuit of the enemy, who were galled by a handful of riflemen under Colonel Stephen, but found protection under cover of the guns of the fort. Woodford declined attempting to storm the works, although strongly urged to it by the bold and ardent Bullet and the enthusiastic wishes of the troops.

In the battle of the Great Bridge every grenadier was killed, and the enemy's killed and wounded amounted to about one hundred. Four officers were killed, one wounded and made prisoner. The affair has been styled "a Bunker Hill in miniature:" but there the loss was very heavy on both sides; whereas here Woodford's troops suffered no loss.

John Marshall, afterwards chief justice, was in this expedition.* Richard Kidder Meade, father of Bishop Meade, was also present at the affair of the Great Bridge. This was the first sc of revolutionary bloodshed in Virginia. On the night following this

---

* An account of his visit to Yorktown shortly after the battle, and his courtship, by John Eston Cooke, is to be found in Historical Magazine for June, 1859.

action the royalists evacuated the fort, and Dunmore took refuge on board of his fleet. Colonel Howe, with five or six hundred North Carolina troops, now joined Woodford, and assumed command at the Great Bridge, with the consent of Woodford, who yielded to the seniority of his commission. Colonel Henry now saw the colonel of the second Virginia regiment, who had refused to acknowledge his command, submitting himself to an officer of no higher rank, and of another colony. He found himself, although invested with the title of commander-in-chief, yet virtually superseded and reduced to the mere shadow of a name. To nullify his superiority of command the committee had only to detach his subordinate officers.

On the thirteenth of December a member of the convention wrote to Colonel Woodford: "I have talked with Colonel Henry about this matter; he thinks he has been ill-treated, and insists the officers under his command shall submit to his orders:" and again, "A commander or general, I suppose, will be sent us by the congress, as it is expected our troops will be upon continental pay." Mr. Pendleton, chairman of the committee, in a letter dated December the twenty-fourth, and addressed to Colonel Woodford, said: "The field-officers to each regiment will be named here and recommended to congress; in case our army is taken into continental pay, they will send commissions. A general officer will be chosen there, I doubt not, and sent us; with that matter I hope we shall not intermeddle, lest it should be thought propriety requires our calling, or rather recommending, our present officer to that station." It appears that Colonel Henry had not owed his military appointment to those members of the committee of safety who conducted the correspondence.* Mr. Pendleton looked upon the appointment of Henry as an "unlucky step." Pendleton and Woodford were both of the County of Caroline.

Late in December, Colonel Henry insisting upon a determination of the question thus raised between him and Colonel Woodford, the committee passed the following resolution:—

"*Resolved*, Unanimously, that Colonel Woodford, although

---

* Wirt's Life of Patrick Henry, 171.

acting upon a separate and detached command, ought to correspond with Colonel Henry, and make returns to him at proper times of the state and condition of the forces under his command, and also that he is subject to his orders when the convention or the committee of safety is not sitting; but that while either of these bodies is sitting he is to receive his orders from one of them."

This decision virtually annulled the power of Henry as commander-in-chief. The clause of the ordinance of convention which authorized the committee to direct military movements is the following:—

"*And whereas* it may be necessary for the public security that the forces to be raised by virtue of this ordinance should, as occasion may require, be marched to different parts of the colony, and that the officers should be subject to a proper control,—

"*Be it ordained by the authority aforesaid*, That the officers and soldiers under such command shall, in all things not otherwise particularly provided for by this ordinance and the articles established for their regulation, be under the control and subject to the order of the general committee of safety."*

It could hardly be said of Woodford and his men that they were marched to a different part of the colony; he and Colonel Henry were still in the same quarter of Virginia, and not far apart. For so numerous a body as the convention, or even the committee of safety, to assume all the functions of the commander-in-chief, was incompatible with the unity, secrecy, and promptitude demanded in the conduct of war. If not, of what advantage was the appointment of a commander-in-chief at all? If the committee, by such a construction of their powers, could virtually annul the authority of the commander-in-chief, he, whose powers were at the least as ample as theirs, might, by a like construction, have repudiated their authority. The conduct of the committee toward Colonel Henry was strongly censured by the people as well as the troops, and they imputed it to personal envy.† Those, however, who approved of the committee's course, attributed it to a want of confidence in Colonel Henry, as deficient in military

---

* Journal of the Convention of 1775. † Wirt's Henry, 178.

experience.* Other mortifications were in store for the man of the people.

Shortly after the battle of the Great Bridge the Provincials, under Howe, took possession of Norfolk, encamped there in the "Town Camp."

---

* And perhaps as unduly familiar with the men under his command. As an instance of this it is said that he was seen among them with his coat off—a grave charge indeed!

CHAPTER LXXXVI.
1775.

Manufacture of Gunpowder—Norfolk burnt—Dunmore's conduct—Henry resigns—Indignation of troops—Troops at Williamsburg—General Orders.

ON Christmas day, 1775, Benjamin Harrison, Jr., having leave of absence from the convention for three days, at the Lower Ferry, on Chickahominy River, was conferring with Jacob Rubsamen, in his broken English, in regard to the manufacture of saltpetre; he having been sent on by the Virginia delegates in congress to superintend the manufacture of gunpowder. Mr. Harrison's father and himself were disposed to "be dabbling in the saltpetre way." Rubsamen afterwards manufactured much saltpetre and powder in Virginia, and was involved in no little trouble in the work, and in getting paid for it.

On the twenty-eighth of December Edmund Pendleton writes to Richard Henry Lee: "If the house of Bourbon mean to join us it will be soon, lest the progress of the enemy should make our connection less valuable by the destruction of our commercial cities."

Dunmore's fleet being distressed for provisions, upon the arrival of the Liverpool man-of-war from England, a flag was sent on shore to enquire whether the inhabitants would supply his majesty's ship? It was answered in the negative; and the ships in the harbor being continually annoyed by a fire from the quarter of the town lying next the water, Dunmore determined to dislodge the assailants. Previous notice having been given to the inhabitants, January the 1st, 1776, a party of sailors and marines landed, and set fire to the nearest houses. The party was covered by a cannonade from the Liverpool frigate, two sloops-of-war, and the governor's armed ship, the Dunmore. A few were killed and wounded on both sides.

A printer's press had been removed from Norfolk some time before this on board the governor's ship, and according to his

(639)

bulletin published after this affair, it was only intended to destroy that part of the town next the water. But the provincials, strongly prejudiced against the place as a harbor for tories, made no attempts to arrest the flames. After four-fifths of the town were destroyed, Colonel Howe, who had waited on the convention to urge the necessity of completing the destruction, returned with orders to that effect, which were immediately carried into execution. Thus fell the most populous and flourishing town in Virginia. Its rental amounted to $44,000, and the total loss was estimated at $1,300,000. It is said that alone of all the civil and military leaders of the colony, General Andrew Lewis opposed the order for burning Norfolk.

In February, the North Carolina provincials defeated the royalists at Moore's Creek Bridge. This well-timed and vigorous blow intimidated the tories, and animated the patriots with new ardor.

Dunmore continued to carry on a predatory warfare on the rivers, burning houses and plundering plantations, and had now rendered himself the object of general execration.

During February John Page wrote to Richard Henry Lee: "I have been always of your opinion with respect to our present commander-in-chief. All orders do pass through him, and we really wish to be in perfect harmony with him." The convention of Virginia having raised six additional regiments, solicited congress to take the Virginia troops on continental establishment. That body, doubtless misled by the intrigues of the same cabal which had already virtually deprived Colonel Henry of his command, resolved to take the six *new* regiments, passing by the first two, so as to exclude Colonel Henry from the chief command, to which he was best entitled. The convention of Virginia, however, interposing at this point, remonstrated against the degradation of the officers of their first choice, and earnestly requested congress, should it adhere to the determination of taking only six regiments into continental pay, to allow the two first raised to stand first in the new arrangement. This request was nominally agreed to, but at the same time when a commission of colonel was forwarded to him, commissions of brigadier-general were forwarded to Colonel Howe and Colonel Andrew Lewis. A commission, dated at Philadelphia, February the 13th, 1776, appointing Colonel Henry to the command of the first Virginia regiment taken upon the continental establishment, was forwarded by congress to the committee of safety.

Colonel Henry felt himself compelled by every sentiment of self-respect to refuse it, and immediately resigned that which he held from the state. The troops encamped at Williamsburg, upon hearing of his resignation, went into mourning, and being under arms, waited on him at his lodgings on the last day of February. In their address they deplored his withdrawal from the army, but applauded his just resentment at "a glaring indignity." Colonel Henry in replying said: "This kind testimony of your regard to me would have been an ample reward for services much greater than those I have had the power to perform." "I leave the service, but I leave my heart with you. May God bless you, and give you success and safety, and make you the glorious instrument of saving our country." In the evening they assembled tumultuously, and unwilling to serve under any other commander, demanded their discharge. Colonel Henry felt himself obliged to defer his departure a while, and he, who was in the following year accused of a desire to make himself dictator, now visited the barracks, and employed his eloquence in allaying these alarming commotions.

Washington, in a letter to Joseph Reed, dated March the seventh, wrote: "I think my countrymen made a capital mistake when they took Henry out of the senate to place him in the field, and pity it is that he does not see this, and remove every difficulty by a voluntary resignation." Mr. Reed, in his reply, dated at Philadelphia, said to Washington: "We have some accounts from Virginia that Colonel Henry has resigned in disgust at not being made a general officer; but it rather gives satisfaction than otherwise, as his abilities seem better calculated for the senate than the field." In the same letter Mr. Reed wrote: "It is said the Virginians are so alarmed with the idea of independence that they have sent Mr. Braxton on purpose to turn the vote of that colony, if any question on that subject should come before congress." Mr.

Reed himself had entertained strong misgivings on the question of independence.

During this month Colonel Henry was addressed by ninety officers at Kemp's Landing, at Suffolk, in Colonel Woodford's camp, and at Williamsburg. In this address they said: "We join with the general voice of the people, and think it our duty to make this public declaration of our high respect for your distinguished merit. To your vigilance and judgment as a senator this united continent bears ample testimony, while she prosecutes her steady opposition to those destructive ministerial measures which your eloquence first pointed out and taught to resent, and your resolution led forward to resist." "We have the fullest confidence in your abilities and the rectitude of your views; and however willing the envious may be to undermine an established reputation, we trust the day will come when justice shall prevail, and thereby secure you an honorable and happy return to the glorious employment of conducting our councils and hazarding your life in the defence of your country." The imputation of envy was aimed at the committee of safety as a body, or what is more probable, at some individual or individuals of it, who were believed to be the secret authors of that series of indignities which had driven Colonel Henry from military life.* The people regarded the indignities shown to their favorite as an effort to pinion the eagle, whose adventurous wing had launched into the storm and cuffed the tempestuous clouds, while others sat crouching in their conservative nests, mute and thunderstruck.

In the mean time the troops remained quartered at Williamsburg.† In a general order issued in March the soldiers were called

---

* Wirt's Life of Patrick Henry, 206.
† GENERAL ORDERS.—*Williamsburg, Headquarters, March 19th*, 1776.

March 23. "The officers are desired to examine strictly into their respective companies that no gaming be carried on of any kind whatsoever. When there is any leisure time from their duties of the camp, every one will be improving himself in the military service, and not pass over in idleness, or business of a worse tendency, the peaceable and precious hours now on hand. The officers will in every respect attend to the morals of their men, and endeavor to train the youths under their particular care, as well in a moral as in a military way of life."

March 27. "The grand squad to turn out at three o'clock on the parade, if

upon to devote themselves to their duty, to exert themselves in learning the necessary discipline, to respect the persons and property of their fellow-citizens; and the officers were exhorted to fit themselves and the men for the high trust of defending the property and liberty of their country.

---

the weather will permit; the awkward squad to turn out at seven o'clock in the forenoon, likewise at three in the afternoon, and to exercise for two hours each time, under the direction of a commissioned officer, sergeant, and corporal, who are accountable for any neglect of duty in management of that squad; those captains who have any awkward men, or men without arms, are to apply to the commanding officer for an order for such arms in the magazine as will do to exercise with, and to be answerable for their return when called for. Captain Cabell's company to draw ammunition to-day for the trial of their rifles to-morrow, between the hours of eight and ten in the forenoon. The men are to provide a target to-day."

R. O. "All the gentlemen cadets* are desired to attend the parade constantly; likewise a list of their names, to be given in to the colonel to-morrow forenoon, specifying the time of their entering, and with what captain. The colonel has thought proper to appoint Matthew Snook as fife-major, and William Croker as drum-major; and they are to be obeyed as such, and are to practice the young fifers and drummers between the hours of ten and eleven o'clock every day, and take care that they perform their several duties with as much exactness as possible. The officers and cadets are to give in their names as is directed in the foregoing orders. A regimental court-martial to sit at twelve o'clock, for the trial of John Hogins, of Captain Massie's company. Captain Johnston, president. Members, Lieutenant Hobson, Lieutenant Burton, Ensign Stokes, Ensign Armistead. Officer for the day, to-morrow, Captain Cabell. Officers for the guard to-morrow, Lieutenant Jones, Lieutenant Garland, Ensign Catlett. Captain Ruffin to find one cadet and fourteen privates." Extracted from MS. Orderly Book, obligingly lent me by Mr. John M. West, of Petersburg.

---

* A cadet was a young man serving in the ranks without pay, in the hope of obtaining a commission.

CHAPTER LXXXVII.

1776.

Patrick Henry, Delegate to Convention—Convention at Williamsburg—Pendleton, President—Corbin's Petition—Wormley's Petition—Nelson's Letter urging Independence—Braxton's Pamphlet—Delegates in Congress instructed to propose Independence—Declaration of Rights—Constitution—Patrick Henry, Governor—George Mason—Miscellaneous.

IMMEDIATELY upon his return to Hanover, Mr. Henry was elected a delegate to the convention which was soon to meet. In a letter, dated April twentieth, Richard Henry Lee exhorted him to propose a separation from Great Britain.*

The convention met on the 6th of May, 1776, at Williamsburg. Edmund Pendleton was nominated by Richard Bland, for the post of president, and the nomination was seconded by Archibald Cary; Thomas Ludwell Lee was nominated by Thomas Johnson, of Louisa, and seconded by Bartholomew Dandridge. Mr. Lee's nomination, made by Mr. Henry's warm supporters, indicates the dissatisfaction felt toward Mr. Pendleton. The last mentioned gentleman, who was admirably qualified for the place, was elected; by what vote is not known. In his address he reminded the convention that the administration of justice, and almost all the powers of government, had now been suspended for nearly two years; and he called on them to reflect whether they could in that situation longer sustain the struggle in which they were engaged. Having suggested certain subjects for their consideration, he exhorted them to be composed, unanimous, and diligent.

John Goodrich, Jr., a suspected person, was confined, by order of the convention, to his room, in Williamsburg, under guard. The court of commissioners for Gloucester having found John Wilkie guilty of giving intelligence to the enemy, his estate was

---

* Convention of '76, p. 8, in note.

confiscated, and Sir John Peyton, Baronet, appointed commissioner to put the proceeds into the treasury. John Tayloe Corbin presented a petition setting forth that in October, 1775, a time when all America, as well in congress as in conventions, was avowing loyalty to the king, he wrote a letter to Charles Neilson, Esq., of Urbanna, who was going to Norfolk, in consequence of which he had been arrested by military warrant, and was now confined in the guard-house. The convention ordered that for the present he should be confined to his room in Williamsburg, under guard. Shortly after he was ordered to be confined to the region between the Matapony and the Pamunkey in Caroline, and give bond in the penalty of ten thousand pounds.

Ralph Wormley, in a petition, apologised for a letter which he had written to Lord Dunmore, communicating his opinions on the state of affairs, and which had excited the indignation of the country against him; declared that he had ever disclaimed parliament's right of taxation over this continent, but that it was his misfortune to differ in sentiments from the mode adopted to obtain a renunciation of that unconstitutional claim, praying to be released from confinement, submitting to the mercy of his country, and promising in future to conduct himself in conformity with the ordinances of the convention. He was ordered to confine himself to Berkley County, and that part of his father's estate which lay in Frederick, and to give a bond with a penalty of ten thousand pounds.

On the eighth Thomas Nelson, Jr., addressed a letter to a member of the convention, in which he says: "Since our conversation, yesterday, my thoughts have been sorely employed on the great question, whether independence ought, or ought not, to be immediately declared? Having weighed the arguments on both sides, I am clearly of opinion that we must, as we value the liberties of America, or even her existence, without a moment's delay, declare for independence. If my reasons appear weak, you will excuse them for the disinterestedness of the author, as I may venture to affirm that no man on this continent will sacrifice more than myself by the separation." He combats the objection that the sentiments of France and Spain should be ascertained previously; because there was reason to hope that their sentiments would be favorable, and because at any rate, in the perilous situation of the colonies, the hazard must be ventured on. France could not fail to understand that the breaking up of the English monopoly of the American trade would enure to her own benefit. The fear that France might be diverted from an alliance by an offer of partition from Great Britain, appeared chimerical, and contrary to the settled policy of the court of Louis the Sixteenth. In any case delay in declaring independence would be ruinous, as without it the soldiers, disheartened, would abandon their colors. Mr. Nelson in conclusion adds: "I can assure you, sir, that the spirit of the people, (except a very few in these lower parts, whose little blood has been sucked out by mosquitoes,) cry out for this declaration. The military in particular, men and officers, are outrageous on the subject; and a man of your excellent discernment need not be told how dangerous it would be in our present circumstances to dally with the spirit, or disappoint the expectations of the bulk of the people.

About this time there was published, at Philadelphia, a pamphlet, by Carter Braxton, entitled "An Address to the Convention of the Colony and Ancient Dominion of Virginia on the subject of Government." It was looked upon as expressing the views of "the little junto from whence it proceeded," and was denounced in a letter by Richard Henry Lee as exhibiting "confusion of ideas, aristocratic pride, contradictory reasoning with evident ill design."

On the fifteenth of May Archibald Cary reported, from the committee of the whole house, a preamble and resolutions which were unanimously adopted. The preamble recited how all the efforts of the colonies to bring about a reconciliation with Great Britain, consistently with the constitutional rights of America, had produced only additional insults and new acts of oppression; and it recapitulated these acts. The first resolution instructed the Virginia delegates in congress to propose to that body "to declare the United Colonies free and independent states;" the second ordered the appointment of a committee to prepare "a declaration of rights," and a plan of government. The preamble and resolutions were drawn up by Edmund Pendleton, offered in committee of the whole house by Thomas Nelson, Jr., and supported by the eloquence of Patrick Henry.* On the next day the resolutions were read to the troops quartered at Williamsburg, under command of General Andrew Lewis; a *feu de joie* was fired amid the acclamations of the people, and the union flag of the American States waved from the capitol, and in the evening Williamsburg was illuminated.

Patrick Henry in a letter, dated at Williamsburg, May twentieth, wrote to Richard Henry Lee: "The grand work of forming a constitution for Virginia is now before the convention, where your love of equal liberty and your skill in public counsels might so eminently serve the cause of your country. Perhaps I'm mistaken, but I fear too great a bias to aristocracy prevails among the opulent. I own myself a democratic on the plan of our admired friend, J. Adams, whose pamphlet I read with great pleasure. A performance from Philadelphia is just come here, ushered in, I'm told, by a colleague of yours, B——, and greatly recommended by him. I don't like it. Is the author a whig? One or two expressions in the book make me ask. I wish to divide you and have you here to animate, by your manly eloquence, the sometimes drooping spirits of our country, and in congress to be the ornament of your native country, and the vigilant, determined foe of tyranny. To give you colleagues of kindred sentiments is my wish. I doubt you have them not at present. A confidential account of the matter to Colonel Tom,† desiring him to use it according to his discretion, might greatly serve the public and vindicate Virginia from suspicions. Vigor, animation, and all the powers of mind and body must now be summoned and collected together into one grand effort. Moderation, falsely so called, hath nearly brought on us final ruin. And to see those who have so fatally advised us still guiding, or at least sharing our public councils, alarms me."‡

There was an apprehension felt by some at this time lest England, in order to prevent France from assisting the colonies, should offer to divide them with her. Patrick Henry in the same

---

* These facts were stated by Edmund Randolph in his address at the funeral of Pendleton. (*Grigsby's Convention of* '76, p. 203.)

† Thomas Nelson, Jr.   ‡ *S. Lit. Messenger*, 1842, p. 260.

letter wrote to Richard Henry Lee: "Ere this reaches you our resolution for separating from Britain will be handed you by Colonel Nelson. Your sentiments as to the necessary progress of this great affair correspond with mine. For may not France, ignorant of the great advantages to her commerce we intend to offer, and of the permanency of that separation which is to take place, be allured by the partition you mention? To anticipate, therefore, the efforts of the enemy by sending instantly American ambassadors to France, seems to me absolutely necessary. Delay may bring on us total ruin. But is not a confederacy of our states previously necessary?" His comprehensive eye glanced from the fisheries of the north to the Mississippi and western lands. "Notwithstanding solicitations from every great land company to the west, I've refused to join them. I think a general confiscation of royal and British property should be made. The fruits would be great, and the measure in its utmost latitude warranted by the late act of parliament."

In the convention a committee of thirty-four, Archibald Cary being chairman, were appointed to prepare a declaration of rights and a plan of government. The declaration was reported and adopted on the fifteenth of June, and the plan of government on the twenty-ninth, (five days in advance of the declaration of independence of the United Colonies,)—both by a unanimous vote. The declaration of rights and constitution were draughted by George Mason.

George Mason, first of the family in Virginia, had been a member of parliament in England, and, at the breaking out of the civil wars, had sided with King Charles the First, although, like Falkland, not wholly approving his course, organized a military corps, and fought on the royal side until the overthrow at Worcester. After this catastrophe he came over to Virginia and landed in Norfolk County, (1651,) and was soon followed by his family. He removed to Acohick Creek, on the Potomac. He commanded (1676) a volunteer force against the Indians, and in the same year represented the County of Stafford in the assembly, being a colleague of the author of "T. M.'s Account of Bacon's Rebellion," who was probably Thomas Matthews, son of Samuel Matthews, some time Governor of Virginia. The County of Stafford had been carved out of Westmoreland in the preceding year, and was so called by Colonel Mason in honor of his native county of Staffordshire, England. His eldest son, George, married Mary, daughter of Gerard Fowke, of Gunston Hall, in that English county. Their eldest son, George Mason, third of the name, also lived in Acohick, and lies buried there. George Mason, fourth in descent, and eldest son of George, last named, married a daughter of Stevens Thomson, of the Middle Temple, attorney-general of Virginia in the reign of Queen Anne. He resided at Doeg Neck, on the Potomac, then in Stafford, now in Fairfax, and was* lieutenant and chief commander of Stafford. He was drowned by the upsetting of a sail-boat in the Potomac. He left two sons and a daughter. One of the sons was George, author of the constitution of Virginia, and the other, Thomson Mason, a member of the house of burgesses, an eminent lawyer, and true patriot. He was elected one of the judges of the first general court. He suffered from the gout, and one of Governor Tazewell's earliest recollections is the having seen him carried into court when laboring under that disease. His son, Stevens Thomson Mason, was a member of the Virginia Convention of 1788, and United States Senator, and his son, Armistead Thomson Mason, was also a Senator of the United States from Virginia. George Mason, fifth of the name, was born at Doeg's Neck in 1726; he married Ann Eilbeck, of Charles County, Maryland, and built a new mansion on the high banks of the Potomac, and called it Gunston Hall.

George Mason was, in 1776, fifty years of age. His complexion was swarthy, his face grave, with a radiant dark eye, his raven hair sprinkled with gray; his aspect rather foreign; nearly six feet in stature, of a large athletic frame, and active step.† His presence was commanding, his bearing lofty. He was fond of hunting and angling. He was a systematic, wealthy, and prosperous planter; indifferent to the temptations of political ambition; devoting his leisure to study. Mr. Madison pronounced him the ablest man in debate that he had ever seen.

---

* 1719.

† His portrait is preserved, and a copy of it is in the hall of the Historical Society in Richmond.

Although a warm adherent of the house of Hanover, and at the first averse to independence, yet he assumed the boldest position and maintained it. In the year 1766 he concluded a letter to the London merchants, on the repeal of the stamp act, thus: "These are the sentiments of a man who spends most of his time in retirement, and has seldom meddled in public affairs; who enjoys a moderate but independent fortune, and, content with the blessings of a private station, equally disregards the smiles and the frowns of the great. His pamphlet entitled "Extracts from the Virginia Charters, with some Remarks upon them," was considered a masterly exposition of the rights of the colonies.*

Of Mr. Mason's sons, George, the eldest, sixth of the name, was captain in the Virginia line of the Revolution, and inherited Gunston Hall. The fourth son was the late General John Mason, of Analostan Island, near Washington City. The Honorable James Murray Mason, United States Senator for Virginia, is a son of the last named.†

The preamble to the constitution, containing a recital of wrongs, was from the pen of Mr. Jefferson, who was at that time attending the session of congress at Philadelphia.‡ George Mason, the author of the first written constitution of a free commonwealth ever framed, was pre-eminent in an age§ of great men for his extensive information, enlarged views, profound wisdom, and the pure simplicity of his republican principles.|| As a speaker he was devoid of rhetorical grace, but earnest and impressive.

Immediately upon the adoption of the constitution, the salary of the governor was fixed at one thousand pounds per annum, and Patrick Henry, Jr., was elected the first republican Governor of Virginia, he receiving sixty votes, and Thomas Nelson, Sr., forty-

---

* Convention of '76, p. 157 † Ibid., 156, in note.

‡ Journal of Convention of 1776; Wirt's Henry, 195; Grigsby's Convention of '76, p. 19.

§ Patrick Henry in a letter to Richard Henry Lee, dated December 18th, 1777, quoted in Grigsby's Convention of 1776, p. 142, in note, states that there was opposition; but the vote appears unanimous on the journal. The persons who opposed it were known, but were so few they did not think fit to divide the house, or contradict the general voice. Ibid., 161, in note. The same persons subsequently opposed the confederation.

|| His statue is to stand on the monument in Richmond.

five. Mr. Henry received an address from the two regiments which he had recently commanded, congratulating him upon his "unsolicited promotion to the highest honors a grateful people can bestow," and they declared, as they had been once happy under his military command, they hoped for more extensive blessings from his civil administration.

The newly-appointed governor closed his reply by saying: "I trust the day will come when I shall make one of those that will hail you among the triumphant deliverers of America." The first council appointed under the new constitution consisted of John Page, Dudley Digges, John Tayloe, John Blair, Benjamin Harrison of Berkley, Bartholomew Dandridge, Thomas Nelson, Sr., and Charles Carter, of Shirley. Mr. Nelson declining the appointment on account of infirm old age, his place was supplied by Benjamin Harrison, of Brandon. It is a remarkable instance of the vicissitudes of fortune, that "a certain Patrick Henry, Jr.," against whom Governor Dunmore had so lately fulminated his angry proclamation, now came to be the occupant of the palace at Williamsburg as governor and commander-in-chief. Although the leaders of the conservative party looked at the contest with Great Britain in a very different light from that in which it was viewed by the movement and popular party, and although the animating motives of the two were so different, yet in the face of imminent common danger they conspired with extraordinary unanimity in the common cause. So the mainmast of a ship of the line, though composed of several pieces banded together, is stronger than if made of a single spar.*

---

* Extract from Orderly Book:—
"WILLIAMSBURG, May, 14th, 1776.
"Parole—Liberty.

"The many applications for furloughs make it necessary for Brigadier-General Lewis to mention in orders as improper in our critical situation, and hopes that no request of this kind for the future, until circumstances will admit, will be made.

"Officer for day to-morrow, Lieutenant-Colonel McClenahan. Officers for guard, Lieutenant Garland, Ensign Barksdale. For guard, 8 p. 1 s. 1 c."

"WILLIAMSBURG, May 17th, 1776.
"Parole—Convention.

"Let it not be forgot that this day is set apart for humiliation, fasting, and prayer: the troops to attend divine service."

CHAPTER LXXXVIII.
1776.

Richard Henry Lee moves a Resolution for a Separation—Seconded by John Adams—Declaration of Independence—Jefferson—General Orders—Thomas Nelson, Jr., and the Nelsons—Benjamin Harrison, Jr., and the Harrisons—George Wythe.

ON the 7th day of June, 1776, a resolution in favor of a total and immediate separation from Great Britain was moved in congress by Richard Henry Lee, and seconded by John Adams. On the twenty-eighth a committee was appointed to prepare a declaration of independence, the members being Thomas Jefferson, John Adams, Benjamin Franklin, and Robert R. Livingston. Richard Henry Lee being compelled, by the illness of Mrs. Lee, to leave congress on the day of the appointment of the committee, and to return to Virginia, his place was filled by Roger Sherman. The declaration, adopted on the 4th day of July, 1776, was composed, in committee, mainly by Mr. Jefferson, but much modified by congress. The Virginia delegates who subscribed it were George Wythe, Richard Henry Lee, Thomas Jefferson, Benjamin Harrison, Jr., of Berkley, Thomas Nelson, Jr., Francis Lightfoot Lee, and Carter Braxton.*

---

* Extracts from Orderly Book:—

"SPRING FIELD, July 17th, 1776.

"General Lewis hopes that the reports of some of the officers gaming to excess is without foundation: he begs that the field-officers will make diligent enquiry into it, and if true, to arrest such officers, that a total stop may be put to so infamous practices.

"Officer for the day LIEUTENANT-COLONEL WEEDON."

"SPRING FIELD, July 24th, 1776.

"The Declaration of Independency is to be proclaimed to-morrow in the City of Williamsburg, by order of the council, when all the troops off duty are to attend."

"WILLIAMSBURG, July 26th, 1776.

"Parole—Stephen.

"A fatigue of one captain, two subalterns, two sergeants, and sixty rank and file, to be warned from the College Camp, to carry on the work intended to be thrown up on the road to Jamestown.

Thomas Nelson, Jr., eldest son of the Honorable William Nelson, some time president of the council of Virginia, was born at York, in December, 1738. His mother was of the family of Burwell. After having been under the tuition of the Rev. Mr. Yates, of Gloucester, he was sent at the age of fifteen to England, where he remained seven years, for the completion of his education. He enjoyed the superintending care of Dr. Porteus,* and was at the school of Dr. Newcome, at Hackney, at Eton in 1754, and at Cambridge. While on his voyage returning to Virginia he was elected (1774) a member of the house of burgesses, being then just twenty-one years of age.† He was a member of the conventions of 1774 and 1775, and displayed extraordinary boldness in opposing the British tyranny. He was afterwards appointed colonel of a Virginia regiment. In 1775 and 1776 he was a member of Congress. There is a fine portrait of him still preserved, taken, it is said, while he was a student at Eton, (by an artist named Chamberlin, London, 1754,) the only portrait of him for which he ever sat.‡

The first of the Nelsons of Virginia was Thomas, son of Hugh and Sarah Nelson, of Penrith, Cumberland County, England. This Thomas Nelson was born in February, 1677, and died in October, 1745, aged sixty-eight. He married, first, a Miss Reid, secondly, a widow Tucker. Coming from a border county, he was styled "Scotch Tom." He was an importing merchant. Yorktown was in his day, and for a long time, the chief sea-port town of Virginia. Of his two sons, Thomas being long secretary of the council, was known as Secretary Nelson. Three of his sons were officers in the army of the Revolution.

William, the other son of the first Thomas Nelson, imported goods not only for Virginia, but at times for Baltimore, and even

---

"Colonel Buckner will please to order a fatigue proportioned to his number of men, to work on the road from Burwell's Ferry to Williamsburg, at such a place as he shall judge proper to fortify. One company of the second regiment to take post to-morrow at Mr. Burwell's, to erect a work at the mouth of King's Creek. The rest of the second regiment to march to-morrow to Mr. Digges's, to fortify there."

* He afterwards sent, by Parson Bracken, a volume of his sermons, a present to young Nelson. The parson liked them so well that he preached them all before he delivered the book.

† Old Churches, of Va., i. 207.

‡ His statue is to stand on the monument in Richmond.

Philadelphia. Negroes were a principal subject of importation; merchants and planters of chief note, some of them leading men in the colony, and patrons of the church, engaged in it; and no odium appears to have been attached to a business in which British capital was so largely interested, which was so constantly encouraged and protected by the British government, and which had been so long an established feature of the colonial system, and so generally concurred in. John Newton, while personally engaged in the slave-trade on board of a Guinea ship, appears to have entertained at the time no scruples whatever on the subject of his employment. It is no matter of surprise that a Virginia consignee of slaves should have received them with a like indifference.

William Nelson married a Miss Burwell, a granddaughter of King Carter. Having been long president of the council, and at one time acting governor, he came to be known by the title of President Nelson. He died in November, 1772, aged sixty-one, leaving an ample estate. His sons were Thomas, Hugh, William, Nathaniel, and Robert. A daughter, Betsy, married, in 1769, Captain Thompson, of his majesty's ship Ripon, which brought over Lord Botetourt. The portion descending to Thomas, oldest son of President Nelson, and who had been associated in business with him, was estimated at forty thousand pounds.

Benjamin Harrison, Jr., of Berkley, was descended from ancestors who were among the early settlers of Virginia. Hermon Harrison came to Virginia in the second supply, as it was called. One of the name was governor of Bermuda. John Harrison was governor of Virginia in 1623. The common ancestor of the Harrisons of Berkley and of Brandon, was Benjamin Harrison, of Surrey. He lies buried in the yard of an old chapel near Cabin Point, in that county.*

---

* The following is his epitaph:—

"Here lyeth
the body of the
Hon. Benjamin Harrison, Esq.,
who did justice, loved mercy, and walked humbly with his God;
was always loyal to his prince,
and a great benefactor to his country.
He was born in this parish the 20th day of September, 1645, and departed this life the 30th day of January, 1712-13."

It was long believed that the Harrisons of Virginia were lineally descended from Colonel John Harrison, the regicide and friend of Cromwell, and one of the noblest spirits in a heroic age. This tradition, however, appears to be erroneous. The first of the family in Virginia, of whom we have any particular record, was the Honorable Benjamin Harrison, of Surrey, who was born in that county in 1645, during the civil war in England. It is certain that he could not have been a son of Colonel Harrison, the regicide. He may have been a collateral relation.

The first Benjamin Harrison (of Surrey) had three sons, of whom Benjamin, the eldest, settled at Berkley. He married Elizabeth, daughter of Louis Burwell, of Gloucester; was a lawyer, and speaker of the house of burgesses. He died in April, 1710, aged thirty-seven, leaving an only son, Benjamin, and an only daughter, Elizabeth.

Benjamin Harrison, Jr., of Berkley, was educated at William and Mary; married a daughter of Robert Carter, of Corotoman;* and was for many years a burgess for his native county, Charles City. In 1764 he was one of the committee chosen to prepare an address to the king, a memorial to the lords, and a remonstrance to the commons, in opposition to the stamp act. Like Pendleton, Bland, and others, he opposed Henry's resolutions of the following year. He was a member of the committee of correspondence, and of all the conventions held before the organization of the republican government. He opposed Henry's resolutions for putting the colony in a posture of defence, but was appointed one of the committee chosen to carry them into effect. He was elected, in 1774, a delegate to the first congress, of which his brother-in-law, Peyton Randolph, (who married Elizabeth Harrison,) was president. In February, 1776, he remarked in that body: "We have hobbled on under a fatal attachment to Great Britain. I felt it as much as any man, but I feel a stronger for my country." As chairman of the committee of the whole house, Mr. Harrison, on the 10th of June, 1776, introduced the resolution declaring the independence of the colonies, and on the

---

* Two daughters of this union were killed at Berkley by the same flash of lightning: a third married a Randolph, of Wilton.

fourth day of July he reported the Declaration of Independence, of which he was a signer. He was six feet in stature, corpulent, and of a florid complexion. He was practical, energetic, frank, epicurean, gouty, good-humored, fearless, and patriotic.*

The sons of the first Benjamin Harrison, of Berkley, were Benjamin, signer of the Declaration; Charles, a general of the Revolution; Nathaniel, Henry, Collier, and Carter H. From the last-mentioned are descended the Harrisons of Cumberland. Benjamin Harrison, Jr., the signer, married a Miss Bassett. Their children were Benjamin, Carter, Bassett, member of congress, and William Henry, President of the United States. One daughter married a Mr. Richardson, a second married first William Randolph, of Wilton, and then Captain Richard Singleton; a third married David Copeland, and a fourth married John Minge, of Weyanoke, afterwards of Sandy Point. So far the Berkley branch of the Harrisons.

The second son of Benjamin Harrison, of Surrey, was Nathaniel. His eldest son was of the same name, and his only son was Honorable Benjamin Harrison, of Brandon, of the council at the same time with his relative and namesake of Berkley at the commencement of the Revolution. This Benjamin Harrison, of Brandon, was father of the late George Harrison, and of William B. Harrison, of Brandon.

George Wythe was born in 1726, in Elizabeth City County, Virginia, on the shore of the Chesapeake. From his maternal grandfather, Keith, a Quaker, he inherited a taste for letters. His ancestor, Thomas Wythe, was burgess for that county in 1718. The father of George was a prudent farmer of estimable character.† George, the second son, losing his father at an early age, enjoyed but limited advantages of school education, and his early tuition was principally directed by his mother; and it is related that he acquired a knowledge of the Latin classics from her instructions.‡ Mr. Jefferson mentions that while young Wythe was studying the Greek Testament, his mother held an English one to aid him in the translation. It has been since inferred, from an examination of his manuscripts, that this last

---

* Convention of 1776, p. 96; Allen's Biog. Dictionary.
† Grigsby's Convention of 1776, p. 125.   ‡ Wirt's Patrick Henry, 65.

was the only kind of assistance that he received from her in the Latin and Greek. He studied law under his uncle, John Lewis, of Prince George; but, upon the death of his elder brother and his mother, becoming master of a competent fortune, he fell into habits of idleness and dissipation. Like Swift, however, he was not one who, having wasted part of his life in indolence, was willing to throw away the remainder in despair; and in the society of Governor Fauquier and Professor Small he imbibed their love of learning; and at the age of thirty applied himself unremittedly to study. He became, eventually, distinguished by his attainments in classical literature; and he pursued other studies with a like success. But he often deplored the loss of so many early golden years. His learning, judgment, and industry soon raised him to eminence at the bar. A member of the house of burgesses as early as 1758, he continued in it until the Revolution. At its dawn Mr. Wythe, in common with Thomas Jefferson and Richard Bland, assumed the ground that the crown was the only connecting link between the colonies and the mother country. In 1764 Mr. Wythe was a member of a committee of the house of burgesses appointed to prepare a petition to the king, a memorial to the lords, and a remonstrance to the commons, on the subject of the stamp act. He prepared the remonstrance in conformity with his radical principles; but it was greatly modified by the assembly. In May, 1765, he, in common with Nicholas, Pendleton, Randolph, and Bland, opposed Henry's resolutions as premature. Mr. Wythe likewise voted (March, 1775,) against Henry's resolutions for putting the colony in a posture of defence; but he was in favor of the scheme of Colonel Nicholas for raising a large regular force. Early in 1775 Mr. Wythe joined a corps of volunteers as a private soldier; in August he was elected a member of congress. He was returned by the City of Williamsburg to the convention of that year; but being in attendance on congress his place was filled by Joseph Prentis. Mr. Wythe signed the Declaration of Independence, which he had strenuously supported in debate.* Mr. Wythe married first a

---

* Convention of '76, p. 122. On his return to Virginia toward the close of the session of the convention then sitting, he was appointed one of a committee to prepare devices for a seal of the commonwealth.

Miss Lewis, and secondly a Miss Taliaferro.* He died childless. He is described as being distinguished for integrity, patriotism, and disinterestedness; temperance and regular habits gave him good health; engaging and modest manners endeared him to every one; his bow was one of most expressive courtesy. His elocution was easy, his language chaste, his arrangement lucid; his frequent classic quotations, smacking a little of pedantry; his style, which aimed at the antique, was deficient in elegance and rhythm. Learned, urbane, logical, he was not quick and ready, but solid and profound. He was of middle size, well-formed, his forehead ample, nose aquiline, eye dark gray, expression manly and engaging. His religious opinions were supposed to be skeptical; but the closing scene of his life is said to have been that of a sincere professor of the Christian faith.

---

* Pronounced "Tolliver," originally an Italian name, Tagliaferro.

CHAPTER LXXXIX.

Richard Henry Lee—Francis Lightfoot Lee—Carter Braxton.

RICHARD HENRY LEE, a signer of the Declaration, was born at Stratford, on the Potomac, in Westmoreland, January the 20th, 1732, about a month before the birth of Washington. The father of Richard Henry was Thomas Lee; the mother, Hannah, daughter of Colonel Philip Ludwell, of Greenspring, of the old family of that name, in Somersetshire, England, who were originally, it is said, from Germany. Richard Henry Lee's early days were passed somewhat after the Spartan manner, his mother, one of the high-toned aristocracy of Virginia, confining her care to her daughters and her eldest son, and leaving her younger sons pretty much to shift for themselves. After a course of private tuition in his father's house, Richard Henry was sent to Wakefield Academy, Yorkshire, England, where he distinguished himself by his proficiency in his studies, particularly in the Latin and Greek. Having finished his course at this school, he travelled through England, and visited London. He returned when about nineteen years of age to his native country, two years after his father's death, which occurred in 1750. Young Lee's fortune rendering it unnecessary for him to devote himself to a profession, he now passed a life of ease, but not of indolence; for he indulged his taste for letters, and diligently stored his mind with knowledge in the wide circle of theology, science, history, law, politics, and poetry. Being chosen (1755) captain of a company of volunteers raised in Westmoreland, he marched with them to Alexandria, and offered their services to General Braddock in his expedition against Fort Du Quesne; but the offer was declined. In his twenty-fifth year Mr. Lee was appointed a justice of the peace, and shortly after a burgess for his county. Naturally diffident, and finding himself surrounded by men of extraordinary abilities, for one or two sessions he took no part in the debates. One of his early efforts was a brief, but strong, elaborate speech in support of a resolution "to lay so heavy a tax on the importation of slaves as effectually to put an end to that iniquitous and disgraceful traffic within the colony of Virginia;" and on this occasion he argued against the institution of slavery as a portentous evil, moral and political.*

In November, 1764, when the meditated stamp act was first heard of in America, Mr. Lee, at the instance of a friend, wrote to England making application for the office of a collector under that act. It was difficult to retrieve so unpopular a step. During this year he brought before the assembly the subject of the act of parliament claiming a right to tax America; and he composed the address to the king, and the memorial to the commons. His accomplishments, learning, courtesy, patriotism, republican principles, decision of character and eloquence, commanded the attention of the legislature. Although a member at the time of the introduction of Henry's resolutions of 1765, Mr. Lee happened not to be present at the discussion; but he heartily concurred in their adoption; and shortly after their passage organized an association in Westmoreland in furtherance of them. When the defalcations of Treasurer Robinson came to be suspected, Mr. Lee, like Patrick Henry on another occasion of the same kind, insisted with firmness on an investigation of the state of the treasury. It was he who introduced the motion (November, 1776,) for separating the offices of speaker and treasurer; and he had a principal agency, together with Henry, in carrying that measure into effect.† A fragment of his speech on this occasion is preserved.

In the succeeding year he vigorously opposed the act laying a duty on tea, and that for quartering British troops in the colonies. He was now residing at Chantilly, his seat on the Potomac, a few miles below Stratford. In July, 1768, in a letter to John Dickinson, of Pennsylvania, Mr. Lee suggested that not only select committees should be appointed by all the colonies, but that a private correspondence should be conducted between

---

* Life of Richard Henry Lee, i. 17. † *S. Lit. Messenger*, August, 1858.

the lovers of liberty in every province. The Virginia Assembly, in 1773, (about the same time with that of Massachusetts,) appointed a committee of correspondence, consisting of six members, of whom Mr. Lee was one. In the next year he was a delegate in the congress that met at Philadelphia. Patrick Henry spoke first, and he was followed by Richard Henry Lee.

He was an active and laborious member of the leading committees, and he composed the memorial to the people of British America—a masterly document.* When Washington was chosen commander-in-chief, Mr. Lee, as chairman of the committee chosen for the occasion, prepared the commission and instructions. He prepared the second address to the people of Great Britain.

In May, 1776, the convention of Virginia passed a resolution instructing her delegates in congress to propose to that body to declare the colonies free and independent; and when those instructions were received at Philadelphia, the delegation appointed Mr. Lee to bring forward a proposition to that effect. He accordingly, on the second of June, made that motion, which was seconded by John Adams. On the tenth Mr. Lee received by express, from Virginia, intelligence of the dangerous illness of his wife; and he, therefore, left Philadelphia on the eleventh, the day on which a committee was appointed to draught a declaration of independence. Had he remained he might have been chairman of that committee, and author of the Declaration of Independence.†

That instrument was adopted on the eighth of July, and shortly afterwards Mr. Jefferson enclosed to Mr. Lee the original draught, and also a copy of it as adopted by Congress. In August Mr. Lee resumed his seat in that body.

He was in person tall and well proportioned; his features bold and expressive; nose, Roman; forehead high, not wide; eyes light colored; the contour of his face noble. He had lost by an accident the use of one of his hands; and was sometimes styled "the

---

* To be found in Life of Richard Henry Lee, i. 119.

† See Randall's Jefferson, i., and a review of his opinions on this subject, by Mr. Grigsby, in *Richmond Enquirer* of January 15th, 1858.

gentleman of the silver hand;" he kept it covered with a black silk bandage, but leaving his thumb free. Notwithstanding this disadvantage his gesture was very graceful. His voice was melodious, his elocution Ciceronian, his diction elegant and easy. His eloquence flowed on in tranquil beauty, like the stream of his own Potomac.* He was a member of the Episcopal church. He married first a Miss Aylett, and the children of that union were two sons and two daughters; secondly a lady named Pinkard, a widow.

Francis Lightfoot Lee, brother of Richard Henry, was born in October, 1734. He was educated under a private tutor. He inherited an independent fortune. He became, in 1765, a member of the house of burgesses, and continued in that body until 1775, when the convention returned him a member of congress, in which he remained until 1779, when he re-entered the assembly. His talents, as an orator and statesman, were of a high order, but it appears that he was never able to overcome his natural diffidence. His seat was Monocan, in the County of Richmond. He married Rebecca, daughter of Colonel John Tayloe, of Richmond County.

Carter Braxton was born at Newington, on the Matapony, in King and Queen, in September, 1736. His father, George Braxton, a wealthy planter, married Mary, daughter of Robert Carter, of the council, and in 1748 represented the County of King and Queen, being the colleague of John (known as speaker) Robinson. Carter Braxton was educated at the college of William and Mary. Inheriting in his youth, upon his father's death, a large estate, at the age of nineteen he married Judith, daughter of Christopher Robinson, of Middlesex. She dying, in 1757, Mr. Braxton visited England, where he remained for several years, and returned in 1760: a diary which he kept while abroad is preserved by his descendants. He married, in 1761, Elizabeth, eldest daughter of Richard Corbin, of Laneville. During his first marriage he built a mansion at Elsin Green, on the Pamunkey, and afterwards another at Chericoke on the same river. He lived in a style of lavish hospitality, according to the fashion of

---

* The motto of his arms was: "Haud incautus futuri."

that day. He was, in 1761, a member of the house of burgesses from the County of King William, and took an active part in the session of 1765. His colleague was Bernard Moore, of Chelsea, son-in-law of Governor Spotswood. Mr. Braxton was, in 1769, a delegate and a signer of the non-importation agreement. He was a member of the convention of 1774. In the following year, when Henry at the head of a party of volunteers had advanced within sixteen miles of Williamsburg, for the purpose of recovering the gunpowder removed by Dunmore, Mr. Braxton interposed his efforts to prevent extremities. In this course Mr. Braxton coincided with the moderate councils of Pendleton, Nicholas, and Peyton Randolph. During this year Mr. Braxton was a member of the assembly, and of the convention that met at Richmond. He was also one of the committee of safety. In December he was elected a delegate to congress in the place of Peyton Randolph, and he was a signer of the Declaration of Independence. The convention having, in June, 1776, reduced the number of delegates in congress from seven to five, Mr. Harrison and Mr. Braxton were not re-elected. According to Girardin,* Mr. Braxton's "Address on Government" was not universally relished, (it was indeed severely denounced, as has been seen,) and his popularity had been in some degree impaired by persons whose political indiscretions, though beyond his control, fatally reacted against him. He was, nevertheless, returned by the County of King William a member of the convention, and if he had fallen under a cloud of suspicion, it appears to have been soon dispersed, for, in October, 1776, the thanks of the convention were unanimously returned to Thomas Jefferson and Carter Braxton, for their ability, diligence, and integrity, as delegates in congress.

---

* Burk's Hist. of Va., iv.

CHAPTER XC.

1776.

Dunmore on Gwynn's Island—Driven thence by General Lewis—Dunmore retires from Virginia—Affairs at Boston—Canada invaded—Howe evacuates Boston—Battles of Long Island and White Plains—Fort Washington captured—Washington retreats—Enemy defeated at Trenton and Princeton—Death of Mercer.

DUNMORE, pressed for provisions, burnt his entrenchments, near the smouldering ruins of Norfolk, and sought refuge on board of his fleet. General Charles Lee devised energetic means for curbing the disaffected in the lower country; and his orders were carried into effect by Colonel Woodford, whose vigor was tempered with humanity. Dunmore with his fleet left Hampton Roads about the first of June, and entrenched himself with five hundred men, including many runaway negroes, on Gwynn's Island, in the Chesapeake, to the east of Matthews County, and separated from it by a strait.*

In the evening of July the eighth, General Andrew Lewis, with Colonel Adam Stephen, reached the camp before Gwynn's Island, and during the night a battery was erected. Next morning the enemy's fleet lying within range, the embrasures were unmasked, and a fire opened upon the Dunmore. This ship, after firing a few guns, cut her cables and retreated, towed off by boats, two batteries playing on her. She was damaged, her cabin shattered, and some men killed. Lord Dunmore himself was wounded in the leg by a splinter, and had his china-ware smashed about him, and exclaimed, as was reported: "Good God, that ever I should come to this!" The other vessels did not escape with impunity, and all retired in confusion to a safe distance. The guns of the batteries were now turned upon the enemy's camp, the shot cross-

---

* There is a tradition that Pocahontas, in swimming across the Pyanketank, was near being drowned, and was rescued by one of the colonists, who received from her, or her father, this island as a reward.

ing each other in the centre of it, and the troops were dislodged. On the next morning Lewis, with the aid of some canoes, captured two small armed vessels, and some of his men landing on the island, the look-outs ran exclaiming, "the Shirt-men are coming!" a panic seized Dunmore's men, so that they precipitately evacuated the island, (before two hundred and fifty of the Provincials could be landed on the island,) and the boats of the fleet, consisting of eighty sail, took them on board. They left valuable stores behind, and burnt some vessels. The inhabitants reported that Dunmore had recently received a re-enforcement of one hundred and fifty tories from Maryland, and some cattle. Part of these last fell into Lewis's hands. A detachment was sent to protect the people on the Potomac. Numerous half-covered graves on the island gave proof of the fatality of the place, and the bodies of negroes were found lying unburied. The small-pox was left as a legacy to the island. Among the graves was one neatly done up with turf, which was supposed to cover the remains of Lord Gosport, who had recently died. Ovens, newly erected, and a windmill commenced, made it evident that Lord Dunmore had contemplated a longer stay there. It was reported that he was sick. The negroes, horses, cattle, and furniture of Mr. John Grymes, a tory, fell into possession of the Provincials. Major Byrd, who was sick, upon their approach was conveyed to Cherry Point in a cart, and embarked there. Dunmore shortly afterwards, despatching the remnant of his followers to Florida and the West Indies, retired to the North, and thence returned to England, where he continued to exhibit himself an untiring opponent of America. He entertained hospitably in London the Virginia refugee loyalists Randolph, Grymes, Brockenbrough, Beverley, Wormley, Corbin, and others. Lord Dunmore was appointed (1786) Governor of Bermuda, and died in 1809.

On the 3d of July, 1775, Washington had assumed the command of the American army, encamped near Boston, and had made his headquarters at Cambridge. His first business was to organize, equip, and discipline his force. The British army, blocked up on the land side, remained inactive in Boston, finding itself, although strongly re-enforced, gradually hemmed in and besieged.

In the mean time, in pursuance of the Quebec act, a Canadian force having been marched into the colonies, and it being the manifest design of the enemy to bring down the savages upon the frontier, a detachment was sent to invade Canada. Marching under command of Montgomery, they crossed Lake Champlain, and laid siege to Fort St. Johns, the key to Canada, strengthened by Carleton, the ablest of the British generals, and strongly garrisoned. During this siege a detachment, penetrating further into the country, captured Fort Chamblee, between St. Johns and Montreal. Carleton, marching to the relief of St. Johns, was met and defeated. St. Johns, after a siege of forty-seven days, in a rigorous season, and in a low and wet ground, where the besiegers slept on piles of brush, covered over with weeds, to keep out of the water, surrendered. November the thirteenth Montreal capitulated to the gallant Irishman, General Montgomery. Arnold, accompanied by Morgan and Greene, rubbing through exposure, hardship, and privation, made his way into Canada by the Kennebec and Chaudière Rivers, and was about to unite his forces with Montgomery's. At this time it appeared as if the whole of Canada would probably soon be reduced, and it was confidently expected that Canadian delegates would shortly appear in congress, and complete the union of fourteen colonies. This brilliant prospect was soon overcast; Montgomery fell in a daring but unsuccessful attack upon Quebec. Re-enforcements of American troops were sent to Canada, but owing to their insufficiency in number and in discipline, the rigor of the climate, and the energy of Carleton, the British commander, the expedition eventually proved fruitless in effecting a conquest; and it was found necessary to evacuate that country. While these reverses occurred by land, it was observed with satisfaction that the colonies abounded in materials and resources requisite for building up a naval force; and in some of the colonies vessels were arming. Richard Henry Lee, in a letter to Mrs. McCauley, of England, compared America on the sea, in that year, to "Hercules in his cradle." The American navy was indeed "nursed in the whirlwind and cradled in the storm."

The British army at Boston, admonished by the scenes of Lexington, Concord, and Bunker's Hill, and finding their position more and more restricted by Washington's lines of fortification, remained in gloomy inaction until March, 1776, when Sir William Howe, who had succeeded General Gage, evacuated that city, and sailed with the troops and many unhappy tory refugees to Halifax.

The American army proceeded to New York. Early in July, 1776, Sir William Howe with his army landed on Staten Island. The commander of the fleet was Lord Howe, brother of Sir William, and these two were constituted commissioners for restoring peace. In the battle of Long Island, which occurred on the twenty-seventh of August, the American army, inferior in number, and without cavalry, fought confusedly and badly, and was defeated with heavy loss, variously estimated. Among the prisoners was Major-General Sullivan. The enemy's loss was by no means inconsiderable. From the commencement of the battle on the morning of the twenty-seventh till the morning of the twenty-ninth, Washington never slept, and was almost incessantly on horseback. The disastrous result of this action cast a gloom over the cause of independence, elated disaffection, and damped the ardor of the American troops. The militia in large numbers quit the camp and went home; and Washington was obliged to confess his "want of confidence in the generality of the troops." He urged upon congress the necessity of a permanent army. On the fifteenth of September he was compelled to evacuate New York, with the loss of his heavy artillery and a large part of his stores, and General Howe took possession of the city.

In a skirmish on Haerlem Heights, a detachment of the third Virginia regiment, which had arrived on the preceding day, formed the advanced party in the attack, and Major Leitch, while intrepidly leading them on, fell mortally wounded.

In accordance with Washington's solicitation congress made arrangements to put the army on a better footing. To obviate the movements of the enemy he moved his forces up the Hudson River. On the twenty-fifth of October the battle of White Plains took place, warmly contested, with equal loss, and without decisive result. In November Fort Washington, on the Hudson, was stormed by the British, and the garrison, consisting of twenty-six hundred men, were made prisoners. Washington is said to have shed tears on occasion of this disaster. The enemy's loss was eight hundred. Early in December Washington, finding his army sadly reduced, retreated across Jersey. They were pursued by a British army, numerous, well-appointed, and victorious. At this conjuncture Major-General Lee was surprised and made prisoner—as is now believed—by collusion with the enemy.* The reanimated spirit of disaffection rendered the American cause still more hopeless. December the twentieth, Washington's army on the west bank of the Delaware, augmented by re-enforcements, amounted to seven thousand effectives; but in a few days all of them, except about fifteen hundred men, were to be discharged upon the expiration of the term of enlistment. Washington became convinced that some bold enterprise was necessary to rekindle the patriotic spirit, and listening to the advice of those about him, resolved to strike at the posts of the enemy, who had retired securely into winter quarters. Crossing the Delaware, a few miles above Trenton, in a night of extreme cold, amid floating ice, he early on the morning of the twenty-six surprised there a body of Hessians, and made one thousand prisoners. Lieutenant Monroe, afterwards president, was wounded in this affair. Lieutenant-Colonel Baylor, of Virginia, aid of the commander-in-chief, carrying the intelligence of this success to congress, was presented with a horse caparisoned for service, and was recommended for promotion. Near Princeton another corps was routed with heavy loss; but the joy of the Americans was mingled with grief for the loss of General Mercer.

Hugh Mercer, a native of Scotland, having been graduated in the medical profession, was present, in the capacity of assistant surgeon, at the battle of Flodden, on the side of the vanquished. Escaping, he came to America, and settled at Fredericksburg, in Virginia, where he married, and successfully pursued his profession. During the French and Indian war of 1755 he was a captain under Washington. In an engagement, being wounded in the wrist by a musket ball, separated from his comrades, and

---

* George H. Moore, Esq., librarian of the New York Historical Society, is preparing an interesting memoir on the subject of General Lee's treasonable conduct.

faint with loss of blood, he was closely pursued by the savage foe, whose war-whoop rang through the surrounding forests. Concealing himself in the hollow trunk of a giant tree, he narrowly escaped. After a journey of more than one hundred miles through an untrodden wilderness, and supporting life on roots and the body of a rattlesnake, he finally reached Fort Cumberland. For his gallant conduct the City of Philadelphia presented him an honorary medal. In 1775 he was in command of three regiments of minute-men, and in 1776 a colonel of the Virginia troops, and rendered important services in drilling and organizing the new levies. In quelling a mutiny in a company of riflemen called, ironically, "Gibson's Lambs," at Williamsburg, whom he disarmed, he displayed that intrepidity and decision for which he was so distinguished. During the same year, being made a brigadier-general in the continental army, he exhibited signal courage and energy throughout a disastrous campaign. On the 3d day of January, 1777, this excellent officer, leading the van of Washington's army, encountered, about sunrise, near Princeton, three British regiments, and while rallying his troops his horse was shot from under him, and he fell dangerously wounded, and died shortly afterwards in a small house near the scene of the encounter. He was attended by Major George Lewis, a nephew of General Washington, who had sent him to perform that duty, and by Dr. Rush.

The death of General Mercer forms the subject of a picture long familiar to the students of the college of New Jersey. He lies buried in Christ Church, Philadelphia.

CHAPTER XCI.

1776.

Death of Richard Bland—Genealogy of the Blands—First Assembly under new Government—Petitions against Church establishment—Memorial of Hanover Presbytery—Rev. Caleb Wallace—Petitions in favor of Established Church—Proceedings of Assembly—Alleged scheme of Dictator—Hampden Sidney—Virginia Navy.

On the 26th day of October, 1776, died Richard Bland, at Williamsburg, aged sixty-six. He was in attendance as a member of the house of delegates at its first session, and was struck with apoplexy while walking in the streets. His intellectual calibre was capacious, his education finished, his habits of application indefatigable. Thoroughly versed in the charters, laws, and history of the colony, he was styled the "Virginia Antiquary." He was a political character of the first rank, a profound logician, and as a writer perhaps unsurpassed in the colony.

His letter to the clergy, published in 1760, and his enquiry into the rights of the colonies, are monuments of his patriotism, his learning, and the vigor of his understanding. He was an ungraceful speaker. It is said that he was pronounced by Mr. Jefferson to be "the wisest man south of the James River." He resided at Jordan's Point, on the James, in Prince George. His portrait and that of his wife were mutilated by the bayonets of British soldiers during the revolutionary war.* His wife had died in 1758, aged forty-six years.

The Blands of Virginia derive their name from Bland, a place in or near Lonsdale, in Westmoreland, or Cumberland, England. William de Bland flourished in the reign of Edward the Third, and did good service in the wars which that king carried on in France, in company of John of Gaunt, Earl of Richmond. Thomas de Bland obtained a pardon from Richard the Second,

---

* The name of Bland ought to be given to a county.

for killing his antagonist in a duel, by the intercession of his friend the Duke of Guyenne and Lancaster. The coat of arms of Bland is quartered by the family of Wansford, of Kirklington, in the County of York, afterwards Lord Viscount Castle-Comer, in the kingdom of Ireland; and the family of Thistlewait, of Thistlewait, bear the arms of Bland for their paternal coat as descended from the ancient family of Bland. Edward Bland, of Burfield, died in the reign of Edward the Fourth; from him was descended Adam Bland, who lived in the reign of Edward the Sixth. John Bland was free of the "Grocers and Merchants Adventurers Company." Thomas Bland, receiver of the rents for Yorkshire in the time of Charles the First, married, secondly, Katherine, sister of Sir Richard Sandys, of Northbourne, in Kent. Giles Bland, collector of the customs for James River, owing to a quarrel with Sir William Berkley, became a partisan of Bacon, and was executed during the rebellion. Edward Bland, a merchant in Spain, (1643,) afterwards removed to Virginia, where he lived at Kimages, in Charles City County. Robert Bland was rector of Weyborough-magna, with the chapel of Sale appendant, in the County of Essex. Richard Bland, of the company of "Framework Knitters," was Lord of the manor of Preston Hall, and Lord Mayor of Preston. Theodorick Bland was some time a merchant at Luars in Spain, but came over to Virginia in the year 1654. He settled at Westover, on James River, where he died April 23d, 1671, aged forty-one, and was buried in the chancel of the church which he built, and gave, together with ten acres of land, a court-house and prison, for the county and parish. His tombstone is to be found in Westover churchyard, lying between those of two of his friends; the church has disappeared long ago. This Theodorick Bland was one of the king's council for Virginia, and was both in fortune and understanding inferior to no person of his time in the country. He married the daughter of Richard Bennet, Esq., sometime governor of the colony. Richard Bland, born at Berkley, son of this Theodorick Bland, married, first, Mary, daughter of Colonel Thomas Swan; secondly, Elizabeth, daughter of Colonel William Randolph, of Turkey Island, on James River. Mary Bland, eldest daughter of Richard Bland, gentleman, of Jordans, born 1704, married Colonel Henry

Lee, of Westmoreland. Elizabeth, second daughter of said Richard Bland, married Colonel William Beverley, of Essex County. Theodorick Bland, Sr., of Cawsons, in Prince George, was clerk of that county and member of the house of burgesses. He married Frances Bolling. The children of that union were Theodorick Bland, Jr., and four daughters, Elizabeth, Mary, Anna, and Jenny. Theodorick Bland, Sr., married, secondly, a widow Yates. Theodorick Bland, Jr., was a colonel of a regiment of horse during the revolutionary war, a member of congress, and of the convention of Virginia that ratified the Constitution of the United States. Patsy, daughter of Theodorick Bland, Sr., married Colonel John Banister, of Battersea, near Petersburg, member of the convention of 1776, lieutenant-colonel of cavalry during the war of Revolution, and member of congress. Frances, another daughter of Theodorick Bland, Sr., married John Randolph, of Matoax, and these were the parents of John Randolph, of Roanoke, the orator, who was born at Cawsons, in Prince George County, the residence of Theodorick Bland, Sr. The mother of John Randolph, of Roanoke, married, secondly, St. George Tucker, judge of the court of appeals of Virginia, and subsequently district judge of the federal court.

The Cherokees, instigated by the English, having made bloody incursions on the Virginia frontier, Colonel Christian, with a body of troops, burnt their towns, and compelled them to sue for peace.

On the 7th day of October, 1776, the general assembly of Virginia met for the first time under the constitution adopted in the preceding July. The house of delegates was composed of the same members as those who constituted the convention which framed the constitution, and who held over without an election, and thus became the house of delegates under the constitution of their own making. The examples which probably guided them were, that of the convention of 1660, which, after calling Charles the Second to the throne, resolved itself into a house of commons; and that of the convention of 1688, which, after settling the crown on William and Mary, also resolved itself into a house of commons. The new senate, however, was elected by the people.* Edmund Pendleton was elected speaker of the house, and Archibald Cary speaker of the senate.

The new declaration of rights asserted that "all men are equally entitled to the free exercise of religion according to the dictates of conscience;" yet it appeared that the assembly intended to continue the old church establishment. This and the circulation of petitions in behalf of episcopacy, as established by law, alarmed the dissenters, and they enquired what advantage then in this great point "shall we derive from being independent of Great Britain? And is it not as bad for our assembly to violate their own declaration of rights as for the British parliament to break our charter?" The Baptists accordingly circulated a counter-petition, which was signed by ten thousand persons, chiefly freeholders. The presbytery of Hanover also presented a memorial to the same effect, pledging themselves that nothing in their power should be wanting to give success to the cause of the country. In the frontier counties, containing one-fifth of the inhabitants of Virginia, the dissenters, who constituted almost the entire population, were yet obliged to contribute to the support of the church as established, and a considerable portion of the inhabitants of the other parts of the colony labored under the same disadvantages. "Certain it is," say the memorialists, "that every argument for civil liberty gains additional strength when applied to liberty in the concerns of religion; and there is no argument in favor of establishing the Christian religion but what may be pleaded with equal propriety for establishing the tenets of Mohammed by those who believe the Alcoran; or, if this be not true, it is at least impossible for the magistrate to adjudge the right of preference among the various sects that profess the Christian faith, without erecting a chair of infallibility which would lead us back to the church of Rome." Religious establishments (they contended) are injurious to the temporal interests of any community; and the more early settlement of Virginia, and her natural advantages, would have

---

* I am indebted to Mr. Grigsby for this statement. His opinions on this point are given fully in a review of Randall's Life of Jefferson, in the *Richmond Enquirer* of January 15th, 1858.

attracted hither multitudes of industrious and useful members of society, but they had either remained in their place of nativity, or preferred worse civil governments and a more barren soil, where they might enjoy the rights of conscience more fully. Nor did religion need the aid of an establishment; on the contrary, as her weapons are spiritual, Christianity would flourish in the greatest purity when left to her native excellence; and the duty which we owe our Creator can only be directed by reason and conviction.

This memorial was composed, in behalf of the presbytery, by the Rev. Caleb Wallace, of Charlotte County, a graduate of Princeton. He was in attendance upon the assembly for six or eight weeks for the furthering of this object.*

The clergy of the established church presented petitions in favor of continuing the establishment, and they were re-enforced by the Methodists as a society in communion with the Church of England. It was urged that good faith to the clergy required that they should not be deprived of their livings, which belonged to them for life, or during good behaviour; that an ecclesiastical establishment was in itself a desirable institution, it being for the benefit of the community that a body of Christian ministers should be thus supported; and that if all denominations were reduced to an equality, the contest for superiority among them would involve confusion, and probably civil commotion; and finally that a majority of the people of Virginia desired to have the church establishment maintained.

---

* In a letter addressed to Rev. James Caldwell, of Elizabethtown, New Jersey, April 8th, 1777, he wrote: "I do not know that we have sinned against the King of England, but we have sinned against the King of Heaven; and he is now using Great Britain as the rod of his anger: by them he is executing just judgment against us, and calling us to repentance and humiliation. I also hope He is bringing about great things for His church." He also adds: "An American ought to seek an emancipation from the British King, ministry, and parliament, at the risk of all his earthly possessions of whatever name; nor is it the fear of danger that has prevented my preaching this doctrine in the army at headquarters." "I meddle very little with matters of civil concern, only to countenance the recruiting business, as far as I have it in my power, and sometimes I have a fight with the prejudices—I would rather say the perverseness—of such as are inclining to toryism among us; but we have reason to rejoice that we have few such cattle with us." (*Hist. Mag.*, i. 354.)

The assembly exempted dissenters from contributions for the support of the Church of England, and repealed all penal laws against any mode of worship, leaving all denominations for the present to support their clergy by voluntary contributions, and reserving the consideration "of a general assessment for the support of religion" to a future session, so that the sense of the people on that subject might be, in the mean time, collected.* This matter was debated for a day or two in the house, and gave rise to some newspaper controversy. Religious freedom was gaining ground; but, although all penal statutes were repealed, the restrictions and penalties sanctioned by the common law remained.

In the struggle that preceded the Revolution more than two-thirds of the Virginia clergy of the established church and a portion of the lay members were loyalists. Of those clergymen who adhered to the patriotic side several were men of note, such as Jarratt, Madison, (afterwards the first bishop of Virginia,) Bracken, Muhlenburg, of the Valley of the Shenandoah, who accepted a colonel's commission, raised a regiment, and served throughout the war; and Thruston, who also became a colonel.

Congress having ordered the army to be augmented to eighty-eight battalions, to serve during the continuance of the war, a quota of fifteen battalions was assigned to Virginia; and to complete them the assembly took measures to raise seven battalions in addition to those already embodied. Attention was bestowed upon the building up of a naval force, and men were transferred from the army to the marine service. Infantry and cavalry, speedily raised and well officered, were sent to join General Washington, and measures were adopted for calling forth the resources of Virginia, and to strengthen her for the exigencies of war. Courts of admiralty were established; entails abolished, the bill for this purpose being framed by Mr. Jefferson; treason was defined, and penalties denounced against such as should maintain and defend the authority of the king or parliament, or should excite sedition in the State; importation from Great Britain was prohibited; loyalist British factors were ordered to

---

* Burk's Hist. of Va., iv. 182.

depart from the commonwealth under a statute of twenty-seventh year of Edward the Third.

Governor Henry, owing to the state of his health, retired, with the concurrence of the assembly, to the country. An effort made at this time by David Rogers, a member of the senate, and some other malecontents in West Augusta, to erect themselves into a separate state, proved abortive. Robert C. Nicholas, resigning the office of treasurer, received the thanks of the legislature for his faithful discharge of the duties of his office. He was succeeded by George Webb. The estate of Lord Dunmore was disposed of, and the proceeds appropriated to the payment of his debts.* Jefferson, Pendleton, Wythe, Mason, and Thomas Ludwell Lee were appointed a committee to revise the laws. By the resignation of Mr. Mason, and the indisposition of Mr. Lee, the duty eventually devolved upon the other three.

Congress, with a view of gaining the alliance of France, appointed three commissioners to that court: Benjamin Franklin, Silas Deane, and Thomas Jefferson. Mr. Jefferson declined the appointment, and it was then given to Dr. Arthur Lee.

Toward the close of this session of the Virginia Assembly, when Washington was retreating through the Jerseys, and when the cause of independence seemed almost desperate, several of the members, it is said, meditated, in imitation of the Roman Republic, the appointment of a dictator. The tradition is, that such was the animosity engendered by this scheme, that they who espoused, and they who opposed it, walked on opposite sides of the street. Who they were that favored it, or where it was concocted, or how developed, does not appear. It is reported, indeed, that Patrick Henry was the person held in view as the dictator; but that he suggested the plan, or favored it, or consented to it, or was in any way privy to it, there is no evidence to prove, nor has it even been alleged. The tradition (resting on no testimony) relates, that Archibald Cary, a man of violent

---

* A number of his books came into Mr. Madison's possession. I remember seeing in Southampton County a Shakespeare with Dunmore's arms. A gentleman in Petersburg has a black-letter Coke, which once belonged to Dunmore, and afterwards to Patrick Henry; it has his lordship's arms, and the orator's autograph.

temper, and a life-long opponent of Henry, sent a message to the governor, (by his brother-in-law, Colonel Syme,) that on the day in which he should accept the dictatorship he should fall by his dagger; and the Colonel has been compared to Brutus—as if the example was worthy of imitation, or as if a dictator appointed by a Virginia assembly can be justly compared to Julius Cæsar at the head of his legions, usurping the government by his sword.

South Carolina invested her governor, John Rutledge, a native of Ireland, with dictatorial powers during the revolutionary war. The Virginia assembly at this session invested Governor Henry with several extraordinary powers, and recommended to congress "to invest the commander-in-chief of the American forces with more ample and extensive powers for conducting the operations of the war." Washington urged the States to clothe their executives with extraordinary powers, and he himself was invested by congress with such. The safety of the people, the supreme law, may demand, in a crisis of extreme danger, the appointment of an officer charged with extraordinary powers, (but who, nevertheless, would be as much the creature of law as any ordinary judge or deputy-sheriff,) "to take care that the Republic shall receive no detriment."

A year or two before the rupture with the mother country, the Presbytery of Hanover established a seminary in Augusta, beyond the Blue Ridge. The Rev. Samuel Stanhope Smith, who had been a teacher of languages in the College of New Jersey, was at this time a missionary in Virginia, and the school was founded upon his recommendation. The superintendent was John Brown, and the tutor William Graham. From this seminary Washington College, at Lexington, arose. By the advice of Rev. S. S. Smith it was determined to found another seminary east of the Blue Ridge, and the funds were raised by subscription; and although it was a period of apprehension and alarm, yet the enterprise was urged with energy and success.* This

---

* The site selected for it was at the head of Hudson's Branch, in Prince Edward County, on a hundred acres of land given for that use by Mr. Peter Johnston. The trustees appointed were Rev. Messrs. Richard Sankey, of Buffaloe, John Todd, of Louisa, Samuel Leake, of Albemarle, and Caleb Wallace, of Cub Creek, together with Messrs. Peter Johnston, Colonel Paul Carrington, Colonel John Nash, Jr., Rev. David Rice, and Colonel James Madison, Jr.

work was accomplished in 1775, amid the throes of revolution, and Prince Edward Academy, the original foundation of Hampden Sidney College, was opened in January, 1776.*

Increased educational means were much needed, all communication with Great Britain being cut off; and educated youth would be wanting to fill the places of such as would soon fall victims of the war. The College of William and Mary was indeed old and tolerably well endowed; but it was near the scene of war and surrounded by noisy camps. In a short time more than a hundred students flocked to the Prince Edward Academy, and their number exceeded the means of accommodation. During the year a military company of the students was organized, Mr. John Blair Smith, Jr., a tutor, being captain. The uniform was a purple hunting-shirt. This company, upon a requisition of the governor for militia from Prince Edward during the following year, marched to Williamsburg, where, however, their services were not required. Some of them became officers in the army, and others enlisted as common soldiers.

In 1775 the convention of Virginia had directed the committee of safety to procure armed vessels, for the better defence of the colony; and the control and management were entrusted to them. The few small vessels and barges in their service were useful in restraining the tories, in protecting property, and in recapturing fugitive slaves. In May, 1776, a board of naval commissioners was appointed, consisting of Thomas Whiting, John Hutchins, Champion Travis, Thomas Newton, Jr., and George Webb. They met for the first time on the eighth of July following, at Williamsburg. About seventy vessels appear to have been in service at some time or other during the war of Revolution—including thirty ships, brigs, and brigantines, and thirty-eight smaller vessels.† Many of the vessels were built at the Chickahominy navy-

---

* Foote's Sketches of Va., 393.

† Among the ships and brigs are found the names of Oxford, Virginia, Loyalist, Pocahontas, Washington, Oliver Cromwell, Marquis La Fayette, Raleigh, Jefferson, Gloucester, Northampton, Sally Norton, Hampton, Liberty, Wilkes, American Fabius. Among the smaller were the Speedwell, Lewis, Nicholson, Harrison, Mayflower, Patriot, Congress, Accomac, Henry, Norfolk, Revenge, Manly, Caswell, Protector, Washington, Page, Lewis, York, and Richmond.

yard, South Quay, Hampton, and near Norfolk. Early in April, 1776, George Mason, of the committee of safety, had charge of the building of two galleys, and of "the American Congress," this last to carry fourteen guns, four and six-pounders, and her complement of marines and seamen being ninety-six men. The look-outs were a sort of winged sentries, and were exposed to hard service. But a small part of the vessels of the Virginia navy were in actual service at any one time; and there was a deplorable want of men, some having not more than one-twentieth of their full number. The vessels usually served separately, but early in the contest Commodore Boucher commanded fifteen sail in the Potomac; and at another time Captain Richard Taylor was in command of a squadron in Hampton Roads. The Virginia-built vessels, although plain and simple in their construction, were very fast sailers. This, together with their lighter draught and familiarity with the waters, often enabled them to escape from the enemy. Of all the vessels of the Virginia navy not one remains.

James Maxwell, Esq., was superintendent of the navy-yard on the Chickahominy, and he was assisted by Captain Christopher Calvert. The former officer commanded the ship Cormorant in 1782. He was father of the late William Maxwell, Esq., Secretary of the Virginia Historical Society. The three commodores commissioned during the struggle were J. Boucher, Walter Brooke, and James Barron. Richard Barron, brother of James, was a captain during the whole war. The Barrons appear to have had a natural proclivity for the water. Lieutenant William Barron, of the continental navy, lost his life by the bursting of a gun on board of the frigate Boston, in bringing to a vessel off the coast of France, in 1778. John Adams, and his son John Quincy, then a boy, were on board of this ship on this occasion. Mr. Adams held the lieutenant in his arms while his leg was amputated. This William Barron had been a lieutenant in the Virginia naval service. Among the captains were Richard Barron, Eleazer Callender, John Calvert, John Cowper, Thomas Lilly, John Pasture, John Harris, James Markham, Richard Taylor, Edward Travis, Cely Saunders, Isaac Younghusband, and John Catesby Cocke. Of the lieutenants may be named Dale, Cunningham,

Chamberlayne, Lewis, Pickett, Watkins, and Jennings. Among the surgeons are found the names of Kemp, Lyon, McClurg, Brockenbrough, Christie, Riddle, Reynolds, Sharpless, Swope, and Pell. Among the seamen were many faithful blacks, who served through the whole war. Most of the Virginia armed vessels were eventually captured at sea or destroyed in the rivers. The vessels commanded by the Barrons were the Liberty and the Patriot. The former was engaged in twenty actions, and was probably the only one that escaped the enemy.

Early in 1776 an armed tender, commanded by the tory Goodrich, was captured off Bowler's wharf, in the Rappahannock. Shortly afterwards the Barrons captured, near the capes, the British transport-ship Oxford, from Glasgow, having on board two hundred and seventeen Scotch Highlanders, who were shaping their course to join Governor Dunmore, whom they supposed to be in Virginia. This ship was destroyed by Arnold in 1781.

Early in July, 1776, Captain Richard Barron captured a sloop, from the West Indies, laden with pine apples, limes, etc., and shortly after the Fanny, an English vessel, laden with supplies for Boston. She had on board numerous presents to the officers in that city. Captain Richard Taylor captured several merchantmen in the Rappahannock. One of them, the Speedwell, was armed, and sent to the West Indies for powder and supplies. In September several large vessels, laden with tobacco, were despatched to the same islands for the like purpose.*

---

* Va. Navy of the Revolution, by Dr. Wm. P. Palmer, Secretary of Va. Hist. Society. (*S. Lit. Messenger*, 1857.)

CHAPTER XCII.

1777.

Commodore Hotham—Proceedings of Assembly—Charges against Richard Henry Lee—He demands an Enquiry—His Defence and Honorable Acquittal.

In January, 1777, when Commodore Hotham was cruising in the Chesapeake, the prisoners that fell into his hands were humanely treated and readily exchanged. In February, the Phœnix man-of-war came to Yorktown with a flag, and sent ashore a party of prisoners, among whom was Colonel Lawson, who had been long in captivity, and who was exchanged for Colonel Alexander Gordon, of Norfolk, a Scotch tory, who had been arrested in 1775 and released on parole. Captain Lilly, in the brig Liberty, captured off the coast of Virginia the British ship Jane with a valuable cargo. Capture Pasture, in the Molly, a small craft, returned from the southward with a supply of gunpowder. The schooner Henry was captured by the British man-of-war Seaford.

When the assembly again met in May, 1777, George Wythe was made speaker of the house of delegates; the oath of allegiance was prescribed; a loan-office was established, and acts passed to support the credit of the Continental and State paper currency. Benjamin Harrison, George Mason, Joseph Jones, Francis Lightfoot Lee, and John Harrison were elected delegates to congress, Richard Henry Lee having been left out. There were no little dissension and animosity in congress between the delegates of the movement party and the moderates; and, added to this, it was believed that an old grudge, harbored in Virginia against Mr. Lee for the prominent part he had taken many years before in disuniting the offices of speaker and treasurer, followed him to Philadelphia. The charges alleged against him by his enemies in Virginia were, first, that he had altered the mode in which his tenants should pay their rent from money to produce, with the design of depreciating the currency of the country; and secondly, that he had favored New England to the injury of Virginia; thirdly, that as a member of the secret committee in congress, he had opposed laying their proceedings before congress— it being thereby intended to insinuate that in so doing he had wished to conceal the embezzlement of the public money.

A letter from Richard Henry Lee to Mr. Jefferson, dated at Philadelphia, November 3d, 1776, contains the following paragraph: "I have been informed that very malignant and very scandalous hints and inuendoes concerning me have been uttered in the house. From the justice of the house I should expect they would not suffer the character of an absent person to be reviled by any slanderous tongue whatever. When I am present I shall be perfectly satisfied with the justice I am able to do myself. From your candor, sir, and knowledge of my political movements, I hope such misstatings as may happen in your presence will be rectified." Early in June, 1777, as well on account of his health as for the purpose of rebutting the charges circulated against him, Mr. Lee returned home; and having been elected to the assembly from Westmoreland, he repaired to Richmond and demanded an enquiry into his conduct.

Mann Page, Jr., and Francis Lightfoot Lee, owing to the proceedings of the house of delegates against Richard Henry Lee, condemning him in his absence without opportunity of defence, addressed a letter from Philadelphia, dated June tenth, to the speaker, tendering the resignations of their seats in congress.

The demand made by Richard Henry Lee for an enquiry into his conduct was acceded to, and the senate on the occasion united with the house of delegates. Several persons were examined, and Mr. Lee was heard in his own defence. It appeared that he had first proposed to make the alteration in the payment of his rents from money to tobacco at a fixed valuation, as early as August, 1775, when the tenants on account of the association could not sell their produce, and when but little paper currency had as yet been issued for the war of Revolution, and, consequently the alteration could not have been proposed for the purpose of depreciating a currency which did not then, to any sensible extent, exist. When in March, 1776, the alteration in the rents was actually made, very little paper money had yet been issued. And it appeared that in August of that year the tenants of Loudoun County themselves petitioned the convention to have their money-rents changed to produce. The truth was, as Mr. Lee declared, certain evil-disposed men hated him for the same reasons on account of which he was devoted to destruction in the British camp, which were, because he had faithfully served his country, and, in concert with other generous friends to human liberty and the rights of America, had contributed to the defeat of the enemy and to the raising of America triumphant over its cruel and vindictive foes.

As to the second charge, that Mr. Lee opposed the laying the proceedings of the secret committee of congress before that body, for the purpose of concealing embezzlement of the public money, it was well known that he had no sort of connection whatever with any commercial business, and, therefore, could not propose to himself any advantage from any such source. But it was very probable that those who themselves entertained designs of peculating upon the public funds, would be glad to get Mr. Lee out of their way. To lay the proceedings of a secret committee before congress would be to defeat its very object and contradict its name. The third charge was that he favored New England at the expense of Virginia and the South. It was known that America could be conquered only by disunion. Mr. Lee called on his accusers to show that he ever had in a single instance preferred the interest of New England to that of Virginia. Indeed, he knew not in what respects their interests conflicted. New England and Virginia had both exhibited a fixed determination against British tyranny, and their guilt was alike in the eyes of the common enemy. The majority of the other colonies had entitled themselves to some hopes of pardon from the tyrant by vacillating conduct. Among the Middle and Southern States there was, in Mr. Lee's opinion, much enmity to Virginia, owing to jealousy of her wisdom, vigor, and extent of territory; but he had ever discovered, "upon every question, respect and love for Virginia among the Eastern delegates." It was his consolation, that "the malignants, who would represent him as an enemy to his country, could not make him so." He gave his enemies credit for more address than he had supposed they possessed, in making use of a good principle—rotation in office—for his ruin; and he believed that the act, limiting the term of service to three years, was framed expressly to fit his case; and thus a malicious slander, uttered in his absence, appeared likely to be successful.* Mr. Lee had been superseded early in the session while absent—a flagrant injustice against which no reputation could be safe. John Banister, although not very fond of Mr. Lee, said of his speech on this occasion: "Certainly no defence was ever made with more graceful eloquence, more manly firmness, equalness of temper, serenity, calmness, and judgment, than this very accomplished speaker displayed on this occasion; and I am now of opinion he will be re-elected to his former station instead of Mr. George Mason, who has resigned."† Mr. Lee is said to have shed tears while speaking on this occasion. The enquiry being ended, the senate withdrew, and in compliance with a resolution of the house, the speaker returned Mr. Lee their thanks for the faithful services which he had rendered his country while in congress. The speaker added his own testimony, and said: "Serving with you in congress, and attentively observing your conduct there, I thought that you manifested in the American cause a zeal truly patriotic; and as far as I could judge, exerted the abilities for which you are confessedly distinguished, to prosecute the good and prosperity of your own country in particular, and of the United States in general." Thus Mr. Lee's vindication of himself was triumphant.

> "Virtue may be assailed, but never hurt;
> Surprised by unjust force, but not inthralled;
> Yea, even that which mischief meant most harm,
> Shall in the happy trial prove most glory."

---

* Letter of Richard Henry Lee to Patrick Henry—among the Lee MSS. I am indebted to N. F. Cabell, Esq., for the use of his transcripts of these interesting MSS., which are deposited in the library of the University of Virginia.

† Life of Richard Henry Lee, 192; Bland Papers, i. 58.

CHAPTER XCIII.
1777.

Battle of Brandywine—Virginia Brigades—Burgoyne's Expedition—His Surrender—Daniel Morgan—Washington at Valley Forge—Frigate Randolph—Treaty with France—Clinton retreats—Battle of Monmouth—General Lee—Anecdote of Colonel Meade—The Meade family—Colonel Baylor—General Clarke.

IN the battle of Brandywine, which took place on the 11th of September, 1777, Sir William Howe again proved victorious; but the action was well contested, and the loss on both sides heavy. The Virginia brigades, under Wayne and Weedon, particularly distinguished themselves. General George Weedon, before the Revolution, had been an inn-keeper at Fredericksburg. The third Virginia regiment, under command of Colonel Thomas Marshall, (father of the chief justice,) which had performed severe duty in 1776, was placed in a wood on the right, and in front of Woodford's brigade and Stephen's division. Though attacked by superior numbers, the regiment maintained its position until both its flanks were turned, its ammunition nearly expended, and more than half of the officers and one-third of the soldiers were killed or wounded. Colonel Marshall, whose horse had received two balls, then retired to resume his position on the right of his division, but it had already retreated. Among the wounded in this battle were La Fayette and Woodford. The enemy passed the night on the field of battle. On the twenty-sixth the British entered Philadelphia.

On the fourth of October occurred the battle of Germantown, in which the American forces, by a well-concerted plan, attacked the enemy at several points early in the morning. The British were at first driven back, precipitately, toward Philadelphia, but at length made a successful stand at Chew's house, garrisoned by five companies of the fortieth regiment, under the command of Colonel Musgrave. Lieutenant Matthew Smith, of Virginia, having volunteered to carry a flag of truce to Chew's house, was mortally wounded, and died in a few days. The Americans being thrown into confusion in a dense fog, Washington, when victory had seemed to be almost within his grasp, was eventually compelled to retreat. A British officer afterwards declared in parliament that Sir William Howe had received information beforehand of the intended attack. The ninth Virginia regiment and part of the sixth were made prisoners. Colonel Matthews, after penetrating to the centre of the town with his regiment, was made prisoner. Major-General Stephen, who commanded the right division of the left wing, was cashiered for misconduct on the retreat, and intoxication. The loss of the enemy was heavy; and congress expressed its approbation of the plan of the battle and the courage displayed in its execution, and the thanks of that body were given to the general and the army.

In the mean time, at the north, Burgoyne, with a well-appointed army, had advanced from Canada, in order to open a communication between that country and New York, and to cut off New England from the rest of the States. Washington, in a letter to General Schuyler, gave it as his opinion that Burgoyne would, eventually, receive an effectual check; that his confidence of success would precipitate his ruin; that his acting in detachment would expose his parties to great hazard, and prophetically adds: "Could we be so happy as to cut one of them off, though it should not exceed four, five, or six hundred men, it would inspirit the people."

After capturing Ticonderoga, Burgoyne moved toward the Hudson, encountering continual obstructions in his route through a wilderness, and harassed by the American troops. A strong detachment was overwhelmed by Starke and his countrymen near Bennington, in Vermont. After a series of engagements, in which he suffered a terrible loss, Burgoyne was at length, on the 17th day of October, 1777, thirteen days after the battle of Germantown, forced to surrender at Saratoga to Gates, who had shortly before succeeded Schuyler. Among those who distinguished themselves at Saratoga was Daniel Morgan, with his Virginia riflemen. He was a native of New Jersey, son of a Welshman, and removed in his youth to Virginia, about 1755, and made his living for a time by driving a wagon. In Braddock's expedition, when about twenty-two years of age, he served as a private, and was wounded. There is a tradition of his having been severely whipped on a charge of contumacy to a British officer.* For some years after he was twenty years of age he was addicted to fighting and gambling; and the reputed scene of his combats, in Clarke County, retains its name of Battletown. When the revolutionary war began he was appointed a captain, and in command of a troop of Virginia horse he marched thence in the summer, with extraordinary expedition, to the American army at Cambridge, Massachusetts. Washington, who knew him well, and had strong confidence in his bravery and patriotism, detached him to join the expedition against Canada; and he exhibited his accustomed courage at Quebec; and when Arnold was wounded the command devolved on him. When Montgomery fell, Morgan was taken prisoner. While in the hands of the British he was offered the rank and pay of a colonel, but he indignantly rejected them. Exchanged in the following year, he rejoined the army; and in command of a rifle corps rendered signal service at Saratoga.

On the thirtieth day of October Gates' victory was celebrated at Williamsburg by a *feu de joie*, joyful shouts, ringing of bells, and illuminations; and all prisoners, except deserters, were discharged from confinement; and a gill of rum was issued to every soldier. The troops were reviewed by General Nelson, by the speakers of both houses of assembly, and by many of the members. Governor Henry, by proclamation, appointed a day of thanksgiving.

In December the American army encamped at Valley Forge, on the Schuylkill, near Philadelphia. The winter was one of extraordinary rigor; the soldiers destitute of clothing, and the hospitals filled with the sick. To aggravate Washington's troubles a cabal formed a design at this time of supplanting him, and making Gates commander-in-chief. But Washington stood unshaken: the angry billows dash in vain against the ocean rock, and fall in empty murmurs at its base.

---

* The Rev. Dr. Hill told Mr. Grigsby that he had seen the marks of the flogging on Morgan's back.

In May, 1778, the American frigate Randolph, (so called in honor of Peyton Randolph, president of congress,) carrying thirty-six guns and three hundred and five men, sailed on a cruise from Charleston. The Yarmouth, British man-of-war, of sixty-four guns, discovered her and five other vessels, and came up with her in the evening. Captain Vincent hailed the Randolph to hoist colors, or he would fire into her; on which she hoisted the American flag, and immediately gave the Yarmouth her broadside, which was returned, and in about a quarter of an hour the Randolph blew up. Four men escaped upon a fragment of the wreck, and subsisted for five days on rain water alone, which they sucked from a piece of blanket which they had picked up. They were rescued by the Yarmouth.*

Early in this month congress received despatches containing a treaty between the king of France and the United States of America. In consequence of Burgoyne's surrender and of the treaty with France, the British army (under command of Sir Henry Clinton, who had relieved Sir William Howe,) evacuated Philadelphia in June, 1778. Crossing the Delaware, they marched for New York. Washington pursued them across the Jerseys, and on the twenty-eighth of June occurred the battle of Monmouth. The result was not decisive; many died from heat and fatigue; the Americans remained on the field of battle, where Washington passed the night in his cloak in the midst of his soldiers. It was during this action that General Charles Lee retreated before the British, who had turned upon him. He was met by Washington, who reprimanded him, ordered the division to be formed, and, with the aid of artillery under Lieutenant-Colonel Carrington, checked the enemy's advance. General Lee was arrested, tried, and convicted of disobedience of orders, of making an unnecessary and disorderly retreat, and of writing disrespectfully to the commander-in-chief, and suspended from the army for one year. Recent developments strengthen the suspicion long entertained that he acted traitorously. It is strange that, conscious of this, he should have remained among those whom he had endeavored to betray. He had previously been signally serviceable in the

---

* Cooper's History of North America, 106.

American cause; and at the time of his suspension there were not wanting divers leading men who thought him hardly dealt with. But a man is never better than his principles, and General Lee's were bad from the beginning. La Fayette said that Washington never appeared to better advantage than in this action, when roused by Lee's misconduct.

Colonel Richard Kidder Meade, the father of Bishop Meade, was one of Washington's aides-de-camp. The following anecdote relative to him is taken from the Travels of Anburey, who was a lieutenant in the British army, and in 1779 a prisoner of war in Virginia, and visiting the lower country on parole: "On my way to this place I stopt and slept at Tuckahoe, where I met with Colonel Meade, Colonel Laurens, and another officer of General Washington's suite. More than once did I express a wish that the general himself had been of the party, to have seen and conversed with a character of whom, in all my travels through the various provinces, I never heard any one speak disrespectfully as an individual, and whose public character has been the admiration and astonishment of all Europe." * * * *
"The colonel (Meade) attributed the safety of his person to the swiftness of his horse at the battle of Monmouth, having been fired at and pursued by some British officers as he was reconnoitering. Upon the colonel's mentioning this circumstance it occurred to me he must have been the person that Sir Henry Clinton's aide-de-camp had fired at, and requesting to know the particular color of his horse, he informed me it was black, which convinced me it was him; when I related the circumstance of his meeting Sir Henry Clinton, he replied he recollected in the course of the day to have met several British officers, and one of them wore a star. Upon my mentioning the observation Sir Henry Clinton had made to his aide-de-camp,* the colonel laughed, and replied, had he known it was the commander-in-chief he should have made a desperate effort to take him prisoner."

The name of Richard Kidder is said to be derived from a bishop of Bath and Wells, who was from the same stock with the

---

* To wit, that he ought by no means to have fired at the American, as he probably might have wished to speak to him and give him intelligence.

Meades of Virginia. Andrew Meade, first of the name in Virginia, born in County Kerry, Ireland, educated a Romanist, came over to New York, and married Mary Latham, a Quakeress, of Flushing, on Long Island. He afterwards settled in Nansemond, Virginia, and for many years was burgess thereof; from which it appears that he must have renounced the Romish religion. He was prosperous, affluent, and hospitable. He is mentioned by Colonel Byrd in his Journal of the Dividing Line run in 1728. His only son, David Meade, married, under romantic circumstances, Susannah, daughter of Sir Richard Everard, Baronet, Governor of North Carolina. Of the sons of David Meade, Richard Kidder Meade was aide-de-camp to General Washington; Everard Meade aide to General Lincoln. Richard Kidder, Everard, together with an older brother, David, were educated at Harrow, England, under the care of Dr. Thackeray. Sir William Jones, Sir Joseph Banks, and Dr. Parr, were at the same time scholars there.

In June, 1778, Colonel Arthur Campbell wrote to the Rev. Charles Cummings, of Washington County: "Yesterday I returned home, the assembly having adjourned until the first Monday in October. The acts passed, and a list of their titles, I here enclose, together with an address of congress to the people of America, for you to publish, agreeable to the resolve. I wish you could make it convenient to preach at the lower meeting-house in this county, if it was but a week-day, as the contents of the address are of the most interesting nature, both as to the moral and political conduct of the good people of America. Providence is daily working out strange deliverances for us. The treaty with France is much more advantageous than the wisest men in this country expected. The Indians the other day were unexpectedly discomfited on Greenbrier. I think the overthrow was something similar to what happened in this county about two years ago. I must give you the intelligence at full length, as the most hardened mind must see and admire the Divine goodness in such an interposition."

The Rev. Charles Cummings, by birth an Irishman, resided for some time in the congregation of the Rev. James Waddell, in Lancaster, and probably studied theology under his care. Mr.

Cummings married Miss Milly, daughter of John Carter, of Lancaster, and in 1773 settled near where Abingdon now stands. His meeting-house was of unhewn logs, from eighty to a hundred feet long and forty wide. Mr. Cummings was of middle stature, well formed, of great firmness and dignity. His voice was of great compass, and his articulation distinct. At this time the inhabitants, during the summer months, were compelled to take shelter in forts for protection against the Indians. The men went to church armed, taking their families with them. The armed congregation, seated in the log meeting-house, presented a singular spectacle of frontier life. Mr. Cummings, when he ascended the steps of the pulpit, deposited his rifle in a corner and laid aside his shot-pouch. He was a zealous whig, and was chairman of the committee of safety of Washington County, formed as early as January, 1775. He was a Presbyterian of the old stamp, a rigid Calvinist, and a man of exemplary piety.

After the battle of Monmouth Sir Henry Clinton occupied New York. The arrival of a French fleet under D'Estaing reanimated the hopes of the Americans. Arthur Lee argued unfavorably of the removal of D'Orvilliers and D'Estaing's appointment. Washington took a position at White Plains, on the Hudson. About this time Colonel Baylor's regiment of cavalry was surprised in the night by a British corps under General Gray. Of one hundred and four privates forty were made prisoners, and twenty-seven killed or wounded. Colonel Baylor was himself dangerously wounded and taken prisoner.

In the year 1778 the town of Abington was incorporated. Virginia sent General George Rogers Clarke on an expedition to the northwest. After enduring extreme sufferings in marching through a wilderness, he and his hardy followers captured Kaskaskias and its governor, Rocheblave. In December, 1778, Hamilton, British lieutenant-governor of Detroit, under Sir Guy Carleton, governor-in-chief, took possession of the post (now the town) of Vincennes, in Indiana. Here he fortified himself, intending in the ensuing spring to rally his Indian confederates to attack Kaskaskias, then in possession of Clarke, and to proceed up the Ohio to Fort Pitt, sweeping Kentucky in the way, and finally overrunning all West Augusta. This expedition was ordered by

Carleton. Clarke's position was too remote for succor, and his force too small to withstand a siege; nevertheless, he prepared to make the best defence possible. At this juncture a Spanish merchant brought intelligence that Hamilton had, by detaching his Indian allies, reduced the strength of his garrison to eighty men, with a few cannon. Clarke immediately despatched a small armed galley, with orders to force her way and station herself a few miles below the enemy. In the mean time, early in February, 1779, he marched, with one hundred and thirty men, upon St. Vincennes: many of the inhabitants of the country joined the expedition; the rest garrisoned the towns. Impeded by rain and high waters, his little army were occupied for sixteen days in reaching the fertile borders of the Wabash, and when within nine miles of the enemy it required five days to cross "the drowned lands" near that river, "having to wade often upwards of two leagues, up to our breasts in water." But for the unusual mildness of the season they must have perished. On the evening of February the twenty-third they reached dry land, and came unperceived within sight of the enemy; and an attack being made at seven o'clock, the inhabitants of St. Vincennes gladly surrendered it, and assisted in besieging Hamilton, who held out in the fort. On the next day he surrendered the garrison. Clarke despatching some armed boats up the Wabash, captured a convoy, including forty prisoners and £10,000 worth of goods and stores. Hamilton, and some officers and privates, were sent to the governor at Williamsburg. Colonel Shelby about the same time attacking the Cherokees, who had taken up the tomahawk, burnt eleven towns and a large quantity of corn, and captured £25,000 worth of goods.

The assembly of Virginia afterwards presented to General Clarke an honorary sword, on the scabbard of which was inscribed: "Sic semper tyrannis;" and on the blade: "A tribute to courage and patriotism, presented by the State of Virginia to her beloved son, General George Rogers Clarke, who, by the conquest of Illinois and Vincennes, extended her empire and aided in defence of her liberties." In his latter years he was intemperate.

CHAPTER XCVI.

1779.

Condition of Affairs—Mason's Letter—Convention Troops removed to Charlottesville — Miscellaneous — Church Establishment abolished — Clergy and Churches—Suffolk burnt—D'Estaing's Siege of Savannah—Lincoln surrenders—Gates defeated at Camden—Sumpter defeated—Battle of King's Mountain—Colonel Campbell—Colonel Ferguson.

WASHINGTON looked upon the early part of 1779 as more fraught with danger than any preceding period of the war, not on account of the strength of the enemy, but owing to the spirit of selfish speculation, money-making, and stock-jobbing that prevailed, the depreciation of the paper currency, the States employing their ablest men at home, the idleness and dissipation of men in public trust, and the dissensions in congress. The demoralizing influences of war were making themselves manifest.*

Colonel George Mercer, of Stafford, who had been compelled to resign the office of stamp collector before the commencement of the revolutionary struggle, retired to England. George Mason, who was related to him, in October, 1778, addressed him a letter, in which he said: "If I can only live to see the American Union firmly fixed, and free governments well established in our western world, and can leave to my children but a crust of bread and liberty,† I shall die satisfied, and say with the Psalmist: 'Lord! now lettest thou thy servant depart in peace.' God has been

---

* From verses supposed to have been written about this time by St. George Tucker:—

"Virtue and Washington in vain
To glory call this prostrate train."

* * "Each eager votary hugs his reams,
And hoards his millions in his dreams.
Ruin with giant strides approaches,
And quartermasters loll in coaches."

† The expression is from Smollet's Ode to Independence.

pleased to bless our endeavors in a just cause with remarkable success. To us upon the spot, who have seen step by step the progress of this great contest, who know the defenceless state of America, and the numberless difficulties we have had to struggle with; taking a retrospective view of what is passed, we seem to have been treading upon enchanted ground."

Washington, in compliance with the resolutions of congress, had ordered the removal of the convention troops of Saratoga, then quartered in Massachusetts, to Charlottesville, Virginia. Congress, whether from distrust in the British prisoners, or from reasons of state, resolved not to comply with the articles of the convention, allowing the prisoners to embark for England on parole, until the convention should be ratified by the English government. Burgoyne had sailed for England in May, and from that time the command of the British troops of convention, quartered at Cambridge, had devolved upon General Phillips. Colonel Bland, with an escort, conducted the prisoners of war to Virginia. Upon their arrival, in December, at their place of destination, on Colonel Harvey's estate, about six miles from Charlottesville, they suffered many privations, being billeted in blockhouses without windows or doors, and poorly defended from the cold of an uncommonly rigorous winter. But in a short time they constructed better habitations, and the barracks assumed the appearance of a neat little town. In the rear of each house they had trim gardens and enclosed places for poultry. The army cleared a space of six miles in circumference around the barracks. A representation of the barracks is given in Anburey's Travels. The officers were allowed, upon giving parole, to provide for themselves lodging-places within a circuit of a hundred miles.* Mr. Jefferson exhibited a generous hospitality toward the captives; and his knowledge of French, his taste for music, his fine conversational powers, and his fascinating manners, contributed not a little to relieve the tedium of their captivity. Governor Henry afforded them every indulgence in his power; and the amiable disposition of Colonel Bland, who commanded the guard

---

* Anburey mentions a Dr. Fauchee as resident at Charlottesville—probably Foushee.

placed over the convention troops, still further ensured their quiet and comfort. General Phillips, described by Mr. Jefferson as "the proudest man of the proudest nation on earth," occupied Blenheim, a seat of Colonel Carter's; General the Baron de Riedesel occupied Colle, a residence belonging to Philip Mazzei, Mr. Jefferson's Italian neighbor; and the Baroness, whose romantic sufferings and adventures are so well known, has given, in her Memoirs, an entertaining account of her sojourn among the picturesque mountains of Albemarle. Charlottesville at this period consisted of a court-house, a tavern, and about a dozen dwelling-houses.*

Anburey has given a graphic picture of the manners, customs, and the grotesque scenes that he witnessed at Charlottesville and in its vicinity.

Violent dissensions convulsed congress; some of the members were suspected of treasonable designs. Early in May, Richard Henry Lee wrote from Philadelphia to Mr. Jefferson, hoping that he "would not be blamed by him and his other friends for sending his resignation to the assembly, and averring that he had been persecuted by the united voice of toryism, speculation, faction, envy, malice, and all uncharitableness," so that nothing but the certain prospect of doing essential service to his country could compensate for the injuries he received. But he adds: "It would content me indeed to sacrifice every consideration to the public good that would result from such persons as yourself, Mr. Wythe, Mr. Mason, and some others being in congress. I would struggle

---

* Colonel Bland, in some verses written during this year, alludes thus to Mr. Jefferson:—

> On yonder height I see a lofty dome;*
> But, hapless fate, the master's not at home.
> His high aspiring soul aloft had towered,
> That like a God he was by men adored.
> But envy now has placed him in Jove's car
> To rule the tempest of the mighty war,
> That he, like Phaëton, may tumble down,
> And by his fall astonish all the town.

---

* Monticello.

with persevering ardor through every difficulty in conjunction with such associates."

In 1779 the legislature rejected a scheme of a general assessment for the support of religion. Patrick Henry was in favor of it. The glebe-lands were also declared to be public property; and thus was destroyed the last vestige of a religious establishment in Virginia. During the Revolution, the loyalist clergy of Virginia who remained, found themselves in a deplorable condition. The prohibition to pray for the king was strictly enforced upon them by the incensed people: some ministers omitted the obnoxious petitions; others abandoned the churches and offered no prayer in public; while a few appeared disposed, if possible, to resist the popular tide, but were compelled eventually to succumb to it. In 1775 Virginia contained sixty-one counties, ninety-five parishes, one hundred and sixty-four churches and chapels, and ninety-one clergymen of the establishment. During the interval of the war part of the parishes were extinguished, and the greater number of the rest were deprived of ministerial help; but few ministers were able to weather the storm and remain at their former posts; the others having been compelled to seek precarious shelter and support in other parishes. Some of the churches, venerable for age and connected with so many interesting associations, were left roofless and dismantled; others used as barracks, or stables, or lodging-places of prisoners of war; and the moss-grown walls of some were pulled down by sacrilegious hands, and books and vessels appurtenant to holy services pillaged and carried off.

Until this year the British arms had been chiefly directed against the Middle and Northern States; but they were now turned against the South. Georgia soon fell a prey to the enemy, and South Carolina was invaded. In May a squadron under Sir George Collier anchored in Hampton Roads, and General Matthews took possession of Portsmouth. The enemy destroyed the public stores at Gosport and Norfolk, burnt Suffolk, and destroyed upwards of a hundred vessels, including several armed ones. The Virginia navy had been reduced previously, and many of the vessels ordered to be sold, and from this time the history of those remaining is a series of disasters.

Upon the approach of six hundred British infantry upon Suffolk, the militia and greater part of the inhabitants fled; few could save their effects; some who remained for that purpose were made prisoners. The enemy fired the town, and nearly the whole of it was consumed: hundreds of barrels of tar, pitch, turpentine, and rum, lay on the wharves, and their heads being staved, the contents flowing in commingled mass and catching the blaze, descended to the river in torrents of liquid flame, and the wind blowing violently, the splendid mass floated to the opposite shore in a conflagration that rose and fell with the waves, and there set on fire the dry grass of an extensive marsh. This broad sheet of fire, the crackling flames of the town, the lurid smoke, and the occasional explosion of gunpowder in the magazines, projecting ignited fragments of timber like meteors in the troubled air, presented altogether an awful spectacle of the horrors of civil war. The enemy shortly after, laden with plunder, embarked for New York.

While Sir Henry Clinton was encamped near Haerlem, and Washington in the Highlands on the Hudson,[*] Major Lee, of Virginia, surprised in the night a British post at Paulus Hook, and with a loss of two killed and three wounded, made one hundred and fifty-nine prisoners, including three officers. Soon after this a fleet, commanded by Admiral Arbuthnot, arrived at New York with re-enforcements. D'Estaing returned to the southern coast of America with a fleet of twenty-two ships-of-the-line and eleven frigates, and having on board six thousand soldiers. He arrived so unexpectedly that the British ship Experiment of fifty guns, and three frigates, fell into his hands. In September, Savannah, occupied by a British force under General Prevost, was besieged by the French and Americans, commanded by D'Estaing and Lincoln.[†] In an ineffectual effort to storm the post the French and Americans suffered heavy loss. The siege was raised, and D'Estaing, who had been wounded in the action, sailed again for the West Indies, after this second abortive attempt to aid the cause of independence. The condition of the South was now more gloomy than ever.

---

[*] August eighteenth.   [†] October ninth.

Clinton, toward the close of the year, embarked with a formidable force in Arbuthnot's fleet, and sailed for South Carolina. In April, 1780, Sir Henry laid siege to Charleston; and General Lincoln, undertaking to defend the place, contrary to his own judgment, and in compliance with the entreaties of the inhabitants, after an obstinate defence was compelled to capitulate.* Shortly after this disaster Colonel Buford's regiment was cut to pieces by Tarleton. Georgia and South Carolina now succumbed to the enemy: it was the bending of the willow before the sweep of the tempest. In June, General Gates was appointed by congress to the command in the South. Having collected an army he marched toward Camden in South Carolina, then held by the enemy. While Gates was moving from Clermont toward that place in the night,† Cornwallis marched out with a view of attacking the American army at Clermont. Thus the two armies, each essaying to surprise the other, met unexpectedly in the woods, at about two o'clock in the morning. At the first onset the American line was thrown into disorder; but a body of light infantry, and in particular a corps under command of Colonel Porterfield, of Virginia, maintained their ground with constancy. This brave officer, refusing to give way, fell mortally wounded. The battle was resumed in the morning, and Gates' army was utterly discomfited: the militia fled too soon; the regulars fought too long. The fugitives retreating in promiscuous disorder, were pursued by the unrelenting sabres of cavalry; and the horrors of the rout baffle description. Thus Gates, verifying General Lee's prediction, "turned his Northern laurels into Southern willows." The defeated general retired to North Carolina to collect the scattered remains of his army. In August, Sumpter was overwhelmed by Tarleton; and for a time the British army were in the ascendant throughout the South.

Cornwallis‡ detached Colonel Ferguson, a gallant and expert officer, across the Wateree, with one hundred and ten regulars; and in a short time tory recruits augmented his numbers to one thousand; and, confident of his strength, he sent a menacing message to the patriot leaders on the western waters. This was,

---

* May twelfth.   † August sixteenth.   ‡ September first.

for the South, "the time that tried men's souls:" many of the leading patriots captives or exiles, the country subjugated, British and tory cruelty desolating it, hope almost extinct,—Marion alone holding out in his fastnesses. The spirit of the hardy mountaineers was aroused, and hearing that Ferguson was threatening to cross the mountains, a body of men in arms were concentrated by the twenty-fifth on the banks of the Watauga—four hundred from Washington County, Virginia, under Colonel William Campbell; the rest from North Carolina, under Colonels Shelby, Sevier, McDowell, Cleveland, and Winston. Crossing the mountains they advanced toward Ferguson, who began to retreat, and took up a position* on an eminence of about one hundred and fifty feet, called King's Mountain. It is situated in the northern part of South Carolina, near the North Carolina line, its sides steep and rocky, a brook flowing at its foot,—the surrounding scenery thickly wooded, wild, and picturesque. It was resolved to pursue the enemy with nine hundred picked men. Near the Cowpens, where Ferguson had encamped on the fourth, and about thirty miles from King's Mountain, the mountaineers were re-enforced by four hundred and sixty men, the greater part of them from South Carolina, under Colonel Williams. Here, at about nine o'clock of the evening, Colonel William Campbell was appointed to the chief command. The mountain horsemen rode on in the night through a rain, with their guns under their arms to keep the locks dry; the leader in front, and each colonel at the head of his troops. In the morning they halted for half an hour to eat a frugal breakfast, and at twelve o'clock, when the sky cleared, they found themselves within three miles of the British camp. They halted, and the order passed along the line: "Tie up overcoats, pick touch-holes, fresh prime, and be ready to fight." At three o'clock in the afternoon of the seventh of October an express from Ferguson to Cornwallis was captured, and his despatches, declaring his position on King's Mountain impregnable, were read to the troops. Galloping off they came in twenty minutes within sight of the British camp. They dismounted on the banks of the little stream, tied their horses to the

---

* October sixth.

limbs of trees, and left them in charge of a small guard. The force being divided, the mountain was surrounded. As each column moved on to the attack it was driven back a short distance by the charge of the British, who were soon compelled to wheel, in order to face another column advancing on the opposite side. Ferguson, finding his troops hemmed in and huddled together on the summit of the mountain, fought with desperate valor, and fell, charging at the head of his men and cheering them on. The white flag was now raised. Of Ferguson's force, amounting to rather more than eleven hundred men, two hundred and forty were killed and two hundred wounded; upwards of seven hundred were taken prisoners, with all the arms, ammunition, and camp equipage. The loss of the patriots was thirty killed and fifty wounded. The gallant Williams was slain, as also was Major Chronicle, and several other officers. The battle lasted one hour. A number of the tories were hung on the next day. The sword used by Colonel Campbell on this occasion is preserved in possession of William Campbell Preston, of South Carolina, the orator, his grandson; it is more than two centuries old, and was wielded by the ancestors of Colonel Campbell in Scotland in the wars of the Pretenders. One of the rifles employed at King's Mountain is also preserved. This battle was the turning-point of the war in the South.

Colonel William Campbell was a native of Augusta County, and removed early to the County of Washington. Fame has awarded him the title of "the hero of King's Mountain." Colonel Ferguson was an excellent marksman, and brought the art of rifle shooting to high perfection. He invented a gun of that kind which was said to surpass anything of the sort before known, and he was said to have outdone even the Indians in firing and loading and hitting the mark, standing or lying, and in no matter what position of the body. It was reported that General Washington owed his life, at the battle of Brandywine, to Ferguson's ignorance of his person, as he was within his reach.* He afterwards, upon discovering the fact, remarked that he was not sorry that he did not know him.

---

* Dodsley's Annual Register for 1781.

CHAPTER XCV.

1780.

Arthur Lee—Deane—Franklin—Madison.

In the year 1780 Arthur Lee returned to America after a long absence. He was born in Westmoreland County, Virginia, on the 20th of December, 1740, being the youngest of five brothers, all of whom became eminent. After passing some time at Eton he entered the University of Edinburgh, where he took the degree of doctor of medicine about 1765. The other students from Virginia there at the same time were Field, Blair, Bankhead, and Gilmer—the earliest pioneers in this profession in the colony, at a time when the apothecary, physician, and surgeon were united in the same person, and when quackery enjoyed full license. Arthur Lee's extreme aversion to slavery and to negroes, and the lamentable state of dependence to which he foresaw that his own country would be doomed for many years, made him dread to return; and he even thought of settling in England, which he looked upon as "the Eden of the world, the land of liberty and independence." Yet he was conscious of such a want of confidence in himself as unfitted him for taking up his abode and embarking in a profession in a land of strangers.* Gladly quitting Scotland, which he disliked extremely, Dr. Lee travelled through Europe, and then returned to Virginia, and commenced the practice of physic at Williamsburg. Here he could not fail to view with interest the stirring events of the day; and although successful in his medical practice, the bent of his genius induced him to return to London for the purpose of studying the law in the Temple, and fitting himself for taking a part in public affairs. At this time he became the intimate friend of Sir William Jones. In London he associated himself with Wilkes, and other oppo-

---

* MS. letter of Arthur Lee, Edinburgh, March 20, 1765.

nents of the government, and prevailed on them to favor the cause of the colonies. In 1768 Dr. Lee was appointed political agent of Massachusetts. In 1769 he wrote the Monitor's Letters, and for some years was a frequent writer in the *Public Advertiser*, over the signature of Junius Americanus; and he held an amicable discussion with Junius on American matters.* That writer remarked of him: "My American namesake is plainly a man of abilities." His writings procured for him the friendship of Burke, Dr. Price, and other leading men. He became acquainted with the celebrated Dr. Samuel Johnson. In 1770 Arthur Lee was admitted to the bar, and he enjoyed a lucrative practice for some years. In the spring of 1774 he set out on a tour through France and Italy; and while at Paris published an "Appeal to the People of Great Britain." During the same year he succeeded Dr. Franklin as agent of Massachusetts; and in the following he was agent for Virginia. The secret committee of congress appointed him their London correspondent; and through the French ambassador there he obtained early assurances of aid from France to the colonies. In August he presented the second petition of congress to the king. He was afterwards made commissioner to France in conjunction with Deane and Franklin; and he joined them at Paris in December, 1776, and assisted in making the treaty of alliance. Discord ensuing between Dr. Lee and the other commissioners, involved them, especially Lee and Deane, in a controversy, which engendered an inveterate hostility, and gave rise to factions in congress, in which the French minister, Gerard, became implicated, and which endangered the cause of independence. Deane, who, in the guise of a merchant, conducted the public business, was subtle and unscrupulous. Mr. Lee had exposed the peculations of some of the agents employed in conducting the commercial details of the public business; and this interference gave rise to many aspersions upon him, which were encouraged by the countenance which congress appeared to lend Deane and those associated with him. Deane, at length, recalled by congress in November,

---

* See Woodfall's Junius, i. 102, where Arthur Lee is erroneously called Dr. *Charles* Lee.

1777, reached America in the following summer, and gave an account of his transactions to congress, making an artful defence against Arthur Lee's accusations. Deane published virulent attacks upon him and Richard Henry Lee, and they retorted with indignant severity.

Congress coming to no determination in the matter, Deane appealed to the public, in December, in an address to the "Free and Virtuous Citizens of America." In 1780 he repaired to Paris to adjust his accounts, but never did so; and after refusing ten thousand dollars offered him by congress to cover his expenses, he fell into pecuniary straits, became alienated from his country, (if he had been true before, which was doubted,) writing home letters representing the American cause as desperate, and favoring immediate accommodation with the enemy. These letters were intercepted by the enemy and published, and his real character was now made manifest. Mr. Jay, who had been his friend and supporter, hearing this at Madrid, took down his portrait and burnt it. Deane appears afterwards to have associated with the traitor Arnold. Deane died in extreme poverty at Deal, England, (1789.) He certainly rendered the colonies great service at one time,* and found a strong party in congress in his support, including men of both sections and of high character. Mr. Paca, of Maryland, and Mr. Drayton, of South Carolina, protested against the further continuance of Dr. Lee in the place of commissioner in France and Spain. Dr. Lee's dissensions with Dr. Franklin resulted in bitter enmity. Dr. Lee charged Franklin with vanity, inflated by French flattery, with overweening and dictatorial arrogance, with connivance at fraud and corruption, and with being under French influence. William Lee and Richard Henry sympathized warmly with Arthur in these disputes. John Adams sided with the Lees. Arthur Lee, in 1780, resigning his post, returned to America, and prepared to vindicate himself before congress, but that body expressed their full confidence in his patriotism. In 1781 he was elected to the assembly of Virginia, and returned to congress, where he continued to represent the State for several years. He was a pure,

---

* Flanders' Lives of Chief Justices, art. JAY.

earnest, incorruptible patriot, love of country being his ruling passion. Of a jealous disposition, and melancholy, discontented temperament; of polite manners and strong passions. He was well skilled in Greek, Latin, French, Spanish, and Italian. He never married. He meditated writing a history of the American Revolution. In a letter to General Washington, dated at Berlin, in June, 1777, he says: "It is my intention to write a history of this civil contention. The share you have had in it will form an interesting and important part. It will be in your power to preserve a variety of materials, papers, and anecdotes for such a work. May I venture to hope that you may think me so far worthy of your confidence as to preserve them for me? Dubious parts of history can be cleared only by such documents, and we shall want every authentic record to vouch against the forgeries which will be offered to the world."*

William Lee, brother of Arthur, was born in Virginia, about the year 1737. Sent to London as Virginia's agent before the Revolution, he took up his residence there. Being a zealous whig, he was elected, in 1773, one of the sheriffs of London. At the commencement of the Revolution he retired to France, and afterwards was appointed by congress their commissioner at Vienna and Berlin. An able man, and an ardent and inflexible patriot, by communicating important intelligence, and by his diplomatic agency, he rendered invaluable services to his country. As a writer he was little inferior to Arthur.

During the year 1780 James Madison took his seat in congress. He was born in March, 1751, O. S., in the County of Caroline, Virginia, on the Rappahannock River, near Port Royal, the son of James Madison, of Orange County, and Nelly Conway, his wife. At the age of twelve young Madison was at school under Donald Robertson, a distinguished teacher in the neighborhood, and afterwards under the Rev. Thomas Martin, the parish minister, a private tutor in his father's family. He was next sent to the College of New Jersey, of which Dr. Witherspoon was then president. Here Mr. Madison received the degree of bachelor of arts in the autumn of 1771. He had impaired his health at

---

* Arthur Lee's Life, i. 88.

college by too close application; nevertheless, on his return home he pursued a systematic course of reading. Shortly after his return he signed resolutions of his county approving of Henry's proceedings in the affair of the gunpowder. He became a member of the convention in May, 1776, and it was during this session that the body unanimously instructed the deputies of Virginia in congress to propose a declaration of independence. He did not enter into public debate during this session. At the next election he was defeated, his successful opponent being Colonel Charles Porter, who was subsequently his frequent colleague in the house of delegates. Mr. Madison was at the ensuing session appointed a member of the council of state, and this place he held till 1779, when he was elected to congress. While he was of the council Patrick Henry and Mr. Jefferson were governors. Mr. Madison's knowledge of French, of which Governor Henry was ignorant, rendered him particularly serviceable in the frequent correspondence held with French officers: he wrote so much for Governor Henry that he was called "the governor's secretary." Mr. Madison took his seat in congress in March, 1780, and continued a leading member until the fall of 1783, when his congressional term expired by limitation. Such was the commencement of the career of this man so illustrious for his genius, his learning, and his virtue, and who was destined to pass through every eminent station, and to fill all with honor to himself and benefit to his country and the world. As a writer, a debater, a statesman, and a patriot, he was of the first order, and his name goes down to posterity one of the brightest of those that adorn the annals of the age in which he lived.*

---

* The Life of Madison, by the Honorable William C. Rives, is a recent important addition to Virginia biography.

CHAPTER XCVI.

1780.

Logan—Leslie's Invasion—Removal of Convention Troops.

In the fall of 1779 Logan, the Indian chief, had again resumed his onslaughts on the banks of the Holston. In June, 1780, when Captain Bird, of Detroit, long the headquarters of British and Indian barbarity, invaded Kentucky, Logan joined in the bloody raid. He was now about fifty-five years of age. Not long after this inroad, Logan, at an Indian council held at Detroit, while phrenzied by liquor, prostrated his wife by a sudden blow, and she fell apparently dead. Supposing that he had killed her, he fled to escape the penalty of blood. While travelling alone on horseback he was all at once overtaken, in the wilderness between Detroit and Sandusky, by a troop of Indians, with their squaws and children, in the midst of whom he recognized his relative Tod-hah-dohs. Imagining that the avenger was at hand, Logan frantically exclaimed that the whole party should fall by his weapons. Tod-hah-dohs perceiving the danger, and observing that Logan was well armed, felt the necessity of prompt action; and while Logan was leaping from his horse to execute his threat, Tod-hah-dohs levelled a shot-gun within a few feet of him and killed him on the spot. Tod-hah-dohs, or the Searcher, originally from Conestoga, and probably a son of Logan's sister who lived there, was better known as Captain Logan. He left children, (two of whom have been seen by Mr. Lyman C. Draper;) so that in spite of Logan's speech some of his blood, at least collaterally, still runs in human veins. Logan's wife recovered from the blow given her by her husband, and returned to her own people.[*]

On the 2d of October, 1780, Major Andre was executed as a spy.

---

[*] Brantz Mayer's Discourse on Logan and Cresap, 66.

Beverley Robinson, a son of the Honorable John Robinson, of Virginia, president of the colony, removed to New York, and married Susanna, daughter of Frederick Philipse, Esq., who owned a vast landed estate on the Hudson. When the Revolution commenced, Beverley Robinson desired to remain in retirement, being opposed to the measures of the ministry, and to the separation of the colonies from the mother country. The importunity of friends induced him to enter the military service of the crown, and he became colonel of the Loyal American Regiment. He was implicated in Arnold's treason, and accompanied Andre in the Vulture. Andre, when captured, was taken to Colonel Robinson's house, which had been confiscated, and then occupied by Washington. Robinson was sent by Sir Henry Clinton as a witness in behalf of Andre.

Prince William Henry, afterwards William the Fourth, was a guest of Colonel Robinson, in New York, during the revolutionary war. Several of his descendants, and those of Captain Roger Morris, have attained distinction. Among them Sir Frederick Philipse Robinson, son of Colonel Beverley Robinson, was an officer of rank under Wellington, and saw hard service in the Peninsular war, and was dangerously wounded at the siege of St. Sebastians. In the war of 1812 he led the British in the attack on Plattsburg, under Prevost.*

On the twentieth of October, a British fleet, in accordance with intelligence which had been communicated by spies and deserters, made its appearance in the Chesapeake. General Leslie was at the head of the troops aboard. Having landed, they began to fortify Portsmouth. Their highest post was Suffolk, and they occupied the line between Nansemond River and the Dismal Swamp. A person of suspicious appearance, endeavoring to pass through the country from Portsmouth toward North Carolina, was apprehended; and upon its being proposed to search him he readily consented, but at the same time he was observed to put his hand into his pocket and carry something toward his mouth, as if it were a quid of tobacco. Upon examination it proved to be a letter, written on silk-paper, and rolled

---

* Sabine's Loyalists, 562.

up in gold-beaters' skin, and nicely tied at each end, so as to be no larger than a goose-quill. The letter was as follows:—

"To Lord Cornwallis :—

"My Lord,—I have been here near a week, establishing a post. I wrote to you to Charleston, and by another messenger by land. I cannot hear with certainty where you are. I wait your orders. The bearer is to be handsomely rewarded if he brings me any note or mark from your lordship. A. L.

"Portsmouth, Virginia, November 4, 1780."

It was a source of mortification to Governor Jefferson and other patriots that the State was unable to defend herself for want of arms. In compliance with the call of the executive, General Nelson made an effort to collect the militia of the lower counties, and to secure at least the pass at the Great Bridge; but his exertions were ineffectual, as the alarmed inhabitants made it their first business to secure their families and property from danger. General Lawson, who had at this time raised a corps of five hundred volunteers to march to the aid of South Carolina, was called on to aid in defending his own State, and General Stevens was preparing to march with a detachment of the Southern army to her aid when* Leslie sailed for South Carolina to re-enforce Cornwallis. Leslie during his stay had abstained entirely from depredation and violence. Many negroes who had gone over to him were left behind, either from choice or from want of ship-room. The chief injury resulting from this invasion was the loss of cattle collected for the use of the Southern army. Another consequence of it was the removal of the troops of convention from the neighborhood of Charlottesville. They marched early in October, and crossing the Blue Ridge proceeded along the valley to Winchester, where they were quartered in barracks. Some of the men occupied a church, and about sixty were confined in jail, probably to prevent desertion. The troops were thence removed to Fredericktown, Maryland, and afterwards to Lancaster, Pennsylvania. The German troops of convention remained

---

* November fifteenth.

longer in Albemarle: they were removed early in 1781, and quartered at Winchester, and the Warm Springs, in Berkley.

The assembly of Virginia was preparing, in the winter of this year, to weather, as well as possible, the storm which was gathering against her; but without Northern assistance she was hardly able to cope with the enemy. She wanted clothes, arms, ammunition, tents, and other warlike stores. Ten millions of paper dollars were issued from necessity, but it was evident that it would be as transient, as a dream at the present, and pernicious in its consequences; yet without it no resistance could be made to the enemy.

CHAPTER XCVII.

1780-1781.

Arnold's Invasion.

TOWARD the close of December, 1780, a fleet appeared within the capes of the Chesapeake, with a force detached by Sir Henry Clinton from New York, under command of the traitor Arnold. A frigate in advance having captured some small vessels, Arnold, with the aid of them, pushed on at once up the James. Attempting to land at Burwell's Ferry, (the Grove Landing,) his boats were beaten off by one hundred and fifty militia of Williamsburg and James City, under Colonel Innes and General Nelson. Nelson, on this occasion, retorted a verbal defiance in answer to a letter with which Arnold had ushered in his invasion.*

Leaving a frigate and some transports at Burwell's Ferry, Arnold proceeded† up the river to Westover. Here landing a force of less than eight hundred men, including a small party of badly mounted cavalry, he marched for Richmond at two o'clock in the afternoon of the same day. Nelson, in the mean while, with a handful of militia, badly supplied with ammunition, had marched up the right bank of the James River, but arrived too late to offer any opposition to the landing of the enemy. Arnold, at one o'clock of the next day after he marched from Westover, entered the infant capital without having encountered any resistance, although his route was very favorable for it. The energetic Simcoe, with a detachment, proceeded a few miles beyond Richmond and destroyed the foundry, emptied the contents of the powder magazine, struck off the trunnions of the cannon, and set

---

* In a series of replies made by Mr. Jefferson to strictures thrown out upon his conduct of affairs at this juncture, the following occurs: "Query—Why publish Arnold's letter without General Nelson's answer? Answer—Ask the printer. He got neither from the executive."

† January 4th, 1781.

fire to the warehouses and mills, the effect of the conflagration being heightened by occasional explosions of gunpowder. Many small arms and a stock of military supplies were destroyed, and five tons of gunpowder thrown into the river. At Richmond the public stores fell a prey; private property was plundered and destroyed; the soldiers broke into houses and procured rum; and several buildings were burnt. Part of the records of the auditor's office, and the books and papers of the council office shared the same fate.

Governor Jefferson used every effort in his power to remove the public stores, and part were rescued by being removed across the river at Westham. Late on the night of the fourth he went to Tuckahoe, and on the next day went down to Manchester, opposite Richmond, where the busy movements of the enemy were in full view. When they advanced upon that place only two hundred militia were embodied—too small a number to make any resistance. The governor, having repaired to Colonel Fleming's, in Chesterfield, to meet Steuben, received there a message from Arnold, offering not to burn Richmond, on condition that British vessels should be permitted to come to it unmolested and take away the tobacco. The proposition was rejected.

The inhabitants of Richmond were, for the most part, Scotch factors, who lived in small tenements scattered here and there between the river and the hill, some on the declivities, a few on the summit. Arnold withdrew from Richmond about mid-day on the sixth, encamped that night, as he had on the march up, at Four-mile Creek, and on the next day at Berkley and Westover.

Arthur Lee wrote, on the twenty-first of March, from Greenspring to Colonel Bland, as follows: "Most certainly you would have heard from me could I have found any conveyance but the tory-post the wisdom of our people has established, or could I have given you a pleasing account of the situation of our affairs here. But in truth, it is impossible to conceive a more hopeless state than what we are in. Laws without wisdom or justice, governments without system or order, complex and heavy taxes to raise money which is squandered away no one knows how, or wherefore, not half the troops being raised, or those which are raised being provided neither with arms, clothes, nor provisions.

Twelve millions were spent in two months, and when the enemy came, there was neither man, horse, musket, cannon, wagon, boat, or any one thing in the world that could be found for our defence. In this situation it need not surprise you that Arnold, with a handful of bad troops, should march about the country, take and destroy what he pleased, feast with his tory friends, settle a regular correspondence with them, which he carried on for some time in vessels sent up the river and unnoticed, till one happening to run aground discovered Mrs. Byrd's correspondence, which, however, will produce neither good to us nor injury to her. I have reason to think she will not be tried at all, means having been taken to keep the witnesses out of the way."*

Mrs. Maria Byrd, of Westover, was a sister of Thomas Willing, Esq., director of the Bank of North America, and partner of Robert Morris, and a strenuous opponent of American independence. A sister of Mrs. Byrd married Captain Walter Sterling, of the British navy. Samuel Inglis, Esq., some time resident in Virginia as factor of the house of Willing & Morris, under the firm of Inglis & Willing, was a decided opponent of independence. He married the daughter of William Aitcheson, Esq., of Norfolk, a Scotch tory, and was brother of Captain Inglis, of the British navy.†

Simcoe, patroling in the night, surprised a party of militia at Charles City Court-house, where, after some confused firing, the militia fled with small loss; some few attempting to escape, were drowned in a mill-pond. Sergeant Adams, of Simcoe's Regiment, was mortally wounded, and dying shortly afterwards, was buried at Westover, wrapped in some American colors taken a few days before at Hoods. Nelson, re-enforced at Holt's Forge by a party of Gloucester militia under Colonel John Page, finding his force not exceeding four hundred men, retreated. On that night‡ the British embarked at Westover, and dropped down the James to Flower-de-Hundred. Here Simcoe was detached with

---

* MS. letter of Arthur Lee in my possession.

† MS. of Colonel Theodorick Bland, Jr. Arnold's visits to Westover are referred to in Edgehill, a novel, by James E. Heath, Esq.

‡ January tenth.

a force to dislodge some militia at Bland's Mills, and after advancing about two miles, the advance guard, in a dense wood, were fired on by some Americans posted at the forks of the road in front. The British lost twenty men killed and wounded; but, charging, put the militia to flight.

Arnold sending a detachment ashore at Fort Hoods, a skirmish ensued with two hundred and forty men in ambuscade, under Colonel George Rogers Clarke. The enemy lost seventeen killed and thirteen wounded at the first fire, when Clarke being charged, found it necessary to retreat. John Marshall was present at this affair. The enemy dismantled the fort and carried off the heavy artillery. Nelson, in the mean time, by a forced march, reached Williamsburg just before the fleet came to off Jamestown. Arnold, however, landed part of his forces at Cobham, on the opposite side of the river, and marched down, his ships keeping pace with and occasionally re-enforcing him. On the next day Nelson paraded about four hundred militia at Burwell's Ferry to oppose the landing of the enemy. Re-enforcements arriving, augmented his force to twelve hundred; but the enemy was now beyond their reach. Colonel Griffin and Colonel Temple, with a party of light horse, had hovered near the enemy's lines at Westover, and followed the fleet as it went down the river. In this party were Colonels William Nelson, Gregory Smith, Holt Richardson, Major Buller Claiborne, General Lincoln's aid, and Majors Burwell, Ragsdale, and others, together with a number of young gentlemen. Arnold returned to Portsmouth on the twentieth of January without having encountered any serious interruption.

Thus it happened that while the regular troops of Virginia were serving at a distance in other States, the militia, after a five years' war, was still so unarmed and undisciplined that no effective resistance was made to this daring invasion.

About the time when Arnold reached Portsmouth, some of his artillery-men, foraging on the road toward the Great Bridge, were attacked, their wagons captured and their officer wounded. Simcoe, with a handful of yagers and Queen's Rangers, was detached for the purpose of recovering the wagons. Ferrying across to Herbert's Point they advanced about a mile, when "an artillery-man, who had escaped and lay in the bushes, came out and informed him that Lieutenant Rynd lay not far off. Simcoe found him shockingly mangled and mortally wounded; he sent to a neighboring farm for an ox-cart, on which the unfortunate young gentleman was placed. The rain continued in a violent manner, which precluded all pursuit of the enemy; it now grew more tempestuous, and ended in a perfect hurricane, accompanied with incessant lightning. This small party slowly moved back toward Herbert's Ferry; it was with difficulty that the drivers and attendants on the cart could find their way; the soldiers marched on with bayonets fixed, linked in ranks together, covering the road. The creaking of the wagon and the groans of the youth added to the horror of the night; the road was no longer to be traced when it quitted the woods, and it was a great satisfaction that a flash of lightning, which glared among the ruins of Norfolk, disclosed Herbert's house. Here a boat was procured, in which the unhappy youth was conveyed to the hospital-ship, where he died the next day."*

---

* Simcoe, 171.

CHAPTER XCVIII.

1781.

Greene, Commander of Southern Army—Morgan's Victory at Cowpens—Arnold at Portsmouth—Battle of Guilford—Re-enforced by Phillips—The Enemy at Petersburg—Devastations—Phillips proceeds down James River—Returns to Petersburg—His Death—Succeeded by Arnold—Simcoe—Virginia Navy—John Tyler—John Banister.

IN accordance with a resolution of congress, passed in November, 1780, General Gates was superseded, and Washington, who was required to appoint an officer to fill the vacant post, selected General Nathaniel Greene, of Rhode Island. He reached Charlotte, the headquarters of the Southern army, early in December. About this time Lee's legion was ordered into South Carolina, to a point west of the Catawba. Cornwallis, whose headquarters were at Winnsborough, detached Tarleton in pursuit of Morgan, who retreated to the Cowpens, and resolved to risk a battle there. Tarleton leaving his baggage behind him well guarded, started, with his accustomed celerity, at three o'clock in the morning,* in pursuit. Before day Morgan received intelligence of his approach, and prepared for action. He drew up his regulars and Triplett's corps, reckoned not inferior to them, and about four or five hundred men, under Howard, on an eminence in an open wood. In their rear, on the declivity of the hill, Lieutenant-Colonel Washington was posted with his cavalry and some mounted Georgia militia as a reserve; and with these two corps Morgan remained in person. The front line was composed of militia, under Pickens. Major McDowell, with a battalion of North Carolina volunteers, and Major Cunningham, with a battalion of Georgia volunteers, were advanced about one hundred and fifty yards in front of this line. Morgan's whole force amounted to eight hundred men. Soon after the troops were disposed, the

---

* February 17th, 1781.

(715)

British van appeared in sight, and Tarleton forming his line of battle, his troops rushed forward to the attack, shouting. Morgan's first line soon retreated into the rear of the second. The British advanced in spite of a firm resistance; Tarleton ordered up his reserve, and Howard's infantry being outflanked, Morgan rode up and directed that corps to retreat over the summit of the hill, about one hundred yards, to the cavalry. The British, now confident of victory, pressed on, in some disorder, and when the Americans halted, were within thirty yards of them. At Howard's order, his men turning, faced the enemy, and poured in, unexpectedly, a deadly fire. Howard, perceiving that the enemy's ranks were thrown into some confusion, ordered a charge with the bayonet, and the British line was broken. The cavalry on their right was at the same time routed by Washington. Howard and Washington pressed their advantage until the artillery and greater part of the infantry surrendered; but Washington pursuing too eagerly, received a temporary check, and sustained a heavier loss in this part of the action than in any other. However, the infantry advancing to support him, Tarleton resumed his retreat.*

In this battle one hundred British, including ten commissioned officers, were killed; twenty-nine commissioned officers and five hundred privates made prisoners. A large quantity of arms and baggage and one hundred dragoon horses fell into the hands of the victors. Morgan lost less than eighty men in killed and wounded.

Tarleton retreated toward Cornwallis, whose headquarters were now twenty-five miles distant. In this action Cornwallis had lost one-fifth of his number and the flower of his army. But Greene was not strong enough to press the advantage; and Morgan,

---

* In the pursuit, Washington advanced near thirty yards in front of his men. Three British officers observing this charged upon him. The officer on his right aimed a blow to cut him down, when an American sergeant intercepted it by disabling his sword arm. The officer on his left was about to make a stroke at him, when a waiter saved him by wounding the assailant with a ball from a pistol. The officer in the centre, believed to be Tarleton, now made a thrust at him, which he parried, upon which the officer retreated a few paces and then discharged a pistol at him, which wounded his horse.

apprehensive of being intercepted by Cornwallis, abandoned the captured baggage, interring the arms, and leaving his wounded under the protection of a flag, hastened to the Catawba, which he recrossed on the twenty-third. The prisoners were sent by General Greene, under escort of Stevens' brigade of Virginia militia to Charlottesville.

In the mean while Arnold, ensconced, like a vulture, was prevented from planning new schemes of devastation by apprehensions that he now began to entertain for his own safety.* Richard Henry Lee wrote: "But surely, if secrecy and despatch were used, one ship-of-the-line and two frigates would be the means of delivering Arnold and his people into our hands; since the strongest ship here is a forty-four, which covers all their operations. If I am rightly informed, the militia now in arms are strong enough to smother these invaders in a moment if a marine force was here to second the land operations."

February the ninth a French sixty-four gun-ship, with two frigates, under Monsieur De Tilley, sailed for the Chesapeake, and arriving by the thirteenth threatened Portsmouth. But the ship-of-the-line proving too large to operate against the post, De Tilley, in a few days, sailed back for Rhode Island. It was a great disappointment to the Virginians that the French admiral could not be persuaded to send a force competent to capture the traitor. Governor Jefferson, in a letter to General Muhlenburg, offered five thousand guineas for his capture; and suggested that men might be employed to effect this by entering his quarters in the garb of friends—a measure not to be justified even toward Benedict Arnold.

After the battle of the Cowpens, Greene, closely pursued by Cornwallis, retreated across the Dan into Virginia. His lordship then proceeded to Hillsborough, then the capital of North Carolina, where he invited the inhabitants to repair to the royal standard. Greene, re-enforced by a body of Virginia militia under General Stevens, soon re-entered North Carolina, where numerous tories were embodying themselves to join Cornwallis. On the twenty-fifth of February, Lee, with his cavalry, by stratagem sur-

---

* January 26th, 1781.

prising a body of royalists under Colonel Pyle, cut them to pieces. On the fifteenth of March occurred the battle of Guilford. Greene's army was much superior in numbers, but consisted mainly of militia and new levies. The cavalry of Lee and Washington was excellent, but the ground was unfavorable for their action. The officers under Greene were mostly veteran. The Virginia militia were commanded by Generals Stevens and Lawson, and by Colonels Preston, Campbell, and Lynch; those of North Carolina by Generals Butler and Eaton. Of the continentals one Maryland regiment alone was veteran. Guilford court-house, near the great Salisbury road, stood on a hill which descends eastward, gradually, with an undulating slope for half a mile, terminating in a little vale intersected by a rivulet. On the right of the road the ground was open, with some copses of wood; on the left a forest. Greene, with not quite two thousand regulars, was posted at the court-house; in the field to the right of the road, the two regiments of Virginia under Huger, the two of Maryland under Williams. Three hundred yards in advance of the regulars were stationed the Virginia militia, crossing at right angles the great road; and as far in front of them and across the same road the North Carolina militia were formed: the Virginia line in the woods; the Carolinians partly in the forest and partly on its edge, behind a strong rail-fence, in front of which lay an open field. Two pieces of artillery, under Captain Singleton, were placed in the road a few yards in advance of the first line. The right flank was guarded by Washington's cavalry, a veteran Delaware company under Kirkwood, and Colonel Lynch with a battalion of Virginia militia. The left was guarded by Lee's legion and Campbell's riflemen. At about ten o'clock in the forenoon, after some firing of artillery, the British, reaching the rivulet, deployed into line of battle, the right commanded by Leslie, the left by Webster. The North Carolina militia, unable to stand the shock, a few excepted, broke, threw away their arms, and fled precipitately through the woods. The Virginia line received the enemy with more firmness, but the greater part of them were compelled to retreat, which was accelerated by the fall of General Stevens, who was wounded in the thigh. The struggle between the enemy and the continentals was stoutly contested, but the second Maryland regiment unexpectedly giving way, Greene was compelled to retreat. Cornwallis pursued but a short distance. The American loss in killed and wounded amounted to thirty officers and four hundred privates. The British loss amounted to five hundred and thirty-two, including several valuable officers. Lieutenant-Colonel Stuart of the guards was killed; Colonel Webster mortally wounded. The total number of Greene's army was forty-five hundred, of whom thirty hundred were actually engaged. Cornwallis' force, according to American accounts, numbered two thousand; according to his statement, to only fourteen hundred and forty-five. After this disastrous victory Lord Cornwallis found it necessary to retire toward Wilmington.

In the mean while Arnold's anxiety for his safety at Portsmouth was relieved by the arrival* of a re-enforcement under General Phillips. This accomplished and able but proud and passionate officer, exasperated by a tedious captivity, upon his exchange had been indulged by Sir Henry Clinton in a desire to invade Virginia, and wreak his vengeance on a State where he had been so long detained (unjustly as he, not without some reason, believed) a prisoner of war. Having united Arnold's force with his own, Phillips left Portsmouth,† and on the following day the army landed at Burwell's Ferry, from which the militia fled. Phillips, with the main body, marched upon Williamsburg, and entered it without serious opposition. Simcoe, with a small party of cavalry, early next morning surprised a few artillery-men at Yorktown, (the rest escaping across the river in a boat,) and burnt "a range of the rebel barracks." The British sloop, Bonetta, anchored off the town. How little did the parties engaged in this little episode anticipate the great event which was destined soon to make that ground classic! The Bonetta, too, was destined to return to that picturesque place to play her part in the closing scene. Phillips, embarking at Barret's Ferry, near the mouth of the Chickahominy, issued "the strictest orders to prevent privateers, the bane and disgrace of the country which employs them;" but these orders were disregarded. When off Westover, he issued further orders, saying:

---

* March twenty-seventh. † April eighteenth.

"A third object of the present expedition is to gain Petersburg, for the purpose of destroying the enemy's stores at that place, and it is public stores alone that are intended to be seized." A body of two thousand five hundred men under Phillips landed at City Point,* and passed the night there; and on the next morning (Wednesday) marched upon Petersburg, by way of Colonel Banister's Whitehall plantation, where they halted in the heat of the day and refreshed themselves. Steuben, with a thousand men, disputed the entry of the town. At about two o'clock the British advanced in two columns by the old road leading by the Blandford Church, and were opposed by a party of militia posted on the heights, just beyond Blandford, under Captain House, of Brunswick, and Colonel Dick. The enemy were twice broken, and ran like sheep, and during two hours advanced only one mile. At length the battalion of Americans posted at the Bollingbrook warehouses, near the Blandford Bridge, being flanked by four pieces of artillery, were compelled to retire over the Appomattox, taking up Pocahontas Bridge as soon as they had crossed it, ten men being killed in ascending the hill. On this hill Steuben had placed some troops and cannon to cover his retreat. The American loss, killed, wounded, and taken, in this affair was estimated at sixty; that of the British probably not less, there having been, according to Colonel Banister, not less than fourteen killed; their wounded were sent down the river in gun-boats. Abercrombie, who commanded the British infantry on this occasion, was the same who afterwards fell in Egypt. Phillips, taking possession of Petersburg, made his headquarters at Bollingbrook, a private residence, on an eminence overlooking the river. He destroyed, next day, a large quantity of tobacco, the people removing it from the warehouses to save it from the flames. One of them was set fire to by a soldier and burnt. The enemy also destroyed several vessels. The bridge over the Appomattox being readily repaired, Abercrombie, with a detachment, passed over on the twenty-sixth, and took possession of the heights opposite the town, known as Archer's Hill. Phillips, with his whole army, crossing on the same day, burnt the bridge, and proceeded to

---

* April twenty third.

commit devastations at Chesterfield Court-house, Osbornes, and at Warwick, destroying the American vessels, and shipping off the tobacco. This being private property, its destruction was in violation of his recent order. At Manchester a detachment destroyed the warehouses and tobacco, and several dwelling-houses, the militia and inhabitants of Richmond being quiet spectators of the scene. Proceeding from Osbornes to Bermuda Hundred, the British embarked there and sailed down the river as far as Hog Island, where Phillips, receiving orders by an advice-boat, returned up the river, as far as Brandon, the seat of Benjamin Harrison, where the troops landed in a gale of wind. Colonel Theodorick Bland, Sr., received the following protection: "It is Major-General Phillips' positive orders that no part of the property of Colonel Theodorick Bland receive any injury from his majesty's troops.

"April 25th, 1781.

"J. W. николь, aide-de-camp Major-General Phillips.

"Major-General Phillips is very happy to show this favor on account of Colonel Bland Junior's many civilities to the troops of convention at Charlottesville."

Notwithstanding this, Colonel Bland's place of residence, Farmingdell, in Prince George County, was plundered by the British troops: his furniture broken to pieces; china-ware pounded up; tobacco, corn, and stock destroyed, and negroes taken off. General Phillips being taken ill, found it necessary to travel in a carriage, which was procured for him by Simcoe.

Part of the troops were sent* to City Point in boats; the rest marched upon Petersburg, arrived there late in the night, and surprised a party of American officers engaged in collecting boats for La Fayette to cross his army.† La Fayette, with a strong escort, appeared on the heights opposite Petersburg, and the artillery, under Colonel Gimat, cannonaded the enemy's quarters. Bollingbrook, where General Phillips lay ill of a bilious fever, being exposed to the fire, it was found necessary to remove him into the cellar, and it is commonly reported that he died while the firing was going on. This mistake appears to have originated

---

* May ninth. † Tenth.

with Anburey, who, in his Travels, mentions that during the cannonade, the British general, then at the point of death, exclaimed, "My God, 'tis cruel: they will not let me die in peace!" Anburey, being himself a prisoner of war, was not in favorable circumstances for obtaining accurate information on this subject. It appears that the cannonading took place three days before the death of General Phillips. He died on the thirteenth. La Fayette, aware that Bollingbrook was headquarters, directed some shot particularly at that house, which, from its elevated site, afforded a conspicuous mark. This proceeding was provoked by the horrid series of devastations which Phillips had just perpetrated in company of the traitor Arnold. Two balls struck the house, it is said, one passing through it. General Phillips lies buried in the old Blandford Churchyard. Miller,* a historian of his own country, observes that it would have been a fortunate circumstance for his fame "had he died three weeks sooner than he did."†

Upon the death of General Phillips the command devolved on Arnold, and he sent an officer with a flag and a letter to La Fayette. As soon as he saw Arnold's name subscribed to the letter he refused to read it, and told the officer that he would hold no intercourse whatever with Arnold; but with any other officer he should be ever ready to interchange the civilities which the circumstances of the two armies might render desirable. Washington highly approved of this proceeding.

Already before the death of General Phillips, Simcoe had been detached from Petersburg to meet Cornwallis, who was advancing from North Carolina. Simcoe, on his route to the Roanoke, captured, some miles to the south of the Nottoway River, a Colonel Gee, at his residence, "a rebel militia officer," who, refusing

---

* Hist. of England.

† Bollingbrook, deriving its name from the family of Bolling, who owned much of the land on which the town of Petersburg was built, consisted of two frame buildings, or wings, standing apart, it having been designed to connect them by a main building, which, however, was never done. The eastern tenement was burned down some years ago, and thus was lost an interesting memento of the Revolution. A representation of it may be seen in Lossing's "Field Book of the Revolution."

to give his parole, was sent prisoner to Major Armstrong. Another "rebel," Colonel Hicks, mistaking Simcoe's party for an advanced guard of La Fayette's army, was also made prisoner. At Hicks' Ford, a captain and thirty militia-men were taken by a *ruse de guerre,* and compelled to give their paroles. Here Simcoe, on his return toward Petersburg, met with Tarleton and his "legion clothed in white."

During this year (1781) Captain Harris, with the little brig Mosquito, after taking two prizes, in a voyage to the West Indies was captured by the British frigate Ariadne, and carried into Barbadoes. The men were confined there in jail and prison-ships: the officers taken to England and incarcerated in Fortune Jail, at Gosport. Driven by cruel usage to make a desperate attempt at escape, they succeeded, and returned to America, and again bore arms against the enemy. Among them were Lieutenant Chamberlayne, Midshipman Alexander Moore, Alexander Dick, captain of marines, and George Catlett, lieutenant of marines. Shortly after the capture of the Mosquito, the Raleigh fell into the enemy's hands, and her crew were no less maltreated. The brig Jefferson, under command of Captain Markham, captured several prizes.

Among those distinguished for their gallantry in the little navy of Virginia was Captain Samuel Barron, (son of Commodore James Barron,) afterwards of the United States navy. Captain John Cowper, of Nansemond County, was in command of the Dolphin brig, with a crew of seventy-five men. Embarking on a cruise, he nailed his flag to the mast-head, and declared that he would never strike it to an enemy. Engaging shortly after with two British vessels, she was seen no more, and it is supposed that she sunk during the action.

John Tyler was born at his father's residence, near Williamsburg, in James City County, in 1748. His father, whose name he bore, was marshal for the colony, and his mother was the daughter of Doctor Contesse, one of the Protestants driven from France by the revocation of the edict of Nantes, and who found a home in Virginia. John Tyler, the younger of the two sons of this union, (the elder of whom died young,) enjoyed frequent opportunities of hearing the debates in the house of burgesses, and heard Patrick Henry in the stormy discussion on his resolutions in 1765, and in the decline of life still related with animation his recollections of that debate. He became so decided an opponent of the tyrannical pretensions of the mother country that his father often predicted that, sooner or later, he would be executed for high treason. Mr. Tyler studied the law under Mr. Robert Carter Nicholas, and while thus engaged formed an acquaintance with Thomas Jefferson which ripened into a friendship terminated only by death. The society of the ardent Jefferson fanned the flame of young Tyler's patriotism, and he became at an early day the advocate of independence. About the year 1774, having obtained his license, he removed to Charles City, where he took up his permanent abode. Successful in the practice of the law, he was after a brief interval elected a delegate from that county. He was re-elected for several years, his colleague for the greater part of that time being Benjamin Harrison, Jr., of Berkley, whom Mr. Tyler succeeded as speaker of the house of burgesses. After the lapse of many years Mr. Tyler's son, of the same name, succeeded General William Henry Harrison, son of Benjamin Harrison, Jr., in the Presidency of the Union. Mr. Tyler, the revolutionary patriot, while a member of the assembly, contracted an intimate friendship with Patrick Henry, for whom he entertained an almost idolizing veneration. They corresponded for many years. Mr. Tyler participated largely in the debates, and on all occasions exhibited himself a devoted patriot, and thoroughbred republican. In subsequent years he was governor of Virginia and judge of the United States district court. In private life his virtues won regard, in public his integrity and talents commanded the confidence of his country.

John Banister was the son of an eminent botanist, of the same name, who settled in Virginia toward the close of the seventeenth century, and devoted himself to the study of plants. In one of his botanical excursions, near the falls of the Roanoke, he fell from a rock and was killed. As a naturalist he was esteemed not inferior to Bartram. John Banister, the son, was educated in England, and bred to the law at the Temple. He was a burgess of the assembly, and afterwards a distinguished member of the convention of 1776. In the following year he was an active member of the assembly. He visited the headquarters of the American army about the time of the battle of Germantown. In 1778-9 he was a member of congress at York, and at Philadelphia, and in September visited headquarters as member of the committee of arrangement. He was one of the framers of the articles of confederation. In 1781 he was lieutenant-colonel of cavalry under General Lawson. The two other colonels in the brigade were John Mercer, afterwards governor of Maryland, and James Monroe, subsequently President of the United States. Lawson's corps was dissolved when Leslie retired from Virginia, and thus the horse commanded by Colonel Banister was lost to the State, at a time when cavalry was so pressingly required. During the invasions which Virginia was subjected to, Colonel Banister was actively engaged in the efforts made to repel the enemy. Proprietor of a large estate, he suffered repeated and heavy losses from the depredations of the British. At one time, it is said, he supplied a body of troops, on their way to the South, with blankets at his own expense.

A miniature likeness of him is said to be preserved by his descendants in Amelia County. Of an excellent and well cultivated mind, and refined manners, he was in private life amiable and upright, in public generous, patriotic, and enlightened. As a writer he may be ranked with the first of his day. A number of his letters have been published in the Bland Papers, and several, addressed to Washington, in Sparks' Revolutionary Correspondence.

Colonel Banister resided near Petersburg, at Battersea, which house he built. Chastellux visited it in 1781. Colonel Banister married, first, Mary, daughter of Colonel Theodorick Bland, Sr. Of this union there were three children; but this whole branch is extinct. Colonel Banister's second wife was Anne, sister of Judge Blair, of the federal court. There were two sons of this marriage: Theodorick Blair, and John Monro. Theodorick Blair Banister married Signora Tabb. Children surviving, (1856:) Monro, Tudor, Yelverton, and two daughters. John Monro Banister married Mary B. Bolling. Children surviving: William C. Banister, the Rev. John Monro Banister, and three daughters.

CHAPTER XCIX.

1781.

Cornwallis at Petersburg—La Fayette retreats—Simcoe's Expedition—Tarleton's Expedition—Cornwallis marches toward Point of Fork—Devastations of the Enemy—Peter Francisco—La Fayette re-enforced by Wayne—Cornwallis retires—Followed by La Fayette—Skirmish at Spencer's Plantation—Action near Jamestown—La Fayette.

CORNWALLIS marched* from Wilmington for Petersburg. To facilitate the passage of the rivers, two boats, mounted on carriages, accompanied the army. Tarleton led the advance. While the army was yet on the left bank of the Roanoke, Cornwallis, who had passed it, upon overtaking Tarleton's detachment, ordered them to be dismounted and formed in line for the inspection of the inhabitants, to enable them to discover the men who had committed certain horrid outrages on the preceding evening. A sergeant and a dragoon being pointed out as the offenders, were remanded to Halifax, condemned by a court-martial, and executed. His lordship was prompted to such acts of discipline not only by his moderation and humanity, but also by a desire to avoid any new exasperation of the people, and by a hope of alluring the loyalists to his standard. On the 19th of May, 1781, he reached Petersburg, and with the remnant of his Carolina army he now united the troops under Arnold, consisting of a detachment of royal artillery, two battalions of light infantry, the 76th and 80th British regiments, the Hessian regiment of the Prince Hereditaire, Simcoe's corps of cavalry and infantry, called the "Queen's Rangers," chiefly tories, one hundred yagers, and Arnold's American legion, likewise tories, the whole amounting to about two thousand five hundred men, which, together with the Carolina army, made his lordship's aggregate force at Petersburg about four thousand five hundred. The

---

* April twenty-fifth.

entire field force now under his command in Virginia was not less than seven thousand three hundred, including four hundred dragoons and seven or eight hundred mounted infantry. He received intelligence from Lord Rawdon of his having defeated Greene, at Hobkirk's Hill. Cornwallis remained three or four days at Petersburg. Light troops and spies being despatched to discover La Fayette's position, he was found posted near Wilton, on the James River, a few miles below Richmond, with a thousand regulars and three thousand militia, the main body of them under command of General Nelson. La Fayette was expecting re-enforcements of militia and Wayne's Pennsylvania Brigade. In compliance with the orders of Governor Jefferson, continental officers were substituted in the higher commands of the militia. Three corps of light infantry, of two hundred and fifty each, of select militia marksmen, were placed under command of Majors Call, Willis, and Dick of the continental line. La Fayette's cavalry comprised only the remnant of Armand's corps, sixty in number, and a troop of volunteer dragoons under Captain Carter Page, late of Baylor's Regiment. General Weedon, not now in service, owing to a diminution in the number of officers, was requested to collect a corps of militia to protect a manufactory of arms at Falmouth, opposite Fredericksburg. Tarleton patroled from Petersburg as far as Warwick, and, surprising a body of militia, captured fifty of them. In the mean while General Leslie arrived at the mouth of the James with a re-enforcement sent by Clinton from New York. Cornwallis, upon receiving intelligence of it, ordered Leslie to repair to Portsmouth with the 17th British Regiment, two battalions of Anspach, and the 43d, to join the main army. His lordship now proceeded with his forces to Macocks, on the James, opposite to Westover, where, being joined by the 43d, he crossed over, the passage occupying nearly three days, the horses swimming by aid of boats, the river there being two miles wide.

Arnold obtained leave to return to New York, "where business of consequence demanded his attendance." The British officers had found it irksome to serve under him. Cornwallis afterwards told La Fayette that as soon as he joined the army in Virginia he took the first occasion to send Arnold down to Portsmouth, and expressed disgust at associating with a person of his character.

The force concentrated by Cornwallis amounted to eight thousand. La Fayette, hearing of this movement of the enemy, crossed the Chickahominy and retreated toward Fredericksburg, with a view of protecting the arsenal at Falmouth and of meeting Wayne. Cornwallis pursued with celerity, but finding La Fayette beyond his reach, gave out the chase, and encamped on the banks of the North Anna, in Hanover. La Fayette, who had been hotly pursued by Tarleton, retreated precipitately beyond Fredericksburg; and it was on this occasion that Cornwallis, in a letter, said of La Fayette: "The boy cannot escape me." The Marquis de Chastellux says: "All I learnt by a conversation with Mr. Bird* was that he had been pillaged by the English when they passed his house in their march from Westover in pursuit of Monsieur de la Fayette, and in returning to Williamsburg, after endeavoring in vain to come up with him. It was comparatively nothing to see their fruits, fowls, and cattle carried away by the light troops, which formed the van-guard; the army collected what the vanguard had left; even the officers seized the rum and all kinds of provisions without paying a farthing for them; this hurricane, which destroyed everything in its passage, was followed by a scourge yet more terrible: a numerous rabble, under the title of Refugees and Loyalists, followed the army, not to assist in the field, but to partake of the plunder. The furniture and clothes of the inhabitants were in general the sole booty left to satisfy their avidity; after they had emptied the houses, they stript the proprietors, and Mr. Bird repeated with indignation that they had taken from him by force the very boots from off his legs." "Mr. Tilghman, our landlord,† though he lamented his misfortune in having lodged and boarded Lord Cornwallis and his retinue without his lordship's having made him the least recompense, could not yet help laughing at the fright which the unexpected arrival of Tarleton spread among a considerable number of gentlemen who had come to hear the news, and were assembled at

---

* Landlord of the Ordinary in New Kent.
† At Hanover Court-house.

the court-house. A negro on horseback came full gallop to let them know that Tarleton was not above three miles off. The resolution of retreating was soon taken; but the alarm was so sudden and the confusion so great that every one mounted the first horse he could find, so that few of those curious gentlemen returned upon their own horses."

From his army encamped in Hanover, Cornwallis detached Simcoe with five hundred men, Queen's Rangers and yagers, with a three-pounder, the cavalry amounting to one hundred. The object of this expedition was to destroy the arsenal lately erected at the Point of Fork, and the military stores there. The Point of Fork is contained between the Rivanna and the James, in the County of Fluvanna. At the same time his lordship detached Tarleton with his legion, and one company of the 23d Regiment, with the design of capturing Governor Jefferson and the members of the assembly, then convened at Charlottesville, and also of destroying military stores.

During the recent incursions of Phillips and Arnold a state arsenal had been established at the Point of Fork, and military stores collected there with a view to the prosecution of the war in the Carolinas. The protection of this post had been entrusted to Baron Steuben, who had acquired a knowledge of the military art under Frederick the Great. Steuben's force consisted of between five and six hundred new levies, (originally intended for the Southern army,) and a few militia under General Lawson. Cornwallis informed Simcoe that the baron's force was only three or four hundred; but Simcoe held the earl's military intelligence in slight respect. Thus he says:* "He had received no advices from Lord Cornwallis, whose general intelligence he knew to be very bad." "The slightest reliance was not to be placed on any patroles from his lordship's army."

Lieutenant Spencer, with twenty hussars, formed Simcoe's advanced guard of chosen men mounted on fleet horses. Simcoe crossing the South Anna, pushed on with his usual rapidity by Bird's Ordinary toward Napier's Ford on the Rivanna. Cornwallis, with the main body, followed in Simcoe's route. No in-

---

* Simcoe's Journal, 226.

habitant of the country coming within view escaped capture. From some of the prisoners intelligence was obtained that Steuben was at the Point of Fork and in the act of crossing to the south side of the James. The baron adopted this measure in consequence of intelligence of Tarleton's incursion. Within two miles of Steuben's camp a patrol of dragoons appeared, was chased and taken; it consisted of a French officer and four of Armand's corps. The advanced men of Spencer's guard changed clothes with the prisoners for the purpose of attempting to surprise the baron at the only house at the Point of Fork. Just as Simcoe was about to give the order to his men to lay down their knapsacks in preparation for an engagement, the advanced guard brought in a prisoner, Mr. Farley, Steuben's aid, who had mistaken them for the patrol which had just been captured. He assured Simcoe that he had seen every man over the James before he left the Point of Fork, and this was confirmed by some captured wagoners. Simcoe's cavalry advancing, plainly saw the baron's force on the opposite side. About thirty of Steuben's people, collected on the bank where the embarcation had taken place, were captured. Simcoe, thus disappointed, employed stratagem to persuade the baron that the party was Earl Cornwallis' whole army, so as to cause the arms and stores that covered the opposite banks to be abandoned. Captain Hutchinson, with the 71st Regiment clothed in red, was directed to approach the banks of the James, while the baggage and women halted in the woods on the summit of a hill, where they made the appearance of a numerous corps, the woods mystifying their numbers, and numerous camp-fires aiding the deception. The three-pounder was carried down and one shot fired, by which was killed the horse of one of Steuben's orderly dragoons. The baron was encamped on the heights on the opposite shore, about three-quarters of a mile back from the river. He had passed the river in consequence of intelligence of Tarleton's incursion, which he apprehended was aimed at him. The river was broad and unfordable, and Steuben was in possession of all the boats. Simcoe himself was now in an exposed position; but his anxiety was relieved when the baron's people were heard at night destroying their boats with great noise. At midnight they made up their camp fires. Soon after a deserter and a little drummer-boy passed over in a canoe, and gave information that Steuben had marched off on the road by Cumberland Court-house toward North Carolina. The drummer-boy belonged to the 71st Regiment; he had been taken prisoner at the Cowpens, had enlisted in Morgan's army, and now making his escape happened to be received by a picket-guard which his own father commanded. On the following day, by aid of some canoes, Simcoe sent across the river Captain Stevenson with twenty light infantry, and Cornet Wolsey with four hussars, who carried their saddles with them. The infantry detachment were ordered to bring off such supplies as Simcoe might need, and to destroy the remainder. The hussars were directed to mount upon such straggling horses as they could find, and patrol in Steuben's wake. Both orders were executed; the stores were destroyed and Steuben's retreat accelerated. Simcoe in the mean while employed his men in constructing a raft by which he might pass the Rivanna. There was destroyed here a large quantity of arms, the greater part of them, however, out of repair, together with ammunition and military stores. The quantity and value of property destroyed were exaggerated by the enemy; as also was Steuben's force. Simcoe took away a mortar, five brass howitzers, and four long brass nine-pounders, all French, mounted afterwards at Yorktown. According to his opinion a small guard left by Steuben would have protected these stores. The disaster was probably owing to a want of accurate military intelligence. Simcoe held Steuben's military qualifications in high estimation; but his opinion of La Fayette was the reverse.

Mean while Tarleton, passing rapidly along the road by Louisa Court-house, met with some wagons laden with clothing for the Southern army, and burnt them. Learning that a number of gentlemen, who had escaped from the lower country, were assembled, some at Dr. Walker's, the others at Mr. John Walker's,* Tarleton, instead of advancing at once upon Charlottesville, despatched Captain Kinloch with a party to Mr. John Walker's,

---

* Belvoir, about seven miles from Charlottesville, and the residence of the late Judge Hugh Nelson. The house has been burnt down.

while he proceeded with the rest to the doctor's mansion, where he surprised Colonel John Syme, half-brother to Patrick Henry, Judge Lyons, and some other gentlemen who were found asleep, it being early in the morning.* Captain Kinloch captured Francis Kinloch, his relative, a delegate to congress from South Carolina, together with William and Robert Nelson, brothers to General Thomas Nelson. There is a family tradition that when this Captain Kinloch was about to leave England, the ladies of his family begged him not to kill his cousin in America, and that he replied, "No, but I will be sure to take him prisoner," which playful prediction was now fulfilled.† A Mr. Jouitte, mounted on a fleet horse, conveyed intelligence of Tarleton's approach to Charlottesville, so that the greater part of the members of the assembly escaped.‡ Tarleton, after a delay of some hours, entered Charlottesville; seven of the delegates fell into his hands, and the public stores were destroyed. Captain McCleod, with a troop of horse, visited Monticello with a view of capturing Mr. Jefferson; but he had about sunrise received information of Tarleton's approach. Some members of the assembly, and the speakers of both houses, who were his guests, hastened to Charlottesville; Mrs. Jefferson and her children hurried off in a carriage, and Mr. Jefferson followed afterwards on horseback, a few minutes before McCleod reached the house. The magnificent panorama of mountain scenery visible there must have afforded him and his dragoons some compensation for the disappointment. While Tarleton was in the neighborhood of Charlottesville, some British and Hessian prisoners of the convention troops cantoned

---

* It is said that as one of the gentlemen, who was rather *embonpoint*, and who in this emergency had found time to put on nothing but his breeches, ran across the yard in full view of the British dragoons, they burst into a fit of laughter at so extraordinary a phenomenon.

† Francis Kinloch, of Kensington, South Carolina, meeting, in passing, with Eliza, only daughter of Mr. John Walker, who was also at Philadelphia attending congress, is said to have fallen in love with her at first sight, she having at the moment just come from her hair-dresser, and he afterwards married her; and Eliza, only daughter of that union, became the wife of the late Judge Hugh Nelson, United States Minister at Madrid.

‡ The general assembly presented him with a horse fully caparisoned and a pair of pistols for his vigilance and activity.

with the planters, joined him. The prisoners of distinction, whom he had captured, were treated with lenity, being detained only a few days on their parole not to escape; "the lower class were secured as prisoners of war." The prisoners of note were released at Elkhill, a plantation of Mr. Jefferson's, where Cornwallis for ten days made his headquarters. This plantation was laid waste by the enemy. Wherever his lordship's army went, plantations were despoiled, and private houses plundered. During the six months of his stay in Virginia she lost thirty thousand slaves, of whom the greater part died of small-pox and camp fever; and the rest were shipped to the West Indies, Nova Scotia, etc. The devastations committed during these six months were estimated at upwards of thirteen millions of dollars.*

Peter Francisco, a soldier of the Revolution, celebrated for his physical strength and personal prowess, lived long in the County of Buckingham, Virginia, and died there. His origin is obscure: he supposed that he was a Portuguese by birth, and that he was kidnapped when an infant, and carried to Ireland. He had no recollection of his parents, and the first knowledge that he retained of himself was of being in that country when a small boy. Resolving to come to America, he indented himself to a sea-captain for seven years, in payment of his passage. On arriving in Virginia he was indented to Anthony Winston, Esq., of Buckingham, and labored on his estate until the breaking out of the Revolution. Being then at the age of sixteen he obtained permission to enlist in the army. At the storming of Stony Point he was the next, after Major Gibbon, to enter the fortress, and he received a bayonet wound in the thigh. He was present in the battles of Brandywine, Monmouth, the Cowpens, Camden, and Guilford Court-house. In the last-mentioned action, where he belonged to Colonel Washington's dragoons, his strong arm levelled eleven of the enemy. His bravery was equal to his strength.

During the year 1781, while reconnoitring alone, and stopping at a house in Amelia, now Nottoway, he was made prisoner by a detachment of Tarleton's dragoons. But availing himself of a

---

* Burk, iv.

favorable opportunity, when one of the British was stooping to take off his silver shoe-buckles, Francisco wounded him with his own sword, and another, and by a ruse frightened off the rest of the party, who fled, leaving their horses, although Tarleton's corps was in full view. This exploit was illustrated by an engraving, published in 1814, a favorite ornament of the drawing-room. Peter Francisco was in height six feet and one inch: his weight was two hundred and sixty pounds: his strength Herculean. He used a sword of extraordinary size. His complexion was that of a native of the south of Europe, his eye dark, his whole appearance massive, unique, and remarkable. An excellent portrait of him was made by Harding. John Randolph, of Roanoke, brought the attention of congress to Peter Francisco's military services in an interesting memoir, and applied for a pension for him. He was in old age made sergeant-at-arms to the house of delegates.*

The condition of affairs in Virginia in the summer of 1781 was gloomy, humiliating, apparently almost desperate. After a war of five years the State was still unfortified, unarmed, unprepared. But it was asked, did not every Virginian possess a gun of some kind, and was it not with such arms that the battles of Bunker Hill and of the Cowpens were fought? Virginia had entered upon the war when she was already loaded with debt, and exhausted by her Indian war, and by her non-importation policy, before the war began. Intersected by rivers, she was everywhere exposed to the inroads of the enemy; and a dense slave population obstructed the prompt movement of the militia. The darkness of the future was relieved by a single ray of hope derived from the uncertain rumors of the sailing of a French fleet for America; but frequent disappointment rendered hope of help from that quarter precarious. The bulk of the people were staunch whigs and well affected to the French alliance; but they were growing despondent, and some were even beginning to fear that France was prolonging the war so as to weaken America as well as Great Britain, and to render the new confederation dependent upon its allies. With the aid of a superior French fleet there could be no doubt of the successful issue of the war; with-

---

* Howe's Hist. Coll. of Va., 207.

out that aid, there was too much reason to fear that the people could not be kept much longer firm, in so unequal a contest.

La Fayette, joined by Wayne's brigade, eight or nine hundred strong, marched toward Albemarle old court-house, where some magazines remained uninjured by the British, and he succeeded in saving them from Tarleton's grasp. La Fayette at this place was joined by Colonel Campbell, the hero of King's Mountain, with his riflemen. Cornwallis, in accordance with advices from Clinton, retired to the lower country, and was followed by La Fayette, who had, in the mean time, above Richmond been reenforced by Steuben with his new levies and some militia. Cornwallis halted for a few days at Richmond; Simcoe being posted at Westham; Tarleton at the Meadow Bridge. La Fayette's army amounted to four thousand five hundred, of whom one-half were regular; and of these, fifteen hundred were veterans; he was still inferior to his lordship in numbers, by one-third, and very deficient in cavalry. Cornwallis, leaving the picturesque hills of Richmond on the 20th of June, 1781, reached Williamsburg on the twenty-fifth. La Fayette followed, and passing Richmond arrived at New Kent Court-house on the day after the British general had left it. La Fayette took up a position on Tyre's plantation, twenty miles from Williamsburg. Cornwallis having detached Simcoe to destroy some boats and stores on the Chickahominy, he performed the service with his accustomed promptness. La Fayette discovering Simcoe's movement, detached Colonel Butler, of the Pennsylvania line, in quest of him. Butler's van consisted of the rifle corps under Majors Call and Willis and the cavalry; the whole detachment, not exceeding one hundred and twenty effectives, was led by Major McPherson, of Pennsylvania. Having mounted some infantry behind the remnant of Armand's dragoons, he overtook Simcoe, on his return, near Spencer's plantation, about six miles above Williamsburg, at the forks of the roads leading to that place and to Jamestown. The ground there, in Simcoe's phrase, was "admirably adapted to the chicanery of action." The suddenness of McPherson's attack threw the yagers into confusion, but they were firmly supported by the Queen's Rangers, to whom the alarm was given by trumpeter Barney, exclaiming: "Draw your swords, Rangers;

the rebels are coming!" Barney himself captured a French officer. Call and Willis having now joined McPherson, a warm conflict ensued; and Simcoe found occasion for all his resources. The advanced party of Butler's corps was repulsed, and fell back in confusion upon the continentals, and Simcoe, satisfied with this advantage, retired. Both parties claimed the advantage in this rencontre, the loss of the British being eleven killed and twenty-six wounded; that of the Americans was not reported, except that three officers and twenty-eight privates were made prisoners; the number of their killed and wounded probably exceeded that of the British.* Lieutenant-Colonel Simcoe considered this action as "the climax of a campaign of five years." Major McPherson was unhorsed, but crept into a swamp, and so escaped. Simcoe, after retreating two miles toward Williamsburg, met Cornwallis with the advance of his army coming to his relief. Colonel Butler, the American commander in this affair, was the same who afterwards fell at St. Clair's defeat.

Late in June, Cornwallis, with an escort of cavalry under Simcoe, visited Yorktown for the purpose of examining the capabilities of that post; and his lordship formed an unfavorable opinion of it. The party was ineffectually fired at from Gloucester Point, and returned on the same day to Williamsburg. After halting here nine days, Cornwallis† marched, and encamped near Jamestown Island, for the purpose of crossing the James and proceeding to Portsmouth. The Queen's Rangers passed over the river in the evening of the same day to cover the baggage which was now transported. La Fayette, as Cornwallis had predicted, now advanced with the hope of striking at the rear-guard only, of the enemy, supposing, upon imperfect intelligence, that the main body had already crossed. Accordingly, about sunset‡ La Fayette attacked Cornwallis near Greenspring, and after a warm conflict was compelled to retreat, having discovered that he was engaged by the main body of the British. Of the continentals one hundred and eighteen were killed, wounded, or taken. Some cannon also fell into the hands of the enemy. The British

---

* Simcoe, 227. Plan of the skirmish opposite 236.
† Fourth of July. ‡ July 6th, 1781.

state their loss at five officers and seventy privates killed and wounded. Cornwallis now crossed the James unmolested and marched* for Portsmouth.

La Fayette, re-enforced by some dragoons from Baltimore, retired to a strong position near the head of York River. The militia had already been discharged.

---

* July ninth.

CHAPTER C.

1781.

Capture of the Patriot—The Barrons and Captain Starlins—Battle of the Barges.

WHILE the British men-of-war and transports were assembled in Hampton Roads, in co-operation with Cornwallis, in the spring and summer of 1781, the small craft were engaged in frequent depredations, going up the James as far as Jamestown, and looking into the smaller streams for plunder. To afford some little relief to the distressed inhabitants, for the most part women, the men being at sea, or in the army, or prisoners, it was determined to employ the only vessel then afloat belonging to the State—the schooner Patriot. She was small, and mounted only eight two-pounders; but she had more than once captured vessels of twice her calibre. Captain Watkins having received his orders, proceeded at once down the James River upon this service. For some weeks a sloop, supposed to be a privateer, had been committing depredations, and Watkins determined to overhaul her. Two young Virginians were on the north side of the James, in the County of Elizabeth City, endeavoring day after day to cross the river and find a safer refuge on the south side of it. Daily emerging from a small house, "in the great gust-wood," where they found temporary shelter, they repaired to the river side, distant about three miles, looking out for some craft to convey them across. In company of the two brothers was a negro, a native of Africa, who had been brought to Virginia in his youth, and had soon evinced an ardent attachment to it. He was an expert pilot, and a devoted "patriot." On a Sunday morning, as the trio stood on the river bank, at a point in Warwick County, they espied the schooner Patriot in chase of the plundering sloop, and apparently gaining fast upon her. The negro, known as Captain Starlins, at this spectacle, gave noisy utterance to his extravagant joy, hopping about and clapping together his uplifted hands. The three hoped soon to witness the capture of the sloop; but it

(738)

turned out that she was purposely retarded in her course by a drag thrown out over her starboard bow, and the Patriot coming alongside of her, there suddenly up jumped fifty marines, and in a moment the Patriot was captured.* The three spectators beheld the catastrophe with intense disappointment. From the zenith of hope Captain Starlins had been suddenly plunged souse down to the nadir of despair. He and the younger of the brothers burst into tears, while the older brother, fifteen years of age, although no less grieved, had more command over his sensibilities. Giving a parting look to the unfortunate schooner as she disappeared in the hazy distance, they retraced their steps. Watkins and those under him were sent off to Charleston, and confined in the provost prison, where he died. The Patriot was taken round to Yorktown. Captain Mark Starlins died a slave a few years after, and just before the passage of a law giving freedom to those men of color who had served the patriotic cause. His slavery, however, appears to have been merely nominal; for his master fully appreciated his noble character, and which was held in high estimation by all worthy citizens, especially by all the navy officers of Virginia. The two brothers were the Barrons, afterwards distinguished in the United States naval service.†

In 1782 Maryland sent out Commodore Whaley, with some barges, to protect the Eastern Shore of that State against bucaneering crafts manned by British sailors, and tories, and negroes. Receiving information of the appearance of a flotilla of such barges in the Chesapeake Bay, under command of a Commodore Kid, a Scotchman, Whaley, deeming them too strong for him, solicited aid from Colonel John Cropper, commander of Accomac County, who, with a party of volunteers, re-enforced him. Colonel Cropper, with several Accomac gentlemen, went on board

---

* Such is the account given by Commodore Barron from his early recollections. It appears, however, that he and his companions were misled by appearances, and that the Patriot was engaged with the British sloop for two hours, and twice attempted to board her, but ineffectually. At length the sloop cut away the Patriot's main halliards, and her main-sail fell to the deck; when, receiving a broadside, and being no longer manageable, the Patriot struck her colors.—[*Va. Navy of Revolution, S. Lit. Messr.*, 1857, p. 147.]

† Va. Hist. Register, i. 127.

the Protector, the commodore's barge. Whaley having requested those in the other barges to support him in case the enemy should make a push at him, they promised to do so, "or all sink together." The enemy's barges were descried in the morning of the thirtieth of November, in Cagey's Straits: they soon hove to, and formed in line. The action commenced at half-past nine o'clock, and lasted twenty-five minutes. The foremost of Whaley's barges having fired a few shot at long distance, retreated. He, nevertheless, with the Protector advanced to within fifty yards of the enemy, exposed to their fire, and returning it warmly. A gunner, in handing an eighteen-pounder cartridge out of the chest, happened to break it, and the spilt powder, although water had been poured upon it, caught fire from the flash of the small arms, and the chest exploded, producing great confusion on board, killing two or three, and causing a number of men, some with their clothes on fire, to jump overboard. The enemy, encouraged by this, pushed on with redoubled fury, and Whaley was deserted by his other five barges, who fled ingloriously, leaving their commander to his fate. Three of Kid's barges were already alongside of him, when a second ammunition chest exploded, renewing the scene of disaster and confusion. Lieutenant Handy enquired of Whaley whether it would not be better to strike: he replied that he should not strike. Colonel Cropper describes the action at this time as "a continual shower of musket bullets, pikes, cold shot, cutlasses, and iron stantials, for eight or ten minutes." The Protector being overpowered by numbers, most of the men being driven from their quarters, she was surrendered, the general cry being for quarter, which, however, the enemy refused. The barge was now boarded by the blacks with brutal cruelty. In this action all the Protector's officers were either killed or wounded. Whaley fell, killed by a musket ball; Captain Handy fell fighting with one arm, after the other had been broken. Lieutenant Handy was severely wounded. Of the sixty-five men that went into action in the Protector twenty-five were killed or drowned, and twenty-nine wounded, some mortally. Of the Accomac volunteers Captain Christian was killed with a musket ball. Captain William Snead, Mr. John Reville, and Colonel Cropper, were wounded. Among those thrown into the water by the explosion was William Gibb, a Scotchman, for many years deputy clerk of Accomac. He could not swim, and was sinking when his friend, Captain Parker, seized him by the hair, and kept him afloat until they both were picked up by the enemy. As long as Gibb lived, which was forty-five years thereafter, he had an annual feast at his house on the thirtieth of November, the anniversary of the Battle of the Barges.*

Colonel Cropper at the age of nineteen was captain of the 9th Virginia Regiment in the continental line: and in 1776 was made major in the 5th Regiment.† He was with Washington in the Jerseys, and present at the battles of Monmouth and Brandywine. For his good conduct in the latter he was promoted.

---

* I am indebted to Dr. Levin S. Joynes for some MSS. relative to the Battle of the Barges.

† Levin Joynes, of Accomac, became at the same time major in the 9th, and Thomas Snead, of the same county, major in the 7th Regiment.

CHAPTER CI.

1781.

Washington—Cornwallis occupies Yorktown—Battle of Eutaw Springs—Henry Lee—Washington invests Yorktown—Capitulation.

In the North, Washington retained a self-possessed mind. So the eagle from his mountain watch-tower looks down and surveys with serene eye the tempest and the storm forming beneath his feet. Re-enforced by the French troops under Rochambeau, and a fleet, he was concerting measures to expel Clinton from New York, believing that in this way he could give the enemy the more fatal blow, and afford the South the more effectual relief. But he resolved, in case he should find this design impracticable, to transfer the scene of war to the South. Cornwallis was advised by Sir Henry to select a post on the Chesapeake, convenient for wintering a fleet—either Yorktown or Old Point. Washington requested La Fayette to endeavor to prevent Cornwallis from marching to Charleston, and Wayne was, accordingly, despatched to the south side of the James to watch his movements.* Cornwallis having selected Yorktown, occupied it and Gloucester Point, on the opposite side of the York, and proceeded to fortify them.

Early in August, Washington received from the Count de Barras the information that the Count de Grasse might be expected shortly to reach the Chesapeake with a formidable fleet. Washington now determined to transfer the war to the South; but to deceive Clinton he made his arrangements secretly, and continued his apparent preparations against New York. Cornwallis concentrated the whole British force in Virginia at Yorktown and Gloucester Point by the twenty-second of August. The latter post was held by the 80th Regiment, the Hessian

---

* August 2d, 1781.

regiment of the Prince Hereditaire, and the Queen's Rangers—the whole under command of the brave and energetic Colonel Dundas, of the artillery. Tarleton, with his cavalry, afterwards passed over to Gloucester Point. La Fayette, in consequence of the movements of the enemy, broke up his camp on the Pamunkey, and drew nearer to Yorktown. Washington, having concerted with the French commanders a plan of operations, with the combined American and French forces, marched for Virginia, the army being put in motion on the nineteenth, and having completed the passage of the Hudson on the twenty-fifth. Sir Henry Clinton did not suspect that the movement was for the South until the third of September.

On the thirtieth of August, De Grasse, with twenty-eight ships of the line and several frigates, arrived from the West Indies, and entered the Chesapeake. At Cape Henry he found an officer despatched by La Fayette with intelligence of the situation of the two armies. On the following day his advanced ships blocked up the mouth of the York. While the French fleet lay at anchor just within the Chesapeake, a squadron was descried early in the morning of September the fifth, consisting of nineteen ships-of-the-line, under Admiral Graves. De Grasse immediately formed his line and put to sea; and a partial engagement occurred. Several ships were damaged, but the result was indecisive. For some days the fleets continued within view of each other, after which De Grasse returned to his moorings within the capes. Here he found* De Barras with a squadron newly arrived from Rhode Island, bringing artillery and stores proper for carrying on a siege. Graves looking in at the capes found the French fleet too strong for him, and returned to New York. La Fayette made his headquarters at Williamsburg, twelve miles from Yorktown.

On the 8th of September, 1781, the battle of Eutaw Springs, in South Carolina, took place. The British army, commanded by Lieutenant-Colonel Stuart, being encamped at that place, Greene marched at four o'clock in the morning, to attack the enemy, seven miles distant. Upon approaching them Greene formed his

---

* September tenth.

first line of militia under Marion and Pickens. The second was composed of continental infantry and the North Carolina Brigade, commanded by General Sumner, on the right; the Virginians, under Lieutenant-Colonel Campbell, in the centre; the Marylanders, under Colonel Williams, on the left. Lee's legion covered the right flank; South Carolinians, under Colonel Henderson, the left; and Washington's cavalry, with Kirkwood's infantry, formed the reserve. Captain Gaines, with two three-pounders, was attached to the first line, and Captain Brown, with two sixes, to the second.

The British were drawn up across the road obliquely,—in a wood, on the heights near the Eutaw Springs, having their right flank on Eutaw Creek. The flanks were protected by infantry and cavalry; and a body of infantry was held in reserve. The British advanced party was soon driven in. The militia, after maintaining themselves firmly for awhile, were compelled to retire before the advancing enemy, and their place was filled by Sumner's North Carolina Brigade, which, supported by Lee and Henderson on the flanks, went into action with great intrepidity. The British fell back to their first ground. Henderson was disabled by a wound. At Sumner's brigade giving way the British rushed forward in some disorder. Greene directed Williams and Campbell to charge with the bayonet, and Washington to bring up the reserve. Williams charged without firing a musket; but Campbell's regiment, chiefly new levies, returned the enemy's fire as they advanced. Lee now ordered Captain Rudolph, of the legion infantry, to turn the enemy's flank, and give them a raking fire. This being done, the British left was broken, and, driven off the field retreated through their tented camp toward Eutaw Creek, where was a brick house, into which a part of them threw themselves. The Americans pursuing closely, took three hundred prisoners and two pieces of cannon.

Washington charging the enemy's right with his cavalry suffered a heavy loss. He himself had his horse killed, and was wounded and made prisoner. The enemy now rallied, and Greene, finding it impossible to dislodge them, retired. It was an extremely hard-fought battle. The loss of the Americans was five hundred and fifty-five, including sixty officers. One hundred and thirty were killed. Seventeen officers were killed, and four mortally wounded. Among the slain was Lieutenant-Colonel Campbell, who fell while leading the Virginia Brigade on to the charge. This excellent officer, on being told just before he expired, that the Americans were victorious, exclaimed, "Then I die contented." The loss of the British was six hundred and ninety-three, of whom eighty-five were killed on the field. Greene made five hundred prisoners. The combatants were about equal in number, and the question of victory was left undecided. Greene was, as a military leader, esteemed as second only to General Washington.

Henry Lee was born in Westmoreland, Virginia, on the 29th of January, 1756, being son of Colonel Henry Lee* and Mary Bland, of Jordans. Henry receiving his early education from a private tutor at home, afterwards pursued his studies at the College of New Jersey, under the presidency of Dr. Witherspoon, and graduated there in 1774, in his eighteenth year. While in college, Dr. Shippen predicted his future distinction. In 1776, when twenty years of age, on the nomination of Patrick Henry, he was appointed a captain in Colonel Bland's regiment of cavalry. In September of the following year the regiment joined the main army, where Lee, by his discipline, vigilance, and efficiency, soon won the confidence of Washington, who selected him and his company for a body-guard at the battle of Germantown. While Lee lay near the British lines, a numerous body of cavalry surprised him in his quarters, a stone house, where he had with him but ten men. Yet with these he made a gallant defence, and obliged the enemy to retreat, after having lost four men killed, together with several horses, and an officer with three privates wounded. Of his own party, besides the patrols and quartermaster-sergeant, who were made prisoners out of the house, he had but two wounded. Washington complimented Lee on his gallantry in this little affair, and congress shortly after promoted him to the rank of major with the command of an independent partisan corps of horse. July 19th, 1779, he surprised the British garrison at Paulus Hook, and was rewarded by con-

---

* For many years a member of the house of burgesses.

gress with a gold medal. Early in 1780 Lee, now lieutenant-colonel, with his legion, consisting of cavalry and infantry, joined the army of the South, under General Greene. In his retreat before Cornwallis, Lee's legion formed part of the rear-guard of the American army. During the retreat, Lee charged successfully upon Tarleton's dragoons. After Greene had effected his escape, he detached Lee, with Pickens, to watch the movements of Cornwallis. Lee, with his legion, by a stratagem surprised four hundred armed loyalists under Colonel Pyle, of whom ninety were killed and many wounded.

At the battle of Guilford Lee's legion distinguished itself. When Cornwallis retired to Wilmington, it was by Lee's advice that Greene moved at once into South Carolina. Lee, detached with his legion, joined the militia under Marion. Several forts speedily surrendered. Lee now joined Pickens, for the purpose of attacking Fort Augusta, which was reduced. In the unfortunate assault upon Fort Ninety-Six, Lee was entirely successful in the part of the attack intrusted to his care. At the battle of the Eutaw Springs he bore a distinguished part; and General Greene declared that his services had been greater than those of any other man attached to the Southern army. As a partisan officer he was unsurpassed. He was a soldier, an orator, and a writer; and in his Memoirs has given a graphic picture of the war in the South. He was about five feet nine inches high, well proportioned, of an open, pleasant countenance, and of a dark complexion. His manners were frank and engaging, his disposition generous and hospitable. He was twice married: first to Matilda, daughter of Philip Ludwell Lee, by whom he had a son, Henry, and a daughter, Lucy; and afterwards to Ann, daughter of Charles Carter, of Shirley, by whom he had three sons, Charles Carter, Robert, and Smith, and two daughters, Ann and Mildred. General Henry Lee resided at Stratford. His statue is to be placed on the Richmond Monument. Among the officers of Lee's legion were Armstrong, Rudolph, Eggleston, and Carrington.

Washington, accompanied by Rochambeau and the Marquis De Chastellux, reaching Yorktown on the fourteenth of September, and repairing on board the Ville de Paris, the admiral's ship, arranged the plan of the siege. By the twenty-fifth, the combined army, amounting to twelve thousand men, together with five thousand militia under General Nelson, was concentrated at Williamsburg. The allies advanced upon York and invested it, the Americans forming the right below the town, the French the left above it, and each extending from the borders of the river, so as to completely circumvent the town. General De Choisy invested Gloucester Point with three thousand men. The enemy's communication by water was entirely cut off by ships stationed at the mouth of the river, some ten miles below Yorktown. Cornwallis, some time before this, finding his situation growing so critical, had anxiously solicited aid from Sir Henry Clinton; and it was promised, but never arrived. Washington was assisted during the siege by Lincoln, Steuben, La Fayette, Knox, and others. The French were commanded by General the Count De Rochambeau. On the twenty-ninth the British commenced a cannonade, and during the night abandoned some redoubts, and retired within the town. Colonel Scammel, while reconnoitring the ground just abandoned by the enemy, was surprised by a party of horse, and, after he had surrendered, received a wound from a Hessian, of which he died in a few days, greatly lamented. On the third of October, in a skirmish before Gloucester Point, Tarleton was unhorsed, and narrowly escaped being made prisoner. The British sent out from Yorktown a large number of negroes infected with the small-pox. On the night of the seventh the first parallel was extended two miles in length, and within six hundred yards of the British lines. By the evening of the ninth, several batteries being completed, Washington himself put the match to the first gun, and a heavy fire was opened, and the cannonade continued till the fifteenth. Cornwallis was driven from Secretary Nelson's house.

Upon the breaking out of the Revolution, the Secretary had retired from public affairs. He lived at Yorktown, where he had erected a handsome house. Cornwallis made his headquarters in this house, which stood near the defensive works. It soon attracted the attention of the French artillery, and was almost entirely demolished. Secretary Nelson was in it when the first shot killed one of his negroes at a little distance from him. What increased his solicitude was that he had two sons in the American army; so that every shot, whether fired from the town or from the trenches, might prove equally fatal to him. When a flag was sent in to request that he might be conveyed within the American lines, one of his sons was observed gazing wistfully at the gate of the town by which his father, then disabled by the gout, was to come out. Cornwallis permitted his withdrawal, and he was taken to Washington's headquarters. Upon alighting, with a serene countenance he related to the officers who stood around him what had been the effect of their batteries, and how much his mansion had suffered from the first shot. A red-hot ball from a French battery set fire to the Charon, a British forty-four gun-ship, and two or three smaller vessels, which were consumed in the night. They were enrobed in fire, which ran like lightning over the rigging and to the tops of the masts. A second parallel was completed, and batteries erected within three hundred yards of the enemy's works. The British had two redoubts about three hundred yards in front of their lines, and it was resolved to take them by assault. The one on the left of the enemy bordering the banks of the river was assigned to a brigade of light infantry under La Fayette, the advanced corps being conducted by Colonel Alexander Hamilton, assisted by Colonel Gimat. The attack commenced at eight o'clock in the evening, and the assailants entered the fort with the point of the bayonet, without firing a gun. The American loss was eight killed and thirty wounded. Major Campbell, who commanded the redoubt, was wounded and made prisoner, with about thirty soldiers; the rest escaped. During the assault, the British kept up a fire along their whole line. Washington, Lincoln, and Knox, having dismounted, stood in an exposed position awaiting the result. The other redoubt, on the right of the British, was taken at the same time by a detachment of the French commanded by Baron De Viomenil. He lost about one hundred men killed and wounded. Of the enemy at this redoubt eighteen were killed and forty-five captured, including three officers.

By this time many of the British guns were silenced, and their works were becoming ruinous. About four o'clock in the morning of the sixteenth, Colonel Abercrombie, with four hundred men, made a sortie against two unfinished redoubts occupied by the French; the British, after spiking some cannon, were driven back, with a small loss on each side. One hundred pieces of heavy artillery were now in full play against the enemy, and he had nearly ceased firing. In this extremity, Lord Cornwallis formed a desperate design of attempting to force his way to New York, his plan being to leave his sick and baggage behind, to cross over the York River in the night to Gloucester Point with his effective force, and, overwhelming De Choisy there, his lordship intended to mount his men on captured horses, and, by forced marches, gain the fords of the rivers, and thus make his way through Maryland, Pennsylvania, and Jersey, to New York. Boats were in readiness under other pretexts, at ten o'clock of the night of the sixteenth, and the arrangements were conducted with so much secrecy that the first division arrived at Gloucester Point unperceived, and part of the troops were landed, when a violent storm drove the boats down the river, and it was not till daylight that they returned to Yorktown. The plan being frustrated, the boats were sent to bring back the soldiers, and they were relanded on the south side during the forenoon. At about ten o'clock in the forenoon of the seventeenth, the British beat a parley, and by a flag requested a cessation of hostilities for twenty-four hours, to settle terms for the surrender of the posts. Washington granted a suspension of hostilities for two hours for the reception of his lordship's proposals in writing. These having been received, the suspension was prolonged. The commissioners for adjusting the terms of the capitulation were the Viscount De Noailles and Lieutenant-Colonel Laurens, in behalf of the allies; and Colonel Dundas and Major Ross, in behalf of the British. The place of meeting was Moore's House, at Temple Farm, in the rear of the first parallel. A rough draft of the articles of capitulation was made on the eighteenth, to be submitted to the respective generals. Washington sent a fair transcript of the articles to Lord Cornwallis early on the morning of the nineteenth, together with a letter restricting the interval allowed for signing the capitulation to eleven o'clock, and that for the actual surrender to two o'clock in the afternoon of that day. His lordship acquiesced, and on the 19th of October, 1781, the British army surrendered. At about twelve o'clock the combined army was drawn up along a road in two lines, about twenty yards apart, and extending more than a mile, the Americans on the right, the French on the left. At the head of the American line Washington appeared on horseback, surrounded by his aids and the American staff; at the head of the French line and opposite to Washington was posted Count Rochambeau, surrounded in the same way. At two o'clock the captive army advanced between the allied lines in column, slowly, and in exact order. Profound silence reigned during this scene,* which recalled to mind the awful vicissitudes of human fortune, awoke commiseration for the captives, and suggested the consequences of this great event. Lord Cornwallis, under the pretext of indisposition, declined being present, and his place was filled by General O'Hara. This gallant officer, mounted on a fine charger, upon reaching the head of the line, mistook Count Rochambeau, on his left, for the commander-in-chief; but quickly discovering his error, flew across the road to Washington, asked pardon for his mistake, apologized for the absence of Lord Cornwallis, and begged to know his further pleasure. Washington courteously referred him to General Lincoln, who had been compelled to surrender at Charleston, for his guidance. Returning to the head of the column, it moved under the guidance of Lincoln to the field selected for laying down the arms. The men manifested their embittered feelings, and Colonel Abercrombie was observed to hide his face when his men threw down their muskets.

The post at Gloucester Point was surrendered about the same time. The command of the British there had recently been assumed by Tarleton, Dundas being required to be present on the south side of the river. Tarleton, before the surrender, waited on General De Choisy, and made known to him the apprehensions which he entertained for his personal safety, in case he should fall into the hands of the American militia, and requested his protection. The danger was imaginary; and the general readily agreed to ensure his safety. Tarleton surrendered his force to the legion of the Duke De Lauzun and Mercer's

---

* Lee's Memoirs, 370. Colonel Lee, despatched by Greene to the North on public business, happened to be present during the siege and at the surrender, and has given a graphic description of them.

corps, the residue of the allied detachment not even being present to witness the spectacle. The number of prisoners surrendered at the two posts was upwards of seven thousand, who, with the artillery, arms, military chest, and stores, were given up to Washington, the ships and seamen to Count De Grasse. The loss sustained by the garrison during the siege of eleven days amounted to five hundred and fifty-two, including six officers. The allied force amounted to sixteen thousand men, being, continentals five thousand five hundred, French seven thousand, militia three thousand five hundred. Loss in killed and wounded during the siege, about three hundred.

In the adjustment of the articles of capitulation, Cornwallis had insisted strenuously upon two points: first, that the prisoners of war should be allowed to return to Europe, upon condition of not serving against the United States or France, until exchanged; second, security for American citizens who had joined the British armies. Both were rejected; but the latter was virtually admitted, by permitting his lordship to send away the Bonetta with despatches to Sir Henry Clinton, free from search. In this way his lordship conveyed away the most obnoxious loyalists securely to New York; but Lord Cornwallis, in soliciting this favor, pledged himself that no officer should go in this way without Washington's consent. In his orders of the twentieth, the commander-in-chief congratulated the army on this glorious event, and declared that it was owing to the assistance of the French allies. He returned his profound acknowledgments to them, mentioning with special honor Count De Rochambeau, the Baron De Viomenil, the Chevalier De Chastellux, the Marquis De St. Simon, the Count De Viomenil, and General De Choisy. The gallant French troops shared in the applause bestowed on the whole army. Generals Lincoln, La Fayette, Steuben, and Knox, together with Colonels Carney, and D'Abbeville, received the highest praise. The services of the gallant and patriotic General Nelson, commander of the militia, were recognized with no less distinction. A general amnesty was granted; and all belonging to the army that were under arrest were pardoned and restored to the ranks, that they might participate in the universal joy. Washington concluded the order in these words: "Divine service shall be performed to-morrow in the different brigades and divisions. The commander-in-chief recommends to all the troops that are not upon duty to assist at it with a serious deportment and that sensibility of heart which the recollection of the surprising and particular interposition of Providence in our favor claims."

Sir Henry Clinton, with a fleet of twenty-five ships-of-the-line, two fifty gun-ships, and eight frigates, commanded by Admiral Digby, and having on board seven thousand chosen troops, appeared off the capes of Virginia on the twenty-fourth—they having sailed from Sandy Hook on the very day of the surrender. Sir Henry finding that he had arrived too late, set sail on the twenty-ninth, from the mouth of the Chesapeake, and returned to New York.

As the drama of the Revolution was opened in Virginia by Henry, so it was now virtually terminated here by Washington and his companions in arms. With this glorious event closes this history of the Colony and Ancient Dominion of Virginia.

INDEX.

Accomac, 55, 261, 305.
Adams, John, 621, 652.
Adams, Samuel, 568, 581.
Agriculture, 349, 614.
Albemarle colony, 258.
Albemarle, Earl of, governor-in-chief, 450.
Alexander, Archibald, 429, 490.
Alexandria, Braddock quartered at, 472.
Algonquin tribes, 269.
Amadas, Captain, 21.
Amsterdam, New, captured by Argall, 111.
Andros, Sir Edmund, governor, 347; charges against him, 356; remanded to England, 357.
Appomattox River discovered, 65, 268, 307.
Appomattox town, 107, 264.
Appomattox Indians, 40, 307.
Argall, Captain Samuel, captures Pocahontas, 107; his expedition against the French in Acadia, 111; reduces Dutch fort at Manhattan, 111; governor of Virginia, 124; his tyranny, 127; departure from Virginia, 129; is knighted, 129.
Arlington, Earl of, 274.
Armada, Spanish, 27.
Arnold, Benedict, invades Virginia, 710; returns to Portsmouth, 713; his position there, 717; joins Phillips in second invasion, 719; succeeds Phillips, 722; La Fayette refuses to correspond with, 722; returns to New York, 727.
Assembly of Virginia first held, 139; petitions the king, 172; the holding of, disallowed by Charles the First, 179; Charles the First desires assembly to be called, 181; declaration of, against restoration of Virginia Company, 200; loyalty of, 213, 251; supreme power claimed by, 238; sends address to Charles the Second, 251; demonstrations of its loyalty, 253; proceedings of, during Bacon's Rebellion, 296-7; journals of, seized, 320; "Bacon's Laws" repealed by, 322; Culpepper calls one; Beverley, clerk of, persecuted, 335; opposes governor's negative, and is prorogued, 339; Nicholson refuses to call, 345; held in college, 364; ceremony of opening, 364; acts of, 376; Spotswood dissolves, 395; Spotswood prorogues, 399; loyalty of, 417; passes relief acts, 507, 509; resolutions of, against stamp act, 540-41; thanks of, given to Washington, 504; remonstrates against proceedings of British government, 543; Botetourt dissolves 557; he calls together, 558; disapproves of Episcopate, 561; proceedings of, 570; Dunmore dissolves, 573; votes thanks to Dunmore for his conduct of Indian war, 594; first under republican constitution, 672; proceedings of, 681.

Bacon, Nathaniel, Jr., his servant and overseer slain by Indians, 286; leader of insurgents, 287; proclaimed a rebel and pursued by Berkley, 289; marches into wilderness and massacres tribe of Indians, 289; elected burgess, arrested, and released, 289; sues for pardon, 290; restored to council, 291; Berkley issues secret warrants for his arrest

INDEX.

and he escapes, 292; re-enters Jamestown and extorts a commission, 293; countermarches against governor, 299; calls convention, 301; exterminates Indians, 307; marches upon Jamestown, 308; puts governor to flight and burns Jamestown, 310; dies, 311; punishment of his adherents, 313, 317, 320, 321, 322.

Bacon, Elizabeth, wife of Nathaniel Bacon, Jr., 312, 329.

Bacon, Nathaniel, Sr., member of council, 292; member of court-martial, 315; auditor, 327; president of council. 344

Bacon, Elizabeth, wife of Nathaniel Bacon, Sr., 344.

Bacon Quarter Branch, 421.

Baltimore, George, Lord, visits Virginia; procures grant of territory from Charles the First, 183.

Baltimore, Cecilius, Lord, patentee of Maryland, employs Leonard Calvert to settle a colony there, 189; character of Baltimore's grant, 191.

Baltimore, Benedict, Lord, 377.

Banister, Colonel John, 725.

Baptists in Virginia, Blair's letter respecting. 554.

Barges, battle of, 738.

Barlow, Captain, 29.

Barradall, Edward, 434.

Barron, Commodore James, 679.

Barron, Captain Richard, 679-80, 738.

Barron, Lieutenant William, 679.

Barron, Captain Samuel, 723, 738.

Batt, Captain Henry, his expedition across the mountains, 268.

Baylor, Colonel, 668, 691.

"Bear and Cub," extract from Accomac records, 261.

Behn, Mrs. Afra, 317.

Bennet, Richard, a non-conformist, removes to Maryland, 212, 215; parliamentary commissioner, 216; with Clayborne reduces Maryland, 222; governor of Virginia, 223; agent at London, 233.

Berkley, seat on James River, 163.

Berkley, Sir William, governor, 200; issues proclamation against non-conformists, 203; captures Opechancanough, 204; visits England, 204; generosity to royalist refugees, 215; surrenders colony, 217; goes into retirement, 222; generous treatment of, 225; elected governor, 242; errors regarding his election, 243; Charles the Second sends new commission to, 248; emoluments of, 252-53; again visits England, 252; superintends Albemarle colony, 267; his statistics of Virginia, 271; his imbecile conduct in regard to the Indians, 281; refuses to give Bacon a commission, 287; proclaims Bacon a rebel, 288; releases Bacon from arrest, 289; issues secret warrants to arrest Bacon, 292; Bacon extorts commission from, 295; summons Gloucester militia, 298; escapes to Accomac, 299; returns to Jamestown, 306; escapes from Jamestown, 310; his recall and death, 223.

Berkley, Lady Frances, 224.

Bermuda Island, Sea-Venture wrecked on coast of, 94.

Bermuda City, 125.

Bermuda Hundred, 107, 112, 117.

Beverley, Robert, clerk of assembly, persecution of, 335-6-8.

Beverley, Robert, author of History of Virginia, 359.

Birkenhead discloses plot, 263.

Blackbeard, the pirate, 396.

Blair, Rev. James, Commissary, procures college charter, 346; president of college, 347; his controversy with Andros, 356; his controversy with Nicholson, 368; his controversy with Spotswood, 400; his death and character, 434.

Blair, John, president, 553; his letter concerning the Baptists, 554.

Bland, Giles, 304, 320.

Bland, Theodorick, speaker, 244.

Bland, John, 264.

Bland, Colonel Theodorick, Jr., has charge of convention troops, 694.

Bland genealogy, 670.

Bland, Richard, his "Letters to Clergy," 509; a burgess, 535; his "Inquiry into Rights of Colonies," 549; member of committee of correspondence, 570; delegate to congress, 630; member of committee of safety, 624; death of, 670.

Bolling, Colonel Robert, marries Jane Rolfe, 122.

Boone, Daniel, 595.

INDEX.   755

Boston, 257; Culpepper visits, 329; port bill, 574; affairs at, 666.
Botetourt, Lord, governor, 556, 558; his death, 559.
Boucher, Rev. Jonathan, his opinions on slavery, 526.
Braddock, Edward, General, his expedition against Fort Du Quesne, 471; defeat, 475; death, 480.
Brandywine, battle of, 685.
Braxton, Carter, interposes to stop Henry's advance, 612; member of committee of safety, 624; his Address to the Convention, 646; signer of Declaration of Independence, 652; sketch of, 662.
Breckenridge, 432, 490.
Brent, Captain, 284.
Bridge, Great, battle of, 635.
Bryan, Butler, Miss, marries Gov. Spotswood, 408.
Bucke, Rev. Mr., 95, 98, 117.
Bullet, Thomas, 501, 594, 635.
Bullet, Cuthbert, 594.
Burden's grant, 428.
Burgoyne, General, surrenders at Saratoga, 686.
Burnaby, Rev. Andrew, his account of Virginia, 502; his opinion on the disputes between assembly and ministers, 511.
Burras, Anne, first Christian married in Virginia, 65.
Burwell, Lewis, President, 450.
Butler's Account of Virginia, 169-70.
Byrd, Captain William, 421.
Byrd, Colonel William, Sr., of Westover, purchases records of Virginia Company, 174; auditor, 341; his generosity to Huguenots, 370; runs dividing line, 414; his opinion of people of New England, 415; plans Richmond and Petersburg, 421; his death, 435; epitaph, 436.
Byrd, Colonel William, Jr., of Westover, commands a Virginia regiment, 500; member of council, 610.
Byrd, Mrs. Maria, of Westover, her correspondence with Arnold, 712.

CABELL, COL. WILLIAM, member of convention of 1776, 624, 626; member of committee of safety, 624; sketch of, 626.
Calvert, Sir George, first Lord Baltimore, 183, 189.

Calvert, Leonard, commands expedition for planting colony in Maryland, 189.
Camden, Gates defeated at, 698.
Camm, Rev. John, opposes "Two-Penny Act," 509, 514.
Campbell, Colonel William, defeats Ferguson at King's Mountain, 699, 700; at the battle of Guilford, 718; joins La Fayette, 735.
Campbell, Lieutenant-Colonel, killed at Eutaw Springs, 745.
Campbell, Colonel Arthur, 690.
Carr, Dabney, 571.
Carrington, Paul, member of committee of safety, 624; sketch of, 624-25.
Carrington, Edward, 625.
Carter, John, 238, 264.
Carter, Robert, President, 412.
Carter, Charles, of Shirley, member of first council under republican constitution, 651.
Carter, Colonel Landon, 509.
Carthagena expedition, 417.
Cary, Colonel Archibald, 555, 646; member of committee of correspondence, 570; reports preamble and resolutions of independence, 646; chairman of committee to prepare declaration of rights and plan of government, 648.
Charles the First, his colonial policy, 175-79; disallows assemblies, 179; desires one to be called, 181; appoints council of superintendence, 187; grants Clayborne a license, 188; reinstates Harvey, 195; his government, 197; his letter to assembly, 201; overthrown at Naseby, 204; executed, 212.
Charles the Second, restoration of, 244; transmits new commission to Berkley, 247; grants territory of Virginia to Arlington and Culpepper, 274.
Charleston, South Carolina, founded, 330.
Charta, Magna, recognized, 237.
Charter granted to London Company, 35; new one, 76; dissolved, 174; Virginia obtains a meagre one, 326.
Chelsea, seat of Austin Moore, 387.
Cherokees, party of, visit Williamsburg, 450; in Sandy Creek expedi-

tion, 490; reduced to submission, 672; invaded by Shelby, 692.
Chesapeakes town discovered, 23.
Chesapeake Bay supposed to have been discovered by Spaniards, 19; Newport enters, 38; Smith explores, 55, 60; discovered by English, 188; explored by Pory, 188; naval action in, 743.
Chickahominy River, 45.
Chickahominies, 110.
Chicheley, Sir Henry, appointed to command expedition against Indians, 280; governor, 328, 332.
Christanna, Fort, 384
Church at Jamestown, 52, 101; of England, conformity to, required, 151; condition of, in Virginia in 1661, 249; laws concerning, 255; in Virginia, Rev. Morgan Godwyn's account of, 277; statistics of, 331; condition of, 354; dissent from, 438; ministers of, oppose "Two-Penny Act," 509.
Clarke, General George Rogers, captures St. Vincennes, 691-92, 713.
Clayborne, Colonel William, secretary of Virginia, effects settlement on Kent Island, 188; his contest with Maryland, 189, 192; convicted of high crimes, escapes to Virginia, goes to England, 192; expels Calvert from Maryland and usurps government, 205; one of commissioners for reducing Virginia, 216; assists Bennet in reducing Maryland, 222; authorized to make discoveries, 225; with Bennet seizes government of Maryland, 230; displaced from office of secretary, 254; burgess, 281; member of court-martial, 315; genealogy, 324.
Cohees, 424.
Coin, current, 350, 444.
Collectors, 351, 354.
College of William and Mary, 345-47, 361-64, 376, 437.
College, Hampden Sidney, founded, 677.
College, Washington, founded, 677.
Commencement at William and Mary, 361.
Commissary, his power, 374.
Committee of correspondence, 570.
Committee of safety, 624.

Commonwealth of England, 212.
Company, Virginia, 175.
Congress meets at Philadelphia, 579, 618.
Constitution of Virginia, 648.
Convention troops quartered near Charlottesville, 694; removed, 708.
Convention called by Bacon, 300.
Convention meets at Williamsburg, 575; second, meets at Richmond, 599, 624; meets at Williamsburg, 644; proceedings of, 644 48; instructs delegates in congress to propose independence, 646.
Convicts, 269.
Convocation, 368, 400.
Corbin, Colonel G., member of council, 610.
Corbin, G., Jr., member of council, 610.
Corbin, Henry, 264.
Corbin, Colonel Richard, deputy receiver-general, 611.
Corbin, John Tayloe, 645.
Cornstalk, Indian chief, 585, 587, 589.
Cornwallis, Lord, invades Virginia, 726; pursues La Fayette, 728; marches to Point of Fork, 729; commits devastations, 733; retires to lower country, 735; pursued by La Fayette, 735; fortifies Yorktown, is besieged and capitulates, 742-45.
Correspondence, committee of, 570.
Council, 351.
Counties, 190.
Court of claims, 351; county courts, 352; general court, 352; courts closed, 620.
Cromwell, Oliver, dissolves Long Parliament, 225; declared Protector, 225; his tolerant views, 231; letters, 230-31; death, 240; Virginia during his protectorate, 242.
Cromwell, Richard, succeeds to protectorate, 240; recognized by assembly, 241; resigns, 242.
Cropper, Colonel, 740.
Culloden prisoners, 340.
Culpepper, Thomas, Lord, governor-in-chief, 328, 331, 333, 336.
Cummings, Rev. Charles, 690.
Curtis, Edmund, 220.
Custis, Martha, Washington marries, 504.

INDEX.

Dale, Sir Thomas, governor, his code of martial law, 104; founds town of Henrico, 105; his expedition up York River, 108; proposes to marry a daughter of Powhatan, 113; takes Pocahontas to England, 116.
Dandridge, Captain Nathaniel West, 409, 418, 422.
Dandridge, John, 504.
Dandridge, Martha, marries, first, John Parke Custis; and secondly, George Washington, 504.
Dandridge, Bartholomew, 644, 651.
Dare, Virginia, first Christian child born in Virginia, 26.
Davies, Rev. Samuel, settles in Hanover County, 446; his zeal and eloquence, 447, 484; visits Great Britain, 482; his allusion to Washington, 483; patriotism and influence, 483, 498.
Dawson, Rev. Thomas, president of William and Mary, 505.
Deane, Silas, 702-3.
Declaration of Rights, 648.
Declaration of Independence, 652; Virginia signers of, 652.
Declaration, Mecklenburg, 615.
Delaware, Lord, first governor of Virginia, 77, 96, 101, 103, 126.
Delaware River, name of, 126.
Delaware City, 126, 313.
Delaware, Lady, presents Pocahontas at court, 119.
Dennis, Captain, commissioner for reducing Virginia, 216; compels colony to surrender, 217.
Dictator, alleged scheme of appointing, 676.
Digges, Edward, governor, 233; agent at London, 236.
Digges, Dudley, 233.
Disputes between colonies and mother country, 530.
Dinwiddie, Robert, governor, 452; dissensions between him and assembly, 454; his correspondence with Washington, 493, 496; letter to Fox, 494; succeeded by Blair, 494, 498.
Discovery, early voyages of, 17.
Dissenters, 202, 211, 371-73, 438, 446.
Dividing line, 414.
Drake, Sir Francis, 24.

Drummond, William, 266, 294, 299, 302-3, 307-8, 316, 321.
Drummond, Sarah, 303.
Drysdale, Hugh, governor, 411.
Dunmore, Lord, governor, 569; dissolves assembly, 570, 573; his Indian war, 582; indignation against, 588; his proclamation, 607; removes powder, 607; his proceedings, 608-10; offers "the olive branch," 618; retires aboard the Fowey, 619; correspondence with assembly, 619; his predatory warfare, 632; driven from Gwynn's Island, 665; retires from Virginia, 665; subsequent career, 665.
Dunmore, Lady, arrives at Williamsburg, 572; retires aboard the Fowey, 612; returns to Williamsburg, 618; embarks for England, 623.
Dutch, the, England at war with, 264.
Du Quesne, Fort, Braddock's expedition against, 471; captured by Forbes, and called Fort Pitt, 502.

Effingham, Lord Howard of, Governor, 336; his corruption and tyranny, 342.
Elizabeth, Queen, names Virginia, 22.
Elizabeth River, 59.
Episcopate, American, 560.
Eutaw Springs, battle of, 744.

Fairfax, William, 435, 457.
Fairfax, Thomas, Lord, 458.
Fairfax, Bryan, 574.
Farmingdale, 122.
Farrar's Island, 104.
Fauquier, Francis, governor, 508; his death, 553.
Ferguson, Colonel, killed at King's Mountain, 698, 700.
Ferrer, Nicholas, deputy treasurer of Virginia Company, 170, 174-76, 187.
Ferrer, John, 171, 187, 226.
Forbes, General, captures Fort Du Quesne, 502.
Fontaine, John, 387.
Fontaine, Rev. Peter, his opinion on slavery, 494.
Francisco, Peter, 733.
Franklin, Benjamin, 473, 652, 702.
Fredericksburg, Smith visits site of, 59; volunteers assembled at, 608.
Free Trade established, 245.

Free Church of Scotland, disruption of, 367.
Fresh, great, 560.
Fry, Colonel, 463-65.

GAP, DUTCH, 105.
Gates, Sir Thomas, governor, 35, 77, 94-8, 102-4, 111.
Gazette, Williamsburg, 419.
Gates, Horatio, serves under Braddock, 472; Burgoyne surrenders to, 686; defeated at Camden, 698.
Geography, physical, of Virginia, 426.
Germans settle valley of Shenandoah, 431.
Germanna, residence of Governor Spotswood, 381, 404.
Germantown, battle of, 685.
Gilbert, Sir Humphrey, 19.
Gilbert, Bartholomew, 29.
Girty, Simon, 593.
Godwyn, Rev. Morgan, his account of church in Virginia, 277.
Gondomar, Count, 19, 169, 176.
Gooch, William, governor, 414; commands Virginia regiment in Carthagena expedition, 417; his character, 449; his interview with dissenters, 440; his measures against them, 441; resigns, 448.
Gookin, Daniel, 164.
Gosnold, Bartholomew, 35; his voyage to New England, 28; his death, 43.
Governor, powers of, 350.
Gravesend, Pocahontas dies at, 120.
Greene, Nathaniel, General, 715.
Greenspring, plundered by rebels, 308; assembly held at, 322.
Grenville, George, introduces stamp act, 538.
Griffin, Rev. C., 384.
Grymes, John, member of council, 446; taken prisoner, 665.
Guilford, battle of, 718.
Gwynn's Island, Dunmore driven from, 665.

HAKLUYT, RICHARD, 115.
Hall, Carpenter's, congress meets in, 579.
Hamor, Ralph, visits Powhatan, 112.
Hampden Sydney College founded, 677.
Hanover presbytery, memorial of, 673.

Hansford, one of Bacon's adherents, executed, 314.
Hariot, Thomas, 23-4.
Harrison, Benjamin, of Surry, 654.
Harrison, Benjamin, of Brandon, member of first council under republican constitution, 651.
Harrison, Jr., Benjamin, of Berkley, member of committee of correspondence, 570; delegate to congress, 681; signer of Declaration, 652; his family, 654-56.
Harrison, John, delegate in congress, 681.
Harvey, Sir John, governor, 182; visits Calvert, 191; gives away large tracts of Virginia territory, 193; his corruption and tyranny, 193; deposed and reinstated 195.
Hatcher, William, 228.
Hawley, Major Joseph, of Massachusetts, 601.
Henrico, town of, 105.
Henry, Prince, 109.
Henry, Rev. Patrick, 521.
Henry, John, father of Patrick Henry the orator, 520; his map of Virginia, 521.
Henry, Jr., Patrick, his speech in "Parsons' Cause," 515; early life and education, 519; his resolutions against stamp act, 538; Mason's opinion of, 573; member of convention, 538-42; member of congress, 579; his resolutions for putting colony in state of defence, 599; his speech, 600; captain of Hanover volunteers, 611; recovers compensation for powder, 612; Dunmore's proclamation against, 613; his popularity, 614; colonel of 1st Virginia regiment, 627; resigns, 641; indignation of troops, 641; member of convention of 1776, 644; elected first governor of independent Virginia, 650; alleged scheme of making him dictator, 676.
Hill, Colonel Edward, (the elder,) speaker, 228; defeated by Ricahecrians, 233; re-elected speaker, 239; disfranchised, 297; his death, 361.
Hillsborough, Earl of, 558.
Hobkirk's Hill, battle of, 727.
Holloway, John, speaker, 415.
Hopkins, William, lawyer, 416.
Horrocks, Rev. James, 562.

INDEX.

Howard, Lord of Effingham, 337, 342.
Howe, Colonel, assumes command of Virginia troops at Great Bridge, 636; occupies Norfolk, 638.
Howe, Sir William, evacuates Boston, 667.
Hudson River discovered, 60.
Huguenots, 369.
Hunt, Rev. Robert, 38, 43, 51, 52.
Hunter, Robert, appointed governor, captured during voyage, 375.

INDIANS, seen at Cape Henry, 39; assault Jamestown, 42; Smith captured by, 46; tribes of, discovered by Smith, 47; Smith erects fort as refuge from, 74; manners and customs and character of, 85; extermination of, 50, 167; general act relating to, 255; number of, in Virginia, 268–69; incursions of, 280, 486, 492; Piscataway besieged, 285; murders committed by, 286; tribe of, massacred by Bacon, 289; Bacon marches against South-side tribes, 307; Spotswood reduces tribes of, 380; Captain McDowell slain by, 431; treaty with Six Nations of, 433; treaty of Lancaster, with, 433; battle with, at Point Pleasant, 584; Logan's speech, 590; Boone's rencontres with, 595–98; Cherokee sue for peace, 672.
Ingram succeeds Bacon, 313.
Innes, Colonel, 469, 496, 632, 710.

JAMES THE FIRST, king, issues letters patent, 35; his cruel treatment of Raleigh, 134, 156; jealous of Virginia Company, 169; death of, 175.
James the Second succeeds to throne, 339; his despotism, 341; abdicates, 342.
Jamestown, landing at, 41; assaulted by Indians, 42; destroyed by fire, 51; scarcity of provisions at, 75; abandoned by colonists, 98; they return to it, 98; church at, 101; condition of, 124; Bacon enters, 293; situation of, 309; burnt by rebels, 310; seat of government removed from, 358.
Jarratt, Rev. Devereux, biographical sketch of, 563.
Jefferson, John, 172.

Jefferson, Peter, 604.
Jefferson, Thomas, meets with Patrick Henry, 524; member of committee of correspondence, 570; his "Summary View," 575; notice of, 603; marries Martha Skelton, 606; author of preamble to Declaration of Rights, 650; author of Declaration of Independence, 652; member of committee of revisal, 676; governor, 708–11; attempt of British to capture, 732.
Jeffreys, Colonel Herbert, governor, 323; his proceedings, 326–28; succeeded by Chicheley, 328.
Jones, Rev. Hugo, 357, 382.
Jones, Joseph, delegate to congress, 681.
Jumonville, M. De, death of, 464.

KEMP, RICHARD, governor, 204.
Kent Island, 196.
Kenton, Simon, 593.
King's Mountain, battle of, 699.
Kinloch, Francis, 732.
Kiquotan, (Hampton,) 66, 104, 139, 319.

LA FAYETTE, MARQUIS DE LA, 722, 735, 737, 743, 747, 748, 751.
Land, grants of, 350.
Lane, Ralph, governor of Raleigh's colony, 23.
Laneville, 611.
Lancaster, treaty of, 433,
Laud, Archbishop, 189, 199.
Lawrence, Henry, 241.
Lawrence, Richard, 259, 294, 298–99, 302, 311, 316, 317.
Laydon, John, 65.
Lee, Richard, 264.
Lee, Richard Henry, his opinions on the "Two-Penny Act," 512; a burgess, 537; proposes separation of offices of speaker and treasurer, 544; sketch of his early life, 577, moves resolution of separation from Great Britain, 652; biographical sketch of, 659; charges against, 681; he demands an inquiry, 682; his defence and honorable acquittal, 682–84.
Lee, Francis Lightfoot, signer of Declaration, 652; notice of, 662; tenders his resignation as delegate in congress, 682.

Lee, Thomas Ludwell, member of committee of safety, 624.
Lee, Arthur, biographical sketch of, 701.
Lee, William, American commissioner at Vienna and Berlin, 704.
Lee, Lieutenant-Colonel Henry, biographical sketch of, 745.
Lee, General Charles, 664, 668, 688.
Leslie's invasion, 707.
Lewis, John, pioneer of Augusta, 428.
Lewis, Andrew, defeats Indians at Point Pleasant, 585–86; sketch of, 588; his brothers, 589; appointed brigadier-general, 641; expels Dunmore from Gwynn's Island, 665.
Lewis, Colonel Charles, killed at Point Pleasant, 585.
Loan office scheme, 539.
Logan, speech of, 590; sketch of, 590–93; his death, 706.
Loudoun, Lord, appointed governor-in-chief of Virginia, 500.
Loudoun, Fort, in Virginia, 494.
Loudoun, Fort, in Tennessee, 492.
Ludwell, Thomas, 264; agent at London, 276; his death, 358.
Ludwell, Colonel Philip, member of council, 291; captures Giles Bland, 306; quarrels with Jeffreys, 327; sent to England to prefer complaints against Effingham, 342, 344.
Lyons, James, attorney for plaintiff in "Parsons' Cause," 516.

MADISON, CAPTAIN, 166.
Madison, Jr., James, biographical notice of, 704.
Makemie, Rev. Francis, 371.
Manhattan, 111, 151.
Manakintown, 370.
Manakin Indians, 289.
Marriage, the first in Virginia, 65.
Marshall, Colonel Thomas, 685.
Marshall, John, (chief justice,) 635, 713.
Mary's, St., in Maryland, settled, 190.
Mary's, Mount, St., settled by Gookin, 164.
Mason, George, draughts non-importation agreement, 558; member of committee of safety, 624; author of declaration (or bill) of rights, 648; author of constitution of Virginia, 648; member of committee of revisal, 676; genealogy, 648.

Massacre of colonists by Indians in 1622, 160.
Massacre of colonists by Indians in 1644, 203.
Massacre of tribe of Indians by Bacon, 289.
Massawomecks, tribe of, 58.
Matthews, Captain Samuel, 209, 212; governor, 234; agent, 234, 236, 238; his election as governor declared void, 238; re-elected, 238.
Matthews, Thomas, 284.
McRoberts, Archibald, 566.
Maury, Rev. James, plaintiff in "Parsons' Cause," 515.
Maynard, Lieutenant, his engagement with Blackbeard, 396.
McDowell, Ephraim, 429.
McDowell, Captain John, 431.
Meade, Colonel Richard Kidder, aid-de-camp to Washington, 689; the Meades of Virginia, 689.
Mechanics, condition of, 350.
Mecklenburg Declaration, 615.
Menendez, Pedro, 18.
Mercer, Colonel George, 487, 543.
Mercer, James, member of committee of safety, 624.
Mercer, General Hugh, mortally wounded near Princeton, 668; notice of, 668–69.
Merchants, 350.
Methodists appear in Virginia, 562.
Middle Plantation, 188.
Minge, James, clerk of assembly, 281, 301.
Ministers, 249, 374, 696.
Monacan Indians, 63.
Monmouth, battle of, 688.
Monmouth's adherents sent to Virginia, 339.
Monongahela, battle of, 474.
Moore, Austin, of Chelsea, 387.
Moore, Bernard, of Chelsea, marries daughter of Governor Spotswood, 408.
Moore, Lucy, married to Speaker Robinson, 548.
Moore's Creek Bridge in North Carolina, battle of, 640.
Morgan, General Daniel, notice of, 686; his victory at Cowpens, 715.
Morris, Samuel, dissenter in Hanover County, 439.
Morrison, Francis, governor, 252; agent, 275.

INDEX.

Morquez, Pedro Menendez, explores Bay of Santa Maria, (Chesapeake,) 18.
Mounds in Virginia, 85.

NANSEMOND, 59.
Navigation act, 218, 248.
Navy, Virginia, 678.
Necessity, Fort, 465.
Neck, Northern, 248, 274.
Negroes introduced into Virginia, 144.
Negroes, number of, in 1649, 206.
Negroes, number of, in 1670, 272.
Negroes, number of, in 1714, 383.
Negroes, number of, in 1756, 494.
Negroes, duty on importation of, disallowed, 412.
Negroes, loss of, during British invasions, 733.
Nelson, President William, 654.
Nelson, Thomas, 653.
Nelson, Secretary Thomas, 651, 653, 747.
Nelson, Jr., General Thomas, his education, 653; member of convention, 653; member of congress, 653; his letter urging independence, 645; signer of Declaration, 652; sketch of, 653; his family, 653-54; commands militia during Arnold's invasion, 710; commands militia at siege of York, 747; notice of him and his family, 653.
Nelson, Judge Hugh, of Belvoir, 731.
Newport, Captain, sails for Virginia, 38; lands at Jamestown and explores the River Powhatan, 41; visits Powhatan, 50; returns to England, 53; arrives with second supply, 61; explores Monacan country, 63; embarks for England, 65.
Nicholas, Robert Carter, elected treasurer, 547; member of committee of correspondence, 624; member of convention, 600, 602.
Nicholson, Colonel Francis, governor, 344; succeeded by Andros, 347; again governor, 358; his tyranny, 358; his complaints against Virginia, 363; his speech to assembly, 365; his controversy with Blair, 368; is recalled, 369; notice of his career, 369.
Non-importation agreement, 558.

Norfolk incorporated, 420; burnt, 640.
Northy, Attorney-General, 367.
Norwood, Colonel, his voyage to Virginia, 213; despatched by Sir William Berkley to Holland, 215.
Nott, Edward, governor, 375.

OHIO COMPANY, 452.
Opechancanough, captures Smith, 46; seized by Smith, 71; visits Jamestown, 124; his hypocrisy, 161; heads a second massacre, 203; taken prisoner by Berkley, and dies, 204.
Opitchapan succeeds Powhatan, 130.
Orders, general, 642, 652.
Ovid translated at Jamestown by George Sandys, 152.

PAGE, JOHN, member of council, 347, 503.
Page, Matthew, 347.
Page, Mann, Jr., 682.
Page, John, of Rosewell, member of council, 614; member of committee of safety, 624; member of first council under the republican constitution, 651; commands party of militia during Arnold's invasion, 712.
Pamunkey, or Pamaunkee, Indian name of York River, 47.
Pamunkey, residence of Opechancanough, 47.
Pamunkey Indians, 298.
Parishes, 371.
Parliament, Long, 199, 215.
"Parsons' Cause," 507.
Paspaheghs, 39, 103; chief of, Smith's rencontre with, 73.
Patriot, the, capture of, 738.
Pendleton, Edmund, his early life and education, 535; opposes Henry's resolutions, 541; member of committee of correspondence, 570; delegate to congress, 575; member of committee of safety, 624; president of convention, 644; member of committee of revisal, 676.
Percy, Captain George, governor, 63, 66, 70, 73, 75, 97, 102.
Petersburg incorporated, 438; skirmish at, 720; General Phillips occupies, 720; his death at, 722; Arnold commands at, 722; Cornwallis arrives at, 726.

Philadelphia, congress meets at, 579.
Phillips, General, prisoner of war, 694; invades Virginia, 719; commits devastations, 720-21; his death, 722.
Pianketank, 59.
Pilgrims land at Plymouth Rock, 144.
Pirates, act against, 360.
Pirate captured, 361.
Piscataway, siege of, 284.
Plague in London, 265.
Plantagenet Beauchamp, 210.
Plantation, Middle, 300, 358.
Plymouth, landing at, 144.
Pocahontas rescues Smith, 48; entertains him with a dance, 62; discloses to him a plot, 67; made prisoner by Argall, 107; John Rolfe marries, 109; baptized, 115; visits England, 116; recommended to the queen by Smith, 118; Smith's interview with, 118; presented at court, 119; her death, son, and descendants, 120, 122.
Point Pleasant, battle of, 582, 584.
Point Comfort, 59, 188.
Population of Colonies, 362, 383, 450.
Population of Virginia, 272.
Porterfield, Colonel, mortally wounded at Camden, 698.
Pory, John, 139, 172, 188.
Post-office, 348.
Potomac River, 56.
Pott, Dr. John, governor, convicted of stealing cattle, 182-83.
Powder, Dunmore's removal of, 607.
Powhatan, name of river and seat, 41, 42.
Powhatan Indians, confederacy of, 269.
Powhatan, Indian chief, visited by Newport and Smith, 41, 49; releases Smith, 48; coronation of, 63; Smith visits, at Werowocomoco, 65; "Powhatan's Chimney," built for him by English, 68; Werowocomoco his residence, 68; consents to marriage of Pocahontas, 109; Hamor's interview with, 112; death of, and character, 129.
Presbyterianism, origin of, in Hanover, 439.
Preston, 432, 491.
Pretender, 437.
Printing in Virginia, 273, 418, 419.

Puritans, English, come over to Virginia, 144.
Puritan ministers from New England visit Virginia, 302.

QUAKERS, 244, 261, 396.
Quiyoughcohanocks, chief of, 39.

RALEIGH, SIR WALTER, his efforts to colonize Virginia, 21; introduces tobacco at court, 25; anecdotes of his using tobacco, 25, 153; notice of his life and death, 132-36.
Raleigh, Lady, 133, 134, 135.
Raleigh, City of, in Virginia, chartered, 26.
Raleigh, the, 573.
Randolph, Sir John, speaker, 420; his death, 424.
Randolph, William, 424.
Randolph, Peyton, king's attorney-general, 535; replied to by Davies, 447; opposes Henry's resolutions, 542; speaker of house of burgesses, 630; delegate to congress, 575; president of congress, 579; member of committee of correspondence, 624; his death, 629.
Randolph genealogy, 629.
Randolph, John, attorney-general, 630.
Randolph, Edmund, 630.
Randolph, Beverley, 630.
Randolph, John, of Roanoke, 630.
Randolph, the frigate, blown up, 688.
Rappahannock River, 57.
Ratcliffe, John, 39, 43, 45, 53, 65.
Read, Colonel Clement, member of convention of 1775-6, 625.
Reekes, Stephen, pilloried, 199.
Revenue, 353.
Revolt threatened, 275.
Ricahecrians, Colonel Edward Hill defeated by, 199, 233.
Rice, Rev. Dr. John H., 82.
Richmond, town of, laid off, 421; incorporated, 433; convention meets at, 599; seat of government removed to, 710; entered by Arnold, 710.
Roanoke Island, 22, 23, 26, 226.
Roanoke River, 24.
Roanoke, or Rawrenoke, Indian shell-money, 56, 113.
Roanoke, John Randolph of, 631.
Robinson, John, president, 449.

INDEX.

Robinson, John, Jr., speaker, 535; his defalcation, 544, 546; his family, 548.
Rockbridge County, first settlers of, 423.
Rolfe, John, marries Pocahontas, 109; member of council, 139.
Rolfe, Thomas, son of Pocahontas, 122.
Rolfe, Henry, 122.
Rolfe, Jane, marries Colonel Robert Bolling, 122.

SAFETY, committee of, 624.
Sandy Creek expedition, 489.
Sandys, Sir Edwin, 144, 149, 151, 176.
Sandys, George, treasurer in Virginia, 151; translates Ovid at Jamestown, 152.
Scarburgh, Edmund, excites disturbances in Eastern Shore, 226; his proceedings as surveyor-general in establishing boundary line, 259.
Scarburgh, Colonel John, 342.
School, East India, 158.
Scotch-Irish settlers of Western Virginia, 423, 429.
Sea-Venture, the, 77, 94.
Secretary, office of, 352.
Shakespeare's Tempest, 99.
Shenandoah River, 389.
Shenandoah valley, 425, 431, 505.
Sheriffs, 353.
Sherwood, Grace, tried for witchcraft, 382.
Shirley, 107, 126.
Silk in Virginia, 158.
Simcoe, Lieutenant-Colonel, 722, 729, 735.
Six Nations, treaty with, 433.
Slaves, baptism of, 267.
Slavery, negro, remarks on, 145, 528.
Smith, Sir Thomas, treasurer of Virginia Company, 37.
Smith, Robert, 264, 266.
Smith, Captain John, his early life and adventures, 30, 34; his life in jeopardy at Isle of Mevis, 38; one of council of Virginia, 39; excluded from council, 41; restored to council, 43; has charge of colony, 44; explores the country, 45; taken prisoner by Opechancanough, 46; rescued by Pocahontas, 48; explores Chesapeake, 55; president, 60; his energetic administration, 64; visits Powhatan, 66; seizes Opechancanough, 71; encounters chief of Paspahegh, 73; builds fortlet on Ware Creek, 74; his efforts to quell disorders, 80; his return to England, 80; descendants still living in England, 83; his epitaph, 83.
Somers, Sir George, 35, 77, 94, 97, 102.
South Carolina solicits aid from Virginia, 391.
Southampton, Earl of, treasurer of Virginia Company, 149, 175-77.
Sovereignty, declaration of, 238.
Spencer, Nicholas, president, 336.
Spilman, Henry, 141.
Spotswood, Alexander, governor, his lineage and early career, 378; dissolves assembly, 379; assists North Carolina, 380; establishes Indian school, 384; visits Christanna, 385; his Tramontane expedition, 387; institutes Tramontane order, 390; his disputes with burgesses, 393-99; he dissolves assembly, 394; complaints against, 398; displaced, 404; review of his administration, 404; manufacturer of iron, 405; subsequent career, death, and family, 404-10.
Stamp act, 534, 538, 543; repeal of, 544.
Staunton incorporated, 438.
St. John's Church, 599.
Starlins, Captain, 738.
"Starving Time" at Jamestown, 93.
State House, Philadelphia, congress meets in, 618.
Statistics, 206, 271, 331, 349, 382, 443, 471.
Steg, Thomas, 216.
"Stint" of tobacco, 265.
Stith, Rev. William, president of College of William and Mary, and author of History of Virginia, 437, 482.
Stobo, Captain, 467-68, 504.
Stone House, the old, on Ware Creek, 74.
Stone, deputy governor of Maryland, 228.
Strachey, William, 102, 106.
Stratford, 577.
Stuart, house of, 243.
Studley, birth-place of Patrick Henry, 519.

Stukeley, Sir Lewis, 122.
Stuyvesant, Peter, Berkley's reply to, 246.
Suffolk burnt by the British, 697.
Summer Islands, 102, 109.
Surrender of Virginia to Commonwealth of England, 217.
Surrender of Burgoyne, 686.
Surrender of Cornwallis, 749.
Swift, Dean, desires to be bishop of Virginia, 377, 562.
Swift Run Gap, 388.
Syme, Colonel John, 519.

TABB, JOHN, member of committee of safety, 624.
Tarleton, Lieutenant-Colonel, 715, 729, 731, 734, 750.
Tayloe, John, member of first council under republican constitution, 651.
Tea, duty on, 568.
Tempest, Shakespeare's, 99.
Temple, Colonel Benjamin, 713.
Thompson, Rev. John, 409.
Tobacco, or Uppowoc, how used by Indians, 24; Lane introduces into England, 25; anecdotes of Raleigh's smoking, 25, 153; culture of, commenced by colonists, 117; new mode of curing, 125; cultivation of, discouraged by government, 151; James the First's aversion to, and his "Counterblast," 153-57; Charles the First affects monopoly of, 180; sole staple of Virginia, 181; "stint" of, 265; low price of, 281, 332; plant-cutting, 333; revenue from, 331; "Two-Penny Act," 507; destroyed by the British, 733.
Toleration act, 373.
Tomocomo, 119.
"Two-Penny Act," 507.
Totopotomoi, 233.
Trade, free, established, 245.
Tuckahoe-root, 75, 87.
Tuckahoe, a seat on James River, 604, 631.
Tuckahoes, a name given to inhabitants of Eastern Virginia, 424.
Tucker, St. George, 672.
Tyler, John, revolutionary patriot, 723.
Tyler, John, President, 724.

UTTOMATTOMAKKIN, 119.

VALLEY OF VIRGINIA, first settlers of, 423, 429, 488.
Valley Forge, Washington at, 687.
Van Braam, Jacob, 461, 466, 468, 504.
Varina, 104-5.
Vernon, Admiral, 417.
Vernon, Mount, 417, 505.
Vestries, 354.
Virginia, state and condition of, 349; opposes stamp act, 538; becomes independent, 648.
Virginia, name given by Queen Elizabeth, 22.
Virginians, habits of, 495.

WADDELL, REV. JAMES, "the Blind Preacher," 521.
Walker, Dr., 731.
Walker, John, 731-32.
Wallace, Rev. Caleb, 674.
Washington, Colonel John, a burgess, 281; commands militia at siege of Piscataway Fort, 285.
Washington, Captain Lawrence, 417, 452; his views on religious freedom, 454; in Carthagena expedition, 417.
Washington, George, his lineage, 457; early life, 457; surveyor, 458-59; major, 460; despatched on mission through wilderness, 461; lieutenant-colonel, 465; surprises French party, 464; surrenders at Fort Necessity, 466; resigns, 470; aide-de-camp to Braddock, 472; heroism at battle of Monongahela, 477; his account of the defeat, 479; commander-in-chief of Virginia forces, 486; visits Boston, 487; Dinwiddie's correspondence with, 496; member of assembly, 503; marries, 503; receives thanks of assembly, 504; reports non-importation agreement, 558; attends meeting of burgesses, 571; member of congress, 575, 580; chosen commander-in-chief by congress, 621; his conduct of affairs during revolutionary war, 665-68, 686-87, 742, 746, 748, 751.
Washington, Colonel William, 716, 718-744.
Washington College founded, 677.
Weedon, General George, 685.

INDEX.

Werowocomoco, 48, 66, 71–2, 108, 129–30.
West Point, 126, 313, 316, 320, 327.
West, Captain John, 195.
West, Francis, Governor, 180.
West, Sir Thomas, Lord Delaware, 96.
Whitaker, Rev. Alexander, 106, 109, 115, 117.
White, Captain John, Governor of City of Raleigh, in Virginia, 26.
Whitefield preaches at Williamsburg, 438, 445.
William and Mary proclaimed in Virginia, 343.
William and Mary College, 345–47, 361–64, 376, 437.
William the Third, death of, 362; succeeded by Anne, 362.
Williamsburg, City of, seat of government removed to, 358; descriptions of, 444, 502; disturbances at, 607; Cornwallis quartered at, 735; La Fayette quartered at, 743.
Winchester first settled, 427, 493.
Wingfield, Edward Maria, first president of council, 41, 43.

Winston, Sarah, mother of Patrick Henry, 519.
Winston, William, 520.
Withe, artist, 23–4.
Wives for colonists, 146.
Woodford, Colonel William, appointed to command second Virginia regiment, 627; sent against Dunmore, 633; refuses to acknowledge Colonel Henry's superiority in command, 633; has command at battle of Great Bridge, 635.
Wormley, Captain Ralph, 214.
Wormley, Ralph, 610, 645.
Wythe, George, a burgess, 537; biographical sketch of, 656.

YEARDLEY, SIR GEORGE, Governor, 117, 180.
Yeardley, Lady Temperance, 180.
Yeardley, Captain Francis, his letter to Ferrar, 226; Roanoke Indians visit, 226; purchases territory in North Carolina, 227.